1994

Major European Governments

The Dorsey Series in Political Science

Major European Governments

Alex N. Dragnich, Ph.D.
Professor Emeritus of Political Science
Vanderbilt University

Jorgen S. Rasmussen, Ph.D.
Professor of Political Science
Iowa State University

Seventh Edition

Brooks/Cole Publishing Company
Pacific Grove, California

ISBN 0-534-10515-7
Former ISBN 0-256-03389-7

Library of Congress Catalog Card No. 85–61898

Printed in the United States of America

10 9 8 7 6 5 4 3

Preface

Those who are familiar with numerology will know that seven is an excellent number. In this case seven means that six previous editions have won acceptance by many people in a variety of schools throughout the United States and, occasionally, abroad. Alex Dragnich originated this text a quarter of a century ago and was its sole author for the first three editions. With the fourth edition in 1974 the text became a collaborative work when Jorgen Rasmussen joined him.

The division of responsibility that has evolved is for Dragnich to concentrate on the Soviet Union and for Rasmussen to deal with the rest of the book, especially the other three sections about specific countries. The text is a collaborative effort—not just the work of two authors between the same covers—because each edition has built upon and developed out of Dragnich's original book. Furthermore, the authors have reviewed each other's revisions, as appropriate.

The basic aim of this text remains as in the past: to present to students the essential features of government and politics in four major European political systems. We try to avoid being either excessively detailed or too simplistic. Since we seek to inform people having little previous familiarity with foreign political systems, much of the book is descriptive. But we also include interpretation and analysis. While this book is not an appropriate place to discuss questions and methods of concern to practicing scholars in comparative politics, our coverage is affected at least implicitly by developments in the discipline of political science.

Studying a new subject usually requires learning a new vocabulary and becoming familiar with new concepts. We have tried to keep unfamiliar terms to a minimum and to avoid needless jargon. We seek to write clear, relatively un-technical prose. We introduce only those terms and concepts that aid fuller understanding of a subject and those that need to be known for further study in comparative politics. While we have not included a vocabulary list, we provide sufficient information when first using a term or concept that readers should have no trouble in defining it. Thus while we want to be helpful, we also pay our readers the compliment of believing them to be intelligent people willing to put some effort into the study of the subject of this book.

Four of the six parts of the book deal with single political systems. Although we compare these systems to others, including the United States, basically we examine each system separately. The Introduction discusses the study of comparative politics without detailed reference to any particular political system. It provides a general guide to the study of any political system. Thus it not only introduces topics that will be the main focal points in the single-country parts of the book and justifies their importance, but it also can aid any study of countries not included in this book. Part Five compares the health of the three democracies we have examined. It provides an opportunity to include some comparative perspectives that may not have been fully developed because of the country-by-country organization of the text. This part also serves as a transition from three systems that are fundamentally the same—democracies—to the one that differs essentially by being a dictatorship.

Although the organization of this edition has been altered only slightly, the book has been extensively revised, as well as updated. While we cannot make this book recreational reading, we hope that its relatively informal approach is sufficiently lively that reading it is not a chore. For this edition we have added more illustrative material and graphics to help clarify or emphasize a particular point being made in the text.

We hope that the clientele of the previous editions of this text will consider this edition a useful and interesting improvement that retains the virtues of previous editions and adds new strengths. We are happy to serve those who appreciate our approach to the introductory study of comparative politics.

While we, of course, bear final responsibility for the book's contents, we want to thank the users and evaluators of previous editions who have provided many useful suggestions over the years. T. Philip Wolf has been especially helpful in this way. We also appreciate greatly the assistance received from the German Information Center in New York, in particular from Hannelore Koehler. Similarly our thanks go to British Information Services in New York and to Caroline Cracraft in Britain's Consulate in Chicago. Robert Worcester of Market & Opinion Research International and Robert Wybrow of Gallup (both in London) kindly have provided useful survey data.

Alex N. Dragnich
Jorgen S. Rasmussen

Contents

List of Figures

List of Tables

PART ONE

INTRODUCTION

Introduction

THE ESSENCE OF POLITICS

You are starting to learn about the government and politics of four large European countries. You know what government is, but your idea of politics may differ somewhat from ours. We like the definition offered many years ago by an eminent political scientist: politics is "who gets, what, when, how." The strength of this definition is that it indicates that politics involves conflict. Indeed, if everyone agreed about everything, there would be no politics. Anyone who deplores the clash of political groups and believes that disagreement should be eliminated from government is either naive or a potential dictator; people *will* disagree on virtually any issue.

People who dislike political conflict, however, are right to some extent. Human beings create governmental structures to channel (not eliminate) conflict, to keep conflict manageable, to keep it from erupting into violence. A 17th-century political philosopher trying to imagine what life would be like without government envisioned a "condition called Warre; and a warre, as is of every man, against every man—[a life] solitary, poor, nasty, brutish, and short." Although the study of politics does not leave out wars, riots, and other disruptive acts, its main concern is with how societies organize to resolve conflicting and competing interests in ways that will not tear those societies apart. The aim is not to avoid conflict but to manage unavoidable conflict. The aim is not to produce universal agreement on issues but to produce policies that the great bulk of a society at least can tolerate, even if many people think the policies are mistaken or undesirable.

3

During the 20th century each of the countries studied in this book has failed at one time or another to varying degrees to keep domestic conflict within peaceful bounds. In Russia the autocratic rule of the tsar was terminated at the time of World War I by a revolution and civil war, only to be replaced by an even more coercive and repressive regime. The communists engaged in systematic execution of countless opponents and even purged hundreds of thousands of members of their own party. The millions of people sent to forced labor camps exceeded even the number confined by the Nazis. Since the death of Stalin in 1953, the level of violence in Soviet politics has declined markedly, although dissidents and various minority groups are still subjected to persecution.

In Germany the brief experience with democracy during the Weimar Republic after World War I was marred by street fighting between political groups and political assassinations. But even this was better than what followed the Nazi seizure of power. Through their secret police and concentration camps the Nazis practiced terror and violence on a scale so vast as to be unbelievable. Disruptive student demonstrations in the late 1960s and extralegal protests against the role of the military and nuclear power at the start of the 1980s caused some people to fear that Germany was returning to the days of Weimar.

In France the serious danger of an invasion of Paris by French paratroopers to seize control of the government brought one constitutional system to an end in 1958 and started the process for a new regime. Ten years later this regime found itself besieged by students and workers who battled police in the streets and from behind barricades, events that contributed significantly to the process of driving the president from office the following year despite the fact that he had served little more than half his term.

Britain has been the most stable, the least turbulent, of the four countries studied in this book. But even there politics has involved violence. Women fighting for their political rights prior to World War I broke windows and set fire to mailboxes. The forced feedings administered to many of these women while they were in prison were not designed to be tortures, but physically they had much the same effect. Full-scale violence was required for Ireland to become independent of Britain after World War I. In Northern Ireland, which remained joined to Britain, the virus of religious discrimination and bigotry remained dormant until the late 1960s when it erupted anew. Thus in the 1970s snipings, fire bombings, and street fighting became common occurrences, and a Catholic young woman even was tarred and feathered because she planned to marry a non-Catholic British soldier who was part of the peace-keeping force in Northern Ireland. In 1984 a bomb planted in a hotel by Irish nationalists nearly killed the British prime minister while she was attending her party's conference and did kill several others, including a member of Parliament.

THE SCIENTIFIC METHOD AND THE COMPARATIVE STUDY OF POLITICS

Clearly, none of the four countries in this book—for that matter no other country, not even the United States—has been able to devise a set of governmental institutions capable of processing conflicting demands for action and assistance without experiencing some resort to violence. Equally clear, countries differ in frequency and level of violence. Russia had a full-fledged revolution; Britain did not. On the other hand, not much has changed in Britain in 50 or 100 years. Some people argue that getting the reforms required to meet the needs of the British people demands at least extralegal, and perhaps violent, action. Why then has the resort to violence been much less common in British politics than in Russian politics in the 20th century? And why is it that the governmental institutions in one country prove much more capable of winning popular support than do those in another? During the past 200 years the French have had over a dozen different regimes—in effect over a dozen different constitutions—during the same time that the United States has had one.

These comments suggest why comparative study of politics is useful. As you begin to learn something about the government and politics of other countries, you are likely to be struck by the differences in political life between them and what you are familiar with in the United States. You may be sufficiently intrigued that you try to explain why things differ elsewhere. Can some pattern of events be discovered, an association or link among them that might suggest a causal relation? Can this hunch—or hypothesis, to give it its more formal name—be supported by evidence that you are able to dig out by detailed study?

This is the process of making scientific discoveries, which are no more than new ways of thinking about familiar things. Such discoveries are desirable either for their practical utility or because their ability to explain why things happen as they do satisfies your curiosity. The familiar things explained are observed regularities—whenever it gets sufficiently cold outside, puddles of water freeze. These observed regularities are only descriptive reports, which do not explain anything. The mere fact that two things always have occurred together or in sequence is no guarantee that they will continue to do so. Thus the process of scientific discovery requires going beyond description to analysis.

The process of analysis separates an event into its component parts to help reveal relations, especially those that might not be readily apparent. This procedure helps to generate hypotheses—tentative solutions to problems, suggestions for interpreting data so that they make sense. The usefulness of these tentative solutions is tested through experiments or observation. The experimental approach is preferable since it tends to minimize the errors or distracting factors that are inherent in unplanned or unmanipulatable observations. By this process of verification, hypotheses are either rejected or transformed into laws.

A scientific law states the form and scope of a regularity. It tells how things known to be connected are related: whether, for example, they increase in size together or whether the one gets larger as the other gets smaller. It tells the circumstances in which the law applies: whether, for instance, it is true only when the temperature is above freezing. The significance of a law is that it implies that the stated relation is a necessary one, thus going beyond the mere report of an observed regularity.

When a number of laws whose scope has been established can be interrelated, the resulting system of knowledge is a theory. A theory's validity depends upon its ability to account for many diverse data simply and economically. The geocentric theory of the universe, for example, was abandoned not because it was disproven—it was not certain that the sun did not revolve around the earth— but because increasingly complex and elaborate explanations were required to make this theory conform with newly acquired information about the movement of heavenly bodies. As the explanations became more cumbersome, the theory became less helpful. A new theory that could explain the available data more simply and would be more productive of useful subsidiary laws was needed.

At this point we have come full circle in describing the process of scientific investigation. A theory helps make a generalization a law by providing reasons for the regularities observed. Furthermore, one can deduce from a theory what relations should prevail if the theory is correct and thus search for regularities not previously discovered. Should these regularities then be found, they can be established as laws, further buttressing the theory's validity.

As we noted, experimentation is a key method in the process of scientific discovery. Unfortunately, it rarely is possible in political science; people, unlike laboratory rats, are not expendable and do not tolerate being manipulated. Therefore, political scientists usually have to settle for observation, for gaining their data from uncontrolled situations and events. In an effort to avoid being misled by the presence of extraneous factors in the research sites they are forced to use, political scientists endeavor to compare political phenomena across national boundaries. If they can discover the same regularity in more than one country, they feel more certain that there is some link between the associated objects and that the relation is not just an accidental one due to mere happenstance. Thus cross-national generalizations are essential for an empirically grounded theory of politics.

We are not just talking about the useless study of a lot of abstract, irrelevant information. As we have already noted, no country has devised a perfect set of political institutions. But all political systems have valuable lessons to teach. Virtually every political system does at least some things effectively, and even if it didn't, it could provide instances of bad examples to be avoided. Thus by studying other political systems we can gain some idea of which political reforms we might wish to adopt in this country and which we would be wise to avoid.

The idea of comparing political systems hardly is new. Aristotle, the Greek philosopher who lived over two millennia ago, sometimes is regarded as the founder of political science because of his attempt to classify the constitutions of the several Greek city-states. In the 1950s some political scientists complained that the study of politics had advanced little since Aristotle's time. They felt that the prevailing practice of concentrating on laws, constitutions, and formal governmental structures, rather than on political processes and group interaction, resulted in mere comparative description, with little analysis. They advocated more systematic and rigorous research with as great precision—typically involving the use of quantitative measures—as existing research techniques would permit. Furthermore, they wished to push the scope for comparison as far as possible, arguing that comparing only three or four countries would do little to avoid the danger of mistakenly attributing causality to mere accidental relationships.

We do not want in this book to become involved in a lengthy discussion of the pros and cons of various methodological approaches. But we do need to explain to you why we have chosen to discuss some things and omit others. Clearly we cannot compare all the world's political systems, past and present. This would produce a book the size of an encyclopedia consisting largely of tables of numbers, something that you would have stopped reading already. Instead, we have chosen to discuss four countries that have some characteristics in common but also exhibit many interesting contrasts—for example, levels of political violence. All four of these countries are major international powers. (Perhaps one should be called a superpower to distinguish its much greater strength internationally.) And three of them are European countries while the Soviet Union is both European and Asian. Thus although these countries differ from the United States in many ways, you should find them more familiar than you would African, Asian, or, perhaps, even Latin American countries. Study of them should be most useful in gaining perspective on American political practices. It also means that the three European ones are more likely to have some elements in their history and heritage in common than they would if we selected a country from each of the corners of the world. This should aid comparison.

We will spend a good deal of time describing the formal status of each country's governmental institutions and also explaining how they operate in fact. We lack sufficient space, however, to be able to provide detailed examples of how decisions have been made in specific policy areas. To that extent we must concentrate more on political machinery than on its output. In addition to the governmental bodies, we will examine political structures seeking to control or influence the government and the means by which people participate in politics. Thus we obviously will go beyond a mere description of each country's constitution.

The key question is how to organize this material. A common approach for textbooks is to focus on one governmental or political institution after another. This approach makes quite clear what is being discussed; you would have no difficulty in knowing what a political party or a legislature is. The problem with this approach is that it might tend to make you believe that all governmental bodies labeled legislatures do basically the same thing. As you will learn from this book, the functions of the British legislature are quite different from those of the U.S. Congress, and the functions of both of these differ considerably from those of the legislature of the Soviet Union. Thus an argument can be made that we should focus on the basic functions that must be performed in every political system and explain to you how the mix of institutions for a particular function varies from one country to another.

The problem with the functional approach as a basis for organizing this text is that were you asked when you had finished reading the British section what are the functions and powers of the House of Commons, you might have some difficulty in answering, since you would have to pull together material from several different chapters to respond. You might well have learned something about the abstraction known as the interest aggregation function or the rule-making function, but probably only at the cost of being somewhat uncertain about what the real institutions such as the Commons and the Cabinet do.

So we have decided to emphasize the reality rather than the abstraction. Although the material for each country is organized by political and governmental institution rather than by function, we will be discussing the functions played by these institutions. You will want to note as your study moves from one country to another how the significant political functions are discharged differently in different national settings. In much of the rest of this Introduction we will discuss these various functions so that you will be familiar with them when you reach the country sections of the book. Thus you will be able to understand the significance of a political or governmental institution having one set of functions rather than another.

DEMOCRATIC AND AUTOCRATIC POLITICAL SYSTEMS

We have observed that social conflict is common and that the attempt to deal with it nonviolently is a constantly pressing concern. Why is this? An ultimate answer would turn on your conception of human nature. Are people fundamentally good and simply corrupted by malignant social structures, as communists assert? Or are they essentially and incorrigibly sinful, as Christians believe? We don't need to go this far to answer the question. You know that even in a prosperous country like the United States, resources are limited and, therefore, not everybody will be satisfied with their share. If deceit and brute strength are not to be the chief means of trying to eliminate such dissatisfaction, if there is to be any community among humans, then some rules, behavioral boundaries, accepted practices must exist to constrain the struggle for redistribution of limited resources.

Someone has to make the rules; someone has to assign the benefits; someone has to be able to apply any sanctions necessary to implement these decisions. A society's government is composed of whatever structures in that society are widely recognized as being properly engaged in these activities and as possessing as well the exclusive authority to set the limits within which force may be used legitimately. Political struggle between various segments of society involves their utilizing whatever power they may possess to try to control the government. Those segments that succeed will be able to make authoritative decisions—those that are binding throughout the society—or alter the procedures for making them.

Thus there are two basic political problems. First, given conflicting individual goals, wants, and needs, how is it possible to maintain social order? How is it possible to get people to obey authoritative decisions that they do not like? Especially, how is it possible to get them to do so voluntarily, assuming an ethical preference for a minimum of coercion? Second, how can the exercise of authoritative power be controlled to prevent the loss of freedom? In ancient Rome the question was put: *Quis custodiet ipsos custodes?* "Who will guard against those who themselves are guards?" How can we ensure that those to whom we entrust the power to settle conflicts nonviolently do not abuse their power and tyrannize everyone? By what means can we call the wielders of political power to account to ensure that the use of authoritative power is responsible?

Whether political decision-makers are accountable, whether political power is responsible—these are the tests for making the most basic distinction between types of political systems. Systems where decision-makers are accountable, where power is responsible, are democracies; those where they aren't are autocracies. Democracy frequently is defined as government by the people. But obviously no country of any size can be run by a mass town meeting of the citizens. So the practical test of democracy becomes whether the people can change by regular, legal procedures the holders of governmental power, replacing one set of leaders with another.

This key procedural criterion for democracy is buttressed by certain basic beliefs and principles. Even though governmental structures vary considerably from one democracy to another, these values are commonly held. At the center of the democratic faith is the belief that individuals are important, that political institutions exist to serve them rather than the reverse, and that the government, therefore, exists by virtue of their consent. Closely related is the belief that individuals can manage their own affairs better than someone else can do that for them. Of course, people do make mistakes, they do at times misconceive their own best interests. Democracy assumes only that in the long run people usually are good judges and can distinguish sensible policies from shortsighted ones and capable leaders from incompetent ones. Furthermore, the mistakes in judgment that the people do make are preferable to paternalist government, however efficient it might be, for without the opportunity to make mistakes and learn from them, human growth would be impossible. People not permitted to think and decide for themselves but allowed only to act on command would no longer be human beings, but animals or robots. So as Winston Churchill, prime minister of Britain during World War II, once said, democracy is the worst form of government except for all other forms.

Despite democracy's concern for the individual, some limits must be placed on behavior or we are back to the brute strength free-for-all that all governmental systems are intended to eliminate. Paradoxically, concern for individuals serves as a basis for justifying limits on individual behavior. In seeking to develop themselves, individuals cannot be permitted to infringe on the rights of others to attempt to realize their potential. This is why democratic government always is in dynamic tension. Individual freedom is tempered by the need for authority to protect the rights of other individuals. Someone once explained it this way: my right to swing my fist stops where your nose begins.

Thus a democratic society is a flexible one, constantly readjusting the balance between freedom and constraint, rather than a fixed order; it is an open society allowing, welcoming change. To some this is an agreeable idea, for they believe that people can be the masters of their fate. But in others, constant change, even the prospect of such change, produces anxiety. They cannot adjust readily to new ideas and new ways of doing things and thus feel threatened by innovation. Taken to an extreme, such feelings are likely to culminate in an authoritarian personality, one which would be more at home in a dictatorial, rather than a democratic, system.

The emphasis on the worth of the individual is expressed politically in democracies through the principles of political equality, majority rule, toleration of opposition, and rule of law. Since it is impossible to insure that everyone has exactly the same amount of political influence, the effort to attain political equality normally is restricted to eliminating all extraneous obstacles, such as religion and occupation, to the right to vote and hold office, and to giving the same weight to each vote. Differences over who should hold government offices and what policies should be implemented are resolved in favor of persons and policies that gain the most votes in honest and frequent elections.

But while the majority is to prevail, it is not to oppress the minority. Minority opinion should not be dismissed cavalierly. Dissenting groups and parties should be free to organize, to assemble, and to speak and write freely as they seek to persuade people to support their programs and policies. At the next election they can offer an alternative set of leaders for approval by the voters. Thus systems in which only one political party can operate freely are not fully democratic. Not all one-party systems can be classified automatically as autocracies, however. In some countries, especially some of the developing ones, a fair degree of governmental accountability and of choice among alternative officeholders exists even though the right to organize politically is limited. The nature of parties, more than the number, is the crucial aspect. Some single-party systems are open to diverse views, while others are more monolithic.

Though the procedures for participating in politics may vary from one democracy to another, the rule of law must prevail in all of them. Sanctions are not to be applied arbitrarily. The rules must be clear and known in advance. Convictions must conform with due process, that is, must be obtained fairly—confessions based on torture are not permitted, for example. Everyone must be subject equally to the law. And the government is not above the law; it must be able to cite authorization for all its actions.

The basic arrangements by which a particular country seeks to implement these beliefs and principles are set forth in its constitution. Constitutions are almost invariably written—Britain is the best-known exception—but commonly augmented as well by certain traditionally established political practices known as usages or conventions (not to be confused with gatherings of people to draw up constitutions or to nominate candidates) that, although unmentioned in the written constitution, are nonetheless an essential part of the country's political system. The U.S. Supreme Court's power to declare a law unconstitutional is an example.

Although constitutions had been written in ancient times, the growth of the idea of limited government a few centuries ago was the main stimulus in convincing countries that they needed a constitution. The original motivation was to limit royal power through a document that spelled out the requirements of natural law. The constitution makers did not claim to be devising new procedures or admit to seeking legal support for their political preferences; they simply claimed to be making explicit certain precepts of justice and right that were said to be divinely established and thus immutable and eternal.

Subsequently, constitutions were justified more pragmatically—an ordered political system with agreed-upon procedures and specified rights seemed likely to minimize arbitrariness, discourage revolutionary disruptions, and thus produce greater stability. This defense came to be questioned as well. Obviously, merely putting words on paper doesn't guarantee anything if the ruling officials refuse to abide by it.

Nonetheless, that even nondemocratic countries feel that they must have constitutions that appear to be democratic illustrates the continued importance of constitutions and of symbols in politics. The quarter of a century following World War II saw a new flurry of constitution writing as political boundaries changed and former colonies gained independence. In Germany and Italy many people felt that dictators had come to power because of defects in the countries' constitutions. Drawing up new constitutions after World War II was very important for them since they believed that if only they could get the right procedures on paper they could avoid another lapse into dictatorship. One need not accept this belief to grant that a constitution can be an ideal statement of a country's political values, and thus can influence political behavior.

The structures and procedures set forth in a country's constitution describe its governmental system. When you add to this the structures for expressing political preferences—parties and interest groups—that, typically, are little discussed in constitutions, you can use the term *political system.* Thus far we have avoided the word *nation,* referring instead to "countries." The reason is that nations and political systems may have different boundaries.

The term *nation* refers to a group of people having a common sense of identity, typically produced by shared customs, culture, language, and history. The German nation today is divided primarily between two political systems—East and West Germany. On the other hand, a single political system may include more than one nation; Britain can be said to include the nations of England, Scotland, and Wales.

The national composition of a political system does not necessarily require a particular type of distribution of power between the central and regional units of government. Britain is a unitary system, while the United States, which despite its diverse population does not include nations in the sense that Britain does, is a federal system. These terms mean that in Britain all the governmental power is constitutionally in the hands of the central government; it decides what regional and local units of government shall exist and gives them whatever powers it wishes. Legally, the British central government can destroy governmental units at all other levels and in the mid-1980s did abolish the major metropolitan governmental structures. In the United States the people, through the constitution, have given some power to the central government and some to the states. The states have an independent existence, which cannot be altered by the central government, and the distribution of power between the states and the central government can be changed only by a procedure that involves both the central government and the states or the people. This establishment of two independent levels of government is the essence of federalism.

Since most Americans know little about other political systems, they tend to assume that American structures and procedures are the natural or right ones, which must be copied closely if a country is to be a democracy. The contrast between federal United States and unitary Britain is simply one illustration that no single set of political and governmental institutions is required to qualify a country as democratic. One of the objectives of this book is to help you understand the contrasts between democratic political systems.

The consensus that stable democracy requires is an agreement on procedures, on the fundamental rules for making political decisions; beyond the basic individual rights we have discussed already, it does not require a commitment to particular policies or goals. Such a commitment is more characteristic of utopian or millenarian dictatorial systems. Democracy does not require any particular type of economic system. Some countries, like Britain and France, have instituted a considerable amount of government ownership of economic enterprises and along with other countries, like Sweden, have established an extensive system of social welfare benefits. This does not make them any the less democratic; in fact, some would argue that they are more democratic as a result. But this requires talking of "social" or "economic" democracy and loses sight of the point made above that democracy is a method. Other than the need to defend the basic principles outlined previously, democracy makes no substantive demands upon a country and leaves the choice of particular political, social, and economic structures up to each country. Some of the resulting combinations work better than others. But, as we have said, one of the hallmarks of democracy is to allow people freedom to make their own decisions and then to assess the results of their choices.

In having had firsthand experience with democracy, you are a very uncommon person. For most of history, even for most people today, life under some form of autocracy, rather than under democracy, has been more common. A brief discussion of the differences among these systems will help to place in perspective the one included in this book—the Soviet Union.

Perhaps the earliest form of autocratic rule was by the chief of a tribe or clan. Such rulers still are to be found in places where tradition-bound societies exist in relative isolation. Greater numbers of people were ruled over by potentates who assumed the title of king or emperor. Various of these rulers assumed an aura of holiness or divinity as a means of legitimating their power. The ruler of Tibet prior to its conquest by China is one of the best contemporary examples.

Autocratic rule in the form of monarchy was important in the history of Europe for most of the past 2,000 years. Modern European monarchies, however, have become constitutional; that is to say, limits have been placed on the powers of the government, and virtually all of the power previously exercised by the monarch has been transferred to popularly elected officials. Elsewhere, however, the power of a monarch often remains virtually unlimited.

The oldest formalized dictatorship, still another form of autocratic rule, was in ancient Rome. A leader often would be given extensive and unchallenged powers to deal with a certain crisis. But, unlike most modern dictators, he was elected rather than self-designated and served for only a limited time, never more than six months. Perhaps the best known of such dictators was Cincinnatus (fifth century B.C.), a farmer who went back to his plow after having dealt with the situation that brought about the emergency grant of power. Modern democracies frequently provide for special reserve powers to meet crises. Their granting extraordinary powers to the executive sometimes is labeled "constitutional dictatorship."

In the modern world there are several types of autocracies. Some, including the quasi-military strong-man type found in some Latin American countries, have only limited aims and can be labeled dictatorships. In such regimes the dictator has complete control of the political and military establishments, and censorship and the police are used to suppress internal opposition. The dictator may have little or no interest, however, in the operation of the economy or in other activities of the society. Thus people are left to pursue their own goals unhindered, so long as these do not constitute a threat to the dictatorship or encroach upon the economic interests of those backing the regime.

The fully developed modern autocracy, however, is totalitarian—a label that usually includes both nazi-fascist and communist types. Such systems are characterized by an official ideology—a system of ideas about the nature, operation, and goals of society. Unlike the democratic faith, these beliefs reject the idea that people can govern themselves, even though the political leaders may claim to speak for the people and to govern in their interest. No other beliefs are permitted to compete for public support. The official ideology, proclaimed and interpreted by those who rule the system, is the sole one.

This ideology is the guide in an effort to remake people and society totally. Totalitarianism, as the word suggests, means that the autocracy concerns itself with everything in the society. Politics comes to include personal, social, and cultural behavior, and all other aspects of life. The rulers seek to eliminate all private spheres of activity concerning the individual alone.

If the ideology is the guide to transform society, the instrument for this process is the single, elite party. It is to protect, propagate, and implement the ideology. Therefore, this form of government sometimes is called "party dictatorship." All other political groups are outlawed and the pronouncements of the party must be accepted unquestioningly. Assisting the party are a variety of auxiliary agencies such as youth groups, women's organizations, and sport clubs. Only those groups approved and controlled by the party may exist. Thus these groups help to ensure that the people are occupied with acceptable activities and can be kept track of easily and mobilized to carry out the will of the state.

To help discourage any opposition, the rulers use terror and repression widely. The way in which victims are selected at times seems irrational, for it often is not clear to them how they have offended the state. This irrationality of sanctions is calculated to sow anxiety among the population and to discourage people from trusting or depending upon anyone. Thus it helps to eliminate all alternative centers of loyalty in the society and makes at least the appearance, if not the fact, of fervent commitment to the party and service to it the only possible hope of safety.

Certain elements of modern totalitarian regimes can be found in earlier authoritarian or despotic systems, but that does not mean that those systems were totalitarian. Unlike modern totalitarian governments, they did not seek to destroy or completely dominate all existing political, economic, and social relationships. They were not bent on undertaking large-scale social engineering with the aim of building a new unity around one ideology—that of the rulers. Totalitarianism is a phenomenon associated with the 20th century's technological advance.

TYPOLOGIES AND TYPES OF VARIABLES

What we have been doing in these last few pages is to outline a simple classification scheme or typology whose main types or categories are democracy, monarchy, dictatorship, and totalitarianism. The criteria for distinguishing among these types were the extent of popular distribution of political power, the security of fundamental rights, and the scope of governmental penetration into the society. Classifying political systems according to basic type is a good way to begin a rigorous study of comparative politics. In addition to the typology just discussed, others frequently used in comparative politics are: one-, two-, or multiparty systems; presidential or parliamentary systems; and federal or unitary systems. We have already discussed the differences between federal and unitary systems; the differences between the categories in the party-system typology are self-evident. Presidential systems, as in the United States, separate the executive and legislative structures of government, with each being elected independently by the people for a set term of office. In a parliamentary system the two branches are fused; the legislature can vote the executive out of office without any need for a national election by the people. In some parliamentary systems the executive has the power to end the term of the legislature by calling for an election early.

Applying these typologies to the countries in this book, Britain usually would be classified as a two-party parliamentary democracy with a unitary division of powers, while Germany would be a multiparty parliamentary democracy with a federal system. Britain never has had even a dictatorial government in modern times, to say nothing of a totalitarian one. Germany from 1933 to 1945, however, provides one of the classic examples of totalitarian government, as does the one-party system that has existed in the Soviet Union since the close of World War I. France, which has had some experience with dictatorial government in both the 19th and 20th centuries, clearly is a multiparty democracy at present, but whether it is parliamentary or presidential is unclear, as we will discuss in detail in the French section of this book.

As this difficulty with labeling France suggests, applying a classification system is not an automatic process, but calls for informed judgments. Some people would argue that Britain has not really been a two-party system for the last decade and others would question whether Germany is a multiparty system. Indeed, it is difficult to state criteria that can distinguish between the party systems of these two countries. (Again, we will discuss this in the country sections.) Others would regard Nazi Germany as highly authoritarian but would question whether it was totalitarian because for much of its rule the regime had the support, or at least the consent, of the bulk of the population. As with any dictatorship, political opponents were suppressed, but the full force of totalitarianism was directed primarily against the Jews rather than against the entire population. On the other hand, although it was not as fully elaborated as the Soviet Union's communism, Nazi Germany did have an ideology that played a role in the effort to restructure the society.

The problem is that any classification system admittedly sacrifices some detailed information by grouping together for the sake of generalization things that are not exactly the same. Given such distortions, why bother trying to classify systems? While no two persons are alike, yet they clearly have enough in common to be grouped together and distinguished from horses. In fact, it is only when we begin to group things according to one or more criteria that we can discover just how much those objects grouped together have in common, and in what regards they differ from each other and from other objects not grouped with them. In other words, similarities and differences spring to view and one begins the process of questioning and seeking answers outlined previously in this chapter.

Once political systems have been grouped according to type, and differences and similarities begin to emerge, where does one begin the search for explanations or reasons? In trying to discover why a country's politics is as it is, both political and nonpolitical factors should be considered. For example, must a country attain a certain level of economic development before it can become a democracy? Or, turning to political factors, does a federal division of powers affect the political party system differently than does a unitary division?

If the basic research question in the study of politics is formulated as: Who governs by what means for what purpose? then we are placing least emphasis on the latter part of the question. We will not be discussing individual motivation to any great extent nor will we proceed very far in examining the impact of societal goals upon the quality of life except where this has particular relevance for the maintenance of the political system.

We will discuss the structures and procedures for the adjustment of conflict, for the making of authoritative (not to be confused with authoritarian) decisions concerning the distribution of benefits and values for each of the four countries we have selected. We also will examine the ways in which individuals and groups can seek to participate in politics and secure the backing of the government for their policy preferences. The political system is not a set of self-contained, insulated structures; it does not operate in a vacuum. Therefore, we have to broaden our discussion to talk about a number of other factors that affect the way in which the political system operates.

ENVIRONMENTAL CONSIDERATIONS

One of the intellectual battles that long has raged in psychology is whether an individual's behavior is affected primarily by environment or heredity—nurture or nature, as the choice is put starkly. Is a personality shaped most by those abilities and capacities with which a person is born or by the situations experienced and the training received after birth? Most psychologists probably now would agree that neither can be ignored. Similarly, in studying a political system we need to consider not only the structures themselves but also the environment in which the system operates.

This needs to be stressed because political science has tended to slight geographic factors, largely as a reaction against geopolitics. This late 19th- and early 20th-century approach to international relations argued that the country that controlled Eastern Europe would dominate the heartland—the Eurasian land mass—and, thereby, the world. The fact that now this approach is largely discredited and considered a pseudoscience should not be allowed to eliminate geographic considerations from politics. A country's location can affect its politics. Where its boundaries are natural ones—rivers, oceans, mountains—rather than an arbitrary line drawn across an open plain, it may feel less threatened by its neighbors and be less likely to build up a strong military establishment and to accept militaristic values. Geographic barriers within a nation's borders can hamper communication and thwart development of a sense of national unity. Finally, a country's location and geographical characteristics will determine its supply of natural resources, which will have a major impact on both its domestic and foreign politics.

The supply of natural resources is an element in a country's level of economic development—to broaden the idea of environment beyond physical geographical factors. In recent years many political scientists have tried to relate various measures of economic development to type of political system. Some have argued that a high level of development in a country affects its politics by making political conflict less ideological and more practical, thus reducing the heat and bitterness of political battle. When the great majority of the people are relatively well off, the conflict over the allocation of resources is presumed to be less sharp, thus facilitating compromise.

Level of economic development also affects the class structure in politically important ways. Industrialization requires a large class of manual, mass production workers, whose values and behavior are likely to differ rather markedly from the rest of the population. But as industrialization becomes fully mature, the proportion of manual workers in the work force begins to decline, and the share composed of service workers rises sharply. In both their lifestyle and economic situation such workers are likely to have much more in common with the middle class than are manual workers. Thus the relative change in these two groups' sizes would seem likely to contribute to greater similarity of outlook in a society and help to reduce the sharpness of political conflict.

Technological advance both requires and contributes to the improvement of a country's communications network. This creates an opportunity for wider circulation of more information about government actions and eases popular communication of political preferences to governmental officials. Improved communications also can help to unify a country through the nationalizing effects of mass media on public opinion. In a more prosperous country more money can be spent to provide mass public education. Raising the educational level makes possible an intelligent use of the greater volume of information supplied by the improved communications network. Mass public education can contribute significantly to a common socialization process in which the predominant values of the society—both political and nonpolitical—are inculcated.

An advanced level of economic development with its necessary concentration of workers in major urban areas also gives rise to a host of complex problems foreign to the simple society of a pastoral economy—problems of transportation, health care, pollution, crime. Many of these can be dealt with effectively only by collective action through government, thus expanding the load of demands and wants that the political structures must process.

The complexity of modern life requires individuals and social structures to specialize to obtain the abilities and knowledge needed to cope with contemporary problems. Efficiency demands that personnel be recruited, retained, and promoted on the basis of merit, rather than kinship or caste. This need to bureaucratize structures is not confined to the economic sector of a society, but is present as well in the political.

Not only do particular structures become more complex but the entire group system becomes more elaborate as new occupational and economic groups are created and grow with economic development. Many of these groups will have political objectives and, therefore, obviously will affect the nature of a country's politics. The advance of technology, coupled with the changes in the bureaucracy just mentioned, enhance the capabilities of governments to control their environments and thus to achieve their goals more readily. Depending upon the orientation of the government, this can mean either greater material prosperity

TABLE I-1   Type of Political System

Economic conditions	Political conditions			
	Democracy	Limited democracy	Limited autocracy	Autocracy
Strong	19	1	0	3
Good	7	5	1	7
Poor	5	4	2	9
Weak	4	5	17	14

and fuller social services for the population or more repressive control of their lives.

The concern mentioned earlier to give comparative politics a worldwide scope led to laborious projects of data gathering, especially during the 1960s. Compendiums of information classifying all the countries of the world on a wide variety of political, economic, and social characteristics were produced.[1] This information was analyzed by a variety of statistical techniques in a search for interesting relationships. Table I-1 provides a very simple example of how this could be done for the topic we've been discussing—the relation between economic conditions and type of political system—by assigning each of 103 countries to one of the 16 cells in the table according to how each was classified on *both* an economic typology and a political typology. The category in which a country was placed in the economic typology depended upon its combined ratings of GNP per capita, stage of economic development, literacy rate, and percentage of the work force engaged in agriculture. For the political typology such characteristics as freedom of the press, constitutionalism, party competition, freedom of political association, and the political role of the police and military were used. The result, for example, was that 19 countries were among *both* the most democratic and the most economically advanced. Statistical analysis of these figures indicates that the grouping of countries obtained is extremely unlikely to occur simply by chance. This means that the relationship is not accidental and is likely to be a necessary one.

What does this prove? Unfortunately, not a great deal. We cannot tell from these figures whether a healthy economy buttresses democracy or whether something about democracy helps to improve economic conditions. Furthermore, whatever the direction of the relation, it is static. The table simply presents the relation between two factors at a single point in time; it does not reveal anything about the dynamic effect of the process of political or economic change. For example, even if a high level of economic development favors a democratic political system, the process of attaining that level may give rise to

---

[1]The best known examples are Arthur Banks and Robert Textor, *A Cross-Polity Survey* (Cambridge, Mass.: MIT Press, 1963) and Charles Taylor and Michael Hudson, *World Handbook of Political and Social Indicators,* 2d ed. (New Haven, Conn.: Yale University Press, 1972). Table I-1 draws upon Banks and Textor.

such conflicts and dislocations and may require such tight social controls that governmental responsibility is lessened in the short run. Many Third World countries faulted for their lack of democracy have responded that their efforts to improve the material conditions of their people did not permit the luxury of the disagreements common in democratic systems.

About all that such tables can do is indicate whether our common sense expectations about how certain factors are likely to be related are grossly mistaken. This is a useful check, since common sense frequently is mistaken in its beliefs about the world and should not be merely assumed to be right.

Part of the problem with the table is that it is so general that it is almost too abstract. Like a skeleton, there is no meat on its bones. It provides no sense of the interplay of politics and economics. It does little more than suggest relations that one might wish to investigate in greater detail while studying particular countries. One aspect of the table deserves to be discussed further along these lines.

You will note that the table has been divided into quadrants, with the upper right and the lower left enclosed with a dashed line. These sections of the table are said to lie off the diagonal, that is, they are deviant cases contradicting the relationship that existed in most countries between economic conditions and the type of political system. In the 11 countries in the upper right, economic conditions were good or better, yet the governmental structures were autocratic to one degree or another. In the 18 countries in the lower left, the political system on balance was a form of democracy despite poor or worse economic conditions.

Why should these 29 countries differ from the other 74? Why are they not on the diagonal with the others? Almost all—nine—of the first group are European nations. In most cases a communist regime has given these countries a dictatorial or totalitarian government despite their economic strength. As we've said before, totalitarianism is associated with 20th-century technological advance. Clearly, we can't assume that economic development alone automatically will make a political system more democratic.

Two thirds of the group in the lower left quadrant—which contains no European nations—are Latin American and African nations. For a variety of reasons, which would have to be ascertained by more detailed studies, they were able, at the time the data were gathered, to operate relatively democratic political systems despite unfavorable economic circumstances. Whether they will continue to be able to do so remains to be seen.

In summary, the table allows us to refine our commonsense view of things to say that, although good economic conditions do seem to facilitate more democratic government, such conditions are neither necessary nor sufficient to attain a system of political structures responsible to the people. Furthermore, only by the extensive study of the deviant cases (far beyond the little we have suggested here) are you likely to gain an insightful understanding of the relationship being investigated.

So studying comparative politics in this fashion has some value, but is of limited use unless it serves as a springboard for further study; analysis of numerical distributions alone is not enough. Because of the extraordinary work involved in gathering data of this type and the limited payoff in research results, the cross-national compendiums of the 1960s have not been updated and other methods of studying comparative politics have been more common.

HISTORY AND POLITICAL CULTURE

At the start of the previous section we used the analogy of the psychologist's interest in an individual's environment and heredity. Having talked about some aspects of political systems' environment, in this section we are going to examine aspects that are rather more like the hereditary.

The major events of a country's history produce a particular mix of values, beliefs, and attitudes, which are passed on from one generation to the next. Of course, you don't inherit these the way you do brown or blue eyes. Nonetheless, talking about a national heritage of feelings about politics does make sense. You can no longer find anyone who lived through the Civil War, and those alive at the time of the American Revolution are long since dead. But both these events continue to have a significant effect upon how Americans think about politics. If you've ever lived in another country for a while, you may well have noticed how the political ideas of its people differed from those you were familiar with in the United States. In some countries government is regarded as a hostile force and contacts with it are to be avoided as much as possible, while in other countries it is seen as a beneficial agency of considerable use in improving the quality of life. In Britain the police are widely respected and generally thought to be incorruptible, while in much of the United States quite the reverse attitudes and beliefs prevail.

Over the years a people begins to build up out of its experiences a body of what may be called "folk wisdom" about government and politics. Political scientists refer to this as political culture, which may be defined more precisely as the sum of (1) individual evaluative attitudes and emotive feelings toward politics and the existing political system and (2) perceptions, feelings, and evaluations of the role of the individual in the political process.[2] In other words, what do people know about the political system, what is their gut reaction to it and their considered judgment, and how do they feel about the political activity and influence which they see the system as permitting them?

While, as we have said, you are not born with these values and beliefs, they are handed down from generation to generation, often without any conscious

---

[2]The classic discussion of the concept of political culture is in Gabriel Almond and Sidney Verba, *The Civic Culture* (Boston: Little, Brown, 1965), especially pp. 11–26. The concept has been criticized considerably. For the authors' reaction see Gabriel Almond and Sidney Verba, eds., *The Civic Culture Revisited* (Boston: Little, Brown, 1980), especially pp. 26–32 and 398–406. The book also contains critical essays and an updating of the country data by other scholars.

FIGURE I–1   Patterns of Political Culture

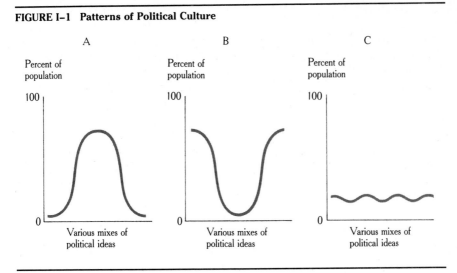

effort to do so. If you want to get the government off our backs, it may be because of comments around the supper table as you were growing up about red
tape and foolish bureaucrats way off in Washington. The process of transmit-
ting political values and beliefs is called political socialization; it helps to provide continuity in ideas about politics from one period to another. The belief
system into which you are socialized is important because it disposes you to regard the political system in a particular way before you have had any firsthand
contact with it. Not surprisingly, when that contact does occur, you tend to interpret it according to what you expected it to be.

While the main elements of a country's political culture can be described, regarding it as uniformly present throughout a country would be a mistake. To
one extent or another, subcultures exist in all political systems. The political culture is the set of values and attitudes that is most common; probably no single
individual will match this mix precisely. More important, certain groups within
a country may depart sharply in their ideas about politics from the common de-
nominator. You can bet that the Jews and Hitler saw things quite differently.
Any study of political culture needs to examine the values and beliefs of major
subgroups—whether they be religious, ethnic, occupational, geographical, or
whatever—to find out just how typical the prevailing political culture is.

Let's consider three contrasting patterns of political culture to see what different effects they might have.[3] Example A in Figure I–1 is of a country with
widespread consensus on political values and beliefs. Political conflict probably

---

[3] In *An Economic Theory of Democracy* (New York: Harper & Row, 1957), pp. 114–32, Anthony Downs discusses the effect of voter distribution upon party systems. While his argument is similar to the one we are making
here, we are not concerned with the specific partisan preferences of the population.

can be waged relatively peacefully there, since political opponents share the same basic values. Political differences are matters of degree, not of fundamental principle, and losing is not too bad since it won't cost you a great deal. Example B is the reverse; a sharp cleavage divides the country into two separate, virtually mutually exclusive political cultures. The potential for hostility and violent disruption of the political system is high. In example C no national political culture exists; each of the various subcultures into which the country is fractionalized encompasses roughly equal segments of the population. Political leaders in such a country will need considerable skills in coalition building as they seek to piece together majority support for some action. Failure to do so may stalemate the political system and, in turn, produce political apathy and alienation among many citizens.

The actual, as distinct from the potential, effect of these patterns is influenced to a considerable extent by the political style that prevails in the country, especially among the political leaders. Style turns on how people conceive of the political process, which affects the disposition they bring to participating in politics and their behavior in doing so.

When their views of the proper political structures, procedures, and policies not only differ but are mutually exclusive as well, when they prefer a politics of redemption to one of convenience, then an explosive situation is the result.[4] The political style characteristic of those who regard politics as the procedure for establishing the true faith is exhortation as they seek to convert the lost souls. Those who see politics as an instrumental process are more likely to employ a political style of bargaining and negotiation as they seek to adjust conflicting desires by a compromise that will satisfy most people at least temporarily. For them governing is not the process of choosing between good and evil but of distinguishing between varying shades of gray.

Political style and patterns of political culture tend to be reciprocally related. A distribution like that of example A helps to encourage an instrumental view of politics. The stakes are relatively limited (penny-ante poker can be enjoyable, but when the cheapest chip costs $1, anxiety sets in); losing the political struggle is no catastrophe, and next time your side may win. But where the pattern resembles example B, the political process may turn into a holy war in which the stakes are survival—lose this time and the game is over forever with no chance to recoup your losses—resulting in dogmatism and distrust—the politics of redemption.

---

[4]The distinction between the politics of redemption and of convenience comes from Glenn Tinder, *Political Thinking: The Perennial Questions* (Boston: Little, Brown, 1970), pp. 108–11. The former is characterized by a belief that politics seeks "a life on earth that is altogether good. . . . Felicity is not a gift of God, and it is not reserved for a heavenly existence or a time after death. It can be attained through human planning and can be attained here on earth." The mood of those who view politics this way is "the impatience and disgust of those who feel that men have betrayed their potentialities. Finding themselves in hell, they have called for the creation of heaven." The mood of those who reject this conception of politics is one "of low expectations and low demands since the world either cannot, or need not, be much improved. Government is not expected to bring salvation but only to enhance the convenience of life."

The reciprocal aspect is that if most of the population practices an instrumental style, this helps to distribute opinions around a single point, as in example A, while style that regards politics as a battle for Truth helps to polarize society into two separate camps, as in example B.

The content and pattern of political culture and the political style of a country are shaped to a considerable extent by the order and nature of major political or social crises and conflicts. Some of the fundamental historical cleavages that have shaped the politics of Western Europe are the conflicts between the church and the state, between primary and secondary producers, and between workers and employers.[5] Whether these crises could be faced one at a time or dealt with simultaneously made a considerable difference. Even if these crises did occur sequentially, if the earlier one had not been resolved by the time the next appeared, then the two would be intermingled in the political process, making it that much harder to deal with either one. The political load to be carried by the transformers of the political system—the magnitude and complexity of the issues to be processed—would be more likely to exceed the capacity of the system. Furthermore, newer issues seldom would be considered on their own merits, since the injection of the still fervent disputes of the past would produce an unthinking conditioned pro or con response. For much of the 20th century one had only to raise the question of the church on any issue in French politics and most of the political participants, like Pavlov's dogs, would froth at the mouth. The result of such intermingling of crises is that nothing is accomplished very well.

These are some of the reasons why we need to examine a country's history to see what cleavage patterns and political culture it has produced. This study is essential to discovering why one people holds one type of political values and another, another; why one type of political structure is viable and effective in one nation and another type in another, or why the same type of structure is functional in one system and not in another.

STRUCTURES FOR POLITICAL PARTICIPATION

Having talked about the environment and heredity of political systems, we need finally to get around to looking at the elements themselves of the political system. The structures for popular participation are a good starting point since if no one wanted anything done but could meet their needs unassisted, a political process wouldn't exist.

To start with needs and wants—inputs, as they are termed by some political scientists—is not to argue that people constantly are clamoring for action. In any political system relatively few people make specific demands upon the gov-

[5]For a rather general, theoretical discussion of crises and cleavage patterns see Seymour Lipset and Stein Rokkan, eds., *Party Systems and Voter Alignments* (New York: Free Press, 1967), pp. 1–64. For more specific application of the approach to particular countries see Gabriel Almond, Scott Flanagan, and Robert Mundt, *Crisis, Choice, and Change* (Boston: Little, Brown, 1973).

ernment. Typically, most people do not want to be bothered by political matters; they prefer to turn over to someone else the job of seeking general social conditions that make life liveable. Yet *some* people do wish to be involved actively in political decision making, and many of the rest wish to be heard on a few occasions when they feel particularly strongly about a matter. The type and amount of political participation that people feel is proper for them is influenced, of course, by a society's political culture and by the subculture of the groups to which an individual belongs. But also important is whether the political structures and practices themselves encourage or discourage participation, whether obstacles exist that make access to decision makers difficult.

Making demands, however, is only one of the two types of political participation; the other is expressing support for the system and its agents. Such expressions may be positive endorsements of particular leaders or policies. Or they may be expressed indirectly. For example, when people vote in an election they not only are expressing their preferences among the contending candidates, but also, unless they vote for antisystem candidates, they are supporting the existing political system. Just as there would be no need for a political system were there no demand inputs, so a political system could not exist unless there were support inputs.

Demands and supports may originate with the public or be stimulated by governmental agencies or by political structures whose apparent primary purpose is simply to communicate public opinion. But almost never is public opinion transmitted in its orignal form to decision makers; instead, as demand and support inputs travel through the channels for political communications, they are altered. The extent to which they are distorted, and public influence upon government thereby lessened, is a key question in the analysis of a country's political process.

Three subsystems of the main political system deal primarily with various forms of participation—the electoral system, the group system, and the party system. In studying the electoral system, you can't be satisfied simply to know the legal regulations; you also need to discover the related behaviors and practices. If night riders call on blacks who vote, if priests can instruct parishioners on how to vote, then neither group of voters really has access to decision makers even if the law provides for universal suffrage.

Access can be drastically affected by the method used to convert the popular vote into office-winners. You will be amazed to learn how inventive the human mind has been in thinking up different kinds of electoral systems. The same number of votes can yield a considerably different share of the seats in a legislature depending upon whether a country employs a single member/simple plurality system, as do the United States and Britain, or a proportional representation system, as does Germany. Still another result would be possible by employing the double ballot system now used in France.

The electoral system may do more than affect access. Some political scientists regard it as the major determinant of what type of party system a country has, while others have gone so far as to claim proportional representation weakened democracy in Weimar Germany and helped to encourage the rise of dictatorship. While these views are extreme, yet party strategies and campaign practices do have to be altered from one type of electoral system to another, and people do decide how to cast their vote differently depending upon the electoral system used in their country.

Voting is only one of the ways in which individuals participate in politics. You may communicate your views to your legislative representative or protest a regulation to a bureaucrat. Most people, however, find that their access or influence usually is so limited that they are much more likely to be successful if they combine their efforts with others. So people sharing a common interest form an organization to advance it. The members of the group may have little else in common. Everyone is familiar with interest groups of this type.

But they are not the only groups involved in the political process. Another type of group is organized for purposes other than influencing the government and yet may devote some of its time to doing just that. Churches are not organized for political purposes, yet various religious groups seek to influence government on a variety of issues. At times, to take another example, a governmental agency itself may operate as an interest group. Some people regard the Army Corps of Engineers as one of the most effective interest groups in the United States, given its success in lobbying Congress for financial support of the various projects it wishes to undertake. Such governmental interest groups may establish close ties with the more familiar type of interest groups; this gives the one the aura of popular support and the other the appearance of official endorsement.

Somewhere between the two types of interest groups that we have discussed so far are the "corporatized" relations that have developed to a considerable extent in Europe between government and nongovernmental organizations. Because of their significance in the society, the government regularly consults with certain groups before taking action that would affect their interests; in some instances the procedure is formalized, and special boards are created with membership shared, for example, by representatives of the government, the leading unions, and the principal manufacturing organizations. This quasi-governmental status for these groups obviously gives them considerable opportunity to influence the government.

Curiously, we also need to mention under the heading of interest groups those segments of the population that hardly are organized at all. In this case, unlike our first type of group, people do not consciously come together to further a shared interest. Instead, they have something in common; they share certain characteristics. They belong to the group by virtue of what they are; they don't have to join anything. The influence of such groups on public policy often is more potential than explicit. In deciding what laws to pass, legislators may consider how certain segments of the society would react, even though no officer of such a group has sought to influence them.

Given the limited organization of such groups, their leaders tend to be self-appointed or created by the mass media. Howard Jarvis was widely recognized as the leader of the Proposition 13 tax revolt that swept out of California to crystallize opposition to government spending and support for lower taxes. Jarvis had developed some organization to assist his efforts in California, but he certainly had no national organization at all. Yet his pronouncements clearly influenced a number of legislators in various states and in Congress, because his efforts appeared to be responsible for California's adoption of Proposition 13. Thus he was a leader of the interest group of taxpayers, a group that was not organized in any systematic way on the national level.

Blacks provide another example of the unorganized interest group. Granted that some blacks, along with some whites, formed various groups, such as the NAACP, to further the shared interest of racial equality. The influence of blacks on public policy, however, extends beyond the efforts of such groups. The influence of Martin Luther King was based not simply on the fact that he headed an organized racial equality group—the Southern Christian Leadership Conference—but more on the willingness of the public to recognize him as a major voice for the unorganized interest group of the general black segment of the American population.

The point of all this is the wide variety of interest groups and the diversity of their means of contacting and influencing governmental officials. The common view that a lobbyist—an interest group agent calling on a legislator in an effort to affect the content of a law—totally encompasses the activity of interest groups is much too narrow an understanding.

Political scientists traditionally have distinguished one type of organized group activity for political purposes from all the other types—the political party. Parties obviously have a good deal in common with interest groups. The difference is that, while interest groups seek to win the support of governmental officials for their views, parties offer candidates in an effort to win control of the government so as to be able to make the policy decisions and supervise putting them into effect. This simple definition needs to be elaborated a bit more, however, to make clear the essential function of parties.

A democratic society has so many groups voicing their views and interests that voters cannot possibly examine the merits of all their proposals and decide which of them are preferable. The purpose of parties is to filter or weed out these proposals and then consider the interrelations of those remaining so that a coherent set of policy proposals emerges rather than a jumbled collection of proposals, each of which may be sound and desirable but which, taken together, are so contradictory that they cancel each other out. Parties simplify and focus policy issues so that voters are presented with a clear choice of alternative programs.

When we were discussing typologies, we noted that a frequently used one turned on the number of parties in a country. You can easily see that politics in a country where only one party legally may offer candidates and communicate with the citizens differs sharply from that of a country where two or more parties compete for support. But why distinguish between two-party and multiparty systems?

The truth probably is that political scientists knew too much about the politics of France, Germany, and Italy relative to what they knew about the politics of Scandinavia and the Low Countries. Looking at the former, they concluded that multiparty systems failed to perform the basic function of parties of focusing the political alternatives as well as did two-party systems, where alternatives had been simplified to only two. In practice this meant that in multiparty systems, no party was likely to control a majority of the seats in the legislature and, therefore, a coalition government would have to be formed. In parliamentary systems where, as discussed, the executive and legislative branches are fused rather than separated, the term *Government* is used to refer to the top leaders of the executive just as in the United States we refer to the president and other top officials collectively as the Administration. In a coalition government the cabinet—the body that includes the principal executive leaders—is composed of people from more than one party.

Obviously, these different parties agree on only some policies. Thus policy conflicts may develop among coalition partners and result in the Government resigning after a short time to be replaced by another tenuous coalition. Rapid turnover of the top executive personnel in this fashion is known as Government or cabinet instability. If the country's leaders are traveling around in a revolving door, they are unlikely to be effective in dealing with the country's problems and hardly can be expected to implement any program requiring a continuing commitment. Even if cabinet instability is avoided, the need for compromise among coalition partners may destroy all coherence in policy. Such a cabinet may implement a series of unrelated measures as it satisfies the desires of first one party and then another of those included in the coalition. Thus, although each party may have presented the electorate with a set of integrated proposals, only bits of each are enacted and no party is able to carry out its program. The voters' opportunity for a clear choice among alternatives is reduced.

Although these problems did occur in the French, German, and Italian multiparty systems earlier in this century, Scandinavian experience at the same time with multiparty systems contradicted any idea that they had to produce unstable, ineffective Governments. The key point was not so much the number of parties but their nature.

Parties may be pragmatic and work together well in devising a coherent compromise program or they may be rigidly dogmatic and refuse to cooperate with each other at all. The result in the latter case is likely to be either a weak and ineffective minority Government—one in which the parties in the cabinet hold fewer than half of the legislative seats—or a divided, and also ineffective, coalition.

Parties may be highly unified or simply loose collections of individuals and local or regional political machines. When parties are organized in this latter way—as the Democratic and Republican parties are—then it is hard to argue that a clear choice has been presented to the voters simply because they have the alternative of voting for one label or another. A multiparty system in which each party was relatively nonideological and highly unified would simplify and focus the policy issues at least as well, if not better, than a system involving two loosely cohering parties.

As you study parties you need to focus on four main aspects—doctrines and policies, supporters, strength, and organization. What does a particular party want to do—what views and actions does it want to make authoritatively binding on the entire population by having them sanctioned by government? Does it have a vision of totally transforming society and human nature or simply a list of preferred policies over which it is willing to bargain and compromise? Is it simply a personal following of an attractive leader and dedicated to attaining power largely for its own sake with little concern for one set of policies or another?

Once you have discovered this you will want to know to whom this type of party appeals. From what groups, segments of society, kinds of individuals does it get most of its support? Is it able, for example, to cut across the main social divisions of a society and thus help to moderate political conflict, or does it tend to reinforce and perpetuate existing divisions by drawing support from only one narrow segment? Are most of its adherents so bound to it by socioeconomic factors that they will continue to support it come what may? If this should be the case, the party may not be very responsive, since it would feel that it could count on continued support regardless of whether it attempted to ascertain or even listen to the policy preferences of its supporters.

Apart from the type of people to whom a party appeals, how many people are willing to vote for it, join it, donate money to it? Is the party just a minor fringe party with no hope of influencing the Government, to say nothing of controlling it, or is it one of the main competitors for political power? In most cases a party's strength is a good measure of its influence in the policy process.

While a party's organization is important because of its impact upon the party's strength, it deserves study in its own right as a crucial factor in governmental accountability—one of the basic democratic characteristics. The way that power is distributed within a party determines whether it can serve as a channel for communicating the views of political activists to the government or whether the leaders so dominate the party that communication is almost entirely from the top down, with party members serving simply to implement the leaders' views. Roberto Michels's Iron Law of Oligarchy maintains that the latter situation must necessarily prevail in all parties however democratic they claim to be. Should this be true, the policy-making process would be even more elite-dominated than it otherwise would be.

Whether you call such a political system democratic depends upon whether you feel that in a democracy people must have an influential role in the policy process and not just in the process of selecting leaders. Some argue that a system qualifies as a democracy so long as the people can select and remove the political elite. In this view the function of political parties is not to assist people in making policies, but to maintain competing sets of leaders who have been tested, apprenticed, and provided with political experience through the parties. The parties thus cultivate the conditions that make democratic politics possible.

Does this view, however, so restrict the scope of citizen political activity as to lose the essence of democracy? Furthermore, popular participation in politics has proven to be an important answer to the question we raised earlier: How do you get people to follow authoritative decisions voluntarily? If people have participated in the making of a decision, they may be more willing to accept the result even if they do not like the substance. They may feel that they had a fair hearing and since they were unable to convince enough others to support them, they should gracefully accept defeat for the time being. Also while participating they may have come to understand better the alternatives to their view and find that these and those who hold them are not so bad after all. Whether these benefits can be obtained when participation involves little more than deciding for whom to vote is questionable.

On the other hand, involving millions of people meaningfully in the policy-making process is a formidable task. No country yet has been able to devise political structures capable of doing this satisfactorily. Even in democracies popular participation in policymaking is limited.

Nonetheless, a society's arrangements for popular participation affect fundamentally the nature of its politics. You must investigate questions of the type we have been discussing to gain an adequate understanding of how accountable to the people is the government of any particular country.

GOVERNMENTAL STRUCTURES AND PROCESSES

Electoral systems, groups, parties: these are the principal structures through which people can support the governmental system and its agents and make demands upon them. The governmental structures are supposed to process these "inputs" and convert them into authoritative rules binding on the entire society. The separation-of-powers idea—well known to all high school civics students—encourages the belief that this process has three main subroutines: legislatures, with some help from the executive, make the rules; bureaucrats, under the direction of the executive, implement the rules; courts adjudicate the conflicts that arise under the rules.

Unfortunately for you, reality is not this simple, and we have a more complicated story to tell. The rules, the law—properly understood—is not just the formal statutes passed by a legislature but the entire body of binding rules for a society. Thus administrators and judges make law just as surely as do legislators. Legislatures often draft statutes in general language with the detailed provisions to be filled in by administrators, whose power to make rules thus is expanded. The vast expansion of governmental activities over the past several decades has given administrators the job of deciding to whom and in what circumstances laws shall apply, since statutes often are ambiguous and the severity of enforcement varies, as you will know if you have ever tried to talk your way out of a highway speed trap.

The power of courts to formulate authoritative rules is most obvious in a country such as the United States, where they have the power to void a rule made by the legislature by declaring it unconstitutional. But even in countries where courts lack this power, as in Britain, the fact that they must interpret the law to apply it to particular cases means that they constantly are deciding the specific details of the law.

Such specific or de facto delegation of legislative authority poses problems for democracy, for few judges and administrators are elected and most have permanent tenure except for malfeasance. How are these wielders of political power to be made accountable so as to attain responsible government? The elected and accountable legislature and executive have the job of surveillance and control of the administrators. In your study of any particular political system, you will need to discover whether the arrangements for doing this job provide sufficient power to control administrators without being so intrusive that efficiency is destroyed. Remember, everyone hates red tape; but red tape simply is the negative name for the procedures used to ensure that administrators are accountable.

In the case of the courts the matter is further complicated by the fact that no one in a democratic system wants to see the courts become partisan organs. Yet doesn't the strict independence of the judiciary threaten to insulate the judges from popular preferences so that all accountability is destroyed? Although right is not necessarily what the majority wants, yet a strong argument can be made that to a considerable extent the courts should follow the election returns.

Some countries use courts or quasi-judicial officials and procedures to try to control administrators. France, for example, in addition to the regular court system has a separate system of courts for the adjudication of conflicts arising from challenges to administrative action. Britain and a few other countries have established an ombudsman—an official to whom complaints about administrative action can be referred—to investigate whether citizens have been treated improperly in their contact with governmental officials. In either case the objective is to provide for people an opportunity for redress or appeal in situations where administrative power may have been abused.

The idea of using one governmental structure to control another is an element in both the separation-of-power and the fusion-of-powers systems, which we defined earlier under the labels of presidential and parliamentary systems. In the presidential, separation-of-powers system, the legislature can refuse to enact the program favored by the executive and may have some powers to block executive appointments. Neither branch of government may end the term of the other, however, simply because of a clash over policy preferences. Thus each branch has an element of independent power, which it can use to limit the action of the other. In the parliamentary, fusion-of-powers system, the legislature's power to control the executive extends to the ability to remove the executive from office simply because of a disagreement over programs and policies. In effect, the executive runs the government so long as it satisfies—retains the confidence of—its controller, the legislature.

In addition to these basic differences, legislative–executive relations are affected by the organization of the legislature. The rules of the procedure may facilitate the passage of laws and create few, if any, obstacles to enacting the executive's legislative program. Alternatively there may be, as in the U.S. Congress, a number of roadblocks providing ample opportunity for ambushing proposed policy. Legislatures may have extensive information-gathering facilities that enable them to examine executive actions knowledgeably, or they may be dependent upon the executive structures for expert knowledge with a consequent lessening of accountability.

The personal characteristics and political style of leaders are important factors as well. Charles de Gaulle was able to dominate the French legislature for many years not so much because of the power vested in the office of president of France as because of his personality, background, and operating procedures. No other political figure in France at the time would have dared to decide on his or her own authority the major issues de Gaulle often did.

How legislative–executive relations operate in practice and the extent to which systems of either basic type achieve the goal of making power accountable depends to a considerable extent upon the nature of the party system and the way in which parties operate in the legislature. Both this influence and that of leaders' personality make clear that important as the governmental structures themselves are, it is the system as it functions—the living body, rather than the bare bones of the skeleton—that matters most.

SYSTEM INSTITUTIONALIZATION AND DURABILITY

The fundamental purpose of the political system as it performs its basic function of making authoritative rules is to enable a society to adapt to, and thus cope successfully with, changes in its environment. To do this the political system itself must survive, must be durable. A political system with staying power is said to be *institutionalized*. This term means that its structures are valued for themselves rather than for the popularity of those who hold positions in them. The Nazi political system proved not to be institutionalized; it could not survive the death of Hitler (granted that losing the war also was a major factor). In the Soviet Union, however, the political system did survive the death of its founder Lenin.

When a system is institutionalized, the society tends to follow known, regular procedures in grappling with public problems. But because a society's environment constantly is changing, the commitment to these procedures has to be tempered with flexibility. Institutionalizing a system does not require engraving it in stone; such monuments are erected to the dead, not the living. A living system needs to be dynamically stable, needs to maintain itself by changing in accordance with established procedures to meet new conditions. Change in any other way becomes merely a contest of brute force and defeats the whole object of creating a political system, which is to make possible human self-government in a civilized fashion rather than an animal existence.

A system that fails to meet the challenge of its environment, that is able to satisfy only a few of the demands made upon it, may, nonetheless, endure for a time. Poor performance may be offset by legitimacy, that is, people may feel that the system is morally sound and conforms to the basic values of the prevailing political culture. Most parents don't throw their children out of the house for coming in an hour late fairly often.

But persistent severe malfunction can exhaust the supply of legitimacy, thus forcing a major overhaul of the system and threatening violence. To speculate about the prospects for a political system, you will need to have some idea of how much legitimacy it has in the bank, how institutionalized it is, in addition to knowing how well it is meeting the needs of its population.

Meeting popular needs might seem relevant to the durability only of democratic systems; after all, dictatorships can maintain themselves by force and don't need to worry about whether people are satisfied with the government. In some senses, however, repression is self-defeating—the more a government uses it, the more it is likely to need to do so. Repression destroys those feelings of legitimacy that are the best buttress for the political system. Without such feelings maintaining the system becomes a matter of force virtually all the time. While we are not suggesting that people armed with rocks can overthrow a regime armed with tanks, still successful dictatorships recognize that force has its limits. As you will see in the Soviet section of the book, the Communists killed many kulaks, but in the long run had to make considerable concessions to the Russian peasants.

The durability of the four political systems in this book should be of interest to you. Many Americans would like to see the Soviet political system collapse. Many of them, reflecting on the past history of political instability in Germany and France, can't believe that these systems really are institutionalized now and thus have some question about how desirable these countries are as allies. As for Britain, it may be the most disturbing of all. The stability of the British political system long has seemed to be a fact of life. The recent poor performance of the system, however, may have produced a run on the bank and left the balance in the legitimacy account dangerously low. And if even Britain faces stability problems, then, perhaps the United States cannot automatically assume that its political system is certain to continue unaltered.

In this Introduction we have indicated what are some of the main topics in the comparative study of political systems. We have pointed out how these topics relate to each other and why they are worth your study. Our aim was to give you an idea of what political scientists in comparative politics do and why.

Even more to the point, we wanted you to know what we are going to do in the rest of this book and why. The topics we have covered in this Introduction provide a general outline for the country sections that follow. Dealing with similar topics for each country makes comparing them easier and will permit you to generalize a bit—even though we will be studying only a handful of countries— about political practices and behavior. In this way you will be able to see which aspects of American politics are unique products of our particular culture and which are common across national boundaries.

We start first with the political system that, because of historical ties and language, is likely to seem less foreign to Americans. Following that we examine the contrasting systems of the other two major Western European powers. Then, to develop the contrast between the various forms of democracy and dictatorship, we conclude with a study of the Soviet Union.

BIBLIOGRAPHICAL NOTE

The following books are suggested as beginning reading for those who wish to pursue further the topics discussed in this section. We don't intend to provide an exhaustive bibliography.

For a general discussion of scientific method and scientific entities see Stephen Toulmin, *The Philosophy of Science: An Introduction* (New York: Harper & Row, 1960). Basic concepts and methods in the study of political phenomena are examined in Robert Dahl, *Modern Political Analysis,* 2d ed. (Englewood Cliffs, N.J.: Prentice-Hall, 1970). The aims and procedures of rigorous investigation in comparative politics are succinctly discussed by Harrow Scarrow in *Comparative Political Analysis: An Introduction* (New York: Harper & Row, 1969). For a functionalist framework for the analysis of politics see Gabriel Almond and G. Bingham Powell, Jr., *Comparative Politics,* 2d ed. (Boston: Little, Brown, 1978).

The basic characteristics of democracy and autocracy are examined in Robert Dahl, *A Preface to Democratic Theory* (Chicago: University of Chicago Press, 1956), and Carl Friedrich and Zbigniew Brzezinski, *Totalitarian Dictatorship and Autocracy,* 2d ed. rev. by Friedrich (Cambridge, Mass.: Harvard University Press, 1965). A rather abstract, theoretical discussion of the concept of the state can be found in Kenneth Dyson, *The State Tradition in Western Europe* (Oxford: Martin Robertson, 1980).

One of the best-known efforts to provide a framework for the comparative study of political parties is Maurice Duverger, *Political Parties,* trans. Barbara and Robert North, 2d ed. (London: Methuen, 1959). For most purposes this now has been superseded by Giovanni Sartori, *Parties and Party Systems* (Cambridge, Eng.: Cambridge University Press, 1976). Some of the basic issues in party structures and party systems are discussed in Leon Epstein, *Political Parties in Western Democracies* (New York: Praeger Publishers, 1967). A concise, clearly written, and rigorous study of the relation between party systems and electoral systems is Douglas Rae, *The Political Consequences of Electoral Laws,* rev. ed. (New Haven, Conn.: Yale University Press, 1971). For an analysis of the extent to which election results are influenced by issues and, therefore, the extent to which the electorate seeks to participate in policymaking through the electoral system see Ian Budge and Dennis J. Farlie, *Explaining and Predicting Elections: Issue Effects and Party Strategies in Twenty-Three Democracies* (London: Allen & Unwin, 1983). Electoral processes are compared in David Butler, Howard Penniman, and Austin Ranney, eds., *Democracy at the Polls: A Comparative Study of Competitive National Elections* (Washington, D.C.: American Enterprise Institute, 1981). The role of leaders is the focus of Robert Putnam, *The Comparative Study of Political Elites* (Englewood Cliffs, N.J.: Prentice-Hall, 1976).

The values and structures affecting political behavior are the concern of Richard Dawson and Kenneth Prewitt, *Political Socialization* (Boston: Little, Brown, 1969), and Lester Milbrath, *Political Participation* (Chicago: Rand McNally, 1965). The latter book makes a special effort to synthesize the results of previous research into a series of basic propositions. Stability and durability are among the concerns of G. Bingham Powell, Jr. in *Contemporary Democracies: Participation, Stability, and Violence* (Cambridge, Mass.: Harvard University Press, 1982).

Among the books dealing with particular governmental structures are Gerhard Loewenberg and Samuel Patterson, *Comparing Legislatures* (Boston: Little, Brown, 1979) and B. Guy Peters, *The Politics of Bureaucracy* (New York: Longman, 1978).

PART TWO

THE UNITED KINGDOM OF GREAT BRITAIN AND NORTHERN IRELAND

Tho' much is taken, much abides; and tho'
We are not now that strength which in old days
Moved earth and heaven; that which we are, we are;
One equal temper of heroic hearts,
Made weak by time and fate, but strong in will
To strive, to seek, to find, and not to yield.

Tennyson

1

The Setting of British Politics

THE INFLUENCE OF GEOGRAPHY

Perhaps it is the influence of Arthurian romance that once led someone to liken the British Isles to a castle surrounded by a moat. The image emphasizes three characteristics of Britain's geographical setting of basic importance to its politics—Britain is a small, maritime nation clearly separated from its most immediate political neighbors.

With a total land area somewhat in excess of 93,000 square miles the country is smaller than 10 American states, Oregon being the most comparable in size. From the northern tip of Scotland to the southern coast of England is just under 600 miles; California is one third again as long. Given an island of this relatively limited area, you will not be surprised to learn that you never are farther than 75 miles from tidal water anywhere in Britain or 110 miles from the ocean proper. Birmingham, located in what the British refer to as the Midlands, is only 95 miles from the sea.

Despite its small geographical size, Britain has a large population. Only a dozen countries exceed its total of 56 million. Most of the population—46.8 million—live in England, with 5.2 million residing in Scotland, 2.8 million in Wales, and 1.6 million in Northern Ireland.[1] Combining small geographical size

---

[1] The United Kingdom of Great Britain and Northern Ireland is composed of four nations. England occupies the bulk of the main island with Wales in the west central portion and Scotland in the north. Northern Ireland is composed of the six counties located in the northeastern tip of the island across the Irish Sea from Great Britain, the term used to refer to England, Wales, and Scotland as a group. The remainder of that island is the Republic of Eire or Ireland, which is completely independent from Britain. Although the United Kingdom of Great Britain

with a large population makes Britain one of the most densely populated countries in the world. It is considerably more densely populated than India and well over 10 times more densely populated than the United States. Furthermore, if England alone is considered—ignoring the more sparsely populated areas of Scotland—the population density exceeds 900 per square mile, far greater than that of Japan.

Associated with the density of population is high urbanization. More than four times as many people in England and Wales live in urban districts (one of

---

and Northern Ireland is the official name of the country we discuss in this section, the term *Britain* is accepted as correct for semi-official purposes and we will use it to refer to the entire political entity. We will refer to the people of the country as British or Britons. You just need to be sure that you do not call a Scotsman or a Welshman, English.

the subdivisions of local government) as in rural districts. Much more so than Americans, Britons are city dwellers. Yet curiously a single city is preeminent and dominates all the rest. London is the political, cultural, and commercial hub of the country; the center for these various activities is not split among a number of cities as it is in the United States. London is preeminent in size as well; an eighth of the entire British population lives in London, which with a population of nearly 7 million is the fourth largest city in the world. The second largest city in Britain—Birmingham—lags far behind with only slightly over 1 million population. And only four other cities exceed a half million.

High urbanization tends to strain governmental capabilities because of increased demands for services. Crime control, transportation, health and sanitation, food distribution, recreational facilities, and the like, which can be handled on a private basis when most people live in rural areas, become pressing public concerns when most people dwell in urban settings. Thus, whatever the political philosophy of the party in power, government must play a more activist, interventionist role in a highly urbanized society than it does in one that is more rural.

The smallness of Britain and the concentration of population in urban areas are a great aid to ease of communication, especially given the excellent rail network that has existed for many decades. A train ride of only an hour and a half takes you to Birmingham. A journey of two and a half hours and you can reach most of the principal English cities, including Exeter in the West Country (the peninsula that juts out into the Atlantic Ocean) and Manchester and Leeds to the north. Even Newcastle, about 45 miles from the Scottish border, can be reached in three and a half hours. And the newer, high-speed trains that make some of the runs can cut these times by about 20 percent.

The rail network enables England to have a national press, something that really has not developed in the United States. People who live in the north or west can read at breakfast the same newspaper, albeit an earlier edition, as do Londoners with their breakfasts. Thus the papers published in the capital city circulate widely throughout the country and help to nationalize opinion. Unlike the situation in the United States, there are no important English regional news media centers.

The smaller a country's area, the less likely to occur are regional differences in geography, climate, lifestyle, occupational structure, social relations. Add to this the national press that we have just mentioned and you sensibly could guess that Britons are likely to react to political events similarly regardless of where they live; you would not expect the contrasts in attitudes from one region of the country to another that you know to be common in the United States.

So great is the contrast with the American political setting in this regard that American students of British politics long have stressed the great homogeneity of Britain and the British people. Although true, compared to the United States, this point has been overemphasized. Customs, food preferences, speech patterns, and the like vary considerably even within England alone, and when Northern Ireland, Scotland, and Wales are considered as well, the contrasts are marked. We hope that you noticed that our comment about a national press referred to England, not to Britain. Most London-published papers can be obtained in Scotland, but their circulation is quite limited. The typical Glaswegian of whatever social class does not read the same paper as does his or her London counterpart. That Scotland has its own media significantly limits British homogeneity.

Granted that some regional differences have little or no political impact, others obviously do. In the late 1960s and the 1970s, political assassinations, bombings, riots, armed conflict between Protestants and Catholics, and extended use of troops to maintain order amply demonstrated that sectarian factors play a much greater role in politics in Northern Ireland than they do in the rest of the United Kingdom. In the rural parts of Wales printing election material in the Welsh language is not uncommon nor is speaking Welsh at campaign rallies. A thorough examination of Scottish political behavior has concluded that Scotland is a distinct political region in Britain, in part because class affected party preference less and religion affected it considerably more than was true in England.[2] During the 1970s the support for the Welsh and, especially, the Scottish nationalist movements, which want Wales and Scotland to separate from Britain and become independent countries, clearly demonstrated the regional diversity of British political patterns. And the results of the 1979 and 1983 general elections exhibited sharp contrasts in party strengths between the north and the south.

Thus while you, viewing things from the familiar perspective of American politics and culture, should see Britons as more alike in their political attitudes and behavior than are Americans, yet you also need to understand that Britons are far from being homogeneous. Despite the smallness of the country and a national press in England, political patterns vary, not only between England, Wales, Scotland, and Northern Ireland, but also between Yorkshire in north England, Cornwall in the west, and Surrey just south of London.

One British characteristic that encourages an American belief that the country is homogeneous is the absence of a sizable minority group. About 8 percent of the population is Catholic and less than 1 percent Jewish, each proportion being less than one third its size in the United States. The number of non-whites—called coloureds in Britain and including Indians and Pakistanis as well as Africans and West Indians—is difficult to ascertain precisely, but can't account for much more than 4 percent of the population. Nonetheless, "colour" has become an important issue in British politics, as we discuss more fully in the next chapter.

Britains reputation for stability derives in part from its geographical situation. Clearly separated from the continent, its boundaries have not altered a

---

[2]Ian Budge and D. W. Urwin, *Scottish Political Behavior: A Case Study in British Homogeneity* (London: Longmans, Green, 1966).

FIGURE 1-1   Travel Times by Regular Rail Service from London to Other Cities

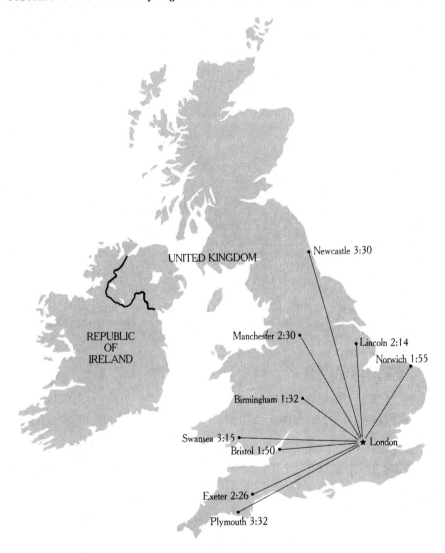

great deal over the years. Wales, which had been an English possession since 1284, formally was united with England in 1535. Scotland became part of the political system in 1707. This expansion of territory was digestible because the Scots assented to it, and the population of England and Wales was about six times that of Scotland. The addition of Ireland in 1800, however, proved to be a problem. Religious differences and economic exploitation, combined with an

Irish population half the size of that of Great Britain, meant that the union never worked. After a long process of violent struggle Ireland (except for the six northern counties) became independent in 1922. Traumatic as this experience was, it meant the loss of only about one tenth the population of the United Kingdom. Given the centuries involved, the changes have been few. The point about boundary stability is that it eliminates the need for major revisions of the political system to accommodate the addition of sizable new territories, and it avoids creating a disaffected or displaced minority if the addition (or subtraction, if the boundary change is a loss of territory) is the result of military action.

The 20-mile-wide English Channel has been a geographical feature of major importance. It has enabled Britain to escape complete involvement in many European wars and has saved it from invasion since the Norman Conquest of 1066. France and Poland, to mention only two examples, doubtless often have wished that 20 miles of water separated them from their neighbors.

The absence of land frontiers has meant that Britain usually has not sought to maintain a large standing army and has preferred instead to develop its navy (referred to in Britain as the Senior Service). In 1832, not many years after the Napoleonic Wars, Britain had only 11,000 troops, an army smaller than the Chicago police force in 1968. Consequently, through most of Britain's history, royal absolutism has been easier to combat than on the continent, for, although a navy is an important weapon in international relations, it is not much assistance in combating domestic challenges to governmental power. The deemphasis of the army also has helped to keep Britain free of the effect of militarism, which often has bedeviled continental politics.

Britain's maritime geographic position also was in large measure responsible for its commercial and military position. The discovery of the New World and the establishment of new trade routes via the Atlantic made Britain the center of world commerce. Industry, cities, and commerce grew apace. Trade and the need to control the waters around the British Isles for defense purposes went hand in hand. At the same time, Britain's dependence on sea power encouraged the growth of the empire. In short, the seas not only became commercial highways but also avenues that led to discovery, exploration, empire, and naval supremacy.

Given Britain's world role, isolationism has not been an important political position in modern British politics. Britain frequently intervened on the continent to maintain a balance of power that would not threaten it. Nonetheless, the British have remained aloof from the continent in some ways. When in the 1960s President Charles de Gaulle of France barred Britain from the European Economic Community (Common Market) with the observation that the British really were not European, there was an element of truth in his position. The British have not traditionally thought of themselves as being an integral part of Europe; they have felt that their history of stable government and gradually expanding liberties has demonstrated a political tradition and competence different from and superior to those of most continental nations.

Thus, on a purely physical level, the idea of a tunnel under the English Channel to connect Britain with the continent has made no headway despite having been discussed for over a century. If you enjoy the type of book known as alternate history, you will be fascinated to learn about the rash of books that appeared in Britain toward the close of the 19th century.[3] The first story of an invasion of Britain through a Channel tunnel (successfully by the Germans) appeared in 1876. From 1882 to 1883 at least eight books were published on this theme with the French usually being depicted as the invaders. While British imagination was running riot in this fashion, the French showed not the slightest interest, to say nothing of anxiety, in speculating about a British invasion of France. These "alarums" eventually blew over, although such stories continued to trickle out in Britain until 1901.[4]

On the political level, the tradition of aloofness from the continent helps to explain why the British have been so skeptical of the Common Market. Had it not been for 20 miles of water and the history associated with it, Britain almost certainly would have been a charter member. As it is, not only was Britain late in joining, but the idea of pulling out of the Common Market remains a hot issue in British politics. British public opinion in the EEC has fluctuated with the phases of the moon. At the start of the 1960s, two fifths favored British membership, one fifth opposed, and one third didn't know. At the start of the 1970s, one fifth favored, three fifths opposed, and one fifth didn't know. Nonetheless, Britain became a member in 1973. In 1975 a referendum was held (the first time such an outrageous innovation had been tried) on whether Britain should remain a member. Although one third of the electorate didn't bother to vote, among those who did the split was two to one in favor. By March 1980, however, opinion had shifted again and only 29 percent supported British membership, with 71 percent opposed. British views on the subject remain volatile. At times in the mid-1980s polls have found more people in favor of continued membership than against, while at other times the reverse has been true.

The British Government was driven to seek membership in the Common Market, despite the country's traditional aloofness, because of the importance of international trade to its economy. Moderate climate together with sizable acreages of good agricultural land enabled the British to produce a large part of their foodstuffs until about a century and a half ago. But as the country industrialized and its population grew, it began to import large quantities of food. Because of advances in ocean transportation and the unsuitability of much of the land for wheat in any case, many food products could be imported more economically than they could be produced domestically.

Furthermore, as the doctrine of free trade prevailed, tariffs were eliminated, and by the middle of the 19th century agriculture was little protected or encour-

---

[3]I. F. Clarke, *Voices Prophesying War 1763–1984* (London: Oxford University Press, 1966), pp. 109–13.

[4]On the other hand, the creator of Sherlock Holmes, Arthur Conan Doyle, published a story only a month before World War I favoring a tunnel. In his story Britain lost a war because a naval blockade of submarines cut off its food supply. Ibid., p. 103.

© King Features

aged. Only between World Wars I and II did British farmers again receive some tariff protection, and only during World War II was an elaborate farm subsidy system developed. As a result of these factors Britain is not self-sufficient in food production and must engage in international trade to feed its population. In addition, since it does not possess many natural resources other than coal and iron, it has to import raw materials for its industries.

Thus Britain's balance of payments is a crucial economic consideration. Selling sufficient manufactured goods to obtain the foreign currencies needed to pay for necessary imports of foodstuffs and raw materials is essential to national survival. Again the point is that whatever the political philosophy of the party in power, considerable intervention in economic affairs is likely to be necessary. Aside from any domestic problems that it might create, continued inflation always carries the danger that Britain will price itself out of its international mar-

TABLE 1-1 **Average Annual Percent Increase in GDP**

Period	Japan	Germany	Italy	Britain	United States
1960–70	10.4	4.4	5.5	2.9	4.3
1970–82	4.6	2.4	2.8	1.5	2.7

kets. Thus British Governments make frequent use of taxation, currency controls, export/import regulations, and similar devices to affect the domestic economy and alter consumption patterns.

Paradoxically, Britain's international trade position has been weakened in part by having been the pioneer of the Industrial Revolution. Coal, iron, good harbors, and urbanized population all helped to make Britain the first industrial nation. This was a major source of world power in the 19th and early 20th centuries. But it also has meant that British industry has hesitated to modernize manufacturing methods. Consequently much industrial equipment suffers from obsolescence, and modern management techniques have been little utilized.

Table 1-1 indicates how Britain's productive efficiency has lagged compared to some other key international economies. Those supporting British membership in the EEC hoped that the economies of scale involved in producing for a larger market and the heightened competitive challenge of no protection from the output of the continental economies would help to strengthen British industry. By the start of the 1980s this had come to seem a pretty forlorn hope or an outright delusion.

Double-digit inflation and balance of payments deficits made the economy Britain's most pressing problem of the 1970s. In 1967 British currency (the pound sterling) had to be devalued by more than 14 percent to the rate of £ = $2.40. In the mid-1970s the pound began an alarmingly rapid drop in value, and by 1976 was worth only about two thirds as much as it had been a decade earlier. Further declines in the mid-1980s reduced its value to just half of what it had been less than 20 years before. Adding to Britain's woes was the recognition that some surprising countries were bypassing it. Not only had West Germany and France long ago moved ahead of Britain with per capita incomes 75 percent and 55 percent greater, so that within the EEC only Italy and Ireland had lower figures than did Britain, but in the mid-1970s East Germany also moved ahead of Britain in per capita income and Czechoslovakia was only $140 per person behind.

Compounding the frustration was the fact that no matter what changed economically, the results continued to be bad. Toward the close of the 1970s Britain's oil fields in the North Sea began major production. Since the country moved rapidly toward self-sufficiency in oil, it was not affected as greatly as were many other countries by the huge increases in the prices charged by OPEC countries. This good fortune gave Britain a balance of payments surplus and greatly strengthened the pound. Fine, you might say if you were the British prime minister. But no, now it appeared that the pound was too strong, that it was overvalued compared to other international currencies and, as a result, British manufacturers had problems competing in foreign markets with goods from other countries.

Furthermore, the methods used to curb inflation, while reducing it somewhat, produced massive unemployment. After World War II unemployment in Britain typically had been about a half million. In 1976 it more than doubled to well over 1.2 million. By the mid-1980s well over 3 million were out of work, a greater number (although a smaller proportion of the labor force) than the record set at the beginning of 1933 in the depths of the international depression.

Little wonder that a Gallup poll in November 1984 found that over two thirds of the respondents regarded unemployment as the most urgent problem facing Britain. When asked which party they thought could best handle the country's most urgent problem, two fifths picked the Labour party, a quarter supported the Conservative party (the party actually in office), and 22 percent confessed that they didn't know. In other words, many Britons were beginning to believe no party could figure out any prescription for their economic ills.

Clearly, the problems and demands that confront the British political system and the way in which it responds to these are greatly influenced by the country's physical setting. Whereas in the past this setting has been a considerable asset in the political development of the country, it is by no means certain that this continues to be the case.

HISTORICAL BACKGROUND

The original population of the British Isles was not, as most people would think, Anglo-Saxon, but Iberian, a people widespread in Western Europe as far as the Caucasus. At an early date various Celtic groups invaded Britain; one was the forerunner of the Scots, another of the Welsh, and a third of the Irish. This was the population mixture that the Romans found when they invaded in A.D. 43.

Although the Roman occupation of Britain lasted about 400 years it had surprisingly little long-range effect upon British political institutions. The rugged Welsh and Scottish countryside prevented the Romans from dominating the entire island. In northern England and southern Scotland they simply built walls stretching across the countryside from one body of water to the other to keep the barbarians—as they regarded the native population—out. The Romans occupied Wales, but really did not settle it. Their presence was little more than a system of forts linked by good roads, and in the mountainous areas their control was tenuous. The area that now is England, however, the Romans settled except for the West Country, the bulk of the peninsula jutting out into the Atlantic Ocean. These differences in type of Roman presence contribute to the regional differences we have already noted.

As their empire crumbled under various barbarian invasions, the Romans were forced to withdraw all military forces from the British Isles and left the population to see to its own defenses. These people—Romanized Celts—were the Britons. With the Roman legions gone, the more militant Celts surged back from the fringe areas into which they had been driven. The Britons hired the Saxons, people living in what now is northern Germany, to help defend against this threat. The resultant upheavals—civil war among the Britons, rebellion by the Saxon mercenaries, and resurgence by the Celts—destroyed the culture that Roman rule had established.

Even before the Romans withdrew, Germanic raiders had been attacking along the coasts. These people—Angles, Saxons, and Jutes—capitalizing on the political chaos, gained control by around 600 of virtually the same areas that the Romans had dominated. The Britons retired in disarray to the fringe areas of the British Isles as any remnants of Roman civilization were destroyed. The significance of these events is that the English legal system did not develop as a Roman law tradition, as is true of the continental political systems, but became a common law system. (We will examine this contrast in more detail when we discuss the British judicial system.) So, in the end, about the only lasting contribution of the Romans to British life was a system of roads; few others were built in Britain during the 13 centuries following the Romans' departure.

The Germanic invaders proved to be more than just raiders, since they began to settle the country. Thus they provide the ethnic foundation of most of the people now living in the United Kingdom. That is to say, the Anglo-Saxons became what we now call the English, while the Celtic Britons became what are now the Welsh, Scots, and Irish. If you had any idea that the British were pure-bred, you can see how mistaken that was.

The Vikings, or Norsemen, got into the act also. Before 800 they began raiding Britain and in less than a century controlled a considerable portion of what now is northeast England. The struggles between the Saxons and the Danes surged back and forth—the Danes actually ruled the country from 1016 to 1042. This contest had not been totally resolved when another group of Norsemen intervened. The Viking raiders had terrorized the continent as well as the British Isles. To buy them off they were given territory in what now is France, an area called Normandy in recognition of their being North-men. These Normans crossed the Channel in 1066 to defeat the English at the battle of Hastings.

One of the reasons William the Conqueror, the Norman leader, was able to establish his rule was that the population of England and Wales was only 1.75 million—less than that of Minneapolis-St. Paul today. The importance of the Conquest lies first in the fact that it unified the country by eliminating the several different dukedoms into which it formerly had been divided. Thus a major step in the essential process of nation building was taken under William's centralized rule.

The other important result of the Conquest was to introduce the feudal system into England. Under the feudal system the rights as well as the duties of the nobility were specified. Although obligated to render certain services in exchange for the lands they were granted by the king, nobles also were to enjoy certain rights so long as they remained loyal. Should disputes arise concerning these rights and duties, they were to be settled in a council of the king and his leading lords. Thus the foundations were laid that eventually supported constitutionalism and parliamentary government.

The gains made under William's rule were almost lost in a period of virtual anarchy following his death. Eventually, however, central control was reexerted. Perhaps the most important fact of English history for several centuries was the country's ability to maintain a balance between feudal anarchy and tyrannical kingship. At any given moment one or the other might be ascendant, but equilibrium was achieved much more consistently than in any other European country.

This was not so much the product of wise rulers' policies purposefully directed toward such an end as it was the serendipitous outcome of variously motivated actions. For example, in the 12th century the Crown developed a policy of sending judges throughout the kingdom to settle disputes other than by resort to arms. The aim was to help unify the country and to increase central revenues by collecting legal fees. But the result was to lay the foundation for the common law, one of Britain's major contributions to constitutional government. In deciding the controversies presented to them, the itinerant judges tended to rely more on tradition, the customs of the local people, and precedent than upon formal edicts or statutes. This practice gave rise to the idea that the judges were bit by bit elaborating a "higher law" more valid than that embodied in any written legal code. This in turn suggested that The Law was above the king and that any rules that he made that clashed with it were unjust and invalid. The concept of limited, or constitutional, government developed from such thinking.

One of the leading governmental structures in controlling royal power was Parliament. Lacking sufficient revenue to finance his policies, King John decided in 1213 to tax the lower nobility, who had not had to bear this burden previously. Since, unlike the higher nobility, there were too many of them to summon them all to the Great Council that would approve the tax, John ordered that a limited number of knights be chosen to attend to represent the many holding such a title. This was the initial step in representative government, since until that time those who participated in the decision-making process were included simply because of their personal eminence and spoke only for themselves. Later in the same century the brief parliament of the rebel Simon de Montfort called representatives of the townspeople as well as of the knights. This practice was legitimated in 1295 when a legal ruler, Edward I, repeated it.

From these feeble beginnings a body of representatives known as Parliament was established. It had very little authority, was not popularly elected, and met only when the king called it. Sometimes several years passed between meetings. Moreover, it was not really a legislature but served as a kind of high court of justice concerned with judicial and administrative matters. The commoners from the counties and the boroughs were not permitted to meet with the monarch and nobles and take direct part in making decisions. In time the gathering of those representing the commoners was allowed to present grievances to the monarch. But not until the 14th century were they told to elect a speaker (to communicate their collective decisions to the monarch) and not until the reign of Henry V (1413–22) did they begin putting their petitions in the form in which they wished them enacted, thus initiating a crude legislative process.

Parliament had not been intended to be a means of controlling the monarch's government. Gradually, however, this is what it came to do. This process developed further as the House of Commons acquired the right of originating all bills for raising or disbursing revenue. This made the support of the Commons essential to the Crown.

Nonetheless, Charles I attempted to rule without Parliamentary support and declined to call Parliament into session from 1629 to 1640. Such high-handed government, which was characterized by illegal taxation, martial law, and arbitrary imprisonment, combined with religious conflict between Protestants and Anglicans to culminate in a civil war during the 1640s. The king was executed, and the monarchy was replaced by a republic, which tended to be an autocracy under General Oliver Cromwell. With Cromwell's death the regime disintegrated, because of factional conflict within the army, and the monarchy was restored. This period of little over a decade more than three centuries ago is the only experience England has had with republican government. The dearth of achievements during that time is one reason why few people in Britain today favor abolishing the monarchy.

The rule of James II raised again the questions of whether Britain was to be a Catholic or a Protestant country and whether ultimate power was to reside with the monarch or with Parliament. In 1688 James was driven from the throne in a bloodless revolution, and Parliament invited his Protestant daughter Mary and her husband William to become monarchs. Since Mary was not the immediate heir to the throne, Parliament had demonstrated its power to determine who the monarch would be. By accepting Parliament's offer, William and Mary were acknowledging its supremacy.

Thus at a time when continental European feudal kingdoms were turning into absolute monarchies, feudal limitations on the royal prerogative in England were developing into parliamentary restrictions on the exercise of Crown powers. The crucial question was whether the monarch could make laws on his or her own without supporting action by Parliament. The Civil War confirmed that the monarch was not above the law and that the common law could be amended only in Parliament. Since 1689 no monarch has challenged the supremacy of Parliament.

This doesn't mean that after 1689 the monarch lost all governmental influence. On the contrary, several of the monarchs were powerful. They had to depend upon Parliament, however, for funds and to determine what would be the law. Nonetheless, the long-term development of the monarchy since 1689 has been a peaceful decline in power and influence.

Parliamentary supremacy meant that the monarch would have to govern through political leaders—ministers—who were acceptable to Parliament. William sought to reduce problems with the House of Commons during conflict with France (which was supporting the deposed James II) by giving some of the principal governmental offices to four leaders having a sizable following in the Commons. Eventually, such maneuvering developed into the practice of selecting the chief ministers exclusively from the party or faction able to control the Commons. While these ministers were supposed to assist the monarch, yet the advice they could give was affected by the views of the group they led in the Commons. Until these groups developed into political parties, the monarch could play one faction off against another, but could not prevail against a united majority in the Commons.

The monarch's small group of chief advisors became known as the Cabinet. During the 18th century the monarch stopped meeting with them as a group. While this temporarily reduced the power of the Cabinet, the ministers remained significant. Since they, as well as the monarch, had to sign all official acts, they came to be regarded as responsible for them.

In the end the Cabinet became, in effect, the executive committee of the party with a majority in Parliament. As the power of the House of Lords declined in the second half of the 19th century and on into the 20th, the political situation in the House of Commons became the more important. The Cabinet's policies could only be those that could command support there. Cabinets advised the monarch what actions their party would accept. The monarch could not take some other action since there would be no majority in Parliament for this, and the result would be the constitutional crisis of monarch defying Parliament that led to the revolution of 1688.

As power within Parliament shifted from the Lords to the Commons, the Commons also became more democratic. Beginning in 1832, in a process that extended for almost a century, Britain permitted more and more of the population to choose the members of the Commons. Thus the country's political leadership became more accountable to the people.

Political parties developed primarily along with the expansion of voting rights. The Whigs and Tories of the 17th century can be called parties only in the loosest sense, since they were little more than factions, based more on personal connections than on shared policy preferences. But they began the process of developing the unified leadership and definite principles that were to characterize their successors. Not until the 19th century, however, did a modern party system, resting on extensive grassroots organization and coherent programs of policies, appear.

At several points in this brief summary of British political history we have noted that a certain basic reform occurred gradually in stages and without each change being consciously planned. We want to stress how important this evolutionary process has been in giving Britain continuity in its political development and a durable political system. The sharpest break in this history was the English Civil War and the republican form of government that resulted from it. But this proved to be only a brief hiatus with little lasting effect. The point is that in Britain, unlike many other nations, reforms have been neither sharp nor sudden. As a result they have won acceptance more readily and seldom have produced enduring extreme political cleavages.

Recently, however, British historians have tended to emphasize the discontinuities, the breaks in British historical development. While British history can't be graphed as an ascending straight line, its development is less jagged than French or American history. British history lacks major watershed events that compare, for example, with the French Revolution. Furthermore, despite periods of reversal or stagnation, British history exhibits a long-term trend toward greater control over governmental power, a trend toward increased responsibility or accountability to the people.

This trend continued until about the half century from 1870 to 1920. During that period several events occurred that suggested that this long-term development may not just have taken a temporary downturn, but may have been reversed. Ironically this apparent reversal occurred during the period in which, in terms of extending the right to vote, democracy was fully realized. We will discuss the factors involved in this paradox in the following chapters. We'll also be looking at the events of the last few years that hint at a move back toward popular accountability, that suggest that the period of greatest accountability in British politics is not passed.

BIBLIOGRAPHICAL NOTE

For a compendium of information on a wide variety of aspects of British life see *Britain [year]: An Official Handbook* (London: HMSO, published annually). Detailed statistics on various social and economic matters appear annually in *Social Trends* (London: HMSO). Geographical contrasts in social and economic conditions are emphasized in B. E. Coates and E. M. Rawstron, *Regional Variations in Britain* (London: Batsford, 1971).

The standard source for British history is the various titles in the Oxford History of England series. Also distinguished is the History of England series published by Longman. Paul Johnson provides an idiosyncratic, but stimulating interpretative overview in *The Offshore Islanders* (London: Weidenfeld & Nicolson, 1972). An even more respected interpretation, which is very well illustrated, is Asa Briggs, *A Social History of England* (London: Weidenfeld & Nicolson, 1983).

2

The Foundations of British Politics

CONSTITUTIONAL ELEMENTS AND PRINCIPLES

As the previous chapter has shown, restraints or limitations on government power have been a feature of British politics for some time. Restraining political power is the essence of constitutionalism. Not only are the powers given government limited, but those that it does possess are to be exercised according to stated rules or principles, not according to the whim of the power-holder. Thus constitutionalism is a matter of both substance and procedure.

Do not confuse constitutionalism with democracy. A country can have a constitutional system without being democratic, that is, the government's powers and procedures may be limited, but the people may have little say in selecting those who decide policy for the country. This, in fact, was exactly the British situation until about the middle of the 19th century.

At this point we are going to discuss the formal, legal limitations on the government, rather than the political restraints growing out of popular values (that is the latter part of this chapter) or involved in the electoral process (that is the first part of the next chapter). Truthfully, however, distinguishing the formal constitutional limitations from the informal political restraints is harder to do in Britain than anywhere else. The limitations do not derive from guarantees in a constitution the way you know they do in the United States. Britain does not have a constitution—that's right, pick up any textbook on U.S. government and turn to the back and there it is, the Constitution; do the same with a text on British government and you will find nothing. Imagine, no Founding Fathers, no original constitutional convention (or, alternatively, just to confuse you a bit, Britain has a permanent, continuing constitutional convention).

Clearly, something is not quite right here. It is not that Britain really does not have a constitution; it is just that it has an unwritten one. That explains everything, right? Not really, since an unwritten constitution sounds rather like a liberal Nazi—a contradiction in terms. What this means is that Britain does not have a single, framework document that allocates power and functions among the various organs of government, prescribes procedures for making decisions, and establishes limits on governmental action. But this does not mean that such limits, prescriptions, and allocations do not exist.

By now you may be expecting us to say: Yes, Virginia, there is a constitution. Unlike Santa Claus, however, the British unwritten constitution is more than just a state of mind. It is composed of four basic elements, only one of which is not actually written. The four are: historical documents, acts of Parliament, judicial decisions, and conventions of the constitution.

Heading the list of historical documents is Magna Carta (1215). This Great Charter was not the result of a popular revolution (how un-English that would have been) and, frankly, contained little that was new at the time. A handful of barons forced King John to sign what they regarded as primarily a statement of existing feudal law in the hope that the king would feel honor bound to stop abusing their rights by autocratic rule. (The English always have placed great faith in signatures on pieces of paper, as Prime Minister Neville Chamberlain showed in his dealings with Adolf Hitler in the late 1930s.)

So what importance does this little skirmish have centuries later? Magna Carta is a constitutional landmark, first, because it contributed to the idea that the monarch was not above certain principles of law and, should he or she disregard them, the nation had the right to force him or her to follow them. Second, although the chief motivation that produced the charter was to protect the barons' privileges, some of its provisions went further—the towns were guaranteed their ancient liberties—and breathed a spirit of basic fairness: "to no one will we sell, to no one will we refuse or delay, right or justice." Third, such provisions and spirit encouraged Britons over the centuries to invoke Magna Carta whenever they felt that a monarch was exceeding royal authority. Thus, totally apart from its specific provisions or original purpose, it has come to serve as the perfect embodiment of constitutionalism. Other historical documents play a similar role, although they cannot match the prestige attaching to Magna Carta because of its great age.

Turning to the second element, not every act of Parliament becomes part of the constitution. Only statutes dealing with fundamental matters such as the distribution of power among various governmental organs, the procedures for making authoritative decisions, or the basic rights of the people are included. Among the acts of Parliament typically considered part of the constitution are the Reform Acts, which extended voting rights, and the Parliament Acts of 1911 and 1949, which reduced the powers of the House of Lords. We say "typically considered part" because nothing explicity distinguishes such constitutional legislation from other laws. Nothing in the statute itself says anything about amending the constitution and no special procedures, such as the extraordinary majorities required in amending the American Constitution, are involved.

Judicial decisions, the third element, form part of the constitution despite the fact that no British court has the power of the U.S. Supreme court to declare laws unconstitutional. Nonetheless, judges must interpret the law as they apply it to the cases that come before them; when these cases involve the same fundamental matters we noted in connection with constitutional statutes, then the judges are modifying the constitution. Their role can be significant because of the tradition that in matters of basic liberties they will interpret the law as narrowly as possible so as to preserve basic rights.

Important as these judicial interpretations are, judicial decisions make an even greater contribution to the constitution through the common law. The common law, one of the world's most influential law systems, is a body of legal rules and principles deriving from judicial decisions, which developed apart from any action by Parliament. Early in English history judges often were presented cases that did not come under any of the statutes enacted by the monarch and Parliament. Since these cases had to be decided to prevent people from taking justice into their own hands, judges looked for a fair solution in the customs and values of the local community. (Centuries later the U.S. Supreme Court, in essence, suggested that the same approach should be used in dealing with pornography.)

As we told you in the previous chapter, these judges were itinerant, sent out by the king to travel throughout the country establishing law and order by deciding conflicts. From time to time these travelers would return to London and get together and discuss their interesting experiences. When, in their subsequent travels, they encountered a case similar to one they had heard about in their London conversations, they were likely to settle it the same way another judge had said he had done. Thus the elaborate body of legal rules that developed was common not only because it was based on the practices of the commoners—the people—but also in that it became uniform throughout the country.

The development of the common law was aided by the medieval notion that law was divinely ordained. Thus governments did not make law, but were only to discover God's law and state it explicitly. (While common law sometimes is referred to as judge-made law, to distinguish it from the statutes passed by a legislature, the judges who developed the common law would have rejected any thought that they were making law.)

Note that the common law was written down—just as were the other two elements of the British unwritten constitution that we have discussed so far, historical documents and fundamental statutes. The records of the various courts would state what judges had decided and why. What didn't exist was any coherent summary of the various cases in a topic-by-topic form. As you can guess, someone eventually got the bright idea that, yes, such a summary might perhaps be of some use now and again. Noted jurists, such as Glanville, Coke (pronounced Cook), and Blackstone, attempted to summarize all the decisions courts had made on a particular subject and a similar set of facts. These collections, or commentaries, as they usually were called, served to "codify," that is, to make uniform and systematic, much of the common law. It is in this body of legal practice and comment that most guarantees of British civil rights are rooted. For that matter, the same can be said about American rights. When the Fifth and Fourteenth Amendments to the U.S. Constitution say that you cannot be put in jail without due process of law, the required procedures are those stemming from the common law.

Conventions of the constitution—the fourth element—are basic practices or traditions; in the United States we would refer to custom and usage. While most of these conventions are not written, this is not the key element in distinguishing them. The basic criterion is whether a particular practice is enforceable, whether it can be the basis for a legal judgment. If so, then the practice is common law rather than a convention. For example, the principle of *stare decisis*—that courts will decide a current case according to the rulings made in previous similar cases—is common law. So also is the supremacy of Parliament—that any law passed by the legislature is valid and cannot be declared unconstitutional—since the courts enforce it. Practices that the courts do not enforce are conventions.

The mere fact that something has been done a certain way for some time does not by itself create a convention, even though the importance of being ancient is high in Britain. A traditional practice also needs logical and normative support; that is, doing things this way makes sense and people feel bound to continue the practice. For example, if the monarch refused to accept as prime minister the person preferred by a majority of the House of Commons, the government could not function, since no other person would have the support necessary to get any legislation approved by the Commons. Thus it is logical and sensible for the monarch to accept the Common's choice. The prime minister must have a seat in the House of Commons not because the law says so, but because it is felt in the 20th century that it would be wrong for him or her to be in the nonelective House of Lords. The prevailing democratic political values provide normative support for this practice and help to make it a convention.

Being used to a formal Constitution with a Bill of Rights, you may not regard the British constitution as offering much protection for basic liberties. Especially is this likely when you recall that the second of the four elements means that Parliament can amend the constitution at will the same way it passes ordinary legislation. (That is why we said earlier that you could think of Britain as having a permanent, continuing constitutional convention.) Frankly, in recent years some Britons have become concerned about this matter as well. Talk about the need for some sort of written bill of rights that could not be altered by Parliament has become common. Part of this concern is politically motivated; some of those on the right of the political spectrum fear that the next time Labour comes to power it might do fearsome things. They fear that if Labour abolishes the House of Lords, as it has said it wants to, then there would be nothing to check a left-wing majority in the Commons.

This probably is an excessively alarmist view. We would argue that basic liberties are at least as firmly grounded in Britain, despite its unwritten constitution, as they are in the United States. As you will see in the section of this book on the Soviet Union, written catalogues of rights do not automatically guarantee anything. The U.S. Constitution could not prevent a strong, determined group from establishing a dictatorship in this country. The success or failure of such an attempt would depend on the public's response. Ultimately, written constitutions, like the British unwritten one and its conventions, rest upon political, not legal, sanctions and supports. Limited government, fair play, and justice are beliefs and values of long standing in the British political culture.

The concern, however, is that this may be changing. Not all of the talk about a bill of rights is the knee-jerk reaction of Colonel Blimps—the British term for right-wing, extremely stuffy traditionalists who believe that nothing should ever be done for the first time. The head of one of Britain's leading public opinion polling firms expressed it this way a few years ago to one of the authors of this book. What has disappeared from Britain, he said, is the idea of "not done," the idea that limits on behavior were perceived to exist and were accepted widely throughout the population, not because one would go to jail for breaking them but because it simply was not proper to do so. This change could be hailed as a new birth of freedom, as a casting off of outdated inhibitions. But it also does raise serious questions about the means of social control. It helps to explain why some people in Britain feel that the time has come to start writing down some of the things that everyone knows, because it now is the case that everyone does not know them.

We are not about to apply for the job of drafting a constitution for the British; however, we would like to give you a summary of the basic constitutional principles. But understand that, given the nature of the British constitution, we cannot provide a comprehensive list that would be accepted by all experts.

1. Liberty of the Citizen.   The rule of law prevails in Britain. This means, among other things, that the government is not above the law; it cannot do whatever it pleases but must be able to cite legal authorization for its actions. All citizens are equal before the law. Convictions for breaking the law must conform with due process; torture, for example, may not be used to secure confessions. The law must be publicly known in advance before it is enforced.

2. Democracy.   As we noted previously, this principle is distinguishable from liberty. It is concerned not so much with seeing that citizens' right to fair treatment is not transgressed as it is with providing an opportunity for them to participate in authoritative decision making. The government is to do what the majority, not the minority, desire. In Britain, as in most mass democracies, this means primarily universal suffrage supported by the ability to form parties and pressure groups and to communicate with one's representatives.

3. Parliamentary Supremacy.   The ultimate legal authority in Britain is Parliament. Since Parliament can alter the constitution at will, its actions never can be declared unconstitutional by any court in the land. All acts of Parliament are legally valid.

4. Constitutional Monarchy.   It follows from principles 1 and 3 that the British monarchy must be a constitutional, limited one rather than an arbitrary or autocratic one. Since the rule of law prevails and Parliament holds final power, the monarch is restrained. Thus, although a hereditary monarch continues to reign over Britain, the occupant of this position does not rule, as we will discuss more fully in a later chapter.

5. Unitary Government.   Unlike the United States and Germany, Britain is not a federal system. In Britain the local governmental units owe their power and existence to Parliament, which can alter them at will. This relation clearly is associated with principle 3, that Parliament is the final authority. Unitary government in Britain was qualified slightly until 1972 by the existence of a separate parliament in Northern Ireland. This body passed domestic legislation for Northern Ireland, although its actions could be supplemented or overridden by the national Parliament meeting in London. In 1972 the Northern Ireland parliament was suspended because of sharp religious conflict between Catholics and Protestants there, and London assumed direct rule.

The increasing strength of the Scottish and Welsh nationalist parties in the 1970s motivated the Labour Government to introduce devolution legislation in Parliament late in 1976. Directly elected assemblies were proposed to be created for both Scotland and Wales. The Welsh assembly was to be limited mainly to supervising administration in Wales, but the Scottish assembly was to be empowered to legislate for Scotland on a wide variety of subjects.

Eventually, in 1979, referenda were held on the devolution proposals. In Wales the proposals were rejected decisively; 80 percent of those voting said no. In Scotland, however, the results were ambiguous. While almost 52 percent of those who voted were in favor of the proposals, 37 percent of those eligible to vote stayed home. Thus only 32.5 percent of the registered Scottish electorate favored the proposals. Turnout was a crucial factor because the opponents of the proposals had amended the legislation authorizing the referenda to provide that the proposals would have to receive the support of 40 percent of the electorate to be put into effect. Therefore, the proposals had to be abandoned, and the question of devolution has been in abeyance ever since. Even had the reform been implemented, it would only have delegated some central power to the subnational level. Britain would have remained a unitary system, not a federal one, since the powers delegated could have been reclaimed by the central government whenever it wished, regardless of the views of the regional government.

6. Parliamentary Government/Cabinet Government.   Unlike the United States, Britain has a fusion, rather than a separation, of powers. The executive structures are not separated from the legislature, but in their origin and maintenance are intertwined with it. Parliamentary supremacy—principle 3—clearly implies the existence of a dependent, rather than an autonomous, executive. The principle of constitutional monarchy is relevant as well, since the Cabinet system has helped to avoid conflict between the monarch and the Parliament. The Cabinet has served as something of a buffer or mediator between the ruler and those political leaders empowered to make authoritative rules for the society. Britain's system is characterized as Cabinet Government also because in the 20th century the Cabinet has become the most powerful element in the British political system. This means, as we will discuss more fully in subsequent chapters, that while Parliament legally is supreme, in practice the Cabinet usually is.

7. Party Government.   If parliamentary government is to produce stable cabinets, well-organized, disciplined parties are essential. The life of British Cabinets was much more tenuous when political groups were based on personal attachments rather than party loyalty. Furthermore, it is difficult to conceive of political process in a mass democracy—principle 2—which would not give rise to a fairly well-developed party system to channel and stimulate demands for governmental action.

BASIC VALUES: UNITING AND DIVIDING

While the values and procedures enshrined in a country's constitution obviously are immensely important, equally crucial, as our discussion of whether the British unwritten constitution can protect liberties suggested, are the values in the hearts of the people and their typical behaviors. We are not going to describe for you the typical Englishman (someone you might envision to resemble Alistair Cooke, unless, heaven forbid, you think everyone in Britain looks like someone from "Monty Python's Flying Circus" or "The Goodies"). This would be the discredited national character approach that deals in stereotypes and prejudices. There may not be a single Briton alive who holds all the values we are about to discuss. What we want to do is to familiarize you with some of the political values and attitudes, each of which is widespread in Britain, however diverse may be the various combinations of them from one individual to the next. As discussed in the Introduction, political culture—the values and attitudes concerning government and politics that are common in a country—varies a great deal from one country to another and greatly influences the way in which the legal, constitutional structures actually function in practice.[1]

Americans tend to think of the British as being very proper and sedate; visualize an Englishman and you can almost hear "Pomp and Circumstance" begin to play. If that is your view, we have a few surprises for you. Prior to the 19th century, Europeans pictured the English as a volatile nation of brawlers (Euro-

---

[1]Gabriel Almond and Sidney Verba, *The Civic Culture* (Boston: Little, Brown, 1965), pp. 30–35, 41–44. Gabriel Almond and Sidney Verba, eds., *The Civic Culture Revisited* (Boston: Little, Brown, 1980), pp. 26–32. 398–409.

peans who have encountered Britons more recently at international soccer matches probably still hold that view). Even in the 19th century lawlessness was at a level we find hard to believe now. When the House of Commons ends its business each night, the policemen on duty pass through the building voicing the traditional cry, "Who goes home?" The origin of this quaint custom was all too serious. As recently as a century and a half ago one was so likely to be mugged on the London streets at night that police escorts had to be formed to get members of Parliament safely home.

But what of political, as distinct from criminal, violence? The Houses of Parliament were destroyed by an accidental fire in 1834. One of the reasons that they were rebuilt in the same place, according to one of the leading political figures of the day, Robert Peel, was "the facility which the [River] Thames offered for escaping from inflamed mobs."[2] Incidents of violence and riots accompanied the widening of the right to vote at the start of the 1830s, and the violence both practiced by and upon the women suffragists in Britain exceeded that which occurred in the United States.

How did such a people ever get a reputation for being sedate? The British response to two major historical events that occurred little over a half century apart is the answer. When France was convulsed with a revolution toward the close of the 18th century—a revolution that claimed to be advancing the cause of the oppressed everywhere without regard to national boundaries—British society and its political system remained intact and unaltered. It would be as though Canada had a bloody communist revolution and we hardly noticed. Similarly, in the middle of the 19th century, revolutions swept the continent but had little impact on Britain. Out of such responses grew the British reputation for political stability and decorum.

While this reputation has been overstated, we wouldn't want you to think that it is completely false. Compared to a country in which any psychotic can buy a gun for less than a day's pay, walk to within 10 feet of the president, and shoot him, Britain is remarkably less violent. The number of murders in New

---

[2]Quoted in M. H. Port, ed., *The House of Parliament* (New Haven, Conn.: Yale University Press, 1976), p. 20.

York City alone in a single year is well over one and a half times the number in all of the United Kingdom. In Britain 1.3 murders occur each year for every 100,000 people; in the United States, 9.7. Furthermore, since guns are tightly controlled, less than 10 percent of all murders are shootings, and only about 7 percent of all robberies involve guns. This is despite the fact, or perhaps because of it, that the British police, except for rare, specially authorized circumstances, do not carry guns. Nonetheless, in the decade ending in 1974 only 11 policemen were killed throughout all England and Wales.

This low level of violence carries on over into the sociopolitical sphere also. Since 1842 only nine people have died in political demonstrations, riots, or industrial confrontations in Britain. No one has died in an industrial confrontation since 1911, and not a single person was killed in a riot from 1919 to 1974.[3] It is true that a British prime minister once was assassinated—back in 1812.

The British have little sympathy for extreme forms of political action.[4] While sizable majorities approve of signing petitions and participating in lawful demonstrations, less orthodox behavior is less acceptable—only 47 percent, for example, approve of boycotts. Even relatively innocuous action such as blocking traffic—82 percent against—is widely opposed. As for real violence, 62 percent strongly disapprove of damaging property and 67 percent strongly disapprove of personal violence; 97 percent say that they would never do either for political purposes.

On things that really matter, the British are a very law-abiding people. Related to this is an attitude toward the police in sharp contrast to the one that prevailed in the United States in the 1960s and 70s. Eighty percent approved of the courts giving severe sentences to protestors who disregard the police, and 73 percent approved of the police using force against demonstrators.[5] When people were asked to rate the honesty and ethical standards of people in various occupations, doctors led the list—73 percent giving them high marks—but police officers were next—51 percent rating them high.[6] By contrast, only 17 percent had this view of business executives. Even more surprising, people about the same age as you—those 15 to 24—had a similar positive view. When they were asked which two or three groups on a list of occupations they had the most respect for, 79 percent mentioned doctors and 54 percent the police.[7] Only a quarter of them cited teachers.

---

[3]Richard Clutterbuck, "Threats to Public Order in Britain," paper presented at the 1977 meetings of the Political Studies Association of the United Kingdom, p. 6.

[4]*Gallup Political Index,* Report No. 290, October 1984, pp. 17–18. Similar results were obtained in another poll a decade earlier. See Alan Marsh, *Protest and Political Consciousness* (London: Sage Publications, 1977), p. 45. Note that Marsh uses these figures and others in his analysis to argue that Britons are more receptive to unorthodox political behavior than our use of figures to discuss opposition to violence might suggest.

[5]Ibid., p. 61. When the same question was asked during the prolonged miners' strike in 1984, only 53 percent approved. *Gallup Political Index,* Report No. 291, November 1984.

[6]Market & Opinion Research Internation (MORI) poll taken in February 1980.

[7]MORI poll taken in August 1979.

While Britons' support for the police seems high, it probably has declined in recent years. It used to be thought that the British police were absolutely incorruptible, but lately cases have come to light of police corruption and abuse of authority. Thus while at the start of the 1980s 71 percent of those having had dealings with the police were very or fairly satisfied, 48 percent of all respondents believed that there now were more corrupt policemen than there used to be (only 29 percent disagreed, since 23 percent saw no change or had no opinion).[8]

Nonetheless, 62 percent said that the last time they had talked with a policeman, he had been friendly and only 4 percent said he had been rude or unfriendly.[9] Even a majority (53 percent) of those 18 to 24 said the policeman had been friendly. Furthermore, only a 10th distrust the police a fair amount or a lot, with only 16 percent of those 18 to 24 having such views. A substantial majority of those middle-aged and older strongly agreed that the British police still were the best in the world. More than a third of those 18 to 24 took the same view with nearly another third tending to agree, so that even among those most likely to have an unpleasant experience with the police two thirds accepted the statement to one degree or another. Finally—and this is really the acid test—nearly two thirds said they would be pleased for their son to become a policeman and only 13 percent would be displeased.

As our comments about attitudes toward unorthodox political behavior and the police suggest, the British in some senses—and attitudes toward political change is one of these—are rather conservative. By this we do not mean that they are right wing in matters of international affairs, economic policy, and moral standards, but simply that tradition is very important in British politics. That something has been done a certain way for some period of time is accepted frequently as sufficient reason for continuing to do it that way.[10] At the very least, it is a strong argument for regarding proposed changes warily and examining them thoroughly. The British, unlike most Americans, do not believe as a matter of faith that the newest always is best. Furthermore, when a case can be made for change, the British prefer to do it gradually, bit by bit over a period of some time.

British preference for the piecemeal approach is related to their taking a more pragmatic than ideological approach to politics. If an ideological approach is defined to include not just thinking about politics in terms of a left-

---

[8]MORI poll taken in February 1980.

[9]MORI poll taken in January 1982.

[10]The political correspondent for *The Guardian,* one of Britain's leading papers, has commented: "Ask the British why they go about things in a certain way and they will examine themselves in great detail, search down into the roots of their long modern experience, and arrive at the conclusion that they do things a certain way because they have always done them that way. The tried is nearly always preferred to the untried, time is much honored; the British pay visits to the past and discover that it works . . . change, even when, as recently, it may be quite rapid and radical, is usually accomplished by sleight of hand. Tradition is viewed not as inimical to change but as the sound basis for change." Peter Jenkins, *The Battle of Downing Street* (London: Charles Knight, 1970), p. 15.

right spectrum, but also to require having a set of stable and integrated attitudes toward public issues, then only a small segment of the British population engages in ideological thinking.[11] Grand, abstract social theories do not impress the British much. This is one of the reasons Marxism has had so little impact in Britain. It matters little to the British that a system has some illogical aspects, so long as it works. Practice, not theory, is the key consideration. Thus they have piled new political institutions on old and altered the original purpose of others all very untidily, but, nonetheless, effectively. By retaining old institutions while shifting power around they have maintained continuity in political development.

The practical, empirical approach that prevails in Britain is reflected in that school of philosophy known as British empiricism. This group of thinkers, including Locke, Berkeley, and Hume, rejected the rationalism of the Frenchman Descartes in favor of a philosophy grounded in experience. This tradition has helped to make it possible in Britain to discuss political issues on their concrete merits rather than on their supposed logical virtues.

In the last several years popular discussions of British politics often have suggested that the ideological level has been rising in Britain. This is to mistake form for substance. As Anthony King, one of the most prominent political scientists in Britain, observed about the years prior to the 1979 election, "The notion that the Tory party had, in some crude way, swung to the right with the election of Thatcher [as party leader] was widely credited; but it was largely false, based on paying too much attention to the leader's rhetoric and too little to the details of her proposals."[12] While the 1979 election may have given voters a clearer choice than they had had in most recent elections, it had none of the bitterness one would expect of a truly ideological clash.[13]

A pragmatic attitude in politics helps to support tolerance for opponents and a willingness to compromise. When one's opponents simply are urging the value of limited, practical reform rather than advocating the virtues of transforming the entire system, then one feels less threatened by their possible victory. As a result, one is more willing to tolerate their views and to attempt to work out some course of action that will be mutually agreeable.

Of course, the British have not always been tolerant, as the religious conflicts of the 17th century demonstrate. This illustrates some of the pitfalls of the national character approach; there is not some inherent characteristic of the British people that makes them tolerant. It simply is the case that the British have for some time been willing to allow unpopular minority views to be expressed freely in their country. They have not sought to outlaw the Communist party nor have they felt the need to create an un-British Activities Committee.

[11]David Butler and Donald Stokes, *Political Change in Britain,* 2d college ed. (New York: St. Martin's Press, 1976), pp. 215–35; and Marsh, *Protest and Political Consciousness,* pp. 90–95.

[12]Howard Penniman, ed., *Britain at the Polls, 1979* (Washington, D.C.: American Enterprise Institute, 1981), p. 69.

[13]Ibid., pp. 302–5; and David Butler and Dennis Kavanagh, *The British General Election of 1979* (London: Macmillan, 1980), pp. 319–20. This was not quite so true of the 1983 campaign. See Jorgen S. Rasmussen, "An American Perspective on the British General Election," *Parliamentary Affairs* 36 (Autumn 1983), p. 385.

The 1960s and 1970s made clear, however, that the British toleration of diversity in political opinions did not extend as readily into racial matters. Although the nonwhite population of Britain is only about 4 percent, its rapid growth during the 1960s and its concentration in a relative few areas has produced many sharp reactions. Some "coloureds" (the British lump Indians, Pakistanis, and West Indians together under this label) have been forced to move from their homes because of pressure from their white neighbors, and others have been discriminated against in employment. Some politicians, the best known of them the right-wing conservative Enoch Powell, have linked nonwhites with crime, disease, and the destruction of British culture. They have favored sharply curtailing or even eliminating further nonwhite immigration into Britain and have suggested that the government pay the immigrants to return to their native countries.

During the last 20 years legislative action on race relations moved in two directions, which some might regard as contradictory, but which the British hope are complementary. Immigration into Britain now is much more tightly restricted than formerly, but racial discrimination against nonwhite residents in Britain is more widely prohibited than it had been. Britons hope that the nonwhites can be more easily assimilated and their rights protected if their number in Britain is kept relatively low. The leaders of Britain's three main parties generally agree on this approach, but many average Britons want stronger actions against nonwhites.

The importance of this emotional issue varies considerably from one time to another. During the 1979 election about a fifth of the population thought it was one of the important issues facing Britain, while little over a year later virtually no one gave this response to opinion pollsters.[14] And during the 1983 campaign, when asked to mention two or three problems on which the politicians should concentrate, only 4 percent said immigration or race relations.[15]

Nonetheless, half the British believe that a lot of prejudice exists against "coloureds" and nearly as many believe that there is more race prejudice in Britain than there was five years ago and that there will be still more five years from now.[16] Furthermore, the racial issue was a point of contention in Parliament in considering a bill altering the requirements for and means of obtaining British citizenship. And Enoch Powell has continued to make speeches predicting racial violence on the scale of civil war.

Several aspects of the "coloured" population have a potential for worsening race relations. "Coloured" Britons are much younger than the rest of the population. Whereas 90 percent of them were under 45 at the time of the 1971 census, only 63 percent of the rest of the people were, and while two fifths of them were under 16, only a quarter of the rest were. This means that the "coloured" pro-

---

[14]MORI panel polls for the *Sunday Times* during April 1979, and *Gallup Political Index Report,* No. 241, p. 4.

[15]MORI poll taken on May 10, 1983.

[16]Roger Jowell and Colin Airey, eds., *British Social Attitudes: the 1984 report* (Aldershot, England: Gower, 1984), pp. 123–4.

portion of the population will continue to increase, as these young people marry and have families, even if immigration were totally prohibited. Second, unemployment hits the "coloured" population much more severely; the rate has been increasing among them about four times more rapidly than among the rest of the population. The drastic increases in unemployment throughout the British work force at the start of the 1980s made the competition for jobs more sharp. Since two fifths of those unemployed were under 25, the relative youth of the "coloured" population meant that they were especially hard hit. Thus the potential for fear, resentment, and conflict is great.

Add to this the fact that by 1971 two fifths of the "coloured" population had been born in Britain, rather than emigrated there. By any reasonable definition of citizenship Britain is their country, yet some Britons talk of sending them home. The sun may have set on the British Empire, but its effect on British politics lingers on in the form of a nonwhite population that the imperial past has ill equipped Britain to deal with.

Despite the occasional successes of Powell and a few other politicians in stirring up the racial issue in Britain, fervent emotionalism is not typical of British politics. Britain has had charismatic leaders, like Winston Churchill, but demagogues have been rare. The British do not lack commitment; they simply do not engage in mass enthusiasms bordering on hysteria. The rather low-key image of bulldog determination is accurate. The chief exception to these comments are the Welsh, who tend to favor a more florid and rhetorical political style. Most English people are uncomfortable with such profuseness and suspect it.

A final important British characteristic having political implications is individualism. This is worth stressing since more Americans seem to regard Britain as a land of socialist collectivism. Our comments about British attitudes toward authority may have served only to reinforce this belief. But recall British tolerance—this is a society willing to make room for the individual eccentric, the screwball. And while Britons may not go as far as Americans in automatically assuming that government action is more likely to be bad than to be beneficial, still skepticism is alive and well in Britain. To take a relatively trivial matter, many more Britons than Americans regard the census as an invasion of privacy and object to cooperating, even though the British census office has never been able to get up the nerve to ask the population to indicate their income. More important, the value placed on individualism means that Britons are no less concerned than are Americans to resist political oppression.

Individualism in Britain is qualified, however, by a social characteristic differing strikingly from the United States. Thus we need to spend the rest of this chapter discussing class solidarity and social division. As we explained in the previous chapter, Britain, on balance, has a more homogeneous population than does the United States. In one regard, however, Americans are less divided from each other than are Britons. Social class separates Britons into distinct groups and for most of the past half century has been the basic cleavage in British politics.

Class differences have long been a part of British life. While the barrier between classes is not so rigid as to prevent all movement on the social ladder, yet British class distinctions are not blurred to the extent that they are in the United States. People are typed according to social status, and the treatment that they receive depends upon whether they are above or below the social position of those with whom they happen to be dealing. Nearly three quarters of the British think that people are very aware or quite aware of class differences and about as many believe that class affects one's opportunities a great deal or quite a lot.[17]

A Briton can tell within a few minutes of beginning to talk with strangers what their social position is, since their speech patterns and accent identify them. Unlike the United States, where a southern drawl may make you the object of fun in another part of the country, in Britain it is the accent of the northerner that stigmatizes one as lacking the proper backgound, breeding, and education.

A number of systems have been used to identify the key classes in British society. For our purposes, commenting on three classes is sufficient. First, the nobility. Americans are aware that the British use titles, that someone is called Lord this or Lady that or Sir whatever. And since these titles do indeed carry some social prestige, Americans may be inclined to believe that these are the people who run the country. Titled persons did occupy, until the 20th century, a large share of the elite governmental positions. But no class has had a privileged legal relationship with the state since the first part of the 16th century, and by the end of the 19th century political power as well had flowed to other groups.

Even were this not the case, having a title is not all that you might think. Many of these titles were created relatively recently and were granted to self-made businessmen or successful politicians. Furthermore, some of the titles are not even hereditary. So a title does not imply centuries of luxury and a home in a castle.

The true governing class in Britain for about the last century has been the upper middle class. Many of these people come from families financially better off than are many holding titles. This group has had a strong sense of the need to justify their existence by serving society. An American parallel would be the Rockefeller family or the Kennedys. In Britain the political relevance of this sense of duty is heightened by the upper middle-class view—in sharp contrast to American attitudes—that politics is a much more suitable and honorable career than is business for someone of this social position.

Within the middle class, occupations and finances vary considerably. And although we can talk of an upper and lower middle class, the dividing line is rather unclear. Therefore, the sharpest break, the point at which one can talk of a gulf separating different lifestyles, is between the nonmanual middle class and the manual workers. The latter are the social class whose accent gives them away the instant they speak.

---

[17]Ibid., p. 194.

One of the key elements productive of a socially divided Britain is the educational system. In the United States education and occupation tend to determine social status; in Britain social status tends to determine education and occupation. Although students may attend the government-supported school system until they are 18, only about a tenth choose to linger beyond the compulsory schooling age of 16; this especially is true in secondary modern and comprehensive schools.

The secondary modern school used to be the main type of school. It provided a general education with some vocational emphasis and was intended for average and weaker students. The more capable students, identified by tests given before the age of 11, were assigned to grammar schools to receive a more academic, college preparatory education. A middle-class child unable to score sufficiently well on the tests to get into a grammar school was regarded by his or her family as an academic failure, an attitude that made the tests a major trauma for many children.

The comprehensive school—the type most similar to an American high school—was devised to bridge the gap between the elite education of the grammar school and the mediocre education of the secondary modern. Although the comprehensive school takes all types of students, its educational programs distinguish between those students planning to go to college and those who are not. Thus, even in this type of school all students do not receive the same training.

The Labour party, in keeping with the egalitarian principles, strongly favored the shift to the American-type comprehensives. Thus they passed legislation requiring all local school boards to "go comprehensive." (The fact that this could be done by action of the national legislature is a good example of what it means to have a unitary rather than a federal system.) The Conservative party opposed this step, arguing that to abandon the grammar schools would dilute the quality of education. Thus, when they returned to power in 1979, one of the first things they did was to repeal the requirement that Labour had imposed.

Despite the political heat that the argument generates, to some extent it is academic. The comprehensive school largely has replaced the secondary modern. Whereas at the start of the 1970s only 3 out of 10 English school children attended comprehensive schools, now about 9 out of 10 of the British children attending government-supported schools go to comprehensive schools and less than 1 in 20 go to grammar schools.

The grammar school remains important, however, because it is a significant entry route from the government-supported school system to higher education. As noted, few students in the comprehensive schools choose to remain on until they are 18, but well over half of the students in grammar schools go on to further education.

If you have been reading carefully, you may have wondered why we have been using this awkward term *government-supported schools*. Why not just say public schools and be done with it? The reason is that what the British call public schools are private. In Britain public schools are supported not by the government but by sizable tuition fees charged to their students. Thus, unless you can win one of the few scholarships available to attend such schools (remember, we are talking about secondary schools, not universities) you can attend only if your parents can afford the fees. Room and board (public schools usually are boarding schools) plus tuition at a top public school can run well over $6,000 a year.[18]

Although about 25 times as many students attend the government-supported schools as do the public schools, the public schools are immensely significant politically and socially. Attending the proper public school enhances (or perhaps we should say, attests to) your social status much more than does graduating from Oxford or Cambridge University—the British equivalent of the Ivy League. Political controversy over the role and status of the public schools exceeds even that concerning the comprehensives and the grammars. The public schools are at the heart of class cleavage in Britain.

The most famous of all British public schools is Eton, founded in 1441. Although it has a student body of little more than 1,000, Eton has produced 18 British prime ministers over the years. Furthermore, of all Conservative Cabinet ministers from 1918 to 1955 well over half (57 percent) had been to Eton and about one quarter of all Conservative members of Parliament during this time were Old Etonians.[19] The old school tie—the bond that men (public schools are not coeducational and those that exist for females do not have the same prestige) who have attended the same public school, however many years apart, feel for each other—is a significant factor in relations among the British political elite. This tie has no American parallel; the link between fraternity brothers is only a pale imitation.

Some members of the Labour party would like to abolish the public schools. More typically, however, Labour has been less concerned to attack the privileges of the elite and more interested in providing equal opportunity for those who merit it among the less well off. Even in the Labour party few people hold the American belief that virtually everyone has a God-given right to attend a university. In Britain higher education is not mass education; only about half a million people attend colleges and universities. The Labour view is that those of demonstrated intelligence should not be prevented by financial constraints from obtaining higher education. Thus about 90 percent of the students attending British universities receive some financial support from the government. Furthermore, tuition charges are below the average for nonresidential public schools, to say nothing of the boarding schools.

This in itself, however, is insufficient to produce equality. Students from working-class backgrounds account for only about a fifth of all those in higher

---

[18]Throughout this book we will be converting the British pound sterling to dollars at the rate of 1£ = $1.25. Thus in this case the charge for room, board, and tuition can exceed £5,000.

[19]W. P. Buck, *Amateurs and Professionals in British Politics* (Chicago: University of Chicago Press, 1963).

education. The entire British educational system remains one that emphasizes the training of an elite. Because of the divisive effect this has on society, education will continue to be an important political issue in Britain.

While class differences in Britain are related to wealth and income, they are not solely, or even primarily, matters of economic disparities. A skilled worker, for example, may think of him or herself as working class while a clerk or teacher may prefer the designation middle class; yet the best-paid skilled workers earn considerably more than the lowest-paid teachers and clerks and do not have the burden of trying to maintain a middle-class lifestyle, such as sending children to public schools. Increased income cannot readily be translated, however, into the manners, speech, social habits, and other class attributes essential for winning acceptance as an equal by the upper classes.

One of the reasons that income is not a major factor in class distinction is that variations in income are not very extreme. The "final income" (after taxes have been deducted and any social security benefits received) for the top 10 percent of all households is less than five times that for the bottom 10 percent; the final income for the middle, or typical, household is less than twice that for the lowest 10 percent. The distribution of wealth, as distinct from income, is more unequal. The top 1 percent of the British population over 18 owns a fifth of all personal wealth in Britain and the top 10 percent owns nearly three fifths. Less than 5 percent of the wealth is owned by the bottom half. While this is much greater inequality than exists in Sweden or Australia, it is not much different than the distribution of wealth in the United States.

Disparities in wealth obviously produce disparities in quality of life. But we stress again that it is not really wealth that is at the heart of social divisions in Britain; it is more a matter of how people relate to each other, how they feel about their place in society. And as we have seen, Britons are much more aware of and feel separated by social divisions than are Americans. Furthermore, a fifth of them believe that class has more effect upon a person's opportunities now than it did 10 years ago.[20] As for the future, they are not overly optimistic—half expect no change in the impact of class and a sixth expect it to have an even greater effect than now, while only a third expect it to become less important.

In short, social class is more a fact of life in Britain than in the United States. Class barriers will continue to exist in Britain until one can relate comfortably to someone from another class as a fellow human being. That time is yet to come to Britain.

BIBLIOGRAPHICAL NOTE

Albert Dicey, *Introduction to the Study of the Law of the Constitution,* 10th ed. (New York: Macmillan, 1961), and Frederic W. Maitland, *The Constitutional History of Eng-*

---

[20] Jowell and Airey, *British Social Attitudes,* p. 194.

land (Cambridge, Eng.: Macmillan, 1908) are considered among the classics of British political literature. Perhaps the most cited work on the British political system is Walter Bagehot, *The English Constitution,* first published in 1867. See the 1963 Fontana edition for an interesting commentary on Bagehot's contemporary relevance by R. H. S. Crossman.

For an extensive discussion of Britain's constitutional structure see E. C. S. Wade and G. Godfrey Phillips, *Constitutional and Administrative Law,* 9th ed., by A. W. Bradley (London: Longman, 1977).

Considerable information on British political values is contained in the Almond and Verba and Marsh books cited in the footnotes. For a discussion of various aspects of class see K. Roberts, F. G. Cook, S. C. Clark, and Elizabeth Semeonoff, *The Fragmentary Class Structure* (London: Heinemann, 1977). Detailed information on the educational background of various social elites appears in David Boyd, *Elites and Their Education* (Windsor, Berkshire: NFER, 1973). The Jowell and Airey book cited in the footnotes is intended to be the first in an annual series of reports of surveys of the views of Britons on a variety of topics. Without doubt the most stimulating recent discussion of British values, along with some insightful comments on the country's economic problems is Samuel H. Beer, *Britain Against Itself: The Political Contradictions of Collectivism* (New York: W. W. Norton, 1982).

The basic source of information on race and immigration in Britain is E. J. B. Rose et al., *Colour and Citizenship* (London: Oxford University Press, 1969). Various studies have appeared since then, a recent one being the Runnymede Trust and the Radical Statistic Group, *Britain's Black Population* (London: Heinemann, 1981). A useful starting point for study of the topic is the essay by Donley Studlar in William Gwyn and Richard Rose, eds., *Britain: Progress and Decline* (New Orleans: Tulane University Press, 1980), pp. 111–28.

3

Individual and Group
Political Activity

THE ELECTORAL SYSTEM

As recently as the 1950s Britain was more democratic than the United States as regards voting rights. Virtually no legal bars to voting existed. No literacy test had to be passed; no poll tax had to be paid; no period of local residency had to be served. Furthermore, social and racial pressures against voting were unknown and legislative districts were much more fairly and equally drawn than was true in the United States. Yet during the 19th century the United States was considerably more democratic, judging by voting rights. To understand this you need to know how the British electoral system developed.

By the beginning of the 19th century, suffrage rules had become confused and chaotic in Britain. In some towns many adult males could vote, whereas in others not even 1 percent could do so. In some towns property determined eligibility; in others, it was membership in the municipal corporation—membership acquired by birth, marriage, or purchase. Moreover, representation in the Commons was not according to population. Each county and each borough, irrespective of its size, was entitled to two Members in the Commons.

The inequities of this situation were worsened by the Industrial Revolution. Despite a rapid growth in population, many of the newer factory towns, like Manchester and Birmingham, were unrepresented in Parliament, while many previously thriving rural towns that had become virtually deserted continued to send two Members each to the House of Commons. Although it had slid into the sea, Dunwich retained two Members in Parliament. The fish at Dunwich were better represented than the people of Manchester. The Members from

70

these "rotten boroughs" often were selected by no more than a handful of free-men, usually nonresidents, who owned a few dilapidated buildings. In such cir-cumstances membership in the House of Commons frequently was bought and sold, with a few men able to swing the balance of power.

The first step in altering this situation to produce greater democratic ac-countability was the Reform Act of 1832. It redistributed the seats in the Com-mons and broadened the suffrage. Representation still was not proportional to population, but many rotten boroughs were eliminated and the more populous towns gained some 150 seats. By providing for uniform suffrage requirements in the towns and by extending the suffrage to certain classes of tenants in the counties, the Act added more than 200,000 voters to the electorate, thereby in-creasing it by about 50 percent. In the United States, by way of contrast, this was the period of Jacksonian democracy, when universal manhood suffrage for whites was widely established. In Britain, even after the Reform Act, only about 7 percent of the total adult population could vote (see Figure 3-1).

Although the franchise was broadened further in 1867, it was not until the re-form of 1884 that most men could vote. Only in 1918 did Britain finally enact universal manhood suffrage. At the same time the vote was extended to women over 30. Only then could a majority of the adult population vote. Finally, in 1928, women between 21 and 30 were enfranchised as well. Thus, electoral re-form required five installments (six if one counts the introduction of the secret ballot in 1872) over a period of a century. This is a classic example of the typical

FIGURE 3–1 Growth of Voting Rights

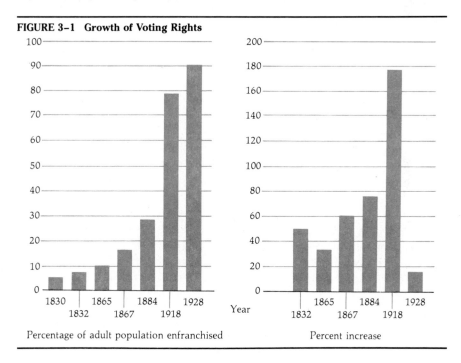

Percentage of adult population enfranchised

Percent increase

British approach to political reform. Nor was the process of extending the franchise ended in 1928, for in 1969 the voting age was lowered to 18.

In Britain, unlike the United States, the government takes the initiative in seeing that those eligible to vote are indeed registered to do so. Every October each household receives a form on which the head of the household is to list all those resident at that address who meet the voting requirements. Failure to return the completed card is subject to a small fine, although this rarely is collected. The registration officer in each constituency compiles a list of registered voters from the information returned and posts the list on bulletin boards in public buildings or other public places. People not on the list, who believe they should be, may protest to the registration officer and, if the decision is unsatisfactory, may appeal to the county court. Similarly, any person may protest the inclusion of persons he or she considers ineligible. The British approach to registration produces a larger percentage of qualified voters than in the United States.

On the other hand, absentee ballots have been much less common in Britain than in the United States, being restricted to those who clearly were unable to get to the polls, such as those physically infirm. Not until 1985 was the law changed to accommodate those who simply were away from home on a vacation on election day. Now they may either obtain an absentee ballot or authorize someone to vote for them. The new law also gave the vote to Britons who are living abroad. For seven years after moving away from Britain they remain on the list of registered voters in the constituency where they last lived. During this time they may vote by absentee ballot or by proxy if they do not wish to return to Britain on election day.

General elections, in which every Member of the Commons stands for reelection, must occur at least once every five years. But, since the date of elections is not fixed, they may occur at any time. In fact, Britain held two general elections in a single year in both 1910 and 1974. On the other hand, even the five-year limit may be exceeded if both Houses of Parliament approve. This was done during both world wars to avoid having an election when the country was fighting for survival.

Despite this flexibility, general elections have been no more frequent in Britain in the 20th century than presidential elections have been in the United States. Through 1984 Britain had held 23 and the United States 22. But do not conclude that this means it makes no difference which practice is followed. Under the British system the scheduling of an election becomes an important consideration in the governing party's electoral strategy. They can wait until unemployment is low, prosperity is growing, or major new policies have been implemented successfully before calling an election in the hopes of capitalizing politically on these developments. Also, British electoral practice makes the mandate theory of elections a bit more plausible. According to this theory the electorate is given a choice between alternative courses of action and approves one or the other. The winning party then is said to have a mandate for its policy. Thus, an election comes to resemble a referendum.

This characteristic, combined with the British tradition of limited, rather than mass, democracy—as we noted in discussing the expansion of voting rights—explains why referenda have not been a part of the British political system. Early in the summer of 1975, however, a referendum was held on the question of British membership in the EEC. This occurred not because political leaders suddenly had been converted to a belief in participatory democracy, but purely for political expediency. The Labour party was divided sharply on whether Britain should withdraw from the Common Market, and the only way that Prime Minister Wilson could think of to hold the party together was to have a referendum and let the people decide. The idea was that whichever side lost would regard the issue as having been settled. Although those who wanted Britain to withdraw were decisively beaten, they did not give up the battle (although they did hold their fire for a time so Wilson's strategy worked in the short run).

The Wilson Government maintained that membership in the EEC was a special issue, and that never again would a referendum be used for any issue. Opponents of the referendum, knowing that in Britain it is getting something done for the first time that really matters, did not have to wait long for their fears to be substantiated. In December 1976 the Government conceded that referenda would be held in Scotland and Wales before any devolution proposals were implemented. As we have discussed, the result of these votes was to kill devolution at least temporarily. Thus while one should not expect frequent use of referenda in Britain, the procedure certainly has become a part of British politics and has important implications for the functions of Parliament, as we will see in a subsequent chapter.

Other than general elections, the only elections for national political office in Britain are by-elections. Whenever a seat is vacant through death or resignation of a Member, an election is called to fill it. Britain does not hold primary elections. Furthermore, never—except in 1979—are local elections held at the same time as national ones.

All this means that the British ballot is simple. No referenda or bond issues clutter the ballot. The only office to be filled is that of representative for the constituency. Voting for the prime minister is impossible unless one lives in the constituency he or she represents. Even then electors are voting for him or her only as a legislative representative and not as prime minister. Thus the voter's only job is to decide which of the typically three to five candidates he or she wishes to represent the constituency.

Candidates' addresses and occupations are included on the ballot, but until 1969 that was all. Not until then were party labels included. Now candidates may use up to six words to describe their party affiliation. Some independent candidates use the label to make a last-minute political statement. In 1970, one candidate styled herself on the ballot as "Stop the SE Asian War." A few prefer a lighter touch as did the candidate in a 1976 by-election who labeled himself "Lorimer Brizbeep, Science Fiction Loony Party." Naturally, the press referred to him for short as the Loony candidate.

Candidates are chosen in private party meetings, not in primary elections. For these choices, or anyone else, to get on the ballot requires only the signatures of 10 qualified voters from the candidate's constituency. This is so incredibly easy compared to the United States that you would guess that there must be some catch. And there is, in the form of a deposit. From its introduction in 1918 the sum always had been £150. Anyone failing to win an eighth of the vote forfeited the deposit, while other candidates had it returned to them after the election. Over the years inflation reduced the value of the deposit so that it no longer served to eliminate all Loony candidates or even eccentrics, like William Boaks, who was a candidate more than two dozen times from 1974 to 1982.

Thus in 1984 the Government indicated that it would have the law amended to increase the deposit to £1,000 ($1,250), while reducing the proportion of the vote a candidate needed to avoid forfeiture to 5 percent. The smaller parties, in particular the Liberals, over half of whose candidates had lost their deposit in the 1979 election, strongly opposed this change. The Liberals were not so much concerned about the possible loss of money—their fortunes had improved considerably in the 1983 election—as they were with having over $750,000 tied up in deposits and thus unavailable at a time when they would be trying to finance a national electoral campaign on already limited funds. They would much more have preferred a substantial increase in the number of signatures required for nomination. They regarded the Government's reform as being motivated more by partisan calculations than by a pure desire to eliminate frivolous candidates.

Certain types of people may not serve in the Commons. (Thus, while they could be nominated, they could not be an MP even if they were elected.) Among these are leading judges; clergy of the Church of England, the Church of Scotland, and the Roman Catholic Church; persons holding an office of profit under the Crown; and those guilty of corrupt or illegal election practices. For years criminals—those who had committed a felony—were barred from the Commons. When the criminal law was revised in 1967, however, the distinction between felonies and misdemeanors was abolished. This had the effect—overlooked at the time—of permitting criminals to sit in the Commons. This error did not create a problem until 1981 when a member of the Irish Republican Army, in jail for terrorist activities, won a seat in a by-election while on a hunger strike to the death. While the Commons could have voted to expel him, this was not a live option since it would only have worsened conflict in Northern Ireland. Since the person starved himself to death, he never actually took his seat in the Commons. The law then was changed to prevent this happening again.

Candidates for the Commons are not required, either by law or by custom, to live in the district they represent. Recall that Britain is a unitary, rather than a federal, system and, while not homogeneous, is less diverse than is the United States. Some candidates do promise that they will move to the constituency if elected. And at times candidates with local connections will refer to opponents lacking these as "carpetbaggers." These strategies usually are not worth many votes.

In contrast with American campaigns, British elections are brief. Legally the campaign does not begin until Parliament is dissolved, less than three weeks before election day. (In 1979 and 1983 the campaigns were longer than usual because holidays occurred during the period; even so the campaigns lasted little more than a month.) At times a party will anticipate the timing of an election (remember, the date is not set, the Government can call the election at any time) and launch an extensive precampaign program. Guessing that the election would be in the fall of 1978, the Conservatives spent over £1 million, mainly on newspaper ads and posters, nearly as much as they spent during the election itself when it finally occurred in the spring of 1979.[1]

Television does not play as major a role in British elections as it does in American elections. Parties and candidates are not permitted to buy time for special broadcasts or spot announcements. Instead parties are officially allotted free media time. The TV programs that they prepare are broadcast over both the government-owned BBC and the commercially operated ITV. Even though British formal campaigns are short, you may be surprised to learn that total time for all parties combined during the 1983 campaign was only about three hours. Labour and the Conservatives had five broadcasts of up to 10 minutes each and the Alliance four of that length. Three other parties, including the National Front, met the requirement of offering at least 50 candidates and thus were given five minutes each. In Scotland the SNP was permitted two programs of 10 minutes each, but Plaid Cymru was allowed only one 10-minute program in Wales.

Of course, television news covers an election.[2] While that may seem obvious now, it was not the practice prior to the 1959 election. Until then one never would have known from watching newscasts that an election was in progress. The British, you see, want to believe that elections are a time for rational choice between partisan alternatives and want to avoid the hype and hoopla that they feel have debased American elections.

In addition to news coverage, various public affairs programs comment on the election and offer discussion or interview programs that give some of the less prominent candidates, as well as the party leaders, a limited opportunity to express their views. At times it is very difficult to accomplish this in Britain because the laws governing equal treatment by the broadcast media are so ambiguous, yet apparently stringent. Some candidates, by refusing to appear on television themselves, have been able to block the appearance of all their local opponents. The Labour party's unwillingness to appear on the same program as the extreme right-wing National Front caused several telecasts to be canceled or altered during the October 1974 election.

---

[1]Howard Penniman, ed., *Britain at the Polls, 1979* (Washington, D.C.: American Enterprise Institute, 1981), p. 216.

[2]For the role of broadcasting in the 1983 campaign see David Butler and Dennis Kanavagh, *The British General Election of 1983* (London: Macmillan, 1984), pp. 147–74.

On most week days during the campaign each of the three main parties will hold a press conference at party headquarters. Various party leaders will be present to make short statements on the issues that are developing during the campaign and to answer questions from the press. The top leaders of the parties usually do not spend much time campaigning in their own constituency. In addition to being in London for several of the press conferences, they will be touring the country making major speeches at various places and engaging in "walkabouts" that give them a chance to shake hands and do something that will get their picture on the evening TV news.

At the constituency level, candidates speak at various meetings, sometimes during the course of an evening talking to three or four small groups meeting in schools or other public places. Occasionally, a national leader will attend one of these meetings in an attempt to boost attendance. But now that almost every British household has a "telly," getting more than a handful of people to attend most meetings is difficult.

So if the voters will not come to the candidate, the candidate and the party must go to the voters. Canvassing is one of the principal activities during the campaign at the constituency level. Candidates and supporters go door-to-door in a constituency seeking support from the voters and inquiring whether they have any questions about the candidate's policies. They hope in this fashion to discover who intends to vote for their party. Then on election day they can check the official record of who has voted to ensure that those who said they would support them actually turn out to vote.

Each candidate may mail one communication to each voter during the campaign free of charge. Typically this "election address" includes the candidate's picture, some biographical information, and a statement of the policies he or she supports (see Figures 3–2 and 3–3).

Each candidate must appoint an election agent (campaign manager) who is required by law to handle the account for *all* election campaign expenses except the personal expenses of the candidate him or herself. No one except the candidate, the election agent, or persons authorized by the agent, in writing, can spend money in an effort to get a candidate elected or another one defeated. Any unauthorized expenditure on behalf of a particular candidate (or against an opponent) for a particular constituency is prohibited. Expenditures between elections are not covered by these regulations.

The amount that a candidate can spend is limited. The figure varies from one constituency to another depending upon the size of the electorate, but typically is under $6,000. Few candidates spend even close to the maximum. In 1983 Conservative candidates averaged less than three fourths of the maximum and Labour candidates less than two thirds, while Alliance candidates spent even a smaller share of what they were permitted.[3]

---

[3]Ibid., p. 266.

FIGURE 3–2   Portions of a 1979 Election Address

My Work for South Hertfordshire

Since I was elected to Parliament, I have tried to serve the interests of all my constituents, regardless of party. Hundreds of you have come to my 'surgeries'. Literally thousands of you have written to me and I have called on many of you in your own homes. In every way open to me I have tried to make myself available to those who need my help or advice and to deal with the problems of my constituents and of South Hertfordshire. I have never allowed my Front Bench duties to interfere with this work and when re-elected I will continue to fight for individual constituents, or for groups of constituents, such as those at Organ Hall Farm in Borehamwood, or those in other parts of the constituency now threatened by the M25.

For three years now I have been Chairman of the Conservative Working Party on Mental Illness and Handicap, an area of vital interest to South Hertfordshire with its five large hospitals.

The State of the Nation

The last five years have been disastrous for Britain. By any of the traditional tests, the Labour Government is a failure:

* Prices have doubled
* Unemployment has gone up from 600,000 to nearly 1.5 million
* The £ has fallen in value against almost every other major currency in the world
* In 1978 124,000 fewer new homes were started than in 1973
* It took 300 years for the National Debt to reach £40 billion. The Labour Government doubled this to £80 billion in only 5 years since 1974

Mr. Callaghan boasts in Brussels that we are now one of the poorest countries in Europe, and he doesn't seem to care.

Stop the Decline in Britain

Conservatives do care. We do not accept that it is inevitable that Britain will become a mediocre, second-rate country. We believe that the British people, given the chance and given the incentive, can stop the steady drift towards mediocrity which is the consequence of Socialism. Our aim is to stop the decline of Britain.

We realise that those who suffer most in a poor country are the elderly, the sick, the handicapped, the children. A mediocre Britain will offer the grimmest future for those least able to take care of themselves. It is for these people in particular that we fight Socialism.

a message from ANN PARKINSON

Over the last five years people and organizations throughout South Hertfordshire have invited me to meet them and hear their views and listen to their problems. This has given me a great opportunity to learn more and more about the hard work of all the voluntary organizations in the area, and to appreciate their efforts on behalf of those often unable to help themselves. I hope to be able to continue to help them in the future.

As a wife and mother, I am delighted that the Conservative Party have elected a woman as our leader. I have met Margaret Thatcher on many occasions. She is a warm, friendly and kind woman, always willing to listen. If there is iron in her, it is an iron determination to see that all the people in this country have a chance to lead a happy and worthwhile life. I wholeheartedly support her and my husband in the forthcoming election.

Ann Parkinson

Win AGAIN with PARKINSON Conservative

Published by Sheelagh Ellis, 11 Stanhope Road, St. Albans
Printed by Nynwood Arts Ltd., Station Close, Potters Bar, Herts.

Election spending by parties at the national level is not limited. The parties must be careful, however, to say nothing that would appear to be an appeal to vote for a specific candidate—including even their party Leader and potential prime minister. This requirement does not preclude using pictures of the Leader in election material, as Figure 3–4 shows. Neither the cover of that leaflet nor anything inside it urged the electorate to vote for Thatcher personally. Were it to do so, the cost of printing would have to be included in her official statement of expenses.

To avoid any possible legal questions on this matter, the custom had been for parties to avoid advertising in newspapers once the formal campaign period began. In February 1974 the Liberal party did run newspaper ads, however, without having individual candidates' official statements of expenses legally challenged. Therefore, in the October 1974 election the major parties followed suit with national press advertising campaigns of their own.

Given the briefness of the formal campaign and the free media time and postage, national parties in Britain spend far less than the vast sums of Ameri-

FIGURE 3–3   A 1983 Election Address

ELECTION COMMUNICATION

Introducing

JOHN ROPER

WORKING TOGETHER FOR BRITAIN

The creation of the SDP and its Alliance with the Liberal Party have profoundly changed British politics. Our two parties are working together because we believe that Britain both needs and wants a credible, realistic alternative to both Labour and Tories. We believe the people of Britain have had enough of the old two party dogfight, and that they want to see Members of Parliament working together for Britain instead of shouting at each other. Only a victory for the Alliance in this vital election offers that prospect.

BREAK SEAL TO OPEN

Alliance
SDP LIB

YOUR
Alliance
Candidate

Our plan to help Britain

● **We'll create jobs for the future**

To restore our economy the Alliance will form a partnership between government and industry, with public money being used to develop the industries of the future. The Alliance budget will provide a million new jobs in the first two years. (It costs £5,000 a year just to keep on the dole a man or a woman who would rather be working.)

● **We'll make taxes fair**

The Alliance will reduce the unfair burden of income tax on the lower paid and cut VAT. We will make the system of taxes and benefits simpler and fairer – so the hard-up will get the help they need and the cheats will get none. But we shall also make sure that the National Health Service and the Welfare State are strengthened so everyone has a fair deal.

● **We'll combat crime**

Everybody is anxious about the record number of crimes – burglaries, assaults, vandalism and hooliganism. We'll put more bobbies back on the beat to crack down crime, and give local people more say in how they are policed, through local liaison committees.

● **We'll bring sense to Defence**

Everybody is concerned about the danger of a nuclear war. Yet getting rid of our nuclear weapons would be irresponsible and dangerous while the Russians still have theirs.

The Alliance will make a much greater effort to negotiate nuclear disarmament on both sides. We insist upon a British finger on the safety catch; a zone free of battlefield nuclear weapons in Europe; and stronger conventional forces so that early resort to nuclear weapons is avoided.

● **We'll reform the Unions**

Trade Union leaders must be made to reflect the good sense of their members. Otherwise the strikes which bring so much hardship, especially to older people, will continue. The Alliance will introduce a system whereby Trade Union executives and principal officers will be elected by secret postal ballots of all their members.

● **We'll educate for the jobs of the future**

Jobs are disappearing as industries change. The Alliance will bring education up-to-date. We'll make sure that as well as teaching children basic academic skills, adults as well as children will be trained for the jobs of tomorrow.

● **We'll give Britain fair elections**

We will change the voting system so that Parliament is truly representative of the electorate. 67% of the population did **not** vote for Mrs. Thatcher and a staggering 74% did **not** vote for the last Labour government. We won't have a stable and representative government until we change the voting system to make sure that every government is supported by at least half the people.

Published by Worsley SDP, 7 Egerton Road, Worsley
Printed by A. Wood & Co., 53 Jordan Street, Liverpool L1 0BP   Tel: 051-709-1143

Councillor		Councillor	
DAVID COWPE	ANDREW BAKER	LYN PICKTHALL	BARRY NEWMAN
35 Maple Grove	7 Egerton Park	75 Withington Drive	26 Farnham Drive
Worsley	Worsley	Astley	Irlam
790 6949	794 6337	Atherton 874207	775 7425

Between now and the election my campaign team and I hope to meet as many of you as possible to explain why we believe you should give me your support. In the short time there is before polling day I will not, unfortunately, be able to get to everyone's home, so if you have any particular question you would like to put to me please come to one of the public meetings I will be holding or telephone one of the people above and I will contact you as soon as I can.

During the period of the campaign I shall continue to hold my regular Advice Centres. Details of these will be in the local press as usual.

Yours sincerely,
John Roper.

ABOUT JOHN ROPER

John Roper has been M.P. for this area for thirteen years, and residents in almost every road of his constituency have had the benefits of his assistance over this period. He now works closely with Social Democrat and Liberal councillors in seeing that the interests of the people of this area are fully protected.

John Roper has made a special study of the problems of the North West and he continues to work to see his ideas translated into action. His other main interests in Parliament have been international affairs, defence and education.

He is Chief Whip for the Social Democrats in the House of Commons and was with the Gang of Four at the founding of the Social Democratic Party in 1981.

Outside Parliament he has gained international recognition. He has served as chairman of a number of Committees of International Parliamentary Assemblies. He is now a member of the Trilateral Commission which brings together people from Japan, North America and Europe. Since 1978 he has sat on the International Affairs Division of the British Council of Churches. He has been decorated by both Belgium and West Germany for his contribution towards improving their relations with Britain.

John Roper served as a National Service Officer in the Royal Navy and taught economics at Manchester University for nine years before entering Parliament. He is married with a fourteen year old daughter.

JOHN ROPER – a man of political vision; a man of experience; a man who will continue to pour his energies into the problems of this area.

FIGURE 3–4   Conservative Election Leaflet

can presidential campaigns. In 1983 the national organization of the Conservatives spent about $4.5 million, Labour less than $3 million, and the Alliance less than $2 million.[4] Given the weakness of constituency parties in the Alliance and Labour, both had to devote a significant share of their spending—Labour about a sixth and the Alliance nearly half—to grants from the national organization to the constituencies. Better constituency party organization relieved the Conservatives of this need, and as a result they were able to outspend Labour about three and a half to one on posters and advertising.

Important as national political activities are, ultimately general elections are 650 local contests. As in the United States, each constituency returns only one representative—the candidate winning more votes than anyone else—regardless of whether this is a majority of the votes cast. Because Britain's population is only about a quarter of that of the United States and the House of Commons is half again as large as the House of Representatives, the ratio of electors to representatives in considerably smaller in Britain—the average English constituency has fewer than 70,000 electors and average Scottish and Welsh ones about 55,000.

The British have made greater efforts since World War II than have Americans to maintain relatively equal constituencies. Extensive boundary changes were implemented in 1950 and further changes were carried out in 1955. The law was amended to avoid such frequent changes and now requires a review of boundaries no oftener than every 10 years and at least every 15. Thus constituency boundaries should have been altered for the 1970 election. This did not occur because the Labour Government feared that implementing the changes proposed by the permanent boundary commissions might cost their party 25 to 30 seats in the upcoming election. With the return to power of the Conservatives in 1970 the changes were implemented. The boundaries were changed yet again prior to the 1983 election. Even with all these efforts sizes still vary. About 7 percent of the constituencies have more than 76,000 electors, while the same proportion have fewer than 52,000.

How much impact all the campaign activities have is uncertain. As we discussed in the previous chapter, in Britain one's party preference had been to a considerable extent a matter of class. Thus deciding how to vote did not require much thought and was not likely to be influenced much by campaign activities. But with the impact of class on politics seeming to weaken and the British electorate becoming more volatile, this seems likely to change. In 1983 more than a fifth of those surveyed said they had decided how to vote during the campaign, while another poll with a research design likely to produce more reliable information about change found that 17 percent had changed their mind about how they would vote at least once during the campaign.[5] A reasonable conclusion is that campaigns tend to have at least somewhat more effect on voting than they used to do.

---

[4]Ibid., p. 267.

[5]BBC Election Survey conducted by Gallup, and Market & Opinion Research International, *British Public Opinion General Election 1983 Final Report,* p. 100. Both figures are slightly lower than they had been in 1979.

FIGURE 3–5   **Percentage of Seats Shifting from One Party to Another at General Elections**

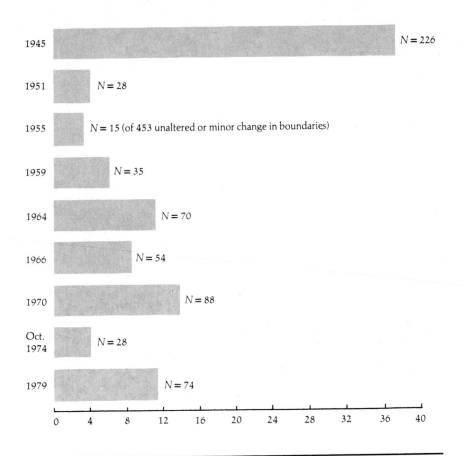

1945	N = 226
1951	N = 28
1955	N = 15 (of 453 unaltered or minor change in boundaries)
1959	N = 35
1964	N = 70
1966	N = 54
1970	N = 88
Oct. 1974	N = 28
1979	N = 74

0   4   8   12   16   20   24   28   32   36   40

Furthermore, campaign activity seems likely to help maintain interest in the election and encourage people to turn out to vote. Turnout in Britain is considerably higher than in the United States. Only once in the 20th century—the first election in which women could vote—has turnout fallen below 70 percent. In one post-World War II election it reached 84 percent. Turnout in 1983 was 73 percent.

These high rates of participation can't be attributed in most cases to doubts about the result in the individual constituencies. From 1955 to 1970, 75 percent of the seats in the House of Commons always were won by the same party. The limited number of seats lost by one party to another at each postwar general election can be seen from Figure 3–5. (The 1950, February 1974, and 1983 elections are omitted because of the extensive boundary changes.)

The simple ballot and the absence of pressures against voting doubtless help to maintain a high turnout. The smaller size of constituencies facilitates contact with the candidates, which also may aid participation. Furthermore, legislative elections usually occur less frequently than in the United States; therefore, voters need not go to the polls as often. Party organization in general tends to be more efficient; up to two fifths of the voters may be canvassed by one party or another.[6]

Also relevant in the past has been a greater sense of partisan commitment in Britain than in the United States. Because of the class nature of British politics many people felt that they would be "letting our side down" if they did not turn out to vote against the party identified with the other class. The classic statement of this view was one voter's comment some years ago to a pollster: "I'd vote for a pig if my party put one up."

As this comment indicates, a candidate's personality doesn't affect the vote much. The British tend to vote for the party, not the person. In 1979 only 16 percent of the respondents to one survey said they voted as they did because they liked the candidate.[7] More than twice as many simply said that they were just voting for the same party as they always had. That explanation and five other reasons having to do with the national parties and their leaders all ranked ahead of liking the local candidate. Probably no more than 3,000 votes are cast for any candidate personally, as distinct from being gained because of his or her party affiliation.

Thus while the basic electoral procedure in Britain is the same as in the United States—single member, simple plurality constituencies—virtually everything else about electoral procedures and campaign practices differs between the two countries.

THE INTEREST GROUP SYSTEM

The British have been slow to admit the importance of interest groups in the British political process. In the United States, particularly in the 19th century, interest groups frequently were involved in political corruption, or at least seemed to pervert the common good in the service of a narrow segment of society. While the British were prepared to agree that such things doubtless happened in the United States, they wanted to believe that Britain's long political history and concern for proper forms of behavior had freed its politics from such disreputable influences. The truth is that not only did interest groups exist in Britain even before the United States became independent, but their role in public policymaking is at least as great in Britain as in the United States.

In any system interest groups focus their efforts at the points where power resides. One of these points in Britain is the electorate. So, like American interest

---

[6]Market & Opinion Research International, *British Public Opinion General Election 1979*, p. 66.
[7]Ibid., p. 52.

groups, British ones devote some time to trying to influence public opinion. Advertisements, speeches, demonstrations—the range of techniques will be familiar to any American.

Another power point is the national legislature; in fact, when most Americans are asked to think about the activities of interest groups, they probably picture a lobbyist talking with a Congressperson. Conflict-of-interest laws force most members of Congress to be very discreet in their relations with interest groups. (We will overlook that handful who are no more intelligent than to run afoul of undercover agents posing as Arab sheiks.) In Britain, however, a direct financial connection with an interest group for an MP is perfectly acceptable. Nearly 60 percent of the Labour MPs elected in 1983 were sponsored by trade unions.

Unions may pay some or all of the campaign expenses of MPs they sponsor. Since this frees the constituency party from having to bear this cost, anyone seeking the Labour nomination who can tell the selection committee that he or she is sponsored has a considerable advantage in being chosen. Sponsored MPs also may be given some financial assistance in meeting their expenses as MPs and even may receive a supplement to their salaries.

While nothing quite the same exists on the Conservative side of the Commons, yet the fact that many Conservative MPs are company directors establishes a quite similar relation. Furthermore, many MPs of whatever party may be honorary officers in an interest group or have some other connection with it, such that when they speak in the Commons they are expressing directly the group's views.

Sponsoring organizations and other such groups cannot order an MP to vote a certain way on particular legislation. Nevertheless, some Labour MPs have gotten into trouble with sponsoring unions because of their votes in the Commons, and unions have withdrawn sponsorship from MPs who they felt were not sufficiently loyal to the policies favored by the unions. Certainly a sponsoring organization may legitimately expect "its" MPs to express its views in Parliament whenever matters in which it is interested come up.

Despite these close ties with interest groups that make MPs of some use, these relationships are not of fundamental importance to major interest groups. Strong party discipline, the limited role of the legislature in initiating and shaping legislation, and the more narrow function of legislative committees (all discussed in detail in a subsequent chapter) combine to make legislative activity less than the most fruitful sphere for interest group efforts.

As we will see, legislative initiative and control belongs to the Government, or the Administration, as we would say in the United States. Thus an interest group that wants a new law must concentrate primarily on convincing the minister of the appropriate department to work for the Government's backing. If money is involved, then the Chancellor of the Exchequer must also be convinced, for proposals to spend money require recommendations from the Government. Of course, if the prime minister can be won to the group's position, that will be a great help, but getting his or her ear is more difficult.

Interest group objectives are not limited to seeking new laws. Modern government intervenes in so many aspects of life that groups are more likely to be concerned with how existing laws are administered, whether they are rigorously applied according to the letter or are implemented in a more selective fashion, either to try to better serve their spirit or to assist a favored group. Furthermore, much contemporary legislation takes the form of rather general framework laws that leave the issuing of detailed regulations to administrators. Thus in many instances administrators have the major role in policymaking. Effective interest groups cannot confine their efforts to contacts with the political elite in Parliament and the Government.

In fact, it is at precisely this point in the policy process that interest groups may play a more important role in Britain than they do in the United States. So closely involved in the policy process are the leading British interest groups that they do not even have to take the initiative. Prior consultation of interests by ministers and administrators is a standard procedure. Before introducing an important bill into Parliament, the relevant government department will discuss its purpose and general contents with interested groups.

While groups are not permitted to see a draft of the bill (this would infringe Parliament's rights), they are given a full briefing. The Government wants to know how they will respond to the proposed legislation—will they cooperate in implementing it or do all they can to hinder putting it into effect? Furthermore, because in many areas the groups have practical experience that the Government lacks, the administrators want to know whether they think the bill actually will work when it becomes law—have those who drafted the law, because they have not had to deal firsthand with the subject, overlooked some crucial aspects.

These contacts give groups a maximum opportunity to influence policy because they occur before the Government has committed itself publicly to all the details of the legislation. Thus it can change the proposals without loss of face. Once the bill actually gets to Parliament the Government is much less likely to be willing to accept a change. Parliamentary activity, although more visible, tends to be a less effective interest group method. Getting your MP to create a fuss in Parliament is simply a last resort when all else has failed, and its object is not so much to gain some concession as it is to make things a bit unpleasant for the Government.

Of course, not every interest group has these valuable contacts with governmental departments. But the major ones do. Groups that have not yet won such recognition may be forced to utilize Parliamentary activities and contacts because that is all they have. The visibility of an interest group's activity probably is inversely related to its strength and effectiveness. The fact that the crucial activities take place behind the scenes helps to explain why the role of interest groups in British politics could be overlooked for so long.

Instead of dealing with a legislator, the agent of a British pressure group is more concerned to maintain close contacts with civil servants. The scope and frequency of these contacts were accelerated greatly in Britain by World War II. Many private groups—for example, producers' associations—became quasi-governmental then in an effort to ensure the most efficient use of resources. The aim was to integrate the productive capacity of the country as tightly as possible into the Government's war plans without having to expand public ownership. The extensive consultation to which both government and interests became accustomed carried on over into the postwar period.

The government recognizes that many of an interest group's staff are experts in a particular field and thus can provide valuable opinions on what measures are practicable. Furthermore, in some cases interest groups will possess much more detailed information about a topic or enterprise than is available to the government. Finally, if compliance is to be voluntary rather than coerced, the government is well advised to consult closely with those who are most likely to be affected directly by its actions. Thus, the government recognizes liaison with interest groups as an essential component of the governmental process. Departments may send draft regulations to interest groups before these orders are issued in their official form. Moreover, some departments have permanent advisory committees, where special interests are represented on a continuing basis.

As you will see in the following chapters, authoritative power is highly concentrated in Britain, not diffuse as it is in the United States. If groups are to relate effectively to this concentration of power, they too must be highly centralized. Thus in Britain, unions, farmers, veterans, and business are each represented primarily by one major interest group, which includes a greater percentage of the relevant population than do the several groups functioning in each interest area in the United States. The Trades Union Congress, for example, encompasses 85 percent of all trade unionists in Britain, while in the United States union members are split chiefly among the AFL–CIO, the Auto Workers, and the Teamsters.

The structure of British interest groups and their relations with government involve the more important of them more directly in the policy-making process than is true of most American groups, although the form of that involvement has tended to obscure their significant influence. Samuel Beer, one of the foremost American students of British politics, has said of one type of group—producer groups—that they "do have sanctions—the denial (in various degrees) of advice, acquiescence, and approval—which can cause, to put it mildly, 'administrative difficulties' and which, by anticipation, endow the group with bargaining power in its relations with government. The source of this power. . . derives from the group's performance of a productive function."[8] Bluntly, if the unions, for example, do not like some legislation, they can act to bring a large segment of the economy, or vital public services, or production of export goods vital to a sound balance of payments to a halt. In short, the power of many groups has reached the point that they may be able to hold the country to ransom.

---

[8]Samuel H. Beer, *British Politics in the Collectivist Age* (New York: Alfred A. Knopf, 1965), p. 331.

This situation has been termed *pluralistic stagnation* and it has been blamed as a major cause of Britain's economic troubles during the 1970s and on into the 1980s. The point is that the government is too responsive to the people's wishes, at least as expressed through interest groups. The various groups seek the benefit of only their members, without thought for the general good of the country. While this usually is true of the great majority of interest groups in any country, the problem in Britain is that the major groups are so intimately involved in the policy process and occupy such key positions in the economy that they are able to block any action not in their members' favor.

Thus Government policy becomes an elaborate compromise resulting from clearing everything with key groups and balancing their contrasting interests. Political leadership comes to consist almost entirely of diplomatic skills and bold, innovative thinking about long-term policy is discouraged. Instead of taking decisive action to solve basic problems, leaders seek not to rock the boat to avoid alienating key groups. Prime Minister Heath sought to break out of these frustrations in February 1974 by fighting an election on the question of "Who Governs?"—the prime minister or the coal miners? He was accused of seeking confrontation (obviously bad) and went down to defeat and eventual loss of the Conservative leadership.

Heath's successor as Leader, Margaret Thatcher, has had to deal with the same basic problem since coming to power in 1979. While she has sought to avoid a stark confrontation with the unions, yet she has devoted herself to changing the style of governing in Britain. She has proclaimed basic goals and remained committed to them even when the immediate policies that she felt were necessary to accomplish them produced distasteful results. She has clung to the actions that she believes are essential to control inflation even when the result has been massive unemployment. As a result, she has been called dogmatic, inflexible, and ideological. That may be true and her policies may be misguided, but her behavior is understandable only in the context of the interest group politics with a vengeance that exists in Britain and her efforts to seek a way out, given the unsatisfactory results that living with the situation has produced.

Thus she was little willing to compromise when in 1984 the miners opposed plans to shut down the least productive coal pits. On the other side, Arthur Scargill, the leader of the miners, constantly demonstrated what the British term *bloody mindedness*. He was at least as concerned to drive Thatcher from office as he was to protect his followers' jobs. The result was a miners' strike that dragged on throughout the year with frequent clashes between pickets and the police. Property damage, personal injury, and even death occurred. Neither side was willing to give ground because the issue had gone well beyond the economic merits and social problems of abandoning a few mines to become a question of the political power of a major group.

You should not think that such problems exist only when the Conservatives are in office. As Labour Prime Minister Harold Wilson once shouted at a major

union leader who was trying to bend the Government's policy to his preferences, "Get your tanks off of my lawn!" In the 1960s the Wilson Government
found that it could not pass legislation that the unions strongly opposed. While
in the 1970s it managed to get the voluntary cooperation of the unions for its
economic policy, this was relatively short-lived, and in the end union refusal to
continue to cooperate led to Labour's loss of the 1979 election.

Currently the unions probably are the interest group whose power is most
visible and which, perhaps, has the most serious effect. But their position is not
unique in Britain. All major groups have the close ties with the government that
we have discussed; all can function as blocking groups to some extent. But why
should groups function as veto groups more frequently now?

In part because, as we have noted, this network of relations really is a product of World War II, so not until the late 1940s did it reach fruition. At that time
Britain's main concern was to rebuild from the war. Then the prosperity of the
1950s—when, as Prime Minister Macmillan told the voters, "You've Never Had
It So Good!"—made it seem that there was more than enough for everyone and
no one had to fight very hard for their particular interests. While prosperity began to slow down, the seriousness of the economic problems did not become
fully apparent until the 1970s. Then, as the expectations that each year should
be better than the previous one were frustrated, interests began to see the need
to flex their muscles to ensure that their members did not lose any ground in the
struggle over declining benefits.

To this should be added a change in attitude. Fewer Britons now than in the
past believe that "the man from Whitehall [the civil servant] knows best." Thus
groups are much more prepared to challenge Government plans than they were
in the past. Furthermore, whereas Britons used to feel that democracy required
no more than a means of representing their interests—through groups and elected
officials—now many of them feel that considerable mass involvement is essential. Britain is moving in an American direction from representative to participatory democracy.

This does not mean, however, that anywhere near a majority of Britons seeks
a highly active role in politics. Britons are not joiners to the same extent that
Americans are and do not tend to think of group strategies in politics as much.
While a majority say that they would sign a petition to try to influence Parliament against passing a law that they considered really unjust and harmful, only
15 percent say that they would take group action, either by raising the matter in
an organization to which they already belong or by forming a group of like-
minded people.[9] Few of them—6 percent—regard group strategies as the most
effective way of influencing the government, while a third think that contacting
their MP (clearly a preference for representative, rather than participatory, de-

---

[9]Roger Jowell and Colin Airey, eds., *British Social Attitudes: the 1984 report* (Aldershot, England: Gower,
1984), p. 169.

mocracy) would have most effect. Nonetheless, the second most preferred method (chosen by nearly a quarter) is to contact the news media, a step that not only requires personal initiative but also ignores representative structures.

Thus various recent developments in British society have made interest group politics even more important than in the past. The interest group system is a source of some concern because the British have yet to devise solutions to the problems growing out of the way in which interest groups are involved in the making of public policy.

BIBLIOGRAPHICAL NOTE

Campaign procedures, issues, and events for each general election since 1945 are discussed in the Nuffield College series of election studies, *The British General Election of [year]*. Since 1951 these books have been authored either individually or jointly by David Butler. A similar series entitled *Britain at the Polls* was begun by the American Enterprise Institute, starting with the February 1974 election. The volume for the 1983 election was edited by Austin Ranney and published by Duke University Press in 1985. After each general election *The Times* publishes a *Guide to the House of Commons,* with all the election results plus brief biographical notes on the candidates and comments on the outcome. While more general in scope, Colin Seymour-Ure, *The Political Impact of Mass Media* (London: Constable, 1974), includes comments on the media in elections.

For a historical overview of groups in British politics see Graham Wootton, *Pressure Groups in Britain, 1720–1970* (Hamden, Conn.: Archon Books, 1975). The Beer book cited in Footnote 8 is a prize-winning analysis of the way in which basic British ideas about how interests should be represented in politics changed from the 19th into the 20th century. The book, especially chapters 12 and 13, stimulated considerable discussion and research concerning pluralistic stagnation. The third edition is published by Norton (1982) under the title *Modern British Politics.*

Among the case studies of particular groups, still interesting and worth reading are Harry Eckstein, *Pressure Group Politics: The Case of the British Medical Association* (London: Allen & Unwin, 1960), and Peter Self and Herbert J. Storing, *The State and the Farmer* (London: Allen & Unwin, 1962).

4

Policy Alternatives

THE PARTY SYSTEM

Visualizing a modern democratic government without political parties is virtually impossible. Where governmental officers are chosen by a broad electorate, ascertaining the will of the people and translating it into effective action requires organization. Political parties provide that organization. They offer the electorate policy alternatives and potential leaders to implement them. They seek to discover the inchoate desires of the people and sort through the diffuse demands of a multitude of interest groups to produce a mutually consistent package of actions. Through this process they enable the electorate to have a choice of political futures. If you have ever had a problem deciding in an ice cream store which of the 31 flavors you wanted, you can multiply that by a thousand to get some idea of how impossible democratic government would be unless parties existed to offer a choice among a relatively small number of policy packages.

Once the electorate has made its choice in an election, parties carry out their function in contrasting ways. The party in power, by defending the policies and actions of its leaders, seeks to convince the people that the country is being governed in the best way possible; the parties out of power, by criticizing the policies and actions (or inactions) of the party running the country, try to convert the people to the idea that they could do a better job. Whether this effort is limited to attacking those in power or includes as well detailed proposals for alternate policies is a matter of tactics. Democratic government is party government.

Although the rudimentary origins of British political parties can be traced back several centuries, many writers prefer to date their origin about 1700, when the two major political groupings were called the Tories and the Whigs. But it was not until well into the next century that a modern party system began to emerge. Only then did loyalty to party doctrine begin to replace personal connections as the basis of party organization. To a considerable extent this was brought about by the parties' need to organize the new electorate as the right to vote was expanded. Membership in Parliamentary factions became more stable and party organization outside of Parliament began to develop. This led in turn to a broadening of party membership beyond a handful of elected officials and party workers, a trend accelerated by the appearance of the Labour party in 1900. Thus at the beginning of the 20th century Britain had a fully developed modern party system.

While the contenders for power have altered over the years—the Conservatives struggled with the Liberals in the 19th and early 20th century and, since then, have had to fight the Labour party—Britain has been classified as a two-party system. Political events in the 1970s, however, raised serious doubts whether such a label was any longer accurate. Even should it be, it probably would mislead you into believing that the British party system basically is the same as the American, which it certainly is not.

In the 12 general elections in Britain from 1945 through 1983, a third of all the candidates for the House of Commons were neither Labour nor Conservative. Taking 1983 alone, the two main parties offered less than half of all the candidates. In the 12 elections 32 percent of all the candidates elected received less than a majority of the vote in their individual district, which clearly means that three or more candidates were seeking election there. Figure 4–1 shows the dramatic change in the nature of electoral contests for the House of Commons in recent elections. From 1951 through 1959 the voters in the majority of constituencies had a choice between only two candidates. In the 1960s three candidates typically appeared on the ballot. By the mid-1970s about two fifths of the constituencies were being contested by four or more candidates, and by the close of the decade three fourths of the constituencies were. While this proportion declined slightly in 1983, nevertheless, every constituency had at least three candidates and most had four or more.

Although candidates from other than the two leading parties have been active in British elections, they have not been very successful. Britain's reputation as a two-party system rests primarily upon party strengths in the House of Commons. Even this measure suggests significant departures from a two-party system during most of the first half of the 20th century, when parties other than the two leading ones were able to win a sixth to a third of the seats in general elections, as Figure 4–2 shows. Since 1945, however, the Labour and Conservative parties always have held between them at least 93 percent of the seats. They have been the only parties that had any prospect of forming a Government.

In the first quarter of the 20th century Britain deviated from a strict two-party system as the Liberals rapidly lost support to the newly formed Labour

FIGURE 4–1 Type of Constituency Contests in Recent Elections

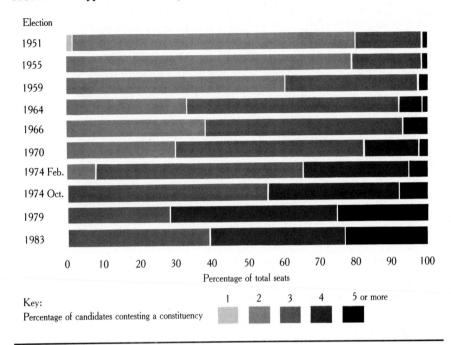

FIGURE 4–2 The Two Leading Parties' Percentage of the Seats in Parliament at 20th-Century General Elections

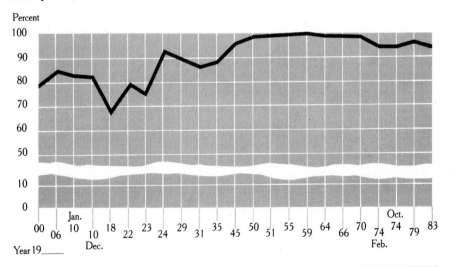

party, which managed to replace it as one of the two leading parties. The Liberals did not disappear, however, as happened when the Republicans displaced the Whig party in the American two-party system. They have continued to contest elections and maintain as extensive a party organization as their finances permit. Although since 1945 their strength in Parliament has been limited, they have had some impact on the policies of the major parties and the political attitudes of the public.

Sectarian conflict in Northern Ireland and the rise of nationalism in Wales and Scotland combined in the 1970s to produce even greater departures from the ideal two-party system. Prior to then the Northern Ireland MPs usually were integrated into the Conservative party and the nationalists were unable to win any representation. Thus in six elections, from 1950 through 1966, only 10 MPs not associated with one of the three leading parties were elected.

But in the early 1970s the Protestant political forces in Northern Ireland fragmented, and the parties that emerged broke all connection with the Conservatives. At the same time many people in Wales and especially Scotland began to feel culturally distinct from the English and favored parties that proclaimed these views. Thus in the February 1974 general election 24 candidates not associated with one of the three main parties were elected and in the next election that October the number increased to 27, the largest number of "minority" Members of Parliament in over half a century.

While these figures may not sound very impressive, they are remarkable given the British electoral system. As we have seen in the previous chapter, whatever candidate gets the most votes wins, regardless of what percentage of the vote that is. The key characteristic of such an electoral system is that the share of the seats in the legislature that a party wins has no necessary relation to the proportion of the popular vote that it received. Unless a party can concentrate its support in a number of constituencies, it could gain a substantial share of the popular vote spread out over the whole country and not win any seats at all.

To a considerable extent this has been the Liberals' problem for the last half century. The pragmatic nature of the British voters has compounded the Liberals' difficulties. Even voters favorable to many of the Liberals' policies realize that the party has little chance of gaining substantial representation in Parliament. Not wanting to waste their vote and seeing little point in a mere ideological gesture (recall our comments abut the low level of ideology in British politics), they choose between the Labour and Conservative parties. Figure 4–3 provides a pre-World War II instance and a more recent example of how the electoral system works to the Liberals' disadvantage and to the benefit of the major parties.

But, you may say, then how did the Labour party, which was the third party early in the century, manage to replace the Liberals as one of the two leading parties? One of the reasons was that the Labour vote then, unlike the Liberal vote now, was concentrated in certain areas—urban working-class districts and mining constituencies. Thus Labour could get more votes than any other party in several places.

FIGURE 4–3   **Relation between Share of Vote and Seats in Parliament**

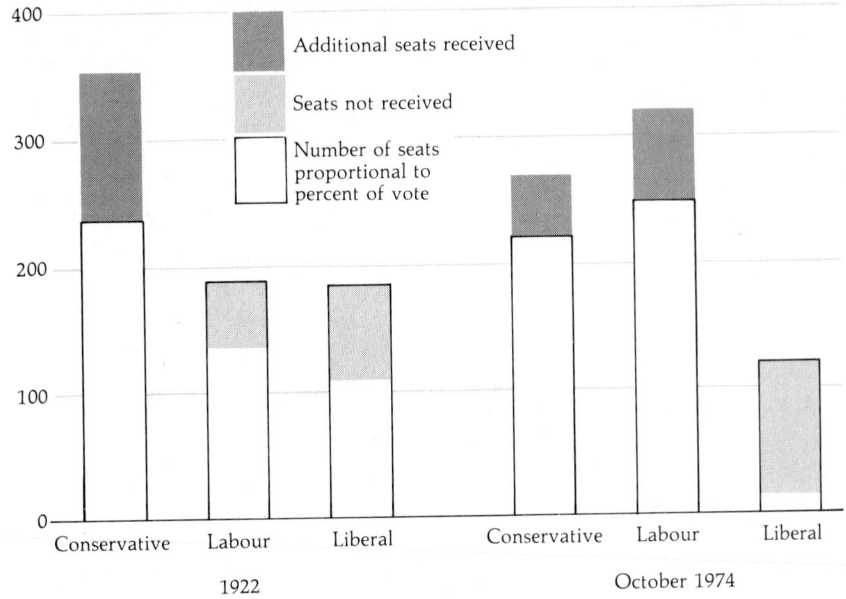

Currently this is relevant to the nationalist parties' situation. Obviously their support is concentrated in their particular nation within the United Kingdom; they are not handicapped by the electoral system to the extent that the Liberals are. In October 1974 the Liberals, with 619 candidates and more than 18 percent of the popular vote, won only 13 seats in the House of Commons. The Scottish Nationalists, contesting only the 71 seats in Scotland, obtained less than 3 percent of the total national vote, but won 11 seats. The crucial difference was that within Scotland the Nationalists received more than 30 percent of the vote, a regional concentration of support nowhere approached by the Liberals.

Third parties, especially nationwide ones, also encounter problems in breaking the strength of the two main parties because of the electoral deposit. Totally apart from campaign expenses, a party must risk hundreds of thousands of dollars in deposits to contest every constituency. Minor parties would have to expect to lose most of this sum. For a small party, whose income is likely to be limited, this presents a major financial burden.

Also helping to maintain the political dominance of only two parties is the allocation of radio and television time. Since time cannot be purchased, parties have only what is officially allotted to them. The fact that the two leading parties get the lion's share of this time not only means that other parties have less opportunity to use these powerful channels of mass communication, but also, in effect, tells the electorate that other parties—such as the Liberals—aren't as important as are Labour and the Conservatives, otherwise they would be given more time.

Formidable as the obstacles of the electoral system, the deposit, and allocation of media time are, they can be overcome. And early in 1981 a new political
development appeared to some to offer the greatest potential in half a century
for changing the party system. Several moderate members of the Labour party
broke away to form the Social Democratic party, which then allied with the Liberals. Should this Alliance prove viable, the nature of the British party system
would be drastically altered. And should the Alliance be able to gain enough
Parliamentary strength to force a change in the electoral system, then the
change in the party system would have a good chance of being permanent.

THE LEADING PARTIES

For the rest of the chapter we will be focusing primarily on the Conservative
and Labour parties with some comments on the Alliance. First, we discuss the
policy alternatives offered by the leading parties and, then, who it is in the population that favors one policy mix or the other. Next, we examine the parties'
strengths—their level of support and prospects. This requires some consideration of the effectiveness of a party's organization. We broaden this discussion
into our fourth consideration of the distribution of power within a party in order to assess its role as a channel for participation in the democratic process.

Party Programs and Policies

Discussing the Conservatives' program is difficult because many Conservatives would question whether such a thing exists. Certainly they would object to
anyone's presuming to study conservative ideology, for they charge that being
doctrinaire is a socialist defect, from which they are free. They would contend
that Conservatism is more an attitude toward society than it is a coherent set of
doctrines. The Conservatives present themselves as the party of governmental
experience, the party composed of the traditional ruling class, obviously best
suited by heredity and tradition to run the country. At times their appeal to the
electorate almost seems to be: Never mind our policies, simply trust our capable
leaders, who will be able to take the proper action whatever the circumstances
may be.

The Conservatives have been identified with support for the traditional elements of British society—the monarchy, the established church, the military,
the existing social structure, the public school system. They have been a party of
the elite, of the status quo. Yet they have not been reactionary nor even conservative, in American terms. They have demonstrated adaptability. While they
have opposed some of their opponents' welfare measures, they have accepted
socialized medicine and have introduced some welfare measures of their own.
The Conservatives have acted similarly with respect to public ownership. Although they are opposed to it in principle, they have reversed very little of what
Labour has implemented. And in fact some government-owned concerns were
nationalized under Conservative Governments.

Thus the Conservatives seek a middle way between the excesses of both individualism and collectivism. They prefer individual freedom to bureaucratic direction and believe that widespread ownership of property is essential to a healthy democracy. Yet they recognize that social considerations may override these views. The party never has supported laissez-faire, but has accepted the idea that governmental action may be necessary to correct economic abuses and stimulate the economy.

The important point is that usually the conservatives do not feel that there is much either that needs to be reformed or that can be. They do not believe that social inequality is bad or can be eliminated. Different people contribute differently to society, so it is only natural that their rewards and political influence should vary as well.

At the same time, however, the Conservatives stress the idea of national unity; they appeal to feelings of community. Despite their association with the elite social and political groups, they see themselves as the only truly national party, representative of all interests rather than just a single section, as they charge Labour is. The Conservatives' ability to win the votes of many workers can be cited in support of this claim. The Conservatives berate socialists for emphasizing class divisions and thus needlesssly stirring up ill feelings. This desire for national unity is related to the Conservatives' concern with national honor. They see their party as the repository of the national interest and at times seem to believe that they are the only true patriots. The British flag often is displayed prominently at Conservative party meetings. For a British party to criticize the country's foreign policy is reprehensible in their view.

Thus, it seems ironic that it was the Conservative party that arranged for British entry into the Common Market, while the Labour party became increasingly hostile to this step. Labour has been more concerned than have the Conservatives about what would happen to the Commonwealth, the contemporary descendant of the British Empire, which always made Conservative hearts quicken with pride. The Conservative leaders have had to cope with some internal party opposition on this issue, but they have been able to win the support of the bulk of the party.

Two issues were central to the Conservatives' 1979 election campaign—the weakness of the British economy and the Labour Government's unwillingness to stand up to the trade unions.[1] The argument that linked these two was the contention that letting the unions demand huge wage increases was fueling a disastrous rate of inflation. Although Labour had reduced inflation from a horrendous 22.3 percent in July 1975 to under 10 percent at the time of the 1979 election, the Conservatives were not reassured because the strikes of the winter of 1978–79 seemed to indicate a new period of union unreasonableness. In any event, when things literally had reached the point that people could not bury

---

[1] Howard Penniman, ed., *Britain at the Polls, 1979* (Washington, D.C.: American Enterprise Institute, 1981), pp. 58–74, 121–28, 320–25.

their dead because the gravediggers were on strike and were picketing the cemeteries to prevent anyone else from digging graves, they had gone too far.

The Conservatives favored cuts in government spending; this would permit reducing government borrowing and enable them to get the money supply under control. The money supply, following the views of economist Milton Friedman of the University of Chicago, was regarded as the key element in controlling inflation. The spending cuts also would permit cuts in income tax. This would restore the incentives for hard work and competition, which the high rates of tax were said to discourage. Thus the economy would become more productive. A tight money supply also meant that employers would need to make more efficient use of their workers to cut labor costs. Thus the Conservatives believed that the free enterprise system of unfettered collective bargaining could be relied upon to limit union wage demands without the need for government action to limit wages and prices.

One final policy was not especially stressed by the Conservatives, but may well have stirred up some popular enthusiasm. This was their plan to permit people living in government-constructed housing to purchase their accommodations. Virtually all public housing in the United States is so ghastly that you may wonder why this was a vote-winner. In Britain, however, public housing typically is quite comfortable. Thus a chance to buy one's accommodation at what would be bargain prices was attractive.

In 1983 the Conservative election *manifesto* (the British term for campaign platform) proclaimed that under their rule "Britain has recovered her confidence and self-respect" and "is once more a force to be reckoned with"—an appeal that should be familiar to you from the American 1984 Presidential campaign, when Republicans asserted that under Ronald Reagan America was back and standing tall. In the British case this was a none-too-subtle reminder that Margaret Thatcher had been responsible for bashing those nasty Argies in the Falklands in 1982. Furthermore, the handling of this conflict showed that the voters could rely on the Conservatives to maintain strong defense forces, contrary to Labour's plans.

Beyond such traditional nationalistic appeals, the Conservatives argued that their policies clearly had worked. Inflation was down to only 4 percent—the lowest level in 15 years. Such success could be maintained only by continuing to keep a tight limit on government spending and preventing unions from making excessive wage demands. To hold down local taxes, various measures would be taken to limit the spending of local government and the major metropolitan units of government—controlled by Labour and accused of spending like drunken sailors—would be abolished. Unions were to be made more democratic, with members to cast ballots on whether a strike should be called and to have increased power to elect their leaders.

Much of Conservative policy of the last few years has not departed greatly from the party's past positions. The real difference has been the new party Leader, Margaret Thatcher. From the beginning she proclaimed her determina-

FIGURE 4–4 Conservative Newspaper Ad—1983 Election

"Like your manifesto, Comrade."

THE LABOUR PARTY MANIFESTO.	THE COMMUNIST PARTY MANIFESTO.
1983	1983

THE LABOUR PARTY MANIFESTO.

1. Withdrawal from the Common Market.
2. Massive increase in Nationalisation.
3. Cancel Trident, remove nuclear defences.
4. Cancel tenants' rights to buy their own council houses.
5. Oppose secret ballots for union members on selecting union leadership.
6. Abolish restraints on union closed shops.
7. Abolish parents' rights to choose their children's school.
8. Oppose secret ballots for union members on strikes.
9. Abolish Immigration Act and British Nationality Act.
10. Exchange controls to be introduced.
11. Abolish Prevention of Terrorism Act.

THE COMMUNIST PARTY MANIFESTO.

1. Withdrawal from the Common Market.
2. Massive increase in Nationalisation.
3. Cancel Trident, remove nuclear defences.
4. Cancel tenants' rights to buy their own council houses.
5. Oppose secret ballots for union members on selecting union leadership.
6. Abolish restraints on union closed shops.
7. Abolish parents' rights to choose their children's school.
8. Oppose secret ballots for union members on strikes.
9. Abolish Immigration Act and British Nationality Act.
10. Exchange controls to be introduced.
11. Abolish Prevention of Terrorism Act.

CONSERVATIVE ☒

tion (some would say her dogmatism) to stick to her policies no matter what. In this she was criticizing the conduct of the previous Conservative Government from 1970 to 1974. Not long after Prime Minister Edward Heath had been in office then, he decided that the economic policies he and the Conservative party had proclaimed were not working. He reversed many of them in what is known as the infamous "U-turn."[2] In contrast, Thatcher continued to pursue her economic policies despite a horrendous growth in unemployment. Many of the traditional elite of the Conservative party (who come from a higher social class than does Thatcher, the grocer's daughter) are bothered by what they regard as her insensitivity to the personal degradation involved in extensive unemployment. These so-called wets fear that she is deflecting the party from its traditional adaptability and concern with national community. Whether they are right in fearing that the Conservative party is being transformed probably will depend upon whether Thatcher is able to win a third term in the next general election.

The basic doctrine of the Labour party is democratic socialism. It has been little influenced by Marxism; rather, its intellectual heritage derives from Christian socialists of the social gospel school and the Fabian Society. In addition the party is greatly influenced, as its name suggests, by being based on the trade unions. Hugh Gaitskell, a former Leader of the party, once said of the Independent Labour party, a forerunner of the Labour party, that its "socialism was derived far more from the Methodist Church and a Christian approach than from Continental revolutionaries."[3] Similarly, the Fabian Society would have nothing to do with Marxist revolutionaries. In an 1896 statement of purpose the Fabians begged "those socialists who are looking forward to a sensational historical crisis, to join some other society."[4]

Sidney Webb, one of the most influential leaders of the Fabians and the Labour party around the turn of the century, once explained the conditions that were essential if political and social reform were to occur in Britain. For change to occur it must (1) come democratically; (2) be gradual, causing no dislocation; (3) not be regarded as immoral; (4) be achieved constitutionally and peacefully.[5] Hardly a cry to man the barricades against the capitalist oppressors! The Fabians believed that sound factual research would be sufficient to establish the case for socialism in the minds of all reasonable people.

The influence of the Fabians has been of great significance in the development of the Labour party's orientation toward politics. The Fabians demon-

---

[2] A year after the election, Mrs. Thatcher told the Conservative annual conference that she would not change her policies despite the massive unemployment they were creating. Punning on the title of a well-known play about the burning of Joan of Arc, Mrs. Thatcher said of herself, "The lady's not for turning."

[3] Hugh Gaitskell, *Recent Developments in British Socialist Thinking* (London: Cooperative Union, n.d. [circa 1960]), p. 4

[4] Quoted in Margaret Cole, *The Story of Fabian Socialism* (London: Mercury Books, 1963), p. 92.

[5] *Fabian Essays in Socialism*, ed. G. Bernard Shaw (Garden City, N.Y.: Doubleday Publishing, n.d.), p. 51.

strated that it was possible to be a socialist without having to use Marxist jargon or swallow an abstract, elaborate theory of history. They made advocacy of moderate reform respectable by showing that one could be for widespread change without having to be a revolutionary.

For about the last two decades the Labour party has been torn between two contrasting views of socialism. The left wing of the party, which believes that it alone is remaining true to the party's basic principles, sees the essence of socialism as nationalization—government ownership of "the commanding heights of the economy," The party has been committed formally to such a policy since 1918. The left has felt that in a democracy large concentrations of economic power must be controlled by government to ensure that they will serve social ends rather than the benefit of a few. The object is to ensure that the working class, through its representatives, exercises power.

For the moderates in the Labour party, nationalization is not a panacea for social ills. They argue that the fairly extensive program of nationalization that Labour implemented from 1945 to 1951 did little to promote greater equality by redistributing the wealth and that this must necessarily be the case unless government is to seize ownership of businesses without compensating their previous owners—an action they reject as tyrannical. For the moderates socialism is not a matter of government ownership of the means of production, distribution, and exchange, but a quest for social justice (not that the left wing is unconcerned with this). Obtaining this requires that the government maintain a floor of basic benefits and services available to all as of right and ensure that everyone truly has an equal opportunity to rise above that floor to the maximum of his or her ability.

This concern with equality is not limited simply to correcting disparities in wealth and income. The values of British society must be transformed to eliminate snobbery and privilege. The class barriers and social inequalities that are obstacles to free social intercourse between people of differing status must be destroyed. Thus socialism is much more than a doctrine about economic relations. The founder of the Labour party, Keir Hardie, observed, "Socialism is at bottom a question of ethics or morals. It has to do mainly with the relationships which should exist between a man and his fellows."[6]

In international affairs Labour has opposed colonialism and been less nationalistic than the Conservatives; they have believed that all workers are bound together whatever their nationality. Despite this view, the party has been suspicious of—at times hostile to—the Common Market (EEC). In this case Labour has been more nationalistic than the Conservative party. The Labour left views the EEC as an alliance of capitalists and faint-hearted socialists that prevents Britain from fully controlling its own economy and thus inhibits socialist reform. They also argue that the Common Agricultural Policy results in higher

---

[6]Quoted in Socialist Union, *Twentieth Century Socialism* (Harmondsworth, Eng.: Penguin Books, 1956).

food prices for the British working class. The growing power of the left within the Labour party resulted in a decision at the 1980 party conference to commit the party, when it returns to power, to pulling Britain out of the EEC.

Although never a majority position, pacifism traditionally has been strong in the Labour party. This belief has combined at times with the left wing's considerable distrust of the United States as a capitalist power to produce neutralist sentiments. At the 1980 party conference Labour adopted a policy of unilateral nuclear disarmament (the same thing has occurred 20 years earlier, but was reversed the following year), which opposed British participation in any defense policy based on nuclear weapons and the siting of the cruise missiles in Britain. On the other hand, the conference voted against a proposal to withdraw from NATO.

Labour's 1979 election campaign was rather schizophrenic. The party's official policy included a number of left-wing measures: more government ownership, a wealth tax on the rich, abolishing the House of Lords, reduced defense spending, and steps against the public schools. Prime Minister James Callaghan and other moderate leaders, however, were busy trying to reassure the electorate that Labour was a safe party that would not think of doing anything adventurous. Their basic appeal was that Labour, unlike the Conservatives, really cared about the life of the common people and would make certain that government helped those who could not adequately help themselves and provided opportunity for everyone of ability to get ahead.

Labour's basic problem during the campaign was to convince the voters that despite all the problems with the unions during the winter of discontent, 1978–79, labor relations and the economy would be better with Labour in power than they would be if the Conservatives won. Labour's most brilliant, but curiously, little-used attempt to do this was the poster that appears in Figure 4–5. What this would immediately call to a British voter's mind was the disastrous confrontation between the Conservative Government and the coal miners in the winter of 1973–74, which resulted in a nationwide three-day work week and widespread power and heating cuts.

Labour's 1983 campaign was even worse than its previous one; it was without doubt one of the most disastrous and incompetently waged in the history of British politics. That Labour managed to lose the election when more than 3 million people were unemployed was due largely to its attacking itself rather than its opponents and its persistence in offering policies clearly unattractive to the electorate. Its manifesto—an extraordinarily large pamphlet of 40 pages— was termed by one of the party's disgruntled right-wing leaders "the longest suicide note in history." It was a laborious compromise that sought to please every faction in the party and as a result irritated them all and alienated the electorate.

In so far as the campaign had any theme, it was that unemployment must be reversed. (See Figure 4–6.) Surprisingly, Labour did not just reprint one of the Conservative ads from the previous election (Figure 4–7) and throw it back in their opponents' face. During the first three and a half years after the Conserva-

FIGURE 4–5   **Labour Party 1979 Election Poster**

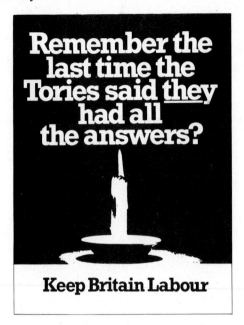

tives returned to power in 1979, unemployment increased at the rate of one per-son *every* minute. (At that point the way in which the figures were calculated was changed.) Labour argued that extensive government spending was needed to create jobs. Wage demands should be kept moderate not by having masses out of work and, therefore, willing to work for low wages, but by closer cooper-ation with the unions. Allowing them an even greater voice in national economic policy was supposed to encourage them to seek only those wage increases that would not fuel inflation and harm Britain's international trade.

On defense the party said that it would institute a nonnuclear policy within the term (that is to say no longer than a five-year period) of the next Parliament. Neither Callaghan (no longer Prime Minister or party Leader) nor Labour's de-fense spokesman Denis Healey supported unilateralism. And both explicitly said so during the campaign. Leaving the current party Leader Michael Foot (who was a unilateralist) to claim that if only people would read the manifesto carefully, everything would be clear, which, of course, it wasn't. In short this, like everything else about the party's campaign, was a shambles.

Immediately after World War II the policy differences between the Labour and Conservative parties seemed to be clear cut; the choice offered the voters appeared much sharper than that provided in the United States by American

FIGURE 4–6   Labour Newspaper Ad—1983 Election

Every day this government hangs on to its job, another 1,395 people lose theirs.

Adding millions more to the country's £17 billion dole bill.

In fact, the Tories spend more on keeping people jobless than they do on keeping people healthy.

Are you going to vote for another 5 years of this nightmare?

Or are you going to think positive and vote Labour?

Only Labour has the experience and the policies to get Britain working again.

The moment you bring Labour back, we will start an emergency programme of investment in industry, in transport, in housing and in essential new technology.

It is a tried and tested method for creating new jobs and for reducing the dole bill.

With jobs again, people can start to buy things again. To produce them, industry then takes on even more people.

We will also encourage the economy to grow by increasing pensions, child benefits, education and health service spending.

But what of the Tory claim that Britain can't afford it?

It's a matter of priorities. Where the Tories waste Britain's vital savings and oil wealth abroad, Labour will invest those resources in Britain again.

You can help us build a healthier society by voting Labour on June 9th.

And sack the Tories before they sack you.

THINK POSITIVE. ACT POSITIVE ✗ VOTE LABOUR.

FIGURE 4-7   Conservative Newspaper Ad 1979 Election

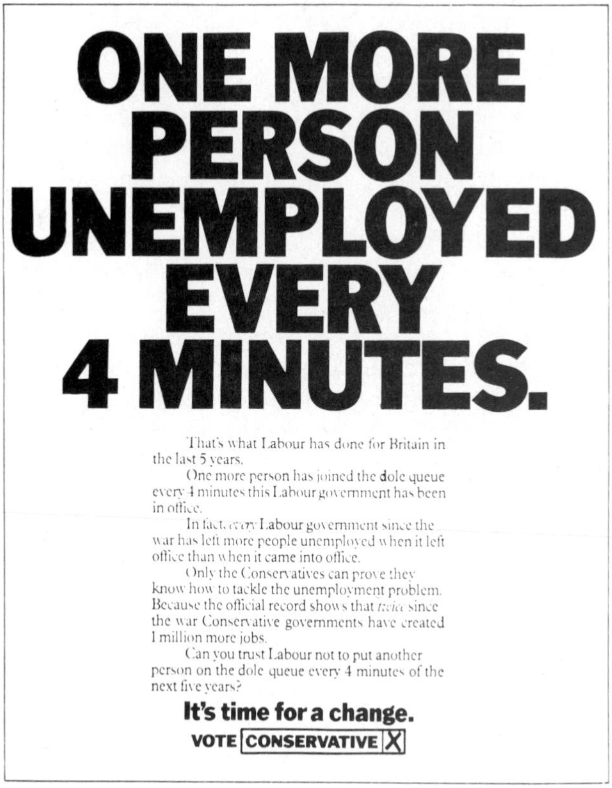

ONE MORE PERSON UNEMPLOYED EVERY 4 MINUTES.

That's what Labour has done for Britain in the last 5 years.

One more person has joined the dole queue every 4 minutes this Labour government has been in office.

In fact, every Labour government since the war has left more people unemployed when it left office than when it came into office.

Only the Conservatives can prove they know how to tackle the unemployment problem. Because the official record shows that *twice* since the war Conservative governments have created 1 million more jobs.

Can you trust Labour not to put another person on the dole queue every 4 minutes of the next five years?

It's time for a change.

VOTE CONSERVATIVE X

parties. During the 1950s and 1960s, however, the two main British parties seemed to converge on policies. The word *Butskellism,* a combination of the names of R. A. Butler, the number-two man in the Conservative party, and of Hugh Gaitskell, the Leader of the Labour party, was coined to suggest how little difference existed between what the parties advocated. Two polls in the mid-1960s found that 40 to 50 percent of the electorate failed to see any important difference between the parties, specifically agreeing that the parties were "all much of a muchness."

The 1970s, however, saw the parties moving apart. The confrontation with the miners, mentioned above, was conclusive proof for Labour that all their charges that the Conservative Government was the most right-wing one since World War II were true. Thatcher's dogmatic and abrasive political style only reinforced such views. At the same time the growing strength of the left was pushing Labour away from the political center. Thus in the 1979 election nearly half of the voters saw a good deal of difference between the Labour and Conservative parties, the largest proportion saying this in at least a decade and a half.[7]

The distance between the two main parties has important implications for the strategy of the Liberal party. When their big rivals seem at opposite ends of the political spectrum, the Liberals offer the voters a moderate, middle way. When the big parties move toward each other and things seem a bit crowded on the center ground, the Liberals claim to provide a distinct alternative no longer offered by the big parties. Clearly in recent years the emphasis has been on the former of these two strategies. The Liberals have charged that both major parties are beholden to limited segments of society, so that neither of them can govern in the general interest. Only Liberals—free from these special interests—can restore good, effective government.

The performance of government is to be improved by structural changes. The electoral system is to be changed so that moderate views—as embodied by the Liberals—will gain seats in the Commons proportional to their share of the popular vote. Regional governmental units are to be created to make government more efficient and closer to the people. A written bill of rights is to protect basic liberties.

As for conflicts between workers and employers, the Liberal remedy long has been co-ownership. A firm's workers would share in the profits and be represented both at the management and governing-board levels. This would ensure that workers would share in deciding how the business would be run and, presumably, make them feel more a part of the business. The Liberals believe that such reforms would help to eliminate class bitterness in Britain and improve productive efficiency.

The Liberals' stress on moderate cooperativeness was given something of a practical test for the 1983 election. In 1981 prominent moderate members of the Labour party broke away in opposition to the party's policies of withdrawal from the Common Market and unilateral nuclear disarmament. Although they formed a separate party—the Social Democratic party—both they and the Liberals recognized that opposing each other in elections would be mutual suicide. Thus the two parties worked out (not without a good deal of acrimony) an Alliance for the 1983 election. Each offered candidates in about half the constituencies, and a joint Alliance manifesto, rather than separate party policy statements, was issued.

The SDP had no great problem in accepting most traditional Liberal policies for the manifesto. The Alliance, like Labour, favored government action to create jobs, but not at the same high level of government spending. Unlike both main parties, the Alliance favored a variety of statutory sanctions to control prices and wages. And on defense the Alliance also took a distinctive course. Although the two parties, especially the Liberals, had some questions about nu-

---

[7] Penniman, *Britain at the Polls*, p. 302, n. 26.

FIGURE 4–8   Liberal 1983 Election Campaign Paper

Campaigner

NEWS from the **ALLIANCE**

YOUR VOTE IS VITAL TO SAVE BRITAIN

It's the most important election of our times — says DAVID STEEL

- DON'T be fooled. You don't have to make a choice between two extremes.

- That's what the Tories and the Socialists would like you to believe.

- Vote ALLIANCE — and we'll bring sanity back to Britain while the extremists kill each other off!

- The Alliance aims to transform our political and economic system.

- We are prepared to *listen* — not to lecture.

- You now have the chance to make a real choice.

OUR CAMPAIGN in this election is different from that of Labour and the Tories. The two major parties will concentrate on what they fondly believe is their devoted and faithful vote.

Their leaders will appear bathed in floodlights at ticket-only political 'rave-ins'. We have a different and much more creative task. Our job is not to rouse the faithful but to convince and convert those who are seeking a new politics.

The style of our campaign will be not "tell the people" but "ask the Alliance". We shall actively encourage the hard, tough, searching questions. We take no vote for granted. Every voter for us is a new voter, to be welcomed, persuaded and convinced.

We shall not harangue or lecture, but listen and discuss. We set this style in Glasgow with the first of our major Alliance Question Times. These are being held in major regional centres and are being presided over not by committee politicians but by Magnus Magnusson and Ludovic Kennedy.

Within this dialogue we should leave people in no doubt that Labour is a rag-bag of Marxist ideas and the Tories are a party of broken promises and doctrinaire dogma.

If the Alliance fails in this election, the price Britain will pay will be high indeed.

Listen to our arguments. Read about our policies. They are sensible and sound. They point the way ahead for Britain.

We must reverse our national decline — says ROY JENKINS

THE SDP and the Liberal Party are fighting this election to reverse a quarter-century of national decline which has now culminated in the highest level of unemployment in our economic history. The old politics has no solutions. Our objective in this campaign is to convince the British people that if the crisis which now faces us is to be successfully confronted, if the tide is to be turned, there must now be a decisive break with the past and the conduct of our national affairs must

be put on a new footing.

We have three basic aims.

First, to break the hold of the two class-dominated parties over our national life. The rhetoric of class conflict fuels the endless, pointless battles between management and unions which have raged on as whole industries have disappeared.

Twenty-five years ago our standard of living exceeded that of Germany. Now it is two-thirds of it. In another twenty-five years time, it will be one-third of it, unless basic

changes are made — reform of the electoral system to produce more constructive policies, industrial democracy, profit-sharing and more democratic trade unions to promote partnership in industry and prosperity in place of impoverishment.

Second, we must have decisive action to bring unemployment down. By next year, one and a half million people will have been unemployed for over a year. A third of those under twenty-five will be out

of work and we shall have a generation without hope.

The social consequences of prolonged unemployment are unacceptable — rising crime, heightened social and racial tensions, increasing deprivation and squalor in our cities, an intensification of poverty. The accelerating slide into social decline and national disintegration must be halted now.

Third, we stand for an open and generous-spirited internationalism

as the basis of our approach to world affairs — solidarity with the NATO Alliance, on which our security rests, firm support for the European Community, on which our exports and livelihood increasingly depend, an awareness of our responsibility towards the less developed countries in an interdependent world. The alternative — narrow nationalism and economic isolation — will undermine our security and impoverish our country.

YOUR VOTE COULD PUT YOUR COUNTRY BACK ON COURSE AGAIN

clear weapons and thus did not embrace them with the Conservatives whole-hearted fervor, yet they certainly did not plan to relinquish Britain's, as did Labour, without getting some reciprocal concessions from the Soviet Union. Thus the Alliance clearly offered a distinctive and coherent policy mix.

The Bases of Party Support

Traditionally, the Conservatives drew their chief support from the landed element in British society. Around the turn of the century, however, many industrialists left the Liberals for the Conservatives. Now the party is strongly supported by business and professional people—including the military—and farmers. Labour's main strength is with the workers and some elements of the lower middle class like teachers. About a fourth of the middle class usually has voted Labour, but this does not offset the one fourth to the one third of the numerically larger working class that usually has voted Conservative.

As an American you probably see little that seems remarkable about these votes across class lines. But remember our earlier comments about class distinctions being much sharper in Britain than in the United States. Recall also that Britain, unlike the United States, has a party—Labour—that in its name and policies claims to represent the workers' interests. Thus that a good many workers do not vote Labour does seem a bit of a puzzle.

An explanation for this behavior that was widely accepted for some time focused on deference.[8] This theory argued that many people of lower social status in Britain believe that intelligence and ability are uniquely inherent to those above them in society and cannot be attained by those not born to them regardless of how much education they might obtain. Those believing this regard voting for people of higher social status as the only sensible behavior since the well-born obviously are the most able and should run the government.

Some scholars, however, could not believe that this picture of passivity accurately described the British working class that they knew.[9] Thus historical changes in the party system were offered as providing a better explanation of voting across class lines. Only many years after the founding of the Labour party around the turn of the century would most voters regard Labour, rather than the Liberals, as the normal alternative to the Conservatives. Until that happened, working-class Liberals who realized that their party had become so weak that continuing to vote for it was pointless would be more likely to switch to the Conservatives than to Labour. Furthermore, when the Liberals and the Conser-

---

[8]See especially Robert McKenzie and Allan Silver, *Angels in Marble* (Chicago: University of Chicago Press, 1968).

[9]David Butler and Donald Stokes, *Political Change in Britain*, 2d college ed. (New York: St. Martin's Press, 1976), pp. 117–38; Alan Marsh, *Protest and Political Consciousness* (London: Sage Publications, 1977), pp. 29–39, 230–34; and Dennis Kanavagh, "The Deferential English: A Comparative Critique," *Government and Opposition* 6 (Summer 1971) pp. 333–60.

vatives were the leading parties, some workers already voted Conservative because the Liberals then represented the industrialists' interests.

A third possible explanation is that improvements in the worker's standard of living since World War II has altered their traditional political preferences. As they become more prosperous, manual workers may acquire middle-class attitudes and thus change allegiance from Labour to the Conservatives. Plausible as this argument sounds, little evidence exists to suggest that the good life by itself is driving workers away from the Labour party.[10]

Labour's internal squabbling and shift to the left, however, have alienated many of their traditional support groups. In 1979 the shift to the Conservatives among the skilled working class was almost twice as great as it was among the electorate as a whole. And in 1983 this shift continued. Thus while in 1974 skilled workers were about twice as likely to vote Labour as to vote Conservative, by 1979 they were as likely to vote for one party as the other, and in 1983 *more* of them voted Conservative than Labour. Labour also has lost ground, although not quite so badly, among unskilled workers. Even among trade union members the proportion voting Labour in 1983 was only 8 percentage points greater than that voting Conservative.

Housing status has come to have a considerable effect upon how workers in Britain vote. (Remember our comments above about Conservative policy of selling public housing to tenants.) Almost half of those workers who were home owners voted Conservative in 1983, with a quarter voting Labour and the other quarter for the Alliance. Nearly half of the workers who rent public housing, however, voted Labour, with a quarter each going for the Conservatives and the Alliance.

Then there are the young voters, a group among which Labour traditionally has been strong. By 1979, however, voters 18 to 24 were no more likely to vote Labour than Conservative, and in 1983 the Conservatives had a 9-percentage-point lead over Labour with this age group.

The Liberal claim not to be beholden to any segment of society has tended to be borne out by the party's pattern of electoral support, and the Alliance with the SDP did not change this. Thus regardless of whether you separate the voters by sex, union membership, age group, or social class, the proportion that voted for the Alliance in 1983 was pretty much the same throughout the electorate.

Except for inner London and the urban industrial areas, the Conservatives have dominated England from somewhat south of Manchester to the southern coast for some time. The last two elections have made even starker this contrast in partisan preference between north and south. Labour has been virtually obliterated as a significant political force in sourthern England, with the Alliance providing whatever challenge there is to the Conservatives. The Conserva-

---

[10]See especially John Goldthorpe et al., *The Affluent Worker: Political Attitudes and Behavior* (Cambridge, Eng.: Cambridge University Press, 1968).

tives won 95 percent of the seats in southern England in 1983 and two thirds of the seats in London and in central England. In northern England, Scotland, and Wales, however, they won fewer than two fifths of the seats.

Since the end of World War II the Liberals' few electoral successes usually have been in the Celtic Fringe—Scotland, Wales, Devon, and Cornwall. This remained largely true in 1983 with 14 of the Alliance's 23 victories coming in these areas. Alliance with the SDP did not help the Liberals break out of the Fringe, and the Alliance's strength in Parliament was concentrated there because the great bulk of the SDP's MPs were unable to retain with their new party label seats that they had won when they had belonged to the Labour party. These defeats were strong evidence that party label continues to be more important than candidate personality to British voters.

Until the 1970s Northern Ireland's seats were virtually an exclusive Conservative preserve. Religious conflict so has fragmented Northern Ireland's politics, however, that now none of the three main parties can win a seat there. As for the Scottish and Welsh nationalists, their support has waned, and in the most recent elections they have been able to win only two seats each.

The basis for political behavior in Britain appears to have altered significantly. Deference, family tradition, and feelings of class solidarity are less important than formerly as more voters pragmatically assess the performance of the parties in deciding how to vote. While the era of Butskellism clearly is over, the harsher rhetoric of the last two elections has not polarized politics. As we have seen, the British electorate has been voting across class lines in record numbers. The volatility of the electorate is what gives the Alliance its main hope; if voters are willing to depart from traditional voting behavior, then a new political grouping may have some future despite the obstacles that the British electoral system requires it to overcome.

Party Strengths

The results of all general elections since 1945 in Britain appear in Table 4–1. After winning an overwhelming victory in 1945, the Labour party just managed to retain power in 1950 and the next year lost control of the Government. This was despite the fact that in 1951 Labour polled more votes than did the Conservatives, more in fact than any party before or since. From 1951 through 1959 the Conservatives won three consecutive general elections, an unprecedented accomplishment. Returned to power by a narrow margin in 1964, Labour won a substantial victory in 1966 but surprisingly was defeated by an unusually large shift of seats to the Conservatives in 1970. Although they received more votes than did Labour in February 1974, the Conservatives did not win quite as many seats and, thus, were driven from office. Labour, although the largest party in the House of Commons, had to form a minority Government since it was several seats short of an absolute majority. Several months later Labour called another election in hopes of winning firm control of Parliament. They were successful, but just barely, gaining only one seat more than an absolute majority.

TABLE 4–1   **Party Strengths since World War II in General Elections**

	1945	1950	1951	1955	1959	1964	1966	1970	Feb. 1974	Oct. 1974	1979	1983
Seats in the House of Commons:												
Conservative	213	299	321	345	365	304	253	330	296	276	339	397
Labour	393	315	295	277	258	317	363	287	301	319	268	209
Liberal*	12	9	6	6	6	9	12	6	14	13	11	23
Others	22	2	3	2	1	0	2	7	24	27	17	21
Percentage of the popular vote:												
Conservative	40	44	48	50	49	43	42	46	38	36	44	42
Labour	48	46	49	46	44	44	48	43	37	39	37	28
Liberal*	9	9	3	3	6	11	9	7	19	18	14	25
Others	3	1	1	1	1	1	2	3	5	7	6	5

*In 1983 Alliance.

The 1979 election saw the Conservatives sweep back to power on the largest shift of votes from one of the two leading parties to the other in the postwar period. Despite their gains the Conservatives polled only 44 percent of the popular vote. (Note that in only one election in the last 40 years has any party managed to get half of the popular vote.) Nonetheless, this was an improvement over the two previous elections in which neither of the two main parties was able to win as much as 40 percent of the vote. Although the Conservatives' support declined slightly in 1983, the collapse of the Labour vote gave the Conservatives a landslide victory—the greatest triumph for any party since 1945. The Alliance came close to beating Labour out for second place in the popular vote, but won only a handful of seats for its efforts.

Labour had not been looking very healthy even before the Social Democrats split away. From the mid-1970s on, in three elections it had been becalmed at about 11.5 million votes, about 500,000 to 1.5 million fewer than it had been polling. The disaster of 1983 reduced it to 8.5 million—a loss of a quarter of its support only four years earlier. In terms of number of votes it was the party's worst result since 1935, and in terms of share of the vote, the worst since 1918.

The severity of the defeat has not done a great deal to reduce factional fighting within Labour. In the past the principal left-wing organization was the Tribune Group. The current Leader of the party, Neil Kinnock, is a Tribunite, as was his immediate predecessor, Michael Foot. Nonetheless, Tribune has been outflanked by the Militant Tendency, an organization of Trokskyites who have been busily trying to take over local Labour party organizations. While not truly revolutionaries, Militant's supporters are willing to engage in extraparliamentary actions to secure their goals.

Internal disputes usually are much less visible in the Conservative party. Currently this is somewhat less true because the previous party Leader Edward Heath has never forgiven Margaret Thatcher for defeating him for the position. Thus periodically Heath will deliver a speech indicating that he thinks her policies are misguided. This behavior does not go over very well in the Conservative party because, unlike Labour, it believes in loyally supporting the leaders. The rank and file in the Conservative party are disposed to follow, in Labour to criticize and berate. On the other hand, once the Conservatives have decided that the Leader is not doing the job, the stiletto is jabbed between the ribs much faster and with less regret than in the Labour party. The defeat of Heath itself is evidence that Thatcher can't assume that her position is secure.

Furthermore, the large majority that the Conservatives won in 1983 has made a number of their MPs restless. They are unhappy with their relatively limited influence and lack of prospects for promotion to Government positions. And they fear that unless something is done about unemployment, they will lose their seat in the next election. This would seem to give the "wet" faction's leaders something to work with. The problem for them is that factional groupings within the Conservative party tend to be temporary, ad hoc alliances, in contrast to Labour's permanently organized groups. Thus internal divisions continue to weaken Labour more than the Conservatives.

Politics obviously is an expensive activity even in Britain. The party with substantial funds clearly has an advantage over poorer rivals. The Conservative party usually enjoys financial resources greater than those of Labour. They claim that such an edge is essential for them to offset volunteer assistance that Labour receives from the unions. Understandably, Labour disagrees and in 1967 passed legislation requiring businesses to reveal their contributions to political parties. Not surprisingly most such contributions go to the Conservatives; anywhere from one third to three fifths of the party's normal incomes comes from business contributions.[11] Probably about a fifth of the national party's funds comes from local party organizations. While the Conservatives claim to have 1.5 million members, the low level of dues collected means that the bulk of local party finances comes from fund-raising activities. In a typical year national Conservative headquarters can expect an income of around $6.25 million, with all the local parties combining to obtain about twice that much.

Despite a financial connection with the trade unions—the overwhelming source of its income—Labour has experienced serious and persistent financial problems. At the national level, income is only about two thirds that of the Conservatives in a nonelection year and local Labour parties manage to raise little more than a third of what their Conservative counterparts do. Perhaps in the past, when voting was more an automatic expression of class status, this financial imbalance was not a great harm to Labour, but with an increasingly

---

[11]Michael Pinto-Duschinsky, *British Political Finance 1930–1980* (Washington, D.C.: American Enterprise Institute, 1981), and *The Economist*, October 22, 1983, p. 67.

volatile electorate it must be a matter of considerable concern. Not only is Labour unable to operate a national headquarters as well organized as the Conservatives', but its organization at the constituency level suffers as well. In contrast to the United States, party organization in Britain does not disappear at the local level between elections. Ideally, in addition to the officers chosen from among party members, each local party would have a salaried full-time agent to direct party activities. While the Conservatives are able to employ such a person in half of all the constituencies in Britain, Labour is able to do so in only about a ninth.

Even Labour's financial situation seems great riches in the Liberals' eyes. During the late 1950s they were trying to run their national party machinery on an annual budget of only $50,000. While the party's finances improved substantially during the 1960s, its leaders had to search constantly for financial angels. This resulted in some financial irregularities that still have not been satisfactorily explained.

There was nothing irregular about a major contribution to the party in 1983 from the British School of Motoring. Nonetheless, the Liberals were a bit embarrassed when this was revealed two years later because the gift—about $280,000 —was nearly twice as big as the largest single gift the Conservatives had received. About a fifth of the money was used to help finance the Liberals' 1983 election campaign with the remainder being spread out over three years to assist with the reorganization of the party. Currently, aside from such special grants, the Liberals must attempt to operate a national organization on only about $333,000 a year, with their local parties raising only about half as much as do Labour's. As a result the Liberals have fewer than two dozen full-time constituency agents.

While initial enthusiasm for the SDP enabled it to raise well over $1 million during its first year of existence, support subsequently declined and reduced it to a level all too similar to the Liberals. After the 1983 election an already small staff at national headquarters had to be cut back. The penury of the two allies was such that the Alliance had no funds for national press advertising in the 1983 campaign.

Party Organization and Power Structure

The modern British party system is the product of the gradual expansion of the electorate since 1832. Before that date, parties were groups of men in Parliament who, on great issues, thought, talked, and, for the most part, voted alike. But even inside Parliament there was no party organization in the modern sense.

Prior to 1832 there was little or no need for party organization. The franchise was so limited and Parliamentary seats were controlled by so few people that there was no need for an organized effort to persuade the public and to seek its votes. When the Reform Act of 1832 enlarged the electorate, however, lists of qualified electors had to be compiled. Each political group sought to be certain that all its qualified supporters were registered and that the names of all un-qualified opponents were removed from the voting lists. Registration societies were formed for these purposes; these were the beginning of party organization at the constituency level.

More than a third of a century passed, however, before these registration so-cieties were brought together in a national party organization supporting candi-dates and offering policies. The second Reform Act, by expanding the right to vote still further in 1867, made national organization necessary if a political group were to compete effectively for power. The National Union of Conserva-tive and Unionist Associations was the first such organization to be formed and continues down to today.

Party organization in Britain may have originated at the grassroots level, but today both main parties are highly centralized, in sharp contrast to the loose structure of American parties. Labour tries harder than the Conservatives to operate democratically, but both parties concentrate considerable power in the hands of the national Parliamentary leaders.

Conservative leaders intended from the beginning that the voluntary, mass party organization outside of Parliament should be the servant of the party in Parliament. The National Union was not to usurp any of the powers of the Par-liamentary leaders. Not only was the party in Parliament to be free of any con-trol by the national mass organization, but the national headquarters of that mass organization was to be directed by the Parliamentary Leader. The Leader appoints the party chairman, two vice-chairmen, and two treasurers, who are responsbile for directing the activities of the national headquarters professional staff. National party organization committees that are of key importance—those dealing with policy, finance, and selection of candidates—are responsible not to the officers of the mass party, but to the Leader. The policy committee, for example, reports to the Leader, who appoints its two main presiding offi-cers. Half of its other members are selected by the Conservative Members of Parliament, thus leaving the mass party a minor influence over its operations.

Thus the National Union is limited to being an aid to the winning of elections and publicizing the party's view on public issues. It provides a channel of com-munication between the Parliamentary elite and the rank-and-file party mem-bers in the country. Most of this communication is downward, but the most ac-tive rank-and-file members are able at times to have the views they express considered in the making of party policy.

The basic organizational unit of the Conservative mass party is the local con-stituency association. To be a party member in Britain one cannot just declare a party preference, as is true most places in the United States, but must formally join a local association and annually pay the small sum required as dues. The Conservatives have been one of the most successful parties in the democratic world in recruiting regular members. During the 1950s their membership rose to around 2.75 million and even now, at about half that, still is quite substantial.

Although the primary function of the local association is to help Conserva-tive candidates get elected to Parliament, and to raise the funds and conduct the publicity that will do that, its most significant role—the function that gives it its only real power—is to decide who will be the Conservative candidate for Parliament in that constituency. The executive council of the local association appoints a selection committee. The committee may invite seven or eight would-be candidates for interviews but ultimately will recommend two or three. These are invited to a special meeting of the council, where they make speeches and answer questions. The council then selects one to recommend to a general meeting of the members of the local party. This meeting almost invariably approves the council's choice.

Early in the selection process the chairman of the local association usually will have requested the party's national headquarters to suggest names of potential candidates. Names that the local selection committee receives by other means are supposed to be cleared with national headquarters. Nonetheless, this does not always occur. The local associations are very jealous of their power to choose whomever they wish as their candidate. If the local party feels that the national headquarters is trying to impose a particular person upon them as their candidate, that is the last person they would select. Thus, although the national headquarters formally has the power to veto a local association's choice for candidate, this never happens. Given the number of safe seats (those consistently won by the same party), the small group of people composing the local executive and the selection committee wield considerable power in determining who holds national legislative office.

At the national level the principal organs of the mass party are the annual Conference, the Central Council, and the Executive Committee. The Conference, which meets yearly for about three and a half days, bears some resemblance to American presidential nomination conventions. That is, it is a gathering of representatives from the local party organizations, each one of which can send seven delegates to the Conference. Thus several thousand party members converge on the seaside resorts (where these party gatherings typically are held) each year early in the fall. Note that, unlike American conventions, the Conference is held annually. The reason is, again in contrast to the American, that the British party gathering has nothing to do with nominating anyone for anything. The sole purpose of the conference is to discuss policy. Resolutions on current political questions are debated and voted upon by the delegates.

The Parliamentary leaders see little harm in letting the delegates talk and pass resolutions, but, as we have already noted in describing the status of the mass party, the leaders are not about to let the Conference make party policy. The resolutions express the delegates' opinions; they do not bind the party itself in any way. The Conference—in the leaders' view—is to demonstrate unified support for the policies the leaders already have been proclaiming. Nonetheless, the resolutions are not meaningless; leaders can be embarrassed by them. The debates at times show such enthusiasm for certain policies that the Parliamentary leaders decide they had better give them some support so as not to alienate their followers.

Not only does the Conference not determine party policy, it is not even recognized as the mass party's governing body. That power is given to the Central Council, which normally meets once a year and is, in effect, a briefer and smaller version of the annual Conference. It consists of the party Leader, all Conservative members of Parliament (including peers), prospective Conservative candidates, members of the executive committee of the National Union, representatives of the National Advisory Committee of the National Union, and four representatives of each constituency organization. Meetings of the Central Council afford constituency representatives an opportunity to express their opinions on any matter that especially concerns them and to get firsthand reports from the leaders.

The Executive Committee of the National Union, with a membership approximating 150, normally meets every other month. It consists of the Leader and other principal officers of the party, together with representatives of the areas, each of which encompasses several constituencies. It concerns itself, in the intervals between the meetings of the Central Council, with matters under the jurisdiction of the Council. Much of the detailed work is performed by the General Purposes Subcommittee. This subcommittee also prepares the agenda for the annual Conference as well as for the Central Council.

We need to stress again that to this point we have been discussing the organizational structure of the mass, voluntary party—the party in the country. We turn now to the more elite portion of the party—the party in Parliament. The key body here is the Conservative Private Members Committee. No one calls it by that name, however, referring instead to the 1922 Committee. In that year a revolt among Conservative Members of Parliament drove the party Leader form his position. The committee then was created to help ensure that the Parliamentary leaders were aware of the views of the average members of the Parliamentary party, and did not get so far out of step with these followers that they again would be forced to walk the plank.

The 1922 Committee does not make policy, but does give the average Conservative member of Parliament a forum in which to question the leaders' actions and policies. Normally votes are not taken at 1922 Committee meetings; the chairman of the group must interpret the "sense of the meeting." The chairman has direct access to the Parliamentary Leader to be certain that he or she can be warned when the Parliamentary party's views diverge from those of its leaders. In some cases the Leader even may need to attend a 1922 Committee meeting in person in order to answer criticism and try to convince the party that his or her policies are the right ones.

Through the 1922 Committee, Conservative Members of Parliament (MPs) are organized into subject matter committees. These party committees should not be confused with the legislative committees of the House of Commons. The scope of these party committees corresponds to governmental departments and ministries. In the committees Conservative MPs discuss in detail current political issues and governmental policies and help to crystallize the party's attitude on them. This process can help to settle internal policy differences in private.

Several times we have referred to the Parliamentary Leader with a capital *L*. The reason is that the Conservative party—whether in or out of power—is headed by a single, clearly designated individual known as the Leader. While we have called this person the Parliamentary Leader, this was to be certain that you understood the distinction between the mass and the Parliamentary parties. In fact, the Leader is the head of the entire party and not just the Parliamentary portion, although he or she invariably is a Member of Parliament. Since American presidents and Congressional leaders may disagree even when they are of the same party and since only one party controls the presidency at any one time, there always is a question in the United States about exactly who really is the head of a party. In Britain such confusion does not exist.

The Conservative Leader is preeminent. National party headquarters is his or her personal machine. He or she is the authoritative voice for the party's policies and is not bound by any policy resolution of the mass party. He or she appoints the chief whip of the Parliamentary party and selects whomever he or she wishes for the Shadow Cabinet, the top leadership group in the party when it is out of power. The Labour Leader has none of these powers.

Despite the Leader's enormous authority over other MPs derived from being either the current or the potential prime minister and thus being able greatly to affect the development of their political careers, the Conservative Leader is accountable. Prior to 1965 the Leader "emerged." This means that when the position was vacant—due to voluntary or forced resignation—the new Leader was chosen in behind-the-scene negotiations before the formal party meeting was called to elect him or her officially. The selection of Lord Home as Leader in 1963 by this process dissatisfied many prominent Conservatives. While Home was the second choice of many, they preferred someone before him. Their lack of consensus on a first preference helped to put Home into the post of Leader.

As a result, the selection process was altered to one of explicit election by Conservative MPs. Special majorities and multiple ballots are provided for to help ensure that the person selected has broad support. The choice of the MPs must be confirmed by a meeting of about 1,000 people—all Conservatives in both Houses of Parliament. Conservative prospective candidates, and members of the Executive Committee. This meeting is unlikely to be anything other than a rubber stamp.

Although the first use of the new procedures went smoothly enough, the next occasion produced surprising results. Having led the party to two electoral defeats in 1974, Edward Heath's position as Leader had been seriously weakened. Few anticipated, however, that Margaret Thatcher, a not especially prominent member of the Shadow Cabinet, would be able to gain more votes than Heath, as in fact occurred. That a party as supportive of tradition as the Conservatives should become the first British party to choose a woman as Leader was amazing.

In summary, the Conservative party is very hierarchically structured, and the apex of the party is the Leader. Yet, despite possessing great strength even when the party is out of office, the Leader can be driven from his or her position by strong opposition from Parliamentary colleagues or the mass party. In fact, in the 20th century Conservative Leaders have suffered this fate more frequently than have Labour Leaders. Although the Conservative party is not democratic, the Leader is responsible to the followers. His or her power is checked by the need to convince the party to accept the policies he or she prefers.

Unlike the Conservative party, which was organized from inside Parliament, the Labour party was organized from the outside. As we have already explained, it was the national Parliamentary Conservatives who saw the need to combine the various local registration associations into a country-wide organization. The Labour party, however, was not represented in Parliament until after the party had organized in the country, with the initiative being taken by people who were not MPs. As a result the Labour party differs profoundly from the Conservatives in structure and organizational values.

The Labour party has regarded itself as a *movement* aimed at voicing the people's interest in the political process. Many Labour members view the Parliamentary Labour Party simply as the instrument through which this objective is to be accomplished. Thus the PLP is to serve the mass party by seeing that its principles are carried into law. This is precisely the reverse of the Conservative party's organizational ethos. In that party the mass party is to serve the Parliamentary party by providing money and personnel to win elections.

The Labour party was founded in 1900 when representatives of the Independent Labour Party, the Fabian Society, various socialists groups, and several of the trade unions met to form the Labour Representation Committee. The key decision was that MPs elected with its support should be totally indepedent of either the Conservative or the Liberal parties. In 1903 the unions took the crucial step of increasing their nominal financial support of the LRC to a substantial regular levy. In 1906 the LRC changed its name to the present one of Labour party. Within 22 years of its founding it had driven the Liberal party (with the aid of factional feuds within the Liberals) into third place in the House of Commons; within 24 years it provided the country's prime minister; within 45 years it won an absolute majority of the seats in the Commons at a general election.

Labour is organized more complexly than are the Conservatives. The mass organization not only coordinates the activities of the local constituency associations but includes as well various related organizations, primarily unions and cooperative societies. Organizations of this type affiliate with the Labour party at both the national and the local level. It is the semifederated nature of the party's organization that accounts for its having two types of membership—direct and indirect.

One may join the Labour party directly by paying dues to a local party association, just as is done in the Conservative party. But of the party's more than 6 million members only slightly more than a quarter of a million are direct members. The great bulk of the members are indirect; they are members simply because the union to which they belong has affiliated with the Labour party and has paid a political levy for each of its members. Thus many indirect members may not really favor the Labour party at all. Should they strongly oppose Labour, as obviously those workers who vote Conservative must do, they can "contract out"—sign a formal statement that they do not wish to have any of their union dues paid to Labour. Approximately 15 percent of those unionists whose unions have established separate political funds refuse to pay the political levy. The proportion paying varies considerably from one union to another. When 98 percent of a union's members pay the political levy—as is true in the National Union of Public Employees—you can bet that considerable peer pressure has been exerted to dissuade members from contracting out.[12] Since the sum that goes to the Labour party is less than a dollar per person per year, alienating your fellow workers in a stand for principle seems pointless. One of the Conservative Government's reforms of trade union law was to require ballots by union members to see whether they wished their union to have a political fund. Since even many trade unionists feel that unions have too much political power, Labour feared that these ballots could further weaken the party's finances. Nonetheless, throughout 1985 members of one union after another voted to maintain these funds.

The local constituency party is governed by a General Management Committee, composed of delegates from ward committees and the affiliated organizations—primarily local branches of unions. Since the GMC meets only annually, effective power is wielded by the executive committee, which is chosen by the GMC and meets monthly.

As in the Conservative party, one of the most important powers of the local Labour association is to decide who will be the Labour candidate for Parliament in that constituency. When a new candidate is to be selected, the executive prepares a short list from among which the GMC chooses one. In recent years this selection power has been a battleground between the left and right wings of the Labour party. The procedure had been that a person currently representing the constituency in Parliament could be dumped as a candidate in the next election only if the local party passed a motion of no confidence in him or her. The left wing felt that this did not give the local party sufficient control over the MP and thus allowed him or her to ignore the policy preferences of "true socialists." They believed that it would be easier to get rid of MPs who refused to do their bidding, if the process of candidate selection were opened to any and all applicants during each term of Parliament. Thus a new candidate could be selected without the need to carry a motion specifically against the current MP.

The left wing has managed to get the rules changed so that now every constituency party must conduct a reselection process during each Parliament. This is an important departure from past practice, which had the effect of continuing an MP as a candidate virtually automatically for as long as he or she wished. Parties that are dissatisfied with their MP will be able to pit him or her against a

---

[12]For detailed information about union finances and the political levy, see *The Economist*, April 4, 1981, pp. 61–62.

field of new applicants. Even constituency parties satisfied with their MP must conduct reselection. What is not clear is whether the executive can eliminate potential nominees to protect the MP and submit to the GMC only the MP's name. While such a practice is discouraged, it has not been formally prohibited and during 1985 many GMCs readopted their sitting MP from a short list of only one—namely, the MP.

By American standards this reform is modest enough. British MPs have been remarkably insulated from accountability to the voters. A handful of local party members—not the voters—decides who the party's candidate will be and that person, if elected, need never be concerned about the bruising primary election fights that have ended the careers of some American politicians. So why have we gone on about it at such length? The substance of the issue is important because it shows how much less accountable to the voters British MPs are than members of the American Congress. More significant, however, is what the issue symbolizes. It is part of the factional fight within the Labour party and is regarded as evidence of the increasing domination of the left wing.

In the selection of candidates for the 1983 election only seven MPs were eliminated by the new rules. Some Labour MPs decided to retire from Parliament, however, to avoid having to endure the reselection process. And still others left Labour to join the Social Democrats. Thus in all somewhere between two and three dozen Labour MPs were affected significantly by the new rules. When reselection began getting underway in the mid-1980s for the next election, several prominent moderates in the party were expected to have serious difficulties being chosen. But, surprisingly, few battles occurred and virtually all MPs who wanted to stand again were reselected.

While the constituency party has the power to select the candidate, the national party organization is more active in the process in the Labour party than in the Conservative. The National Executive Committee must have an opportunity to comment on the short list before the constituency party makes its choice. Furthermore, this choice is not official until endorsed by the NEC. And in by-elections the constituency party must share the power to select the candidate with the NEC.

The national governing body of the mass party is the annual Conference. Well over 1,000 delegates from local associations and affiliated organizations attend these gatherings, whose principal business is to discuss and vote upon the various policy resolutions that these groups have submitted. When formal votes, called card votes, are taken on these resolutions, heads of the various delegations hold up cards indicating how many members their organization has in the party. Thus, regardless of the number of delegates present in the hall at the time of the decision, votes totaling 6 or 7 million are not uncommon.

The policy-making power of Conference is a matter of some dispute and considerable importance. Various party documents and leaders have said from time to time that Conference is the ultimate authority in the entire party and thus controls the Labour Members of Parliament. Were this true, Labour MPs would be accountable not to the voters but to Conference, an apparent short-circuiting of democracy in the British political system. The power of Conference is limited, however, by not being able to dictate to Labour MPs how they must vote on specific bills in Parliament. Furthermore, although the principles endorsed by Conference are to be carried out as soon as practicable, the party's constitution does not say who is to determine this practicability. Thus, while Labour leaders cannot defy Conference, they have some discretion about when and how its decisions are to be implemented and in some instances they may decide that the time never is suitable.

Such procrastination may be risky, however, for the Leader must report annually to Conference on the work of the PLP (Parliamentary Labour Party) during the preceding year. When the delegates debate this report, they may challenge the Leader on why their previous resolutions have not been heeded.

Whatever the power of Conference over the PLP, it is clear that it directs the National Executive Committee, which is responsible for the work of the mass party when Conference is not in session. The NEC's duty is to enforce the party's constitution, rules, and standing orders. It is empowered to expel members from the party. Furthermore, should a constituency association continue to support the candidature of an MP expelled by the NEC, the NEC can disaffiliate the local party and replace it with a newly organized Labour party in that area. The NEC directs the party's national headquarters and its professional staff. In contrast to the Conservative party, Labour national headquarters is not the Labour Leader's personal machine, but the servant of Conference and the NEC.

The Leader, Deputy Leader, Young Socialist delegate, and general secretary (the head of the professional staff) all are ex-officio members of the NEC. The remaining 25 members are chosen at the annual Conference. Of these, 12 are elected by trade union delegates to Conference, 7 by delegates from the constituency parties, and 1 by delegates from socialist and cooperative organizations affiliated to Labour. Five places on the NEC are reserved for women, and these are elected by Conference as a whole. The same is true of the party treasurer.

Since the trade unions always have a huge majority of Conference votes, they are able to select a majority—18 (12 union seats plus 5 women plus the treasurer) —of the NEC. Furthermore, under long-standing Conference procedure each delegation casts all of its votes as a single block. The block vote of the six largest unions is well over a majority of total Conference voting strength. Thus when the main unions agree, they determine what policies Conference supports and who controls the NEC.

During the 1940s and 1950s union leaders usually were politically moderate and not very assertive. The policies of the Parliamentary leaders were acceptable to them. In fact, the Parliamentary leaders found the union leaders useful allies in fending off attacks from extremist delegates from the constituency parties. Furthermore, since most union leaders were interested mainly in industrial relations and not in a political career, the majority of the NEC's members were MPs.

Beginning in the 1950s, however, struggles over policy so divided the PLP that having a majority of MPs on the NEC was no guarantee of control by the Parliamentary leaders. More important, the new generation of union leaders frequently were more militant than their predecessors on foreign affairs as well as domestic. Relations between them and the Parliamentary leaders were worsened further because Britain's economic problems forced Labour Governments to take action that the unions didn't like. Thus instead of being able to count on the union block vote to save them at Conference from the left-wing enthusiasms of the constituency parties, the Parliamentary leaders now frequently find several unions allied with the left. The task of leading the Labour party, difficult at best, has become an even more onerous job.

As we noted in discussing party policy, in the 1979 election campaign the Parliamentary leaders tried to soft-pedal Labour's official left-wing policy. In the postmortem of defeat the left vowed that it would not let the leaders sell out again. The struggle has taken the form of a dispute over how the party's election *manifesto* (the term used by British parties to refer to their election platform) shall be drawn up. The demand was to give the NEC, as the guardian of Conference policy decisions, the final word. Although the 1979 Conference voted in favor of this, the 1980 one reversed the decision by narrowly defeating a resolution that would have given the NEC control over the manifesto, with the PLP only being consulted. This, in fact, was about the only thing that the moderates won at the 1980 Conference.

Turning from the organization of the mass party to the Parliamentary party, Labour MPs are organized into two sets of overlapping committees—area groups and subject groups. The former are used in party management to help ensure that Labour MPs attend important debates in the Commons and vote as the party wishes. The latter are similar to the Conservatives' functional committees. They provide some opportunity for MPs of little prominence to have some input into the party's policy-making process. The committees are less important when the party is in power—when the Cabinet makes party policy—and even when the party is out of power the committees' influence is limited and depends to a considerable extent upon the amount of status within the party that a particular committee chairman possesses.

The PLP selects a chairman to preside over its regular meetings. This person occupies a position similar to that of the chairman of the Conservatives 1922 Committee. Furthermore, when Labour is in power this person heads a specially created liaison committee intended to keep the Labour Government informed of the views of the rank-and-file Labour MPs. Also when Labour is out of office, the PLP annually elects a Parliamentary Committee of 12 MPs. These 12 along with three representatives from the Labour party in the House of Lords, the PLP chairman, the chief whip, the Deputy Leader, and the Leader are in effect the party's Shadow Cabinet. While the Leader may add other members to the Shadow Cabinet, he or she basically has to work with those MPs that the PLP has chosen.

Given its conception of itself as a democratic movement of the people, the Labour party was slow to designate someone Leader. The PLP had a chairman in its early years, but this was simply because someone had to preside over PLP meetings, Certainly the position was not intended to carry any special authority or power. During the first two decades of the party's existence, six men held the post and four years was the longest unbroken term. When the party finally reconciled itself to having a Leader, it had the misfortune of a traumatic experience in 1931 with the first man to hold that title—Ramsay MacDonald. Without going into the historical details, suffice it to say that the Labour party believes that MacDonald betrayed the movement by forming a coalition government that, although he was its prime minister, was dominated by the Conservatives.

While the party office of Leader survived, the experience reinforced the suspicions already widespread in the party that a taste of power was sufficieint to make those at the top of the party sell out party interests and personal principle for personal gain and glory. One of the ways in which a Labour Leader can attempt to counteract these suspicions is to reassure the party that he or she is a true socialist. Someone has observed that the Labour party can be led only from the left of center. This is why Harold Wilson and Clement Attlee were more successful as Leaders than Hugh Gaitskell.

When Labour is out of power the Leader is elected annually. Most of these elections have not been real contests, since usually no one stands against the Leader. Until 1981 the PLP elected the Leader. Now the Leader is elected at the annual Conference, with the unions having 40 percent of the votes and the PLP and the constituency parties 30 percent each. Thus once again the left wing has managed to reduce the power of the Parliamentary party.

The position of the Labour Leader contrasts with that of the Conservative Leader in several ways. To summarize them: (1) the Labour Leader does not choose the bulk of the Shadow Cabinet or appoint the chief whip, the PLP does; (2) Labour headquarters is not the personal machine of the Leader, but is directed by the NEC; (3) the Labour Leader is not empowered to make policy on his or her own authority; (4) the Conservative Leader is not required to report to the party's Conference annually on the work of the Parliamentary party; (5) the Labour Leader is elected by a much larger group than just the Parliamentary party.

Despite these restraints and the complications that they produce in the process of party leadership for the Labour Leader, the fact remains that he or she is the most powerful figure in the party just as the Conservative Leader is. And when Labour is in power, the Leader, who then becomes prime minister, functions basically as the Conservative counterpart does when that party controls the Government. The Labour prime minister can pick a Cabinet as he or she chooses, and the Cabinet runs the Government. Of course, a Labour prime minister cannot afford to ignore strongly held views in the party, but no Conservative Leader, for all his or her power, can do that either. And if the most important evidence of power is the ability to retain one's office, then the Labour

Leader is stronger than the Conservative. For, as previously noted, in the 20th century, intraparty revolts have driven Leaders from power more often in the Conservative than in the Labour party.

A classic study of British parties has argued that despite contrasts in party rhetoric, founders' intentions, and pattern of development, both of the main parties have the same fundamental power structure.[13] Supposedly the constitutional structure of British government required and supported one type of party power structure. The Leader of each main party either is prime minister or the alternative candidate for the post; thus he or she is powerful whatever party constitutions provide. Parliamentary democracy requires responsibility to the voters, so Parliamentary parties must be free of control from mass parties, in which only a fraction of the electorate participates. Until recently a reasonable argument could be made that Labour did indeed operate in practice as did the Conservatives—the Parliamentary leaders were in command and the MPs were responsible to the voters. Events in the Labour party at the start of the 1980s make this much less certain. Labour may now differ fundamentally in structure from the Conservative party.

The Labour left sees this difference in structure as essential to ensuring a fundamental contrast in policy. Certainly at the start of the 1980s Labour policy had moved far from the Conservatives on many issues. Yet we do not want to leave you with the impression that Labour and Conservative are polarized the way right-wing and communist parties are in some continental European countries. The political alternatives in Britain are not so stark, the stakes of electoral competition so high, that the political game is transformed into a struggle for survival. Politics in Britain is characterized by some excitement, not by anxiety.

One aspect of the Liberal party's organization deserves comment: the Liberals have gone far beyond what even the Labour party now is beginning to do in democraticizing the process of selecting a Leader. Until 1976 the Liberals used the same procedure as the other parties—Liberal MPs selected one of their number to be Leader of the entire party. This method came to seem faintly ridiculous in the 1950s, when the Liberals were reduced to only six members in the Commons.

While the matter never became a factional fight, as we've seen that it has in the Labour party, the Liberal MPs did not want any change that would jeopardize the autonomy of the Parliamentary party. Thus when the procedure was changed, it was agreed that the Leader had to be an MP and that only MPs could nominate candidates for the election of the Leader. The power to elect, however, was shifted from the Parliamentary party to the mass party. Each constituency party is allotted a number of votes, depending in part on Liberal electoral strength in the area. Each constituency party holds a meeting open to all its members. This meeting decides how to cast its vote for the nominated candidates—the party's allocation is not given in a block to the top preference but is

---

[13]Robert McKenzie, *British Political Parties*, 2d ed. (London, Mercury Books, 1963).

divided among the candidates in the same proportion to the vote they received among the members attending the meeting. In July 1976 each of the Liberal constituency parties phoned in their vote to London on the same day. David Steel received 12,541 votes to defeat John Pardoe with 7,032.

Since the Liberals have not changed Leaders since then, this is the only experience with the system. It certainly worked smoothly; whether this would be the case were there more than two candidates (when the rules require a preferential voting system) is unknown. The point is that had Labour really wanted to be democratic, rather than to wage a factional feud further, it might have devised a system closer to that of the Liberals. Furthermore, the Liberals can claim, as they enjoy doing on matters of public policy, that they are the innovators and that only later do the ponderous, old-fashioned large parties get around to doing what the Liberals already have done.

The SDP has gone even a step beyond the Liberals. While their candidates for the position of Leader must also be MPs nominated by MPs, election is by a mail ballot of all party members. Thus they are the only party to use a system of one person, one vote.

OTHER PARTIES

The Conservatives, Labour, the Liberals, and the SDP are not the only parties organized on a country-wide basis in Britain. There is a Communist party, but it never has gotten even as much as 1 percent of the vote and recently has polled less than 0.1 percent. A more recently organized party is the National Front, a neofascist group whose chief appeal is a strong racist position. Despite contesting nearly half of the constituencies in 1979, it received only 0.6 percent of the vote. In 1983 it did even worse. An Ecology party has offered some candidates in recent elections, but has obtained little more than 1 percent of the vote.

As for regional parties, the Welsh nationalists—Plaid Cymru (pronounced *plied come ree*)—and the Scottish Nationalist party now appear to have been a phenomenon primarily of the 1970s. As Table 4–2 makes clear, neither party was of political consequence prior to then and in the 1980s have almost fallen back to that level.

Their success in the 1970s can be attributed in part to Britain's economic problems—many Welsh and Scots concluded that things hardly could be run any worse, and that if they were allowed to manage their own affairs they might be more prosperous. Further fueling this feeling in Scotland was the discovery of extensive oil fields in the North Sea. The SNP campaigned widely on the slogan, "It's Scotland's Oil." They argued that Scotland could be wealthy if it alone received oil profits.

The ultimate aim of the nationalist parties is complete independence from the United Kingdom. Since they know that the majority of the population in neither Wales nor Scotland favors this, they sometimes try to make the break seem less drastic by describing their goal as Commonwealth status. Only when one bothers to reflect that this is the position of fully independent nations such

**TABLE 4–2   Liberal and Nationalist Strength in Wales
and Scotland in Recent General Elections**

	Wales			
	Seats		Percent of vote	
	Liberal*	PC	Liberal*	PC
1966	1	0	6	4
1970	1	0	7	12
February 1974	2	2	16	11
October 1974	2	3	16	11
1979	1	2	11	8
1983	2	2	23	8

	Scotland			
	Seats		Percent of vote	
	Liberal*	SNP	Liberal*	SNP
1966	5	0	7	5
1970	3	1	6	11
February 1974	3	7	8	22
October 1974	3	11	8	30
1979	3	2	9	17
1983	8	2	25	12

*Alliance in 1983.

as Canada and Australia and that the nationalists also talk of control over foreign affairs and defense and of obtaining seats in the United Nations does one understand that what they seek goes far beyond the Liberals' federal proposals.

The nationalists do take stands on other issues. Plaid Cymru is especially concerned with defending Welsh language and culture. The Scot Nats devote little time to such issues, emphasizing instead economic policy, particularly measures to fight the poverty that exists in many parts of Scotland. This contrast probably is due to the fact that few Scots can speak Gaelic, but around a fifth of the Welsh can speak Welsh. Given this difference, it is a bit surprising that the SNP has been so much more successful than the PC, even to the extent of surpassing the Liberals (for that matter, the Conservatives as well at one point) in their region. The 1970s saw ethnonationalist movements rise to prominence in several countries—Canada and Belgium, for example—and this experience seemed to suggest the importance of being able to play upon a grievance about language. British experience with ethnonationalism suggests that economics is more important than language.

The 1979 election reversed the rise of nationalism. As we discussed in the preceding chapter, devolution proposals had been unsuccessful in a referendum held shortly before the election. Perhaps this forced the Scots and Welsh to think about nationalism as a serious change rather than as an emotional ideal. Then, too, the SNP has suffered internal conflicts between those favoring a socialist-type economic policy and those wanting to concentrate almost entirely upon nationalism. Furthermore, the referendum itself divided the nationalist parties. The devolution proposals did not go as far as they wanted, but to oppose an offer to shift some powers from the central government to the regional level seemed contrary to the nationalists' championing of more freedom for their people.

The formation of the Alliance appears to have hurt the nationalists in Scotland much more than in Wales, with the SNP losing a third of its vote in 1983. Thus any extensive changes in the British party system are more likely to come from the Alliance than from the nationalists.

BIBLIOGRAPHICAL NOTE

The classic study of British parties is the McKenzie book mentioned in footnote 13. For the Liberal party, which McKenzie ignores, see Jorgen Rasmussen, *The Liberal Party* (London: Constable, 1965). McKenzie and Silver, cited in Footnote 8, contains an excellent summary of Conservative beliefs.

Labour's fundamental values are well summarized in H. M. Drucker, *Doctrine and Ethos in the Labour Party* (London: Allen & Unwin, 1979). Labour's recent troubles are examined extensively in Dennis Kavanagh, ed., *The Politics of the Labour Party* (London: Allen & Unwin, 1982) and Paul Whiteley, *The Labour Party in Crisis* (London: Methuen, 1983). History, principles, party organization, strength—all are covered in Philip Norton and Arthur Aughey, *Conservatives and Conservatism* (London: Temple Smith, 1981.) For the policy positions of the parties in the 1979 election see the Penniman book cited in Footnote 1 and for 1983 the next book in the series, edited by Austin Ranney, *Britain at the Polls 1983* (Durham, N.C.: Duke University Press, 1985). Samuel Beer, *British Politics in the Collectivist Age* (New York: Alfred A. Knopf, 1965), discusses party development in terms of British political values and social change. Richard Rose's *Do Parties Make a Difference?*, 2d ed. (Chatham, N.J.: Chatham House, 1984) thoroughly examines the question of whether the rhetorical and value differences between Labour and Conservative make any practical differences in public policy.

The best studies of the process of candidate selection are Austin Ranney, *Pathways to Parliament* (London: Macmillan, 1965), and Michael Rush, *The Selection of Parliamentary Candidates* (London: Nelson, 1969).

A good source for election results and a great deal of other political and social information is David Butler and Anne Sloman, *British Political Facts, 1900–1979*, 5th ed. (London: Macmillan, 1980).

The benchmark study of voting behavior is David Butler and Donald Stokes, *Political Change in Britain,* 2d coll. ed. (New York: St. Martin's Press, 1976).

5

Representation and Accountability

The political parties present policy alternatives to the people. The voters decide who will represent each of the constituencies into which the country is divided and, more important, thereby determine which party will control the House of Commons. The Commons, more than any other political institution, seems to embody the essence of British government. It appears to be the focal point of the political process, the showcase of democracy in action. Increasingly, however, a number of observers have complained that the Commons is virtually all show and very little substance, that what happens there largely is irrelevant to the governing of the country, to the making of national policy. In this chapter we will concentrate mainly on form and procedure to give you a feel for the atmosphere of Parliament—its show—and an understanding of how it works. In the first part of the next chapter we will do basically the same for the executive. Then in the latter part of that chapter we will be able to build upon this information to discuss power relations between the executive and the legislature and assess the balance between show and substance in the Commons.

THE HOUSE OF COMMONS

The Chamber and Its Members

The House of Commons meets in a small—68 feet by 45 feet—room. Although the Commons has half again as many members as does the U.S. House of Representatives, its meeting room is only about one fourth as large. The Commons' chamber is too small, in fact, to seat all its members; less than two thirds of them can squeeze onto its green leather-covered benches at any one time. The members do not have desks or even assigned seats. MPs sit on tiers of benches with the two main parties facing each other across a wide aisle running lengthwise down the center of the chamber. You can see the detailed arrangements in Figure 5-1, which presents an aerial view of the main floor of the Commons and its balcony as though you were looking straight down from the roof.

In its long history the Commons has met in a variety of places. It has been located in its current site since 1852. In May 1941, however, a Nazi bomb destroyed the nearly century-old chamber. (During the next several years the Commons met in the House of Lords chamber, and the Lords met in the monarch's Robing Room, which tells you something about the hierarchy of power in Britain.) After World War II the Commons chamber was rebuilt along its old lines except for more modern lighting, a voice-amplification system, air conditioning, leather-covered foam rubber on the benches, and a less ornate design of interior decoration. So why, you must wonder, given such an opportunity, would any sensible people build a meeting room for their legislature too small to hold all the members?

Britain's wartime Prime Minister Winston Churchill spoke for many in offering two reasons. He believed that a small chamber was essential to preserve the conversational style of speaking that characterized Commons' debates. A large chamber would encourage bombastic rhetoric rather than reasoned discourse. Furthermore, if the chamber were large enough to seat every Member, then "nine tenths of its debates will be conducted in the depressing atmosphere of an almost empty or half-empty chamber."[1] (The accuracy of this belief is shockingly evident to first-time visitors to the U.S. House of Representatives.)

Churchill wanted the rectangular shape to be retained because he was convinced that this helped to preserve a two-party system. Crossing the floor (that is, switching parties) was made to be a clear break that required serious consideration (although he himself had done it twice, whatever the deterrent of the chamber's shape) in contrast to a semicircular arrangement permitting members to move easily from one to another of several political groups. (Never mind that both houses of the U.S. Congress and most state legislatures seat members in a semicircle and still maintain a two-party system. Churchill was thinking only of continental European politics.)

At the head of the chamber is a large, canopied chair. Here sits the presiding officer of the Commons, the Speaker, still wearing the traditional garb of knee breeches, wig, and long black gown. In front of him at a long table sit the clerks of the House, also wearing wigs and gowns, recording the proceedings. On the table are receptacles to hold the Mace, the jewel-encrusted club that symbolizes the monarch's authority.

---

[1] Winston Churchill, *The Second World War: Closing the Ring* (Boston: Houghton Mifflin, 1951), p. 169.

FIGURE 5–1   Arrangement of Seating in the House of Commons

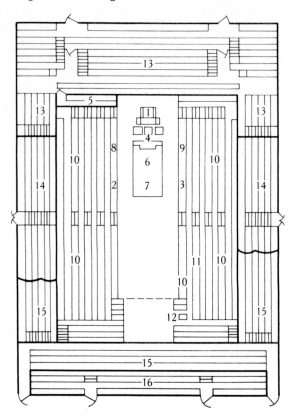

1. The Speaker.
2. Prime minister or Government spokesman.
3. Leader of the Opposition or Opposition spokesman.
4. Clerks at the table.
5. Civil servants in attendance.
6. The table.
7. The mace.
8. Government front bench, occupied by ministers.
9. Opposition front bench.
10. Backbenches.
11. Other opposition parties.
12. Serjeant-at-arms.
13. Hansard and press gallery.
14. Members' side galleries.
15. Special galleries, including peers', "distinguished strangers," diplomatic and commonwealth galleries.
16. The public gallery.

Turning from the chamber to the Members, while one need be only 21 to be an MP, most are well into middle age.[2] The median age of the Conservatives elected in 1983 was 47 while for Labour it was 51. Only 10 Conservatives and one Labour MPs were under 30. Most MPs are experienced legislators; somewhat more than a fifth of those elected in 1983 either were entering the Commons for the first time or had done so in a by-election from 1980 to 1983. At the other extreme, less than a tenth of the Members had first been elected before 1960.

The occupational background of the Members differs considerably between the major parties. Among Conservatives the largest group is company officials (about a quarter of all Conservative MPs) with barristers (trial lawyers) providing about a seventh. Journalists and other businesspeople are other sizable groups. In the Labour party the largest single group—a quarter—is teachers at whatever level of education. Next come skilled workers, with miners and other types of workers also being sizable groups.

Over the long term the percentage of Conservative MPs with business backgrounds has declined while the proportion from professions has increased. The proportion of working-class Labour MPs has dropped (although this decline did not continue in 1979) while the percentage from the professions has increased for Labour as well. Thus both parties have been moving away from their traditional class base in the occupational composition of their Parliamentary parties and are becoming more like each other. Both parties have been choosing professional types as candidates. Despite the considerable shift in partisan strengths in 1983, the distribution of occupations changed little.

Educational contrasts are more marked. Nearly half of the Conservative MPs went to Oxford or Cambridge, while only a seventh of the Labour MPs did. In keeping with the comments on education and the class system in Chapter 2, the differences in secondary schooling are more striking still. Seventy percent of all Conservative MPs attended public schools, while little more than a seventh of Labour MPs did so. Furthermore, a sixth of Conservative MPs attended either Eton, Harrow, or Winchester. Only three Labour MPs attended one of these schools. Even among what could be called the political elite, social class differences between the two parties are sharply etched.

Prior to 1911 MPs were not paid. While the salary established then has been increased over the years, the British have been niggardly in helping MPs meet the expense of public service. They feared that if MPs were paid a decent salary, some rotter would try to make a good thing of it and stand for Parliament just for the money. The salary is to be increased until it reaches £18,500 ($23,000) in 1987. Then it will be set at the level of a civil servant who was earning £18,500 in 1983. In addition to the salary, MPs who do not reside in London are given a

---

[2]The information in this and the next three paragraphs is derived from David Butler and Dennis Kanavagh, *The British General Election of 1983* (London: Macmillan, 1984), pp. 232–7.

supplement of about $6,000 to pay for the cost of rooms when they are attending Parliament.

Not until 1969 were MPs allowed to use the mails for constituency business without having to pay postage. And only then did they get money for secretarial assistance. While the approximately $15,000 a year they receive for that purpose now allows them to obtain a person or two to deal with their correspondence and files, it clearly cannot finance the veritable army of research assistants than an American Congressperson enjoys. Expenses of traveling to and in the local constituency now are covered also. And in a show of great munificence the British provide 15 travel vouchers a year for an MP's spouse to come to London for a visit.

Incredible though this inadequate level of compensation is, you have not yet heard the topper. MPs could not even count on having office space. It used to be that when you visited the Palace of Westminster (the large building in which the chamber of the Commons is located) you would see MPs sitting on the stone benches dictating letters to secretaries they had paid out of their own pockets. If they had managed to ferret out an empty room somewhere in the Palace of Westminster, they could establish squatters' rights, or they might share an office (and perhaps a secretary) with another MP. Even then space was not available for everyone. While things have improved through acquisition of office space in nearby buildings, MPs have nothing like the elaborate suites enjoyed by members of the U.S. Congress.

The material returns for being an MP hardly are great. One must have either a high sense of public service or a strong desire to be near the seat of power to undertake this career. And unless he or she is independently wealthy, some other source of income such as part-time journalism or partnership in a legal firm may well be necessary.

Powers and Procedures

The powers of the House of Commons can be stated briefly: Parliament is supreme. This means that the Commons—given the concurrence of the Lords or an overriding of their opposition—literally can do whatever its Members want. No matter how outrageous it may be, any law passed by Parliament is valid.

Each fall a new session of Parliament begins (unless the occurrence of a general election has altered the usual schedule) with the Speech from the Throne. The monarch delivers this speech from a throne in the House of Lords, with the Lords seated as usual and Members of the Commons standing crowded together at the foot of the chamber. The Cabinet has drafted the speech for the monarch, who has nothing to say about its contents. The speech outlines the Governments legislative plans for the coming Parliamentary session. Thus it is the equivalent of the president's State of the Union Message in the United States, although it is much shorter than those usually are.

For about the next week the Commons discusses the contents of the speech. Then it begins to consider specific bills that the Government has submitted to it.

With various holiday recesses, the session continues until the following fall. Usually the Commons comes back from summer vacation for about a week to wrap up loose ends. Again the monarch delivers a speech in the House of Lords, this time summarizing the accomplishments of the session. The session formally closes, and all bills and motions still on the books and which did not get acted upon now die. Then a new session of Parliament is opened and the cycle begins again.

The daily sittings of the Commons begin at 2:30 Monday through Thursday and usually end at 10:30. Longer sittings are possible, however, and sometimes the Commons does not adjourn until the wee hours of the morning. In fact, a sitting even can last for more than 24 hours, thus running on over into the next day's business and forcing it to be rescheduled. On Fridays the Commons meets from 9:30 to 3:00 to enable MPs to leave London early enough for weekend visits to their constituencies.

As we noted in discussing the rebuilding of the Commons chamber, the ideal procedure is reasoned debate. A number of customs have grown up over the years concerning such things as how MPs are to refer to each other. Thus MPs may speak of "my gallant friend"—a member of the same party with a distinguished war record—or "the learned lady"—a woman with a college degree. On the other hand, an MP may not refer to another MP as a swine, jackass, stool pigeon, or guttersnipe, among other things.

The responsibility for seeing that name-calling does not occur and that the Commons does not get carried away with emotion lies with the Speaker. The Speaker, lacking the gavels and bells used by presiding officers in legislatures elsewhere, merely stands up when tempers flare and says "Order, order." This usually is sufficient. If an individual MP is the cause of a disturbance and refuses to obey the Speaker, then the Speaker can bar him or her from the Commons for several days. If the disorder is more general, the Speaker can suspend the sitting for a period of time until the Members calm down. Such measures are rare because the Speaker is accorded great respect and authority, except from Labour MP Dennis Skinner, who specializes in getting himself "named" (suspended), thereby demonstrating, no doubt, that he is a true man of the people.

The Speaker's salary indicates the importance of the position. At £48,750 (1981), the Speaker is topped only by the attorney general and the highest judges.

One of the main reasons for the Speaker's honored position is that, unlike the Speaker of the U.S. House of Representatives, the Speaker of the House of Commons is nonpartisan. While Speakers are selected by the leaders of the governing party, they then are formally elected by the Commons, usually without dissent by the opposition parties. As a rule, those chosen have not been prominent partisans. Furthermore, once elected, Speakers divorce themselves from their party's activities. This means, for example, that a Speaker may not even make a partisan speech when standing for reelection to the House of Commons. In a spirit of fair play, the custom had been that parties would not offer candidates against the Speaker in a general election. This practice appeared to lapse beginning in the mid-1960s, although in the 1979 election only the National Front and Plaid Cymru ran candidates against the Speaker.

Since the daily sittings of the Commons run without break for at least eight hours and frequently longer, the Speaker obviously needs assistance in presiding over the meetings. Furthermore, the Speaker does not preside when the Commons meets in Committee of the Whole. When the Speaker is absent, the Commons is presided over by either the chairman or one of the two deputy chairmen (despite the title, women have held one of these positions) of the Ways and Means Committee. Although these three officers of the House, unlike the Speaker, do not sever their ties with their parties, they are expected to be just as impartial as is the Speaker. To help insure this, they do not vote in any of the divisions of the House of Commons. Since everyone understands that those who preside over the House must be absolutely impartial and fair to all, it is not surprising that the Speaker and the other three officers are selected from the opposition parties as frequently as from the Government party, a practice that would be totally unheard of in the United States.

While the Speaker is to ensure order and fair play in the Commons' deliberations, MPs are not to be prevented from expressing their views fully. To be certain that this is the case, MPs have no legal responsibility—cannot be sued for slander—for statements they make in the House of Commons. And to prevent hampering them in their duties, they are immune from arrest arising from civil suit and exempt from jury duty.

The legislative process begins when a member of the Government (the typical way) or an ordinary MP introduces a bill. In the latter case this is referred to as a private member's bill. Bills of limited application relevant only to specific localities are known as private bills, while those of general application and public importance are termed public bills. We will be concerned only with the procedure for passing public bills; the procedure for private bills differs in some ways.

All bills must go through three readings plus consideration by a committee and usually a report stage as well. The first reading in merely a formality to get the bill into the legislative process; no debate occurs at this time. The second reading is unquestionably the most crucial stage for any bill. The essence of this stage is a debate on the main principles of the bill. Amendments are not in order; the Commons must either kill the bill or continue it on its way.

If a bill passes second reading, its final passage is extemely likely. Nonetheless, it must now go to committee for detailed consideration and amendment in light of the views expressed in the Commons during the second reading debate. It is important to note that the committee stage in Britain comes later in the legislative process than is true in the United States. In the Congress, bills are sent to committee immediately after first reading and before the legislature as a whole has had an opportunity to express its views on the subject in the bill. In Britain, when a committee receives a bill, the House of Commons already has approved the bill in general. Thus a Congressional committee may spend weeks on a bill only to see it killed on the floor when finally it is reported out of committee.

This virtually never occurs in Britain, where committees can carry out their work guided by general approval and suggestions for alteration already voiced by the Commons.

The most controversial bills, as a rule, go to Committee of the Whole—that is, to the House sitting as a committee. This makes the rules of procedure more informal and permits many more Members to participate. Obviously, however, it is much more time-consuming than is the standing committee route. Thus at times, especially in the 1970s, taking a bill in Committee of the Whole has been a means of forcing the Government to make significant concessions in the content of legislation or to abandon a bill entirely.

If a bill has not been amended in Committee of the Whole, it goes directly to third reading. When, more typically, it has been amended or has been considered by one of the standing committees, then it returns to the Commons for report stage before going on to third reading. Report stage offers a last opportunity for amendments of substance, since the vote on third reading, except for possible minor technical changes, is on the entire bill.

In part because the committee stage occurs at a different point in the legislative process, British standing committees are structured and function differently than Congressional committees. Commons' committees are not designated by topic or subject, but simply by letters of the alphabet. Despite what the label standing committee would suggest, they have no permanent membership. When a bill is sent to committee, the Committee on Selection appoints 16 to 30 MPs to serve on that committee to deal with that bill only. Thus although standing committee A may deal with several bills—totally unrelated to each other—during a given session of Parliament, the membership of the committee will change completely from one bill to the next.

The Committee of Selection is chosen annually by the Commons. In staffing the standing committees, it tries to appoint MPs with knowledge relevant to the particular bill being considered. Length of service in the Commons has little to do with appointment to a committee, since there is no seniority system as in the U.S. Congress. This applies as well to committee chairmanships. The Speaker of the House selects chairmen. Since they, like the Speaker, are to preside impartially, an MP from an opposition party may be appointed chairman. Since committees do not have permanently assigned topics and since they cannot kill legislation, MPs unually do not compete for appointment to committees.

Unlike Congressional committees, gathering information is not one of the functions of Commons standing committees. They do not hold public hearings on proposed legislation; they do not call expert witnesses to testify for or against a bill. If someone feels that he or she possesses information the committee would find helpful, that person must communicate the information to a committee member who can relay it to the committee. Thus while an interest group would want to have one of "its" MPs on a committee dealing with a bill of interest to it so that it would be informed about new legislation, it would not be mounting an extensive campaign to lobby the committee, as it would in the United States.

Since the Commons already has accepted a bill in principle before it goes to committee, the committee to which it is sent cannot kill or mutilate it out of recognition. The committee's job simply is to give the bill the detailed consideration for which the Commons did not have time and to make those changes that second reading debate indicated that the Commons desired.

The absence in Britain of permanent subject matter legislative committees is an important contrast with the United States. The British system does not provide for constant surveillance of the actions and proposals of the executive by small groups of legislators who have built up a fund of expertise in a variety of delimited subjects. We have already seen that most MPs cannot afford a sizable research staff; now we see that they cannot call upon such assistance even collectively. Thus the Commons frequently is not well informed on the subjects with which it must deal; it is unable to challenge the Government's proposals because, based as they are on the expertise of the civil service, they appear to be justified by superior knowledge.

In an effort to remedy the problem, the Commons in the late 1960s began experimenting with specialist select committees. These committees could call expert witnesses and hold public hearings. Their function was solely informative, however; no bills were sent to them. It was as though the British had taken the functions of Congressional committees and split them in two, with one set of committees dealing with bills and another set gathering information on which to base a report to expand the legislature's knowledge in certain areas.

The current set of specialist select committees dates from late in 1979. Fourteen committees with 11 members each (except for Scottish Affairs, which has 13) were established with subject matters corresponding to particular government departments. Each committee is able to hire a few people—typically three or four—to serve as expert advisors.

Several problems associated with the new committees have yet to be resolved. While they can call Government ministers and civil servants to testify, they do not have a statutory right to compel them to provide information. Thus some ministers have not been very cooperative in answering committee questions. Civil servants called to testify have been told by their supervisors not to discuss a long list of subjects, including "questions in the field of public controversy." The Government has been reluctant to permit even such a simple thing as creation of subcommittees; only a few of the 14 may do so.

As for the Commons itself, it really has not been able yet to figure out what it wants to do with these committees. No procedure has been established to ensure regular discussion by the full House of the reports of the committees. Thus their investigations may wind up informing only the dozen MPs who are on a given committee.

Early in 1981 the Commons began another committee experiment. One of the standing committees (the ones that deal with legislation, not the specialist select committees we have just discussed) was permitted to call witnesses while dealing with a bill in committee stage. This is the closest the British have moved yet to the Congressional system. But note that even though this experiment combines information gathering and shaping of legislation, the committee involved is not a subject matter committee and has no permanent membership.

You may wonder why the British have made reform of the Commons' committees such an involved process. Apart from the fact that, as you have already learned, the British change things only bit by bit over some years, the slowness is because a fundamental issue concerning the ultimate location of power in the British system is involved. The Commons wants to be better informed, so that it can exert greater control over the Government; the Government does not want to give up any of its power and wants to avoid any reform that would make it beholden to the Commons. Thus the basic issue is one of executive–legislative relations, which, as we indicated at the start of the chapter, we will discuss more fully in the next chapter.

While not part of the legislative process as such, another form of information gathering may produce proposals for legislation. From time to time the Government appoints Royal Commissions to study a topic of public importance such as the criminal justice system, control of the mass media, or gambling. Typically, the Government appoints 8 to 16 people chosen for wide experience and diverse knowledge. The Commission is well provided with research staff and can take testimony from governmental officials as well as private organizations and individuals. When it completes its work it issues a report of its findings and recommendations.

While the operation of Royal Commissions does allow for more input from interest groups than has been possible with the Commons committees, yet testifying before a Royal Commission hardly is a major interest group strategy. Commissions are created too infrequently—an average of less than two a year during the 20th century and closer to one a year recently—to do most interest groups much good. Furthermore, despite their high-powered membership and impressive title, Royal Commissions are not very highly regarded. Creation of a Royal Commission usually is regarded as a delaying tactic—a way of appearing to do something without actually taking any action. Since Royal Commissions take so long to produce a report, a Government creating one usually can count on at least two years during which it can claim that it is waiting for a report before considering whether to propose any legislation on a subject. Thus while the Commons occasionally will have the benefit of a Royal Commission report relevant to legislation it is considering, the Commissions are not a satisfactory substitute for an effective legislative committee system.

Every democratic legislature must face the problem of how debate can be limited to avoid dogmatic obstruction without trampling on the rights of those favoring unpopular views to gain a full hearing for their position. In Britain, closure, the proposal to end debate and take a vote on an issue, requires only a simple majority vote of the Commons provided that at least 100 Members vote to end debate. The Speaker may refuse a motion for closure, however, if he or she feels that some significant views have not been adequately heard yet. The

Speaker's impartiality and considerateness, mentioned above, are essential to ensuring that neither the will of the majority nor the rights of the minority are violated in the legislative process.

To ensure that the business of the Commons is processed promptly, the Speaker, on his or her own initiative, may ignore amendments proposed by small, atypical segments of the Commons. This power is referred to as "kangaroo" closure. During the report stage of a bill he or she, in effect, hops over insignificant amendments, calling for action on only those amendments that he or she thinks are supported by substantial sections of the Members. The chairmen of Ways and Means and of the standing committees possess this power as well.

Another form of closure utilized in the Commons is the "guillotine." Officially it is referred to as "allocation of time orders." A guillotine is used when a bill is likely to arouse lengthy and fierce opposition. The guillotine sets time limits for each state (committee, report stage, and third reading) in the consideration of a bill. Moreover, it makes dilatory and adjournment motions out of order, and it removes other impediments (such as time regularly set aside for the consideration of certain subjects) to speedy action. To prevent guillotine motions themselves from delaying the Government's legislative program, debate on them is limited to no more than three hours.

In addition to these limits on debate for the Commons as a whole, the rules limit individual MPs also. Except when the Commons is in Committee of the Whole, MPs may speak only once on any motion. Furthermore, they must be relevant or the Speaker can order them to stop speaking. Unlike the well-known example of Huey Long in the U.S. Senate, MPs cannot filibuster by reading recipes for creole cooking. Since reading prepared speeches is prohibited, the difficulty of speaking for very long without violating the requirement of relevancy operates as something of a time limit. A formal time limit as such does not exist, except that in 1980 the Commons tried as an experiment permitting the Speaker to limit backbenchers (MPs not part of two main parties' leadership group) to 10 minutes during second reading debates occurring between 7:00 to 9:00 P.M.

Some votes in the Commons simply are by voice. When a record of each Member's vote is desired, however, as on major legislation, the Commons uses a method sharply distinct from the roll call of American legislatures. The Speaker calls for a division of the House. Members then have six minutes to enter one or the other of the two "division lobbies" around the Commons' chamber. Each party's whips make certain that late-arriving MPs enter the proper lobby. As Members file out of the division lobbies, they give their names to clerks, who check them off the list of Members, and are counted by tellers. After all the Members have left the lobbies, the tellers and the clerks make certain that their total for the ayes (and in the other lobby, the noes) agree and the results are reported back in the chamber to the Speaker.

You may regard calling a division as another of those quaint practices that by now you have come to expect of the British and that any sensible country would abandon for more up-to-date methods. The procedure does give rise to snide comments about Members being herded through the lobbies like sheep. None-theless, a division in the Commons consumes only about 10 minutes, less than that required by the U.S. House of Representatives with only two thirds as many members and electronic voting. The apparently silly, traditional ways do have something to be said for them at times.

Calling the Government to Account

The House of Commons devotes more floor time to its business than any other legislative body in the world. In a typical year it meets for 150 to 180 days and averages well over 1,500 hours of sittings. This is almost five times as many hours as that spent by the German Bundestag and one third longer than the U.S. Senate. Yet, not counting the time spent in discussing financial matters, the Commons devotes only about two fifths of its time to debating and passing legislation.

Furthermore, as we will see in the next chapter, strong party discipline has moved the center of decision making from the Commons to the Cabinet. The Cabinet makes policy; the Commons does little more than ratify. The most important function of the Commons, therefore, is not policymaking, but calling the Government to account. The Government is forced to defend and justify in the House its actions and proposals. The Commons provides an arena for this debate and for criticizing the Government and ventilating grievances against it.

But to what purpose? In normal circumstances the Opposition does not expect to defeat the Government in the Commons or even to get it to modify its policy in any important respect. Actually, the Opposition in the Commons is playing to the public at large. By challenging the Government in the House it seeks to persuade enough voters to give it a majority at the next election. The Opposition is trying to convert not the Government and its MPs, but the electorate. If, as occasionally occurs, the Government modifies or even withdraws proposals because of criticism in the Commons, that is an unexpected bonus for the Opposition.

By criticizing the Government, the Opposition can develop policy alternatives during the periods between elections and not have to rely on the campaign alone to inform the electorate on how the parties differ. By being forced to explain and defend its actions, the Government clarifies for the public its program and plans. Thus each side has an opportunity to work out a coherent set of policies and to get some indication of public response to them.

While the Government obviously expects to be challenged in the Commons by the Opposition, debate may reveal as well complaints and doubts among Government MPs. Such evidences of discontent require prompt response or they may grow into a major defection. In terms of producing immediate changes in Government action, dissent among Government MPs is more effective in calling the Government to account than is the challenge of the Opposition.

One of the best known means of calling the Government to account is question time. Four days a week (no questions on Fridays) one of the first things the Commons does as soon as it meets is to hear replies by Cabinet ministers to questions that have been submitted at least two days in advance by nonministerial Members. Each MP may submit two questions addressed to those ministers in whose sphere of responsibility the matter inquired about falls. The prime minister is required to reply to questions twice each week. Questions may be designed to embarrass a minister, call attention to minor injustices in the bureaucracy, or simply obtain information. In the hands of skilled MPs this procedure has been a potent weapon in the past. More recently, however, a number of people have become skeptical about the power of question time to control the Government.

Ministers have experts in their department to prepare answers to questions. Once an answer is made to a question, however, any Member may ask a supplementary question, provided it is related (the Speaker will not permit unrelated ones), and the supplementaries must be answered at once. At this point the minister is on his or her own, although civil servants may be in the box (a row of seats at the end of the House to the right and behind the Speaker, no. 5 in Figure 5-1.) The box is separated from the House chamber by a low partition and technically is not a part of it. Because no messengers are used, conversation and notes pass over the partition if the minister needs help. The minister's Parliamentary private secretary, a Member of the House, is present also to assist, if necessary. If the minister is a member of the House of Lords, questions in the Commons relative to his or her department are handled by the Parliamentary secretary of the department, who is a Member of the Commons.

A minister may refuse to answer a question on the ground that to do so would injure the national interest—for example, questions about delicate foreign negotiations in progress. The Government usually tries to avoid such a reply so that it does not appear to have been embarrassed or to be hiding something. A minister inadequately informed or unable to think on his or her feet is a liability to the Government. Careers may be jeopardized and reputations broken by consistently poor performances during question time.

Occasionally the Government uses question time by getting its supporters to ask questions, the response to which can correct false or misleading information or quell rumors. Early in the 1970s this standard procedure was abused. Some ministers had their civil servants prepare large numbers of innocuous questions, which were submitted by Government supporters. This clogged up the Commons question agenda so that questions submitted by the Opposition did not have to be answered in the House. Question time ends at 3:30, and all questions scheduled for that day that have not been answered receive only a written reply. An MP who wants an oral reply—the only way that supplementaries would be possible—would have to get the question rescheduled, probably a week or two later when its political impact might be greatly reduced.

While this abuse was ended, questioners still faced the problem that ministers are very skilled in not telling the Commons anything that they do not wish

MPs to know. Question time is useful, but probably highly overrated as a means of calling the Government to account. Nonetheless, some MPs devote considerable time to questions. During the 1979–80 session of Parliament one MP submitted nearly 1,400 questions. The typical MP, however, submitted fewer than 100. The specialist select committees may breathe new life into question time by providing MPs with the detailed information necessary for asking more searching questions that the Government could not evade as easily.

In addition to question time, MPs have a special opportunity to call the Government to account at the end of each sitting. At 10:00 P.M. the Commons' regular business is halted for an adjournment debate. (If this is a sitting that is to continue beyond the usual 10:30 closing, then the adjournment debate does not occur until whenever the end of the sitting is.) During the next half hour before the House automatically adjourns, MPs can discuss a particular grievance or aspect of Government policy. At times an MP who feels that he or she did not receive a satisfactory reply from a minister during question time will have an opportunity to pursue the matter further during an adjournment debate.

The end-of-the-sitting adjournment debates, like question time, provide a chance for individual MPs to call the Government to account on detailed matters that may be of limited interest to most MPs. Another type of adjournment debate deals with issues of wider concern. After each sitting's question time, an MP may move that the Commons adjourn on "a specific and important matter that should have urgent consideration." If the Speaker agrees that the subject meets these criteria and the request, if opposed, is supported by 40 MPs, a special three-hour debate is scheduled for the following day immediately after questions. Alternatively, if the Speaker feels that it is necessary, he or she can schedule the debate for 7:00 P.M. on the day of the request. When the debate occurs (typically from one to four times per session), the House does not argue the merits of whether it should go home, but discusses the urgent topic that the MP had raised.

At times the Government itself may move immediately after questions that the House adjourn. This is not because the Cabinet ministers are unprepared and want a day off. Under the Commons' rules of procedure virtually any topic is relevant on a motion to adjourn. Thus such a motion permits a wide-ranging debate on some topic of current interest without having to worry about whether the Speaker needs to rule some MP out of order for not being relevant. The Government arranges such debates in consultation with the Opposition, so the latter has some influence over the topics that are discussed.

The Opposition has even more control over the topic for the 19 Opposition Days scheduled during each session. For these the Opposition decides what subject will be debated and what form of motion will be the basis for the debate. Until 1985 these Opposition Days were totally controlled by the largest Opposition party. Thus the Alliance could determine the topic on which the Government was to be challenged only through the grudging charity of Labour in granting it some of the Opposition Days. The changes in the British party system finally were recognized by providing that the second largest Opposition party should be granted three days of its own. Thus the Liberals would qualify and could share their days with their Social Democratic allies.

When an Opposition party wants to challenge the Government as aggressively as possible, it can submit a motion of censure against or lack of confidence in the Government. Such motions usually cite an alleged failing of the Government, but the resultant debates tend to have a broad scope. We will discuss such motions in more detail in the next chapter.

The point of all these procedures is that in Britain it is possible to have public, face-to-face discussions by the top political figures of current political issues precisely at the time they are of greatest prominence. The fact that the government cooperates with the Opposition in arranging these debates is evidence of the great importance attached in Britain to fair play, free speech, and responsible government. For those in power to help provide their opponents with opportunities to drive them from power is a remarkable rarity among the world's nations. Furthermore, in order to ensure a viable Opposition, financial aid is provided for parliamentary parties not belonging to the Government. The amount given to them is determined according to the number of seats and votes that they received in the previous general election. In 1985 the sum was set at about $550,000 for Labour, more than $100,000 for the Liberals, and not quite $80,000 for the Social Democrats.

Many students of Parliament and MPs themselves have become concerned, however, that strengthened party discipline and increasing complexity of public problems and government policy have robbed the Commons in the 20th century of the ability to control the Government despite its possession of procedures that were effective in the 19th century. The accountability of the Government has been declining. To that extent democracy has been attenuated despite (some would argue because of) the expansion of the right to vote to the mass of the people at the end of the 19th century and early in the 20th.

THE HOUSE OF LORDS

Turning now to the upper house of Parliament—the House of Lords—we examine briefly a huge legislative body with a potential membership of around 1,200. None of them is elected and most of them are entitled to membership simply because they have inherited a title from their forebearer. Those who have not inherited membership have been appointed because of their eminence in various fields. In addition, the Lords includes 26 bishops of the Church of England and 9 Lords of Appeal in Ordinary, who are the leading judges of the land.

Granting excuses to those Lords who indicate they do not care to attend reduces the body's effective size to 900. Its working size of active members is smaller still—about 300. To help improve the quality of the Lords' active members by recruiting capable people who objected to a hereditary aristocracy, Parliament passed a Life Peerages Act in 1958. This made it possible to appoint people to the Lords for their lifetime only. When they die their title and membership in the Lords do not pass on to their oldest son. Life peers now make up about 30 percent of the total membership of the Lords and an even larger proportion of the active membership.

The Lords meet less frequently than the Commons and their meetings are shorter, about six and a half hours a sitting on average. Procedure is more informal than in the Commons; there are no standing committees and no closure. The lord chancellor, a member of the Government, presides over the Lords. Unlike the Speaker in the Commons, he takes an active part in debate. Many members of the Lords are not active in any political party, but enough of them are to give the Conservatives a permanent majority in that House.

Given this political situation the powers of the Lords are of some importance. A major constitutional crisis the Lords' powers to be limited in 1911. These were reduced further by the Parliament Act of 1949. To become law, a bill must pass both Houses of Parliament. When the Houses disagree, a bill can be shuttled back and forth in an effort to modify it into a form acceptable to both. Unlike the U.S. Congress, no joint conference committee composed of members from both chambers is set up to work out a compromise.

If the efforts to get a consensus fail and the Lords refuse to pass the bill, then it cannot become law. The Commons may, however, override the Lords. If the bill is reintroduced the following year and passed in exactly its original version, then it becomes law, regardless of whether the Lords still object. Furthermore, should the Speaker of the House of Commons rule that the bill in question involves financial legislation—creation of a new tax, for example—then the bill becomes law 30 days after passage by the Commons despite any opposition from the Lords.

The power of the Lords to delay the passage of legislation can be important at times, especially near the end of a Government's term. If it loses the election, then it will not be able to reintroduce a bill that the Lords opposed and the Lords' suspensive veto will, in effect, become a permanent one. This is not to suggest that the Lords and the Commons constantly are at odds. Typically, if the Commons insists on having legislation in a particular form and will not accept the changes that the Lords want, then the Lords will give in and not block passage of the bill. Nonetheless, the frequency of Government defeats in the Lords has been growing. During the 1970–74 Parliament such defeats averaged 7 a year, while for the 1979–83 Parliament the figure had grown to 11. Then in the single session of 1983–84, the Government suffered 18 defeats in the Lords.

This may make it appear that Gilbert and Sullivan were right when they wrote of the Lords' action during the Napoleonic Wars, "The House of Lords did nothing in particular and did it very well." The Lords, however, play a useful role in considering amendments that the Commons did not have time to discuss. The diverse membership of Lords enables it to hold informative debates by nonpartisan experts on topics of public interest. And the Lords can help to prevent possible abuses from delegated legislation, provisional orders, and other such executive decrees.

As we have mentioned earlier, much contemporary legislation simply states general provisions and procedures and leaves the details of implementation up to the bureaucracy. The framework legislation authorizes the executive to issue detailed regulations to achieve the goals set by the legislature. The power to issue such rules—typically called statutory instruments in Britain—must be controlled to ensure that the executive does not become a law unto itself. Parliament needs to be certain that the executive does not abuse this grant of power.

Lack of time prevents the Commons from discussing more than a handful of the approximately 2,500 statutory instruments issued each year. While the Joint Committee on Statutory Instruments (composed of seven Members from each House) and the Commons' Standing Committee on Statutory Instruments do manage to discuss a good number of them, still most statutory instruments receive little scrutiny by Parliament before going into effect. The House of Lords makes the situation somewhat more tolerable than it otherwise would be. The Lords has more free time than does the Commons, it has people with legal training, and, since its members need not be concerned to attract attention to help get reelected, it has people willing to work on matters generally regarded as dull or unspectacular. Thus in this area as well the Lords makes a worthwhile contribution.

Perhaps the best brief assessment of the Lords is that offered by Herbert Morrison, a prominent figure in Labour's 1945–51 Government, who wrote, "The fact that the House of Lords has many irrational features is not in itself fatal in British eyes, for we have a considerable capacity for making the irrational work; and if a thing works we tend rather to like it, or at any rate to put up with it."[3] A more quintessentially British comment would be hard to find.

Nonetheless, changes in the Lords powers and membership have been discussed for some time. In its manifesto for the 1979 election the Labour party declared that it would eliminate the power of the Lords to delay bills. Those on the left wing of the party want to go farther and abolish the Lords entirely to produce a unicameral legislature. Those on the right of the political spectrum in Britain fear that this would permit a left-wing dominated Government to take radical action that would be irreversible. This conflict is intertwined with the question we discussed in a previous chapter of whether Britain needs a written constitution. While the outcome of the struggle in the Labour party is too uncertain to permit any detailed prediction about the future of the House of Lords, the history of political reform in Britain suggests that an upper chamber is likely to continue to exist, although some change in its membership is quite possible.

---

[3]Lord Morrison of Lambeth, *Government and Parliament,* 3d ed. (London: Oxford University Press, 1964), p. 205.

BIBLIOGRAPHICAL NOTE

Philip Norton, *The Commons in Perspective* (New York: Longman, 1981), provides an excellent analysis of the Commons' functions, as well as a great deal of factual information. Eric Taylor, *The House of Commons at Work,* 9th ed. (London: Macmillan, 1979), is extremely helpful on details of Commons procedures. For interesting comparisons with the United States, see Kenneth Bradshaw and David Pring, *Parliament and Congress* (London: Constable, 1972).

Bernard Crick, *The Reform of Parliament,* rev. ed. (London: Weidenfeld & Nicolson, 1968), and A. H. Hanson and Bernard Crick, eds., *The Commons in Transition* (London: Fontana/Collins, 1970), provide the background for understanding the concern about the declining power of the Commons. Proposals for reform are examined in David Judge, ed., *The Politics of Parliamentary Reform* (London: Heinemann, 1983). For perspective on the evolving role of specialist select committees, see Alfred Morris, ed., *The Growth of Parliamentary Scrutiny by Committee* (London: Pergamon Press, 1970), and Anne Davies, *Reformed Select Committees: The First Year* (London: The Outer Circle Policy Unit, 1980).

6

The Executive and Policymaking

As we have seen, the idea of limited government has had a long history in Britain. One of the reasons that the struggle to establish this doctrine in Britain was so protracted is that while many of the royal powers were derived from acts of Parliament, many powers, rights, immunities, and privileges of the monarch were based on common law—on legally enforceable custom and tradition. Rather than try to abolish all royal prerogatives—the Crown powers—some of which were essential to the proper functioning of any government, the British instead eventually established the doctrine that the decision to exercise these powers belonged not to the monarch, but to the Government's ministers. The ministers in turn were made answerable to Parliament for their acts. Thus the Cabinet is the center of power in the British political system, and its relation with the Parliament is the key aspect of accountability. Before dealing with these topics, however, we need first to explain the role and powers to which the monarch now is limited.

THE ROLE OF THE MONARCHY

Queen Elizabeth II can veto legislation, designate whomever she chooses as prime minister and make other key Governmental appointments, summon and dissolve Parliament at will, and, having received advice from her ministers, decide what her Government's policy and actions will be. While none of these actions would violate statutory law, in practice none of them are powers of the monarch and for the monarch to attempt to exercise any of them probably would be regarded as unconstitutional.

The British, in typical fashion, have shifted power around within the governmental system by custom rather than by statute. Dissolution of Parliament, for example, remains a Crown power, but the monarch uses the power only when told to do so by the prime minister. Not for more than a century has a monarch refused to dissolve Parliament when the Government desired it. A monarch has not vetoed a bill for well over two and a half centuries. Nor for almost a century and a half has a monarch dismissed a Government because he or she disliked its policies.

Furthermore, the monarch has no discretion in designating the prime minister. General elections determine who will be prime minister; the Leader of the party with the largest number of seats in the House of Commons is entitled to that office. Each party, as we have seen in Chapter 4, has a formal procedure for choosing a new Leader should their current one die or resign. And should they be in power, it would be that new Leader who would become the prime minister. The parties would not permit the monarch to select their Leader for them by picking a prime minister.

Nor does the monarch have any greater power in selecting other members of the Government. The prime minister assigns government offices without any assistance from the monarch. And as for the government's policies, these are decided by the Cabinet. The Cabinet does not advise the monarch what to do; the monarch, at best, can only suggest to the Cabinet what it might do.

Should a government be defeated in Parliament and resign instead of dissolving the Commons, the monarch must call the Leader of the Opposition to let that person attempt to become prime minister by forming a Government. This must be done without seeking anyone's advice, for not to do so could only be interpreted as an effort to keep the recognized Leader of the Opposition out of office.

For a monarch to do any of the things we have mentioned would violate conventions of the constitution and involve the ruler personally in partisan politics—the actions could not fail to aid one party and injure others. Such an effect a monarch must avoid at all costs. The monarchy has survived in Britain and indeed has become a respected institution, because of its successful transition from a position of dominating power and authority to one of political neutrality.

The political neutrality of the monarch stems from changes begun by the Reform Act of 1832. This and subsequent legislation expanding the right to vote made Cabinets dependent on the vote of the people, not on the favor of the monarch. Collective responsibility (which we discuss later in this chapter) enabled the people's representatives in the Commons to call the Government to account for the way in which the country was being run. Thus the monarch was spared responsibility for shortcomings and relieved of being involved in political struggles.

You easily can see that if the queen were to identify herself with a particular group of party politicians or a specific political program, she would become a politician, subject to criticism and attack like all other politicians. She could not appeal to the people against the Cabinet without expecting the Cabinet to appeal to the people against her. Not only *is* the queen impartial but, what is perhaps more important, the public at large *believes* her to be so. They rarely did so until the 20th century; Queen Victoria, for example, was perceived (and rightly) as a political partisan during many years of her reign.

Despite recent monarchs' withdrawal from politics and the monarchy's limited real power, the monarch is not totally irrelevant to the policy process. A monarch's influence on policy is affected by the ability, the capacity for hard work, and the personality of the particular ruler, as well as the political climate of the times. Given perceptiveness, a monarch can accumulate much information and experience over the years. Cabinet minutes and papers, Foreign Office telegrams, and other official papers are sent to Buckingham Palace daily. In addition, a monarch may ask for information and may talk with experts and dignitaries. A monarch who is willing to read, to study, and to ponder questions of public policy, can be very well informed, always a firm foundation for exerting influence.

Outside opinions free of political partisanship often are useful to a prime minister, when they come from one with long experience and sound knowledge. Queen Elizabeth, just entering her 60s, already has been served by eight different occupants of the office of prime minister. Thus she can provide a continuity in government and an active recollection of previous decisions not available from anyone else in the Cabinet. None of the members of the Conservative Cabinet that came to power in 1979 were Cabinet members when Elizabeth became queen in 1952 and most of them, including Prime Minister Thatcher, had not even won their first election to the Commons then.

The value and impact of the queen's opinions should not be exaggerated. She has little personal contact with average Britons and is insulated from the normal concerns of life. Furthermore, no government can abandon major elements in its party's program just because the queen gets a good idea. The queen can influence her ministers only to the extent that her views are considered sound and provided they do not clash with important party aims and policies.

Thus the queen's most important function is not as a policymaker, but as the ceremonial or symbolic head of state. As such she can relieve the political head of state, the prime minister, and his or her colleagues of many time-consuming duties such as meeting foreign dignitaries on arrival in Britain, dedicating important buildings or monuments, and other ceremonial functions. While this is useful, the role has a more important aspect.

The monarch provides an apolitical focus for national loyalty. Queen Elizabeth personifies the state; she is a *living* symbol of the nation and thus is able to stir patriotic feelings of national pride more successfully than a flag or a song. The strength of such feelings was amply demonstrated in 1977 by the outpouring of genuine enthusiasm for the queen on the 25th anniversary of her accession to the throne. Nor are these feelings confined to Queen Elizabeth alone. The public showed very warm sentiments for Queen Elizabeth's mother, the wife of the former king, when she celebrated her 80th birthday in 1980. And the marriage of Prince Charles, the heir to the throne, in the summer of 1981 was a very popular event, as have been the birth of his children.

Apparently not all Britons, however, stand in awe of the monarchy. In mid-1985 a British finance company sent a warning letter to Buckingham Palace accusing the Queen of being £4,000 behind in the payments on a tractor being used on her farm at Windsor. To make matters worse, the letter was addressed to "Mrs. Elizabeth Regina." The Palace took this in stride; the letter was returned with a handwritten note saying, "unknown at this address."

Over a century ago in a classic study of British government, Walter Bagehot argued that the head of state—the monarch—played a dignified role, while the head of Government—the prime minister and his Cabinet colleagues—performed an efficient function. The Cabinet was to run the government behind the scenes, while public ceremony suggested that the monarch actually was in charge. In his view monarchical pomp so awed the public that it would accept laws and regulations; if people were to discover that politicians made the decisions, they would be less willing to obey.

Such an idea seems pretty far-fetched in the closing decades of the 20th century. Yet as recently as the 1960s a public opinion poll suggested that there was still some truth to it. People were asked whether the views of the queen or of the prime minister *would* prevail if they conflicted on a matter of policy, and which *should* prevail. A substantial majority not only believed that the queen's views would triumph, but that they should.[1] Thus the monarch may still help to encourage popular feelings of the political system's legitimacy.

Distinguishing between a head of government and head of state enables the monarch to have this effect. In the United States, where the president combines both roles, criticizing the president as a partisan head of government without appearing to be attacking him as the symbolic head of state is difficult. The former clearly is legitimate, but the latter is not. Thus people are reduced to comments such as, "I respect the office, but not the man." The British system clearly offers a symbolic focus for loyalty whatever the shifts in partisan control of the government.

Finally, it can be argued that the monarch serves something of a lightning-rod function. People frequently desire a certain amount of charisma in their politics. If an unscrupulous politician with such an attribute were to gain power, he or she would pose a serious threat to democracy. Rather than try to banish charisma from government, the British allow for its channeling through the monarchy. This presents no danger because the monarch's powers have been reduced to virtually nothing. Thus the monarchy can help to discharge popular passions that otherwise might be used to jeopardize the system. The role of the monarchy in system maintenance should not be ignored.

---

[1] *The Queen* (Harmondsworth, Eng.: Penguin Books, 1977), p. 13.

Whatever the reasons, the British remain strongly attached to the monarchy. Nearly two thirds believe that it is very important for Britain to be a monarchy, while another fifth feels that it is quite important. Only 3 percent want to abolish the monarchy.[2]

THE CABINET AND THE PRIME MINISTER

Unlike the American political system, British Cabinet Government fuses the legislature and the executive. The electorate votes only for legislative representatives, not for any executive. The leaders of the largest party in the House of Commons are joined by leaders of the same party in the Lords to form the executive. This group of about 100 people—all of whom continue to serve in Parliament as well—is called the Government. The Government is responsible for making all the basic policy and administrative decisions necessary to run the country.

Within the Government, the directing group is the Cabinet. Despite its key position, the Cabinet is little mentioned in British law. Its powers, functions, and composition are almost wholly a matter of custom (the unwritten constitution again). The Cabinet's size is not set nor is there any list of governmental positions whose holders must be included in the Cabinet. In fact, the law does not even require that Cabinet members have a seat in Parliament.

In recent years the Cabinet has numbered from 17 to 24, depending entirely on the prime minister's wishes. Political leaders holding key offices, like foreign secretary (the equivalent of the American secretary of state) invariably are included in the Cabinet. Most of the Cabinet members will head one or another of the various government departments or ministries (hence the term *minister* to refer to them). Not since before World War II has someone not having a seat in Parliament been a member of the Cabinet, apart from a brief interim exception.

In selecting the members of the Cabinet, the prime minister will be influenced by political considerations. Several of his or her party colleagues will have to be included because of their experience and popularity within the party. Most of those chosen will have served in the *Shadow Cabinet,* a term applied to the Parliamentary leaders of a party when it is out of power. Some will have served in the Cabinet the previous time the party was in power. Thus the prime minister's choice will be somewhat circumscribed; people that the prime minister really would prefer to leave out may have to be included to ensure unified support from the party in Parliament. In fact, because of collective responsibility (more about this in a moment), including a known dissident from one's party in the Cabinet may be a more effective strategy for a prime minister than leaving that person out to run free in Parliament stirring up dissent.

---

[2]Roger Jowell and Colin Airey, *British Social Attitudes: the 1984 report* (Aldershot, England: Gower, 1984), p. 30.

The prime minister's choice also is limited by the Ministers of the Crown Act (1937), which requires a minimum number from the House of Lords. The Act groups ministers into two lists and sets a maximum number from the House of Commons for each. Even apart from this limitation, the prime minister would want to have some ministers in the Lords to speak for the Government. Usually the most important ministries are headed by members with seats in the Commons, but exceptions do occur. For example, in the early 1980s the foreign secretary was in the House of Lords. When this happens, the undersecretary or secretary (these are not clerical staff) must be in the Commons to present and defend the Government's policies where the people's elected representatives are.

By now you should not be surprised to learn that the Cabinet has no legal, statutory power. It makes decisions, which are implemented, because of custom and party discipline, by those who do have legal authority. The Cabinet decides what the country's policies shall be and what legislation needs to be introduced into Parliament to implement these policies. If there is to be any coherence in the Government's actions, if there is to be any planning to attain long-range goals, it must occur in the Cabinet. The Cabinet needs to be certain that a number of policies each of which individually seems desirable are not at cross-purposes to each other. Furthermore, the Cabinet is responsible for seeing that once decisions have been taken they are implemented as intended by the bureaucracy.

Traditionally, the Cabinet operated very informally; there were no agendas, no minutes, no record of decisions that than a letter sent to the monarch by the prime minister reporting on meetings. The result, as you would expect, frequently was confusion. While tolerable in peacetime, such a system would not be permitted to endure during World War I. A Cabinet secretariat was created in 1916 and now is firmly institutionalized in the Cabinet Office. The secretariat issues notices of Cabinet meetings and Cabinet committee meetings, prepares the Cabinet agenda (under the direction of the prime minister), circulates memoranda and documents relevant to items on the agenda, and takes minutes of Cabinet discussions and decisions.

This latter record is called Cabinet Conclusions. Initially these provided a full summary of each Cabinet meeting. Now they offer only a general outline of the main points made in the meeting without attributing these to any particular minister. The Conclusions state all the points agreed upon by the Cabinet. They are circulated to all ministers regardless of whether they are in the Cabinet. Ministers are expected to implement any decision relevant to their administrative responsibilities. The Cabinet Office is responsible for verifying that the respective departments act in accord with the Cabinet Conclusions.

The Cabinet meets regularly for about two to three hours one morning each week, although it can be summoned whenever the prime minister chooses and additional meetings are not uncommon. Since the relevant ministers or a Cabinet committee are expected to have discussed an issue in some detail before it comes to the Cabinet, lengthy debates on a single topic are unusual. Thus the Cabinet can cover a good number of matters in a typical meeting.

Formal voting in the Cabinet is extremely rare. Instead, when the prime minister feels a subject has been discussed adequately he or she will "collect the voices." This procedure involves having Cabinet members in turn briefly state their final views on the subject. The prime minister sums up by stating what he or she takes to be the sense of the meeting, which then becomes Government policy.

While they may differ in the secret confines of the Cabinet room, members of the Cabinet are obligated to tell the same story in public. Any one of them who does not resign is responsible for all aspects of the Government's policies. Similarly, those ministers outside of the Cabinet, who have had no direct voice in making most of the Government's policies, must be prepared to defend all Cabinet decisions or else resign from the Government. No member of the Government can reject criticism at a later time on the ground that he or she had not originally agreed with the decision. This is the doctrine of collective responsibility. Thus when Parliament challenges a minister on the policies implemented by his or her department, it is attacking the entire Government. To censure the minister would be to drive the entire Government from office.

At the same time, the Cabinet need not defend a minister's errors of judgment or faulty administration. Collective responsibility extends only to matters of policy. Each minister is responsible individually for the proper operation of his or her department. Should he or she be forced to resign for mistakes of this type, the Cabinet would remain in office.

The doctrine of collective responsibility had been so well established in Britain that it virtually had the status of a constitutional principle. The only exception had been in the 1930s during a period of coalition Government. In the 1970s, however, two further exceptions occurred, and not just to keep differing parties in the same Government, but to prevent the fall of a Government controlled by only one party. The Labour Government's policy in 1975 was to continue British membership in the EEC, but many Labour supporters, including some Cabinet ministers, wanted Britain to withdraw. Thus as the 1975 referendum on the issue approached, Labour's leaders decided that Cabinet ministers could oppose the Government's policy in speeches around the country and even could vote against it in the House of Commons. They were not permitted, however, to speak against the Government's position in the Commons, thus maintaining the fiction that the Government had a single official view. Thus collective responsibility clearly was violated.[3]

At the time it was said that the issue was an exceptional one, and that such a departure from collective responsibility would not occur again. But in 1977 exactly the same exception was made on the issue of direct election of the EEC

---

[3]For the relevant documents see Harold Wilson, *The Governance of Britain* (New York: Harper & Row, 1976), pp. 191–97.

Parliament. Thus collective responsibility has become a weapon for dealing with relatively manageable dissent within the Government—if the dissidents are few or insignificant, they must accept the majority view or resign. But the doctrine no longer has much vitality in dealing with sharp cleavages within the Government—when the minority is quite sizable and includes prominent party leaders the Government may permit an exception to collective responsibility so as not to split the party and drive the Government from office.

A number of Cabinet committees, such as the Legislation Committee, which is in charge of seeing that Government bills progress through Parliament on schedule, exist. Technically, these all are secret; not only is there no list of their members, they themselves are not even acknowledged to exist. Despite the activity of such committees, modern government is so complex and time-consuming that Cabinets can find only limited opportunity to discuss general policy and long-term goals.

Although the Cabinet is headed (some would say dominated) by the prime minister, such a position does not even exist in British law. The law literally states no qualifications that one must possess to hold the office. In fact, not until 1937 was a salary provided for the prime minister.

In practice, one becomes a potential prime minister by being chosen Leader of a party. When that party holds the largest number of seats in the House of Commons, the Leader is summoned by the monarch to become prime minister and form a Government. Constitutional practice has firmly established that the prime minister must have a seat in the House of Commons. There has not been a prime minister from the House of Lords since Lord Salisbury left office in 1902.[4]

Given the fusion of executive and legislative branches in Britain, you will not be surprised that British prime ministers have considerable legislative experience before attaining that office. Of the 17 people who have become prime minister in this century, the least that anyone had served in Parliament prior to becoming prime minister was 14 years, and the mean length of prior service was 25 years. Winston Churchill had been in Parliament 38 years before he became prime minister. By way of contrast, 9 of the 15 men who have become president of the United States in the 20th century have had no prior Congressional experience at all. The mean period of service for the six having had this experience was only 14 years.

The route to the top political post in Britain is much narrower than it is in the United States. One must work one's way up in the party through service in the legislature. There are no alternative routes such as being governor of a large state, war hero, or prominent in business, which have been among the means to

---

[4]In 1963, the Earl of Home was made prime minister, but this was after the passage of the Peerage Act, 1963, which permits a peer to give up a title. Lord Home promptly gave up his title, became Sir Alec Douglas-Home, and was elected to the House of Commons, where he had served for a number of years before he had become a peer.

presidential nomination in the United States. Thus one's political future in Britain would seem to be much more dependent upon the favor of party leaders. If one rebels against the leaders, one is not likely to receive appointment to the subsidiary offices in which one can demonstrate having the abilities necessary for top political office. Nevertheless, four of the nine people who have served as prime minister since the end of World War II had been party rebels at earlier stages in their careers. Despite stepping out of line, they were able, for a variety of reasons, to survive and advance.

Given the length of legislative service that most prime ministers have, clearly a person cannot be especially young upon reaching the post. The mean age on first becoming prime minister of the 17 people holding the post in the 20th century is 59. Margaret Thatcher, who was not yet 53 when she became prime minister, was the second youngest in this century. For the 15 men who have become president of the United States in the 20th century, the mean age at inauguration is 54 (the average would be 53, were it not for President Reagan's exceptional age).

The prime minister appoints, and can dismiss, the top executives, presides over Cabinet meetings, coordinates and directs Government policy. Traditionally, the prime minister was said to be *primus inter pares*—first among equals. Regardless of whether that phrase ever accurately described the prime minister's position, some experts have argued recently that it is totally misleading now. They argue that the power, prestige, and authority of the prime minister are so great that just as power earlier passed from Parliament to the Cabinet, now it has continued on into the prime minister's hands. According to them the correct label for the British system is not Parliamentary Supremacy or even Cabinet Supremacy, but prime ministerial Government.[5] The basis of the prime minister's strength is domination of the Cabinet, the civil service, and the party machine.

The prime minister has considerable control over the political careers of his or her colleagues. The prime minister can dismiss a minister from the Cabinet or shift him or her to a less important department. By controlling the Cabinet agenda the prime minister can determine what issues will be discussed and when. The prime minister formulates the Cabinet Conclusions, which then become the official record of what the Cabinet decided. Cabinet committees are created by the prime minister, who determines who will serve on them and what their rules of procedure will be. Should the prime minister announce a new policy the Cabinet is committed to it even if he or she did not bother to consult Cabinet members beforehand. Individual ministers, on the other hand, may be disowned should they initiate a change without having consulted the Cabinet and the prime minister.

---

[5]For a brief statement of these views see Richard Crossman. *The Myths of Cabinet Government* (Cambridge, Mass.: Harvard University Press, 1972), especially Lecture II.

In the bureaucracy the prime minister decides who will be the top civil servant in each department. Especially important is the prime minister's ability to decide which civil servant will head the Treasury and which will be secretary of the Cabinet.

The personalities of the main parties' leaders have come to play a larger role in British elections. Posters such as that in Figure 6–1 are much more common than in the past. (The Conservatives made considerable use in 1979 of posters with Thatcher's picture, even though it was clear that she was much less popular than was Prime Minister Callaghan.) Insofar as a prime minister is an electoral asset, his or her position as party Leader is strengthened. No sensible party would want to lose or weaken someone who can help them gain votes. Thus a popular prime minister can be expected to be able to direct the party machine, which in turn will help to strengthen his or her position as prime minister.

On the other hand, a prime minister lacks the huge staff of an American president, has nothing equivalent to the Executive Office of the president. While the National Security Council, for example, is part of the Executive Office of the president in the United States, the similar Defence Committee in Britain is under the Cabinet. The total number of employees in the prime minister's private office, counting not only clerks and typists, but messengers and cleaners as well, is under 100. Including those in the non-civil service political office, the policy unit, and the press office would add only a handful more.

Former Prime Minister Callaghan certainly would question the belief that a prime minister dominates the party machine. He persistently found the left-leaning National Executive Committee of the Labour party opposed to his views and frequently was defeated in its votes. Nor did he have any greater success with Labour's annual Conference.

Furthermore, prime ministers lack the constitutional powers and position of an American president. Since a prime minister is not elected for a fixed term, he or she must work constantly to retain the support of colleagues and followers. An American president can ignore dissent within the Cabinet with relative impunity, but a prime minister cannot. Resignation of key Cabinet members could cause the Government to fall, so the prime minister must win rather than coerce their support. Since 1885 the terms of office of British prime ministers have ranged from a half a year to eight and two-thirds years, with the median slightly more than three years. During the same period American presidents have served from 2½ to 12 years, with the median 4¼ years. Were it not for assassinations and death in office of American presidents—neither of which occurred to British prime ministers during this period—the gap would be even larger.

The point is that on the one hand prime ministers lack presidents' security of tenure and thus may tend to be more cautious in exercising their power. Second, a prime minister has less time than does a president to have some impact upon the political process by implementing his or her program fully. This again implies a limit upon the power of the prime minister.

FIGURE 6–1   Conservative Party 1979 Election Poster

The absence in Britain, however, of a separation of powers system with checks and balances greatly strengthens the executive as a whole vis-à-vis the legislature. Thus, although within the executive branch the American president is more powerful than the British prime minister, the British executive as a whole is more powerful than the American executive. The following section's discussion of executive–legislative relations in Britain will make this clear.

LEGISLATIVE–EXECUTIVE RELATIONS

The Government dominates the legislative process. The Cabinet decides what legislative program will be presented to Parliament and how the available time will be allocated to the various bills and other matters demanding Parliamentary action. Those things that the Cabinet chooses for action always get first priority. While the Government permits the Opposition at times to decide what the subject of a Commons debate will be, the Opposition does not introduce bills and attempt to pass them. As for individual MPs, while they can introduce bills, they have little hope of getting them enacted. Only 12 Fridays are set aside to deal with all stages beyond first reading of bills introduced by backbenchers. Remember that in Britain a bill does not go to committee until after it has passed second reading. Thus, unless an MP can get his or her bill on the agenda for a second reading debate, there is no hope for its survival. So scarce is the available time that MPs actually hold a lottery to determine which MPs will be able to use some of the time on the 12 Fridays for their bills. Thus with few exceptions, and those usually for bills of relatively limited importance, the laws that Parliament enacts are those that the Cabinet has proposed.

The power of the Government is enhanced further because, unlike the American practice, only ministers can propose the raising or spending of money. A bill authorizing expenditure, even though it does not appropriate money, requires a recommendation from the Government. Motions to increase expenditures are contrary to the Commons' rules of procedure. While a motion to reduce expenditures would be in order, it would be regarded as tantamount to a motion of censure. Such motions—for example, one to cut a minister's salary by £50—are used as a means to hold a debate about the success or failure of the Government's policy on the subject with which that minister is concerned. Were such a motion to pass the significant result would not be that the minister would be paid a bit less, but that he or she probably would have to resign because, in effect, the Commons had voted no confidence in the minister.

While the Government as a whole exercises the initiative in the raising and spending of money, the Treasury and its head, the chancellor of the exchequer, play a major role. All departmental requests for money must undergo Treasury scrutiny. The power of the chancellor of the exchequer requires firm support from the prime minister for maximum effectiveness. Once, however, the Government's financial proposals reach Parliament, everyone in the Government must support them because of collective responsibility. While Cabinet members will have a general idea of what is being planned for taxes and government spending, they will not have been told the detailed proposals prior to the chancellor's announcing them in the Commons. The fact that this procedure still prevails despite frequent complaints from Cabinet members is one of the things cited by those who argue that the British system is prime ministerial Government.

The job of seeing that the Government's legislative program progresses expeditiously through the Commons falls on the leader of the House, who is designated by the prime minister. While the leader is responsible for overseeing the business of the House in general, the detailed day-to-day arrangements are made by the Government party's chief whip. He or she consults with the Opposition chief whip, who receives advance notice of how the Commons' agenda is being arranged. These contacts—referred to in the Commons as the "usual channels"—help the Government get its proposals through the Commons without denying the Opposition a chance to criticize them and to make a case for alternative policies.

The Government chief whip is assisted by a deputy chief whip and by a varying number of junior whips. All the whips are members of Parliament, and most of the Government whips receive additional salaries. The chief whip has an office at 12 Downing Street (No. 10 is the residence of the prime minister), where there are accommodations also for the junior whips. The main Opposition party has several whips as well. The Government even pays an official salary to three of them. This is additional evidence of the importance the British attach to having a loyal Opposition prepared to challenge the Government and offer an alternative set of leaders.

The main concern of the Government whips is to be certain that MPs belonging to the Government party are present when votes are taken in the Commons and that the MPs vote in support of the Government's proposals. The whips also serve, however, to inform ministers of the misgivings and complaints of the backbenchers. The whips must be certain that the party's leaders know the mood of the followers even if (or especially when) that mood is opposed to some Government policy.

Each Thursday when the Commons is in session the leader of the House announces the business that will be brought before the House the following week. The next day each party mails to all of its MPs a document called the whip. This document not only includes the schedule as announced by the leader, but also may indicate who some of the main speakers will be for the various debates and, most importantly, indicates the relative significance to the party of each item of business. A matter of limited importance will be underlined once. Fairly important matters are underlined twice. A three-line whip means that one or more votes are certain to occur during the discussion of that business and that the party expects (you could really say "requires") every one of its MPs to be present, unless ill or unavoidably absent. At times even these two excuses are not sufficient. MPs have been brought from hospital beds on stretchers to the precincts of the House of Commons so that their votes could be counted in important debates, and ministers have had to break off negotiations in foreign countries to fly home to London for a vote. While votes on a motion of censure always will be designated a three-line whip, many other items of business involving the Government's legislative program also will be put in this category.

Strictly speaking, the whip is no more than instructions to MPs of when they are to be certain to attend the Commons. In fact, of course, their party is concerned not just to have the pleasure of their company, but to have them vote and not just vote, but vote as the party wants. MPs are expected to vote the party line regardless of their personal views or of any arguments made during the debate. Abstaining is about as far as an MP can go in refusing to support the party's line, and even that can get him or her in trouble at times. On some issues— those involving morals or conscience, like the death penalty—parties usually will permit a free vote: not take a position and permit MPs to vote as they wish. But when, as usually is the case, a party takes a stand, an MP must fall in line or suffer the consequences.

If an MP rebels on an issue of sufficient importance or frequently enough, he or she may have the whip withdrawn. In the Conservative party this power is vested in the Leader, while in the Labour party it requires a majority vote of the Parliamentary Labour Party. The result is to expel an MP from the party in Parliament. In the Labour party the action is reported to the National Executive Committee, which may decide to expel the offender from membership in the Labour party. Thus rebels risk ending their political careers.

To Americans, used to seeing a coalition of Democrats and Republicans passing legislation in opposition to a group of other Democrats and other Republicans, such a draconian concern with party discipline may seem almost totalitarian. You may conclude that British MPs simply are a group of cowardly sheep terrorized by their leaders through their brutal whips. But the whips rarely bully or coerce; reasoned persuasion is their typical approach.

This method can be highly effective because of the fundamental difference in legislative-executive relations between Britain and the United States. Unlike the American president, the British prime minister has no fixed term; in Britain the executive can be voted out of office at any time by the House of Commons. If the Commons passes a motion of censure or of no confidence in the Government, the prime minister must either resign, letting the Opposition party come to power, or call a general election, which the Opposition may win.

Thus if enough MPs vote against their party when it is in power, they are likely to drive it out of office and permit the Opposition to come to power. Obviously, whatever their quarrel with their own party they must regard bringing the Opposition to power as a worse alternative or they would be members of that party. Furthermore, British MPs perceive the role of legislator differently than do members of the American Congress. The typical MP recognizes that he or she has not been elected because of any personal abilities or magnetism, but because of the party label. People vote for an individual in order to give a particular party the majority in Parliament needed to carry out its policies.

To the extent that Britain is more homogeneous than the United States, political issues are more national instead of regional. Thus, unlike a member of Congress, an MP has neither the opportunity nor the necessity to deviate from the party line. Being less likely to be subject to regional pressures, an MP is less likely to disagree with national leaders. For the most part his or her constituents will not be clamoring for stands at variance with the national leaders. And precisely because this is likely to be true, an MP will have little opportunity to win local popularity by defying the national leaders.

The whips do not need to do anything to the MP who persistently rebels; his or her local party is likely to warn that unless this behavior ceases they will find another candidate for the next election. Usually dissent is tolerated only when it moves an MP away from the opposition parties and toward the fringe of the political spectrum. Especially in the Labour party, local party activists tend to be farther from the center of the political spectrum than are the national party leaders. Thus an MP who voted against the party's policy because it was too moderate would be unlikely to be disciplined by his or her local party.

Also helping to maintain party unity in votes in the Commons is the influence that backbench party committees can have on proposed legislation before it is submitted to Parliament. Thus the views of the Government's MPs will have been taken into account before the debate occurs in the Commons. At that stage in the legislative process, a bill has progressed too far for major changes to be possible. As we saw in the previous chapter, the executive has close contact with the relevant interest groups in deciding upon the details of proposed legislation. When a bill arrives in the Commons it is likely to be an elaborately worked out set of compromises not permitting any extensive alteration. Furthermore, since no person can be expert on more than a few matters, on any given issue most MPs will be uninformed or uninterested. Why, in such circumstances, should they be expected to do anything other than vote as the whips tell them to do?

The result of all these factors is extremely high party cohesion—the disciplined voting of MPs in the same party in the same way. When a party wins a working majority of Commons seats in a general election, it can count on getting its legislative program through Parliament. Its proposals do not have to hurdle a number of obstacles or fear being ambushed by a hostile committee chairperson. The Government knows that it has the votes to pass the bills. This is why, as we discussed in the previous chapter, interest groups, although regarding contacts with MPs of some use, are mainly concerned to develop their links with various executive departments.

A strong case can be made for a political system that concentrates power as the British system does. Such a system concentrates responsibility as well. A British Government never can argue that its program was thwarted by the perversity of a handful of strategically placed legislators. Under the British system not only does the same party control the executive as controls the legislature, but the same section of a party controls both. Unlike in the United States, there are not congressional Democrats and presidential Democrats responsible to contrasting constituencies and thus perpetually at odds with each other despite nominally belonging to the same party. Thus when things do not get done or when that which does get done is objectionable, the voters know whom to blame. And at the next election they can remove them from power and give their opponents a chance.

The cost of such a system, however, is that Parliament is reduced to little more than a rubber stamp for the Government's plans and the individual MP is greatly devalued. The typical backbencher has little freedom in deciding how to vote in the Commons, has little chance to introduce possible legislation, and does not even have much chance to speak in the House, given the large number of members and the priority that the Speaker gives to the chief party leaders. Why should an MP's constituents think that such a person is of any importance at all?

The Commons has the power to remove the executive from office, but virtually never uses it. In the last century only four votes of no confidence or of censure have been carried against the Government. On a few other occasions votes in the Commons have changed the Government. In 1940, for example, the Government carried an adjournment motion by 81 votes but resigned because its potential majority was around 200. Since many of its supporters had abstained or even voted against it, Prime Minister Chamberlain felt that he no longer had the confidence of the Commons. Therefore, he resigned and Winston Churchill became prime minister. Nonetheless, such displays of the Commons' power were all too rare.

By the 1960s the ineffectiveness of Parliament had reached the point that many scholars and politicians were discussing a variety of ideas for the reform of Parliament. Of the many experiments that were tried, the one that seemed to win the most support was the reform of the Commons' committee system to create specialist select committees. As we explained in the previous chapter the root of the problem was diagnosed as the MPs' lack of expertise. The reformers seemed to believe that MPs could swallow a few select committee reports like Popeye gobbling a can of spinach and their muscles would bulge for a knockout punch of the Government.

The error of this proposal was to concentrate on institutional change and ignore behavior. The reformers failed to understand that the real problem was not that MPs were ignorant, but that they were not motivated to oppose the Government, for the reasons we already have discussed in explaining party cohesion. No matter how much information MPs have, if they are not willing to vote against their own party's Government more often, the Commons will remain weak.

More significant, then, than institutional reform of the Commons was the change in MP behavior that developed during the 1970s. Although not beginning to approach the American level, MPs did begin to vote against their party's line much more frequently than in the past. Discovering the reasons for this change is difficult, but a key factor appears to have been the personality and policies of Prime Minister Heath.[6] Heath's failure to communicate adequately with his backbenchers and his unyielding commitment to policies that were unpopular with them caused many Conservative MPs to vote against their own party's Government. Dissent even reached the point of defeating the Government on a three-line whip. Such an event was unprecedented, especially as the Government did not resign.

Until then most scholars and politicians had believed (they had no way of knowing for certain since Britain does not have a written constitution, as you know) that a defeat on major legislation would force the Government to resign just as surely as a defeat on a motion of censure or no confidence. But suddenly the scales fell from MPs' eyes and they realized that only a defeat on a question of confidence or censure would force the Government out. Thus the argument of the whips that MPs must support their Government on votes on legislation or it would have to resign no longer had much influence. Clearly, the Government could tolerate some defeats and continue in office.

This became even clearer under the Labour Governments of the 1970s. Admittedly, these Governments were in a minority in the Commons most of the time, and thus some have argued that they were not expected to meet the same requirements as Governments controlling a majority of the seats in the Commons. Nonetheless, the fact was that they lost a number of votes in the Commons and did not leave office. Only when Prime Minister Callaghan's Government was defeated by a single vote in March 1979 on a motion of no confidence did Labour call an election and, having been defeated in the election, leave office.

Not since the Chamberlain vote of 1940 had a Government been driven from office by a vote in the Commons, and not since 1924 had a Government been defeated on a matter of confidence or censure. Thus the House of Commons had demonstrated that, despite the many years since it last had exercised the power, it still could determine the fate of the Government.

When the Thatcher Government came to power in 1979 with a majority of more than 40 over the combined strengths of its opponents in the Commons, some observers expected a return to the party cohesion of the 1960s. But Conservative MPs soon showed that they had not lost their willingness to vote against their own Government, and that they were able in some instances to get it to change its plans. This became even more true when the election of 1983 gave the Thatcher Government a majority of more than 140 over its opponents. Clearly, with such a large margin the Government hardly was likely to lose even if two or three dozen of its MPs defected on any given vote. Thus rebellion threatened the Government's life little more than it would in a system with a specified term for the executive, as in the United States.

---

[6]Philip Norton, *Conservative Dissidents: Dissent within the Parliamentary Conservative Party 1970–74* (London: Temple Smith, 1978), pp. 217–55.

The change in MPs' behavior may also be due to the change in their backgrounds. Some evidence suggests that new MPs (who would not have years of socialization into the old ways of not making a fuss about anything) and MPs with middle-class backgrounds (who would be less likely to find fulfillment in the idea of membership in the Commons as an activity to occupy the time of the idle rich or to provide a pleasant retirement for elderly trade union officials) are more likely to dissent.

Dissent does not have to defeat the Government to be effective. Despite the change in MP behavior it remains true that the main purpose of debate in the Commons is not to defeat the Government, but to force it to defend its actions. A Government must be able to make a convincing case for its policies; if it frequently appears to be incompetent or callous, its support is likely to dwindle among both the electorate and its followers in Parliament. MPs do not enjoy appearing to be blind loyalists; they expect their Government to have a case that they can defend to their constituents without looking foolish. At times the Government may not appear to be influenced by Commons debates precisely because it already has been concerned to draw up proposals that can be defended as logical and generally fair.

Thus in the 1980s the British Government continues to dominate the Commons well beyond what the typical president can do with Congress. The influence of the Commons, however, is greater than it seems at first. Furthermore, the experiences of the 1970s have changed MPs' attitudes toward the Government and self-perceptions of their role in the policy process. The Commons now is more influential than it had been a quarter of a century ago. If recent trends are developed further, the Commons will be seen to play a more essential role in the British political system.

BIBLIOGRAPHICAL NOTE

The following are useful sources on the monarchy: Frank Hardie, *The Political Influence of the British Monarchy,* 1868–1952 (London: Batsford, 1970); Kingsley Martin, *The Crown and the Establishment,* rev. ed. (Harmondsworth, Eng.: Penguin Books, 1965); and Sir Charles Petrie, *The Modern British Monarchy* (London: Eyre & Spottiswoode, 1961). The book cited in Footnote 1, a varied and uneven collection of material, contains some worthwhile information. Although it is a popular treatment, Jerrold M. Packard, *The Queen and Her Court: A Guide to the British Monarchy Today* (New York: Charles Scribner's Sons, 1981) can answer most questions Americans typically ask about the Royals.

The standard work on the Cabinet is John Mackintosh, *The British Cabinet,* 2d ed. (London: Stevens, 1968). For views from the inside from those who were members, see the Crossman book cited in Footnote 4 and Patrick Gordon Walker, *The Cabinet,* rev. ed. (London: Cape, 1972). The Wilson book cited in Footnote 2 is not as informative as one would expect from someone who has been prime minister, but it does provide some information. For a good summary of the role of the prime minister, see Richard Rose, "British Government: The Job at the Top," in Richard Rose and Ezra Suleiman, eds., *Presidents and Prime Ministers* (Washington, D.C.: American Enterprise Institute, 1980).

For a discussion of the role of Parliament in the light of some of the recent proposals for reform, see Jorgen Rasmussen, "Was Guy Fawkes Right?", in ed. *Is Britain Dying? Perspectives on the Current Crisis,* Isaac Kramnick (Ithaca, N.Y.:Cornell University Press, 1979). The leading authority on dissent in Parliament is Philip Norton. See "Conclusions" in his *Dissension in the House of Commons 1974–1979* (Oxford: Clarendon Press, 1980).

7

Implementing Policy

THE CIVIL SERVICE AND ITS POLITICAL SUPERVISORS

So the parties have presented their programs, the voters have made their choices, the legislators have been elected, and the Cabinet has presented a coherent legislative package, which has been enacted. That's it, right? Hardly. Now somebody has to decide what these rather general laws really were intended to accomplish when applied to specific cases—cases involving not abstractions, but real people. At this point the governing process directly affects you and me. Yet we have no direct voice at all in selecting these somebodies who are going to do this to us. How can this be in a democracy?

But reflect for a moment. Do you really want the extent to which the law is applied to someone to depend on whether he is a buddy of the chief of police? Do you really want someone's tax to be assessed on the basis of whether she has a friend in the IRS? Do you really want someone who is a nice guy and, perhaps, has some good ideas, but lacks the ability to organize a scrap paper drive to administer the law? We want the law to be applied fairly to all regardless of who they may be and to be done so efficiently and competently. We need administrators selected for ability, not popularity or whom they know. Once selected, they need to be protected from powerful interests that would pressure them to apply the law unfairly.

The problem is that these various needs are mutually exclusive to some extent. Take efficiency and accountability, for example. The well-known bureaucratic red tape is nothing other than the detailed records that must be kept to justify administrative action should the legislators—functioning as watchdogs for the people—demand that particular behavior be explained. The endless forms that governmental agencies fill out and file away could be disposed of almost entirely if bureaucrats never were to be called to account for their actions. In that case, however, democracy—popular control over government—would be weakened greatly.

An effective way to obtain popular control is to replace all administrators each time one party replaces another in power. But the prospects for efficient, experienced administration would not be bright in such circumstances. Since responsibility can be obtained only at the cost of efficiency and vice versa, political systems must devise some sort of compromise between the two. The balance struck in Britain differs significantly from that preferred in the United States.

Staffing the Bureaucracy

In the United States the Jacksonian period popularized the slogan "To the victor belong the spoils" and established the system of rotation in office—bureaucrats came and went in accord with election results. The result was not only considerable administrative incompetence but also appalling political corruption.

While Jacksonian ideas played no part in British politics, Britain, as well as the United States, practiced a patronage system in government employment for much of the 19th century. Merit or ability had nothing to do with getting a government job. Government employment was something in the nature of unemployment relief for otherwise unoccupied aristocrats. So far were the British from notions of rotation in office that the holder of a government position acquired property rights to his job. He could sell it; he could will it; if it were abolished, he was entitled to compensation.

Overcoming this obstacle to the establishment of a civil service system was not as difficult as in the United States, where both patronage and rotation in office were impediments. Once Britons were convinced that administrators should be an aristocracy of *talent* rather than of *inherited title,* support was available for a professional civil service system. Thus in 1870, 13 years prior to similar action in the United States, the principle of open competition for governmental jobs was established and the various governmental departments were unified into a single civil service system.

The British civil service system was created by an Order in Council under the prerogative powers of the Crown. These powers are the residue discretionary authority legally remaining to the Crown. As the previous chapter noted, the exercise of Crown powers rests with the Cabinet; despite their name they are not subject to the personal decision of the current sovereign. The significant point rather is that the operation of the civil service still is governed chiefly by various Orders in Council and the regulations made under their authorization. Parliament could act, but it has passed little legislation regulating the internal organization of the civil service.

Little more than 600,000 people work for the national government in Britain. One of Prime Minister Thatcher's goals has been to reduce the size of the civil service, and by 1984 it had reached its lowest level since World War II. Still further cuts are planned through 1988, by which time she will have eliminated about a fifth of the bureaucracy that existed when she came to power. Most of these cuts, however, have been of the so-called industrial civil servants, people working for government enterprises such as the Royal Ordnance factories and the Royal Dockyards. (Workers in nationalized industries, however, are not counted as civil servants.) Nonetheless, the people you usually would think of as bureaucrats—those of varying responsibilities who fill a department's basic positions and provide its services—number only half a million. Furthermore, more than three fourths of these would occupy relatively routine positions, so that those having even a limited role in policymaking are relatively few.

Until 1971 the civil service was divided into three hierarchical categories. The Fulton Report, produced by a committee appointed by the Government to study the civil service, charged that these divisions prevented recruiting and promoting the best persons. The Government accepted many of the Fulton Report's recommendations. Implementing them was far easier (at least on paper) than in the United States because, as we've already told you, the British civil service is governed largely by Orders in Council, which the Government can issue with a relatively free hand.

Thus a variety of occupational groups—such as secretarial, data processing, and legal—exist now. Perhaps the most important of these is the administration group, which provides the organizational skeleton for the civil service. Recruitment into various levels of this group continues to depend upon a person's educational achievements. The current structure, however, provides greater opportunities for promotion. Even one who has entered at the bottom with limited education can progress up the ladder with suitable abilities.

Lower-level civil servants—those doing manual or clerical work—are recruited separately by the various ministries. Middle- and upper-level recruits, however, are obtained for all departments by the Civil Service Commission. Furthermore, in response to the Fulton recommendations, the top five grades in the civil service are covered by an open and unified structure, regardless of the particular duties associated with a given post. This facilitates shifting civil servants from one ministry to another to produce an integrated rather than a narrowly segmented civil service. Thus top civil servants should have greater breadth and be concerned with the impact of a policy beyond just their particular department.

Despite these reforms, the Fulton Committee's goals have not been attained. Tradition—and those having a vested interest in supporting it—proved too strong. For higher-level positions the civil service uses both written examinations and oral interviews. The written examination tests general knowledge, proficiency in English, and knowledge of two or three academic subjects chosen from a large number of alternatives. The British have sought to recruit civil servants on the basis of general ability and not on the basis of preparation and training for a specific job. They feel that top minds can quickly learn specific job requirements after they have been appointed to their position. In any event, they remain convinced that a knowledge of classical Greek is excellent preparation for life and admirable training for being in charge of public affairs. This stress upon the amateur was criticized by the Fulton Report, which favored a greater effort to recruit people for specific jobs.

The Fulton Committee was concerned not only with the rigid distinctions between levels within the civil service, but also with those between functions or specialties at the same level. The latter distinction had the effect of relegating the subject-matter expert merely to supplying technical information to the amateur or generalist, who alone could make the decisions that really shaped policy. This part of the Fulton Report was not implemented, and thus the impact of two other recommendations was nullified.[1]

Furthermore, the reforms have done little to alter the class composition of the civil service. A disproportionately low number of people with working-class backgrounds enter the civil service; the typical civil servant in a responsible position continues to be a person who went from a public school to Oxford or Cambridge. Many people—particularly Labour supporters—feel that the oral interview is part of the reason. They believe that the interviewers are looking for people with the proper social background.

Few would deny that the top British civil servants are highly intelligent, extremely able people. The question is whether their academic backgrounds are such that they know too little of science and technology and of management techniques. In so far as this is the case, the efficiency, even the competency, of the civil service is hampered. The restricted class nature of the civil service produces a second type of narrowness. Here the problem is not efficiency, but accountability. As we have seen, calling any bureaucracy to account without harming efficiency and introducing undesirable partisanship is difficult. In Britain the problem is compounded further—how can a civil service, so few of whose shapers of policy have had direct experience with the type of life lived by most people, adequately consider the people's needs and concerns? Is not such a civil service likely to require being called to account even more than one rather more representative of the population? Thus, although Britain can be termed the mother of civil services, even more than it has been called the mother of parliaments, serious problems of both efficiency and accountability have yet to be solved there.

Treasury Control

Although Britain long has had a Civil Service Commission to recruit administrators, the Treasury actually controlled the civil service. A 1920 Order in

---

[1]On the ambushing of Fulton by the generalists see Peter Kellner and Lord Crowther-Hunt, *The Civil Servants: An Inquiry into Britain's Ruling Class* (London: Macdonald and Jane's, 1980).

Council empowered the Treasury to supervise the standards and conditions of work in the civil service.

This meant that the Treasury had two important links with other departments and ministries. One link, a financial officer, was responsible for regularity in accounting and in scrutinizing proposals for new expenditures. The other, the principal establishment officer, was responsible for office organization and for matters affecting the staff, regardless of whether this was related to financial policy. Thus other departments appeared to be subordinate to the Treasury; its power was both financial and psychological.

The Fulton Report thought that Treasury control was an illogical arrangement. So in 1968 Prime Minister Wilson created a Civil Service Department to recruit administrators *and* manage the civil service. In 1981, however, Prime Minister Thatcher, as part of her effort to reduce the bureaucracy and cut government spending, abolished the CSD and restored to the Treasury much of its former powers.

The Treasury controls manpower and pay in the civil service. It designates an accounting officer in each department, usually the chief financial officer of the permanent secretary. This officer is responsible, through the minister, to Parliament for departmental expenditures. Moreover, he or she is personally and pecuniarily liable to the Treasury for unauthorized or irregular expenditures, unless he or she has protested to the minister in writing and has received authority from the minister to incur such expenditures.

The civil service responsibilities not returned to the Treasury now belong to the Management and Personnel Office in the Cabinet Office. The MPO sets policy for recruitment and training of civil servants (the Civil Service Commission and the separate ministries simply are the agencies that implement these policies) and for organization, management, and efficiency in the civil service.

What's important about all this? First, as already discussed, the preeminent position of the Treasury within the British administrative structure: It almost exercises veto power over new policies anywhere within the government. The second important point concerns the role of the prime minister. The prime minister is both First Lord of the Treasury and Minister for the Civil Service. While Prime Minister Thatcher delegates day-to-day supervision of the civil service to another Cabinet minister, she remains ultimately in charge. Furthermore, she appoints both the permanent secretary of the Treasury and the secretary of the Cabinet, who are the joint career or professional (that is nonpolitical) heads of the civil service. All of this helps to ensure that the civil service follows the prime minister's wishes. The arrangements are yet another element in the argument, which we discussed in the previous chapter, that British government no longer is Cabinet government, but has become prime ministerial government.

Organizing the Bureaucracy

The principal activities in implementing the Governments' policies are carried out by some two dozen departments and ministries, whose political heads

---

FIGURE 7–1   Typical Administrative Structure of a British Ministry

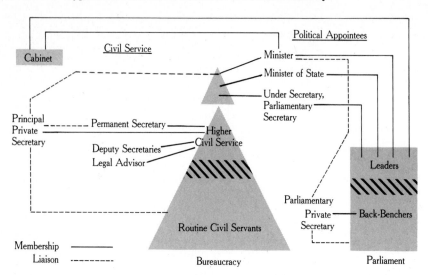

are responsbile to the House of Commons. Each ministry and department is staffed by permanent civil servants headed by the permanent secretary, (see Figure 7–1). Above this hierarchy are a handful of political appointees—typically, the minister and two to four associates—to give political direction to the department. The minister serves at the pleasure of the prime minister, as do the minister's associates, whom the prime minister has picked in consultation with the minister.

Policy and administration fuse at the ministerial level. Ministers, as Members of Parliament and of the Government, are both policymakers and administrators. Clearly, they can devote only part time to the latter job, even though they are responsible to the Commons for it. Ministers must spend much time in the Commons for its debates, must keep in touch with constituents, and must be involved in party activities. Much time is required also for meetings of the Cabinet and its committees.

Ministers can delegate some tasks to the political appointees who assist them—variously titled minister of state, undersecretary of state, and parliamentary secretary. These persons also are members of the Government party and have seats in either the House of Commons or the House of Lords. When a minister is in the Lords, his or her immediate assistant must be in the Commons to defend the department's policies in the legislative body that can censure the Government. Ministers of state rank above secretaries and undersecretaries in that they have some discretionary powers. The secretaries relieve ministers of less important duties. By learning the business of administrative departments, secretaries qualify themselves for eventual promotion to ministerial rank. Secretaries cannot determine policy on their own; they cannot override the opinions of permanent civil servants, but must refer these views to their minister.

A minister is assisted as well by a Parliamentary private secretary (PPS). A PPS, also a Member of Parliament, is not technically part of the Government; he or she receives no administrative salary, as do the others we have mentioned, in addition to MP's pay. PPSs perform a variety of tasks for their ministers. They are expected to know the temper of the House so that a minister does not encounter an unexpected revolt against a ministry's policies. They convey both the ministers' views to the party's backbench supporters and the backbenchers' grievances to the ministers.

Only the minister is responsible to the Commons for what happens in a department. Civil servants do not have to answer publicly for administrative errors or misjudgments. The British do not believe that civil servants should be dragged into the political arena; only the politicians should face that occupational risk. Therefore, the minister is to shield the civil servants from blame and, in return, receive from them faithful service and absolute loyalty. This is why, for example, civil servants called to testify before the Commons new specialist select committees are instructed not to give evidence about advice they have given to their minister.

Privately, a minister will criticize those civil servants responsible for administrative failures in implementing or formulating policy; publicly, he or she must accept the blame personally. A grave mistake may require the minister to resign as political head of the department and leave the Government. If he or she can assure the Commons that knowing about the action before it was carried out was impossible and that steps have been taken to ensure that it cannot happen again, then a mere apology to Parliament may be sufficient and the minister will be permitted to remain in office. These customary procedures are known as individual ministerial responsibility (as distinguished from the doctrine of collective responsibility, discussed in the previous chapter).

Although the requirements of individual responsibility clearly are understood by those to whom they apply, they do not seem to be practiced often. From 1946 to 1984 only 17 ministers resigned on grounds of individual responsibility.[2] Furthermore, many of the recent cases have involved personal scandals, rather than bad administration. That was not true, however, when Lord Carrington and two associates resigned from the Foreign and Commonwealth Office in April 1982 on grounds that they had failed to perceive the seriousness of the Argentine threat to the Falkland Islands. On the other hand, this hardly seems to have been a case of civil servant error for which supervising politicians had to pay the cost. So while these were instances of individual responsibility, they weren't classic cases. Thus they had only limited effect in breathing some vitality into the old doctrine.

---

[2]Calculated primarily from David Butler and Anne Sloman, *British Political Facts 1900–1979,* 5th ed. (London: Macmillan, 1980), pp. 82–83. During the same period of time half again as many ministers resigned on grounds of collective responsibility.

The doctrine also appears to have lost much of its importance because cases have occurred in recent years that seemed to require a minister to resign, yet that didn't occur. For example, in 1983, 38 members of the terrorist Irish Republican Army, in jail for various criminal activities, escaped. Although the subsequent investigation cited a wide range of failures at the prison and recommended 73 improvements in security, the relevant minister, James Prior, declined to resign. Furthermore, in contrast to past practice, he did not even argue that he was staying in office because he had made changes that would ensure that such a thing could not happen again—he specifically said that he couldn't guarantee this.

Thus Cabinets tend either to treat a colleague's poor administration as a matter of collective, rather than individual, responsibility or to overlook it entirely and thus spare the minister the embarrassment of resigning. This development weakens the accountability of administrative power. If the minister really is not responsible and the civil servants are insulated from public responsibility so as to guard their efficiency, then no one is accountable. Abandoning the doctrine of individual ministerial responsibility destroys the effective solution that the British had devised to the basic problem of public administration—how to reconcile efficiency with accountability.

Further questions about responsibility and the neutrality of the civil service were raised early in 1985 when a civil servant was acquitted of violating the Official Secrets Act. He had leaked confidential documents relating to the question of whether the Argentine ship, the *Belgrano,* had been sunk unnecessarily—for political rather than military reasons—during the Falklands conflict. Had he simply given the documents to a journalist, he probably would have been convicted. He gave them instead to an MP. Parliament was investigating independently what had occurred in the sinking. The jury acquitted him on the grounds that his primary responsibility was *not* to bureaucratic superiors *nor* to the minister in charge of the department, but to Parliament.

Since Watergate few people in the United States are willing to condone governmental coverups, and many in Britain thought that in the case of the sinking the relevant members of the executive were trying to cover up. And British constitutional doctrine certainly makes clear the essential role of Parliament in securing accountability. Yet the question remains whether this decision will create suspicion between ministers and civil servants and open the floodgates to a torrent of revealed confidential documents, not just a few leaks. Surprisingly, for a system that seemed to have solved the problem effectively, Britain faces serious accountability questions.

The Policy Role of the Civil Service

While the minister is the political head of a department or ministry, the non-political head is the permanent secretary—a career civil servant who is the true administrative chief of the agency (see figure 7-1). He or she is responsible for the general organization and efficiency of the agency and for the advice given to the minister on behalf of its permanent civil service. Staff are not to deal directly with the minister without the knowledge and approval of the permanent secretary. Given the fact that in most cases he or she will have been at the top of the department much longer than the minister has been, the permanent secretary is in an excellent position to have considerable influence on policy formation.

The British believe that really capable people cannot be recruited to and retained in the civil service unless they see some prospect of eventually reaching a position where they can have an effect. The structure of the British civil service facilitates this because, in contrast to the American administrative structure, the top positions—often referred to as the Higher Civil Service—extend much higher into the policy process.

Usually, the officials who work most closely with a minister are the permanent secretary and the principal private secretary. The latter is a promising young civil servant whom the minister has designated as a special assistant. The principal private secretary shields the minister from unnecessary engagements and needless paperwork. He or she also has the delicate task of maintaining good relations with both the permanent secretary and the medium-level civil servants in the department. The idea is to help ensure that the permanent secretary is not filtering out of reports to the minister views and doubts about current policy that should be considered. In an effort to make the department seem completely agreed on advice to the minister or to make a decision easier by limiting the options, a permanent secretary may not report conflicting views. Furthermore, medium-level civil servants may be more willing to talk with the principal private secretary since he or she is not their superior in the chain of command and thus does not have direct control over their career prospects.

A department's legal advisor and a few deputy secretaries also will have some contact with a minister. These civil servants, along with the permanent secretary and the principal private secretary, are the only ones able to influence important policy matters directly. They are expected to serve each succeeding minister loyally whatever their own political views. Only by keeping out of the political arena, through such devices as individual responsibility and acting like faceless mandarins, can they play this role. British practice contrasts sharply with both American and French; in the United States, turnover in top posts within a department is high from one Administration to another, while in France a minister brings along a personal group of trusted advisors for protection from the civil servants.

When the Labour party came to power in 1945, having won a majority of seats in the Commons for the first time and thus fully controlling the Government, many of its adherents feared that an unsympathetic civil service would sabotage the party's nationalization program. This did not occur; the civil servants loyally assisted their political supervisors in implementing Labour's economic and industrial policies. With equal loyalty six years later, when the Conservatives had returned to power, the same civil servants helped denationalize the iron and steel industry, which they had aided Labour in taking into public ownership.

One might have thought that this demonstration of civil service political neutrality and willingness to serve whoever wins elections would have put Labour's fears to rest. But concern continues to linger. Almost invariably the top civil servants, as career merit personnel, will have been with a particular department considerably longer than the minister, whose service will depend upon the shift of electoral fortunes and changing power relations within a party. Thus the civil servants may know more about a topic than does the minister; they certainly are likely to think that they know the practical complexities better. Furthermore, since ministers come and go, the civil servants feel that they will be the ones that will have to clean up any mess resulting from a mistake in policy.

As a result the civil service tends to be cautious, suspicious of innovation; it is too willing to argue that something cannot be done simply because it never has been. Richard Crossman, Cabinet minister in the Labour Governments of the 1960s, was especially concerned about the problem this attitude produces for a reformist party like Labour. He saw the civil service as opposed to change not because they were Conservative partisans, but because change disrupted past patterns of activities. It was resisted because it was inconvenient. Top civil servants were more concerned, in his view, to tell a minister why a certain policy could not be implemented than to find ways of carrying out reform. A determined minister could avoid having a program sabotaged, but any signs of indecision and the civil servants would be managing the minister rather than the reverse.

A few quotes from a permanent secretary may help to summarize the relation. In the 1960s the Labour party had among its aims reducing the price of building land so as to prevent windfall profits and encourage construction of new homes. Evelyn Sharp was permanent secretary of the Ministry of Housing at the time. Ten years later in a TV documentary Baroness Sharp (she had been given a peerage when she retired from the civil service) revealed what occurred. Speaking of the top civil servants in her department she said, "so okay we had to accept that there should be a Land Commission. We didn't think it was a good idea . . . we started to work out, as I think departments always do during election periods, how the incoming government, assuming it was to be a Labour government, could best give effect to the things they had said . . . we came to the conclusion that it really couldn't be done the way it was said."[3] So the civil service tried; it was not involved in a Conservative plot to thwart Labour. Yet the advice to the minister was that it could not be done.

On the other hand, Baroness Sharp also commented, "I've known ministers who, when you have said 'I don't believe this will work and I don't see how this can be made to work,' who have said, 'You jolly well go away and make it

[3]Draft script of Granada TV broadcast, "The State of the Nation: Party in Power, Labour and Land," May 1976.

work,' and that's been that." Sharp's comments tend to support Crossman's views—a determined minister can win, but it is likely to be a struggle. Thus for probity, loyalty, discretion, and intelligence the British civil service probably is unsurpassed. Whether it is the ideal instrument for reform of whatever type is questionable.

CONTROL OF ADMINISTRATIVE DISCRETION

Although implementing the laws necessarily involves administrators in some rulemaking, such activity has increased greatly as government has expanded into economic and social fields. Parliament has tended to pass laws in a skeletal form, entrusting to administrators the authority to fill in the details. Two major problems have arisen as a result: (1) providing adequate safeguards so that rule-making authority will be exercised in conformity with the basic statute, and (2) ensuring that administrative boards or tribunals do not violate citizens' rights, especially when they have no recourse to appeal in the courts.

Parliament has little alternative to delegating rule-making authority to administrators; it cannot cover in legislation all the details of every situation that may arise. Furthermore, as we have seen, pressure upon the Commons' time usually does not permit full discussion of technical details, and in any event the Commons really is not organized in such a way as to scrutinize such aspects of bills. The Commons' strength lies in debating the general policies that lie behind particular bills.

Even were it possible for laws to detail individual cases, it would not be desirable. Such laws would be too rigid; some flexibility to deal with changing circumstances and human variability is desirable. So bureaucrats must be given some leeway to make rules adapting the general principles of the law to practical circumstances of everyday life.

On the other hand, administrators' discretion must be limited. They are not elected; people have no way of replacing them if they do not like the rules they are making. The problem is more acute in Britain than in the United States because no constutition limits the British legislature and the role of the courts is far more modest than in the United States. British courts cannot inquire whether Parliament has the right to legislate and, consequently, to bestow rule-making power. They merely can decide whether the rule-making body is acting in accordance with the procedural framework prescribed by law.

The British have attempted to deal with the problem through certain safeguards. First, ministers are able to make rules and regulations that have the effect of law only when authorized to do so by statute. Second, all rules made in a department must be confirmed by a minister. Third, an increasing number of statutes require consultation with advisory committees prior to the making of regulations. All departments in the economic and social sphere use advisory committees. Their effectiveness depends, however, upon how willing the minister is to consult and the extent to which advisory bodies are representative of the interests affected.

As a further safeguard, Parliament is given a role in the process. We explained in Chapter 5 that the Joint Committee on Statutory Instruments and the Commons' Standing Committee on Statutory Instruments manage to discuss some of the rules made by administrators, as does the House of Lords on occasion. Direct Parliamentary power over such rules varies from one type to another. In some cases a rule goes into effect unless one house of Parliament or the other votes against it within a stated period of time. In other cases Parliament must vote in favor of a rule before it can go into effect. Thus, in one way or another, Parliament does have a check upon delegated legislation, but in practice this probably serves only to catch blatant cases of abuse of administrative discretion. Parliament will not be able to prevent some undesirable regulations from going into effect.

The increasing number of rules made by administrators has caused concern for individual rights. To resolve conflicts between governmental agencies seeking to implement a policy and citizens alleging that their rights have been invaded, various ministries have established administrative tribunals. These tribunals are staffed by experts possessing the special experience or training related to the relevant field. Because the tribunals operate less formally than the regular courts, they tend to be speedier and cheaper.

Nonetheless, the tribunals have drawn criticism precisely because they do not follow all the rules that would apply in a court of law. For example, the lack of an opportunity to cross-examine those who testify at a tribunal may make it difficult to refute their comments and to establish the validity of one's own case. Furthermore, since the head of a department appoints the members of the administrative tribunal that will deal with questions arising out of that department's actions, it almost appears that the department is being permitted to be a judge in its own case.

To meet some of the criticism of administrative tribunals, Parliament passed the Tribunals and Inquiries Act in 1958. The purpose was to provide for some measure of appeal from the tribunals to the courts. In addition to certain procedural reforms, the Act established the principle of judicial scrutiny on points of law. Moreover, it set up a council to review and report on the workings of some 30 designated administrative tribunals.

Despite these reforms, some people continued to be dissatisfied with the tribunal system. They even charged that Britain's ancient liberties were being snuffed out by a powerful bureaucracy hiding behind weak and overworked ministers. Therefore, in 1967 Britain decided to try an approach similar to that utilized by Scandinavia and New Zealand and create an ombudsman, or Parliamentary commissioner, for administration.

The commissioner's powers are more limited, however, than those usually associated with an ombudsman. He or she is an officer of Parliament and is permitted to consider only those complaints that come through its Members. This procedure was liberalized somewhat in 1978. Instead of merely returning the letters that people wrote to him directly and suggesting that they contact their

MP, the ombudsman reviewed them and passed on to MPs those cases that seemed worth investigating, asking the MPs to refer the case back for action. Parliament has declined, however, to go beyond this and permit direct access to the ombudsman except in the case of the National Health Service. When this was added to the ombudsman's jurisdiction in 1973, patients were permitted to go directly to the ombudsman with complaints.

Initially, the commissioner was limited to examining only matters of maladministration and was not permitted to question any discretionary decision that was made in accord with proper procedures. A Select Committee was created in the House of Commons to supervise the commissioner's work and to follow up on any reforms which his or her reports showed were needed. As suggested by this committee, the commissioner in 1968 extended the scope of his jurisdiction somewhat. He would now examine as well cases where administration action was so "thoroughly bad in quality" that it suggested the existence of bias or perversity. And he would accept cases where, despite correct application of the rules, considerable hardship and injustice had been visited upon a person. In such cases the commissioner would investigate whether the department concerned had reviewed adequately the applicable rule to see what changes needed to be made to prevent such results in the future.

Even with this expanded scope, most complaints referred to the commissioner have been rejected for being outside his authority. In some instances this has been because the complaints concerned matters of general policy, while in others the complaints dealt with excluded subjects such as nationalized industry and foreign relations.[4]

Furthermore, the ombudsman is restricted to investigating and reporting to Parliament; he or she only can recommend redress, not order it. Despite the limitations on the office, the commissioner has had some success. During the first four years of operation the ombudsman's investigations and reports resulted in over 60 people receiving a total of more than a quarter of a million dollars in compensation for administrative mistreatment. Assisted by a staff of around 90, the ombudsman investigated nearly 3,000 cases during the first decade that the office existed. While the ombudsman had been finding the bureaucracy at fault in about 20 to 25 percent of the of the cases, toward the close of the 1970s the rate rose to 40 percent.[5]

At the end of the 1970s the number of complaints received by the ombudsman (both those coming through MPs and those sent—mistakenly—directly to him) dropped off. The general view seems to be that people still do not fully un-

---

[4]Local government is among the excluded subjects. Therefore, in 1974 a system of ombudsmen was established to deal with complaints of that type. A three-member Commission for Local Administration was created for England, (A similar commission was set up for Wales, but in Scotland there is only a single commissioner.) Complaints must be referred to the ombudsman for a particular area of the country by a member of a local government council.

[5]High as the latter figure was, it was exceeded for the cases investigated by the ombudsmen for local government, in which the proportion in which maladministration was found was half again as great.

derstand how the commissioner operates and, perhaps, do not regard the office as likely to be of much assistance. Thus while the Parliamentary commissioner is a useful supplementary safeguard against administrative abuses, the office is not a complete solution to the problem.

ACCOUNTABILITY IN THE NATIONALIZED INDUSTRIES

Government control of the economy and regulation of business can be distinguished from direct management and ownership of specific enterprises. In this sense nationalized industries—government-owned concerns—are not a part of the regular administrative structure. Yet they must be administered by governmental agents. Thus, this chapter on the structures for implementing governmental policies cannot close without some attention to the public corporation—the device used in Britain for managing nationalized, or publicly owned, industries.

Although the Labour party is closely identified with nationalization, it did not originate public ownership in Britain. London Passenger Transport, domestic telegraph, telephones, transmission of electricity, foreign air service, and radio all were taken into public ownership by non-Labour Governments. Nonetheless, considerable scope for further public ownership remained when Labour first won an absolute majority in the House of Commons in 1945. From 1945 to 1951 Labour extended nationalization in aviation, electricity, and communications and introduced it in the financial system, coal, transportation, gas, and iron and steel. Despite this expansion, publicly owned firms employ less than a tenth of the British work force and produce only about a tenth of the gross domestic product; contrary to widespread misconception in the United States, Britain remains largely a private enterprise economy. The Labour party never has intended to collectivize all commercial activity down to the corner fish-and-chips shop. They felt it sufficient for the government to acquire only the essential industries, the so-called commanding heights of the economy.

In deciding what type of administrative structure should run the nationalized industries, the government was influenced by the fact that these industries, unlike governmental departments dealing with foreign relations and defense, were commercial operations. A clearly identifiable product or service was available to specific individuals willing to pay for it. Efficient management of such an operation seemed to require greater flexibility in day-to-day operations than is possible in a government department that must keep a record of all decisions to reply to any inquiries to justify its actions. On the other hand, the principle of responsibility to Parliament had to be preserved.

The organizational form chosen to attempt to comply with these conflicting objectives was the public corporation. These corporations are under the jurisdiction of various ministers, each of whom is responsible to Parliament for their work. But the corporations have considerable latitude in making many decisions without reference to a minister. Ministers are not responsible for all of the corporations' decisions.

Although nationalized industries vary in the details of their structures, public corporations share five basic features. Their finances are self-contained, that is, their accounts are kept separate from those of the regular government. They are run by specially appointed boards, whose members normally serve for fixed terms. Neither the members of the boards nor those who work in nationalized industry are civil servants. The boards governing the industries do not seek to make a profit, but to provide the best service; a nationalized industry is supposed to break even over a period of years. No political figure exercises day-to-day control over the managerial activity of the board.

The board of a public corporation is appointed by the appropriate minister, who has power to remove members and is responsible to Parliament for the appointments. He or she also determines the salaries and conditions of service of the board members. While the minister is given certain powers of control and direction, the board has the duty of operating and managing the industry in the public interest. The minister is required, however, to approve the borrowing and the capital investments the board wishes to undertake. Also, he or she has to approve programs of research and development. Finally, the minister is required to lay before Parliament the annual report and statement of accounts of the corporation.

To help make public corporations responsive to their customers, consumer councils were established. Through this machinery the views of consumers are to be brought systematically to the boards and the relevant ministers. The consumer councils are appointed by the minister. As a general rule, he or she is obligated to consult representative consumer groups, often specified by statute, before making the appointments. In practice, the minister asks for a panel of nominees from which most of the members are chosen, although some (for example, civic leaders) are his or her personal appointees. Most councils have representatives from the board or corporation governing the industry. The size of the councils varies from 3 to 30. Some councils exist on the national level only, while some are regional and local only. None exists on all three levels. On the average, they meet about six to eight times a year; the national councils meet less often than regional or local ones.

The councils are to consider matters of consumer interest raised by consumers themselves, referred to a council by a minister, or initiated by a council, and recommend action. Whether these recommendations are implemented is up to the minister. Some councils are informed of the general plans for their industry and can have some influence on policy by commenting on these. The typical council, however, has little impact.

The reason is in part that consumer interest groups are less well organized in Britain than in the United States. And those that do exist are likely to find other channels for exerting influence—departmental advisory committees and direct meetings with a minister, for example—more effective than working through the consumer councils. Since the councils depend upon the ministries for information and cooperation in implementing recommendations, they tend to avoid challenging the ministers.

Creating a semiautonomous public corporation significantly altered the old doctrine that ministers were responsible for every administrative act in their departments. They are not held accountable for the actions of a public corporation board unless their consent was required or they could have voided the decision. Borrowing and capital investment are examples of actions for which ministers remain accountable.

Ministers can issue general instructions or policy directives to boards, but they rarely do so because that would be regarded as questioning the board's competence. Typically, ministers express their wishes informally and boards comply to avoid receiving a directive. This obscures responsibility; since a directive was not issued, Parliament cannot question the minister about the action, and the board's annual report need disclose nothing about how the decision was made.

The problem is not that public corporations are a power unto themselves. In addition to the guidance that the relevant minister gives, a board also must respond to Treasury inquiries concerning income and expeditures. The concern is that, although public corporations are subject to Government direction, the Government escapes having to answer fully for the policies that it instructs the corporations to pursue.

Parliament debates some of the annual reports of the boards operating the nationalized industries. But it finds time for only about two or three a year. Since there are nearly two dozen nationalized industries, some time passes between one Parliamentary scrutiny of an industry to the next. As for other Parliamentary control, the Commons' Public Accounts Committee does examine the finances of the public corporations. But since it is responsible for scrutinizing the full range of government spending, it cannot devote much time to the public corporations only.

For almost a quarter of a century the Commons' Select Committee on Nationalized Industries monitored these enterprises to keep the Commons informed of their aims, activities, and problems. While the committee issued a number of well-done reports, these usually attracted little attention, and thus it did not contribute greatly to Parliamentary control over the industries. When the new crop of specialist select committees was established at the close of 1979, the Select Committee on Nationalized Industries was abolished. If the department that one of the new committees is scrutinizing is responsible for a nationalized industry, then the committee can investigate it, as well as the regular activity of the department. This means that the operation of the nationalized industry can be seen in the context of related functions and activities. It may also mean, however, that the committee is so concerned with the typical functioning of a department that it devotes little time to examining any nationalized industry. Thus there may be even less surveillance by Parliament than in the past.

A satisfactory solution to the problem of attaining both commercial flexibility and political accountability has yet to be worked out. The nationalized industries undoubtedly are more subject to governmental control than they were before they were taken into public ownership. Yet, despite their being owned by the public and operated in its name, they clearly are not responsible to the electorate even in the limited sense that the Government and MPs are. This short-circuiting of accountability is made more unpalatable by a growing feeling that government could exercise just as much control over industry through legislation as it does through outright ownership. Nonetheless, some Labour party members continue to regard nationalization as *the* distinct element in their party's ideology. For them this is a symbolic issue: the capitalists must be dispossessed. At the other end of the ideology spectrum, the Thatcher Government in the mid-1980s was engaged in a vigorous program of privatization, that is, selling nationalized industries. The idea was to increase the government's income, reduce the sums needed for capital investment in nationalized industry, and to increase efficiency by making the industries more subject to the economic pressures of the free market. The government sold considerable portions of its holdings in British Petroleum and British Telecom, among other businesses. During the mid-1980s such sales were planned to run more than $2.5 billion a year.

Nonetheless, industries owned by the government will still be substantial, so public ownership will continue to be an issue in British politics. The need to devise some means of reconciling flexibility and accountability will remain a pressing problem.

BIBLIOGRAPHICAL NOTE

The Kellner and Crowther-Hunt book cited in Footnote 1 is essential reading on the values and behaviors of the civil service and, fortunately, is one of the few books on administration that will not put you to sleep. For an even more critical insider's view of the civil service's lack of interest in reform and efficiency see Leslie Chapman, *Your Disobedient Servant: The Continuing Story of Whitehall's Overspending* (Harmondworth, Eng.: Penguin Books, 1979). Douglas Ashford presents an academic analysis of some of these problems, along with some relevant readings, in chapter 2 of *Policy and Politics in Britain* (Philadelphia: Temple University Press, 1981). In *No, Minister: An Inquiry into the Civil Service*, (London: British Broadcasting Company, 1982) Hugo Young and Anne Sloman draw on a radio series in which top politicians and bureaucrats discuss the fundamental problems of the civil service.

Richard Pryke, formerly a defender of nationalized industry, finds serious faults in several respects in *The Nationalised Industries: Policies and Performance since 1968* (London: Martin Robertson, 1981).

8

Resolving Conflicts

As we suggested in the Introduction, the entire political process—the election of representatives to make rules and supervise those entrusted with implementing them—is an effort to resolve conflicting needs and desires without resort to violence or coercion. But just as the political process does not end with the passage of a law, so does it not end with its implementation. Bureaucrats may apply the law improperly. Furthermore, conflict is not just a matter of the individual against the government. Equally significant is the conflict between individuals. In those cases the government's role is to provide a means of resolving the dispute that is fair to all. The government maintains a system of courts so that the people do not have to engage in feuds. Thus any assessment of a political system's success in achieving its fundamental purpose of resolving conflicts fairly and peacefully is incomplete without considering the legal system.

THE ROLE OF COMMON LAW IN BRITISH JUSTICE

In Chapter 1 we referred briefly to the early development of the English judicial system and the evolution of common law. We touched on the common law again in the discussion in Chapter 2 of the constitutional foundations of British politics. The common law system is worth further comment in this chapter because it, along with the Roman law system, are the most extensively copied legal systems. The common law system spread from Britain through most of the areas that were under British influence at one time or another, including, of course, the United States. Roman law is the prevailing system on the European continent and in Japan and Turkey. Interestingly, Scottish law is in the Roman tradition and, therefore, Scotland's court system is distinct from that of England and Wales.

You will recall that common law is based on judicial decisions; Roman law is founded on legal codes. Legislatures may be reacting to court cases in passing certain laws, but the point of distinction is that in the Roman system statutes, rather than judicial decisions, are at the heart of the system. Conversely, to say that a country is a common law system does not mean that its legislature does not pass laws; the point is that judicial decisions, not legal codes, are the backbone of the system. Thus, typically, judges in a Roman law system turn to the legal code in deciding cases, while judges in a common law system seek their ruling by examining previous judicial decisions.

In the early history of British courts, the royal courts were simply one of several types, including private feudal courts. Because the royal courts provided better justice, however, they came to be preferred and, eventually, superseded the others. By the end of the 14th century, the royal courts were staffed by professional judges appointed by the monarch from among the practicing lawyers. These courts were known as common law courts to distinguish them from the ecclesiastical courts and other special tribunals.

As you can readily see, these courts did not attempt to lay down legal rules on a subject, but waited until specific cases arose. Even then the purpose was to decide the case itself rather than to elaborate general legal principles. Thus many topics were untouched by the law simply because cases requiring a decision had not arisen. In essence the law developed accidentally, although its growth was most rapid in precisely those areas of most concern to people because they generated the most cases.

Leading legal scholars, such as Coke and Blackstone, attempted to produce some order in the haphazard development of common law by grouping together several cases of the same type and indicating what type of ruling was typical. Such collections or "commentaries" revealed obvious defects in the law. In some instances the prevailing common law rules failed to distinguish sharply enough between cases that were only somewhat similar; in other cases conflicting rulings existed for cases that were quite similar. Furthermore, the doctrine of *stare decisis*—the holding in a previous similar case should determine the decision in subsequent cases—resulted over the centuries in the common law losing a good deal of its former flexibility. Excessive devotion to precedent was hindering the common law from promoting justice and preventing injustice.

For example, under common law, contracts made under threat to life and limb were invalid, but those affected by other distorting influences, such as alcoholic drinks, were valid. Turning to remedies, often all one could do at common law was to seek damages. But a payment of money could not replace a large shade tree that had been cut down or bring back to life a pet animal.

How was the law to keep flexible enough to provide justice without becoming so irregular as to be arbitrary or capricious? The solution in England was for the lord chancellor to function as the monarch's conscience to prevent the suffering in individual cases that would result from a rigid devotion to precedent. Gradually, a whole system of legal rules known as equity (or chancery) developed out of the lord chancellor's decisions in cases appealed to the monarch in an effort to gain relief from common law decisions that seemed unjust. By the early part of the 19th century, equity had taken its place alongside the common law as a humanizing element. Equity dealt with civil controversies, not criminal cases, and established the practice of issuing an injunction to prevent threatened injury or nuisance.

Until late in the 19th century, the equity courts were separate from the regular law courts. The Judicature Acts of 1873–75, however, ended the separation of law and equity, and provision was made that *all* courts should apply and use both sets of rules. In case of conflict between them, equity was to prevail. Where statutes are applicable, however, they supersede both the common law and equity.

Prior to 1832 the typical British court case did not involve laws passed by Parliament. Increasingly, however, Parliament legislated in areas previously covered only by common law or equity. The purpose usually was not to repeal case law, but to provide rules to cover expanding governmental activities. Although statutes have modified both criminal and civil law extensively, judge-made law is still basic in most areas of British jurisprudence.

THE ORGANIZATION OF THE JUDICIARY

Like so many other institutions of British Government, the court system was shaped and altered by usage over a period of years. One-time itinerant royal commissioners, who were concerned mainly with looking after the king's financial affairs, eventually became itinerant judges. As royal commissioners, they had little judicial authority; as itinerant judges their main function became judicial. These itinerant judges visited each country three or four times a year to determine whether charges of serious crimes—the lesser offenses were handled by the sheriff and, later, by justices of the peace—were accurate.

Consequently, the practice of hearing almost all criminal cases in the country where the crime was committed became well established. In civil cases of any importance, however, the proceedings were held at Westminster, which meant that participants, witnesses, and others with an interest in the case had to travel to London for the trial. Because of the hardship imposed by such travel in those days, some decentralization became necessary. Justices of the Assize Courts, who were the best available justices, were sent to the countries to hear cases. The points of law, however, were argued mainly at Westminster and the formal judgment was rendered there.

Perhaps the greatest strides in the systematization of the British judicial system were made during the reign of Henry II (1154–89). At that time the system of royal writs, which are the root of common law procedure, was inaugurated. These writs required that disputes be brought before royal authorities for settle-

FIGURE 8–1 The British Court System

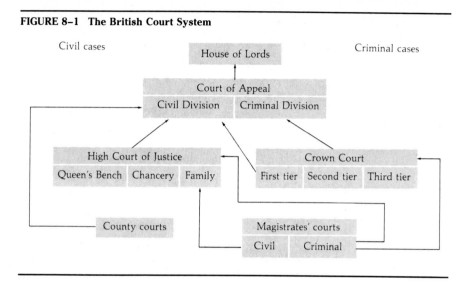

ment. Moreover, Henry II adopted and perfected the system of itinerant judges. In addition, he established the principle of the king's peace—that is, a crime should no longer be considered a wrong against the individual but rather a wrong against the state. Finally, he asserted the exclusive jurisdiction of the Curia Regis in the case of all serious crimes, and he hastened the demise of the older methods of trial (such as ordeal or battle), which led to the development of trial by jury.

Although the British legal system was unified into a national system both in its structure and its appointment procedures, it remains divided to some extent into separate judicial hierarchies. The rules that courts apply can be placed in two categories: those regulating relations between individuals and the government, and those between individuals alone. The first is called public law, and the second, private law. Public law is subdivided into constitutional, administrative, and criminal. Thus civil cases include not only private law but portions of public law as well.

Criminal law deals with offenses against the state and those offenses considered sufficiently serious (such as murder and arson) to be offenses against society as a whole. In Britain, in contrast to the United States, courts dealing with criminal cases are to a considerable extent separate from those hearing civil cases (refer to Figure 8–1 as you read this discussion of the court system).

About 98 percent of all criminal cases are heard in magistrates' courts. These cases involve summary offenses—minor violations that do not require an indictment and are not decided by a jury, with a maximum sentence of six months or $1,250. While these courts are concerned primarily with criminal cases, they do have some limited civil jurisdiction, primarily on some family law matters.

Magistrates' courts also function like American grand juries; for indictable offenses (serious crimes) they decide whether sufficient evidence exists for a case to be tried.

Approximately 24,000 magistrates (judges) staff about 700 of these courts. Magistrates usually are unpaid laypeople appointed by the lord chancellor. They sit in groups of three and are advised on points of law by a legally trained clerk. In large urban areas, however, magistrates typically are full-time, legally trained judges, who sit alone in hearing cases.

Appeals go from the magistrates' courts to the High Court of Justice if a point of law is involved. If the question in a criminal case is whether a guilty verdict was correct or whether the sentence was too severe, the appeal is to the Crown Court. The civil case appeals go to the Family Division of the High Court of Justice.

In addition to hearing appeals from the magistrates' courts, the Crown Court is where trials of serious crimes begin. For the most serious cases a judge from the High Court of Justice presides alone. For less serious ones, such as assault or forgery, a circuit judge presides, or even a part-time recorder, assisted by from two or four magistrates. In either case juries are used.

The Crown Court has about 90 centers grouped into three tiers. The first tier centers are located in the largest cities. In addition to criminal cases, these centers have some limited civil jurisdiction. The second tier centers are in smaller cities, but still can hear serious criminal cases. The third tier centers, about half of the total, are in towns and deal only with the less serious criminal cases within the jurisdiction of the Crown Court. Appeals from the Crown Court go to the Court of Appeal, in most instances to the Criminal Division of that court.

Turning to civil cases, the lowest level is the county court, of which there are about 300. The maximum damage that a plaintiff can seek in a county court is $6,250. The lord chancellor assigns circuit judges to the county courts. Typically, they sit alone and no juries are used. Appeals from these courts go directly to the Court of Appeal.

More important civil cases begin in the High Court of Justice, located in London and 23 other cities. The High Court has about 80 judges. They preside alone for cases being heard for the first time, but when the case is an appeal, two or three will hear it together. The High Court has three divisions: Queen's Bench, dealing with commercial law; Chancery, wills and estates; and Family, divorce and guardians for minors. Appeals go to the Court of Appeal.

The Court of Appeal to some extent joins the separate criminal and civil law systems, yet even it has two divisions corresponding to type of case. The Court of Appeal has 22 judges.

You probably will be surprised to see in Figure 8–1 that the court of last resort in Britain, to which appeals from the Court of Appeal are taken, is the House of Lords. Although technically, all peers are eligible to hear cases, by custom the Lords' judicial business is dealt with by only a few members. The prime minister gives life peerages to nine people who have demonstrated outstanding legal ability. These lords of appeal in ordinary (usually called law lords) hear the cases reaching the Lords. Should the work load be so heavy that they need assistance, they can call on the lord chancellor, retired law lords still living, or peers having held high judicial office.

Since the House of Lords itself is the court, the law lords cannot hear cases when the Lords are in session as the upper House of Parliament. To avoid this problem, the device of appellate committees was established in 1948. Three or five justices actually hear a case. Their decision is accepted by the other law lords as though it had been made by all nine, just as the House of Lords accepts the decisions of the law lords as though they had been made by the entire House. A majority vote in an appellate committee is sufficient to decide a case. In addition to the main opinion explaining the reasons for the decision, concurring and dissenting opinions can be written.

Since ample opportunity is provided in the British judicial system for appeal before a case could reach the House of Lords, no one has an automatic right to appeal his or her case to the Lords. Cases reach the Lords only if the Appeals Committee of the Lords requests them or the Court of Appeal refers them. When the Lords hears a case the only issue is questions of law, never matters concerning the facts involved in the case. The Lords leaves to the lower courts the job of clarifying what really happened in the case, and it simply decides how the law should be interpreted and applied to the facts that already have been established through judicial proceedings.[1]

Until 1966 the House of Lords could not reverse its decisions in previous cases. Now it may do so, provided there are compelling reasons for departing from earlier rulings. Although the House of Lords is the ultimate authority on what is the correct interpretation of the law, you need to remember that, as we explained in Chapter 5, Parliament is supreme. Not even the law lords have the power of U.S. Supreme Court justices to check a statute against a constitution to see whether it is valid. All laws passed by Parliament are valid; none can be declared unconstitutional. The law lords do interpret the law, as do other judges. These interpretations are not final; Parliament can reverse them simply by passing a new law. There is no need, as there would be in the United States, to go through an elaborate process of constitutional amendment when the highest court in the land interprets basic government powers and duties in a way that many people dislike. The other side of this coin, however, is that British judges cannot go as far as American ones in protecting people from arbitrary government action. True, until the law is amended, its provisions are what the British judges say they are. But a majority in Parliament has the power to alter the law. As we have discussed in Chapter 2, this has made some people in Britain concerned about the adequacy of defense for basic freedoms.

---

[1]What we have described is the court system that exists in England and Wales. As we noted, Scotland has a different legal system and, therefore, a different court system. Describing it as well would be excessively detailed. Suffice it to say that appeals from the Scottish judicial system come to the House of Lords only in civil cases. For criminal matters the High Court of Justiciary in Scotland is the court of last resort.

COURTROOM JUSTICE

While British justice has a deservedly high reputation for fairness and reliability, some problems exist. These start even before an offense gets to the courtroom. The police have no legal power to hold a person for questioning, yet they regularly do so. People taken into custody for this purpose are said, in a classic British phrase, to be "helping the police with their inquiries." As Michael Zander, professor of law at the London School of Economics, has said, this really means that they are "being held illegally by the police while they decide whether there is enough evidence to charge [them] with some offence." While 75 percent of the suspects are dealt with in six hours or less and 95 percent in 24 hours or less, yet in some cases the police will hold a person for several days without laying any charges against him or her.

Applying for a writ of habeas corpus has done little to prevent abuses. The writ is an order by a court to bring a detained person before a judge to justify continued detention. For a suspect the justification would have to be that he or she had been charged with a specific crime. But fewer than 10 percent of the applications for habeas corpus in Britain are successful. When a lawyer seeks the writ for a person being held by the police solely for questioning, the courts tend to adjourn the hearing, thus giving the police still more time to question the suspect and to figure out some offense with which to charge him or her.

The Police and Criminal Evidence Act passed in 1984 modernized and clarified the power of the police in a number of areas, including detention. Now most people can be detained without being charged for no more than 24 hours. But in the case of serious arrestable offenses, the period is 96 hours. At the end of 36 hours, however, a magistrate must decide (in a full hearing with the detainee present and legally represented) whether to continue the detention, and a second such proceeding is required at the end of 72 hours.

Of course, even 24 hours is a long time to be held by the police if you are the person being held, especially if you have not been told precisely what it is that they think you may have done wrong. What is even more bothering is that during this first period of detention (24 or 36 hours as the case may be) the police can hold you incommunicado—they are not obligated to inform anyone where you are, and whether you can contact even a lawyer is murky.

The Judges' Rules (guidelines for police conduct) state that anyone detained by the police has the right to consult a lawyer at any time. This apparent right is qualified by the proviso that such consultation must not cause unreasonable delay or hinder the process of investigation. Two studies prepared for the Royal Commission on Criminal Procedure in 1979 found that the police refused up to 75 percent of the requests for legal advice. The new law specifically says that a person may, *on request*, consult with a lawyer. The police are *not* obligated by law to advise detainees that they have this right, although the police code of conduct states that they should do so. Even the limited right of access to a lawyer may be denied by a senior police officer during the first 36 hours for detainees suspected of having committed a serious arrestable offense.

The most positive aspect of this part of the new law is the plan to expand funding of the service that makes lawyers available on a 24-hour basis at police stations. The cost of this service is to be provided under the legal aid system without regard to whether a client meets the financial eligibility tests for such aid. Thus lawyers will not lack the incentive, as they had, of going to the police station because they might find on arrival that they could not claim payment from legal aid.

Another problem concerns illegally obtained evidence. The American exclusionary rule does not apply fully in Britain. While confessions are admitted as evidence into British trials only if they were obtained voluntarily, other evidence is admissible regardless of whether it was obtained by improper means. For example, if the police in Britain search your home without having a warrant to do so and find evidence suggesting that you have committed a crime, the fact that they obtained that evidence improperly does not mean that the judge will prevent the evidence from being used in your trial. If the police search your home on the basis of a warrant indicating suspicion that you have committed one type of crime and find nothing related to it, but do come across something that suggests you might have committed another type of crime, the evidence can be used in trying you, even though again it was obtained improperly.

Until 1979 British judges were permitted under the common law to exclude improperly obtained evidence from trials, if they felt it would make the proceedings unfair. A case in the Lords greatly restricted the judges' discretion, however, by holding that improperly obtained evidence could be excluded only when its prejudicial effect on the defendant's case was greatly outweighed by its probative force. In short the English view is that evidence is evidence and the guilty should not be allowed to go free simply because the police use a few bad methods—a view that certainly would recommend itself to law-and-order advocates in the United States.

What the Police and Criminal Evidence Act did was to restore the situation in effect prior to the Lords' 1979 decision. Thus once again British judges may, *if they choose*, exclude from trials evidence improperly obtained. The judges are expected to use this power sparingly, just as they had prior to 1979.

Remember that the American exclusionary rule is a constitutional interpretation and thus does not depend upon the discretion of the particular judge who happens to hear your case. Remember also that when you are arrested in the United States you have a right to one phone call—usually to a lawyer or to someone who will get a lawyer for you. Thus defendants and suspects tend to be better off under the American legal system than under the British. Whether that means that the United States coddles criminals, is a matter of opinion. But it does indicate that a country can have a reputation for fair justice, as Britain does, without providing all the rights that the United States does.

Whether a person must stand trial for a relatively serious crime is decided by a magistrates' court functioning as a grand jury. If all parties agree, this can be done routinely in only a few minutes. Should the defense claim, however, that the evidence is too weak to justify a trial, a more elaborate procedure involving a statement from the prosecution and the calling of witnesses is used. This second procedure involves a couple of potential penalties for the defense. Since the prosecution clearly wants to go to trial, it makes the defense appear to be dilatory by not accepting the rubber stamp procedure. But worse is the fact that opting for the second procedure results in a delay of weeks or even months before the matter is decided. Unless the defendant is out on bail, he or she will spend this time in jail until it is eventually decided whether there should be a trial.

A single lay magistrate, assisted by a legally trained clerk, decides whether a person should be committed for trial in the Crown Court. Given the magistrates' limited legal knowledge, they tend to commit for trial almost automatically—only about 2 percent of the people brought before them are discharged. Yet when cases are tried in the Crown Court, acquittals run from 40 to 50 percent. This suggests that the magistrates are not doing a very effective job of reviewing the evidence and that they are imposing the costs and stigma of a trial on people who should not be subject to them. Furthermore, it means that the police are not discouraged from seeking committals for suspects for whom they really lack sufficient evidence. Thus slipshod police work is encouraged.

Mentioning the police in the committal process brings out a significant contrast between the British and American legal systems in criminal prosecutions. In Britain, in the great majority of cases, the police decide whether to prosecute and they are responsible for the conduct of the prosecution. They will either conduct the case in court themselves or hire a lawyer to do so.

While Britain does not have a system of public prosecutors comparable to American district attorneys, there is a director of public prosecutions. The DPP is assisted by a professional staff of about 70. For certain offenses—for example, treason, murder, bribery of officials, possession of explosives—only the DPP or the attorney general can decide to prosecute. Another group of offenses—for example, those relating to obscene or indecent publications—must be reported to the DPP so that the DPP can prosecute instead of the police, should that seem to be desirable. In either case the DPP's decision is discretionary. The DPP prosecutes in only about 3 percent of all the cases heard in the Crown Court. In addition, in about 5 percent of the cases the DPP advises the police to prosecute. So one way or another the DPP is involved in only about 8 percent of the indictable offenses.

In a 1980 speech the DPP commented that "the fact that there is sufficient evidence to sustain a prosecution does not necessarily mean that there ought to be a prosecution. I always have a *discretion* as to whether to prosecute, and it is my duty to exercise that discretion by considering the facts and background circumstances of the particular case."[2] Some people are concerned that this element of discretion may protect prominent people from the disgrace which may be imposed on ordinary people. In 1981, for example, a former British diplomat involved in some child pornography activities was not prosecuted by the

---

[2] *The Guardian,* June 2, 1980, p. 7.

DPP despite clearly having violated the postal laws. Furthermore, unlike others involved, he was not called as a witness during the committal proceedings, and all reference to him during the proceedings used a fictitious name. At the police level discretion tends to result in blacks more likely being regarded with suspicion. In one case, for example, the police got a young black man to confess (without using violence) to the theft of some models, which he in fact had purchased. They took him in for questioning because they saw him walking late at night with a sack in his hand. Only after he had been persuaded to confess did it become clear some time later that he had missed the last bus home and had a sales slip for the models. Although these and other such cases are the exceptions, they do indicate that British justice is not always even-handed.

A person committed for trial will have to wait some time before the case actually is heard. Delays of three months are common in most areas for the Crown Court and in London a wait of six months is likely. At the end of the 1970s some 14,000 cases were awaiting trial in London and the southeast. A case may consume some time, as well, once it actually begins. Whereas it used to be that even the longest trial in a Crown Court would not exceed 50 days, now some last more than 100. One aspect of the British judicial system does help, however, to give it an edge over the United States in securing effective justice with some dispatch. Typically, only a single appeal is possible in Britain. The interminable appeals that drag out judicial proceedings in the United States and postpone implementing sentences are not part of the British system.

Obtaining a lawyer differs somewhat in Britain from the United States. The British legal profession is divided into solicitors and barristers. Solicitors usually do not present cases in court. They advise clients and prepare the material for the trial. Then they turn the material over to the barrister whom they have engaged, the courtroom lawyer who argues the case in court. One cannot be both a solicitor and a barrister at the same time. Nor may a solicitor and a barrister enter into partnership. Standards of professional ethics are set for solicitors by the Law Society, the professional organization for solicitors. For barristers the Inns of Court, their professional organization, has this responsibility.

Not everyone, of course, can afford the cost of judicial proceedings. Shortly after World War II a system of legal aid and advice was established to try to deal with this problem. The government finances this program, which is administered by the legal profession. The idea was to provide the services of solicitors and barristers free or at a reduced rate, depending on a person's financial situation.

Unfortunately, the program's benefits have declined. Whereas in 1950, 80 percent of the population could qualify for civil legal aid, a quarter of a century later only 40 percent could, and in the case of married couples only 20 percent. To receive aid without having to pay anything one must have disposable income of under $5,600 and disposable capital (excluding a house) of less than $3,400. Thus only the poor qualify. Middle-class and even skilled working-class people must bear the costs themselves, which often means that they simply cannot afford to go to court. A further problem of legal aid is that a disproportionate amount of the total costs of the program are devoted to cases arising out of divorce, such as child sharing and maintenance payments.

In the case of criminal cases the financial requirement for legal aid is not as much a problem. The cost of defending against a serious criminal charge is so great that virtually no defendant can afford it. Thus some 95 percent of the trials in the Crown Court are financed by legal aid.

The problem of responsibility or accountability mentioned in the last chapter in connection with administration is relevant as well to the judicial system. Insofar as judges exercise political power, they should be subject to popular control in order to maintain democracy. Thus at the state level in the United States it is not unusual for judges to be elected and to serve only short terms before they must stand for reelection. Yet at the same time most people feel that judges should be objective, that they should not be swayed by political considerations in reaching their rulings. The law should not be just a matter of transient majority opinion. Paradoxically, then, people want judges to be both above and subject to politics.

Although British judges are not elected, it might appear at first glance that they are to some extent involved in politics. The head of the legal system, the lord chancellor, is a member of the Cabinet, appointed by the prime minister. He or she has no fixed term and always is replaced immediately when the Opposition forms a new Government. Most British judges are appointed on the advice of the lord chancellor. A few of the top judicial appointments are even made by the prime minister, usually after consulting with the lord chancellor. Unlike the situation in the United States, no legislative approval for these appointments is required.

Nonetheless, the British judiciary is independent of rather than subservient to the political interests of the Government. In order to keep the monarch from controlling the judiciary, the Act of Settlement of 1701 provided that judges serve not "at the pleasure of the Crown," but "during good behavior." In effect this means permanent tenure. A judge can be removed from office only by vote of both Houses of Parliament. This occurred only in 1830, when a judge had misappropriated funds.

Judges are appointed because of their professional competence and not for their political opinions or activities. Until 1972, when the Courts Act of 1971 went into effect, only barristers were eligible for appointment as judges. They were required to have at least 10 years' experience before they could become circuit judges. Under the Act solicitors can become recorders, part-time lower-level judges. After three years' experience in this position, they are eligible for appointment to the circuit bench of full-time judges. Despite this change, former barristers still greatly outnumber former solicitors among judges. As for the lowest courts, since magistrates are not required to have legal training, they do not need to be either barristers or solicitors.

Although judgeships are not partisan appointments, some people are concerned that the class background and age of judges may make them conservative. Clearly, a typical working-class child is unlikely to be able to afford a legal education. While progressive views are not unknown among the middle and upper classes, yet by the time that one establishes a legal practice and then progresses up the judicial hierarchy, one is likely to have lost youthful idealism before becoming a high judge.

Part of the concern is related to the somewhat different role of the British judge compared to the American one. While in Britain, as in the United States, the burden of proof is on the prosecution, the judge is not just a referee, but plays an active part in the trial. British judges may comment on the evidence as it is presented as well as on the failure of the defendant to testify.

At the same time, however, the atmosphere of British courts does tend to be more formal and sedate than often is true in the United States. While the Perry Mason stereotype has little validity in the American courtroom, it is even less applicable in Britain. Blustering or hectoring is rare; quiet questioning prevails. Both judges and barristers are attired in robes and wigs to lend dignity to the proceedings. On the other hand, this may make them seem like representatives of the established elite to a poor defendant, who may conclude that there is little prospect of justice being done to one clearly belonging to a lower class.

Thus, although British judges are not involved in partisan politics (and, therefore, are not really accountable), their background is such that their views are not likely to be representative of the public (just as is the situation with the civil service) and they may be disposed unconsciously to favor one element of society over another. So what is the solution to the problem of unaccountable power? The basic answer in Britain is to grant judges considerably less power than is done in the United States. No British judge can declare a law unconstitutional. British judges cannot overturn what the representatives of the people have enacted into law. To the extent that they are less powerful than American judges, the problem of making them accountable is less pressing. We would not claim that this is a perfect solution. Some decisions of British judges do have political impact. But the problem of freedom from popular accountability would be much greater if British judges, like American, had the power of judicial review.

This is a point that those in Britain who have been advocating a written constitution have not adequately considered. A written constitution would end Parliamentary supremacy; it would provide that Parliament could not do certain things. Someone would have to decide whether certain controversial actions of Parliament transgressed these prohibitions. Thus something like a supreme court would have to be established. Some judges (the law lords?) would have to wield significant political power. For while these matters might be raised in the form of court cases, as occurs in the United States, yet one person's legal/constitutional issue is another person's political issue. Furthermore, if the U.S. system were to be followed, then not only the law lords would be involved. Although the U.S. Supreme Court is the final authority on the meaning of the Constitution, even lower courts can refuse to enforce a law because they believe it to be unconstitutional.

Thus constitutional reform in Britain would make the question of how to balance judicial accountability and objectivity a more pressing problem than it is now by destroying the current workable, however imperfect, solution.

Looking back over the British political system as a whole, you can see that it is beset by a number of substantive and structural problems. While many countries encountered economic problems during the 1970s, in Britain these seemed to have had a much more adverse impact. No solution has yet been found and current efforts have resulted in almost intolerable levels of unemployment and in seriously curtailing capital investment. Unemployment and economic stagnation only add fuel to the smoldering fire of race relations. The British rapidly are running out of time for dealing with race unless they want to endure the American experience of the 1960s.

The question of accountability is a significant one at several points in the political structure. Are MPs sufficiently accountable to their constituents and their supporters? Can the Commons continue the process of regaining some ability to call the executive to account? Within the executive is the prime minister too dominant, too free from some check or even guidance by his or her colleagues? Are the top civil servants so free from any form of popular control that they run the country as they wish without having to account to anyone? Is industrial power—whether in the form of big business or big unions—totally irresponsible?

Perhaps the basic structural issue is whether the consensus on political values, which in the past seemed to be the hallmark of the British political system, has dissipated so much that a constitution must be written to articulate what in the past was taken to be understood by everyone. And yet if basic agreement has disappeared, how can proclaiming a constitution be anything other than one side imposing its values on the other?

Serious as these problems are, you should not conclude that the British political system is on its deathbed. The British system holds the world record for durability and adaptability. We have no crystal ball to predict how Britain will solve these problems, but, given the well-demonstrated British talent for governing, we anticipate that it will.

BIBLIOGRAPHICAL NOTE

A good deal of information concerning legal proceedings in Britain is presented in nontechnical language in Marcel Berlins and Clare Dyer, *The Law Machine* (Harmondsworth, England: Penguin, 1982). Concerns about the quality of British justice are discussed in Patricia Hewitt, *The Abuse of Power: Civil Liberties in the United Kingdom* (Oxford: Martin Robertson, 1982). For the view from the other side of the bench, see Alan Paterson, *The Law Lords* (London: Macmillan, 1982), the result of extensive interviews with top judges.

PART THREE

FRANCE

9

The Setting of
French Politics

GEOPHYSICAL AND SOCIOECONOMIC DIVERSITIES

Although France is geographically the largest country in Western Europe, it is considerably smaller than the state of Texas. Thus the area is compact, and there are no formidable mountain barriers inside the country. Navigable rivers, an extensive network of canals, and a railway system provided the country with a superb system of internal communication long before the coming of the airplane. On the north, west, and south, France is surrounded by water, while the Alps and the Pyrenees offer partial protection to the southeast and southwest. The Rhine River and the open country of the northeast constitute the one break in the natural protection pattern.

While this geophysical configuration has helped to give French people a very highly developed sense of national identity, ease in communication has produced neither homogeneity of customs nor nationalized opinion. Significant regional differences are common. One of the principal ones is the contrast between north and south, which some people trace back to the effect of the Romans in the south contrasted with the influence of Germanic tribes in the north. Instead of contrasting the France north of the Loire River (which enters the Atlantic Ocean at Nantes) with that south of the Loire, some experts contend that the contrasts between "two nations" can be sharpened by dividing the country east and west of a line running from Caen on the English Channel to Marseilles on the Mediterranean Sea. However the line is drawn, the point is that the south/west portion is largely a rural area of conservative farmers and population decline, while the north/east section is an area of large factories, modern farms, and dynamic growth.

Another frequently cited contrast is that between Paris and the provinces. Paris has played a dominant role in the history of modern France. At times it has seemed to be all of France, while on occasions it has appeared to be distinct from and at odds with the rest of the nation. Whatever its relation to the values and culture of France, Paris clearly monopolizes many aspects of French life—national administration, banking, industry, and intellectual life. More than one third of all industrial and commercial profits are earned in the Paris area, while more than half of the turnover of French business occurs there. In several important industrial and commercial sectors of the economy Paris employs a majority of the workers.

Paris is the model for contemporary urban life, with a population of about 10 million (2 million within the official city limits). The next largest city—Marseilles, on the Mediterranean—is less than a million. France has only six cities with populations over 500,000—only about half as many as in Germany and a third as many as in Britain. Thus while well over half of the British live in cities of a half million or more, only a third of the French do. Outside of Paris, France is typified by the small market town. The hectic, hurried life of Paris gives way in the provinces to what many French would regard as the true spirit of the people—a more deliberate, less hustled, and philosophical attitude.

An important element in the provincial mind is a feeling of attachment to the soil. The average French peasant's (the term usually used for farmers) particular piece of land has been in the family for generations. Thus it is a family heirloom, not just a piece of ground. This strong family tradition has been an obstacle to improving the productivity of the land. The desire to farm in the same way as previous generations did has meant resistance to modern agricultural techniques.

By the 1960s some of these feelings were beginning to change. Especially important was the merging of about one fifth of the land previously in small, less efficient farms into larger, more productive units. Thus in the quarter of a century from 1955 to 1980 the proportion of farms consisting of less than 86 acres was almost cut in half. Nonetheless, such farms still accounted for more than a third of all French farms.[1] The average French farmer has only 75 acres, only about half the area needed to do well at farming. With the merger of small farms many farmers left the land. The number of farms was cut almost in half from 1955 to 1980. While in 1960 more than a fifth of the French labor force was engaged in agriculture, by 1980 only 8 percent was. Even so this proportion remains substantially larger than in most industrial countries—in both the United States and in Britain only 2 percent work in agriculture. And French farmers remain a sizable group—about 2.5 million—a fact of both economic and political significance.

Despite French slowness in modernizing agriculture, the country's abundance of fertile soil (85 percent of its total area arable or wooded), variety of cli-

---

[1] John T. S. Keeler, "The Corporatist Dynamic of Agricultural Modernization in the Fifth Republic," in eds. William Andrews and Stanley Hoffman *The Impact of the Fifth Republic on France,* (Albany: SUNY Press, 1981), p. 145.

mates, and adequate rainfall have combined to yield a productive and diversified agricultural sector. France provides more than a quarter of the EEC's agricultural output. A good supply of natural resources has helped to balance the total economy. A base for industry was provided by the abundance of iron ore, bauxite, and potash.

Nonetheless, France long remained a nation of small farmers, artisans, and shopkeepers. While Britain led the Industrial Revolution, France was slow to follow. Change was hampered by the attachment to the soil already mentioned, the artisan or hand-crafting conception of manufacturing, and the achievement of a balanced and prosperous economic order prior to the Industrial Revolution.

The French were slow to adopt power-driven machinery in many industries. As artisans they took great pride in conceiving and creating quality individual products. They abhorred the idea of mass producing the exact same item over and over again with machines. Quality and craftsmanship were preferred over quantity and standardization.

Having achieved a prosperous and balanced economy, the French saw little reason for change. During the 17th and 18th centuries, agriculture, commerce, and handicraft production were the dominant features of economic life in France. Soil, climate, and industrious peasants made France relatively self-sufficient. Manufacturing was limited to a few people and tended to emphasize luxury goods. But this balance was to be upset in the 19th century, which became the century of coal, iron, and applied science, with an emphasis on mass-produced consumer goods. Large-scale enterprises left the craftspeople behind. The French economy resisted change at the time that technical advances were enabling foreign agriculture and foreign industry to compete successfully with its own counterparts.

France entered the 20th century a comparatively rich nation, largely self-sufficient, and still maintaining a nice balance between agriculture and industry. Instead of responding to competition, both at home and abroad, with more effective production, however, the policy followed was one of cartels, tariffs, and subsidies. While the French pay lip service to individualism and the profit motive, the basic characteristic of their economy has been corporate or collective. Individual enterprise has been curtailed considerably. Cartels have protected industrialists from domestic competition, while high tariffs and restrictive quotas have shielded them from foreign competition. Peasants have demanded subsidies so they can buy the expensive French-produced goods, while workers have sought wage supplements and other benefits. Prior to the formation of the Fifth Republic, which reduced subsidies, approximately one third of the French national budget went for direct or indirect subsidies.

French business tended to take an uncapitalistic view of commercial enterprise.[2] Most businesses were relatively small, family enterprises that aimed rather

---

[2]These comments are based on Jesse Pitts, "Continuity and Change in Bourgeois France," in *In Search of France,* Stanley Hoffmann et al. (New York: Harper & Row, 1963), pp. 244–54. But see also the qualifications and more extensive discussion of the French economy by Charles Kindleberger in the same volume.

more at perpetuating the family name than at making profits. Competition was the reverse of cutthroat, since to drive a competitor from business was to ruin a family, a result desired by no responsible person of principle. Similarly, there was little willingness to risk capital in some new venture, since this was to risk ruining the family's status. Profits tended to be small and merely withdrawn rather than reinvested. Little money was spent to replace obsolete machinery. Limited production runs resulted in high unit cost because of a lack of economies of scale. The multiplicity of small businesses meant that capital was not effectively concentrated to support innovative production methods requiring sizable initial expenditure.

The result was economic stagnation despite France's great potential for balanced economic strength. In 1938 France's gross national product was only slightly higher than it had been just prior to World War I; the country had grown hardly at all in a quarter of century. It had sought to maintain itself as a nation of villagers in a world of cities. It had been unable or unwilling to submit unproductive ideas and institutions to external competition, from which they long had been protected. Modern industry, as well as industrial workers, had been regarded as foreign intruders. In brief, France tried to remain aloof from the real world of the 20th century.

France's relatively late industrialization has affected its occupational structure in politically significant ways. Industrial workers are a smaller proportion of the work force in France than in Britain. Mass unionization in France, although at about the same level as in the United States, is low by European standards. Thus about half of the British workers are unionized and over a third of the German are, but less than a quarter of the French. On the other hand, about half of the French union members belong to the Communist-dominated CGT and about a fifth to the leftist socialist CFDT. Frequently, the workers' desires have a political impact disproportionate to the workers' numbers. As for business, France has a greater percentage of economic units involved in distribution than does any other industrialized nation. The large number of middlemen means that each receives only a small profit. This, combined with high unit costs for many manufacturers, has helped to produce a large number of marginal and disaffected business people.

During the late 1940s and the 1950s the Fourth Republic began to strengthen the French economy. These efforts had some success—from 1953 to 1958 the average annual GNP growth rate for the United States was 1.8 percent, for Britain 2.3, while for France it was 4.8.[3] Germany, however, grew at the rate of 6.9 percent a year. The return of Charles de Gaulle to power and the creation of the Fifth Republic produced a dramatic change.

The government promoted scientific research and technical education, improved rural public utilities and trade and distribution channels, and reformed

---

[3]Bela Balassa, "The French Economy Under the Fifth Republic, 1958–1978," in *Impact of the Fifth Republic,* Andrews and Hoffmann, p. 138.

tax and investment laws. New resources were developed, including oil, electricity, and nuclear energy. Industrial enterprises were merged to produce more efficient units and became less reluctant to employ modern technology. The political stability of the Fifth Republic helped to give business and capital greater confidence by eliminating the financial instability and foreign exchange crises that had characterized the last years of the Fourth Republic.

By 1963 industrial production was double what it had been in 1952, and in 1972 it was 70 percent greater than it had been in 1962. In agriculture, too, more advanced methods and techniques were introduced. In the late 1960s and early 1970s the value of agricultural production increased by 40 percent in only five years. Ever since the start of the Fifth Republic the French economy has grown more rapidly than has the German. Thus, as Figure 9–1 shows, by the 1980s not only had France long surpassed Britain, but it was catching up with the United States and Germany as well. Among major industrial nations only Japan was expanding more rapidly than France. And while this expansion was associated with some inflationary problems, the French managed to handle this better than did the British—an average annual rate of inflation from 1970 to 1982 of 10.1 percent compared with one of 14.2.

The French population has changed as well. With a population of 55 million, France is somewhat smaller than Britain and considerably smaller than Germany. This was not true in the past, for in 1800 France was the most populous

FIGURE 9–1   Relative Economic Strengths

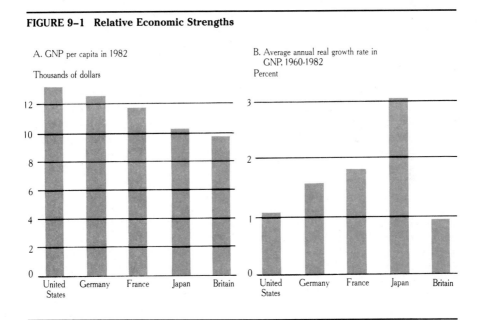

A. GNP per capita in 1982

Thousands of dollars

B. Average annual real growth rate in GNP, 1960-1982

Percent

Source: *World Development Report 1984*, p. 219.

country in Europe, well over twice as large as Britain. Just as the economy stagnated, so population growth lagged behind that of other European countries. In 1940 France had only a couple of million more people than it had had in 1860. From 1930 to 1940 the total population (not the growth *rate*, but the absolute numbers) actually declined.

A major explanation for these figures is the great number of Frenchmen killed in World War I—1.5 million. The United States, which then was twice as populous as France, lost only 115,000 in World War I. And in World War II, when the U.S. population was 3.5 times as great as France's had been in 1914, we lost only 400,000. One of the effects of this human disaster was that, while France had as many men of military age as did Germany in 1870, in 1940 it had only half as many. This helps to explain why the overt, regular French military resistance to Germany collapsed so early in World War II. Another effect concerns the quality of political leadership in France between World Wars I and II. In many cases France had to rely disproportionately upon the old or second-raters for leaders; many of the middle-aged men of quality who would have led the nation were dead.

Because of the declining birth rate and the war losses, France was seen four decades ago as a country of old people. But after World War II the birth rate began to climb, a trend that lasted through the 1950s. Now the fertility rate seems to have leveled off at 1.8, somewhat below the 2.1 that demographers believe is necessary to maintain France's population. Nonetheless, France remains a young country—nearly a third of its population is under 20.

The large number of young people plus extending the age for compulsory schooling to 16 has put a considerable strain on the French educational system. France has one of the highest school enrollment rates in the world, with nearly 13 million pupils in primary and secondary schools. As for higher education, in 1950 only 136,000 students were enrolled in universities; now there are over 860,000. Any student who has taken the college preparatory course in secondary school and passed the school leaving exam is entitled to attend a university. Furthermore, university education is free of charge.

That young people can be a significant political force was demonstrated in May 1968 when student demonstrations initiated a process that ultimately led to the president's resignation. The number of university students in the Paris area alone at that time—over 100,000—was more than there were in all of France in 1945.

Income is another factor dividing the French. About the only other industrialized, democratic country with a distribution of income more unequitable than France is—the United States. The top 5th of all French households receive 46 percent of all disposable household income and the top 10th get 31 percent. Both shares are about 6 percentage points higher than they are in either Britain or Germany, but a few percentage points lower than in the United States.

On religion France appears to be (although it really isn't) united because it is overwhelmingly Catholic. About 40 million people have been baptized into the

Catholic Church, while Protestants number only about a million and Jews about three fourths of a million. But for most of the French, Catholicism is more nominal than practicing. They are Catholics mainly at only four moments in their lives—birth, first communion, marriage, and death. Furthermore, anticlericalism is a strong tradition of long standing. The revolution that created the first republic was directed against the Church as well as the monarchy. Throughout the 19th century the Church continued to oppose republican institutions. Therefore, in 1904, Church and state formally were separated.

But this does not mean that the Church is of little importance and lacks political influence. About a sixth of primary and secondary school pupils attend Catholic schools. In September 1951 the Church managed to have enacted a law *(loi Barangé)* providing government subsidies for the Catholic schools. In 1959 a subsequent law *(loi Debré)* offered Catholic schools a choice, if they wished to continue receiving subsidies.[4] They could sign an "association agreement," which would obligate the government to pay teachers' salaries and other expenses of running the school but would require the school to teach according to the regulations and curricula of public schools. Or they could sign a "limited agreement," which would give the government some control over teachers but no influence over curricula, with only the teachers' salaries being paid by the government.

The great bulk of the Catholic primary schools signed limited agreements, with most of the secondary ones preferring association agreements. About 6 percent of the primary schools and about a fifth of the secondary preferred to have no agreement at all despite the loss of subsidies. Since the limited agreements were to be for a trial period only, further action was required about a decade later.

Under a 1971 law the limited agreements in the primary schools were made permanent. Association agreements continued as before at both levels. But for secondary schools limited agreements were ruled out after 1979. Thus, although the Church has had to concede some control over parochial education to the government in order to obtain financial support, yet it continues to operate a separate school system, educating a substantial segment of the population at public expense.

In 1984 the Socialist Government proposed to integrate the Catholic schools more fully into the state system. Confronted with nationwide dissent, including a protest march of up to 1.5 million people in Paris, it quickly had to drop these plans. Thus religion continues to affect politics in France more than in the United States or in Britain except for Northern Ireland. Many people remain concerned about the role of the Catholic schools because of their ability to shape basic values, which in turn frequently affects political attitude and behavior.

---

[4]Jack Hayward, *The One and Indivisible French Republic* (London: Weidenfeld & Nicolson, 1973), pp. 193–95.

Another major influence on political attitudes is the mass media. France lacks the mass circulation newspapers of other countries. Perhaps its best known and most respected paper, *Le Monde* has a readership of only 1.5 million. Only two other Paris dailies—both tabloids—surpass a million. These figures may be a bit misleading since all three papers have a circulation—as distinct from a readership—of less than half a million. The paper with the greatest circulation—three quarters of a million—is a regional paper selling in Brittany (the peninsula that juts out into the Atlantic) and surrounding areas. Furthermore, the Paris dailies—about a dozen papers—have been declining in circulation. For the country as a whole the circulation of the daily press has declined to little more than 200 copies per thousand people, compared to nearly 400 per thousand in Britain.

Weekly newsmagazines have not been any more successful. The best known, *Paris-Match,* prints little more than 800,000 copies a week, followed by *L'Express* at less than 650,000.

The nationalizing effect of print media, which we discussed as a factor in British homogeneity, is not present in France. What, then about the even more important electronic media? France has four television channels. All are owned by the national government—three entirely and one partially—although one is a network of regional stations. The channels buy a substantial minority of their programs—a fifth to a third—from one or another of the more than a dozen private companies producing film and video materials. Virtually every household in France (95 percent) has one or more TV sets. The French, however, do not watch television nearly as much as do Americans, averaging little more than two and a half hours a day.

More than a third of total TV programming is news, with about an eighth being documentaries and performing arts. Although broadcasting is supposed to be independent so as to ensure free expression of opinion, it has a long history in France of being political, subservient to the government. Despite frequent claims that the system is being reorganized or reformed so as to be fair to all, this has not happened. Whatever parties have controlled the government have seen that what is broadcast is to their advantage. At times this has been blatant—taking broadcast time without allowing opponents an equivalent right of response—at other times more a matter of slanting content. In Britain government-directed broadcasting has a reputation for unparalleled fairness, in France government monopoly has produced spineless toadies. About the only relief is the fact that some radio stations located just outside of France—Radio Luxembourg, for example—can be heard in various parts of the country. President Mitterrand has announced that he wants to authorize about 80 new TV stations that would be affiliated with two or three *privately owned* networks. Whether such a development would do anything to make French television less politically subservient remains to be seen. Mitterrand may simply believe that a shift to some private ownership of television is inevitable, so it would be best for this to occur while he was in power and could ensure that those controlling commercial television were not hostile to the Socialists.

HISTORICAL BACKGROUND

France was one of the first countries in Europe to develop a sense of national unity, symbolized by the monarchy. Unlike Britain, however, France did not make steady strides toward stable and effective parliamentary democracy. Progress of this type came later than in Britain and was characterized by a number of interruptions and reversals. Moreover, the transitions—notably the Revolution of 1789–were more violent and more disruptive of political unity than those experienced by the British. In brief, a sense of national unity was not accompanied by an evolving agreement concerning the nature of the nation's political institutions. Evidence of this lack of agreement is the fact that in less than 200 years the basic form or type of government in France has been altered over a dozen times. This lack of continuity in regime means that people are less likely to feel a traditional attachment to the existing government structures than they are in Britain and, perhaps, even less likely than in Germany.

France of the *ancien régime* (from about 1000 to 1789) was governed by a king, who wielded his powers through secretaries of state personally selected and directed by him. They, in turn, exercised their authority through a centralized bureaucratic machine, which was several centuries in the making and which was perfected under King Louis XIV. After Louis XIV (d. 1715), however, the political structure lacked cohesion, being characterized by weakness and division.

A type of representative assembly, called the Estates General, had come into being in France in the 14th century. It was to represent the three estates (classes). The first two, the clergy and the nobility, were by far the most powerful, although they represented only about 5 percent of the population. The third estate was a catchall in which the middle class (bourgeoisie) was the most important. The feeble attempts of the Estates General to limit the monarchy were singularly unsuccessful. The irrelevance of the Estates General to the political system is clear from the fact that it did not even meet from 1614 to 1789. Obviously, this body could not evolve into an effective check on the monarch in the way that the British Parliament was doing at that time.

What the Estates General did not do in the way of limiting royal authority, was attempted, to a degree, by the *parlements,* of which France had a number, the most important being the *Parlement* of Paris. *Parlements* were primarily law courts that had exercised some advisory powers in the medieval period. Because royal decrees were promulgated by registering them with *parlement,* the *parlement* became able to criticize and even refuse to register them. For strong monarchs this was merely a nuisance, since they could overrule such refusals. Under weaker rulers, however, *parlements* became centers of opposition and were regarded by many as guardians of liberties. Ironically, *parlements* often opposed needed reforms, and thus contributed in part to the ineffectiveness and stagnation of the political system.

The king's decision in 1788 to suspend *parlements* and to call a meeting of the Estates General for May 1789 was a confession of defeat, signifying the end of absolute monarchy. But the privileged classes, which had sided with the *parlements,* had not counted on the possibility of the Third Estate's taking over the revolt and turning it to its own ends. Similarly, the Third Estate set in motion certain forces it could not control. Within a brief span of time, the constitutional struggle turned to civil war and a profound social revolution.

The French Revolution had a tremendous impact, especially in Europe, raising the hopes of peoples in the struggle against monarchical regimes. On the other hand, it disappointed many of its supporters, not only because of the excesses (such as arbitrary executions) but also because it seemed unable to produce a stable political order. For France it ushered in a century of political turmoil, which culminated in the establishment in 1875 of the Third Republic, a tentative compromise that few expected to last, but which proved to be the most durable political system that France has tried from the Revolution down to today.

The revolutionaries at first attempted to establish a constitutional monarchy. But Louis XVI was unwilling to accommodate himself to reality in the fashion of British monarchs and refused to accept a new status of limited power. His constant intrigues against the constitutional government's officials soon led to the creation of a republic and to his execution. So great were the social and political dislocations of this period that France had to endure virtual anarchy. The Convention—the legislative body that was the supreme governmental organ—proved too weak and inexperienced to govern the country effectively. The system rapidly moved toward increasing executive dominance, especially as Napoleon Bonaparte gained prominence. Finally, in 1804, Napoleon was able to have himself declared emperor, thus ending the First Republic and replacing it with the First Empire.

This was not a triumph of the old order. Napoleon had perverted the revolution, but he had not destroyed it. He was not from an aristocratic background, and his opportunity to rise to political power would not have occured had it not been for the Revolution. Furthermore, he did not abolish all the Revolution's institutional reforms. While he did effect a reconciliation with the Church, its leaders did not return to the positions of political dominance they formerly had occupied. Nor did the nobility recoup its losses. And Napoleon did at least pretend to consult the citizens through the frequent use of plebiscites. So thorough and valuable were his modifications of the bureaucracy that the Napoleonic system provided the basic structure for French administration on into the closing years of the 20th century and even then seemed impervious to reform efforts.

Military defeat ended Napoleon's rule and brought the old Bourbon ruling house back to the throne. In a classic phrase it is said that the Bourbons had learned nothing and forgotten nothing. They governed entirely as though the Revolution never had occurred. Once again they demonstrated their inability to adapt to changed conditions. Their high-handed rule produced another revolution—this one more moderate—in 1830. A new king, one willing to accept the position of a constitutional monarch, was placed on the throne.

By now, however, revolution had come to be seen as virtually a regular part of the political process. Thus in 1848 unemployment and discontent in Paris combined with conflict over extension of the franchise to topple the monarchy and create the Second Republic. Napoleon's nephew Louis was elected president. He quickly parodied his uncle by making himself emperor in 1852, a move sanctioned by 97 percent of the voters in a plebiscite.

As with his uncle before him, Louis Napoleon's rule was ended by military defeat—in the Franco-Prussian War in 1870. Thus the Third Republic was proclaimed to replace the Second Empire. A sizable majority of those elected to the National Assembly in 1871, however, were monarchists. Reacting against this and the ending of the war, Paris set up its own government—the Commune. Putting down this attempted secession produced the bloodiest civil war in French history, with 20,000 people killed during the last week of fighting. Marxists subsequently developed the myth that the Commune was a self-conscious proletarian uprising. And a century later they continue to honor the Communards as martyrs.

The National Assembly elected in 1871 to agree to peace terms with Prussia did not disperse even after the Commune had been put down and a treaty had been agreed to. Instead, it governed France for five years and drew up the organic laws that were to serve as the constitution for the Third Republic. Since that system was to last for 65 years, a century of political turmoil had been brought to an end for a time.

But this conclusion was a tentative, uncertain one. Unlike the English Revolution of 1688, which established (without bloodshed) the supremacy of Parliament, the French Revolution had succeeded only in *asserting* the democratic ideal of popular sovereignty. No lasting agreement had been achieved on how this ideal was to be embodied in governmental institutions. The question of where responsibility for political acts was to rest was not adequately answered.

In these circumstances everyone was surprised that the Third Republic proved to be more than a stopgap political system. Instead of soon being replaced by a restored monarchy, as many anticipated, it became the longest-lived of any French political system since the Revolution, surviving World War I and the depression, to be ended by France's defeat by Germany in 1940. Although the Third Republic as a system or regime was quite stable, its executive was very unstable. Premiers frequently fell from power and Cabinets often were reconstituted.

Early in its life the Third Republic was threatened by a right-wing coup. Conservatives feared that a republican government was too weak to provide effective national leadership, and chauvinists despaired that the government was not seeking revenge against Germany for the defeat of 1870. These groups, along with supporters of the Church and military officers, focused their hopes in the late 1880s on General Feorges Boulanger, minister of war. He won great popularity by advocating *revanche* against Germany and revision of the constitution to strengthen the executive. Eventually he organized the National party, financed largely by those who wished to restore the monarchy. Despite his personal ambition, he did not seek to use the Paris mobs to overthrow the government. Nonetheless, the republicans feared he was an antidemocratic threat and planned to arrest him for conspiring against the government. He fled France and was convicted in his absence. Two years later he committed suicide in Brussels.

Boulangism is an excellent example of the French tradition of the man-on-horseback—the military figure whose popularity and political ambition threaten democracy. We will discuss this at greater length in the next chapter. In terms of historical developments, rather than values, however, the importance of Boulangism ironically was that it helped to strengthen the Third Republic. The republican leaders had demonstrated that they could be decisive, strong in a time of apparent crisis. Furthermore, the affair (and certain aspects of Boulanger's private life) served to discredit conservatives and royalists.

Hardly had the dust settled from the Boulanger affair, when politics was polarized by an issue that festered for over a decade. In 1894 a Jewish captain of artillery, Alfred Dreyfus, was convicted in a secret court-martial of selling military secrets to Germany. His sentence was life imprisonment on Devil's Island off the northern coast of South America nearly on the Equator—the most infamous penal colony until the Gulag Archipelago. Hysterical anti-Semitism swept France. Again royalists, clericals, chauvinists, and conservatives were arrayed on one side against liberal republicans on the other.

After a long-drawn-out public campaign it was eventually established in 1906 that the whole case against Dreyfus was unfounded, that the evidence against him had been forged, and that the legal proceedings had been a gross injustice. He was freed, given the rank of major, and awarded the Legion of Honor. Once again royalists and clericals were discredited. The republican leaders were strengthened by being able to gain greater control over the military, which had continued to be the preserve of the heavily royalist upper classes.

Thus the Third Republic acquired the strength to survive World War I and the depression. In fact, had France not been defeated by Germany in World War II, the Third Republic well might exist still today. Initially, after their victory, the Germans occupied only the north and west parts of France. The rest of the country was governed by a puppet government located in Vichy, a small town in central France northwest of Lyon. As part of the surrender arrangements, the French Parliament voted full power to Marshal Henri Pétain, France's most prominent hero of World War I. While hardly dashing at age 84, Pétain provided another example of the man-on-horseback. He issued constitutional decrees giving himself full legislative and executive powers and dismissed Parliament. He required all high officials to swear personal loyalty to him. Thus the Third Republic was replaced with a dictatorship.

Following the military liberation of France, the population voted overwhelmingly for a new political system rather than a revival of the Third Republic. When the constituent assembly submitted its proposed constitution to the people, the nation, which consistently and frequently had given virtual unanimous approval to anything the two Napoleons had proposed, rejected it. A revised constitution subsequently was approved—but only barely. While it was bad enough that the vote was only 9 million for to 8 million against, the result was made disastrous by the fact that another 8 million abstained. Thus throughout the Fourth Republic the supporters of Charles de Gaulle, who adamantly opposed the constitution as providing for too weak a government, taunted those in power with the fact that their political system had the approval of only 37 percent of the population. Crippled by such a birth defect and the obvious availability of de Gaulle to lead an alternative political system, the Fourth Republic was unlikely to enjoy a long life.

The Fourth Republic's life expectancy deteriorated further because it came to resemble the Third Republic, only more so. The same executive instability, the same governmental ineffectiveness, the same dissatisfaction soon were rampant. The average life of a Cabinet was even shorter in the Fourth Republic than it had been in the Third—now less than six months. During 1951 and 1958 the average length of Government crises, the time from the resignation of one Government to the agreement upon its successor, was two and one half weeks.

The fatal flaw of both the Third and the Fourth Republic was the party system. The country not only was politically divided but each group deeply distrusted its opponents. Conservatives believed that socialists and communists wanted a Marxist dictatorship, while the left saw the right as committed to a repressive, neofascist regime. Clericals expected anticlericals to persecute the Church, while anticlericals anticipated that clericals would try to establish a Jesuitical regime. The electoral system, PR in the Fourth Republic, faithfully reflected these social divisions in the legislature.

Despite the cleavages between political groups, parties in the legislature—with the exception of the Communists—rarely were cohesive. Thus the executive, which was responsible to Parliament, rarely could command an effective majority and was unable to act decisively. The Fourth Republic was ineffective because it was unable "to give clear priority to the task of economic and social transformations, because its institutional set-up allowed distracting tasks (such as colonial wars) and social groups that were being squeezed out by the new policies . . . to interfere with the modernization."[5] Government's "expectation of staying in office beyond a few months could be fulfilled only by following a most cautious course. The expectation of governmental instability endowed every new government with a basic weakness."[6]

In January 1958 a public opinion poll asked a sample of the population, "What would you do if there were a coup?" Only 4 percent said that they would actively oppose it, and the majority responded that they would do nothing. Not suprisingly, four months later the Fourth Republic collapsed under a virtual coup. The system would probably have survived if it had not been for the government's inability to maintain the French colonial empire. Economic conditions at home had improved greatly in 1953–57. Paradoxically, the increasing prosperity seemed to magnify the reverses in the foreign field, which were pull-

---

[5]Stanley Hoffmann, "The Fifth Republic at Twenty," in *Impact of the Fifth Republic,* Andrews and Hoffmann, p. 287.

[6]Ezra Suleiman, "Presidential Government in France," in *Presidents and Prime Ministers,* eds. Richard Rose and Ezra Suleiman (Washington, D.C.: American Enterprise Institute, 1980), p. 96.

ing France's international prestige downhill, and which had consumed much of her material and human resources.

The immediate circumstances leading to the downfall of the Fourth Republic can be summed up in one word—Algeria. The French settlers there, numbering at least 1,500,000, were determined to resort to violence, if need be, against what appeared to be the helplessness of the government in Paris to cope with the Moslem nationalist movement in Algeria. In this attitude they were supported by professional army officers, partly because of the humiliating defeat in Indochina and a no less humiliating withdrawal from Suez in 1956. Moreover, it was apparent that certain army units in Algeria and in France meant business. The threat of a military revolution was real.

The government was undercut further by the fact that many people in France itself sympathized with the Algerian settlers and the army. Furthermore, while many other people, particularly the younger generations, cared little about Algeria, they were equally apathetic about defending the established political system, given its general aura of ineffectiveness.

The French Government concluded that the only acceptable way of avoiding an almost certain military dictatorship was to call upon the country's World War II hero, General Charles de Gaulle, to form a Government. On June 1, 1958, he was made premier—the last one of the Fourth Republic—and was empowered, as he had insisted upon, to rule by decree for six months and to revise the constitution drastically. The only apparent difference between 1958 and 1940 was that this time no German soldiers were in the country.

Instead of summoning a constituent assembly, de Gaulle turned the task of drafting a new constitution over to a handful of his supporters who could be trusted to devise a document embodying his views on the proper form of government, in particular the need for a strong executive. When the proposed constitution was submitted to a referendum, the population reverted to their voting patterns under the Napoleons. Eighty percent voted in favor of it, with only 15 percent abstaining. Thus, unlike the Fourth Republic, the Fifth began life with the approval of two thirds of the electorate, apparently vindicating the Gaullists' jeers at the Fourth.

During the next 10 years de Gaulle's actions amply demonstrated his predominance within the French political process. He extracted France from the Algerian dilemma, demonstrated French domination of the Common Market by vetoing British membership, and gained an enhanced international prominence for France through the development of a nuclear force and a measure of detente with the Soviet Union. Then in May 1968, the arrest of an extremist student leader mushroomed without warning into a confrontation between the government and the students, which eventually included the workers. While de Gaulle was able to ride out this storm, it is clear in retrospect that his authority had been weakened fatally.

The following April a referendum was held on the question of reorganizing the government so as to strengthen regional structures and to transform the

Senate and further reduce its powers. As he had done for previous referenda during his decade of power, de Gaulle threatened that were his proposals for reform not approved by a substantial margin he would resign. The technique that in the past had worked so well now backfired; 53 percent of those voting said no. Some analysts have argued that the negative vote represented not so much a rejection of the substance of the reforms as it did a refusal to allow de Gaulle to continue to govern in a high-handed fashion. Unbending as ever, de Gaulle resigned as president.

The years that have passed since his resignation have provided a partial answer to the question asked almost from the inception of the Fifth Republic: *Après* de Gaulle? Contrary to what he sometimes had predicted—*Après moi, le déluge*—his departure was not followed by chaos. The system that was drawn up to his specifications has endured even beyond his death in 1970.

Yet, in some senses, the Fifth Republic's durability still has not been tested fully. For nearly the first quarter century of its existence, despite various occupants in the office of president, the Fifth Republic did not see a change in the segment of society that controlled the government. Only in the presidential election of 1981 did someone from the opposition, from the left, gain the office. And that victory was followed immediately by parliamentary elections that gave the left firm control of the legislature, as well. True, the Fifth Republic proved to be established sufficiently to adapt to the alternation in power of contrasting political forces. But as the parliamentary elections of 1986 approached, the question was being asked whether control of the legislature by political forces opposed to the president (as seemed likely) would stalemate the system. And stalemate it to such an extent as to create a constitutional crisis. How many people did you hear voice this concern in the United States in 1984, when, despite President Reagan's reelection, the Democrats continued to control the House of Representatives? The fact that the answer is none indicates that American political institutions are more firmly established than are French ones, that the durability of the Fifth Republic can't just be taken for granted.

BIBLIOGRAPHICAL NOTE

For discussion of various social and economic aspects of France see parts II and III of Andrews and Hoffmann, cited in Footnote 1. For a survey of these subjects after a decade of the Fifth Republic see John Ardagh, *The New French Revolution* (New York: Harper & Row, 1969). A valuable essay on social change in France is Laurence Wylie's contribution to the Hoffmann book mentioned in Footnote 2.

A great number of French histories are readily available. Gordon Wright, *France in Modern Times* (New York: Rand McNally, 1960), is reliable and comprehensive. A standard, relatively brief source is David Thomson, *Democracy in France since 1870*, 4th ed. (London: Oxford University Press, 1964). Philip Williams was a leading authority on the Fourth and Fifth Republics. His study of the Fourth is *Crisis and Compromise* (Garden City, N.Y.: Doubleday Publishing, 1966). For the Fifth he collaborated with Martin Harrison on *Politics and Society in de Gaulle's Republic* (Garden City, N.Y.: Doubleday Publishing, 1973).

10

The Foundations of
French Politics

THE REPUBLICS' CONSTITUTIONAL TRADITIONS

Given the great variety of governmental systems that France has had since the Revolution, it is difficult to speak of a single constitutional tradition. Between the Revolution and the establishment of the Third Republic the French experimented with about a dozen constitutions. The relative durability of various French political systems is indicated in Figure 10-1. Although the average lifespan of each was brief, these constitutions usually were elaborate, long, and detailed documents. But, as history has demonstrated, the care and precision with which a constitution is drawn has no relation to its survival. Nor does practice in drafting constitutions guarantee their workability.

The most durable of French constitutions was that of the Third Republic. Since it, along with the Fourth Republic, which, contrary to the intentions of its founders, came to resemble its predecessor so closely, spanned a total of 77 years (two fifths of France's history since the Revolution), discussion of their basic constitutional principles is necessary. This also will help to clarify how greatly the Fifth Republic's basic provisions depart from previous tradition.

The constitution of the Third Republic consisted of three laws drawn up in 1875 (thus Figure 10-1 gives 65 years for the Third Republic, even though a republic was declared in 1870) as a temporary expedient by a monarchist assembly that could not decide which of two royal families should rule France. This was a compromise that neither faction wanted and neither side believed would endure. The three laws do not resemble a constitutional document. The Law on the Organization of the Public Powers vests legislative power in a Chamber of

FIGURE 10–1   Regime Instability

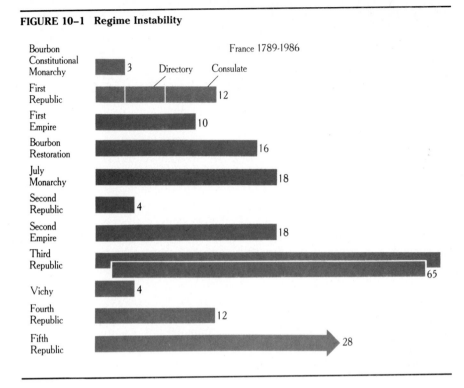

Deputies and a Senate, provides for a formal executive (president), prescribes that ministers are responsible to both houses of the legislature, and provides for a method of amending these arrangements. The Law on the Organization of the Senate prescribes in more detail the organization and the powers of that body. The Law on the Relations of the Public Powers, passed several months after the other two, seeks to regulate more precisely governmental procedures involving the legislature and the executive.

The essential point to remember is that these three laws provided a mere structural framework, with the actual operation of the system to be worked out in practice. These laws did not place any limitations on the powers of government except that the republican form of government would not be subject to amendment. The two houses, acting together, could presumably legislate about anything when and as they wished. And since there was no judicial review in the American sense, they had no fear of being overruled. Furthermore, this meant that formally amending the constitution was unnecessary.

More in accord with French tradition, the constitution of the Fourth Republic was detailed and logical, but, in the main, it ratified the political practices that had evolved under the Third. Some efforts were made to remedy the most serious shortcomings, primarily the relatively rapid turnover of Cabinets. Spur-of-the-moment votes of confidence, which had brought down so many Governments in the prewar period, were eliminated. A cooling-off period of 24 hours was required and only the prime minister was permitted to ask for a vote of confidence. The Cabinet was required to retain the support of only the lower house. Furthermore, it was not forced to resign on either a vote of confidence or a motion of censure unless an absolute majority voted against it. And to give the Cabinet a weapon against the legislature, it was empowered to dissolve Parliament and call for new elections.

For historical reasons, however, the power to dissolve Parliament was virtually unusable. The president had had this power in the Third Republic, subject to the consent of the Senate. In 1877 President MacMahon, attempting to obtain a more conservative Government personally acceptable to him, dissolved the Chamber of Deputies and called for new elections. Since the prime minister and his Government had effective Parliamentary support at the time, MacMahon's action was considered a virtual coup d'etat by those who favored a democratic political system, and they raised a storm of protest. Thus dissolution came to seem an antidemocratic measure and was never done again until some 80 years later toward the close of the Fourth Republic. Even then it still was regarded as a controversial act. So during the Third and Fourth Republics the Government could not attempt to whip its nominal followers into line by threatening to call new elections.

This was a particular weakness because of the party system. Unlike Britain, Third and Fourth Republic France had several major parties plus a number of smaller ones, all electing members to Parliament. A Cabinet could obtain the support of a majority in Parliament only by including members from several parties. Every Cabinet, therefore, was a coalition of divergent views. On crucial issues the governing parties seldom agreed. Cabinets could not implement decisive party pledges and did all they could to avoid having to act on anything of real importance. When the evil day could no longer be postponed and something had to be done, the typical result was the breakup of the coalition and the fall of the Government.

Although Cabinets were short-lived, instability was not as pronounced as it appeared on the surface, because a number of members of an outgoing Cabinet would always be found in the succeeding one. Certain men served in Cabinet after Cabinet, in the same or different posts, which meant that there was a great deal more continuity and experience in Cabinets than surface impressions indicated. Nonetheless, decisive action seldom occurred on major issues.

The prime minister could not function as a strong leader since his role was that of a broker seeking to formulate a compromise that the divergent groups in the Government would accept. Often one or more of these groups saw more advantage in voting against the Cabinet, even though some of their own party members were in it, than in supporting it. Such action enabled them to avoid responsibility for decisions that might prove to be politically unpopular. At times they were unwilling to vote for the policies of a Cabinet to which they belonged because they anticipated gaining a larger share of the seats in the new Cabinet that would be formed following the breakup of the current one. The parties could play this game of political musical chairs with impunity because they did not need to anticipate a new election, which might have cost them seats in Parliament.

Certain aspects of Parliamentary procedure also weakened the Cabinet. In contrast to the British practice, the French Cabinet could not determine how Parliament's time would be spent; it could not even insist on priority for its own legislative proposals. It lacked financial control; Parliament could increase expenditures without providing new funds to cover it—legislative irresponsibility prohibited in Britain. The Cabinet was at the mercy of Parliamentary committees. Cabinet measures often were buried, or so rewritten that they resembled the original version only faintly.

Although France under the Third and Fourth Republics had a parliamentary system, it clearly differed from the British parliamentary system. France lacked strong executive leadership. To distinguish between the two systems, some people have termed the French system assembly government, indicating the predominant power of the legislature, in contrast to the label of cabinet government used in Britain. Michel Debré, the chief drafter of the Fifth Republic's constitution, identified the main problems of assembly government as ministerial instability and legislative infringement on administrative action.[1]

Debré and his colleagues intended the Fifth Republic's constitution to "correct the inadequacies of the Republic's institutions which had been apparent for nearly a century." A key part of the remedy was to create "a parliamentary system, meaning on one hand a cabinet backed by a majority within an assembly and thus able to guide this majority as well as head the administration, but also on the other hand, a parliament that could carry out its legislative duties and act as a control without infringing on the executive." In addition, there would be "an executive with its own authority stemming from both its mode of selection and its powers."[2]

Specifically, Parliament's policy-making powers were limited, and its ability to vote a Government out of office was circumscribed. The formerly powerless head of state, the president, was given substantive powers, especially in times of crisis. The resultant system has been regarded as a hybrid—parliamentary in some ways and presidential in others. Debré himself has argued that either interpretation is correct. Whether the one view or the other is more accurate at any given time depends upon the political situation in Parliament. A strong majority in Parliament supportive of the president makes the system more presidential; when this does not exist the system is more parliamentary. And, obvi-

[1]Michel Debré, "The Constitution of 1958, Its Raison d'Être and How It Evolved," in *The Impact of the Fifth Republic on France,* eds. William G. Andrews and Stanley Hoffmann (Albany: SUNY Press, 1981), p. 8.
[2]Ibid., p. 7.

ously, the personalities of the president and the prime minister also affect the nature of the system.[3]

In part to keep Parliament within the new bounds of its power, the Fifth Republic's constitution introduced an innovation for France. A Constitutional Council with some powers of judicial review similar to those of the U.S. Supreme Court was created. We will discuss the details of this arrangement in subsequent chapters.

The procedure for altering the constitution is much more formal under the Fifth Republic than it was in the Third. Amendments may be proposed by the president, by the prime minister, or by members of Parliament. In each case a proposed amendment must obtain a majority in each house of Parliament. After passage by the two houses, the proposed amendment, if initiated by members of Parliament, must be submitted for ratification by the people in a referendum. If the proposed amendment is initiated by the president or the prime minister, however, ratification (after passage by the two houses) may, at the discretion of the president, be achieved by either popular referendum or a three fifths majority vote in a specially called joint meeting of the two houses of Parliament.

Despite these detailed provisions, in 1962 the constitution was amended by a different procedure. It is illustrative of President de Gaulle's conception of his role and authority that, when he found it inconvenient to follow the rules set forth in the constitution drawn up to his instructions, he employed other means that he found more congenial. De Gaulle had his prime minister propose amending the constitution to provide for direct election of the president. Instead of sending this proposal to Parliament—whether the proposal had sufficient legislative support to pass was doubtful—he submitted it directly to a referendum. Popular approval was deemed to be sufficient to implement the proposal. Thus, strange as it sounds, the French constitution was amended unconstitutionally. This simply is one evidence of the fact that in France, as on the continent generally, constitutionalism—the idea that certain rules of the game must be observed and can be altered only by special procedures—is not firmly established.

THE SEARCH FOR CONSENSUS

As we have seen, France has changed socially, economically, and politically in the last quarter of a century. Change in fundamental political values tends to occur more slowly, however, and to lag behind other shifts. Furthermore, you cannot fully understand the significance of value change unless you are familiar with the basic content of the traditional value system.

---

[3]Ibid., pp. 10–11, and "Appendix: Dialogue, Michel Debré and Conference Participants," in *Impact of the Fifth Republic,* Andrews and Hoffmann, p. 331.

The French Revolution was a civil war, not a revolt against a foreign colonial power. The values of the Republic were neither widely nor rapidly embraced by the population. For many the Republic was associated with chaos, with arbitrary imprisonment and even execution. When this ceased to be true, the Republic's leaders often seemed weak and indecisive. Furthermore, the Republic seemed to be, and often was, antireligious. Many people wanted at least an end to persecution of the Church, if not a larger role for religious values in public life, and many wanted stronger leadership, if not a return to the monarchy. Furthermore, the frequent changes in regime (see Figure 10–1) at the close of the 18th and in the first two thirds of the 19th centuries made fundamental change in the political system a live option, not just the nostalgic dream of grandparents. The Third Republic was created not because the people clamored for it, but because of defeat in war and unresolved competition between claimants for any throne.

As a result French politics involved not only the usual conflicts over short-range policy preferences, but also clashes on fundamentals. These basic cleavages frequently were injected into the debate over immediate goals. Thus the political stakes seemed quite high and dogmatism and hostility were encouraged. Political debate was very ideological; politics was a matter of faith rather than effectiveness. The main goal was not to negotiate a compromise but to convert your benighted opponents. Distrust and suspicion between political opponents were great because each regarded the other as seeking a fundamental change in the political structure.

Such values combined with an undisciplined multiparty system and assembly government to produce immobile, ineffective government in a stalemate society.[4] One way of dealing with this problem is to unify society through a movement of charismatic nationalism.[5] Personal magnetism combined with patriotism can give the various fragments of society a temporary sense of shared purpose. The rules of both Napoleons are examples. During the Third Republic such movements did not come to power, but Boulangism and the presidency of MacMahon seemed to threaten such a development. The democratic system was preserved, but it failed to provide stable, effective leadership.

The 65 years of the Third Republic did little to reconcile satisfactorily the principle of aristocratic command with the principle of democratic consent. Nor was a solution to the governmental counterpart of this dilemma—an equitable balance between the legislature and the executive—worked out. A basic paradox in French political culture thwarted any resolution. On the one hand, assembly government is unattractive because it results in immobility. That dissatisfies not only reform elements in France, as you would expect, but conservatives as well. They want a strong executive to restore France to a position of in-

---

[4]The term, as well as several of the points in this discussion, is from Stanley Hoffmann, "Paradoxes of the French Political Community," in *In Search of France,* Hoffmann et al (New York: Harper & Row, 1963), pp. 1–117.

[5]Gabriel Almond, "Comparative Political Systems," *Journal of Politics* 18 (August 1956), pp. 391–409.

ternational leadership and grandeur comparable to that the country had in the days of the monarchy.

So everyone can agree on the need for a stronger executive, whether for domestic reform or international prominence? No, not really, because many of the progressive political elements have feared that strengthening the executive would be the first step toward destroying the Republic. They have been haunted by the specter of the man-on-horseback—the leader who rises to power because of his military exploits and whose commitment to democracy appears to be questionable.

This fear of French democrats has been related to an inconsistency in their thinking about the political role of the people. On the one hand, they have tended to contend that the popular will always is right—French democratic thought shows little concern for minority rights and favors instead unlimited majority rule. For this reason they opposed any constitutional or judicial limits on Parliament, because it was the instrument of the popular majority. The legislature, in fact, was the only organ through which popular sovereignty could be expressed; even a popularly elected chief executive was not conceded this role.

French democrats were unwilling to trust popularly elected executives; they feared that they would attempt to subvert the democratic system as both Napoleons did. In other words, the people, whose will always was right, could not be trusted to vote for a chief executive. They would fail to perceive the danger of a charismatic leader; they would be taken in by the glamour of a famous name and would elect a man who would destroy the Republic.

So the traditional preference of the French democrats was for an executive beholden to the legislature as the only means of ensuring the survival of democracy. Yet thereby they not only condemned themselves to a system usually too weak to implement the reform policy they desired, but they also made democracy less attractive to conservatives because of its inability to strengthen France as a nation. In the name of defending democracy they undercut it.

We already have mentioned that fundamental political values of this type change very slowly. One would have thought, for example, that 65 years of the Third Republic would have been sufficient to establish that political system. Admittedly, it was replaced by the Vichy regime because of military defeat. Yet because Vichy provided for a strong executive and gave a prominent place to religious values, many of the French happily supported it as an improvement on the Third Republic. De Gaulle's return to power in 1958 stirred considerable controversy because it seemed to be another classic example of the man-on-horseback. These feelings were reinforced four years later when de Gaulle unconstitutionally amended the constitution to provide for direct election of the president. Traditional political leaders vigorously opposed this change not so much because of its content but because of what it symbolized—directly elected executives were a threat to democracy.

Despite the strength of these views in the early 1960s, by the 1980s they had dissipated. One of the factors contributing to President Giscard d'Estaing's failure to be reelected in 1981 may well have been the monarchical airs that he increasingly had seemed to assume. Yet no one regarded him, or his predecessor Pompidou, as a threat to democracy. And while the new president, François Mitterrand, was expected to reduce some of the grandeur of the office, he obviously did not intend to dismantle the office in the name of a return to true Republican values. Regardless of whether the acceptance may be a bit wary, French democrats have come to terms with a powerful elected executive.

In part, this may be because the old stalemate society has been destroyed and the country has been converted to growth and material progress.[6] The distrust and suspicion of others of the past seems to have been erased. A recent poll found that the overwhelming majority of the French believed that their fellow citizens were very or fairly trustworthy.[7] The proportion expressing this view differed little from the level of trust found in Britain and was only slightly below the German level.

Nonetheless, some residues of past problems continue to linger. The Fifth Republic seems to have reconciled the political right to the political and social order. With rare and tiny exceptions, the right no longer is a source of intransigent opposition to the Republic. The other side of the spectrum, however, has seen only partial success. The working class is not fully integrated into society; a sizable proportion does not accept the capitalistic system or the existing institutions for dealing with conflict. The problem is most pronounced at the elite level. In France the "range of disagreements within the political class is obviously greater than in West Germany, in Britain, or in the United States."[8]

Polls taken in EEC countries on attitudes toward the way in which society should develop provide an example of this. On nine separate occasions from 1976 through 1980 people were asked to choose among three statements: one a revolutionary option, another a reformist one, and another a status quo one. With one exception (when Italy was first), the proportion of French respondents selecting the option "The entire way our society is organised must be radically changed by revolutionary action" always was the highest of the nine EEC countries (Belgium tied France once).[9] While the proportion favoring this option in France was not huge—it ranged from 8 to 15 percent over the years—it was substantial. In Germany, by way of comparison, support for this option varied only from 1 to 4 percent. Furthermore, if you consider only the opinion leaders—the 10 to 15 percent of the population who discuss politics and try to persuade others—the proportion favoring the revolutionary option rises to about 20 percent.[10]

---

[6]The following discussion draws on Stanley Hoffmann, "The Fifth Republic at Twenty," in *Impact of the Fifth Republic,* Andrews and Hoffmann, pp. 281–327.

[7]Norman Webb and Robert Wybrow, eds., *The Gallup Report* (London: Sphere Books, 1981), p. 90.

[8]Andrews and Hoffmann, *Impact of the Fifth Republic,* p. 310.

[9]Webb and Wybrow, *The Gallup Report,* p. 84.

[10]Ibid., p. 83.

These figures become less surprising in the context of French history. During the past two centuries reforming the French governmental system along more democratic lines or protecting what democracy existed often has required armed domestic conflict. An ultimate resort to violence has seemed justifiable. Thus those not fully supportive of the existing system can advocate extreme measures without feeling that they are violating French democratic tradition. Especially is this true when there is reason to believe that such action is more a rhetorical flourish than a serious intent.

Furthermore, the existing political institutions lack in France the widespread support that they have in other leading democracies. A 1984 poll asked people in various countries which items on a list of characteristics they regarded as their country's strong and weak points in getting ready for the coming years. In Britain, the United States, and Germany more than half said that the country's political institutions were a strength, while in France only a third thought this. Nearly half of the French (45 percent) regarded their political institutions as a weakness for the coming years.[11]

French attitudes toward authority long have puzzled scholars by their apparent contradictoriness. Even after 20 years of the Fifth Republic, one scholar noted the persistence of "the traditional style of authority, with two components: resort to superior authority to solve conflicts and the fear of arbitrariness and resulting resistance to superior authority."[12] One scholar whose work has greatly influenced students of French government has argued that the French fear face-to-face relationships because these involve personal dependence.[13]

One of the few studies to focus on French behavior toward authority focuses on the relations between children and teachers in the secondary schools.[14] It suggests that French children do not learn in their families or primary schools to set self-limitations on behavior, and that they develop an idea of legitimacy based on the perceived forcefulness of superiors. Forcefulness should not be confused with physical coercion or punishment. Forcefulness is attributed instead to those who give the appearance of being in command and being totally certain they are correct. When a forceful person's authority is challenged, he or she does not respond with emotional threats but behaves calmly to suggest that no control has been lost and authority relations will continue as they have been.

What this eventually produces is a system in which people obey not because they are given detailed orders, but because they feel they have no choice but to obey. The French feel constrained to discover what their superiors want them to do and to do it, but they do not like having to behave this way. They will not express this discontent, however, to the superior within the organization to which

---

[11]*Gallup Political Index,* Report no. 285, p. 39.

[12]Andrews and Hoffmann, *Impact of the Fifth Republic,* p. 288.

[13]Michel Crozier, *The Bureaucratic Phenomenon* (Chicago: University of Chicago Press, 1964).

[14]William Schonfeld, *Obedience and Revolt: French Behavior Toward Authority* (London: Sage Publications, 1976). While his argument is closely integrated see, in particular, pp. 113–17.

they belong. Instead they will engage outside the organization in rhetorical condemnation of the system or, perhaps, join some other organization proclaiming values opposed to the first organization. They will not actually rebel so long as the superiors in an organization seem to be effective in achieving a goal of importance to the followers and do not actually issue a lot of specific directives for behavior. Thus they usually are not dominated by authority but feel that they are, because they have learned to try to please superiors. They fawn—in part because the absence of detailed directives gives them little to rebel against—but complain about having to do so.

Again, EEC polls provide an example of this. On four occasions from 1973 through 1980 respondents were asked whether they were satisfied "on the whole . . . with the life you lead?" Except for Italy, France always had the lowest level of satisfaction among the nine countries, ranging only from 10 to 15 percent who were very satisfied.[15] Giving a political focus to the question did not improve the responses much. On three occasions from 1973 through 1980, only 36 to 41 percent said that they were "satisfied with the way that democracy works in France."[16]

While in part these responses can be seen as rhetorical complaints that help the French to deal with their feelings of constraint in authority relationships, they also raise important questions of legitimacy. One scholar who frequently has attempted to draw up a balance sheet of the Fifth Republic finds evidence of doubts about the legitimacy of the economic system, the educational system, and even, to some extent, the political system.[17] This is why the victories of Mitterrand and the Socialists in 1981 were so important for the durability of the Fifth Republic. They offered an opportunity to integrate into the system those workers who had remained on the fringes. Legitimacy will be enhanced by evidence that the political system is not the property of only a portion of the political spectrum.

France has a strong democratic tradition. When, between World Wars I and II, European problems and turmoil drove Germany and Italy from democracy to authoritarian systems, France managed to survive as a democracy. But democratic values are challenged in France by a competing tradition. Not sufficiently repressive to be termed authoritarian, this value system has been labeled the administrative tradition—government "through an elite, supported by a powerful and centralized bureaucracy."[18] The Fifth Republic originated in this tradition. As we will see in greater detail when we discuss the functioning of the legislature and its relations with the executive, much of the life of the Fifth Republic has remained in this tradition. The question for the 1980s is whether the development

---

[15]Webb and Wybrow, *The Gallup Report,* p. 81.

[16]Ibid., p. 82. Of the nine EEC countries only Italy was lower (persistently) and Belgium (once). In Germany satisfaction with democracy went from 44 percent in 1973 to 80 percent in 1979 and 73 percent in 1980.

[17]Andrews and Hoffmann, *Impact of the Fifth Republic,* pp. 308–12.

[18]Nicholas Wahl, *The Fifth Republic* (New York: Random House, 1959), p. 28.

of the Fifth Republic's institutions under President Mitterrand can give the system an equal footing in the representative tradition. The Fifth Republic may be able to bridge these two traditions in political consensus.

This will not be easy because such a development will seem like the sloppy compromises that are more typical of British political development. The French tend to value highly critical, analytical thinking. But the rational approach can be carried too far (imagine, college professors telling you that). A nice illustration was the difficulty of deciding upon the final resting place of France's unknown soldier. A location associated with the Revolution would have been offensive to those who never had accepted its transformation of the political system. As for a chapel, there was no proof that the unknown soldier was even a Christian, to say nothing of a Catholic. In England no one considered the theological implication of burying that country's unknown soldier in Westminster Abbey. At times in France a bit more pragmatism and a bit less rationality would be helpful politically.

Nothing that we have said should make you think that the French are not proud of their country. They are intensely loyal to the nation and its culture. The problem is that because of their attitudes toward authority and two centuries of competing political traditions, their commitment to the political system is not as strong. The 1980s, however, may finally change that by producing in France a broad-based acceptance of the political institutions of the Fifth Republic, thus giving France the fundamental consensus for which it so long has sought.

BIBLIOGRAPHICAL NOTE

In addition to the Hoffmann essay cited in Footnote 4, see the Goguel essay in the same book. Schonfeld, cited in Footnote 14, briefly summarizes the various interpretations of French political authority on pp. 137–42 and comments on Crozier on pp. 174–82. The principles in accord with which French politicians appeared to operate in the Fourth Republic are discussed in Nathan Leites, *On the Game of Politics in France* (Stanford, Calif.: Stanford University Press, 1959). For an interesting effort to assess the impact upon political culture of socioeconomic change in Fifth Republic France, see Harvey Waterman, *Political Change in Contemporary France* (Columbus, Ohio: Charles E. Merrill Publishing, 1969). The Hoffmann essay cited in Footnote 6 brings the assessment up to date through the second decade.

11

Individual and Group
Political Activity

ELECTORAL SYSTEM TRADITIONS

Given the many changes we have told you about in the French basic political system, you will have a hard time believing that the French have altered their electoral system even more frequently. (Be of good cheer; we are not going to discuss all of these.) A French electoral system usually has not endured beyond two elections without some significant alteration in procedures. The French constantly have tinkered with electoral procedures not because they were striving to satisfy some idealistic abstract conception of electoral justice; instead, the changes have been partisan attempts by those in power to strengthen their own position and weaken their major challengers.

The electoral system has been altered only slightly, however, during the life of the Fifth Republic. The system is similar to one first introduced in 1852 and used off and on since then for a total of almost 100 years. This will surprise some people since a common belief is the mistaken idea that the typical French electoral system is some form of PR (proportional representation)—a system that distributes the seats in the legislature in accord with a party's share of the popular vote. Prior to World War II France made only rare use of such a system and never in a pure form. Thus only from 1945 to 1958—for only five elections and two of these for constituent assemblies—did France use PR.

This needs to be stressed because some people have argued that PR helps to produce a multiparty system. France had several competing parties, however, long before it adopted PR. Thus, whatever the impact of PR on French politics, it did not create the multiparty system.

PR is a general type of electoral system, not a single form. Some forms of PR favor large parties and others, small ones. Initially in the Fourth Republic a system favoring large parties was used. But as the time for a national election in 1951 approached, the parties in power feared that the Communists and the supporters of de Gaulle (then regarded by many as antidemocratic right-wingers) would gain a majority of the seats and paralyze the political system through an unholy alliance of the left and the right. So in accord with hallowed practice, the governing parties rigged the electoral system.

In each of the constituencies parties could declare that they were allied. The allies did not have to offer a joint, agreed set of candidates. Each ran its own candidates as in the past and simply declared formally that they were allied. The alliance clearly was in name only. In every constituency where the vote for the separate allied candidate slates totaled more than 50 percent when combined, the allies were given *all* the seats in that constituency (several members represented each constituency) instead of only their proportional share. Furthermore, in a few areas where the Communists and Gaullists were known to be particularly strong the PR system was altered to a form that favored small parties rather than large ones.

The result of these manipulations was to give the Gaullists 26 seats fewer than they otherwise would have received and the Communists 71 seats fewer. The strategy was successful in preventing the left and the right from getting a majority of legislative seats between them. It did little, however, to strengthen people's belief in the moral virtues of democracy.

When de Gaulle returned to power in 1958, he decided to change the electoral system to a double ballot system similar to the one used for much of the Third Republic. Interestingly, the leaders of the party organized to support de Gaulle, the Union for the New Republic, did not favor this system. They felt that it would be difficult for the new political faces in the Union for the New Republic to defeat the better-known candidates of the old parties. De Gaulle did not want the Union to gain a massive victory, however, since he did not want to be beholden to any political group, even one organized to support him.

In the 1981 parliamentary election campaign, the Socialists pledged to alter the double ballot system—which had helped to keep the left out of power for entire life of the Fifth Republic—and replace it with PR. When they unexpectedly won a landslide victory, under the existing system, few people believed that they would redeem this pledge, having found that the system could be as kind to them as it had been to the right in the past. And certainly the Socialists had a number of more pressing reforms to enact.

Increasingly in the mid-1980s, however, their thoughts began to turn to PR. As had so often been true in the past, the reason was not an idealistic concern with electoral justice. Rather the Socialists' popularity had declined to the point that it appeared that they could be reduced to only a tenth of the seats in parliament in the 1986 elections. On the other hand, various types of PR systems (remember PR is not a single procedure, but comes in many varieties) could give them up to a quarter of the seats. Thus yet another change in the electoral system had come to seem quite possible.

And indeed in April 1985 the Cabinet did introduce legislation to change the electoral system to PR. The distribution of seats proportional to a party's share of the popular vote would occur not at the national level, but at the local, that is, the department, level. Any party failing to receive at least 5 percent of the vote in a given department would not be entitled to any seats there. Parties clearing this hurdle would receive a share of the department's representatives proportional to their popular vote. Depending upon the size of its electorate, a department would have between about 6 and 30 representatives. In Chapter 19, in the German section of this book, we explain in detail the actual working of one type of PR system. For the remainder of this chapter, however, we will discuss the French electoral practices that have existed for virtually the entire life of the Fifth Republic.

CURRENT ELECTORAL PRACTICES

France has four types of elections for national governmental units. General elections choose all the members of the National Assembly, the lower house of the legislature, and partial elections fill some vacancies in its membership. Indirect elections select members of the Senate, the upper house of the legislature. Popular elections choose the president. We will discuss the two types of elections for the National Assembly first.

National Assembly Elections

France is divided into single-member constituencies, unlike the multimember ones used for PR in the Fourth Republic. A candidate who receives more than 50 percent of the votes cast is elected. Given the number of parties in France, this usually does not occur. The high point was in 1968, when a third of the constituencies were won on the first ballot. In the three previous elections the proportional never had exceeded one fifth. Since 1968 only about a seventh or an eighth of the constituencies have been won on the first ballot. But in 1981 the proportion of first-ballot winners rose to about one third. The chief reason was the agreement reached between the Gaullists and the Giscardiens not to run candidates against each other in most constituencies on the first ballot. Since the vote of the right and the center was not divided, they tended to win constituencies on the first ballot that they otherwise would not have won until the second.

In constituencies where no candidate has received an absolute majority, another election, or second ballot, is held a week later. In this election the candidate receiving the most votes is elected regardless of whether that is a majority. In the interval between the two ballots, candidates may drop out as parties negotiate. The idea is that parties relatively close together on the political spectrum want to agree upon a single candidate best placed to defeat the candidate(s) of parties farther away from them. No one who did not run in the constituency on the first ballot may do so on the second ballot, and anyone failing to win at least 12.5 percent of the total electorate (not just of the vote cast) on the first ballot is barred from the second ballot.

As a result of the regulations and the political maneuvering, only two candidates run for election on the second ballot in the vast majority of constituencies. If one considers supporters of the Government (whatever their party affiliation) as one party and members of the Opposition (regardless of party) as another, then France resembles a two-party system on the second ballot. The electoral choice has been simplified and is relatively clear cut.

In some senses, then, the French double ballot system tends to work something like American primaries. The first ballot establishes who the candidates will be in the decisive second ballot. On the first ballot voters tend to vote for the party they most prefer regardless of its chances of winning. Such a strategy is costless because a candidate from a party that one strongly opposes cannot be elected unless he or she manages to get more than half of the votes. Thus dividing the support of the left, for example, among several candidates will not permit the right to win simply by gaining more votes than any single candidate of the divided left. Should the right win because its candidate gained a majority, it would have done so even had the left offered only one candidate, since that candidate, obviously, would have had to receive less than half the vote.

You might want to think of the double ballot system as going one step beyond opinion polls. The first ballot makes clear exactly what each party's strength is in each constituency—there is no need to take a poll to find out; instead of a sample of the voters telling a pollster how they would vote, the voters actually have demonstrated their preferences. Thus the parties have fairly reliable data as they plan their best strategy for the decisive ballot. Of course, some people may vote on the second ballot who abstained on the first, and vice versa. Furthermore, the deals that the parties make cannot be imposed on their supporters. For example, a Socialist candidate may get fewer votes on the first ballot than a Communist candidate, and so withdraw in the latter's favor. But some of the people who voted for the Socialist may be so hostile to communism that they vote for a center or right-wing candidate on the second ballot. Despite these uncertainties, the parties do tend to see the first ballot as a chance to test their relative strengths. The parties supporting the Government in 1981, for example, spoke of having "primaries," meaning that each of them offered candidates in many constituencies on the first ballot, allowing the electorate to determine which party would provide the jointly supported candidate on the second ballot.

Although the French electoral system differs significantly from the American and the British, and although France in the past has used PR, you must understand that there is nothing even remotely proportional about the double ballot system. In 1958, for example, about 7 million Communist and Socialist voters elected 54 members of the National Assembly, while about 4 million voters for the Union for the New Republic returned 212 members. In 1968 the left political parties got the same share of the vote as did the Gaullist, but received less than one third as many seats.

Candidates must be French citizens and at least 23 years old. They do not need to live in the constituency where they run. They must deposit 1,000 francs (about $1,100), which they forfeit if they fail to receive 5 percent of the votes cast. Each candidate must have an alternate, usually called a *suppléant*. Should a member of the National Assembly die or resign because of joining the Cabinet (as required by the constitution), the *suppléant* serves the remainder of the term.

Should a seat in the National Assembly become vacant for any other reason, an election is held to fill that seat. Several such elections usually are held at the same time, and these are called partial elections. Such elections cannot be held during the last year of the National Assembly's maximum term.

As in Britain, the legislature has a maximum term of five years, but general elections may occur more frequently at irregular intervals. The National Assembly can be dissolved for new elections at any time the president chooses, except that elections must be at least 12 months apart. Thus President Mitterrand, seeking to follow up his electoral victory in the spring of 1981, called for new legislative elections even though the maximum term of the National Assembly still had almost two years to run.

Legally, election campaigns are brief, about the same as in Britain. Taking 1981 as an example, candidates had the week of May 25–31 in which to file. The campaign formally opened on June 1 with the first ballot on June 14 and the second on June 21. Of course, just as in Britain preparations for the campaign and political maneuvering may begin weeks or months earlier. This was less true in 1981 because had President Giscard been reelected, then legislative elections would not have been held. Only when Mitterrand won the presidential election on May 10 was it clear that legislative elections would occur shortly afterward.

Television plays an important role in the campaign. Not only does a substantial portion of the electorate regard it as a useful media in helping them to reach a voting decision, but a substantial majority thinks it is the most important of a wide variety of communications media in influencing their vote.[1] Parties and candidates are barred from buying time on TV. Instead, the parties supporting the Government are given a total of an hour and a half before the first ballot, with the same amount going to the Opposition parties. Each side then distributes this time to the parties, according to their strength in the National Assembly. Parties not represented in the National Assembly, but which contest at least 75 constituencies, are given two broadcasts of seven minutes each. Between the first and second ballots, each side receives a total of 45 minutes, and parties not

---

[1]Roland Cayrol, "The Mass Media and the Electoral Campaign," in *The French National Assembly Elections of 1978,* ed., Howard Penniman (Washington, D.C.: American Enterprise Institute, 1980), p. 148.

in Assembly get one broadcast of five minutes. These broadcasts go out at prime evening time on weekdays simultaneously on radio and all TV networks.

These arrangements certainly seem equitable. The question is whether they offset the bias that characterizes government-controlled radio and television when campaigns are not in progress. At those times Government officials are covered in detail while the speeches of leaders of other parties hardly are reported at all. Most significant has been the president's practice of intervening in the campaign. For example, on the night before the first ballot in the 1978 legislative elections, President Giscard broadcast a talk telling the voters to support the Government parties. Since the campaign already was over, the Opposition party leaders had no way in which to respond. Given the closeness of the vote in 1978, this intervention may have been a crucial factor in preventing a victory by the left.

Neither candidates nor parties are limited in what they can spend on campaigns. In 1978 the Communists and the RPR both claimed to have spent about $2 million with the Socialists reporting $6 million. The true figures are estimated to be anywhere from 2 to 20 times higher.

As for individual candidates, the government limits the size and number of posters and allocates officially designated sites for them. The government reimburses every candidate receiving at least 5 percent of the vote for the cost of posters and for printing and mailing election material to every voter. This is supposed to cover the candidates' election expenses, although they are not prohibited from spending additional funds of their own for campaign purposes.

The government prepares lists of eligible voters, which it updates annually. France did not enfranchise women until after World War II, but now suffrage is universal at age 18. Mail ballots were abolished in 1975, but in 1977 a system of proxy voting was established. Persons absent from their constituency on election day or who lived permanently abroad can authorize someone to vote for them. A voter can cast up to five such proxy votes. People living abroad can have their vote cast in any town having a population of at least 30,000. Shortly before the 1978 election sizable numbers of French voters living outside the country began to register in marginal constituencies. The Government apparently attempted to organize proxy voting so as to win some constituencies where a close contest was expected. As a result a few of the 1978 elections were invalidated and new elections were held. Little was heard about any potential abuse of proxy voting in 1981.

Shortly before going to the polls, each French voter receives in the mail a packet containing a number of ballots. Each candidate prints his or her own ballot, although it must conform to a standard approximately 4-by-6-inch size. Other than including the names of the candidate and the *suppléant,* what the ballot says varies a good deal. Some will include the name of a nationally recognized party and others will not. Some will include the age and occupation of the candidate and *suppléant* and others will not. A voter either takes one of these ballots along to the polling station on election day or picks up the desired one at the polling station. The voter puts the ballot of the candidate for which he or she wishes to vote in an envelope provided by the election officials and drops the envelope in a ballot box.[2]

French elections are held on Sundays to help produce a high turnout. Generally, in the Fifth Republic turnout has been around 80 percent. The 83 percent attained in 1978 was the best ever for legislative elections. In 1981 apathy resurged; turnout plummeted to only 71 percent. Only in 1962 had a smaller proportion of the voters participated in an election in the Fifth Republic. Perhaps having gone through two rounds of Presidential voting only a few weeks earlier, the French were tired of voting. Perhaps they assumed that the Socialist tide that had carried Mitterrand to the presidency would continue to flow, with the results a foregone conclusion. If that was their guess they were making it without the help of last-minute opinion polls. Since 1977 French law prohibits publishing, distributing, or commenting upon the results of opinion polls within one week of an election.

Senatorial Elections

For administrative purposes France is divided into 96 departments. Each department is entitled to one senator, and those with a population of more than 154,000 receive additional ones for every 250,000 people or fraction thereof more.

Senators are elected indirectly by an electoral college. This college, which meets to cast its votes, is composed of all the department's members in the National Assembly, the members of the departmental legislative body, and representatives from local government (the number depending upon the size of the town). The total number of people in all the electoral colleges is about 110,000. Considerably fewer than this participate in any given senatorial election, however. The French Senate, like the U.S. Senate, is a continuing body, that is, only a third of its seats come up for election at any one time. In France, however, senators have nine-year terms, so the process of replenishing the Senate takes longer than in the United States.

Senatorial candidates must be French citizens who are at least 35 years old. In departments having fewer than five senators, the electoral college uses the double ballot system—absolute majority on the first ballot and relative majority on the second. Where there are five or more, PR is used. Votes are cast for one or another of a slate of candidates. Each slate is given a number of seats comparable to its share of the vote.

A sizable proportion of those eligible to vote for senators comes from small towns or rural communities. That, along with the prolonged renewal of membership and age requirement, has tended to make the Senate more conservative than the National Assembly.

---

[2]See Penniman, *French National Assembly Elections,* pp. 221–27, for examples of ballots.

Presidential Elections

Originally in the Fifth Republic the president was chosen by an electoral college very similar in composition to the one that continues to elect senators. As we explained in Chapter 10, in 1962 the constitution was unconstitutionally amended to provide for direct election of president. De Gaulle insisted on this change in part because of attempts on his life. He felt that while he had sufficient personal magnetism to make the office a strong one, no one else did. Thus, were he to be assassinated, his successor would have great difficulty in preventing a return to the tradition of weak executives of the Third and Fourth Republics. A president who had won the direct support of a majority of the electorate might, however, be in a sufficiently strong position to be able to resist the encroachments of the legislature. This is to say that while De Gaulle felt no need of a popular mandate to legitimate his rule, he believed that the mere mortals who would come after him would need this to be effective.

Presidential elections are supposed to occur every seven years. This has not always happened because France lacks the office of vice president. If the president is incapacitated temporarily, the president of the Senate acts as president of France. If the president dies, resigns, or is incapacitated permanently, the president of the Senate also acts as president of France, except that a new election must be held within 50 days. While acting as president of France, the president of the Senate can utilize the normal presidential powers except that he or she is not permitted to call a referendum.

French citizens who are at least 23 years old may be nominated as a candidate for president. In a futile effort to reduce the number of candidates, the nomination procedures were tightened in 1981 to require the signatures of at least 500 sponsors for nomination. Only members of the National Assembly, Senate, or departmental legislatures or mayors of towns could serve as sponsors. Furthermore, the sponsors had to come from at least 30 different departments. Finally, nomination forms were mailed to potential sponsors only a month before the deadline for returning them. As in the past each candidate was required to deposit about $1,100, which would be forfeited by failing to receive at least 5 percent of the vote cast.

After the closing of nominations, the names of the candidates are announced, and the formal campaign period of only two weeks begins. Each candidate receives two hours of television time and two hours of radio time free of charge. Although this time is supposed to be used by the candidate personally, he or she is permitted to share it with designated supporters. Official billboard sites are allocated to the candidates by the government, and one circular is distributed to each voter free of charge. In addition, each candidate polling at least 5 percent of the vote is given about $27,000 to help pay campaign expenses.

If one candidate receives a majority of the votes cast, he or she is elected. If not, a second election is held. The procedure differs from National Assembly elections, however, because the first and second ballots for president are separated by two weeks, instead of one, and only two candidates are permitted on the second ballot for president. Normally this would be the two leaders on the first ballot, although either may withdraw, to be replaced by the next highest candidate.

In the two weeks between the first and second ballot, both candidates again are given two hours of radio and two hours of television time. Since on the second ballot there are only two candidates, someone will be elected with a majority. All French citizens who are 18 may vote in presidential elections.

The first presidential election under the amended popular system occurred in 1965, when de Gaulle's first term expired. This was the first direct election of a French president since 1848 and turnout was high—85 percent. To everyone's surprise, de Gaulle was not reelected on the first ballot. He received only 44 percent of the vote, with his main challenger being Mitterrand with 32 percent. On the second ballot de Gaulle defeated Mitterrand, 55 percent to 45.

The resignation of de Gaulle in 1969 forced an early election. Georges Pompidou, who had served de Gaulle as prime minister for some years before falling into his disfavor, did as well as de Gaulle had done with 44 percent of the vote, although turnout declined to 78 percent. Mitterrand chose not to run and so the main challenger turned out to be Alain Poher, a little known senator, who had won prominence suddenly by being president of the Senate when de Gaulle resigned—thus he had become acting president of France. On the second ballot Pompidou won with 58 percent of the vote.

Five years later Pompidou died and Poher again became acting president. He did not run again, but 12 other candidates were nominated. Mitterrand, back in the fray, was first with 43 percent, followed by Valéry Giscard d'Estaing with almost 33 percent. Giscard had been minister of finance and economic affairs under de Gaulle and Pompidou. A surprisingly distant third—due largely to factionalism within the movement—was the Gaullist candidate, former Prime Minister Jacques Chaban-Delmas, with 15 percent. Giscard managed to pick up enough of the Gaullist vote plus some from minor candidates to nose out Mitterrand on the second ballot with 50.8 percent of the vote. The turnout rate—88 percent—was the highest ever recorded.

The 1981 election provided a rematch—Mitterrand (labeled by one reporter the most experienced loser in France) against President Giscard. Giscard led on the first ballot with 28 percent compared to Mitterrand's 26 percent. Compared to the 1974 election, Mitterrand would appear to have lost considerable support. In 1974, however, the Communists had not run a candidate of their own but had supported Mitterrand. In 1981 a separate Communist candidate polled 15 percent of the vote. Since most of these of votes would go to Mitterrand on the second ballot along with those from minor left-wing candidates the result obviously would be close again.

Giscard had lost much of the freshness that had made him an attractive candidate seven years earlier. He had become increasingly aloof and seemed to take on monarchical airs, such as making a point of having himself served first at state dinners as the Bourbon monarchs had done. His image had been tarnished by accepting a gift of diamonds from an African head of state. Giscard eventually claimed to have sold them and given the money to charity, but this seemed to have been done only after public opinion objected to his keeping them. Finally, the Government's economic austerity measures designed to cope with inflation were unpopular.

Mitterrand won the second ballot with 52 percent of the vote; turnout declined only slightly compared with the second ballot in 1974 to 86 percent. Even the first ballot turnout for the presidential elections—81 percent—was considerably better than the 71 percent participation in the first ballot of the legislative elections less than two months later. Thus the 1981 elections in France continued the past pattern of greater participation in presidential elections, especially on the decisive second ballot. The contest between two nationally known figures seems to stir more interest than does a series of contests between a number of less prominent candidates.

Mitterrand's prolonged, but steady, progress to the presidency is revealed in Figure 11-1. On his first try in 1965, he led de Gaulle in only 24 departments. De Gaulle, in addition to strength among the middle and upper classes, had sizable support among the working class. Thus all of Mitterrand's 24 departments were in the southern half of France and, while they did include the area around Marseilles, his support tended to come from the economically less-modern sections of the country.

Then in 1981 Mitterrand expanded again. He continued to be ahead in every one of the 44 departments (except for Var on the Mediterranean) where he had been in 1974, and he added another 22 departments, thus leading Giscard on the second ballot of 65 of the 96 departments. The new gains were mainly in areas either of Gaullist strength or where no party in the past had had a decisive lead. Those areas in the north that resisted Mitterrand even in 1981 were concentrated primarily in the east and west. These sections have a strong Catholic tradition and long have been on the right of the political spectrum. As for the south, the main area that Mitterrand failed to get is an area with personal associations with Giscard.

Another element entered into the growing support for Mitterrand. In 1981 a fifth of the electorate were young people voting in their first presidential election. All polls showed them to be overwhelmingly on the left. Thus with the aura of reform and freshness gone from Giscard, Mitterrand was able to gain considerable support from the young, even though at 64 he was 10 years older than Giscard.

THE ROLE OF INTEREST GROUPS

French political philosophy, influenced by Rousseau's concept of the general will, regards interest groups as intruders in the relation between the citizen and the government. In practice, of course, interest groups have been as active in the

FIGURE 11–1   Support for Mitterrand in Presidential Elections

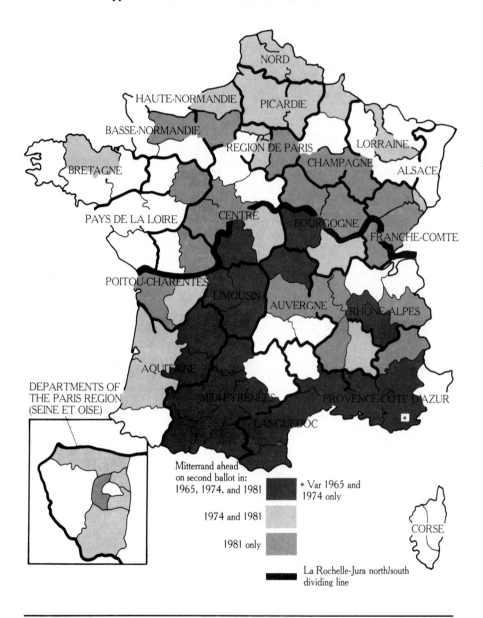

DEPARTMENTS OF
THE PARIS REGION
(SEINE ET OISE)

Mitterrand ahead
on second ballot in:
1965, 1974, and 1981

1974 and 1981

1981 only

* Var 1965 and
1974 only

La Rochelle-Jura north/south
dividing line

CORSE

political process in France as they have been in other democracies. The role of such groups was recognized formally in the constitution of the Fourth Republic by creating an economic council whose members were chosen by trade unions, business associations, and agricultural organizations. A similar institution, the Economic and Social Council, was established by the constitution of the Fifth Republic. The powers of both councils were advisory only. The CES has about 200 members, 70 percent of whom are nominated by organized interests and the rest by the government. Although the CES is little known to most French, it does provide an opportunity for interest groups to discover what the government is planning, how committed to the plans it is, and how other interest groups feel about this. Thus it formalizes consultative procedures even if it does not permit a great deal of influence.

Although not the central element in the relation, the CES is typical of "'neo-corporatism,' the complicated symbiosis between the state on the one hand, organized social groups on the other, which allows the state, as the dispenser of subsidies, favors and power, to orient these groups and to carry out policies which cannot be enforced by bureaucrats alone."[3] The benefits derived from neocorporatism involve serious costs.

On the one hand, for example, the leading farmers' organization "has had the means not only to *influence* policy through privileged access, but also to *implement* and even *formulate* policy at the sub-national level. Authority to administer many aspects of [the agricultural] modernization policy has been devolved to a network of co-management . . . institutions . . ., in most cases, dominated" by it.[4] But the result is that the organization's leaders seem to be working so closely with the government that the members of the group frequently feel that the leaders have sold out and are not defending group interests adequately. This tends to create disillusion with the whole democratic process.[5] Furthermore, those farmers who, for whatever reason, have chosen not to join the leading farmers' interest group tend to be denied any significant influence in the shaping of public policy. When Mitterrand's first minister of agriculture, Edith Cresson, attempted to reform this by including small, left-wing farmer organizations in the negotiating process, she enraged the large, conservative interest group that had monopolized this process. It egged the farmers on to protest demonstrations, which culminated in a mob chasing Cresson across a muddy pasture and having to be rescued by helicopter. Finally, the whole question of the nature of the relation between groups and the government has been complicated by the Fifth Republic's Gaullist view that "the state is the sole definer or diviner of the national interest."[6]

---

[3]Stanley Hoffmann, "The Fifth Republic at Twenty," in *The Impact of the Fifth Republic on France,* eds. William G. Andrews and Stanley Hoffmann (Albany: SUNY Press, 1981), pp. 286–87.

[4]John T. S. Keeler, "The Corporatist Dynamic of Agricultural Modernization in the Fifth Republic," in *Impact of the Fifth Republic,* Andrews and Hoffmann, p. 154. See the entire essay. pp. 139–59, for the other points made in these comments.

[5]Hoffmann, "The Fifth Republic at Twenty," p. 303.

[6]Ibid., p. 288.

The role of interest groups in the agricultural sphere may be a bit atypical. Leaders of farm interest groups tend to desire more than do other group leaders, not only to be consulted by the government but to have a role in implementing policy.[7] They also are more likely than other leaders to believe that a basic consensus exists between themselves and the government. This may simply be evidence of their success in dealing with the government during the past quarter of a century.

Generally, interest group leaders tend to be wary of possible government control and manipulation. Nonetheless, they feel that interaction with the government is essential. Their primary aims are to voice their members' views—regardless of whether this produces a response from the government—provide the government with information about the group's interests and situation that the government is likely to lack and gain information from the government, and help to influence policy. Despite the reports appearing occasionally in newspapers about protest activities of interest groups, few interest group leaders regard protest as an important activity for their group. Although the great majority of leaders do feel that their groups manage to influence governmental actions, they also complain that they frequently are listened to without being heard. They feel that group and government relations are too stiff, too rigid. They would like more real dialogue. Thus, although the role of interest groups in France has progressed farther toward neocorporatism than in the United States, the attitudes of interest group leaders correspond for the most part more closely to the pluralistic group role prevalent in the United States.

The influence of labor in France has been weakened because workers are divided (the less than 25 percent who do belong to a union) among several competing and frequently mutually hostile trade union federations. The largest, the CGT, is essentially the industrial or economic arm of the Communist party. Thus the CGT's influence upon policy has tended to be no greater than that of the PCF. While the other union federations also have political orientations, none of them are as closely related to a party as is the CGT. The second largest union, the CFDT, is socialist oriented without being linked directly to any party. Its main goal is to introduce *autogestion* into French industry. Under such a system the workers would elect the plant managers and draw up the production, sales, and investment plans for them to follow. Thus the workers would control industry and be, in effect, their own bosses. Although the Socialists indicated some sympathy with such steps in the 1981 elections, the labor legislation which they introduced after coming to power moved little in this direction. The CFDT, then, has not had appreciably more influence during the first quarter century of the Fifth Republic than has the CGT.

Of course, unions can influence the economy and thus the government by striking. The one-day general work stoppages that they have organized from

---

[7]This paragraph and the next are based on Frank L. Wilson, "French Interest Group Politics: Pluralist or Neocorporatist?" *American Political Science Review* 77 (December, 1983), pp. 895–910.

time to time have received considerable press coverage and make them appear quite strong. But this really is not a very effective weapon. Since such a small proportion of the labor force is unionized, unions tend to have limited funds. Thus prolonged strikes are unattractive. This has been even more true recently when unemployment has been higher than usual in France. If unions were to become less ideological and politically partisan, they probably would be able to increase their influence.

The fractionalization of the French party system has produced a number of small, narrowly based parties that are rather difficult to distinguish from interest groups. Perhaps the best example of such an organization was the Poujadists. This movement was organized in 1953 by Pierre Poujade to defend the interests of small, marginal businesses that were being injured by economic change as France sought to modernize the economy. The most dramatic of the Poujadists' activities were their clashes with tax officials. The Poujadists objected to these officials inspecting shopkeepers' books in order to assess their taxes; they wanted the government simply to accept the shopkeepers' word, which by long tradition greatly understates their amount of tax liability. So the Poujadists physically barred tax agents from shops and assaulted tax offices. (That was a real taxpayer's revolt.)

When the 1956 election was called, the Poujadists decided to expand their activities by running a number of candidates for Parliament. Despite their political inexperience and short existence, they managed to poll 2.5 million votes—12 percent of the total cast—and win 52 seats in Parliament. Rapidly changing economic and political conditions soon made the issue for which the Poujadists had organized less important and the group rapidly disappeared as a political force. Although it has had no importance during the Fifth Republic, it illustrates the difficulty of drawing a sharp distinction between pressure groups and political parties.

As we explained in Part One, agencies of the government themselves sometimes function as interest groups. The army has been a group of this type in France. The military's role in the fall of the Fourth Republic was a crucial one. The rationale used to justify this role seems capable of supporting a similar subverting of the Fifth Republic.

The army reasoned that since a modernized fighting force could not cope with a guerrilla force having strong indigenous ties, the only way to end conflict in Algeria was to exterminate the rebel organization by whatever means, however extreme, and replace it with a new political structure. Since the nation's political leaders did not seem to the army to grasp the necessity of this strategy, they had to be educated. At first, the army sought merely to ensure that its views were heard adequately. While the government conceded some of the action the army sought, it did not embrace fully a military solution. The army responded by arguing that while the civil and military authorities should work together, in a subversive war the army had to be the final judge of what policies were essential.

Soon the army went even further. Some army officers declared that the civil administration was swayed by partisan political considerations, thus so weakening the government's resolve to act effectively that the rebels would be encouraged to hold out until France capitulated. Only the army, which was above political influences, could act fully in the national interest. Thus the army, in effect, was seeking to *be* the government.

Although the army was instrumental in bringing de Gaulle back to power, he did not implement—to many people's surprise and the army's disillusionment—their ideas. When in 1959 de Gaulle proposed self-determination for Algeria, a number of French army officers (some active and some retired) and their sympathizers made several desperate bids to prevent Algerian independence. These involved forthright efforts to defeat referendums, open rebellion in Algeria (and the seizure of power there in some areas for a brief period), as well as the creation of the Secret Army Organization (OAS), whose aim was to overthrow de Gaulle. These actions, as well as the attempt to assassinate President de Gaulle, ended in failure.

Currently the army's activities are not so visible or dramatic. Nonetheless, it should be obvious that there remain in the military a number of officers who believe that their forces should play an active political role, especially when the regularly elected officials seem to be ineffective or misguided. France is not at present involved in any conflict like Algeria that seems to demonstrate military impotency. Futhermore, President Mitterrand has indicated his full acceptance of the French independent nuclear deterrent. Thus there would not appear to be any reason for the military to feel challenged or lacking in support by governmental leaders. Nonetheless, a small doubt lingers about the role the military might wish to play in a major crisis.

BIBLIOGRAPHICAL NOTE

For a fairly comprehensive, yet brief discussion of French electoral laws (and election results), Peter Campbell, *French Electoral System and Elections since 1789,* 2d ed. (London: Faber, 1965), is very useful. Philip Williams, *French Politicians and Elections 1951-1969* (Cambridge, Eng.: Cambridge University Press, 1970), discusses the campaign and the results of each of the early elections of the Fifth Republic. For coverage of more recent elections see Howard Penniman, ed., *France at the Polls: The Presidential Election of 1974* (Washington, D.C.: American Enterprise Institute, 1975), and the Penniman book cited in Footnote 1.

For a detailed discussion of the impact of Algeria on French politics, as well as of de Gaulle's various maneuvers to keep the army in line, see Roy C. Marcridis and Bernard E. Brown, *The De Gaulle Republic: Quest for Unity* (Homewood, Ill.: Dorsey Press, 1960), as well as their *Supplement to the De Gaulle Republic* (1963). Also see William G. Andrews, *French Politics and Algeria: The Process of Policy Formation, 1954-1962* (New York: Appleton-Century-Crofts, 1962). Two works concerned with the role of the army in French politics are John Ambler, *Soldiers Against the State* (Garden City, N.Y.: Doubleday Publishing, 1968), and George Kelly, *Lost Soldiers* (Cambridge, Mass.: MIT Press, 1965).

Other works examining interest groups include: V. Lorwin, *The French Labor Movement* (Cambridge, Mass.: Harvard University Press, 1954); James M. Clark, *Teachers and Politics in France: A Pressure Group Study of the Federation de l'Education Nationale* (Syracuse, N.Y.: Syracuse University Press, 1967); and John Sheahan, *Promotion and Control of Industry in Post-War France* (Cambridge, Mass.: Harvard University Press, 1963). Three shorter studies of particular value are Bernard E. Brown, "Pressure Politics in France," *Journal of Politics* 18 (November 1956), pp. 702–19; "Alcohol and Politics in France," *American Political Science Review* 51 (December 1957), pp. 976–94; and "Pressure Politics in the Fifth Republic," *Journal of Politics* 25 (November 1963), pp. 509–25.

12

Policy Alternatives

A MULTIPARTY SYSTEM

Traditionally, European political parties have been much more ideologically oriented than have American and British parties. This is less true now in France than earlier in the century. Furthermore, the extent of emphasis on ideology varies considerably from one French party to another. Nonetheless, the lack of political consensus and the existence of sharp cleavages over basic issues such as the role of the Church have encouraged French parties to appeal to the electorate in a style more ideological than that of American parties.

The greater a party's emphasis on ideology, the narrower its appeal is likely to be. When a party merely stands for a particular mix of policy positions on short-range issues, people who like most of what it offers usually will be willing to accept some objectionable policy stands. But when the appeal is more doctrinal, support requires a greater degree of commitment, which is unlikely to be given unless the entire program is acceptable. The more ideological a party's appeal, the more it attempts to present an integrated series of doctrines relevant to many aspects of life, the more difficult it is to secure the agreement of a large number of people.

Add to this ideological approach the tendency of French pressure groups to convert themselves into parties, plus the existence of a fairly rigid class structure, and one begins to expect the French party system to be a multiparty one. This clearly has been the case (see Figure 12-1). Since World War II the combined share of the vote obtained by the two leading parties has ranged only from 40 to 60 percent. In past elections national parties sometimes have numbered

FIGURE 12–1   The Two Leading Parties' Percentage of the Vote in Legislative Elections in the Fourth and Fifth Republics

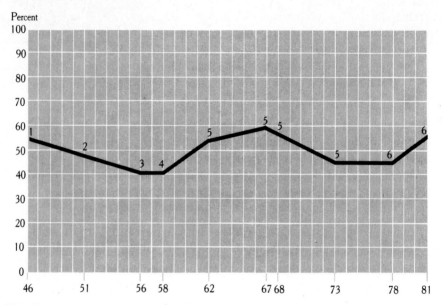

Year 19_____

Key:
1 = PCF and MRP.
2 = PCF and Gaullists.
3 = PCF and Socialists.
4 = Independents and Gaullists.
5 = Gaullists and PCF.
6 = Socialists and Gaullists.

between 10 to 20, in addition to a number of purely local or regional parties. For example, in 1978, 11 minor parties, in addition to the main ones already represented in the legislature, qualified for free radio and television time by running at least 75 candidates.

The number of parties and diverse political approaches in France is due in part, to an absence of consensus or a common understanding concerning the basis and form of government. When political parties formed in the United States and in Britain, the form of government in those two countries was not really in question. The differences that divided people into parties were primarily over the policies that government should follow. In France, on the other hand, political parties formed before agreement on the nature of the system of government. Differences over the question of how the state should be organized could not help but creep into party positions. Moreover, by the time the Third

Republic was organized and a certain consensus achieved (1875–85), parties organized along class lines had appeared (first the Socialists and, in this century, the Communists). In other words, just when Republicanism had become respectable, a new source of division had arisen to perpetuate the multiparty system.

French governmental practices helped to perpetuate these divisions and maintain a variety of parties. Under assembly government little Parliamentary discipline existed; deputies could do as they pleased politically and be secure for at least the full term of Parliament. The electoral system did not encourage any merger of political groups since it did not penalize a failure to concentrate electoral support as does the Anglo-American system. Furthermore, France, unlike the United States, had no single important national office—a powerful president—that could be obtained only by those fractionalized political forces willing to merge their efforts.

An obvious result of a multiplicity of parties is a fractionalization of the vote. The Gaullists far outstripped the success of any other political party since the end of World War II by gaining almost two fifths of the vote in 1968, only to decline considerably in subsequent elections. In 1981 the Socialists came close to duplicating the Gaullists' 1968 success. Even the most successful parties, then, have not begun to approach winning a majority of the vote.

The political composition of Parliament has reflected the fractionalization of partisan support with no single party usually being able to control a majority of the seats. The Gaullists managed to do this only from 1968 to 1973. This indicates why the Socialists' success in 1981 was so remarkable. Since such triumphs remain the exception, the process of coalition building in France differs considerably from that in the United States. In the United States diverse interests compete for influence within institutionalized parties prior to elections as two abroad, opposing coalitions are built up. In France this process occurs later in another arena; coalitions are constructed *in the legislature between* parties *after* the election.

The multiplicity of French parties is matched by their diversity in organization and politics. Politically, they range from parties that emphasize rigid adherence to principle, such as the Communist party, to parties that espouse no principle and are the personal followers of an individual. Organizationally, they vary from the tight discipline that the Communists and Socialists have imposed to the largely unorganized groups on the far right. Some Parliamentary groupings have little or no organization in the country other than a number of personal electoral machines.

Another characteristic of French parties is their fluidity. New parties skyrocket into prominence, bursting on the political scene in a dazzling display of pyrotechnics only to shimmer rapidly out of sight, leaving not a trace. Usually these parties do not embody significant shifts in political opinions and tendencies. Studies of French voting behavior indicate considerable stability over time, with political tendencies passed on from one generation to the next. Primarily what changes are the party labels. It's rather like an advertising campaign for a "new and improved" soap—the contents of the box hardly differ from what they used to be, but the box itself looks different.

The French constitution says that "political parties and groups may compete for votes. They may form and carry on their activities freely. They must respect the principles of national sovereignty and of democracy." The last sentence provides a justification for possible action against antidemocratic parties. In 1959 the Govenment dissolved the small Nationalist party, an extreme right-wing group formed with the avowed aim of opposing the democratic political system. The Government also has banned about 150 newspapers at both ends of the political spectrum. While no action has been taken directly against the Communist party and its publications, some protest meetings scheduled by Communists or their sympathizers have been banned, as have some similar meetings by right-wing groups.

THE LEADING PARTISAN GROUPINGS

By the latter part of the 1970s four principal political forces had emerged in the French Parliament—the Communists, the Socialists, the Giscardiens, and the Gaullists. In the 1978 election each of these four was able to gain a little more than a fifth of the vote. The remaining one fifth was fractionalized among a number of minor political groups. The 1981 elections shifted the balance of strength among the four main groups, but did not destroy any of them. In discussing French parties we will concentrate primarily on these four groups, moving across the political spectrum from left to right.

Doctrines and Policies

The French Communist Party (PCF) clings closely to basic Marxist doctrine. The nature of this ideology is examined fully in Part Six on the Soviet Union, and thus is not elaborated here. Suffice it to say that the PCF has been perhaps the most hard-line Communist party operating in a democratic, Western political system. This does not mean that it is a highly subversive, revolutionary force. The student and worker street demonstrations in 1968, for example, were organized almost totally apart from the Communist party, which became involved only at a relatively late date and after considerable doubt and hesitation. The point rather is that the PCF has been extremely dogmatic in its policies and rigid in its rhetoric. Furthermore, the PCF has been the Western party most loyal to Moscow.

Toward the close of the 1960s, however, the party appeared to alter its stance. Many French Communists criticized the Russian invasion of Czechoslovakia in 1968, and in 1972 the PCF formally condemned the political trials of the deposed Czech leaders. Even more surprising, a few years later the PCF criticized the Soviet Union for its treatment of dissident Russians—imagine, telling the vanguard of the proletariat that it was wrong in its internal affairs.

Bad feelings between the Soviet Union and the PCF deteriorated into a childish game of tit-for-tat. In 1974 the PCF joined with the Socialists to support Mitterrand for president. During the course of the campaign the Soviet ambassador to France, Tchervonenko, called on the conservative candidate, Giscard, but had no time to see Mitterrand. The Communists felt that the Soviet Union deliberately had undercut them. Since then Georges Marchais, the leader of the French Communists, has refused to see Tchervonenko. When Kirilenko of the Soviet Politburo attended the French Communist party congress in 1976, he was not allowed to speak. Furthermore, Marchais refused to attend the meeting of the Soviet Communist party in Moscow in February 1976, thus breaking with past custom. When Leonid Brezhnev paid a state visit to France in June 1977, he talked with several political leaders but not with Marchais. Just who was avoiding whom is not clear.

These events in the PCF were part of a larger European development referred to as Eurocommunism. The basic idea of Eurocommunism was that communism was not a monolithic international movement directed from Moscow. Communist parties would interpret Marx's ideas in the context of the political situation in their respective countries. The most important implication of this approach was that in Western democracies communists would accept the democratic process and not attempt to install a dictatorship.

As evidence of their commitment to democracy the PCF in 1975 issued a detailed Declaration of Freedoms. Although in earlier days the PCF had talked about establishing a dictatorship of the proletariat, by the late 1960s they largely had abandoned such rhetoric. Then in January 1976 Georges Marchais announced that the party officially would drop the phrase. This step was approved by the party Congress that met the following month. The Congress also specifically acknowledged that the electorate should remain free to vote the Communists out of office, should they attain power.

In 1972 the PCF reached agreement with the Socialists on a Common Program of broad economic and social reform. This program was the basis for both parties' campaign in the legislative elections of 1973. In anticipation of the next legislative elections in 1978, the parties began in 1977 to prepare an updated version of the program. The PCF took an extremely hard line in these negotiations, demanding much more extensive government ownership of business. The negotiations collapsed and the PCF offered a separate program of its own in both the 1978 and 1981 legislative elections.

The break over renewal of the Common Program seemed to signal a shift in the PCF back to its dogmatic loyalism to Moscow. Unlike the Italian Communists, who condemned the Soviet Union's invasion of Afghanistan in 1979, the PCF not only refused to do so, but its leader, Marchais, defended the Russian action. Thus the party's apparent moderation and independence of the Soviet Union during the 1970s seems to have been an aberration. Like relaxing in a pair of old, worn-out slippers, it has returned to its old doctrinaire stance. In domestic affairs: virtually total government control of the economy, a reduction or elimination of profits, and confiscatory taxing of the rich to provide benefits for the workers. In foreign affairs: loyal support of the Soviet Union combined with strong anti-American and anti-German views and condemnation of NATO.

Despite (according to them, precisely because of) the PCF's opposition to NATO, it regards France's nuclear weapons as a vital, nonnegotiable element essential to the country's security and independence. (In France virtually everyone is a Gaullist on nuclear weapons and the PCF is no exception.) This stance poses a bit of a problem for the PCF's relations with the Soviet Union, which professes to believe that French weapons are a threat to it and which long has insisted that negotiations to reduce the number of nuclear weapons must include the British and French weapons and not just the American and Russian ones.

The French Socialists' rhetoric has been farther to the left than that of either the German socialists or the British Labour party. The mainstream of the French Socialists party (PS) has more in common with the left wing of either of those parties than it does with their mainstreams. The party has been more willing to talk to class struggle and even revolution. The PS has said that it aims to replace capitalism, not transform it. In 1972 the PS and the PCF agreed upon a Common Program that included a pledge to take into government ownership banking, insurance and credit, and nine of France's largest private companies. The PS also advocated *autogestion*—management of industry by the workers themselves. In noneconomic matters the PS wanted to redress the balance of power between the legislature and the executive and favored eventual elimination of the Catholic schools.

The extent to which these views are something more than rhetoric is ambiguous. On the basis of the record over the past third of a century the French Socialists are more social democratic than Marxist. The PS accepts the mixed economy and has been concerned mainly to ensure that sufficient welfare programs are available along with some redistribution of wealth to aid the lower middle class and the workers. As we noted above, the PS refused to agree to the PCF's demand to extend the government-ownership commitments in the Common Program to include a much greater number of companies.

Part of the uncertainty about the PS's position is because the party is divided into three or four factions, known as "currents." In 1980 François Mitterrand led a center group supported by somewhat less than half the party's members. About a fifth followed Michel Rocard, considered to be on the right of the party and having views that can be labeled social democratic. Rocard wished to be the PS candidate in the 1981 presidential election, an ambition for which Mitterrand—who intended to be the candidate himself—never has forgiven him. Rocard had some support from Pierre Mauroy, who led a current of about a sixth of the party. To fend off Rocard's challenge, Mitterrand sought the support of the Ceres current. This left-wing faction, organized around the Center for Socialist Studies, Research, and Education, had a good deal in common with the PCF on economic policy. Only with the help of Ceres was Mitterrand able to maintain control of the PS.

While Mitterrand and the PS are not synonymous, yet as the founder of the party in its present form and its foremost leader, his policies to a considerable extent are the PS's policies. Among his first actions after becoming president of France were to require another week's paid vacation for workers, to increase pensions for retirees, to raise the family allowances paid to those having children, and to begin reducing the standard work week to an eventual 35 hours. A new tax was imposed on those with great wealth, the death penalty was abolished—yes, France still was using the guillotine until then—and laws discriminating against homosexuals were reformed. Perhaps most dramatic was the extension of nationalization. Almost all private banks, steel producers, a major armaments firm, and several French multinational corporations were taken into government ownership. In an effort to end the recession and reduce unemployment, Mitterrand's government increased public spending by about 25 percent even though this produced an unprecedented deficit.

This attempt to reflate the economy produced serious problems. While the rate of inflation was declining in the rest of the EEC, it continued to grow in France. And the large deficit in France's international trade forced the franc to be devalued three times. Thus after only about a year in office Mitterrand had to reverse policy to austerity measures—*riqueur* in French. These measures included a four-month freeze on wages and prices, despite strong dissent from the trade unions.

The Mitterrand Government's swing to the right produced a good deal of rumblings within the PS, especially from Ceres. Ceres preferred a package of reflation and strong growth based on devaluation of the franc and protection of industry from foreign competition along with greater governmental intervention in the economy.

As for foreign policy, the PS at its 1983 congress used the slogan "Keeping the balance to preserve the peace." According to Mauroy, this meant that every time the United States has threatened the balance of power, such as in Chile, Nicaragua, and Grenada, France has said no. And the Congress deleted from a policy statement a point that said France should feel closer to the United States than to the Soviet Union. But here, as in other matters, Socialist policy in practice will tend to be more moderate than in word, certainly as long as Mitterrand is in charge.

In his pursuit of the presidency and eventual service in that office, Valéry Giscard d'Estaing developed a political base that came to be referred to as the Giscardiens. Recently in elections and in the National Assembly they have used the label Union for French Democracy (UDF). Not only is the UDF, unlike the PCF and the PS, a grouping around an individual rather than around a doctrine, it is not a single party, either, but an alliance. The largest party within the UDF is the Republican party (PR). The PR is a descendant of an economically right-wing party of the Fourth and early Fifth Republics, known by various names, but usually Independents or Independent Republicans. The Independents opposed state interference in economic affairs except for subsidies to farmers and protective tariffs for business. The party also supported the Church and government aid to Catholic schools.

In the 1960s the party split with the relatively more liberal but also pro-Gaullist faction following Giscard d'Estaing. Giscard established this faction as the Republican party. Although generally willing to support Gaullist Governments, the PR sought to maintain its separate identity. Giscard used the well-known phrase "yes, but . . ." to indicate the qualified nature of his party's commitment to Government policy.

The alternative to Gaullism that the PR offered to voters on the right of the spectrum lay in two main areas. The PR was much more in favor of European unity that were the Gaullists, and it wanted to strengthen Parliament so that it would not be completely subservient to the executive. Giscard himself strongly emphasized liberal reform; this included a greater concern for civil liberties and for social policies like easier divorce and abortion.

As with Mitterrand and the Socialists, however, Giscard and the PR were not synonymous. Even though the PR had left many of its most conservative adherents behind when the Independents split in 1962, still many in the PR were not as liberal as Giscard. Furthermore, Giscard himself seemed to become less liberal during the latter half of his presidency. Granted that the UDF, to say nothing of the PR itself, was nowhere near to a majority in the National Assembly, yet Giscard did not try very hard to strengthen Parliament and the bias of government-owned broadcasting and government tapping of telephones continued under him largely as they had before.

Following his defeat for reelection in 1981, President Giscard went into mourning for a time. This enabled Raymond Barre, who had been his prime minister, to emerge as a possible candidate for president in 1988. Although Barre had been elected to the National Assembly under the UDF label, he is not associated closely with any political party. Barre wants to return to private ownership the businesses nationalized by Mitterrand, favors cuts in government spending, and stresses law and order. Differences between him and Giscard are more personal than substantive.

Nonetheless, following Giscard's active return to politics with a victory in a partial election for the National Assembly in 1984, a difference of some importance emerged. Giscard indicated that should the right win the 1986 Parliamentary elections, it should try to cooperate with President Mitterrand. Barre, apparently reversing what had been his stand, said that this would be contrary to the spirit of the constitution and that in such circumstances Mitterrand should resign. Thus Giscard seemed to be seeking the support of the more centrist segments of the UDF, while Barre was appealing more to those on the group's right.

The other major element within the UDF is the Center of Social Democrats (CDS). Contrary to what the name would seem to suggest, the party has nothing to do with socialism and rather is what in other European countries would be called Christian democrat. Christian democracy emerged as a major political force in Europe following World War II. The idea was to bring religious values to bear upon the revitalization of the continent and prevent authoritarianism from becoming dominant again. Religious parties, primarily Catholic ones, had existed prior to then, but they usually had been conservative ones opposed to social and economic reform. The new Christian democrats were reformists. Although anti-Marxist and opposed to class war, they also criticized capitalism. While these parties usually were Catholic, they were independent of the Church and included Protestants among their supporters.

Given the tradition of anticlericalism in France, the French version of this political development did not dare to call itself Christian democrat, selecting instead the label Popular Republican Movement (MRP). The MRP made a tremendous impact at the start of the Fourth Republic. In one of the 1946 elections it polled almost 30 percent of the vote, more than any other party including the Communists. In part this was because the MRP was widely thought to be de Gaulle's favorite, since no Gaullist party then existed. The formation of a Guallist party in the late 1940s hurt the MRP considerably; for the remainder of Fourth Republic it obtained less than half as much support as it initially had, eventually dropping to little more than one tenth of the vote.

A major emphasis of MRP policy was support for European unity. Eventually, the party split between those willing to support de Gaulle despite his stress on French nationalism and those who felt he was too anti-European unity. The MRP was formally dissolved in 1968 with the pro-Europe remnant establishing the Democratic Center (CD) in its stead. The CD split on whom to support for the 1969 presidential election. Since both factions found Giscard acceptable in the 1974 election, they managed to reunite in 1976 to form the CDS.

The CDS remains the most pro-Europe of any French political party. They are more actively in favor of social reform, except in such areas as divorce and abortion, than are the bulk of the Republicans. Despite their support for Giscard in 1974, the CDS threatened not to attend a national meeting of the UDF in November 1982 if Giscard were to be imposed as leader upon the alliance. In the event the CDS did attend and, there being no challenge, Giscard was acclaimed as UDF leader. Within the UDF group in the National Assembly, the CDS is led by Jean Lecanuet.

The Gaullist movement has changed its name many times since the end of World War II. The current name—the Rally for the Republic (RPR)—was adopted in 1976 when Jacques Chirac reorganized the movement. The Gaullists have stood more for loyalty to a person than for particular policies. Although they agreed on the need for de Gaulle's leadership, they were divided on exactly what role he should play. Furthermore, while they believed that France needed a national renewal, they were vague regarding what specific goals this involved and divided on the means of achieving them. They were, however, clearly opposed to the existing political system and desired reform of the constitution to provide for stronger executive leadership.

The Gaullists never have called themselves a political party, claiming instead to be a movement of the people. In this the group reflects de Gaulle's enduring contempt for the political parties that, by squabbling among themselves, in his view, so weakened France that it collapsed under German attack. The fact that the Gaullists typically have called themselves a union or a rally is not just a matter of semantics, but of basic political attitude.

Perhaps the Gaullists are best characterized as nationalistic rather than conservative. Traditionally, these two positions have been distinct in France. Nationalists frequently have been willing for a strong executive to act to improve workers' living standards. This has been seen as a means of cementing together the various classes of the nation and thus strengthening it. The Conservative party in Britain has a similar tradition stretching back to Disraeli in the latter part of the 19th century. Thus, the Gaullists have supported some economic and social reform, such as government support for housing and social services. Unlike right-of-center parties in most democracies, they have not opposed governmental economic intervention, but have seen this as necessary at times to ensure that the nation has the strength required to carry influence internationally. For Gaullists international independence has meant the French nuclear striking force and suspicion of the Common Market and NATO as possible infringements on French sovereignty. Finally, only a strong executive and a weak legislature can ensure the decisive action and consistent policy necessary for France to have a major role in international affairs. Thus the Gaullists oppose any change in the existing political system.

In the jockeying for the 1988 presidential election Chirac has been moving to the right. Reversing his earlier position, he has come out against free abortions—that is, the present practice of paying for such procedures under government-financed medical benefits. His reason for doing so is even more right-wing—color prejudice. He argues that easily available abortions result in a falling population, which soon will make stemming the flow of immigrants from North Africa to France impossible. While this is a new position for him, the popularity of such views among the French working class and the supposed implications for French national strength suggest that such a position is rather in keeping with the Gaullists' basic political tradition.

Party Appeals and Supporters

A number of factors help to explain Communist strength in France. There is a tradition of voting for the revolutionary left in France, partly because the left was the historical defender of republican institutions, and partly because it was the antirepublican forces that brutally suppressed the workers' uprisings in 1848 and 1871. The Communist party inherited the leftist position and thereby became the beneficiary of the leftist voting tradition. In addition, the Communists usually have received a good share of any protest vote cast by those discontented with various social and economic conditions. Such voters for the Communists are not necessarily convinced that the party would solve the problems; they simply wish to vote for the most vocal opponent of the system to show how dissatisfied they are.

The PCF devotes a great deal of time and effort to its organizational and pro-paganda drives. It sponsors youth groups and discussion and protest meetings, and puts out numerous publications. Despite being out of the Government from 1947 to 1981, the PCF has been able to demonstrate that it is a party of action and not just of words. It has organized cooperatives to sell goods cheaply to members and has provided poor tenants with legal aid against landlords. Furthermore, its extensive organization permits it to offer posts of responsibility and power to a number of people. Thus it can provide those whose social origins might otherwise deny it to them an opportunity to gain a sense of personal accomplishment.

You need to understand that the French are not as fearful of communism as are Americans. A 1978 poll asked people in France whether having Communists in the Government would be a good or bad thing for five different areas such as freedom and stability of the Government. Although in each case more people thought Communists in the Government would be bad than thought it would be good, yet the proportion thinking it would be good ranged from 28 to 34 percent and 21 to 27 percent had no opinion. [1]

A major element in the PCF's strength is its control of a large part of the trade union movement. It has convinced many workers that the Communist party is *the* working-class party. These workers are not really interested in the Soviet Union; they are disturbed by the real or fancied injustices of French society. By controlling major unions the Communist party has been able to mobilize workers to vote, to contribute to the party treasury, and to participate in Communists-organized demonstrations. Well over a third of the manual workers vote Communist as do about a fifth of the white-collar workers. [2]

The Communists are more successful than any other party in appealing to the younger voters. More than a quarter of those under 35 vote Communist.

Analyzing support for parties according to its geographical distribution is a well-established scholarly tradition in France. As a couple of practitioners of this approach have said, "In France voting patterns are truly as much the result of geographically entrenched political tradition as the result of social conditions . . . electoral geography brings us back to a consideration of history and to the political traditions which are passed on within given regions from generation to generation . . . only electoral geography allows us to estimate the importance of the unconscious feelings of fellowship which condition voting in both space and time." [3]

---

[1] Jérôme Jaffré, "The French Electorate in March 1978," in *The French National Assembly Elections of 1978,* ed. Howard Penniman (Washington, D.C.: American Enterprise Institute, 1980), p. 75.

[2] For these figures on support of various groups for PCF and similar figures elsewhere in this section, see Jaffré, "The French Electorate," pp. 69–71.

[3] Marie-Thérèse Lancelot and Alain Lancelot, "A Cartographic Approach to the Presidential Election, May 1974," in *France at the Polls,* ed. Howard Penniman (Washington, D.C.: American Enterprise Institute, 1975), pp. 154, 155. See also Jaffré, "The French Electorate," pp. 64–68.

A word of caution, however, about interpretation. Since population and geographical size do not go hand-in-hand, maps of party strengths make a party with support in rural areas appear to be stronger than it actually is.[4] In France, for example, more than a quarter of all the seats in the National Assembly are concentrated in the Paris region and the two departments immediately north of it—Picardie and Nord.

The Communists are particularly strong around Paris (but not in Paris itself) and in France's northern industrial areas, as you can see from Figure 12-2. The party has another band of strength along the Mediterranean coast from Italy to Spain, which includes Marseilles. Finally in central France, in the largely rural areas to the north and west of the Central Massif, the party does well. Support in this area comes in part from poor farmers and farm workers, but it also is based on a tradition of leftism in some rural areas.

Although the Communist party lost considerable ground in the 1981 elections, the areas where it did best in 1981 were almost exactly the same as those of its greatest strength in 1978. Were there room to present additional maps showing Communist strength back into the Fourth Republic, you would see that the pattern would change little. Whatever the flux and instability of some aspects of French government and politics, some things have altered little over time.

Historically, the Socialists were the party of the workers. But once the Communists broke away after World War I to form a separate party, the Socialists gradually lost ground among the working class to them. Since the Socialists were in power part of the time during the Fourth Republic, they were unable to compete effectively with the Communists for the vote of disaffected workers.

In terms of members, the Socialists clearly are a middle-class party, with only about a seventh of its members being manual workers. Nor has the party been able to do as well as the Communists in getting the votes of this class—only about a quarter of them. On the other hand, the Socialists gain electoral support from about a third of the white-collar workers—nearly half again as many as the Communists get. Furthermore, the Socialists do slightly better than the Communists among the poorest French households.

Unlike the other main parties, support for the Socialists is not affected by age or sex. Equal proportions of men and women support the Socialists as do different age categories.

Support for the Socialists had been concentrated in the north and along the southern coast, with the party especially weak in and around Paris. In 1978, however, the PS managed to make some inroads into conservative, Catholic areas and obtained a somewhat regionally, less-concentrated pattern of support. The party's 1981 triumph was a national victory as Figure 12-3 indicates. Those areas not swept up in the Socialist tide were largely isolated spots scattered throughout the country, and even here the Socialists hardly could be said to be weak.

---

[4] Lancelot and Lancelot, "A Cartographic Approach," p. 140.

FIGURE 12–2   Communist Strength in Recent Elections

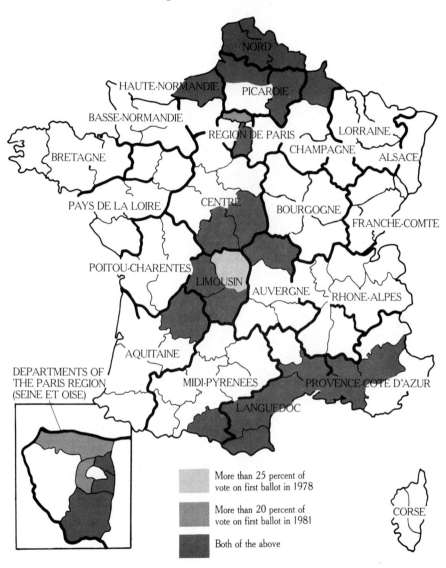

The Giscardiens' support is fairly diverse, since each party in the alliance has its own clientele. Supporters of the Republicans have included both the wealthy and the lower middle class. Industrialists and businesspeople (including shopkeepers) along with bankers and managers have joined with farmers and some civil servants to back the party. The CDS appeals primarily to the lower middle

FIGURE 12–3 Socialist Strength in Recent Elections

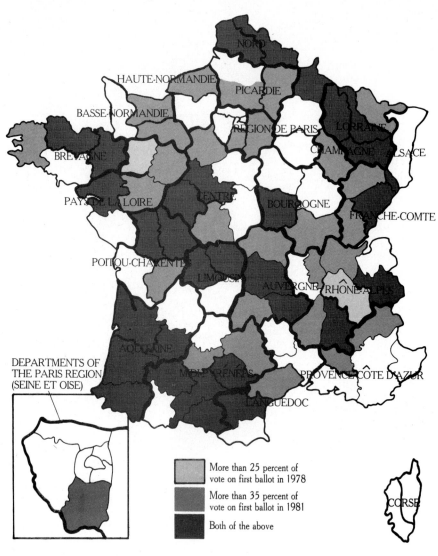

DEPARTMENTS OF
THE PARIS REGION
(SEINE ET OISE)

More than 25 percent of
vote on first ballot in 1978

More than 35 percent of
vote on first ballot in 1981

Both of the above

class—salaried workers, civil servants, and middle-level professionals. The party
also has some limited support among industrial workers, in part attributable to
Catholic trade union organization efforts.

Figure 12–4 indicates how the Socialist landslide in 1981 cut into the Giscardiens' strength. The pattern also is affected by the agreements between the Giscardiens and the RPR not to oppose each other in most constituencies on the

FIGURE 12–4 Giscardiens' Strength in Recent Elections

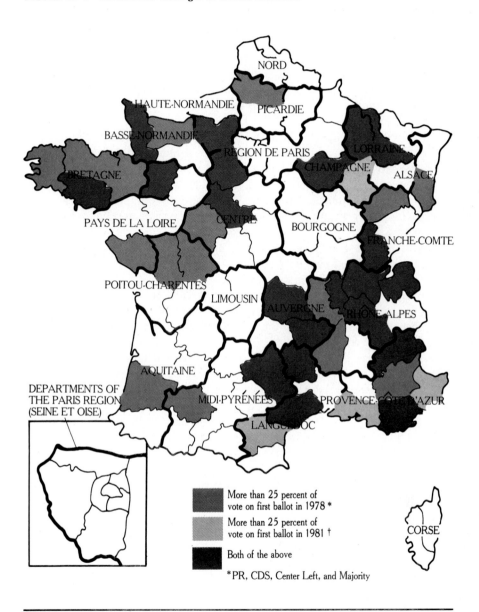

NORD

HAUTE-NORMANDIE   PICARDIE

BASSE-NORMANDIE

RÉGION DE PARIS   LORRAINE

CHAMPAGNE   ALSACE

BRETAGNE

PAYS DE LA LOIRE   CENTRE   BOURGOGNE

FRANCHE-COMTE

POITOU-CHARENTES   LIMOUSIN   AUVERGNE   RHÔNE-ALPES

AQUITAINE

DEPARTMENTS OF
THE PARIS REGION
(SEINE ET OISE)   MIDI-PYRÉNÉES   PROVENCE-CÔTE D'AZUR

LANGUEDOC

More than 25 percent of
vote on first ballot in 1978 *

More than 25 percent of
vote on first ballot in 1981 †   CORSE

Both of the above

*PR, CDS, Center Left, and Majority

first ballot in 1981. Although naturally a party would not agree not to offer a candidate where it was particularly strong, yet the agreements meant that in many constituencies a Giscardien did not stand and this makes identifying a geographical pattern of strength more difficult.

Nonetheless, you can note some strength for the Giscardiens in the strongly Catholic east and west. Other strength appears east of the Central Massif, an area, as we noted in the previous chapter, having personal associations with Giscard. Also notable is the absence of strength in the north and around Paris—the urban, industrial areas.

The Gaullists appealed to all those who were dissatisfied with the Fourth Republic for whatever reason. They also gained the support of apolitical voters for whom stability and prosperity were uppermost. While de Gaulle remained on the scene the party's support was well distributed—nationally, in the sense of having few geographical weaknesses, and socially, in having reasonable strength in all classes and groups. Furthermore, the party appealed to the young as well as the old.

All this is considerably less true of the RPR. The party's support is concentrated among business people (whether managers or shopkeepers), professionals, and farmers. The RPR is stronger among the latter occupation than is any other party. Only about a seventh of the manual workers vote for the party and support among white-collar workers is little better.

The geographical reflection of this can be seen in Figure 12–5. Although retaining some strength in and near Paris (Chirac *is* the mayor of Paris, after all), the RPR lacks the strength which the Gaullists used to have in the industrial area north of Paris. Note that for the most part despite a slight decline in support in 1981, the RPR's areas of strength did not change a great deal. Compared with the earlier years of the Fifth Republic the party has been pushed back into the Catholic areas of the northeast and northwest along with the rural areas on the west of the Central Massif. This pattern is related to the fact that about a third of those who are more than just nominal Catholics indicate that they prefer the RPR.

While we do not intend to stereotype, we would note that some evidence suggests that on the whole religion is more important to women than to men. Thus the support that active Catholics give to the RPR may help to explain the imbalance in support between the sexes. The proportion of women favoring the party is about a fifth greater than the proportion of men—the Communist party tilts in almost exactly the opposite direction. Religion may explain the age imbalance as well, if we assume that younger people usually are not as fully involved in the Church as are their elders. Among those under 35 support for the RPR is only about two thirds as great as among those 36 or over.

Thus in the early years of the Fifth Republic the Gaullist movement became a national political force in a way that its predecessors in the Fourth Republic had not been. Now the movement is declining from that status, but in so doing it is not returning to what it had been. In the Fourth Republic the Gaullists were a movement of the industrial north; now they are shifting to becoming a party of conservative, rural France.

FIGURE 12–5   Gaullist Strength in Recent Elections

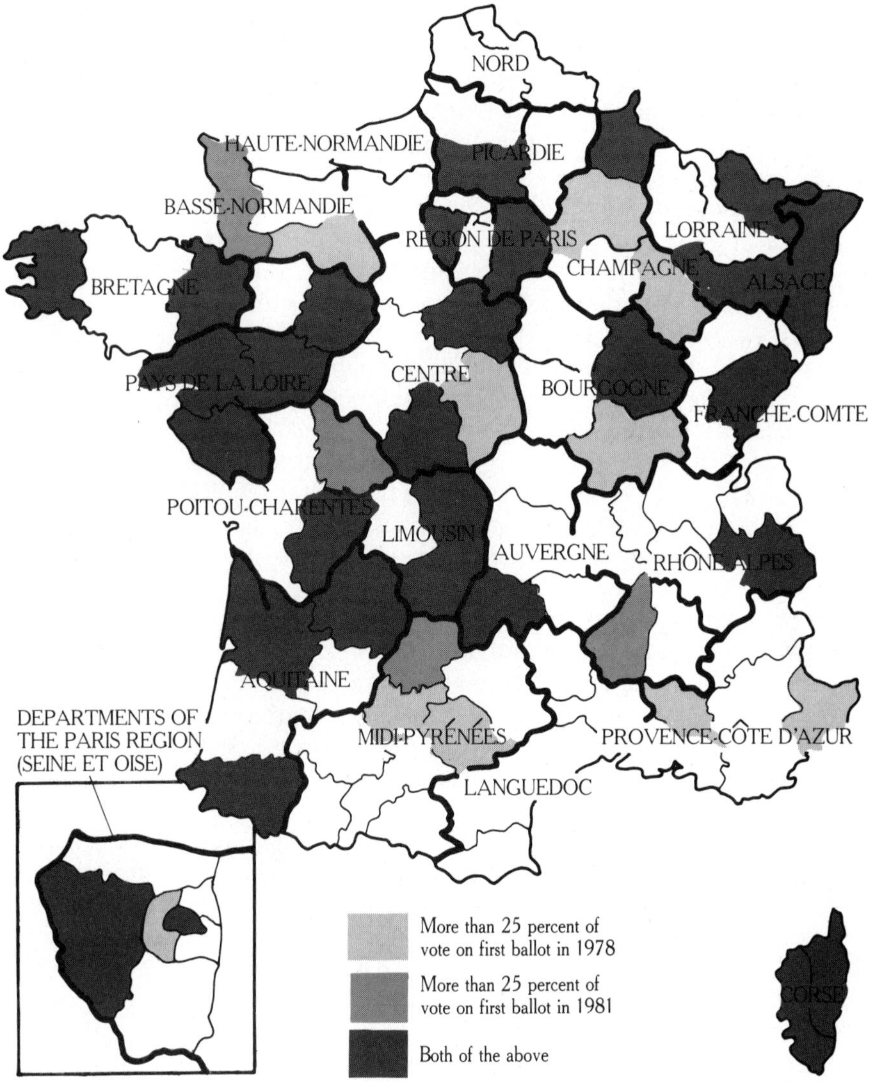

NORD
HAUTE-NORMANDIE   PICARDIE
BASSE-NORMANDIE
LORRAINE
RÉGION DE PARIS
CHAMPAGNE
BRETAGNE   ALSACE
PAYS DE LA LOIRE   CENTRE
BOURGOGNE
FRANCHE-COMTE
POITOU-CHARENTES
LIMOUSIN
AUVERGNE   RHÔNE-ALPES
AQUITAINE
DEPARTMENTS OF
THE PARIS REGION
(SEINE ET OISE)
MIDI-PYRÉNÉES   PROVENCE-CÔTE D'AZUR
LANGUEDOC

More than 25 percent of
vote on first ballot in 1978

More than 25 percent of
vote on first ballot in 1981

Both of the above

CORSE

Party Strengths

The Communist party, after its founding in France in 1920, gradually gained strength to emerge after World War II as the largest single party in the country. During the Fourth Republic it always polled more than a quarter of the popular vote and had at least one sixth, and usually more, of the seats in the lower house of Parliament. In the first election of the Fifth Republic in 1958, however, the Communists lost considerable support, especially to the Gaullists, and fell below one fifth of the vote. Furthermore, since no other party would cooperate with them, the revised electoral system worked against them to cut their strength in Parliament even more drastically—they received only 10 seats. This was far too few to be recognized as an official group. Thus they were deprived of committee assignments and could not introduce censure motions by themselves.

In subsequent elections during de Gaulle's presidency, the Communists recovered slightly and increased their share of the vote by 2 to 4 percentage points over what it had been in 1958. More important was their greater representation in Parliament. Depending upon what cooperative arrangements the party was able to make with other parties, it won from 34 to 86 seats. Although the party had recovered, it clearly was not the major political force in Parliament that it had been during the Fourth Republic. But it must be emphasized that this was not because its appeal to French voters had declined sharply. Except for 1958, its share of the vote was only a few percentage points lower than it had been.

This is why the 1981 results were such a trauma for the PCF. While some of the Socialists' gains came from other parties, the bulk of them were at the expense of the Communists. With only 16 percent of the popular vote on the first ballot, the Communists not only were behind the Socialists—as had happened for the first time in either the Fourth or Fifth Republics in 1978—but even had less than half as many votes as did the Socialists. The Communists had lost about a quarter of the support they had had three years earlier; 1981 was their worst showing since 1936. As for Parliamentary representation, the PCF lost half of its seats, being reduced to only 44. Whereas in 1978 the PCF had more than 20 percent of the vote in 45 departments, in 1981 it obtained that level in only 25 departments.

Immediately after World War II the PCF expanded rapidly to over a million members. Then, like other French parties, it began to have difficulty retaining them and fell in the 1960s to a claimed membership of 400,000. Many experts felt that the true figure was closer to 150,000. Among those members that remained, many were dissatisfied that the PCF was not modernizing like the Italian Communists and permitting some internal discussion of party doctrine. In 1972 the PCF expelled its most vocal dissident, despite his long years of service to the party. One of the leaders in this step was the PCF's new general secretary, George Marchais. Yet at the same time the party proved cooperative enough to sign a Common Program with the Socialists.

The Common Program soon proved a serious threat to the Communists. They found that their dealings with the Socialists had blurred their own image as an adamant party of opposition. Having lost their distinctiveness, they began to lose support to the Socialists, who, the opinion polls suggested, had for the first time moved ahead of the Communists in popular support. Clearly the PCF needed to reemphasize its separate identity, but how? By stressing its differences from the Socialists it would appear to be becoming a dogmatic, working-class party again, exactly what the Common Program was supposed to prove that is was not.

So in the mid-1970s the PCF stressed that party membership was open to everyone, including even such unlikely people as businesspeople, Christians, and Gaullists—it was not for workers only.[5] In doctrine, the PCF became Eurocommunist—criticizing the Soviet Union and abandoning such Marxist doctrines as the dictatorship of the proletariat, as we have explained earlier in this chapter. The party's membership did expand to over two thirds of a million. But in the 1978 elections the PCF vote remained exactly where it had been, while the Socialists gained yet again and passed the Communists.

The strategy had not had its desired results. Even before the election the Communists had begun to back away from it by their intransigence over the updating of the Common Program. Thus at the close of the decade the PCF returned to its Stalinist traditions. Apparently such cynical, opportunistic maneuverings were too much for the voters, who abandoned the party in record numbers in 1981.

To make matters even worse, in the elections for the European Parliament in June 1984 only a 10th of the voters supported the PCF. Marchais came under even heavier attack, especially within the Central Committee. There were even those who dared to complain about democratic centralism and to argue that the party should move toward real internal democracy. On the other hand, within the leadership elite Marchais' severist critics were those who felt he was too moderate—that is, they were the most Stalinist of all. Thus while some change may occur within the PCF, it is unlikely to take the party nearer to the center of the political spectrum.

You should delay, however, before ordering a coffin for the PCF. Communist activists are nothing if not tenacious. One of the party's greatest strengths has been to organize these committed members into a highly disciplined force. The party machine provides during a time of siege a bailiwick from which the loyalists can sally forth when their opponents weary. The strength of the party machine is buttressed by control of major trade unions. Thus despite their current reverses the Communists have sufficient core strength to remain a significant political force in French politics.

Immediately after World War II the Socialists polled a quarter of the vote. They soon declined, however, and by the latter stages of the Fourth Republic were obtaining less than a sixth of the vote. This decline in popular support continued into the Fifth Republic. By the close of the 1960s the Socialists had only about half the Support they had had immediately after World War II. Although the Socialists were the party which introduced dues-paying, card-carrying mass

---

[5]Georges Lavau and Janine Mossuz-Lavau, "The Union of the Left's Defeat: Suicide or Congenital Weakness?", in *The French National Assembly Elections of 1978* ed., Howard Penniman, (Washington, D.C.: American Enterprise Institute, 1980), pp. 121–22.

membership into French politics, the party at its high point in 1946 had only 350,000 members. By the close of the 1960s this figure had declined to less than 80,000. The party experienced serious financial problems and found maintaining an adequate national party organization difficult. In short, by 1971 the Socialists appeared about to wither into irrelevancy as had the once great Radical party before it.

Ten years later, however, the Socialists enjoyed the second greatest triumph in French electoral history. What happened? We are going to give you some good reasons, but let's be honest—we would not have dared to predict such a result even as little as six months before it happened. No one could have foreseen the Socialists' triumph and yet it is understandable.

One important factor was summed up in a cartoon that appeared in *Le Monde* the day after the voting on the first ballot for the 1981 legislative elections. General de Gaulle is sitting on a cloud in heaven reading a newspaper that tells of the Socialists' success. With a smile on his face he says, "It is the triumph of the Institutions." The system that he had constructed is so sound that it called forth the legislative election results needed to prevent a deadlock between the president and the Parliament. The office of president is so predominant, the Parliament such a mere appendage, that the president's coattails can determine the election results.

Perhaps a more accurate assessment of the impact of the institutions would be to say that, while they cannot produce an election result to order, they can thwart a result that otherwise would have occurred. Thus in some senses the surprise is not that the Socialists won in 1981, but that the left failed to do so in 1978. A major factor in the defeat was the intervention from the Olympian heights at the last minute by President Giscard, warning the nation that French civilization would end if the left won. In 1981 there no longer was a President Giscard—Mitterrand had taken care of that a month and a half earlier by winning the presidential election. Mitterrand did not need to intervene to get the result he desired in the legislative elections—all that was necessary was that the institutions were not used to deflect the normal flow of political opinion.

The basic argument here is that in the 1970s the political trend was flowing to the Socialists. In 1969 Guy Mollet, the dead weight of the past, gave up the firm, the old Socialist party (SFIO), that he had run into the sands, to anyone who wanted it. Heading those in receivership of this bankrupt operation was François Mitterrand, even then an old war horse of the Fifth Republic, who had not even been a member of the SFIO. Mitterrand brought together a number of socialist and left political groups to found a new Socialist party (PS) in 1971.[6] The idea that he constantly stressed was the need for unity on the left—including cooperation with the Communists—as the only means of driving Gaullism from power.

---

[6]Technically, the PS was founded in 1969. But only with the Congress of Unification at Epinay in 1971 did Mitterrand and his colleagues join, thus giving the PS its decisive form.

Against all expectations the PS began to succeed. A Common Program was agreed upon with the Communists for the 1973 legislative elections. The PS received half again as much of the popular vote as had the SFIO in 1968 and doubled the number of Socialist deputies in the National Assembly. Membership grew, reaching 130,000 by the mid-1970s and 180,000 by 1981.

The PS came to match the electorate's views of itself. In a 1978 poll 52 percent of the respondents indicated that they considered themselves to be center or moderate left in politics. And 73 percent of the respondents placed the PS in one or the other of those categories.[7] The electorate was quite favorably disposed toward the PS. In a 1977 poll 59 percent said their opinion of the PS was positive—more than 20 percentage points higher than the proportion positive for any other party—and only 27 percent had a negative opinion—the lowest for any party.[8] Thus on a balance the electorate was favorably disposed by a net 32 percentage points; the PS was the only party to have such a strength.[9]

Although the Socialists always had had more seats in the National Assembly during the Fifth Republic than had the Communists, they always had trailed in popular vote until 1978. At the level of the individual constituency the shift had occurred earlier. In 1967 and 1968 the Communists had been the leading party on the left in the majority of electoral districts, but in 1973 the PS led the PCF in most cases. By 1978 the PS was the leading party on the left in more than two thirds of the constituencies.[10]

Thus the trend was to the Socialists, but the left did not win in 1978. As we pointed out, in part this was due to Giscard's efforts. But another factor was the breakdown of cooperation with the Communists. In 1978 the reasons for the failure to renew the Common Program were ambiguous. Some thought that the Communists' intransigence was due to their unwillingness to see the left win if they themselves were not the largest party. On the other hand, some felt that Mitterrand and the PS made an issue out of points that could have been compromised because they were willing to kick the Communists in the face once they had used their shoulders to climb to the top of the wall.

The Stalinist behavior of the PCF from 1978 to 1981, however, must have convinced many uncertain voters about who really was responsible for any lack of cooperation on the left. Thus those who wanted a reform Government saw little reason to vote for a party—the PCF—concerned more with its own fortunes than with public policy reforms. Beyond that was the changed political situation. A victory for the left in 1978 meant a Socialist party strongly dependent on the Communists—Giscard's warning raised some legitimate concerns.

---

[7] Jaffré. "The French Electorate," p. 52.

[8] Jaffré. "The French Electorate," p. 43.

[9] The net scores for the other parties were: Republicans, plus 4; MRG, plus 3; RPR, minus 1; CDS, minus 7; and PCF, minus 21.

[10] Jaffré. "The French Electorate," p. 59.

In 1981, however, the risks had been reduced considerably for now there appeared to be a prospect of electing the PS to power on its own. Contrary to what de Gaulle, Pompidou, and Giscard had told the people over the years, it was possible to get reform without revolution. The dikes were opened and the Socialist tide came in to inundate much of France.

The Socialists received 36 percent of the vote—more than half again as large a share as they had received in 1978—and 267 seats in the National Assembly. The surge to the Socialists was nationwide. In 1978 the Socialists had more than 25 percent of the vote in only about a third of the departments—33. In 1981 they had more than 30 percent of the vote in 82 departments and more than 35 percent in 59.

Following the electoral triumph, party membership rose above 200,000 and, in a show of unity, the various "currents" within the party ceased their activities—although Ceres did not disband. As we have seen in discussing party policy, disillusion soon set in. For many in the PS Mitterrand's *riqueur* looked like the rigor mortis of socialism and Ceres quickly took the responsibility for trying to galvanize the corpse. True, the leader of the Ceres current, Jean-Pierre Chevènement, did reenter the Government in 1984 after a time out of office. Mitterrand remains in charge, but a serious electoral reverse for the PS in the 1986 Parliamentary elections is likely to weaken his control. On the other hand, the exit of the Communists from the Government in 1984 has demonstrated that the Socialists can run the Government without having to rely on the influence of the PCF within the trade unions. Thus although the PS is enjoying its greatest success, it looks vulnerable.

Historically, the French right never was organized into a single major party. Following World War II a small number of right-wing deputies, mainly from poor, strong Catholic areas, formed a Parliamentary group. This group, which eventually became known as the National Center for Independents and Peasants (CNIP), became a sizable political force. In the first election of the Fifth Republic the CNIP gained over a fifth of the vote, the largest of any political group. With 120 seats in the National Assembly they were second only to the Gaullists, while in the Senate they were the largest group.

The CNIP soon split, however, on the question of support for de Gaulle's policies. The anti-de Gaulle faction has continued to use the same name and has declined to virtually no popular support or seats in the Parliament. The pro-de Gaulle faction under Giscard became the Republican party, after some name changes.

From 1967 through 1978 the Republicans ranged from 42 to 67 seats in the National Assembly. This success was due primarily to electoral alliances with the Gaullists, since the PR's share of the popular vote ranged from only 6 to 11 percent. In the Senate the Republicans were consistently the largest party, although never controlling as much as a quarter of the seats.

Giscard's election to the presidency may have been of some assistance to the Republicans, since their support in 1978 did increase somewhat over the 1973 level. Nonetheless, Giscard was not able to take his party into the major Parliamentary force that the Gaullists have been. During his presidency his party was only about a third less than a half as large in the National Assembly as were the Gaullists.

In the 1981 legislative elections, although the PR did not lose much popular support, its seats in the National Assembly were cut in half to only 33. The CDS, the other significant element in the UDF, received only about 4 to 5 percent of the popular vote. In 1981 it lost almost half of its seats in the National Assembly, declining to only 19. While the UDF is not a political party as such, a few candidates did run in 1981 with no party label other than UDF. Nine of these were elected.

Both the UDF and the PR are primarily personal vehicles for Giscard. He clearly wishes to run for president again in 1988 and in the meantime is intimating that he would be an excellent prime minister following a victory for the right in the 1986 Parliamentary elections. So long as Giscard remains a viable presidential candidate his groups should hold together. Should Barre begin to outdistance him by a substantial margin in the opinion polls, however, a split within the UDF and, perhaps, even the PR would be likely.

The Gaullists did not exist as a party at the start of the Fourth Republic. But they did fight the 1951 election, winning over a fifth of the vote and gaining more seats in the National Assembly than any other party despite having the electoral system rigged against them. After de Gaulle disowned the party in 1953, it rapidly declined. Although the Gaullists had to start from scratch, then, at the beginning of the Fifth Republic, they again polled a fifth of the vote and obtained well over two fifths of the seats. Throughout de Gaulle's presidency the party increased its share of the vote and strength in the National Assembly. The Gaullists reached their peak in 1968 with nearly two fifths of the vote and three fifths of the seats—a victory unprecedented in French history.

By 1973, however, scandals in the government and other embarrassments—such as the Gaullist prime minister's using loopholes in the law to avoid paying income tax—began to erode its support. Furthermore, de Gaulle's personal magnetism no longer was available to attract people to the party. The movement has managed to survive de Gaulle's passing from the political scene, but without him it has been weakened by factionalism.

In 1976 Jacques Chirac reorganized the movement, under the label of the Rally for the Republic (RPR). Chirac is a man of boundless energy and ambition with a considerable capacity both to mobilize and alienate people. Some people are active in the RPR because it is the Gaullist movement, not because they have any affection for Chirac. For example, Michel Debré, de Gaulle's long-term associate, who drew up the constitution of the Fifth Republic, apparently believes that he embodies the honor of de Gaulle, just as de Gaulle believed that he embodied the honor of France. Debré does not take kindly to an upstart—Chirac—who takes over *mon General's* heritage. Thus he felt compelled to run in the 1981 presidential election even though Chirac was a candidate. Debré's reward was a derisory 1.7 percent of the vote, eighth of 10 candidates.

Then there are the social-reform Gaullists like Jacques Chaban-Delmas, former prime minister and president of the National Assembly from 1978 to 1981. Chaban was elected to the latter office, despite the fact that Chirac and the RPR favored someone else. Relations between Chaban and Chirac have not been cordial since 1974 when Chirac's support for Giscard in the presidential election helped to destroy Chaban's candidacy. Any closeness between Giscard and Chirac expired, however, when Giscard forced him out as prime minister in 1976. Chirac repaid the compliment by running for president in 1981, when Giscard was trying to be reelected. Furthermore, once the election field had been narrowed to Mitterrand and Giscard, Chirac did not tell his supporters that they now should vote for Giscard. Giscard and Chirac supposedly were reconciled at a meeting late in 1982 to agree upon a united right-wing challenge to the left in the upcoming local elections. Actually a reconciliation between the two is as likely as one between Jerry Falwell and Larry Flynt, since both (the first pair, not the second) want to be president in 1988.

The maneuverings within the Gaullist movement—and we have mentioned only a few of them—are so medieval that the older generation of prominent Gaullists who were closely associated with the General himself for some years are referred to popularly as "barons." It is all rather like a big happy Carolingian royal family, each member looking for the opportunity to murder the others.

Chirac has had some success in developing the grassroots organization of the RPR. Within a year of its founding it was claiming half a million members, and now it is supposed to have up to three quarters of a million. The RPR did not lose much popular support to the Socialist tide of 1981, still managing to poll more than a fifth of the vote. Its seats in the National Assembly, however, were cut by about 40 percent to 84. Furthermore, 1981 was the third election in a row in which the Gaullists' share of the popular vote and their representation in the National Assembly had declined. Thus Chirac will need all his energy to defend his control of the RPR from internal challenges and prevent the Gaullist movement from fractionalizing as it did in the Fourth Republic.

OTHER PARTIES AND ALLIANCES

Ground between the upper (until 1981) millstone of the right and nether millstone of the left, the French political center (sometimes referred to as *marais,* the swamp) has been ground into splinters. Here are the remnants of the great party of the Third Republic—the Radicals.

The Radicals were so called because when they were formed in the 19th century they supported the republican system—universal suffrage, civil liberties, Parliamentary preeminance, and hostility to the role of the Church in public affairs—pretty extreme positions in their day. Eventually, however, they came to be described as a radish—red on the outside, white on the inside, and always on the buttered side of the bread.

As first the Socialists, and then the Communists, displaced them on the left of the political spectrum, the Radicals came to occupy a pivotal center position. Thus, although the party usually had little more than a tenth of the seats in the National Assembly, it provided 7 of the 17 men who served as prime minister during the Fourth Republic.

The party always was very loosely organized both inside and outside of Parliament. Its external organization consisted largely of a network of committees usually headed by *notables*—politicians of local prominence and status. The party was little more than an alliance of personal political machines. It is almost impossible for such a party to be cohesive in Parliament. On almost any key issue the Radicals would be divided into three groups—yes, no, and abstain. Some Radical members of Parliament did not even hesitate to vote against a prime minister who belonged to their own party.

The Radicals appealed primarily to small business people, shopkeepers, and farmers, along with country doctors and lawyers. The largest single occupational group was farmers, which accounted for about a third of the party's support. The Radicals were closely identified with static southern agricultural interests. In some ways it appealed to those who were not yet fully reconciled to 20th-century society.

In the early years of the Fifth Republic the Radicals had about 8 percent of the vote and about 35 seats in the National Assembly. In 1967 and 1968 the Radicals, who continued to decline in strength, were allied with the Socialists in the Federation of the Democratic and Socialist Left (FGDS). In 1971 the question of whether the party should break this alliance and move to the right came to a head and the Radicals split.

Those who wished to remain to the left of center formed the Leftist Radical Movement (MRG) in 1972. The MRG joined the Communists and Socialists in support for the Common Program. In 1977, however, it adamantly refused to agree to the PCF's plans for updating the program and was an important factor in the collapse of these negotiations. Since then the MRG has maintained a close electoral alliance with the PS. What little electoral success it enjoys is due mainly to the willingness of the PS not to run candidates against the MRG in a few places where Radicals traditionally have had strength. The MRG obtains only a couple of percentage points of the popular vote and in 1981 won only 14 seats, but this was more than it had had since 1968.

Few policy differences exist between the MRG and the right wing of the PS. Primarily, the MRG is a bit more skeptical about expanding government ownership. Thus the continued existence of the MRG is largely a matter of the personalities involved.

The more right-wing Radicals continued under the party's traditional name. For a time in the 1970s they formed an alliance known as the Reformists with the Democratic Center (discussed under the Giscardiens above). Such cooperation with a Catholic group would have shocked 19th century Radicals. With the passing of the Reformists, the Radicals became part of the Giscardien UDF. In 1981 the Radicals were reduced to only two seats in the National Assembly.

Several ecologist groups combined to offer a candidate in the 1981 presidential election and fielded some candidates in the following Parliamentary elections. They obtained little support, as also does the extreme left Workers' Struggle party, a Trotskyite group. Not quite that far to the left is the Unified Socialist party (PSU). The PSU is primarily a group of middle-class intellectuals who enjoy talking about social revolution but really do not want to get directly involved with the grubby workers they might encounter were they to join the Communists. Also they regard the Communists as authoritarian bureaucrats and they favor decentralization of political power—management of industry by the workers themselves, for example. In 1981 the PSU candidate for president did even worse than did the Trotskyite one—last of 10 candidates.

In the mid-1980s the growing strength of a party on the far right began to have an impact on French politics. The National Front was founded by Jean-Marie Le Pen in 1972. For a time Le Pen wore a black patch to cover an eye lost in a street fight. While he holds a number of right-wing views such as anticommunism and restoration of the death penalty, the issue which has swelled his support is immigration. By the end of 1983 there were 3.5 million immigrants in France, of which nearly half came from North Africa—that is to say, had skins of a somewhat darker color and had different customs and religion. Le Pen argues that he is not a racist, but merely is pointing out the striking coincidence that France has 2 million foreign workers in the country and 2 million unemployed. If only the foreigners were sent back where they belong, then all French could have jobs. Furthermore, just to be certain that there never is any room for the foreigners to return, the birth rate should be expanded. (But won't that lead to unemployment of *Frenchpeople*? Yes, but don't bother me with the facts.)

In the elections for the European Parliament in 1984, the National Front got about a 10th of the vote, doing nearly as well as the PCF. In some areas of the country in local elections it has fared even better. The National Front may be just one of those skyrocket parties that we mentioned at the start of this chapter, not uncommon in France. Le Pen has firsthand experience with such phenomena, since he was elected to Parliament about 30 years ago as a Poujadist. (See the discussion of the Poujadists in the interest group section of Chapter 11.) Nonetheless, the National Front's success has led Chirac to begin to sound like a civilized version of Le Pen, as we have seen. Thus the National Front's impact does not depend solely on its ability to win seats in the National Assembly.

A single election, of course, cannot by itself offer conclusive evidence of change. In any event the 1981 triumph of the Socialists did little more than produce a situation that the mirror image of that which resulted from the Gaullist landslide in 1968. Thus, although somewhat less fractionalized than it was during the Fourth Republic, the French party system remains basically unchanged—a multiparty system. Some of the actors have changed (or at least acquired new stage names), but the basic nature of the system has not been altered. The center is more divided and ineffective than ever; the right is more unified than in the past, but of uncertain durability now that it has been deprived of the cement of office; the left remains bifurcated.

Some people have argued that one of the reasons the United States has a two-party system is because of the presidency. This is the supreme political prize in American politics. Therefore, considerable party activity is directed toward attempting to win this office. Since only a broadly based national party can have any hope of success in this contest, American parties are forced to be coalitions of diverse, even discordant, interests united primarily by their desire to win the ultimate victory. This quest for a winning coalition prohibits the luxury of small, programmatic parties, each appealing to a narrow segment of the electorate.

In France also the presidency clearly is the supreme prize. As will become clear in the following two chapters, the French president dominates the policy process even more than does the American president. Yet the quest for this office seems to have had only limited impact on the French party system. Certainly both the Socialists and the Gaullists are coalitions of diverse groups and interests; in this regard they tend to resemble Amercian parties. Yet neither has been able to encompass the full breadth of support of American parties. In France the old cleavages, doctrines, and habits of the past continue to affect the party system.

BIBLIOGRAPHICAL NOTE

Among the best sources on parties and politics in the Fourth Republic are the Williams book mentioned in the Bibliographical Note for Chapter 9 and Duncan MacRae, Jr., *Parliament, Parties, and Society in France, 1946-1958* (New York: St. Martin's Press, 1967). See also the various essays covering the Fifth as well as the Fourth Republic in the Williams book mentioned in the Note for Chapter 11. The most recent, comprehensive study of French parties is J. R. Frears, *Political Parties and Elections in the French Fifth Republic* (London: C. Hurst, 1977).

A number of studies of particular French parties have been written. Especially useful is Jean Charlot. *The Gaullist Phenomenon,* translated by Monica Charlot and Marianne Neighbour (London: Allen & Unwin, 1971), which includes the Giscardiens as well as the regular Gaullists. Frank Wilson, *The French Democratic Left, 1963-1969* (Stanford, Calif.: Stanford University Press, 1971), examines the problems of trying to reform the Socialist party into an effective left political force. The problems that electoral success brought the Socialists are examined in John Ambler, ed., *The French Socialist Experiment* (Philadelphia: Institute for the Study of Human Issues, 1984).

13

Legislation and Accountability

THE CHAMBERS AND THEIR MEMBERS

The French Parliament is divided into two houses. The popularly elected National Assembly consists of 491 deputies—474 from France proper, 11 from overseas departments, and 6 from overseas territories. The Senate's 315 members are elected indirectly. We discussed election procedures, qualifications for office, and term of service in Chapter 11.

The National Assembly meets in the Palais-Bourbon on the Seine not far from the Louvre. The original building was built in 1722 for a daughter of Louis XIV. During the Revolution the palace was confiscated and served as the meeting place for the lower house of the legislature. As regimes came and went so did control of the palace until in 1843 the government bought the entire property. Even so legislative bodies met in various places until 1879, when the Chamber of Deputies (the lower house in the Third Republic) settled into the Palais-Bourbon. Except for 1940–44, when the Germans occupied the building, the lower house of the French Parliament has met there ever since.

The meeting chamber itself is arranged like that of the U.S. Congress, rather than the British House of Commons. The deputies sit in a semicircle on curved benches behind desks facing the rostrum. Each row is raised slightly as in an amphitheater. Given the number of parties represented, no clear-cut separation between Government and Opposition exists. Deputies sit according to political association, however, from the far left (presiding officer's left) to the extreme right.

Seating arrangements have at times caused some controversy. At the beginning of the Fifth Republic the Gaullists favored an arrangement like that of the

British House of Commons. But they were unable to win the support of any other political group for this and were not sufficiently strong themselves to carry it. Nonetheless, they won their demand that they be allowed to occupy the central seats, thus demonstrating to the electorate that they were not a reactionary party of the right.[1]

The reduction of Communist strength in the National Assembly in the Fifth Republic has had a significant impact on the social composition of the house. Whereas in the Fourth Republic manual workers had made up 13 percent or more of the lower house, during de Gaulle's presidency the proportion of workers was only half this great for just a brief period and usually was much lower than even that. Following the 1981 election, only 3 percent were workers. The Socialists had only 2 and even the Communists only 13—less than a third of their total delegation. A major share of the deputies are civil servants—usually about 25 percent. Teachers, lawyers, and doctors are other important occupational groups. The average deputy is a man in his early 50s. Women are grossly underrepresented. Early in the Fourth Republic they were about 5 to 6 percent of the deputies. The proportion then declined and has fallen even further in the Fifth Republic; usually only about 2 percent of the deputies have been women.[2] In 1981, however, the proportion expanded to 5 percent.

The first Parliament of the Fifth Republic saw a considerable number of new faces in the lower house. Less than 30 percent of those deputies who stood for reelection were successful. While it would not be quite true to conclude that most of the deputies elected were inexperienced—most of them either had been active in local politics or unsuccessful candidates for Parliament in previous elections—yet this is evidence of the extent to which the electorate was turning its back on the national politicians of the Fourth Republic. Even after the next elections in 1962 almost half—45 percent—of the members of the lower house had never served in that body before. By the 1970s this had changed; nearly two thirds of the deputies elected in 1978 were serving their second term.

One characteristic of recruitment patterns that did not change with the founding of the Fifth Republic was local government experience. As had been true in both the Third and Fourth Republics, well over a majority—three fourths in 1958—had been members of local government councils prior to being elected to the national legislature. In fact, the typical deputy is likely to continue such local service while belonging to the National Assembly, since nothing prohibits holding more than one elective office simultaneously. Many nationally prominent political leaders serve as mayor of a town or city while also sitting in the National Assembly. Deputies are not very well supported. The monthly sti-

---

[1]Philip Williams, *The French Parliament* (New York: Praeger Publishers, 1968), p. 36. This is the source for some of the other information in these paragraphs.

[2]Monica Charlot, "Women in Politics in France," in *The French National Assembly Elections of 1978*, ed. Howard Penniman, (Washington, D.C.: American Enterprise Institute, 1980), p. 181.

pend is modest and, like British MPs, but in contrast to members of the U.S. Congress, they have no staff.

Unlike the practice in the United States, Britain, and Germany, in France both houses of the legislature are not in the same building. The Senate meets in a separate location some ways across Paris from the Palais-Bourbon. The Palais-Luxembourg was built early in the 17th century and then remodeled in a Florentine fashion for the widow of Henry IV. During the Revolution it served as a prison. Subsequently, Napoleon lived there for a short time. The Senate began meeting there in 1801 and despite some breaks in tenure has continued to do so ever since. Behind the Palais-Luxembourg are attractive formal gardens, including a reflecting pool where children sail toy boats. The seating arrangements in the Senate's meeting chamber are similar to those for the National Assembly.

In keeping with its more rural and conservative electorate, the Senate usually has contained few workers, but it has had a sizable number of farmers. The differing electorate also explains why, unlike the National Assembly, the first Senate of the Fifth Republic showed little change from its Fourth Republic predecessor. Of those members of the upper house who sought reelection when the Fifth Republic began, 84 percent were successful. Furthermore, many of those newly elected to the Senate simply were experienced national politicians who had been unable to retain their seats in the earlier election for the new National Assembly. The new Senate proceeded to elect as its president the man who had presided over the upper chamber since 1947.

POWERS AND PROCEDURES

In contrast with the constitutional documents of the Third and Fourth Republics, that of the Fifth spells out Parliament's powers and, by stating in other areas that the Government can set policy by decree, seeks to limit them. As we have explained in previous chapters the basic idea behind the political system of the Fifth Republic was to strengthen the executive and curtail the ability of the legislature to infringe upon executive action.

Within the sphere of powers granted to the legislature, areas in which it can make detailed regulations are distinguished from those in which it can set only general or basic principles. Parliament can legislate in detail on: civil rights and obligations; nationality, contracts, gifts, and inheritance; crimes and criminal procedures, taxation and currency, electoral systems; public institutions; economic plans, including nationalization and denationalization of enterprises. But Parliament can establish only the policy outlines and must leave to the executive the filling in of details on: general organization of national defense; education; property rights; employment, unions, and social security; administration of local government units. In all other areas, except for declaring war, ratifying treaties, and voting the budget, the constitution says that Government may legislate by decree.

Furthermore, under Article 38 the Government may ask the legislature to delegate to it for a limited time even those powers specifically given to the legislature. If the Parliament grants this request, any decrees issued by the Government—which needs only to consult with the Council of State before doing so—are effective immediately. They become null and void, however, should the Government fail to submit to Parliament a bill for their ratification within a date specified in the request for decree powers.

This procedure was fairly common—some 15 times—while de Gaulle was president, much to the dismay of the left. The General's successors, trying to show that they were not as imperious as he, did not avail themselves of this procedure. Shortly after the Socialists won power in 1981, however, they asked Parliament to authorize decree powers for three months so that the labor laws could be amended. The Government claimed that this step was necessary because its extensive program of reforms had created a backlog in Parliament, which prevented prompt action to help the unemployed. When the Government felt in 1983 that additional austerity measures were needed, it once again used the Article 38 procedure. The left's willingness to use, when in power, those procedures that it criticized, when in opposition, made it seem a bit hypocritical.

Since the Parliament's enumerated powers appear quite broad, the specification of its sphere may not seem to be a serious limitation. And as for legislation by executive decree, this long has been a French tradition. The difference is that in the past such *cadre* laws always were based on grants of authority to the executive from the legislature, grants that could be revoked at any time. This now is only partially true. Most of the executive's decree power now comes from the constitution, and thus is not subject to control or alteration by the Parliament. In addition, the new step of limiting the Parliament's competency to only those areas specified is part of a deliberate effort to restrict it and make it subject to the executive.

In addition to its legislative function, Parliament is supposed to have a role in the amendment of the constitution. But, as discussed in Chapter 10, this has been circumvented on one occasion. Thus, Parliament's power and status in that area was undercut as well.

Turning to the distribution of power between the two houses of Parliament, in the Fourth Republic the upper chamber was a weak body, quite in contrast to the Senate of the Third Republic, known as the Council of the Republic. In returning in the Fifth Republic to the old name for the upper house, an effort was made to restore that chamber to much of its former power. This was a deliberate political tactic. The Gaullists were uncertain of their ability to control the lower house, but were confident that they would have an ally in the conservative upper house. Therefore they sought to give it considerably more power than that possessed by the Council of the Republic in the Fourth Republic.

With a few exceptions the formal powers of the Senate equal those of the National Assembly. Finance bills must be submitted to the National Assembly first. But should the lower house fail to act within 40 days, then the Government can introduce the bill in the upper house. If the two houses cannot agree on a bill, it dies unless the Government intervenes to call for a conference committee composed of members chosen from each house. Even if this committee formulates a compromise acceptable to the representatives from both houses, its agreed draft can be submitted to both houses only if the Government approves and only with those amendments that the Government favors. If the committee fails to agree, then the Government can ask the National Assembly to act. Its decision is final regardless of the views of the Senate.

Presumably, if the Cabinet and Senate were of like mind and the Assembly hostile, the Senate could be employed to exercise a veto power in legislation. On the other hand, the Senate can be overruled if the Cabinet and the Assembly agree. Thus, the Senate can serve as a check upon the Assembly but not upon the Government.

The conference committee (*Commission Mixte Paritaire*) is called for about 12 percent of the laws. The Government never has used the option of rejecting the report of a CMP. Slightly more than a quarter of the time (72 out of 257 cases during the first 20 years of the Fifth Republic) the Government has asked the National Assembly to make the final decision because the CMP could not work out a compromise agreement.[3]

Contrary to their expectations, the Gaullists never have been very strong in the Senate. Usually, they have been only the fourth or fifth largest political group in the upper house. Thus during the presidencies of de Gaulle and Pompidou the Senate often was a sharper critic of the Government than was the National Assembly. Under Giscard this changed because his closest allies were stronger in the Senate than in the National Assembly.

The election of Mitterrand as president altered the situation once more. Although the senatorial elections of 1980 had made the PS the largest party in the Senate, yet it held little more than a fifth of the seats. Even adding other left and left-center Senators to this total failed to bring Mitterrand even close to a majority in the upper house. The Senate's hostile majority was not a major problem, since the chamber lacks the power to vote the Government out of office. Nonetheless, it did produce some troubles for Mitterrand. The Senate voted against the Government's nationalization bill. While this became law anyway with the support of the Socialist-controlled National Assembly, the Government did decide to modify its bill to decentralize French government in order to avoid yet another defeat in the Senate. And in 1984 Mitterrand and the Senate clashed on amending the constitution. When Mitterrand was forced by public demonstrations to withdraw the Socialists' proposals to integrate the Catholic schools more fully into the state education system, he sought an alternate means of accomplishing this so as not to alienate Socialists clinging to the party's tradition of secular education. He proposed amending the constitution so that there

---

[3]John R. Frears, "Parliament in the Fifth Republic," in *The Impact of the Fifth Republic on France*, eds. William G. Andrews and Stanley Hoffmann (Albany: SUNY Press, 1981), p. 51.

could be referenda on what were termed *basic public liberties*. The Senate, fearing that Mitterrand might use this power frequently to enhance his popularity, voted against the proposal. Since in amending the constitution the Senate's powers equal those of the National Assembly, the adverse vote killed Mitterrand's plan.

The present constitution deals with legislative procedure in greater detail than have past ones. Here again the basic idea has been to curtail the legislature. The easiest way to control a legislature, of course, is to keep it from meeting. So Parliament has been limited to only two sessions a year, each of which cannot exceed three months. Special sessions, not to exceed 12 days, can be called at the request of the prime minister or a majority of the Assembly to deal with a specific agenda of items.

In 1961 during a period of emergency rule, however, President de Gaulle refused to summon a special session of Parliament even though the members of the National Assembly wishing such a session had complied with all the required procedures. Although his actions clearly seemed to violate the constitution, Parliament could do nothing. Once again de Gaulle had demonstrated his refusal to abide by the rules, even those drawn up under his guidance, whenever doing so was inconvenient for him.

Thus the first special session occurred in March 1979, when President Giscard complied with the request of a sizable majority of the National Assembly. The Government was subjected to strong criticism of its economic policies, but basically emerged unscathed. Another special session was called immediately after the Socialists' 1981 victory to begin work promptly on their reform program.

The interminable debates that used to occur on the budget and other bills have been sharply reduced because the constitution gives the Government great control over Parliamentary time and financial matters. To be certain that the legislature does not manage to claw back any of its lost power, the constitution provides that Parliament's standing orders on procedure cannot become effective until they have been examined by the Constitutional Council to be certain that they conform with the constitution.

Although the Government has ultimate control of Parliament's timetable, the National Assembly does have a committee that deals with these matters. The Conference of Presidents, composed of the leaders of all recognized political groups, the chairpersons of the committees, the six vice presidents of the National Assembly, and its president, sets the agenda and allots the amount of time to be spent in debating each item. Voting in the Conference is on the basis of formal group strength in the National Assembly. Given the power of the Government in these matters, however, the Conference votes only infrequently. It serves more as a channel for communicating the views of the various political groups to the Government and a means of negotiating with the Government and, at times, persuading it to change its mind on matters of legislative priorities.

Each chamber is presided over by a president. French presiding officers remain members of their respective political parties, unlike the Speaker of the House of Commons, and do not have the Speaker's unchallenged authority. In the past, they were elected to their posts annually, but the constitution now provides that the president of the Assembly is elected for its duration, while the president of the Senate is elected every three years—that is, after each partial renewal of its membership. Moreover, the standing orders now give the presiding officer more authority in controlling debate and in calling members to order than his or her predecessors had.

The president of the National Assembly is assisted in presiding over the debates and in organizing and directing its activities by the Bureau. The Bureau is composed of the 6 vice presidents, 12 secretaries, and 3 *questeurs* (members in charge of the administrative and financial arrangements of the Assembly). These positions are distributed among the various political groups according to their strength in the Assembly.

To be recognized as a political group requires the support of at least 30 deputies. During the first four years of the Fifth Republic, this requirement served to deny the Communists any formal role in the National Assembly's procedures despite their having received a fifth of the popular vote. The leaders of political groups are required to submit an official declaration of their group's policy. All members and affiliates of a group are required to sign this statement, but usually it is so vague as to be virtually meaningless. Special debating privileges are granted to the leaders of recognized political groups. In recent years there have been four to six such groups in the National Assembly.

Part of the apparent confusion in the French party system stems from the fact that the political groups in the National Assembly do not necessarily correspond to various political parties. As we explained in discussing French elections, candidates may give themselves a label on the ballot that is not the name of a party. The labels used frequently prove to be not very good predictors of what group a successful candidate will join in the National Assembly. In addition to this confusion, parties that fought the election separately may join together to form a recognized group in the National Assembly in order to increase their influence in directing its activities. Thus parties may have no counterpart among the Assembly's groups, and groups may have no counterpart among party organization outside of the legislature.

The number of committees has been reduced from 19 in the Fourth Republic to 6 for two reasons: to reduce the authority of committees and to avoid the time-wasting practice of submitting identical matters to several committees. Under the Fourth Republic committees were independent centers of power, just as they are in the U.S. Congress. The committees were numerous enough so that each could build up a fund of expertise in a specialized area. The chairpersons of committees became virtual shadow ministers, able to keep a close watch and considerable control over the members of the Cabinet. In a multiparty system having no single party as the Opposition, this was an important element in legislative dominance of the executive.

The smaller numbers of committees in the Fifth Republic mean that committees are larger and less specialized. Two of the committees have about 120 members and the other four 60 each. They are prevented from being unwieldly largely by absenteeism. Only those members particularly interested in the bill being discussed are likely to attend a given session. Nonetheless, the larger size of the committees has meant that it is more difficult than it had been in the Fourth Republic for a pressure group to secure a majority in a committee and thus get it to recommend legislation that it favors.

Special committees consisting of not more than 30 members with no more than 15 from any single permanent committee may be created on an ad hoc basis to deal with a particular bill. These have not been used to any great extent, particularly in recent years. Also possible are committees of inquiry, comparable to select committees in the House of Commons.

Only recognized political groups are entitled to members on the committees. Party strengths vary from one committee to another, even though the initial allocation of seats corresponds to the relative strength of political groups in the National Assembly. The groups trade seats with each other in order to maximize their strength on those committees dealing with subjects of special interest to them. Once its allocation for a particular committee finally is determined, each group decides which of its members will fill the seats.

When the 1978 session of the National Assembly began, President Giscard wanted the left to be given two of the six committee presiding positions. While his supporters in the National Assembly were willing to give one, the Gaullists opposed giving any. The result was that the previous pattern of four for the Gaullists and two for the Giscardiens was continued and the left got none. Following the 1981 election, the Socialists offered to let the right preside over some of the committees. Just to prove how strongly they opposed the new Government, the right refused this offer.

Typically, committees meet all day on Wednesday and in the morning on other days. The Assembly usually meets on Tuesday, Thursday, and Friday afternoons. No quorum is required for debates in the National Assembly, but at least half of the deputies must be present for a valid vote. If not enough are present, the vote is postponed for an hour, at which point it is valid regardless of the number present. Deputies may not speak for more than five minutes except in organized debates. The Conference of Presidents allocates the time for such debates to the various political groups, and they in turn decide which of their members will speak for how long.

The Government's legislative business goes on the priority order of the day and is dealt with first. Once this has been completed, bills introduced by the deputies can be taken up on the complementary order of the day, but this does not happen very often. During the first 20 years of the Fifth Republic 87 percent of all legislation originated with the Government and only 13 percent with Parliament.[4] Although during the Fourth Republic more than twice as much of all

---

[4] Ibid., p. 49.

legislation originated with Parliament, the Fifth Republic figure is not markedly different from the situation in Britain.

Usually in the Fifth Republic about 8 to 10 percent of the legislation introduced by deputies passes.[5] Again, this does not differ markedly from the situation in Britain. In addition, nearly a fifth of all the amendments to bills adopted by the National Assembly are originated by deputies. Deputies cannot propose on-the-spot amendments to bills during debate on the floor of the National Assembly. The Government can reject from consideration any amendment that was not submitted during the committee stage of a bill. Thus it cannot be caught off guard by an apparently innocuous amendment proposed unexpectedly that actually has an impact not readily clear.

A bill returns from committee in exactly the same form as when it was sent to committee. The committee's report indicates the amendments that the committee favors. This is of great assistance to the Government; no longer does it have to try to piece together various majorities to try to restore to something like its original form a bill mangled by committee. Those who want to make changes have the problem of trying to get a majority for them.

The Government is empowered to decide how a bill will be voted upon. It can decide that only certain sections or only the bill as a whole will be voted upon. In this way it can avoid a vote on unpopular provisions and get them enacted as part of a popular bill. This power was used relatively frequently when Pompidou was president, but subsequently declined to only about four times a year.[6]

Power over financial matters may be the most important political power. Thus you will not be surprised that the Fifth Republic's constitution weakens Parliament here also. If Parliament does not pass the budget within 70 days of having received it from the Government, the Government implements it by executive decree. This means that while Parliament can pass a budget that the Government does not like, it cannot hold up the budget indefinitely as a means of getting some concessions from the Government. Furthermore, should the Government be having any problems piecing together a majority in the Parliament, it does not need to worry. If it cannot get its budget passed, it can be implemented by decree. The ability of Parliament to pass the budget in a damaged form opposed by the Government is limited because the constitution now bars deputies from introducing bills that would either reduce revenues or increase expenditures.

LEGISLATIVE RELATIONS WITH THE GOVERNMENT

We already have touched at various points in this chapter on executive–legislative relations. We have noted the limiting of the Parliament's sphere of competence and the corresponding expansion of the Government's, the ability of

---

[5]Ibid., p. 50.
[6]Ibid., p. 52.

the Government to play one house off against the other, and the Government's greatly enhanced control over Parliament's procedures. For a Government to exercise powers of this type in a parliamentary system is not unusual, provided that it is responsible to a popularly elected legislature for the way in which it exercises its authority.

Since the French president is not responsible in any way to Parliament, the Fifth Republic is a major departure from the parliamentary system. The extent to which this is significant will be clear in the next chapter when we discuss the president's substantive powers. At this point we want to focus on that part of the executive that is supposed to be accountable to Parliament. Fifth Republic France has not completely abandoned the parliamentary system but retains an element of fusion of powers along with separation of powers.

One element in the ability of a parliament to call a Government to account is the power to force the Government to justify its actions. Questioning of the Government in France can take a variety of forms. Under oral questions without debate, a deputy has up to two minutes for a question, a minister replies, the deputy then comments for up to five minutes, and the minister can respond again. These questions have little impact because a month passes between the time the deputy submitted the question and the time it is taken up in Parliament. Furthermore, these questions are scheduled on Friday, when absenteeism is high.

Oral questions with debate bear little resemblance to question time in the British House of Commons. The questioner speaks for a half hour, followed by other members for up to 20 minutes each. Then a minister makes a responding speech and the original questioner can reply. Although this procedure continues to be used in the Senate, it no longer is in the Assembly.

Taking its place since 1974 in the Assembly have been Questions to the Government. One day a week all the ministers attend, and any deputy may question any minister. Half the time is allocated to supporters of the Government and half to the opposition parties. A deputy makes a short speech and receives a reply from a minister but is not allowed any response.

We commented earlier that question time in Britain probably is not nearly as effective in controlling the executive as has been claimed. In France questions of whatever type have even less impact than in Britain.

The ultimate weapon in a parliament's ability to control the executive is its power to vote the Government out of office. During the Third Republic the Government had to please both houses of Parliament, although adverse votes in the Senate came to mean less and less in terms of the Government's survival. In the Fourth Republic only the lower house could dismiss the Government. As we have mentioned repeatedly, the Government had few weapons with which to defend itself during the Third and Fourth Republics, and thus frequently either was voted out of office or resigned because it could not get Parliament to pass its legislative program. The Fifth Republic was deliberately designed to break free from this tradition of Assembly dominance.

Article 49 of the constitution states: "The Prime Minister, after deliberation in the Council of Ministers, may pledge the responsibility of the Government to the National Assembly with regard to the program of the Government, or with regard to a declaration of general policy, as the case may be." In the early years of the Fifth Republic this was interpreted to mean that when a prime minister formed a Government a policy statement would be made in the National Assembly, which could reject the Government by a simple majority and force it to resign. This was in keeping with the investiture practice of the Third and Fourth Republics by which Parliament indicated its willingness to accept a new Government.

After this procedure was followed for the first three Governments, however, prime ministers ceased to ask the National Assembly for a vote of confidence when they formed a Government, although they usually did make a statement of what their policy would be. Apparently, French presidents were trying to demonstrate that the Government really was more responsible to them than it was to Parliament. President Giscard appeared to revive the original practice when in 1974 he had his first prime minister, Jacques Chirac, ask the National Assembly for a vote of confidence on the new Government's policy. But the next prime minister, Raymond Barre, did not ask for a vote of confidence until he formed his third Government.

When Mitterrand was elected president, he dissolved the National Assembly and called for new legislative elections almost immediately. Thus no Parliament was in session from which Pierre Mauroy, the first Socialist prime minister, could seek investiture. Following the Socialists' victory in elections for the Assembly, Mauroy formed a new Government and did ask the Assembly to approve a statement of its program. The same procedure was followed when Mauroy formed a third Government in 1983 and when Laurent Fabius (pronounced fah-bee-you) became prime minister in 1984.

Thus investiture is not a regularly established procedure. On the other hand, 8 of 19 Governments in the Fifth Republic (including all of the most recent ones) have sought such evidence of Parliamentary support at the start of their time in office. In each case the Government has won the vote.

In addition to the investiture requests, Governments have asked the Assembly to express confidence in a policy statement on eight other occasions. Here again a simple majority vote against would be sufficient to drive the Government from office, but this never has happened.

Besides asking the Assembly to support its general policies, the Government can request such backing for a text—that is to say, it can make passage of a particular bill a matter of confidence. When a prime minister stakes the life of the Government on a particular bill, the Government is assumed to have the confidence of the National Assembly unless a censure motion is filed within the next 24 hours. Filing such a motion requires the signatures of at least one tenth of the deputies in the National Assembly. Once the motion is filed, the Government is given 48 hours in which to mobilize its Parliamentary supporters before the motion is voted upon. Should a majority of the *total* membership of the National Assembly vote to censure the Government (only votes for censure are counted), then it is forced to resign. If the motion fails to obtain this absolute majority, then the bill to which the government committed itself is considered approved.

Under this procedure a bill can become law even though *a majority of those present* have expressed their disapproval, because a censure motion fails unless it receives *a majority of the total membership.* In fact, unless a motion of censure is moved, a bill can become law without ever having been voted upon at all. The general effect of this procedure is that the Cabinet can go on with its program unless the Assembly is willing to turn it out of office.

On 20 occasions the Government has staked its life on a particular bill; four times the National Assembly did not respond and the bill passed without a vote. The procedure seemed for a time to be falling into disuse because only two instances occurred from June 1967 until late 1979. Then four instances within a month raised a storm of controversy.

Conflict between the Gaullists and Giscardiens in the National Assembly had deprived Prime Minister Barre of a working majority. In October 1979 the Government was defeated on the budget when the Gaullists abstained. In another instance they actually voted with the Communists and Socialists to reject Government proposals for changes in the income tax rates because they believed these would hurt people who were lowly paid. Thus Barre in November and December on four occasions made passage of the budget and of social security reforms a matter of confidence. The Communists and Socialists responded with a flurry of seven motions of censure. All of these fell short of getting the support of an absolute majority of the National Assembly, however, because the Gaullists could not bring themselves to vote the Government out of office.

Jacques Chaban-Delmas, the Gaullist president of the Assembly, referred to the Constitutional Council, however, the question of whether the budget could be passed in this fashion. On Christmas eve the Constitutional Council filled Prime Minister Barre's stocking with coal—it ruled the budget "unconstitutional and invalid." But this was not really a victory for the National Assembly. The Council did not object to combining the budget with a vote of confidence. They invalidated the action because the revenue raising and expenditure sections of the budget had been passed simultaneously, while the constitution required that this be done separately. Thus the Government was able to correct the problem with only a little inconvenience.

Since coming to power the Socialists have used the procedure of making passage of a text a matter of confidence for bills freezing wages and prices for four months, on education, and on newspaper ownership. Perhaps the most interesting use was for a bill to grant amnesty for generals who had been involved in the Secret Army Organization (OAS) conspiracy to overthrow the Government and even kill President de Gaulle because of his policies in Algeria. This proposal initially was defeated when Socialist deputies rebelled against their own Government. But neither they nor the Gaullist deputies (who also opposed it) offered a censure motion when the Government made its passage a matter of confidence. Thus it went into effect without a vote.

The Government's Parliamentary opponents do not need to wait for it to raise a question of confidence. A motion of censure can be moved whenever at least one tenth of the deputies so desire. The founders of the Fifth Republic did not intend, however, to permit Parliamentary dissidents to make life unpleasant for the Government by using this power as a propaganda or obstructionist device. Therefore, if a motion of censure initiated by the deputies fails to pass, then none of those (at least one tenth of the total membership) who signed the motion in order to get it on the agenda may sign another such motion for the remainder of that session of Parliament. (This limit on the signing of censure motions does not apply in those cases when the Government has initiated the process by staking its life on a bill.)

Once the motion is on the agenda, there is a delay of 48 hours before the vote. An absolute majority is required to pass it. Only one of the nearly two dozen such motions that have been introduced has passed. The National Assembly censured the Government when de Gaulle bypassed Parliament in amending the constitution to provide for direct, popular election of president. Instead of having the Government resign, de Gaulle dissolved Parliament, held new elections, and used a referendum to amend the constitution precisely as he had intended. Both the elections and the referendum were substantial victories for de Gaulle. The results did not exactly make moving censure motions look attractive.

Adding together all the motions of censure of whatever type and the times the Government has asked for confidence on policy statements produces a total of 56 votes of confidence of one type or another. This is an average of just over two a year. Furthermore, recall that the Government has lost only one of these 56 votes. Clearly, the power of the National Assembly to harass the Government has altered drastically from what it was in the Third and Fourth Republics.

Graphic evidence of this change appears in Figure 13–1. In 12 years the Fourth Republic had 22 prime ministers; in its first 12 years the Fifth had only 4, and even after 26 years it had had only 9. While prime ministers in the Fourth Republic averaged only six months in office, in the Fifth they have averaged three years. Thus some have concluded that the constitutional reforms of the Fifth Republic have been a great success.

But the significant increase in executive stability in France is due not so much to constitutional changes as to changes in the party system. Only during the first four years of the Fifth Republic, when de Gaulle was the predominating power as president in any event, and the last two years of Giscard's term, did the Government lack an assured working majority in the National Assembly. Had prime ministers in the Third and Fourth Republic had this kind of support in Parliament they would have headed much more durable Governments also.

Since greater stability would have occurred even in the absence of constitutional reform, it is especially important to assess what the costs of reform have

FIGURE 13-1   **Number of Years Served in Office by Each Prime Minister, 1946–84**

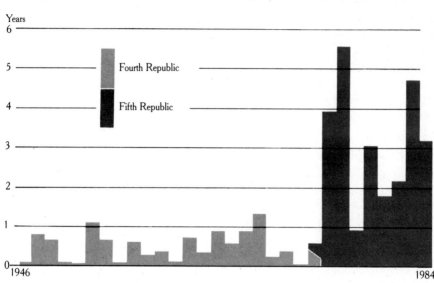

been. In trying to cut Parliament down to size in the ways that we have explained, what have the founders of the Fifth Republic produced? At about the end of the first decade of the Fifth Republic, Philip Williams, one of the foremost students of French politics, assessed Parliament's status. He granted that Parliament performed its legislative function more efficiently than ever before. But he also concluded:

> Parliament is sadly inefficient as a forum for popular grievances, as a check on the administration, as a defender of the liberties of the subject, or as a political sounding-board for the opposition (or indeed government) to appeal to the electorate . . . In the old regime Parliament dominated the Government and denied effective leadership. In the new regime the government dominates Parliament and denies itself effective criticism.[7]

A decade later another prominent student of French politics, John Frears, drew up his balance sheet. Like Williams, he found that "the first of our requirements for a modern parliament—that it should direct itself to scrutinizing and improving legislation rather than initiating or impeding it—is reasonably well fulfilled." But when it came to his other requirements, having to do with

---

[7]Philip Williams, *The French Parliament*, p. 118, and "Parliament Under the Fifth French Republic Patterns of Executive Domination," in *Modern Parliaments: Change or Decline*, ed. Gerhard Loewenberg (Chicago: Aldine-Atherton, 1971), p. 109.

Parliament's ability to control the executive and call it to account, again, like Williams, his evaluation was negative. "France remains a country where executive power remains almost totally immune from parliamentary scrutiny, especially the sort of power exercised by the technocratic elite in ministerial *cabinets*. . . . The government in France . . . is still much too safe from scrutiny and control."[8] The coming to power of the left in 1981 has done little to alter these verdicts. Thus, successful as the Fifth Republic has been, the fundamental problem of French politics—establishment of a balanced relation between the executive and the legislature—remains unsolved.

BIBLIOGRAPHICAL NOTE

The Williams book cited in Footnote 7, despite its brevity, contains much useful information on both the law and practice concerning the National Assembly in the Fifth Republic. The Loewenberg book mentioned in the same Footnote contains, in addition to the essay by Williams, an article on Parliament by François Goguel. The Frears contribution to Andrews and Hoffmann, Footnote 3, is an invaluable update. For comparison of the Parliament in the Fourth Republic, see D. W. S. Lidderdale, *The Parliament of France* (London: Hansard Society, 1951).

---

[8]Frears, "Parliament in the Fifth Republic," pp. 54, 62, 63.

14

Policymaking Structures

The constitution of the Fifth Republic provides for a dual executive—president and prime minister. This is a typical pattern in monarchies that have become republics. The president functions as ceremonial head of state with the prime minister exercising the real political power. This was the situation in the Fourth Republic, except that, given the weak executive, the prime minister did not have much power either. The constitution of the Fifth Republic sought to strengthen the executive not only by making the prime minister less beholden to Parliament, but also by creating a president independent of Parliament and having substantial powers. The result is a hybrid system with elements both of parliamentary and presidential systems. In the previous chapter we examined the parliamentary aspects of this system—how the Government relates to the Parliament. In this chapter we need to examine the president's role, how that office relates to the rest of the executive, and the implications of both of these for overall legislative–executive relations in France.

FORMAL POWERS AND DUTIES OF THE PRESIDENT

The French president is designated the head of state, while the prime minister is to be the head of the Government. This does not mean that the president is to be simply a ceremonial figure like the British monarch. The president is to be the guarantor of national independence, of the integrity of the territory, of respect for international treaties and agreements. The president is entrusted with the task of protecting the constitution and to this end is to use the power of the office to "arbitrate" among political forces and governmental bodies to insure the regular functioning of the state and its continuity. This responsibility is so vague that it is hard to know precisely what action it authorizes; at times de Gaulle seemed to feel that it justified his taking whatever action he felt necessary.

The president's powers are impressive. Some of them, such as the power to pardon, the appointment of ambassadors, and nominations to civil, army, and judicial posts, require the signature of the prime minister (and possibly another minister), in true parliamentary form. But a number of substantive powers are exercised by the president alone, without any reference to advice from those who can be held politically accountable in Parliament.

The president designates the prime minister and, while the National Assembly can vote the Government out of office, its approval is not necessary, as we have explained, for the prime minister to take office. The president may dissolve the National Assembly and call new elections, although not more often than once a year. The only other limit is to consult with the prime minister and the presidents of both houses of Parliament before acting. On the other hand, the president can refuse to grant the prime minister's request for new elections. The power to propose a referendum lies with the Government or the Parliament, but the president can refuse a request to hold one.

The president can ask the Constitutional Council (three of whose members he or she appoints and whose president she or he designates) to rule on the constitutionality of bills and laws. If the prime minister agrees, the president can ask Parliament to reconsider a bill that it has passed. While this forces Parliament to take the bill through its stages again, no special majority is required to repass it; thus the French president lacks the veto power of the American president.

As you can see, the Fifth Republic does create a system of some checks and balances. The one area where this is not so, where the president truly becomes dominant, is the emergency powers. "When the institutions of the Republic, the independence of the nation, the integrity of its territory, or the fulfillment of its international commitments are threatened in a grave and immediate manner," says Article 16 of the constitution, "and the regular functioning of the constitutional governmental authorities is interrupted, the President of the Republic shall take the measures required by these circumstances." If ever there were a blank check, this is it. The president needs only to consult the prime minister, the presidents of both houses of Parliament, and the Constitutional Council. Having done so, the president may rule as he or she chooses. True, the nation must be informed of what is being done and Parliament cannot be dissolved or adjourned, but these hardly are limitations. The measures taken "must be prompted by the desire to ensure to the constitutional governmental authorities, in the shortest possible time, the means of fulfilling their assigned functions." But this hardly differs from the motives expressed by military officers staging a coup in a banana republic. In any event, no time limit is set and the president can continue to exercise emergency powers as he or she wishes.

While Parliament does meet when the emergency powers are in effect, it apparently is prevented from censuring the Government. At any rate, no censure motions were allowed during the five months in 1961, which is the only period in which Article 16 has been invoked. The supporting reasoning was that were the Government to be censured, it might be deemed desirable to dissolve Parliament and call for new elections in an effort to determine whether the public supported the Government or the Parliament. But, since Article 16 prohibits dissolution of the Parliament during the use of emergency powers, it would be impossible to call an election. Therefore a motion to censure should not be allowed to create such an impasse. Thus in yet another way the powers of Parliament were restricted.

Given the ambiguities and elasticity of this system, its actual operation turns to a considerable extent upon the personalities of the two main political executives. Since the Fifth Republic is a young system—little more than a quarter of a century old—the personalities of these executives and their relations with each other are of major significance in establishing traditional conceptions of the roles of the top two executive offices. Given his dominance of French life and the fact that the Fifth Republic's constitution was drawn up to his specifications, the attitudes and actions of de Gaulle have been of immense significance in determining how the system operates in practice. Therefore, we need to discuss this topic in some detail.

DE GAULLE'S CONCEPTUALIZATION AND SHAPING OF THE OFFICE

During the first dozen years of the Fifth Republic the system was dominated by Charles de Gaulle from the office of president. So much was this the case that some observers referred to France during this period as the de Gaulle Republic.

Although often seeking to convey the impression that he stood above the partisan battles of the political arena, de Gaulle was the prime mover in the politics of the Fifth Republic during his presidency. In exercising personal leadership he often violated both the spirit and the letter of the constitution. But since he arrogated to himself the power to interpret the meaning of the constitution whenever he believed it important or necessary to do so, no serious challenge to his personal rule arose prior to the crisis of 1968. His actions evoked criticism, however, and made him the subject of political controversy, precisely what the ceremonial head of state in Britain seeks to avoid.

De Gaulle exercised his personal leadership in several ways. First of all, through visits to foreign heads of states and their visits to him, and through declarations of foreign and domestic policy, he became the spokesman for the nation. His insistence on pomp and ceremony caused the limelight to focus on him. Second, through his employment of the referendum, he sought to buttress his authority by demonstrations of popular approval. The constitution does not give the president the right to initiate referendums, only to refuse to call for them when asked to do so by the Government or by Parliament. Nonetheless, he obviously was the initiator of those that were held. The National Assembly opposed, to no avail, the referendum that amended the constitution to provide for popular election of the president. Despite the illegality of this action, even the Constitutional Council was powerless to prevent it.

Many of the French were most disturbed, given the past abuse of plebiscites discussed in Chapter 9, to be told by the president that the referendum had become a normal feature of government—a way, in effect, of circumventing Parliament. Although in the early years of his tenure de Gaulle used the referendum effectively (in disposing of the Algerian question), demonstrating that a vocal opposition often constituted but a minority, an unsuccessful referendum led to his downfall in 1969.

Third, de Gaulle actively sought to determine Government policy in fields he considered vital. At times he made policy and simply told the Government rather than asking its advice. Relying on technical committees or personal advisors, he often bypassed ministers. Sometimes he contradicted policy statements of the prime minister, who was forced to "change his mind" publicly. He would appoint to the Government only those people he approved, regardless of the prime minister's preferences, and would require them to resign when he was dissatisfied with their work, again regardless of the prime minister's views.

Some students of the French system developed the doctrine of reserve powers and open areas to explain de Gaulle's conception of the office of president. Under this interpretation, defense and foreign policy were reserved for presidential action. The constitution does make the president commander of the armed forces and says that he "shall preside over the higher councils and committees of national defense." On the other hand, it also says that the prime minister "shall be responsible for national defense." But in de Gaulle's view defense and foreign policy clearly affected the whole nation; therefore, they must be the concern of the president, given his duty to guarantee national independence, the integrity of the territory, and the continuity of the state. Thus, although a General Secretariat of National Defense reported to the prime minister and he appointed an Inner Defense Committee, they had little to do with defense policy. The president made such policy in the Defense Committee (which, at least, did include the prime minister and several other ministers) and simply informed the Government.

Domestic policy was an open area where discussion of policy alternatives could be carried on more freely by the rest of the executive. These matters were likely to lack the exalted importance of defense and foreign policy and thus be beneath the president's dignity; they were, as de Gaulle once contemptuously dismissed them, "decisions concerning the price of milk." Yet even in domestic matters the president's views were understood to be decisive, should he care to intervene. Despite this qualification, de Gaulle himself never accepted the doctrine of reserve powers and open areas. He felt that such a conceptualization was too restrictive—his policy area should be unlimited.

Finally, in the exercise of the president's emergency powers, de Gaulle insisted that he was the sole judge of the propriety of all Governmental actions for the duration of the emergency. He thus refused to permit the convocation of a special session of the National assembly during such a period, even though a majority of the deputies demanded one in accordance with constitutional provisions. The manner in which the president conducted himself during the five months of emergency rule in 1961 at the time of the military insurrection in Algeria was in many ways reassuring. But whether the situation in Algeria met the constitutional requirements for emergency rule was questionable.

De Gaulle was able to exert personal leadership in these various ways because of his success in appealing to French national pride. On matters such as the future of NATO, the development of the Common Market, and relations with the Soviet Union, de Gaulle forced other countries to recognize that France's views must be given considerable weight. Domestically, he was willing to attack any and all established institutions if he felt it necessary. He did do something about housing. He did do something about university reforms, particularly in the establishment of new technical universities. He successfully fought the Catholic hierarchy in the matter of adoption and child care laws.

De Gaulle's exit from power was characteristic of him and illustrated his conception of the office of president. In mid-1968 student protests over centralized, outmoded, and overcrowded universities resulted in demonstrations at most French universities and even at some high schools. The student demonstrations and the excessively brutal police response to them triggered worker protests. Within a few days more than half of France's industrial work force was out on strike and workers had occupied hundreds of factories. When the Government promised university reforms, the workers demanded greater economic benefits, and were not in a mood to accept partial concessions by the Government and the management. Virtually everything came to a standstill. The economy seemed to be approaching paralysis. The French Government seemed helpless to deal with the crisis. De Gaulle waited, then announced plans for a referendum in June that would empower him to deal with economic and university reforms, presenting the whole matter as a choice between him and chaos. It soon became apparent that the chances of a successful referendum were dim.

We now know, from Prime Minister Pompidou's posthumously published memoirs, that for perhaps the only time in his life de Gaulle panicked. He fled Paris without leaving a forwarding address—Pompidou did not know where to find him. At the time it was thought that de Gaulle had gone to Germany to assure himself of the support of the French troops stationed there in any confrontation between himself and the protestors. While he indeed had gone to Germany, his purpose was to arrange to go into exile there. Only when the general in charge of the French troops in Germany persuaded him to return to Paris did he do so.

Upon his return, he dissolved the National Assembly, calling for new legislative elections. This show of leadership—so far as the public knew at the time, de Gaulle had once again demonstrated his decisiveness and coolness under fire—

rallied the public, which had grown exasperated with disorder. De Gaulle and Pompidou (the true architect of the triumph) managed to pin much of the blame for the widespread disorder on the Communists, even though the PCF actually had accused the students of anarchism and juvenile radicalism. In the electoral campaign the party tried to disassociate itself and the workers from the breakdown of law and order, but to no avail. The election became a means of expressing disgust with the rioters, many of them not students, who had taken over after the initial demonstrations. The result was a landslide victory for the Gaullists.

De Gaulle declined to reappoint Pompidou as prime minister—you surely didn't think he was the type of man who would express gratitude to anyone, want to feel indebted to them, did you? The General once again seemed firmly in control. Early in 1969, however, de Gaulle again sought to amend the constitution by way of the referendum. One proposal was to make the French Senate an advisory body. Another proposed change was to strengthen regionalism by replacing the 96 departments with 21 regions. These regions were to be governed by locally elected assemblies with significant powers, including taxation. De Gaulle had sketched out these ideas for regional reform prior to the 1968 crisis.

Although de Gaulle stated clearly that he would not remain in office if the referendum failed, the electorate rejected his proposals, 10.5 million yes to 11.9 million no. De Gaulle promptly declared that he was ceasing to exercise his functions as president of the Republic.

De Gaulle had not needed to make the threat of resignation nor was he obligated to carry it out once the referendum was lost. But clearly, for a man as concerned with honor as he was, there was no alternative. He felt repudiated by the French people and, as he had done 23 years earlier when they had rejected his advice, he turned his back on them and left them to work out their destiny by themselves. No one can say whether the French really did intend to reject de Gaulle or whether they really believed he would carry out his threat if the referendum failed. Perhaps the best interpretation is that they had grown weary of his high-handed style of government and, just as adolescents seek to establish themselves as people not subject completely to their parents' values and plans for them, rebelled. The other relevant factor was that for the first time in the Fifth Republic many of the French felt that an alternative was available. Whereas in the past the choice, as de Gaulle himself often had posed it, was either de Gaulle or chaos, in 1969 a competent replacement for de Gaulle was available— Pompidou. Had de Gaulle not made the mistake of dismissing Pompidou as prime mimister, despite his importance in helping the Gaullists to win the 1968 elections, Pompidou might not have made it so clear that he was quite prepared to succeed de Gaulle in the president's office. Pompidou had demonstrated in May 1968 that he could act coolly and effectively. Thus, the French decided to defy their guardian's instructions, relatively secure in the knowledge that the bogeyman really would not get them for their transgression.

THE PRESIDENCY SINCE DE GAULLE

Unique as de Gaulle's presidency was, events since then have demonstrated that the governmental structures created to his specification have a vitality of their own beyond what his personality gave to them. Already when Mitterrand entered office the Fifth Republic had spent more time under presidents other than de Gaulle than it had under de Gaulle himself. De Gaulle probably would have regarded the continuing effectiveness of "his" constitution as a satisfying memorial, for, despite his arrogance, he sought not his own glory but the revitalizing of France.

His successor, Pompidou, did not have much opportunity to put his mark on the office, since death shortened his term to only five years. Ironically, although Pompidou had been irritated by the way de Gaulle treated him as prime minister, he himself functioned as president much as de Gaulle had. The grandeur of the office and the dominant role of the president were maintained or even enhanced. In fact the photos that appear in Figure 14–1 seem to have been taken at one of those amusement arcades in which you have your picture taken with your head thrust through a piece of plywood painted to show a funny scene or character. The background and the body appear to be the same and only the head has changed.

The election of Giscard in 1974 seemed to offer a less regal presidency. His campaign seemed to be trying to project the same image that had made John Kennedy president of the United States about a decade earlier. He stressed his age—he was the youngest of the major candidates—and dynamism. His four children bicycled around France leading groups of teenagers wearing T-shirts emblazoned with the slogan *"Giscard à la barre"*—Giscard to the helm. It was all very American and would have appalled the General.

Although he came from a party on the right of the political spectrum, Giscard projected the image of a reformer. He wanted to liberalize France's abortion and divorce laws and to end the political bias of governmental controlled broadcasting, for example. Furthermore, he claimed an interest in humanizing the office and developing closer contacts with the common people. He announced that he would accept dinner invitations from private citizens, and for several years actually did eat with "typical" families two or three times a year. But these soirees eventually disappeared from view. Despite the fact that the President and his wife arrived unescorted, the president driving his own car, and stayed after dinner for a few hours of conversation, the whole idea was too contrived to be effective. While some people no doubt believed that the president's effort was sincere, general reaction probably is best summed up by the fact that one could buy in Paris specialty shops plasticized aprons with a caricature of Giscard's face and the words, "Guess Who's Coming to Dinner Tonight?"

Then there were some—if not scandals—actions that did not seem quite right. Perhaps the most widely discussed was the "diamonds affair." The dicta-

FIGURE 14–1   Presidents of the Fifth Republic

Charles de Gaulle 1958–69

Georges Pompidou 1969–74

Valery Giscard d'Estaing 1974–81

Francois Mitterrand 1981–

tor of a former French colony in central Africa gave diamonds to Giscard—among others—apparently in appreciation for French military and financial aid, which helped him to keep his control over the country. In the United States gifts beyond those of the most minimal value received by the president and other such officials from their counterparts in other countries must be turned over to the government. The idea is that the gift has been given to the office itself rather than to the current holder of it and, in any event, retaining a valuable gift would raise questions of attempted bribery. Giscard appeared, however, to regard the diamonds as his own personal property. He did not reveal having received them—it was left to a satirical French magazine to do so some time later. Giscard tried to claim that they were very small diamonds and not worth a great deal, but the story refused to die. Eventually he claimed that he had sold them and given the money to charity (recipients unspecified). The General would not have been pleased.

Finally, he did not leave office with much grace. As you know, in the United States an outgoing president is a lame duck for two and a half months after the election, since the new president does not take office until January 20. The new president appoints a transition team, which works closely with the outgoing Administration trying to prepare everything for effective use of power once the new president is inaugurated. None of this occurred in the shift from Giscard to Mitterrand.

Part of the problem was that no one was quite certain just when Giscard should turn over the office of president to his successor. No previous president of the Fifth Republic had served a full term after being directly elected—de Gaulle resigned and Pompidou died. So no one knew whether Giscard's term expired seven years from the day of the previous election or from the day that the results had been announced officially or from the day that he took up residency in the Elysée Palace, the presidential residence. In any event, Giscard broadcast his farewell to the nation seven years to the day after he had been elected, and two days later formally transferred power to Mitterrand. Thus Mitterrand took office only 11 days after the second ballot in the presidential election. Giscard's attitude throughout these proceedings seemed to be one of pique that the voters had dared to deprive him of a personal possession and bestow it upon an interloper.

Thus by the end of his presidency Giscard had become at least as aloof and regal as de Gaulle had been. One almost wonders whether the office itself produces such behavior, totally apart from its holder's intentions and desires. Mitterrand's presidency provided the first opportunity to see what the office does to a man on the left of the political spectrum. He came to office regarded as a reformer and opposed to an "imperial presidency."

On the other hand, Mitterrand never has been known for personal warmth, and he enjoys solitary pursuits. For someone who has been in politics as long as he has, he is a remarkably private man. He is quiet, even taciturn, and his great love of nature and the countryside causes him to spend a good deal of time out

FIGURE 14–2   The Château

of the public eye. He has shown within the Socialist party that he can be quite ruthless politically. He is a shrewd political tactician, a manipulator, who attaches great importance to unquestioning personal loyalty—remember what he has done to Rocard. A good American parallel for all this would be President Lyndon Johnson.

It was not long before people were saying the Mitterrand's press conferences resembled in style the legendary ones of de Gaulle—let me have your questions for the answers I have prepared. He was regarded as an authoritarian and was nicknamed Uncle Napoleon. Conflicts within the Government would be resolved by a phone call from the "château," as insiders came to call the Elysée Palace. For policy advice Mitterrand relies not so much on the Government as a group, but on one-to-one contacts. Even more important is his own staff of personal advisors for such matters as African affairs and intelligence.

As regards policy, Mitterrand is a pragmatist, little committed to ideology. His socialism is more a socialism of the heart; he scorns the power that wealth bestows and is committed to social equality. But his knowledge of economics is weak and he is little interested in economic collectivism. On defense he is even more of a hawk than was Giscard, and he tends to be more sympathetic to the United States and critical of the Soviet Union than were any of his predecessors, despite his complaints about U.S. policy in Central America and high U.S. interest rates.

The Government's austerity measures have taken their toll of Mitterrand's popularity. In mid-1982, polls showed that as many people were satisfied with him as were dissatisfied. By August 1984 only a third were satisfied—he had become the most unpopular president in the Fifth Republic's history. And in November 1984 the proportion satisfied declined further to only 26 percent—the first time ever the figure had been below 30 percent.

But at that time Mitterrand was only halfway through his term. He still had ample opportunity to recoup his popularity and demonstrate whether the French president can provide leadership without being the imperious figure that the de Gaulle heritage seems to have cloned.

THE GOVERNMENT AND ITS RELATIONS WITH THE PRESIDENT

During the Third and Fourth Republics, the prime minister and his colleagues usually were referred to as the Cabinet, although their official name was the Council of Ministers. They deliberated informally, presided over by the prime minister. In such a capacity they were known as the Cabinet Council. In order for their acts to be valid, however, they had to meet as the Council of Ministers, over which the president of the Republic presided. These were brief meetings to give legal form to what had been hammered out at length in the Cabinet.

Early in the Fifth Republic the Cabinet Council continued to function, meeting about once a month.[1] Meetings then became less frequent, and now it has virtually ceased to exist. Thus the only full, general purpose Government body (as distinct from a variety of subject matter executive committees, including only some of the ministers) is the one provided for in the constitution—the Council of Ministers.

The Council of Ministers is composed of the prime minister and an unspecified number of ministers (the constitution does not list those who are to be included). The Government also includes a number of junior or assistant ministers, called secretaries of state. Prior to 1981 the Council usually numbered about 20, with about another 20 serving as secretaries of state. At times some of these secretaries would be included in the Council—there is no rule or consistent practice on this.

When the Socialists came to power a new position was added—minister delegate. While these ministers ranked ahead of the secretaries of state, like them they were to assist particular ministers by focusing on a specific area within a given ministry. So long as Mauroy was prime minister, the Council numbered about two and a half dozen, mainly ministers, but included the relatively few minister delegates as well. About a dozen secretaries of state brought the Gov-

---

[1]William G. Andrews, "The Collective Political Executive Under the Gaullists," in *The Impact of the Fifth Republic on France*, eds. William G. Andrews and Stanley Hoffmann (Albany: SUNY Press, 1981), p. 17.

ernment up to a total in the low 40s, as had been standard in the past. Under Fabius, the Council was to be slimmed down to fighting trim to combat France's economic problems. The number of ministers was cut and the minister delegates were dropped from the Council. The result was a Council composed of the prime minister and 16 ministers. The Government as a whole, however, continued to number in the low 40s.

The incompatibility rule in Article 23 of the constitution prohibits a member of the Government from serving in Parliament. This probably is why the Government in France is so much smaller than in Britain—much less than half as large—while the British Cabinet and the French Council of Ministers are about the same size. When French deputies become members of the Government, they must resign from the legislature. Despite no longer being a member of it, they are permitted (as a member of the Government) to address either house and engage freely in the debates. The main disability is that they are prohibited from voting in the legislature. Thus again in contrast to Britain, the French Government does not have the automatic "payroll" vote of about 100 members—about a sixth of the total Commons membership—whose support it can count on in Parliament. This is an argument in favor of giving the French Government additional procedural devices to help get its program through the legislature.

With the incompatibility rule you can see once again the hybrid nature of the French system. The hallmark of the parliamentary system is the fusion of powers. Typically, this means that members of the executive not only are drawn from the legislature, but continue to serve there simultaneously with their service in the executive, as is the British practice. Although breaking with this practice, France has not embraced the U.S. system of complete separation of powers—members of the Government continue to have floor privileges in the legislature, something denied to U.S. Cabinet members.

The idea behind the incompatibility rule, as with virtually everything else in the Fifth Republic, was to strengthen the executive. You will recall that in the Third and Fourth Republics, the ministers played musical chairs. Once a Government fell the ministers who did not manage to find a place in the next one could continue in Parliament waiting for their next turn, which probably would be in about six months, given the typical life of a Government. Thus the fall of a Government might cost a minister something, but it was not a major career setback. He or she lacked any major incentive to make an all-out effort to marshal all friends to support a challenged Government. But when a Government falls in the Fifth Republic, ministers are not only out of executive office, they are without a seat in Parliament as well. Increasing their personal stake in a Government defeat was seen as a means of strengthening their commitment to the Government. Thus they would be more likely to use their influence to get their friends in Parliament to vote for the Government.

In contrast to Britain, French Governments are overwhelmingly composed of civil servants. Typically during the Fifth Republic the proportion has run from two fifths to two thirds. The sharpness of the contrast is reduced some-what because in France a civil servant can be elected to Parliament and hold both positions simultaneously. Thus despite containing a high number of civil servants, every Government has had a majority of legislators and some have been entirely legislators (in the sense of having held seats in Parliament before the incompatibility rule required giving them up).[2] Nonetheless, such legislators are a very different type of person from the career elective politician who makes up the bulk of the British Cabinet.

French Councils in the Third and Fourth Republics were weak, resulting in general Governmental instability. What is the Fifth Republic's answer to assembly government? Is it the establishment of a strong Council along British lines, or is it the foresaking of parliamentary traditions and the inauguration of presidential government along American lines? The aim of the framers of the new constitution was to strengthen the executive and to produce greater stability, but the French political system is neither *presidential* nor *parliamentary* as these terms are generally understood in Britain and in the United States.

As for the prime minister in the Fourth Republic, unlike his British counter-part, he was not necessarily the leading figure in the Government. At times he simply was one of several leaders of a small center party that was well placed on the political spectrum to serve as a focal point for a coalition. He frequently had to compromise on policy. His ability to appoint members to the Government was limited because certain parties were recognized to have claims on particular posts and he would have to accept whomever they wanted for that job.

The Fifth Republic's constitution provides that "the Government shall determine and direct the policy of the nation." Furthermore, as explained in the previous chapter, the constitution empowers the Government to regulate by decree those areas for which Parliament has not been given specifically power to legislate. And with Parliament's consent, the Government can regulate by decree even those areas normally within the legislative domain. During the period for which Parliament has granted such power to the Government, it has denied itself power to pass any laws on those particular subjects. But it is not the Government as a collectivity nor even the Council of Ministers as a group that really decides how to wield such powers.

We have seen that concern exists in Britain that the prime minister may be becoming too dominant. Nonetheless, the British Cabinet is not just a rubber stamp; it does provide a forum for collective deliberation and decision making. This is not the case with the Council of Ministers.[3] A good share of the meetings is devoted to what in elementary schools would be called "show-and-tell," Dissent is rarely permitted and discussion is in name only. The sessions amount to

[2] Ezra Suleiman, "Presidential Government in France," in *Presidents and Prime Ministers*, eds. Richard Rose and Ezra Suleiman (Washigton, D.C.: American Enterprise Institute, 1980), p. 123.

[3] Andrews, "The Collective Political Executive . . . ," pp. 19, 25, 27–29. Ezra Suleiman, "Presidential Government in France," p. 113. Françoise Giroud, *La Comédie du pouvoir* (Paris: Fayard, 1977).

little more than a highly formal report of important decisions that have been taken elsewhere.

The atmosphere of Council meetings is encapsuled in the following incident. President Giscard had maneuvered his prime minister, Jacques Chirac, into resigning. That Chirac was doing so was generally known, but it so happened that a Council meeting was scheduled for the day on which he was publicly announcing his resignation. Giscard decided to go through the regular Council meeting just as though nothing unusual were to occur. Then at the end he turned to Chirac and said, "Mr. Prime Minister, I understand you have something to tell us."

On paper the Fifth Republic has strengthened the prime minister, but his or her actual power depends on relations with the president. The role of the prime minister has varied from being little more than an agent of the president—for example, Couve de Murville—to being an initiator of policy—Pompidou from 1966 to 1968.[4] Barre at times was able to insist on a particular course of action and get Giscard to accept this.[5] In part, this was because Giscard trusted Barre more than he had his predecessor, Chirac. Barre, unlike Chirac, clearly was not at that time a potential challenger for the office of president. Chirac's frequent disagreements with Giscard also had raised doubts in the president's mind about whether Chirac could be trusted to faithfully execute Government policy.

The division of responsibility between Giscard and Barre was somewhat similar to that which had existed between de Gaulle and Pompidou. Giscard concentrated on defense and foreign policy with Barre working on domestic policy. Giscard sought to establish the idea that he was concerned with long-term issues that could best be dealt with by someone above the political battle, leaving to Barre the short-term matters requiring political in-fighting.

Specifically, given France's economic difficulties toward the close of the 1970s, Barre was to figure out how to halt inflation and increase productivity. In effect, Giscard used Barre as a shield. When the tough measures necessary to deal with inflation aroused public discontent, Barre had to take the blame—he became the most unpopular prime minister in the history of the Fifth Republic. Had the economic medicine been successful, however, then Giscard would have taken the credit. Barre was more than just a front man, however, because Giscard did give him a relatively free hand in economic matters.

Mitterrand and his personal assistant meet each Tuesday morning at breakfast with the prime minister and the head of the Socialist party. Don't think that this is like the weekly meeting in which the British prime minister tells the queen what's going on. While these meetings in France do give those dealing firsthand with the National Assembly an opportunity to tell the president what the mood

[4]Michel Debré, "The Constitution of 1958, Its Raison De'être and How It Evolved," *in The Impact of the Fifth Republic on France*, eds. William G. Andrews and Stanley Hoffmann (Albany: SUNY Press, 1981), pp. 10–11. Suleiman, "Presidential Government in France," pp. 112-9.

[5]Suleiman, "Presidential Government in France," pp. 119-21.

of the deputies is, the object really is for the president to tell them what he wants done.

The nature of the relationship can be seen in the proposal to alter the government of Paris so that it would have 20 mayors, rather than just one (who happened to be—coincidence—Chirac). Mitterrand and the Minister of the Interior (the old political war-horse Gaston Defferre) drew up this plan in secret without telling, much less consulting, the prime minister or the Socialist party.

Nor is Mitterrand content simply to direct policy; he also concerns himself with Government style or procedure. At one point while Mauroy was prime minister, the Minister of the Interior, Defferre, publicly dissented from what the Minister of Justice, Robert Badinter, had announced were the Government's plans for reforming police powers. Mauroy made light of the disagreement, saying that Socialists ran a more democratic-style Government than had the right in the past and that ministers should be free to express contrasting views. From on high, Mitterrand issued the pronouncement that ministers could speak outside the Council of Ministers only if in so doing they did not harm the Government's coherence and cohesion (which, obviously, in this case they were doing).

During the Fourth Republic the general secretary of the Government (a staff position, rather than a political one) attended Council meetings to take minutes. Now meetings are attended as well by the general secretary of the presidency.[6] The secretary of the Government submits draft minutes to the secretary of the presidency for the president's approval. The minutes are confidential, and the only copy is kept in the presidential archives.

Except for vacations, the Council meets about once a week.[7] Meetings last about two or three hours. The general secretary of the Government drafts an agenda under the supervision of the prime minister. The president and the prime minister then discuss the agenda, and the secretary of the Government and of the presidency draw up a second draft in the light of the discussion. This, then, is presented to the president for any final changes. So although the prime minister has some influence in this process, the president controls the agenda for the Council.

When the Council meets, the president, not the prime minister, presides. "In earlier republics, presidents had chaired the council formally, but, in fact, prime ministers had exercised greater control over its business. De Gaulle and Pompidou transformed formal leadership into effective and virtually complete control."[8] Complete control means exactly that.

The president decides what the relation will be with the prime minister and he always has been the dominant figure. "The President of the Republic is the real head of the Government even though a necessary division of labor grants the

---

[6] Andrews, "The Collective Political Executive . . . ," p. 21.
[7] Ibid., pp. 21–26.
[8] Ibid., p. 31.

Prime Minister certain 'frontline' tasks such as responding to parliamentary criticism and coordinating the work of the different ministerial departments."[9] But this simply is the way in which the system has developed in practice; it is not constitutionally required. A future president might conceive of the office as that of ceremonial head of state, and thus allow the prime minister and the Government to exercise most executive power. Alternatively, had de Gaulle chosen in 1958 to be prime minister rather than president, the balance of power between the two offices obviously would have been reversed from what it now is. The only constitutional advantage that a president would appear to have is the ability to invoke emergency powers and a set term of seven years, in contrast to the prime minister, who can be voted out of office at any time by the National Assembly or replaced by the president.

Thus far, the Fifth Republic has operated more as a presidential than a parliamentary system, even though the Government is responsible to the National Assembly. The new powers given to the Government have not so much strengthened it as they have the president, who has been the dominant executive to this point. Not only do the precedents seem to be hardening in favor of a presidential system, but a quarter century of the Fifth Republic seems to have weakened, and perhaps destroyed, traditional French hostility to a strong executive.

One question remains, however, about the workability of the system. What happens when the president comes from one segment of the political spectrum and the majority in the National Assembly, and, therefore, the prime minister, come from another? The question was posed at the time of the 1978 legislative elections when it appeared that the left might win. Since it did not, finding the answer became less pressing until the presidential elections of 1981. When Mitterrand won, it momentarily appeared that the question might need an answer, since his opponents controlled the National Assembly. But he immediately called for new elections and his Socialist party swept to a majority in the National Assembly. Thus the Fifth Republic never has dealt with the situation in which the legislature is politically out of phase with the president. Could the system function effectively in such circumstances?

Divided control of the Congress and the presidency in the United States does not provide much of a guide. The French situation is more complicated because the system includes elements of parliamentary government absent in the United States. France has a dual executive, one portion of which is accountable to the legislature. How can the prime minister please a legislature of one political orientation and a president of another? How effective a leader can the French president be without majority support in Parliament? As we noted in the previous chapter it is majority support, not the various constitutional changes, that really explains the strengthened executive in the Fifth Republic.

The question is an important one, which is likely to become pressing after the legislative elections in 1986. At that point President Mitterrand may have the in-

---

[9] Jean Massot, quoted in Suleiman, "Presidential Government in France," p. 112.

teresting experience of discovering whether the apparently well-established Fifth Republic can weather a basic political stalemate.

BIBLIOGRAPHICAL NOTE

In addition to the Andrews and Suleiman papers cited in Footnotes 1 and 2, see Suleiman, *Politics, Power, and Bureaucracy in France* (Princeton, N.J.: Princeton University Press, 1974). The Giroud book cited in Footnote 3 is the jaundiced view of a former Council of Ministers' member. Also useful are Malcolm Anderson, *Government in France: An Introduction to the Executive Power* (Oxford: Pergamon Press, 1970), and chapters 1 and 3 of F. Ridley and J. Blondel, *Public Administration in France* (London: Routledge & Kegan Paul, 1964).

15

Policy-Implementing Structures

The outstanding characteristic of French public administration is centralization. Like Britain, France is a unitary state; yet French administration, which retains a great deal of the absolutist tradition, is more centralized. What the British call local government is more appropriately referred to in France as administration. The centralized bureaucracy of Napoleon's time has survived and has played an important role in French public life largely because of the weakness and instability of the political executive. Stability in administration in the midst of political instability was no doubt recognized and appreciated by the French people.

Paradoxically, administration in France also can be characterized as dispersed or loosely integrated. At the national level (as distinguished from the national–local relation mentioned in the first paragraph), departmental integration tends to be less advanced than in Britain.

STAFFING THE BUREAUCRACY

Not until the Fourth Republic did France establish a single, unified civil service system. The principle of selection of civil servants by merit had been instituted prior to that time, but individual government departments had a relatively free hand to recruit staff by their own procedures. As a result, personnel seldom moved from one ministry to another. Civil servants acquired a highly specialized knowledge of their own ministry but lacked a broad view of government operation. Recruitment was unified by law after World War II, with general conditions established to govern promotion and discipline. But even then some areas remained outside the civil service code (for example, nationalized enterprises and technical branches such as mining and engineering).

While the post-World War II recruitment procedures have not resulted in dramatic changes in the class composition of the civil service, they have produced greater uniformity in the training of personnel. This in turn helps to facilitate transferability of staff.

To centralize the recruitment of top administrators and to provide them with the skills needed in their work, the National School of Administration (ENA) was created by executive order in 1945.[1] The ENA is under the office of the prime minister with its day-to-day operations supervised by a director chosen by the Council of Ministers.

The school is open to two groups of people: those with university degrees who are not yet 25 years old and civil servants under 30 who have worked for the government for at least five years. The two means of entry were provided in an attempt to "democratize" the civil service—reduce the class bias that has been a problem in France just as it has in Britain. Making young civil servants without a university education eligible for entry was to be a means of permitting people from lower economic levels to rise to positions of responsibility if they were capable.

Admission to the ENA is highly competitive. Students must take a long and difficult series of written examinations. Civil servants must take written exams also, but these are easier. Those from either group who do sufficiently well then are given a series of oral exams. Applicants then are ranked and the top ones— usually only about 150 a year—are admitted. Despite the intended aim of democratization and the easier exams for civil servants, usually about two thirds of those admitted are students. Civil servants without university education or upper-class background do not do well on the type of exams that are given for admission.

The Communist Minister for Civil Service in Mauroy's Government attempted to democratize the ENA slightly. Under his reforms people who "have shown their devotion to public service"—trade unionists, local government councillors, and members of community associations—may take a special entrance exam slightly different from the usual ones. Furthermore, they are guaranteed an interview with the admissions committee. (Strangely, in Britain the oral interview in civil service recruitment and promotion is regarded as a means of being able to discriminate against the lower classes, while in France it is considered a means of giving them entry into the recruitment channel.) And those taking these exams and interviews are guaranteed 10 of the 150 places for admission to ENA.

Training begins with a year's internship at an important administrative office. The assigned duties are not errand-running but involve discretionary deci-

[1]William Schonfeld, *Obedience and Revolt: French Behavior Toward Authority* (London: Sage Publications, 1976), pp. 229–43.

sion making. The internship is followed with a 17-month program of study back in Paris at the school itself. The ENA is located on a rather dingy side street. Unless you know exactly where to look, you easily can walk right by the brass plaque identifying the ENA on the pillar next to the doorway leading into the courtyard around which the school's classrooms are grouped. The courses are organized as small seminars. The ENA has no regular faculty, but instead uses, on a part-time basis, people who hold relatively high positions in the civil service.

An elaborate grading system covering all aspects of work during the program is used to rank the participants. Each person in the class then can choose in turn whichever of the available government positions he or she wishes. One needs to be among the top 15 to 20 to have much hope of getting one of the "plums"—a position with the *grand corps*. The *grand corps* is the term used to refer to the elite sections of the civil service and includes the Council of State, the Court of Accounts, and the Inspectorate of Finances.

It is difficult to overestimate the importance of the ENA. This is not because of the quality of the instruction it provides for its students. The ENA "is a machine for mixing and ranking. It is hardly a machine for teaching."[2] Its importance is not that it prepares future administrators to function effectively, but that it creates a pool of recruits for top governmental positions, all of whom have had a similar socialization experience, which should facilitate their interrelations.

Although the total number of ENA graduates is not great—around 3,000— they occupy key positions not only in the bureaucracy but also in the Government. A high point was reached in Pierre Messmer's Government in 1974, when half of the ministers were ENA graduates. Graduates included not only such prominent figures on the right as Giscard and Chirac, but also such leading Socialists as Prime Minister Fabius and ministers Rocard and Chevènement. Although it is an overstatement, someone has coined the term *enarchy* to suggest that France is ruled by an elite produced by the ENA.

THE IMPACT OF BUREAUCRATIC STRUCTURE UPON PUBLIC POLICY

National Administration

As in Britain, political ministers direct the administrative system through a number of ministries. The organizational structure of these ministries is quite diffuse. The basic unit is the bureau, headed by chiefs. Related bureaus are combined in *directions,* or divisions, which are headed by directors. But French

---

[2]François Bloch-Lainé, quoted in Ezra Suleiman, "Presidential Government in France," in *Presidents and Prime Ministers*, eds., Richard Rose and Ezra Suleiman (Washington, D.C.: American Enterprise Institute, 1980), p. 122.

bureaucracy lacks an official comparable to the British permanent secretary to coordinate the various divisions.

Thus, contrary to what some have argued, Government instability was important. Some have suggested that, although ministers came and went with great rapidity, this made little difference because the civil service went on as usual and could keep government operating efficiently. But the lack of a permanent secretary on the British model made coordination and continuity of policy more difficult to maintain. The result was less coherent, consistent policy than otherwise would have been the case.

The impact which the bureaucracy had on policy tended to be negative. That is, in the absence of adequate coordination, preventing something from getting done was much easier than implementing a new program. The brief tenure of ministers in the Third and Fourth Republics encouraged civil servants to take a new minister's desire for policy or procedural innovations less than seriously. One simply could drag one's feet for awhile, and the minister who was making waves would be gone to be replaced by a new minister who might prefer a quiet life, or who at least might have other ideas. There was little need to try actually to implement a minister's ideas. While in some ministries, notably foreign affairs, where the same person held the same ministerial post in several successive Governments, this situation was less prevalent, it was not entirely absent. Thus ministers came, with good reason, to distrust the bureaucracy of their respective ministries. Had ministries been structured as in Britain, the civil service would have had positive as well as negative influence upon policy. The problem of making policymakers accountable to the electorate would have been even greater than it was.

Because of this distrust and the lack of coordination, French ministers appoint a group of about a dozen people or fewer who enjoy their absolute confidence and share their outlook. These groups are called ministerial *cabinets*. A *cabinet* advises and assists the minister and acts as intermediary between the minister and the career civil servants.

Heading the group is the *directeur de cabinet,* a senior civil servant, usually from the *grands corps,* personally selected by the minister. The *directeur* is the equivalent of the British permanent secretary; he (virtually never she) supervises the operation of the ministry, in particular coordinating the various divisions. Dealing with the political aspects of the ministry's work is the *chef de cabinet,* typically a close political friend of the minister—a British equivalent would be a PPS. The *chef* handles relations with Parliament, arrangements for political speeches, and matters of that type. Assisting the *chef* are several *attachés.* The *cabinet* also will include some technical staff, junior-level civil servants recruited from other ministries, like Finance.

In the Third and Fourth Republics the bulk of the members of *cabinets* were bright young people who had just completed a university degree in law or politics. The experience they gained in a *cabinet* was a means of launching a political career. In keeping an eye on the work of the civil servants and trying to ensure that they implemented the minister's policies, the *attachés* learned a good deal about practical government and politics and demonstrated their loyalty and usefulness to their political mentor, the minister.

In the Fifth Republic this has changed; the overwhelming majority of the members of *cabinets* are senior civil servants. Their primary concern now is not relations with Parliament, but coordination of policy with other ministries. This development, along with the changed composition of the Council of Ministers, which we mentioned in the previous chapter, has produced a gain, but at a serious price. The bureaucracy and the executive now are so intermeshed that the Fifth Republic has seen "the end of the relation of mutual tension between a cabinet composed essentially of politicians supervising the bureaucracy, and professional civil servants removed from politics."[3] Furthermore, a French Government does not face the problem of a new American Administration of trying to locate people who are something other than birds of passage for top jobs. The French "President can therefore surround himself with competent advisors, who are legitimate in the eyes of the community that they serve, who belong to a permanent and stable set of institutions, and, finally, who are linked to a wide network in the public sector and beyond."[4]

The price for these developments is, first, that civil servants selected by a minister for a *cabinet* "continue to be paid by the corps to which they are attached. A public institution thus continues to pay the salary of a civil servant who no longer works for it and who is taking some form of political apprenticeship."[5] This is just one aspect of a general politicization of the civil service that has become prevalent under the Fifth Republic.[6] Anything approaching the British idea of political neutrality in order to be able to serve Governments of whatever political hue has been destroyed.

Finally, there is the question of Parliamentary control. Reversing the usual pattern in a parliamentary system of the legislature putting its members in the executive to supervise the bureaucracy, in the Fifth Republic the executive/ bureaucracy has been "colonizing" the legislature. Political careers no longer are developed from grassroots electoral support to national office, but from national administrative positions to legislative and local influence. You should have no trouble understanding why one scholar, as we mentioned in an earlier chapter, places the Fifth Republic in France's "administrative tradition."

More stable Governments in the Fifth Republic have meant greater life expectancy in office for ministers. Thus the coordination provided by ministerial *cabinets* has been able to serve as an effective means of producing integrated,

---

[3]Stanley Hoffmann, "The Fifth Republic at Twenty," in *The Impact of the Fifth Republic on France,* eds. William G. Andrews and Stanley Hoffmann (Albany: SUNY Press, 1981), p. 306.

[4]Suleiman, "Presidential Government in France," p. 126.

[5]Suleiman, "Presidential Government in France," p. 124.

[6]Suleiman, "Administrative Reform and the Problem of Decentralization in the Fifth Republic," in *Impact of the Fifth Republic,* Andrews and Hoffmann, p. 71.

coherent policy. The structural reforms instituted since the end of World War II—centralized recruiting of civil servants and establishment of the ENA—have helped to produce greater interdepartmental integration. Intradepartmental integration also has been achieved to a considerable extent, but in the case due to changed patterns rather than structural alteration.

The Prefectorial System in Transition

Centralized administration has characterized nation—local government relations in France since at least the time of Napoleon and in some ways since the heyday of the Bourbon monarchs. Contrary to what those who believe that socialism seeks to concentrate all power in a central government would expect, one of the first tasks that the Mitterrand Government set itself was to decentralize French administration. This reform was potentially more far-reaching and significant than any other step taken by the new Government, including expanded public ownership of industry. At stake was the total transformation of the nearly-two-centuries-old prefectorial system. Since the success of this reform effort still is not clear—the changes began going into effect in March 1982—and because its radical nature can be understood only in the context of what existed before, we need to explain in detail how the prefectorial system operated.

France is divided into regions, departments, arrondissements, cantons, and communes or townships. For administrative purposes the key unit was the department (not to be confused with the departments or ministries of the national government's administrative structure), of which there are 96.

Each department has a popularly elected general council, which is something like a legislature in possessing some budgetary and rule-making power. These powers, however, are much more limited than those exercised by local government in Britain or the United States. Councils meet for only a few days each year. Nonetheless, many deputies and senators are candidates in council elections as they seek to establish or maintain a local power base.

The councils' power is limited because all subnational units of government in France are dependent completely upon the national government for their power and existence. The national government, quite in contrast with the situation in the United States, can reorganize or abolish the subnational units at will. There are no states' rights in France. The local units of government, then, simply are one branch of a single, unified state. This is not just a matter of some subnational units of government serving as administrative agents for some national programs, as can happen in the United States. Instead, in France, a direct line of administrative responsibility extends from the national government to the local level. So highly centralized is this relationship that it differs from the one that exists in Britain, even though both Britain and France are unitary systems.

Characteristic of the centralization of French public administration is the fact that one ministry, the Ministry of the Interior, supervises implementation of all national laws throughout France. To realize the far-ranging powers of the minister of the interior, you must visualize central control of everything from the police to the supervision of elections. To maintain this direct, centralized control the minister of the interior appointed a national civil servant, the prefect, to head each department. Thus although each department general council selects one of its members to be its president, the executive officer at the department level was not this person, but the prefect.

Prefects were to keep the national government informed on what was happening in "their" departments and to coordinate and supervise all governmental activity and services there. They were assisted by a staff that included experts in particular subjects, such as welfare and housing. These individuals, however, were not responsible directly back to their home ministry in the national government, but to the prefect. The prefect was controlled by *décrêts d'application,* instructions issued by the Council of Ministers on how the laws should be applied, and by regulations of the Ministry of the Interior. The minister of the interior could remove a prefect at will. Therefore, a prefect's independent discretion was limited; nonetheless, it did exist. Furthermore, prefects were in charge of extensive powers.

Not only did the prefect prepare the budget for action by the departmental council, the council could consider only those matters referred to it by the prefect. The prefect attended council meetings and, should he or she dislike the way in which the discussion was developing, could walk out, thus preventing the council from making any legally recognized decisions. The important decisions concerning the department were made not by the council but by the prefect.

The popularly elected councils at the commune level also were tightly supervised by the prefect. If a commune council did not balance its budget, the prefect could raise taxes to do so. If it failed to provide for mandatory services specified by the national government, the prefect included these services in the budget and raised taxes to cover them. In France at the local level the power of the purse does not exist. Communes are required to build and maintain schools, but have no control over the hiring of teachers or of what is taught. For a long list of subjects commune councils were not permitted to make final decisions without the prefect's prior approval.

This system of controls was referred to as *tutelage,* a term that aptly describes the relation between the national and subnational levels of government. Such tight control is understandable when one recalls that the Revolution and the Republic have had to battle for acceptance for years in France. Such a centralized system of administration helped to ensure unified Republicanism throughout the country. Local control of education, for example, might have allowed too great a clerical influence in some areas. More recently, local control of the police might have raised problems of potential Communist subversion in the late 1940s in those areas where the Communists were the strongest party.

The picture that we have presented probably sounds more extreme than it actually was. Prefects were not petty dictators. Prefects who tried to order and coerce were not very effective and were unlikely to last very long; persuasion and manipulation were more the style of the successful prefect. "The prefect can only effectively run his department with the acquiescence of the local notables, the mayors of the communes and the departmental councillors. To win this support, he must in return espouse their causes and so he is converted into the conciliator and champion of local interests as the price for which the local leaders will prevent opposition to his authority."[7] The prefect's relation with the mayors, in particular, was an interesting and complex one.

Although the mayor is a political figure, selected by the commune council from among their number, and not an administrator, he or she has the same status at the commune level that the prefect had at the departmental level. That is, the mayor is the final link in the administrative chain that stretches from Paris to every locality. Furthermore, the mayor functions like the prefect in that the commune council, like the department one, exercises little influence. The members of commune councils tend to be locally prominent people who regard being elected as a matter of social recognition, rather than as an opportunity to help make policy. Thus they are ready to agree to the mayor's view that they should serve primarily as a rubber stamp of his ideas in order for the commune to appear united in its struggle with the national administration to secure as much as possible of grants and other benefits. And—most important—many mayors are not just small town politicians, but national political figures. A substantial number of deputies in the National Assembly and an even larger number of senators are mayors, some of them quite prominent—both Giscard and Mitterrand were mayors before being elected president and Chirac is mayor of Paris. Thus in some instances a town may regard its mayor, rather than the department prefect, as its contact, its intermediary, with the national government.

In addition to the mayors, several members of a department council may be deputies or senators. National legislators in Paris for meetings of Parliament may in fact spend a good deal of their time away from their chambers contacting ministries about the needs of their departments or communes. On the one hand, these contacts could be a means of controlling a prefect who was at odds with a department or commune. More likely for a skillful prefect, it could be a means of enlisting additional support and political pressure upon the national government to get the assistance that the prefect requests through administrative channels. As you would imagine, whether these contacts of whichever type were effective depended to a considerable extent upon whether the political affiliation of the deputy cum mayor or councillor matched that of the national Government. During much of the life of the Fifth Republic it paid to have a Gaullist mayor.

The French system of centralized administration in local—national relations makes obtaining uniform and consistent policy throughout the entire country easier than it is in the United States. Purely local interest groups tend to have

---

[7] Jack Hayward, *The One and Indivisible French Republic* (London: Weidenfeld & Nicolson, 1973), p. 20.

less influence and to be filtered out of the policy process. Groups need to be sufficiently well and widely organized to affect national ministries if they are to have some hope of achieving their aims. But on the other hand, the French system also results in a less open, less participatory policy process. Policymaking is more bureaucratized than democratized. Furthermore, administration tends to be more partisan, the implementation of the laws tends to be affected by political considerations.

In the early years of the Fifth Republic several steps were taken to improve the administrative system. To facilitate cooperation among the departments and to promote the national government's plans for economic growth, the departments were grouped in 21 economic regions. For the most part these groupings conform to the historic regional areas (for example, Normandy, Burgundy, Brittany). The Government designated superprefects to act as coordinators, mainly for the regional economic programs. Moreover, prefects were given increased responsibility for management, arbitration, and coordination of economic activities in their respective departments.

To facilitate cooperation among communes and among departments, the old regulation prohibiting lateral communication—intercommunal or interdepartmental—has been modified. The prohibition was motivated initially by the desire to avoid any danger of concerted opposition to the national government. Now two or more communes can associate more easily to establish joint services or to plan and implement joint public works programs. In large population areas, urban districts that involve several communities may be created to perform necessary services that the localities may not be able to perform individually. This may be done by local initiative or by request of the national government. Also, the consolidation of small communes has been made easier.

Other measures were designed to reduce the extent of national supervision and make local fund-raising more flexible. Budgets for departments no longer need national approval, if they are balanced and the interest due on loans does not exceed 10 percent of the department's tax revenues. Financial supervision of communes with populations exceeding 9,000 has been reduced. A number of taxes yielding only small sums have been abolished, and more flexible tax systems better adapted to present economic conditions have been introduced. Land assessments have been revised, and the local system of business turnover taxes has been modified. The acute problem of operating deficits for public transportation systems, due in part to conflicting jurisdictions and the refusal of some communities to invest in necessary modifications, was alleviated.

Special reforms were implemented for Paris. One of these was the creation of the Paris Area Authority, which seeks to deal more effectively with the enormous problems of this vast concentration of people, comprising one fifth of the population of France and affecting several units of administration. The Central Markets (*Les Halles*), which were inefficient, unhygienic, and monopolistic, constituted one of the most serious problems of the Paris area. The Paris Area Authority decentralized and reorganized many of the Central Markets' operations, and subsequently moved them from the center of the city. (What was built in its place—a cultural center, which resembles a cross between a factory and a petroleum refinery—may be regarded by some as contributing to visual pollution.) Paris continues to have a popularly elected council, but not until 1977 was this council again permitted to choose a mayor for Paris. The position had been abolished in 1871 when the Paris Commune was overthrown; the idea was to eliminate a possible focal point for the supposedly radical views of Parisians. The new mayor, however, is to have no more power than mayors in other towns. To a considerable extent Paris was governed by two prefects, both of them under the minister of the interior.

The basic aim of these reforms was to make a highly centralized administrative system more rational and efficient rather than transfer real power to the subnational level. Thus these changes differed fundamentally from what the Mitterrand Government attempted. The prefects' powers have been reduced and they now are called commissioners of the Republic.

At the regional level the councils are to be elected directly. The council is to promote the region's development in economic and social affairs, health, culture, science, and environmental planning. The commissioner, designated by the Council of Ministers, heads the national government's regional services in that area and serves as the representative of each national minister. Only the commissioner can speak for the national government before the council. The commissioner is responsible for national interests and respect for law within the region and oversees the performance of the regional authorities.

The department now is to be administered by the council rather than the prefect. The president of the council becomes the executive agent and is in charge of departmental services. This includes implementing the council's decisions, being responsible for income and expenditure, and exercising police power relating to the management of the department.

Should a political stalemate deadlock the council so that it cannot function, the Council of Ministers can dissolve it (a not unknown action in the past). While the president of the council then becomes responsible for day-to-day affairs in the department, his or her decisions can be enforced only if the commissioner agrees. Under normal conditions the commissioner will function at the department level largely as does the commissioner at the regional level. The departmental prefect is the only person, however, authorized to take action concerning public order in an area larger than a single township.

What this reform amounts to, then, is a shifting of the prefect's powers to the mayors of the communes and the president of the department council. Furthermore, the prior control that the prefect exercised over local authorities has been abolished in favor of postaction review of legality by an administrative court. Nonetheless, the prefects remain in the guise of the commissioners as the national government's representative in a given area, even though they now are to be a mere advisory link. While the system has been democratized and decentralized in some ways, some see an aspect of the reform reinforcing centralization.

The explicit designation of the commissioner as the national government's sole representative is regarded as likely to reduce the powers of those local functional specialists who had short-circuited the prefect by going directly to the relevant ministry in Paris. In any event there is the question of whether it is possible to alter fundamentally a system that has endured as long as the prefectorial one had. The French have a cliche, *plus ça change, plus c'est la meme chose*—the more it changes, the more it's the same. However good Mitterrand's intentions, that may well be the most accurate verdict on the decentralization reform.

BIBLIOGRAPHICAL NOTE

A thorough study of French administration is the Ridley and Blondel book mentioned in the Bibliographical Note for the previous chapter. Two works by Brian Chapman, *Introduction to French Local Government* (London: Allen & Unwin, 1953), and *The Prefects and Provincial France* (London: Allen & Unwin, 1955), are penetrating studies of local government and administration in France. Other useful specialized studies are Roger Gregoire, *The French Civil Service* (Brussels: International Institute of Administrative Services, 1965), and Margherita Rindel, *The Administrative Functions of the French Counseil d'Etat* (London: Weidenfeld & Nicolson, 1970). A study more concerned with the politics than the structure of local government is Mark Kesselman, *The Ambiguous Consensus: A Study of Local Government in France* (New York: Alfred A. Knopf, 1967). Finally, an interesting analytical study from the point of view of organizational theory is Michel Crozier, *The Bureaucratic Phenomenon* (Chicago: University of Chicago Press, 1964).

16

Judicial Structures

THE NATURE OF FRENCH LAW AND JUDICIAL PROCEEDINGS

The French judicial system is based on Roman law. Because of its systematic codification under Napoleon, French law is often referred to as the Napoleonic Code. In the British section we noted that common law is largely case law as modified by legislative enactments. Roman law, on the other hand, is primarily code law. Carefully drawn statutes enable the Roman law judge to turn to the law for every case, instead of seeking to find it in the decisions of previous cases, as is often the case in common law. Interpretation of previous cases can be used to provide some flexibility in Roman law systems, but this practice is not essential as in common law systems. The trademark of the common law is *stare decisis* (adherence to decided cases); in other words, previous cases decide present ones. Roman law systems have in recent decades made some use of precedent, especially in France, but there is no acceptance of the principle that precedent is binding in future cases.

French judicial procedure is labeled an *inquisitorial* system, as distinguished from the *accusatorial* or *adversary* system followed in the United States and Britain. The chief difference is that the inquisitorial system emphasizes the rights of society and seeks to repress crime promptly, while the accusatorial system stresses the rights of the accused and attempts to safeguard him or her from possible injustice. The difference is a matter of priorities and, in principle, one system is no more fair or just than the other.

A person taken into custody by the police in France may be held for 24 hours without any charge being brought. The public prosecutor may authorize up to

307

48 hours, however, but in that case the detainee must be visited by a doctor. Once a charge is brought, the prisoner can be held in preventive custody for up to four months (even longer for repeat offenders) for crimes carrying a sentence as little as two years. While France does not have habeas corpus, as in the United States and Britain, those in preventive custody may apply to a judge for release and get a ruling within five days. Nonetheless, several thousand people have been jailed for some time, only to be released ultimately because the evidence against them was insufficient.

Eventually the accused is brought before an examining magistrate—*juge d'instruction*—who decides whether a prima facie case exists. The magistrate examines witnesses, including the arrested person (in the presence of his or her lawyer), and studies other pertinent information. Neither the accused nor his or her counsel is present at the examination of witnesses, although a confrontation in court subsequently is a fairly regular practice. However, the defense counsel has access at all times to the dossier the examining magistrate is compiling. The record compiled mixes facts and rumors that may tend to incriminate the accused, and may include a survey of the accused's past. If the examining magistrate decides that there is a case, the accused is committed for trial; otherwise he or she goes free.

At the trial, the presiding judge does not act as an umpire of a duel between two opposing sets of lawyers. Rather, the judge conducts the trial from beginning to end. He or she has the complete dossier and is familiar with it. He or she interrogates the witnesses, beginning with the accused. The sole aim is to discover the truth. During the trial, witnesses are able to talk at length and there is no rule of evidence that excludes irrelevant eloquence on their part. Lawyers do not directly cross-examine witnesses; they only suggest questions to the judge, who propounds them. There is no summing up of a case in the British-American manner.

A basic French historical document, *The Declaration of the Rights of Man*, asserts that accused are innocent until proven guilty. Despite this element in France's political tradition, scholars disagree sharply on whether the presumption of innocence is adhered to in practice in French courts. Illustrative of one view are the comments that being held without charge before trial effectively neutralizes the presumption of innocence. "When a trial begins, defence and prosecution are formally on an equal footing but it is preceded by a protracted phase during which a *prima facie* case is prepared by the police and the examining magistrate. French procedure is directed at securing a confession of guilt. Generally, the examining magistrate is not concerned at how the confession has been obtained by the police, even though the person brought before him shows obvious signs of having been beaten up."[1] Another view agrees that most defendants are convicted, but notes that not all cases go to trial. "There is a lengthy

---

[1] Jack Hayward, *The One and Indivisible French Republic* (London: Weidenfeld & Nicolson, 1973), p. 13.

pretrial investigation by police magistrates, in which the various due-process guarantees are applied and in which the suspect may be able to use counsel."[2] Yet another view asserts that "the defendant in a criminal trial is presumed innocent and the burden of proof is clearly on the court insofar as conviction is concerned . . . careful attention is given to the admissibility of evidence. Guilt or innocence is determined by secret ballots."[3]

Given such diverse interpretations of French justice, perhaps about all that we can say is that it would appear in France that being required to stand trial carries with it a bit more of a tendency to believe that a person has done something wrong than does an indictment in the United States. An indictment is supposed to mean only that the evidence appears to be sufficient to justify holding a trial to establish clearly whether a crime was or was not committed. Even under the American legal system many people are inclined to regard an indictment as an indication that the accused indeed probably has done something wrong.

Whatever the situation regarding presumption of innocence in practice, the difference between the French and American systems can be seen in the treatment of the accused in one regard. In the United States—given the stress upon protecting the accused from injustice—the defendant does not have to take the witness stand to be questioned. In France—given the concern to discover the truth and protect society—the accused must stand examination.

In France a case may involve both criminal and civil proceedings. An injured party may seek damages in addition to the government's prosecution on criminal charges. The two actions may be separate or the injured party may join the criminal prosecution, being represented by his or her own counsel. Such linked proceedings can produce a curious result—a person may be ordered to pay damages for killing someone whom he or she has been acquitted of murdering.

On the whole, French courts are free from many of the technicalities characteristic of the Anglo-American system. Justice tends to be accessible because France has a large number of courts geographically well distributed. While judicial proceedings are not inexpensive and those who are wealthy do have an advantage, yet costs probably are not as great a problem in France as in Britain and the United States. Legal aid is provided without charge to those who cannot afford it.

STAFFING AND ORGANIZATION OF THE COURTS

Another difference between Roman law and common law systems is the contrast in judicial careers. In the common law system judges are drawn from the legal profession. In the Roman law system, a person interested in a legal career

---

[2]William Safran, *The French Polity* (New York: David McKay, 1977), p. 239.
[3]Lowell Noonan, *France: The Politics of Continuity in Change* (New York: Holt, Rinehart & Winston, 1970), p. 398.

must decide at a relatively early age to become a judge or a lawyer. In France the judiciary is part of the civil service. Judges are trained for a career on the bench through the Ministry of Justice.

Judges are recruited from law graduates under 27 years old who have passed a competitive examination and who then spend three years in training at the National Center of Judicial Studies, which was created at the start of the Fifth Republic. The Center is designed to do for the judiciary what the ENA was intended to do for the bureaucracy—namely, produce a highly competent, respected judiciary. Before completing the program at the Center, students must decide whether they wish to become a judge or a prosecutor. It is worth noting that the fact that both professions are trained in the same school may make judges feel a kinship with prosecutors that they do not feel with defense attorneys.

Judges are appointed not by the minister of justice, but by the president. The president acts on the basis of recommendations from the High Council of the Judiciary. The president presides over the High Council, which is composed of the minister of justice and nine others appointed by the president for four-year terms. The High Council itself presents names for appointments to the Court of Cassation and for the first presidents of the courts of appeal. In the case of other judicial appointments the High Council comments on names proposed by the Ministry of Justice. In addition to these duties the High Council also acts as a disciplinary council for judges. And the president must consult the High Council before pardoning persons sentenced to capital punishment, and may consult it in cases of petition for reprieve of sentence.

"Although in theory the judiciary is independent of the executive, it tends in practice to be subordinated to the government."[4] This is not because judges are removable, but because of the discretion of the minister of justice in promoting them. Judges who have shown a willingness to favor whatever position is desired by the government, advance in their careers, while those who do not are less likely to do so. "The virtual subordination of the bench to the prosecutors in turn leads to the dominance of the police, whose minister of the interior is much more powerful than the minister of justice."[5]

The constitution of the Third Republic did not refer to the judiciary or a judicial system. In practice, a dual system of courts developed—ordinary courts and administrative law courts. This judicial system, as it evolved, was virtually unaltered by the constitution of the Fourth Republic. In the early years of the Fifth Republic, however, a number of changes were made. These sought: (1) to modernize a court system which originated at a time when 75 percent of the population was rural; (2) to improve rules of procedure and to clarify jurisdictions; (3) to improve training of judges (in the Center already mentioned); and (4) to establish the Constitutional Council, mainly as a check on Parliament.

---

[4]Safran, *The French Polity*, pp. 237–38.

[5]Hayward, *The One and Indivisible French Republic*, p. 128. On pp. 128–30 he provides some examples of executive pressure on the judiciary.

We will discuss the Constitutional Council in the final section of this chapter. But first we explain the structure of the judicial system, beginning with the ordinary courts and then turning to the administrative law ones.

At the bottom of the ordinary court system are the courts of first instance (*tribunaux d'instance*), which replace the justices of the peace of the Fourth Republic. There are 457 of these courts, so they are quite accessible. Each court has several judges, who are required to reside in the place where the court is located in order to be attuned to local values. Cases are heard and decided by a single judge sitting alone. As is common in Europe, the French separate civil jurisdiction from criminal. The courts of first instance deal with civil cases in which the sum involved is no more than about $500 or $600.

At the next level in the civil court hierarchy are the courts of major instance (*tribunaux de grande instance*), of which there are 172. The jurisdiction of each of these courts extends throughout a department, although the larger departments may have more than one such court. These courts try the more important civil cases for the first time and also have some appellate jurisdiction, not only from the courts of first instance, but also from the special labor and commercial courts. Three judges preside over cases in the courts of major instance, and decision is by a majority vote.

Turning now to the criminal courts, the lowest level is the police court, which is as widespread as are the civil courts of first instance. These deal with petty offenses with a maximum sentence of two months in jail.

Above the police courts are the correctional courts. Here the maximum sentence can be as much as five years in jail. The judges staffing the correctional courts are the same as those for the courts of major instance. The same system of three judges and majority verdicts also is followed in the correctional courts.

The most serious criminal cases originate in the assize courts. Each department has an assize court, which is called into session each quarter. An assize court receives its cases on the basis of an indictment from the court of appeal in the area or from the Court of Cassation. Three judges preside over an assize court with the main one, called the president, coming from the court of appeal in that area. These three judges are joined by nine lay people in a jury. A two-thirds vote of these 12 people is required to convict. Decisions of the assize court are final. Even though the cases it hears are being tried for the first time, they may not be taken to a higher court on appeal. The Court of Cassation can be petitioned, however, to review the decision to see whether the law has been interpreted correctly.

The divided civil and criminal jurisdictions are merged in the 27 courts of appeal, one for each of the judicial regions into which France is divided. The courts of appeal hear appeals from the decision of the criminal courts (except for the assize courts), the civil courts, and the various special courts such as farm lease courts, commercial courts, and the like. In civil cases the review deals both with matters of fact and matters of law, while in criminal cases the only issue is whether points of law were decided correctly when the case was originally tried. A court of appeal also may have a case referred to it by the Court of Cassation when that court objects to a decision of another court of appeal.

At the top of the judicial hierarchy is the Court of Cassation. It has three sections: the criminal chamber, the civil chamber, and the chamber of requests. Each section has a president and 15 judges. Criminal cases go directly to the criminal chamber, but civil appeals are funneled through the chamber of requests, which forwards only those appeals that it believes contain substantial grounds for reversal. Like the American highest courts, the Court of Cassation does not finally dispose of an appealed case. A reversal of a lower-court decision—that is, a successful appeal—merely means that the case is sent back for retrial. In retrying the case the lower court is to act in accord with the reasoning of the higher court in sending the case back. If the lower court does not do so, however, and the case comes back to the Court of Cassation yet again, then the entire court deals with the case. If it remains convinced that it is right in its interpretation of the law, it returns the case of another lower court of the same level with instructions for decision that must be followed. Thus in this fashion the way in which the law is interpreted will be consistent throughout the country.

Apart from the regular court system is the High Court of Justice. The High Court can try the president or other members of the Government for high crimes and misdemeanors. It is composed of deputies and senators elected in equal number by the National Assembly and the Senate. For a case to be tried by the High Court of Justice both the National Assembly and the Senate must vote indictments by a majority of their total membership.

Also separate from the regular court system is a fully developed system of administrative law courts. In the course of providing a public service, governmental agencies may damage some individuals. In other instances bureaucrats may misinterpret, deliberately or inadvertently, the power that the law gives them and act beyond what is authorized. In such instances an agent of the government is acting not in the capacity of a private citizen, but in a public capacity. To prevent or rectify the results of abuse of administrative power, to deal with maladministration requires judicial action not against the bureaucrat as a private individual, but against him or her as an agent of the government.

The rules applied in such cases are administrative law. Administrative law deals not only with the rights and liabilities of citizens in their relations with agents of the government, but also with the relations between bureaucrats and the government. The administrative law court system is intended to provide an inexpensive, accessible, and efficient means of redress for people injured by governmental action. Of fundamental importance is the fact that under this system private citizens can sue the government without first having to obtain the government's approval to do so. Interestingly, although French administrative law includes various statutory rules and regulations, it also makes considerable use of the decisions made in previous cases. Thus administrative law in France comes closer to the case law approach of Anglo-American justice than do criminal and civil proceedings there.

The administrative law system in France seems to have originated in the French Revolution and the events that preceded it. Even the *ancien régime* had been subjected to intolerable restraints by the law courts. With the coming of the Revolution, all parties were agreed that the courts would be a stumbling block to the new order, and all were determined to change things. A revolutionary law of 1790 declared that judicial functions must remain distinct from the administrative ones, while the constitution of 1791 forbade the courts from engaging in actions that would infringe upon the administrative field.

These actions were in line with Montesquieu's interpretation of the separation of powers as understood by the French—that is, the courts must not interfere with the freedom of administrative action. Theoretically, under this philosophy, the government can do anything it pleases without any fear from the ordinary courts. The undesirability of freeing governmental action from all legal controls quickly became apparent to the French. Over the decades safeguards evolved in the form of administrative law courts. The result is a system that makes government responsible for its acts and protects individuals from administrative excesses.

Administrative courts do not function like regular courts. When one feels wronged by administrative action, he or she files a petition indicating the objectionable action and specifying the remedy sought. The court then functions like an investigating committee to ascertain the facts of the matter. The petitioner does not need to hire a lawyer, since it is up to the court to be certain that all relevant points of law are brought out. After all the relevant information is gathered, the court announces its findings. Then in closed session it decides whether there is a basis for voiding the action taken by administrators in this particular case.

One advantage of this system is that costs are extremely low even if one loses a complaint. Thus, even those with little money are not prevented from seeking redress from maladministration. The administrative courts have a high reputation for fairness; many, in fact, feel that justice is more likely to be done here than in the regular court system. The administrative courts have been losing, however, one of their former advantages—that of speedy disposition of cases. Delays—as much as two years between petition and decision—are no longer uncommon, especially in important cases.

The impact of the system is limited by the fact that only administrative acts, and not other governmental actions, are subject to control by administrative courts. Actions by administrative agencies may be nullified only if the agency or administrators in question were not empowered to do what they did or sought to do, if prescribed forms of procedures were not observed, if power was abused (that is, legal acts performed for purposes not contemplated by the law), or if there was an error in the law. In short, an administrative court may not challenge the right of a law to exist, but only the way it is being implemented.

In recent years, however, decisions have tended to expand the scope of review, to emphasize merit instead of merely technicalities in deciding cases.

Nonetheless, the system's ability to protect civil liberties is restricted because action by judges and the police cannot be challenged in administrative courts. Arrests and searches, for example, are not under the administrative courts' jurisdiction. Because in recent years government has expanded into matters where the ordinary law already applied (such as nationalization and the protection of property rights), the line of demarcation between private law and administrative law has become less clear. If government does violence to the right of property or public freedom, it may be subject to the jurisdiction of the ordinary courts.

Should a dispute arise concerning whether a case should be heard in the regular court system or in the administrative law courts, the matter is referred to the Court of Conflicts. The Court of Conflicts consists of the minister of justice plus three members of the Court of Cassation, three members of the Council of State, and two from either of these two bodies. Although normally the Court of Conflicts simply decides where the case should be heard, in exceptional circumstances it may decide the case itself.

Thirty-one administrative law courts of general jurisdiction are distributed throughout the country. Each one has a staff of a president and several councillors. Cases are heard by a group of three. In addition to these courts a number of specialized courts are part of the administrative court system. Among these are the Court of Accounts, which verifies the accounts of all persons who handle public funds, and the Superior Council of National Education, which deals with complaints against decisions in the school system.

At the top of the administrative court system is the Council of State. Its approximately 180 members are divided into five bodies or sections, only one of which deals with judicial business. But it is this section that has given the Council of State the high public prestige that it has. Despite the fact that its members are appointed by the Council of Ministers, acting on the recommendation of the minister of justice, the Council of State is free from domination by the Government. If there is any bias in its decisions, it is in favor of the citizen.

Members of the Council of State have no specified term of service; they can be removed only for malfeasance. Typically its members make service a life career, although some may take a leave of absence to serve in Parliament or in a position in the executive branch. Most members are chosen by competitive examination, and the ENA is the predominant source of candidates. To be certain that the Council can deal adequately with changing conditions, a small number of members can be appointed for one-year terms because of their expertise in special subjects that may have come to attract the Council's attention.

The Council of State hears appeals from the various administrative law courts, and in addition has original jurisdiction in some cases. When a case reaches the Council of State it is heard by five councillors. If the administrative exercise of discretionary power is challenged, the Council of State will require the ministry concerned to state its reasons for its actions. The Council is empowered to call for documents and files relevant to the case. The Council endeavors to insure that administrative actions are reasonable, while preserving to administrators the discretion of action that properly belongs to them. The Council is the ultimate umpire to determine whether administrators exceeded the power vested in them. Despite its difficult task, the Council has struck a balance that has gained the confidence of both the administrators and the citizens. The existence of such a body empowered to redress grievances helps to make administrators act more responsibly.

The other four sections of the Council of State act in a consultative capacity to the Government on administrative questions. In some instances the Government is required to consult with the Council—on decree laws, nonlegislative decrees, and before submitting a bill to Parliament, for example. The Council can take the initiative and suggest to the Government areas where legislative or administrative reforms would be desirable. As a means of protecting its interests, each ministry designates an official of high rank who participates in all meetings of the Council when matters relevant to the ministry are being considered.

The advice of the nonjudicial sections does not bind the judicial section in any case that comes before it nor does it bind the Council of Ministers. For example, the Council of State wanted the Socialist Government to modify its bill to nationalize the banks. The Government had attempted to avoid any international problems by excluding from the bill foreign-owned banks in France. The Council of State felt that this raised constitutional problems by not treating all banks equally. The Government rejected this advice and went ahead with the bill as it was. Nonetheless, so great is the Council of State's prestige that Governments usually follow its advice. Thus many people feel that the Council helps to check arbitrary action in its consultative capacity as well as in its work as the top court in the administrative law system.

Considerable delay may occur before the Council of State completes action on a case. Furthermore, even though it often is disposed to help the citizen, it cannot overturn a law. If the proper procedures have been followed, it may not be able to give the citizen any redress. Therefore, the French decided to create an ombudsman, but only after considerable hesitation, since they felt that the administrative law courts should have been able to cope with matters that typically are referred to ombudsmen in other countries that lack administrative law courts. The French ombudsman is called the *Médiateur*. He or she is appointed for a nonrenewable six-year term.

Like Britain, which it used as the model for its system, France has been more cautious than Sweden in creating this new position. A French person with a complaint against an administrator cannot go directly to the *Médiateur*. Instead he or she must communicate with a member of Parliament, who will decide whether the complaint has sufficient merit to be passed on for action by the *Médiateur*. Nonetheless, the French now have the opportunity to seek redress for maladministration in some cases without having to go through even the quasi-judicial procedures of the administrative law courts.

The French legal system provides a number of protections for the individual; in theory there is nothing unjust about the system. In practice, as we have seen, there are areas of legitimate concern. This, however, is an outside observers' judgment. What do the French people themselves feel? In four public opinion polls taken from September 1962 to February 1971 in France, the proportion of respondents saying that the French judicial system works rather badly or very badly ranged from 48 percent to 60 percent.[6] Only once on these four occasions did the proportion drop below 50 percent and that time, because some people questioned did not have an opinion, only 35 percent said that the judicial system worked rather well or very well. Clearly, the French themselves are not satisfied with the quality of justice they receive.

The minister of justice in the Mauroy and Fabius Governments has sought to improve that quality, to humanize the system without in any way reducing its effectiveness. He has attempted to make the system more concerned with protecting the individual, rather than with protecting the government. In some instances he has been successful, in others less so because of the opposition of the conservative minister of the interior, who heads the police. Thus Robert Badinter has achieved the goal to which he was passionately committed of ending capital punishment, but he has been less successful on identity checks.

Identity checks by the police generally were illegal until the Giscard presidency. During his last year in office the law was changed to permit such checks to avert threats to law and order. While a judge needed to approve this practice, this did little to restrain its use by the police. In practice the power tended to be used to harass those with dark skins—once again the tensions in France produced by sizable numbers of immigrants from North Africa. Badinter planned to revise the law so that identity checks could be made only when a crime had been committed or the police had evidence that a crime was being planned *and* objective signs indicated that the person to be checked was a suspect for the crime. While this reform was made, a major loophole was included as well. The new criteria did *not* have to be observed by the police in cases where they perceived an immediate security threat. Thus it appears that despite the change in procedure, the police still are using identity checks in a discriminatory fashion.

The important point illustrated by this example is that in France the balance that any judicial system must strike between authority and individual liberty is tilted much more toward the former than it is in either Britain or the United States.

THE STATUS OF JUDICIAL REVIEW

Traditionally, France, like most other European countries, has not had the American equivalent of judicial review. Courts could not question the right of the legislature to legislate on anything it wished. This was due, perhaps, to the fact that French constitutions have been unlike the American. They did not impose specific limits on what the legislature could do; there were no prohibitions,

---

[6]Hayward, *The One and Indivisible French Republic*, p. 130.

and no powers reserved to subordinate units such as the states. The very concept of judicial review did not arouse much enthusiasm or support.

The constitution of the Fourth Republic established a Constitutional Committee to determine whether the laws passed by the National Assembly implied amendment of the constitution. While the Committee could not nullify acts of the legislature, it could return for reconsideration bills it thought implied amendment of the constitution. If Parliament persisted, the law could not be promulgated until the constitution was amended. Since the Parliament by itself could amend the constitution, however, no one regarded the Constitutional Committee as a judicial hurdle to the aims and desires of the legislature.

As we indicated in Chapter 13, the Fifth Republic's constitution departs from French tradition by specifying, and, therefore, limiting, the powers of Parliament. Since Parliament no longer is completely free to legislate as it chooses, some form of judicial review is needed. the question now *can* be raised whether Parliament has overstepped the bounds of its power. The principal mechanism for determining this is a new Fifth Republic institution, the Constitutional Council, although the Council of State also is involved to some extent.

The basic membership of the Constitutional Council is nine people appointed for nine-year terms. Three of these are chosen by the president of the Republic, another three by the president of the National Assembly, and the final three by the president of the Senate. Former presidents of the Republic also are members. The Council has a number of functions. For example, it is in charge of supervising elections. If the Government asks it to do so, it decides whether the president is so incapacitated that his or her powers should be exercised by the president of the Senate. But its primary duty is constitutional interpretation.

As you may have concluded from Chapters 13 and 14, disputes about the boundary line between the executive's and the legislature's policymaking powers under the Fifth Republic's constitution can occur easily. To compound the confusion, the laws of the Fourth Republic, passed under a different constitutional allocation of power between the executive and the legislature, did not cease to exist simply because a new constitution went into effect. So who has the power now to alter Fourth Republic laws that are still on the books? If the law to be modified is in the legislature's field, then a new amending law will have to be passed. But if the law now falls in the executive's field, then it can be changed simply by decree. The Council of State decides whether the law falls in one field or the other. Like other decisions of the Council, this opinion, although usually followed, is only advisory.

In the case of laws passed since the beginning of the Fifth Republic in 1958, the decision lies with the Constitutional Council. The Government can ask the Council to rule that the subject of the law actually falls within the executive's decree power rather than in the Parliament's sphere. Should the Council agree with this contention, then the Government can alter the law by decree.

More typically, the Constitutional Council is involved before a law is passed. Should it appear to the Government that a bill being discussed in Parliament infringes on the executive's decree power, the Government simply declares that item out of order for Parliamentary consideration. The president of whichever house of Parliament is involved must indicate whether he or she agrees with the Government's view. If the president disagrees, the matter goes to the Constitutional Council for decision. The constitution does not provide for Parliament to object should it feel that the executive has issued a decree in an area that seems to have been placed within Parliament's sphere of action. As noted in previous chapters, the Fifth Republic tilts the power balance decisively in the executive's direction.

The Constitutional Council is not really declaring a law unconstitutional in these circumstances. Instead it simply is relieving the Government, if it agrees with it, of having to alter a disagreeable law by having new legislation passed and permitting it to make the changes itself. In another type of situation, however, the Constitutional Council can void a law as unconstitutional.

The president, the prime minister, the president of either house of Parliament, 60 deputies, or 60 senators can question the constitutionality of a law during the 15-day period between final passage and promulgation. If the Council agrees with the challenge, the law cannot go into effect. Should no one raise the question within the specified time and the law is promulgated, then it is valid regardless of whether it seems to violate the constitution. No procedure exists for subsequently challenging its constitutionality.

While this is a form of judicial review, it differs considerably from procedures in the United States. In the first place the Constitutional Council is not the final appellate court for the regular court system as is true of the American Supreme Court. Second, the decision in France on constitutionality is being made in the abstract. In contrast with American law, there is no case or controversy involved; no effort has been made to apply the law. Thus the Constitutional Council is giving something like what in American law is called an advisory opinion. This the U.S. Supreme Court will not do. In its view one must have an actual legal conflict between opposed parties to be able to ascertain the full ramifications of a law; rights cannot be specified in the abstract. Given the Anglo-American emphasis on the case law approach, this position is understandable. Similarly, given the French preference for the Roman or code law system, it is understandable that the French feel that issues of constitutionality are best decided in the abstract when a general, rather than a specific rule, can be laid down and when the details of a particular case are not allowed to get in the way of deciding issues of basic principle. Somewhat less easy to understand is why the power to challenge a law's constitutionality should be prohibited to the average citizen. To this extent American citizens have a much stronger defense of their basic rights than do French citizens.

In the first decade of the Fifth Republic the Constitutional Council appeared to be little more than the Government's lap dog. A Gaullist majority on the Council supported the Government's efforts to obtain constitutional interpretations that would expand executive power at the expense of Parliament. In

1961 the Council refused to rule on the question of whether a motion of censure can be introduced in the National Assembly during the time that the emergency powers authorized by Article 16 of the constitution are in effect.

The following year the Council backed away from a confrontation with the president over the question of amendment of the constitution. As mentioned in a previous chapter, de Gaulle resorted to a referendum to change the constitution to provide for direct election of the president instead of using the procedures for amendment set forth in the constitution. When the matter was referred to the Council after the referendum, the Council held that it lacked jurisdiction. It interpreted its powers to apply only to laws passed by Parliament and not to what the people had done in a referendum. Had they decided otherwise, the result would have been a major constitutional crisis. Yet the decision also demonstrated the unwillingness of any governmental organ to attempt to thwart de Gaulle in the pursuit of his goals. What made the Council appear especially spineless was the fact that in any advisory opinion prior to the referendum it had said that the procedure violated the constitution.

In the 1970s, however, the Council appeared to acquire some backbone. Especially notable was a 1971 ruling. The Government had attempted to pass a bill limiting freedom of association by giving prefects the power to refuse to register, and thus legally recognize, any group that the prefect *thought would engage in illicit activities.*[7] Thus a group would be condemned not for something it had done, but for what a governmental official guessed that it might do. The president of the Senate referred the law to the Constitutional Council before it was promulgated, and the Council ruled it unconstitutional. On other occasions the Council has ruled against the Government on the question of whether a bill fell outside Parliament's sphere of competence and on whether existing laws could be changed by decree. Also by 1978 it had ruled all or part of a law unconstitutional on 6 of 19 occasions.[8]

When the Socialists passed their extensive nationalization program in 1981, opposition legislators took the matter to the Constitutional Council, which declared the law unconstitutional. The Council held that the private owners of the firms involved had not been compensated adequately. While greatly angered, the Government revised the method for determining how much the owners would be paid and blustered that the Council had better not void this version as well. For whatever reason, the Council found the second plan acceptable. Thus the number of workers employed in state-owned enterprises nearly doubled (although still amounting to only about a 10th of the labor force) and the percent of industrial sales derived from state-owned enterprises went up from 16 to 29.

The Constitutional Council has provided some defense of liberties and has helped to prevent the legislative–executive balance from being totally one-sided.

---

[7]Hayward, *The One and Indivisible French Republic*, pp. 122–24.

[8]J. R. Frears, "Parliament in the Fifth Republic," in *The Impact of the Fifth Republic on France*, eds. William G. Andrews and Stanley Hoffman (Albany: SUNY Press, 1981), p. 52.

Nonetheless, it shows no signs of developing into the powerful institution that the U.S. Supreme Court is.

The Fifth Republic has succeeded well beyond what many people anticipated when it was founded in 1958. It has become the second most durable political system of modern French history. It has solved the enduring French political problem of executive instability and ineffectiveness, and has done so without the absolutism and antidemocratic measures that characterized past remedies. Nonetheless, the balance of power between the legislature and the executive is tilted too far in one direction. In some ways France simply has been lucky. Had a contemporary version of Napoleon I or III appeared and gained control of the Fifth Republic's executive, democratic institutions in France could have been threatened. Thus some adjustments to the basic constitutional structure still are needed before all doubts and concerns can be laid to rest. And apart from these anxieties the question remains of whether this system can function when the president lacks a majority in the National Assembly. France has developed an interesting hybrid, but the product is still being tested.

BIBLIOGRAPHICAL NOTE

Discussions of French law and legal philosophy may be found in René David and Henry DeVries, *The French Legal System: An Introduction to Civil Law Systems* (New York: Oceana Publications, 1958), and Sir Maurice Sheldon Amos and F. P. Walton, *Introduction to French Law*, 3d ed. (Oxford: Oxford University Press, 1967).

For a comparative view of the administrative law system, see Bernard Schwartz, *French Administrative Law and the Common-Law World* (New York: New York University Press, 1954).

PART FOUR

THE FEDERAL REPUBLIC OF GERMANY

In Germany they came first for the Communists, and I didn't speak up because I wasn't a Communist.

Then they came for the Jews, and I didn't speak up because I wasn't a Jew.

Then they came for the trade unionists, and I didn't speak up because I wasn't a trade unionist.

Then they came for the Catholics, and I didn't speak up because I was a Protestant.

Then they came for me, and by that time no one was left to speak up.

Pastor Martin Niemoeller
WW I U-boat commander and
Nazi concentration camp victim

17

The Setting of German Politics

THE INFLUENCE OF GEOGRAPHY

Germany's geographical position places it astride the center of the European continent. The Federal Republic of Germany (to give it its official name) lies to the east and north of France and stretches from the northern boundary of Switzerland to the North Sea and the southern boundary of Denmark. About half the size of pre-World War II Germany, the area of the Federal Republic is comparable to that of Britain, or about half the area of France.

Germany lacks well-defined geographical frontiers except for the seacoast in the north, and even that is interrupted by the Jutland peninsula. Most of the main rivers either rise on foreign soil or leave Germany for other countries. The Rhine, for example, originates in Switzerland and flows into the sea in Holland.

This fact of geography has had an immense impact on German history, most of it adverse. The absence of geographical barriers meant that little impeded the spread of the German language beyond the political boundaries of Germany. Germans obviously felt a kinship with people of German language and culture in neighboring countries and often saw no reason why areas inhabited by such people should not be incorporated in Germany even when the other countries involved did not want to relinquish the area. Thus at times geography encouraged Germany in aggressive attitudes toward its neighbors.

But, equally, geography has put Germany on the receiving end of aggression. Given Germany's location, almost any European war of any importance was certain to involve German territory. Until German-speaking areas strengthened themselves by unifying, they were the regular battleground of Europe. As you can imagine, the Germans eventually got tired of this and decided it was time to show some muscle simply for self-protection. To some extent Germany's belligerent international attitudes in the late 19th and first half of the 20th century were the product of having been bullied by other countries for some centuries before then.

More positively, Germany's location made possible the development of great ports, such as Bremen and Hamburg, on the North Sea coast, and the development of international trade. Unfortunately, even this had a negative aspect. Had Germany not been a seafaring nation, then the late 19th-century tensions with Britain over naval armaments would not have developed and the world wars of the 20th century might have been avoided.

Germany is rich in natural resources, especially those essential for a modern, industrialized society. Iron and coal are plentiful, along with other important minerals. The many rivers, in addition to facilitating domestic and even international transportation, have been a source of energy.

Farm land would appear to be an abundant resource as well, since 53 percent of Germany's territory is devoted to agriculture. Nonetheless, the Federal Republic is not an agricultural country. The traditional German agricultural areas were in the east; since the end of World War II these areas have been within the boundaries of Poland or the German Democratic Republic (East Germany). Little more than 5 percent of the German work force is involved in agriculture, fishing, and forestry combined. Since the mid-1960s the number of farms and the number of people employed in agriculture have declined by about a third. Agriculture accounts for only 2.4 percent of the German GNP.

Thus Germany, like Britain, cannot feed itself; international trade is essential for survival, to say nothing of prosperity. Many German employees work in export industries, and exports account for a quarter of GNP. The significance of this figure becomes obvious when compared with the United States, where exports are only 7 percent of GNP.

One of the really important keys to the growth of Germany as an international power was its rapid transformation in the latter half of the 19th century from a primarily agrarian country to a modern industrial nation. Economic growth was particularly phenomenal after unification. German coal production jumped from about 30 million metric tons in 1871 to more than 190 million tons in 1914. Similarly, from a low of a few hundred thousand tons in 1850, Germany forged ahead in iron extraction to more than 8 million tons in 1900, equaling that of Britain, and, then, more than doubling the output of Britain before World War I. By 1913, Germany had also become Britain's rival in merchant shipping. Considerable progress was made in organic chemistry and the consequent development of such products as synthetic drugs and dyes. Moreover, Germany developed a sizable electric power industry.

By the late 19th century, then, Germany had used the advantages of its geographical setting to jump from a precapitalist economy to a mature capitalistic one with heavy corporate concentrations and cartels (monopolies). Germany's

FIGURE 17-1   Germany before and after World War II

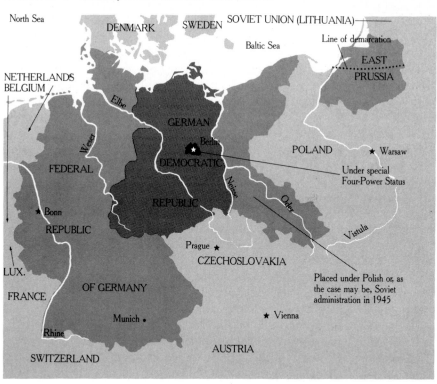

rapid industrial and commercial expansion was facilitated by a banking system purposely designed to promote economic growth. The German economic empire extended far beyond the country's borders. Large enterprises evolved into cartels, which were able to fix prices, regulate markets, and avoid competition. Typical of these developments was the I. G. Farben enterprise, which was virtually an arm of the political system in two world wars.

Germany's position as the industrial leader of Europe was not greatly affected by World War I; in that case geography stood the country in good stead. Most of the fighting did not occur on German soil and, since long-range bombing was little developed, hostilities did not damage German property. World War II obviously was a totally different situation with many urban, industrial areas obliterated. Yet paradoxically, Germany recovered more rapidly and soundly than after World War I. To some extent, American aid accelerated recovery after World War II, but the Germans deserve the primary credit. Hard work and determination were esssential elements in the recovery.

While no sensible person would want to have his or her country's industry bombed into rubble, yet the destruction proved to be a long-term asset in one sense. The Germans had no choice after World War II but to adopt new productive equipment and techniques. These in turn helped to reduce production costs. Thus, while Britain—which did not suffer damage as extensive and total as did Germany—continued to produce with increasingly obsolete machinery. Germany industry of necessity was introducing more efficient methods. Furthermore, in the early postwar period, the victors severely limited German military expenditures. Thus scarce capital was not diverted from industrial recovery. Nor did Germany grant aid to underdeveloped countries to the extent that Britain and France did.

The recovery was an economic miracle. By 1953 Germany had achieved an industrial output that was 59 percent larger than in 1936. By 1956, its gold and dollar reserves were larger than Britain's. Its exports quadrupled between 1952 and 1961, in part because of the heavy investment in the production of goods for export. In many areas, Germany's share of the export market exceeded that of Britain or the United States. Twenty percent of the world's manufactured exports come from German shops and factories. By 1965, Germany was producing every 12th ton of steel and every 14th ton of coal of the world's output. Germany's total national income surpassed that of France in 1960. And its GNP rose to third largest in the world until Japan overtook it in 1968.

Germany's economic recovery may have been aided by a burden that proved to be a blessing in disguise. During the immediate post-World War II years, Germany was almost inundated with a flood (some 13 million all told) of refugees and expellees from communist countries to the east. While most of them were similar to the country's population in having a Germanic background, yet they clearly differed in feeling dispossessed and disaffected. The government sought to integrate these people into the population by means of a number of measures, only some of which were economic. But certainly a key economic measure was the "equalization of the burden" law passed in 1952.

Under this law all able people were to contribute half of what they possessed for redistribution to refugees and others who had suffered major losses during the war, in order to equalize the burden of recovery. Certain public organizations, such as the central banks and religious and charitable institutions, were exempt. The tax base of the lean year 1948–49 was used to determine a person's worth, and individuals and companies were given the opportunity of spreading their payments over 30 years. Out of the fund thus created, the refugees, as well as other Germans who had suffered war damages or who were wiped out by the currency reform, were assisted (according to a complex formula) through grants or loans for housing, furniture, and pension payments.

Such measures were extremely influential in preventing the huge group of refugees from becoming an ocean of malcontents ready to be whipped into a tidal wave of dissent by some demagogue. Not only did Germany avoid this, but by making most refugees feel at home in the Federal Republic, the country managed to channel the determination and energy of these people in ways that speeded economic reconstruction.

Even though Germany was able to integrate successfully millions of refugees into the rest of the population, it remains a country of considerable diversity. As we will explain in the next section, Germany unified into a single country relatively late. Thus a variety of customs and dialects exists in various areas. Just as in the United States, regional stereotypes are common. A south German, for example, usually is expected to be more emotional and fun-loving than a north German, who is regarded as more austere and sober.

But a sense of identity with a subnational level is not as strong as in the United States. The equivalent of the pride of being a Virginian or a Texan would be unusual in Germany. Germany, like the United States and in contrast to both Britain and France, is a federal system. Few German states (land—singular, laender—plural), however, have a long historical tradition. When the current political system was created after World War II, the boundaries that were drawn up for the laender rarely corresponded to those that had existed in the past. In part, the aim was to discourage strong subnational loyalties that might interfere with commitment to the new national political system.

But although past land boundaries were ignored, no attempt was made to produce uniform laender. Thus although Germany has only 10 laender, they differ considerably from each other. Two of them—Bremen and Hamburg—are city-states; it is as though New York and Chicago were to be made separate states in the United States. Even if these two laender are ignored, the remaining eight still differ considerably in size, as Figure 17–2 shows.

Partially related to regional differences are religious differences. Germany divides almost equally on religious preferences, Protestants having only a slight majority over Catholics. Prior to World War II, Protestants had outnumbered Catholics two to one. The balance shifted because the areas now in East Germany and Poland were overwhelmingly Protestant. Although now equally strong at the national level, the strength of the two religions varies by region. Catholics tend to be more prevalent in the south with Protestants dominant in the north.

While religion has some political impact, as we will discuss in subsequent chapters, it does not divide the country into hostile sects. Suspicion and dislike of other segments of society is more likely to be the product of class differences. Traditionally Germany has lacked a sizable small-business middle class, given the rapid transformation into a corporate industrial economy, which we already have discussed. Thus it has been easier in Germany, than in the United States, to believe that the economic system pitted the proletariat against the capitalists and their toadies. Income distribution has been less equal than in either Britain or Scandinavia, although better than in France. Furthermore, educational opportunities have been limited. Children from working-class families have found rising to a new status or more prestigious occupation difficult.

FIGURE 17-2   Area and Population of German Laender

A. Area (000 of square kilometers)

B. Population (000,000)

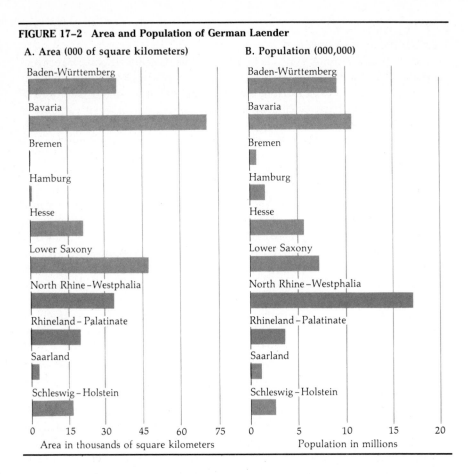

Although class conflict and bitterness have not been totally eliminated, the prosperity that Germany has enjoyed for most of the post-World War II period has reduced such feelings considerably. The average skilled industrial worker in Germany earns about $14,000 a year.[1] Four families in 10 have their own home and eight have a car.

We noted at the start of the chapter that Germany was only slightly larger than Britain in area. But with a population of over 61 million it is almost 10 percent more populous. Like Britain, therefore, Germany is densely populated. In fact, with more than 640 people per square mile, the Federal Republic exceeds the United Kingdom (less than 600 per square mile), although it is much less dense than England alone (over 900). Germany has faced the added problem,

[1]This is at the exchange rate of 1 DM (deutsche mark) equals $0.45 that prevailed at the time.

however, of a dramatically expanded population. Prior to World War II the portion of Germany that now is the Federal Republic had a population about two thirds the number that now live there. In part the great increase was due to an influx of refugees, which we mentioned previously. In some senses, then, the territory that now is Germany is being required to support nearly half again as many people as it did a few decades earlier.

Like Britain, Germany is highly urbanized; a third of the population lives in cities of more than 100,000 and only a quarter in communities of 10,000 or less. Germany is even more of a country of big cities than is Britain. With a population of 1.9 million West Berlin is the largest city, but it is not fully integrated into the political system and does not overshadow other cities the way London does in Britain or Paris in France. Hamburg's population is 1.7 million and Munich's 1.3. Furthermore, nine other cities have populations of a half million to a million. The current capital, Bonn, has a population of only 300,000 and was a sleepy college town until becoming the capital after World War II. It never has dominated German politics in the way that Paris does French politics or that Berlin did in pre-World War II Germany.

As we commented in the British section, city life calls for an activist government. Dense, urban populations give rise to problems that cannot be left to benign neglect. Here again, as we have noted several other times, Germany's physical setting, its geographical characteristics, have important political implications.

You probably have read so much about overpopulation and hunger in third world countries that you will be surprised to learn that Germany faces problems due to declining population. The German birth rate is only 1 per 100 inhabitants—one of the lowest in the world and about 40 percent lower than it was a quarter of a century earlier. Half of Germany's families have no children and of those families with children only half have more than one. This has produced an extremely high old-age dependency ratio; there is one retired person in Germany for every two workers. If current trends continue, in a half century, retired people will come close to equaling workers. Such developments raise serious questions about the ability of the employed to finance the retirement and medical benefits that people have come to expect governments to provide for older citizens.

The size of the work force already has produced problems. The work force was decreasing in the 1960s at the same time as industrial expansion demanded additional labor. So Germany recruited the *gastarbeiter*, the guest worker, from Italy, Turkey, or Yugoslavia to fill the gap. The number of such foreign workers rose to about 2 million. They and their dependents—nearly 3 million more—brought different customs and languages into Germany that were not especially welcomed. Furthermore, when the economy slowed down in the 1970s, the guest workers were resented by many people, who considered them to be a cause of unemployment for native German workers.

HISTORICAL BACKGROUND

Germany is a prosperous, well-educated, Western nation—all characteristics that various studies have found to be associated with democratic political systems. Yet some lingering doubt remains whether democracy is established firmly in Germany. The problem is not like that of France, where other political traditions challenge the democratic tradition. Instead it is the absence in Germany of any democratic tradition at all. Since the formation of the present political system in 1949, Germany has experienced nearly three times as many years of parliamentary democracy as in the whole of its previous history. A brief survey of that history will help to make that clear.

During the latter part of the Middle Ages, the Holy Roman Empire (despite its name, basically a Germanic political system) was the leading European political structure. In the 13th century its significance began to wane, and by the 14th century it was more facade than reality. A unified German nation did not exist. The ties that did remain among Germans were weakened when the Reformation and the religious wars of the 16th century split the Protestant north from the Catholic south. Following the Thirty Years' War in the 17th century—which devastated German areas and greatly reduced the population—the Peace of Westphalia (1648) formally recognized the independence of the various German princes. This so fractionalized Germanic areas that in 1800 314 separate German political units existed, some good sized, but most small.

By smashing this conglomeration of small political units, Napoleon unintentionally facilitated German unification. Austria and Prussia struggled for leadership in this process. Prussia's rulers, especially Frederick the Great (1740–86), raised it from a weak principality to one of the strongest countries in Europe by combining ruthless military action with economic modernization. Nonetheless, Napoleon dealt Prussia a disastrous defeat in 1806. Determined not to be humiliated again, Prussia swept away lingering feudal institutions, modernized the bureaucracy, and introduced military conscription. The regenerative process that would result in German unification by military prowess was under way.

The German response to the impact of France upon central Europe at the turn of the 18th century sharply reduced the number of German political units. At the Congress of Vienna (the international gathering of statesmen in 1814–15 that marked the end of the Napoleonic wars and attempted to restore the old 18th-century political systems) the German Confederation, a loose combination of 38 states, was established. At this point Austria still predominated, although Prussia was able to seize the lead eventually.

This switch was of immense significance for Germany's political development; Prussia was not a liberal monarchy, but a militaristic society. Its political system was not even remotely democratic. An attempted democratic revolution in 1848 was repressed, driving many of the democratic middle class to migrate, especially to the United States. Unlike the situation of comparable groups in

Britain, these Germans could see no hope of liberalizing the political system from within. Thus political leadership among the middle class, those who in many countries played a key role in the movement toward democracy, was weakened greatly.

Certain virtues, however, must be conceded to the Prussian system. The rulers did not live in the luxury of the French Bourbons, but preferred a rather austere or Spartan existence. Administration was scrupulously honest; there was not a hint of corruption. And the system's legal codes were adhered to rigidly, which meant that arbitrary governmental action was extremely rare. Thus, for all its lack of democracy the system was attractive to many.

The person who capped the unification efforts, and who, in a real sense, was the unifier of Germany, was Otto von Bismarck (1815–98). At the age of 47, he was made minister-president of Prussia. He was to guide the nation's destinies, and to a large extent Europe's destiny as well, for three decades. From the outset, he made it clear that he was no democrat. His method would be force, "blood and iron." In two quick wars, against Denmark in 1864 and against Austria in 1866, he established Prussia's dominance, after which he set up the North German Confederation (1867), a union of 22 states and principalities. The unification was made complete after the rapid defeat of France in 1870 and the subsequent ceding to Germany of Alsace and a part of Lorraine. In January 1871, the North German Confederation was abolished and a German empire, consisting of Prussia and the north and south German states, was proclaimed. By "blood and iron" Germany had been unified.

The unified Germany was called the Empire or the Second Reich (the Holy Roman Empire being considered the first one). The Empire lasted longer than any subsequent German political system (see Figure 17–3). Although the Empire supposedly was organized as a federal union of 25 states, one of these, Prussia, held a predominant position in the federation, being able to veto any amendment of the constitution. Moreover, although powers not delegated to the central government were in theory retained by the states, more and more powers were transferred to the central authorities.

FIGURE 17–3   German Regimes since Unification, 1871–86

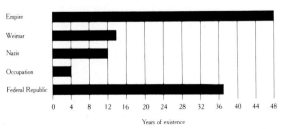

Bismarck did more than unify the nation. For the next 20 years (1871–90), he manipulated and guided the social forces in the Empire and made Imperial Germany a power among the nations of Europe. In domestic policy, he is best known for his actions against, first, the Catholic Church and, then, the Social Democrats. The first, known as the *Kulturkampf* ("fight for civilization"), was not so much an antireligious campaign as it was an effort to undermine the moral and intellectual authority of the Church. Bismarck's memory of his conflicts with Catholic France and Catholic Austria were still fresh, and he suspected the political loyalties of German Catholics in a possible war of revenge. His actions against priests, nuns, and monks, and his expulsion of the Jesuits, together with the confiscation of Catholic Church property, no doubt contributed significantly to the formation of the Catholic Center party. But when this party became reconciled to the German Empire in its existing form and when its political demands turned out to be exceedingly moderate, Bismarck readily repealed the anti-Catholic laws. More than that, he sought to enlist the Catholics in what he had come to regard as a more important struggle—his campaign against the Social Democrats.

Bismarck apparently feared that the Paris Commune of 1871 could have a German counterpart. Two unsuccessful attempts by extremists to assassinate the kaiser (the German monarch) in 1878 gave Bismarck a pretext. He had enacted laws prohibiting socialist groups and meetings and suppressing socialist newspapers and pamphlets. The police were to supervise unions and expel anyone thought to be a socialist. The laws were so extreme and arbitrary that they threatened the liberties even of nonsocialist liberals.

The fact that other political groups joined with the socialists in opposing the laws may explain why they proved to be only a temporary setback for the Social Democrats, rather than destroying them as a party. In 1890 the Social Democrats doubled their support, polling 20 percent of the popular vote. We can only conjecture whether Bismarck would have wanted to pursue even more repressive measures in response, because that year he left office. Kaiser Wilhelm II, newly come to the throne and just past 30 years old, was determined to rule, rather than be a figurehead, and was unwilling to limit himself by allowing Bismarck a major role in policymaking. Thus although Wilhelm regarded the socialists as enemies of the state, he allowed the ban on them to lapse and refused to support Bismarck. Bismarck long had thwarted parliamentary democracy by maintaining that as chancellor (the German prime minister) he was responsible not to the popularly elected legislature but only to the kaiser. Therefore, once the kaiser wanted him out of office, Bismarck had no choice but to resign.

Bismarck had sought a strong and united Germany through a balance of social forces, notably an alliance between the middle class—too weak to achieve power on its own—and the military aristocracy of Prussia. Neither the kaiser nor the military were willing to relinquish any of their powers, and Bismarck certainly did not want to weaken the military might that had unified Germany and guaranteed its international position. So he sought instead concessions for the middle class, such as their appointment to important administrative posts and to positions in the Prussian Cabinet.

Simultaneously, he tried to convince the Prussian aristocracy that they must learn to live with liberal, middle-class government ministers and reconcile themselves to the growing wealth and power of the cities. Similarly, he attempted to persuade the middle class to be satisfied with these modest concessions, arguing that the international situation did not permit weakening the military or the kaiser. Despite his hostility to the socialists, Bismarck tried to win the working class to the grand balance of social groups through an extensive program of social legislation. This included the first system of national health insurance anywhere in the world (a good fact to recall when you hear someone damn a government-financed system of health care as socialist—Bismarck would have been amazed).

Thus Bismarck managed to construct an equilibrium, however delicate, among the social forces; with his departure in 1890 this collapsed. Real power now was in the hands of Kaiser Wilhelm. Neither he, nor his several chancellors, sought to make meaningful concessions to the middle class or to come to terms with the growing political strength of the workers. By the eve of World War I the Social Democrats were polling over a third of the popular vote, more than double the second largest party.

The political system did not move toward true parliamentary democracy. Occasionally, some political groups were consulted about the measures that the Government introduced into the Reichstag (the national legislature). But generally the Reichstag influenced public policy only slightly at best. It had little or no control over financial matters and could not call the Government to account. As we have noted, the chancellor was responsible to the kaiser, not the Reichstag, and as for the other members of the Government, they were chosen for their administrative abilities rather than for any political support that they could muster in the Reichstag.

In view of the failure of many previous efforts to wrest parliamentary democracy from the government, it is ironic that such a political system finally was initiated without a struggle. At the end of September 1918 the military leaders told the kaiser that World War I was lost. He appointed Prince Max of Baden as chancellor and indicated he would accept reform of the politican system. The imperial constitution was revised quickly to provide that the chancellor was accountable to the Reichstag and responsible for all political acts of the kaiser. Thus the imperial system became a parliamentary democracy. But it had no chance to develop further for with the abdication of the kaiser the system collapsed.

In January 1919 Germany embarked on its first real experiment with democracy by electing a constituent assembly for a republic. The delegates, who included some of the best constitutional scholars in Germany, met in the city of Weimar. The parliamentary system that they drew up organized Germany on federal basis with 17 laender. Remembering Prussia's dominance of the imperial federation, they made certain that it could not overshadow the other laender in the new system. They also made the central government considerably stronger than the American national government was at that time.

Unfortunately, the democratic system created at Weimar, which went into effect in mid-1919, lasted less than a decade and a half (see Figure 17-3). As was true of the Third Republic in France, the Weimar Republic experienced considerable cabinet instability. In 14 years there were 20 different Cabinets, which hindered effective government action to deal with the problems facing Germany. To many Germans the government seemed weak and indecisive compared with what they had been used to under the Empire. And at the time of the Weimar Republic weak government was a particular liability.

The old order was crumbling in Germany. In a country where the family traditionally had been a very hierarchical, even authoritarian structure, children no longer respected their parents. The father's generation was seen as having brought defeat in the war. Furthermore, with the economic collapse of 1929 many fathers were unable to support their families. By 1932 almost one third of the working force was unemployed. Another pillar of the old order—the monetary system—was falling apart. After World War I the mark finally stabilized at a rate of 4.2 trillion to the dollar. This wiped out pensions and savings and hit hardest at the middle class—the segment of the population often regarded as the foundation of a democratic political system. In 1929 economic collapse made it appear to Germans that they would suffer this financial chaos yet once again. Anyone who has collected German postage stamps of the Weimar period is familiar with this financial turmoil. Stamps constantly were being surcharged—reissued with new higher values printed over them—as the value of the mark plummeted.

Thus, to many Germans life came to appear meaningless, to be without order. Sociologists term this mental state *anomie*. And they suggest that the behavior typically associated with anomie is to seek a savior. One searches for someone who can eliminate the aimlessness of existence by stating authoritatively rules and guides for life. No democratic politician or structure was able to satisfy this felt need.

Into this vacuum stepped the perfect charismatic leader—Adolf Hitler—who spoke as one having authority. Hitler told the Germans exactly what they wished to hear at that point: that it was not their fault that they had lost the war, for the democrats, particularly the Jews, had betrayed the army. He denounced the Treaty of Versailles, hated by all Germans for the harsh terms it imposed on Germany in ending World War I, and promised that he would make Germany strong enough to ignore its terms. Germans were a superior people, he proclaimed, and must be restored to their former greatness. He used the business interests' fears of communism and their hostility to the trade unions to get financial support from the pillars of society. Thus he was able to create a political organization and make an electoral appeal equal, if not superior, to that of the other parties.

In general, the Weimar Republic never succeeded in creating a political consensus. The country was torn ideologically between the far right and the far left, which represented sizable elements of the population that did not believe in a democratic order. The country was also torn economically and politically; to many, Weimar became synonymous with poverty, national humiliation, and fruitless debate in the Reichstag. The climate of fear and frustration that Hitler sought to dramatize and exacerbate was, in the end, to help him get to power. But before the existing discontents could be shaped into a political force, it was necessary to have a leader and an efficient organization. These Hitler and the Nazis provided.

Given the rising tide of nationalism in Germany in reaction to the harshness of the peace treaty and the general dissatisfaction on economic and other matters, it is not surprising that by 1930 about one third of the electorate was voting for extremist parties. And then in 1932 Hitler's Nazi party polled 14 million votes, leading all other parties and winning almost 40 percent of the seats in the legislature. Originally attracting demobilized soldiers who could not adjust to civilian life, the party soon had gathered a motley crew of social misfits, cranks, political adventurers, criminals, and some idealists. By 1930, it drew strong support from the lower middle classes, from the youth, and from the militarists. It also received the support of significant financial and business circles. Organized along military lines, the Nazi party stirred up delirious demonstrations and carried violence into the streets and into the gatherings of the other parties.

Hitler came to power legally. In the mist of the political, economic, and social chaos, President Hindenberg invited him to form a Cabinet of "national concentration" in which the Nazis and the Nationalists would share power. At that point the only possible majority grouping in the parliament included the Nazis. The only alternative to Hitler would have been a Government ruling without regard to parliament, precisely the failing with which democrats had charged the old imperial system. The army feared that attempting to return to that system might produce civil war. Ironically, Hitler was put in charge of the government in an attempt to avoid civil war and illegality.

Although Hitler retained only three Cabinet positions for the Nazis, they were key ones which helped to ensure control of the government. In March 1933 he called for a Parliamentary election. The Nazis curbed their opponents' use of radio, press, and assembly and looted and destroyed the offices and organizations of other parties. In the end they and their allies, the Nationalists, won over half of the seats in the legislature. On March 24, 1933, in an atmosphere of indescribable frenzy, coercion, and terror, an Enabling Act was passed that became the "constitution" of Nazi totalitarianism in a system called the Third Reich. This title recalled the international prowess of Germany under the Empire and the grandeur of the Holy Roman Empire.

Hitler rapidly consolidated his dictatorship through the process of *Gleichschaltung*, or coordination. Literally everything was to be under his control. The Nazi party had a key role in enabling him to achieve this. The exact relation between the party and the state, however, was extremely complex and defies unraveling. When President Hindenburg died in 1934, Hitler merged that office with that of chancellor, which he held. Thus he headed both the government and the party, and used both to control the country.

Nonetheless, the party clearly was supreme. Should a government employee receive conflicting instructions from a party superior and a governmental superior, the former was to be obeyed. The party's principal tasks were intended to be educating the public at large about Hitler's values and goals and recruiting, training, and placing in governmental positions his loyal and able followers. But since the governmental bureaucracy—a very cohesive and traditional structure in Germany—was not always as responsive as Hitler wished, some functions that in most political systems would be performed by the government were turned over to an agency of the party.

This development was most clear in the case of control agencies. In addition to the usual police forces, several party organizations were created. These included the Gestapo (the secret state police), the SS (an elite political police and military organization), and the SA or storm troopers (a paramilitary organization) that grew from 300,000 in 1933 to a million in 1939. To some extent these groups were intended to be a mutual check upon each other, in addition to controlling society at large, to ensure that no coup could topple Hitler.

Specifying the exact status of the party also is complicated by the many organizations it created for purposes that in a democracy would fall outside the realm of politics. Party groups existed for virtually all important social groups—doctors, lawyers, teachers, students, women, and others. These were both a means of indoctrination into party ideology and a means of control by keeping tabs on the members. Thus the line between politics and other activities—sports and art, for example, since there were party groups for these as well—between public and private life was blurred.

This was the totalitarian element in the system; nothing was outside the concern of the Nazi party. Hitler proclaimed his concern for and his demands upon the entire individual. He sought not just to govern but to remake or purify the German people. The *Volkgeist*—the spirit of the common people—was to imbue the entire nation. This mystical force would restore the Germans to their natural superiority and enable the country to fulfill its destiny.

This new faith was to be the Germans sole guide for behavior. If one accepted this, if one were not a Jew, a gypsy, or a nonconformist, if one were happy to follow orders, then life under the new order could be quite pleasant. For those who posed no threat to the regime, who were not bothered by injustice so long as it affected only others, the system was a relatively open one. One could travel to other countries, and tourists were welcomed in Germany.

But one had to remember that first—no, only—loyalty went to the *Führer* (leader). Neither religion nor family ties could be allowed to compete with dedication to or adoration of Hitler. When a man entered the army he took an oath not to the political system or even the Fatherland, as had been traditional, but to Hitler personally. As for opponents, the secret police rooted them out. Political parties were abolished and newspapers shut down. Concentration camps were filled with not only non-Nazi politicians, but also with union officers, artists, religious leaders—anyone who opposed or was imagined to oppose the Führer.

Seeming to suggest that these sufferings were not major is almost obscene. But they pale into insignificance compared with what was to come. In the 1930s the deaths were numbered in the thousands; in the 1940s, in the millions. Persecution of the Jews—denial of employment, seizure of property, and other measures—began almost immediately under the Third Reich. But time to get out remained for those willing to abandon everything they owned. About half of Germany's half million Jews left before World War II started. Those that remained suffered the same fate as Jews living in the areas that Germany overran in the war. Hitler's "final solution" exterminated nearly three quarters of the Jews in these areas—a total of 6 million people.

In the end the geographical vastness of the Soviet Union and its inexhaustible supply of military personnel combined with the economic strength of the United States to defeat Nazi Germany. Portions of what had been Germany even before Hitler began his expansion were taken away, and the territory that remained was divided into four occupation zones—one each for the United States, the Soviet Union, Britain, and France. Berlin, located inside the Soviet zone, similarly was divided into four sectors. These arrangements were intended to be transitional only until an acceptable government could be established in Germany. The inability of the occupying powers to agree upon the form of this government, however, produced a divided Germany.

The Soviet Union installed a communist system in its zone, which became the German Democratic Republic. The three Western powers merged their zones into another political system. Under the guidance of occupation officials, delegates chosen by the land legislatures drafted a constitution. Since they did not want to accept the division of Germany into two political systems, the document was called the Basic Law, rather than a constitution, and provided that it would be replaced by a newly drafted constitution as soon as Germany was reunited. This now is little more than a forlorn hope.

Thus, with the Federal Republic created by the Basic Law, Germany began its second experience with democratic government. Although young by American standards, the system now has endured nearly three times as long as did the Weimar Republic. German economic prosperity, Cabinet stability, and decline of ideological conflict all proclaim that "Bonn is not Weimar." A tradition of democratic parliamentary government is developing in Germany; only the past history of the country makes one hesitate to affirm that democracy is firmly established there.

BIBLIOGRAPHICAL NOTE

Studies useful as introductions to Germany are: Michael Balfour, *West Germany* (New York: Praeger Publishers, 1968); Ralf Dahrendorf, *Society and Democracy in Ger-*

many (Garden City, N.Y.: Doubleday Publishing, 1967); and Robert E. Dickinson, *Germany, A General and Regional Geography* (New York: E. P. Dutton, 1953).

A standard history is Marshall Dill, *Germany: A Modern History* (Ann Arbor: University of Michigan Press, 1961). More specialized studies of particular periods include John Conway, ed., *The Path to Dictatorship 1918–1933: Ten Essays by German Scholars* (Garden City, N.Y.: Doubleday Publishing, 1966); Franz L. Neumann, *Behemoth, The Structure and Practice of National Socialism 1933–1944*, 2d ed. (New York: Oxford University Press, 1944); Alan Bullock, *Hitler: A Study in Tyranny*, rev. ed. (New York: Harper & Row, 1970); Peter Merkl, *The Origin of the West German Republic* (New York: Oxford University Press, 1963); Richard Hiscocks, *The Adenauer Era* (Philadelphia: J. B. Lippincott, 1966); and Alfred Grosser, *Germany in Our Time: A Political History of the Postwar Years* (New York: Praeger Publishers, 1971).

Gold and Iron: Bismarck, Bleichroder, and the Building of the German Empire by Fritz Stern (New York: Alfred A. Knopf, 1977) deals not only with the formation and development of the Empire, but also with basic German values, and thus is relevant to the second part of the next chapter as well as to this one.

Alex de Jonge, *The Weimar Chronicle: Prelude to Hitler* (New York: New American Library, 1978), is an interesting popular survey of the atmosphere of the time. What mainly recommends the book, though, is the fine selection of pictures. If you really want to know what adulation of the *Führer* meant, look at the eyes of the people in the photo on p. 194.

18

The Foundations of German Politics

CONSTITUTIONAL HERITAGE

Since the constitution of the Empire remains the longest-lived of all constitutions of modern Germany, any discussion of German constitutional traditions must mention it. The system could claim some elements of democracy. In addition to extensive social legislation like old age pensions and national health insurance, it enfranchised all men 25 or older. Britain, long considered a model democracy, did not make the right to vote this extensive until 1918, nearly a half century later. But the Empire was not a parliamentary democracy because the powers of the legislature (Reichstag) were so insignificant that it was unable to develop into a genuine instrument of the popular will and served mainly as a debating society. The center of political gravity was the Bundesrat, whose members were controlled by the separate laender. Since Prussia had 17 votes out of a total of 48 (no other land had more than 6), it clearly was in command. The Prussian king was the German kaiser and the Prussian prime minister was the German chancellor.

The kaiser and the chancellor wielded the executive power. Although the kaiser could not veto laws passed by the Reichstag, almost the only ones of importance that did pass were those initiated by the chancellor, the kaiser's appointee. Bismarck as chancellor never really formed an imperial cabinet, but governed Germany from his position as prime minister of Prussia.

The chancellor could dominate the Reichstag because it could not compel him to resign. Other ministers, chosen from members of the high bureaucracy rather than from Parliamentarians or party leaders, were only assistants to the chancellor and personally responsible to him. Because the Reichstag was more openly critical of certain governmental policies in the post-Bismarck period, and because it insisted on more budgetary powers, Bismarck's successors thought it desirable to make political bargains to get their budgets adopted, while at the same time not acknowledging responsibility to the Reichstag.

Since World War I supposedly had been fought to make the world safe for democracy, the victors decided that Germany must have a democratic constitution, and war hysteria against the German kaiser meant that the system would have to be a republic. The constitution for the Weimar Republic was regarded as a very progressive document for its time. The legislature was made up of two houses, the Reichstag, which was elected by universal, equal, direct, and secret suffrage, and the Reichsrat, whose members were appointed by the Governments of the member states. Since a two-thirds vote in the Reichstag could override the decisions of the upper house, the popularly elected lower house had the bulk of legislative power.

Even the public at large was given a role in the legislative process. Deadlocks between the two houses were to be resolved by referendum. Furthermore, legislation could be launched by popular initiative, a novel procedure that had been pioneered at the state level in the western United States by the Progressive movement. This was thought to make the greatest possible provision for popular participation in the governmental process. Furthermore, the electoral system was felt to be quite democratic and just. It was a form of proportional representation in which the number of seats in the legislature was not predetermined. A party would receive one seat for every 60,000 votes it gained. Thus all interests and opinions would be represented in the legislative process.

A new office of president was created, filled by popular election. The president was not just a figurehead like the British monarch or the president of France in the Third Republic. Instead, he wielded real power, being able, among other things, to dissolve the Reichstag and dismiss the Cabinet. The office of chancellor was retained. Despite the legislature's delegating considerable authority to the executive in the postwar crisis years (1919–23) and during the years of economic depression (1930–33), the chancellor's position never was very strong. In part this was because as in Third Republic France no single party had a majority in Parliament. All Cabinets were coalitions, usually short-lived, representing varying political views. This added to the president's power by allowing him considerable choice in selecting a chancellor.

Perhaps the president's most important single power was contained in Article 48. This provision had been intended to provide the government with extraordinary powers to defend itself in a constitutional crisis. When the president felt that such a situation had arisen he could permit the Cabinet to do whatever was necessary to restore order. This sounds rather similar to Article 16 of the present French constitution. Unlike the French, however, the Germans did attempt to include some safeguards on these emergency powers. The grant of power to the Cabinet was to lapse as soon as the emergency was over. All actions taken under this power had to be submitted to Parliament, which could void them. Furthermore, the constitution was not to be infringed. The importance of this protection was compromised, however, by the fact that some basic rights—for example, free speech, free assembly, and the right to habeas corpus—could be suspended under the emergency powers.

Some observers have blamed Article 48 for the downfall of the Weimar Republic. By 1930, 10 parties were able to gain over a million votes each and the electoral system insured that each received substantial representation in Parliament. As a result, constructing a majority coalition became virtually impossible. When lack of majority support in the Reichstag prevented passage of the Government's budget, an emergency was declared within the provisions of Article 48. Frequent resort to these provisions from 1930 on made government in Germany largely a matter of rule by decree. Thus Hitler's initial actions did not seem very different from what people had become used to under a democratic system.

Regardless of whether Article 48 and proportional representation contributed materially to the collapse of democracy in Germany in the 1930s, both the Western Allies and the Germans themselves were very conscious of such elements in Germany's previous constitutional history. Thus, when it came time after World War II to draw up a new constitution that was to seek once again to bring democracy to Germany, deliberate efforts were made to rectify the supposed shortcomings and loopholes of the Weimar constitution. The drafters of the Basic Law sought to make the position of chancellor more secure, for example, so that he or she could not be toppled by a temporary alliance of Parliamentary dissidents.

While the Basic Law does not specify a particular electoral system, the delegates who wrote the constitution also drafted an electoral law, which went into effect after the occupation authorities modified it, partly at the request of the ministers president (prime ministers) of the laender. Although detailed provisions have been modified subsequently, the basic form of the law is unchanged—a complicated form of proportional representation aimed at fairness while avoiding the supposed defects of proportional representation. We will explain the details in another chapter. The point here simply is that the present German constitution and related fundamental statutes have been influenced greatly by the German past. The Germans live in a haunted house and continue to fear that they will be harmed by their Amityville horror—Adolf Hitler.

In addition to the provisions already mentioned, the constitution organizes the country along federal lines. The central government (Bund) is given the exclusive right to legislate in such fields as foreign affairs, citizenship, currency and coinage, railways, posts and telecommunications, and copyrights. The central government and the laender have concurrent powers for civil and criminal law, laws relating to the economy, labor, agriculture, public welfare, ocean and coastal shipping, and in "the prevention of the abuse of economic power" (antitrust actions). In other areas, notably education and cultural affairs, the laender exercise primary responsibility. In case of conflict between laws of the Bund and those of the laender, the national laws prevail. The Bund also is given sufficient powers to ensure that laender fulfill their duties as prescribed in the Basic Law.

In at least two areas—taxation and education—the trend has been toward strengthening the powers of the Bund. The laender (especially the richer ones) wanted as much independence as possible in tax matters, while the Bund wanted to equalize major tax revenues between rich and poor laender. After much opposition and delay, the Bund finally won in 1969. The Basic Law was amended to increase the Bund's financial powers and its ability to redistribute tax revenues among the laender. At the same time other amendments increased the Bund's responsibilities for educational planning. The goal was to improve education and make it more uniform throughout the country so that people moving from one laender to another would not be handicapped by varying educational requirements.

The Basic Law may be amended by a two-thirds vote of the members of each house of Parliament. Some provisions, however, are unamendable. These include those portions of the Basic law that affect the organization of the Republic into laender as well as those sections that provide the basic form of democratic organization, including the protection of fundamental civil liberties.

Under American influence, the Basic Law sets up a Federal Constitutional Court, with powers to annul acts of the legislature or the administration if they violate the Basic Law. The court is also authorized to forbid unconstitutional parties if such action is recommended by the Cabinet. On the basis of such requests, it banned a neo-Nazi party in 1952 and the Communist party in 1956.

The most significant amendment to the Basic Law thus far came two decades after the start of the present system and dealt with the touchy and hitherto unresolved question of emergency powers. This amendment, consisting of 17 articles, is commonly called the emergency constitution. Ten years of discussion and debate preceded its adoption. Because the emergency powers of the Weimar constitution had been used to bypass Parliament and ultimately to destroy democracy, the Germans were wary of any emergency powers. Yet they realized that a need might arise for them. Consequently, the major concern in drafting the amendment was the protection and survival of the democratic order in times of crisis.

The existence of any emergency must be recognized by the Bundestag (lower house) with the approval of the Bundesrat (upper house). In both cases a two-thirds vote is required and in the Bundestag this two thirds must include at least a majority of its total members.

In the event that insuperable obstacles prevent the Bundestag from meeting, or if the situation demands immediate action, an emergency parliament, called a Joint Committee, will act. The Joint Committee, by a two-thirds vote consisting of at least a majority of its members, decides if the conditions are such that it should act. The Joint Committee is made up of 33 members, two thirds of whom are Bundestag deputies and one third Bundesrat members (one from each of the laender). The 22 members from the Bundestag are selected so as to represent the political parties in proportion to their Parliamentary strength, but members of the Cabinet may not be included.

The emergency constitution specifies in considerable detail various procedural and substantive safeguards. Among other things, the dissolution of the Bundestag during a period of emergency is forbidden. The Constitutional Court cannot be tampered with. Moreover, the Bundestag, with the approval of the Bundesrat, can repeal laws of the Joint Committee and can declare an emergency at an end at any time.[1]

BASIC VALUES: AUTHORITARIAN OR DEMOCRATIC?

Until the end of World War I German political life was characterized by autocracy. The lack of progress in adopting democratic institutions contrasted sharply with the rapid strides Germany was making in industrialization. It contrasted as well with the liberal political developments occurring in other West European countries.

The revolutionary tide that swept across Europe in the mid-19th century achieved little democratic reform; the impact in Germany was even slighter than elsewhere. Politics continued along an authoritarian path, especially after Bismarck came to office in Prussia in 1862. Nonetheless, democracy did make some inroads. Bismarck was forced to accept a moderately free press, political parties, and a popularly elected legislature, despite openly denouncing parliamentary democracy. Although the legislature was relatively powerless, the German people were learning some of the rudiments of the democratic process.

Support for parliamentary democracy was undermined, however, by a feeling that the Prussian parliament had contributed nothing to German unity. It had, in fact, seemed to hamper this development—contrary to the desires of the great majority of Germans—by opposing the strengthening of the Prussian army. Yet it was precisely this instrument that accomplished what all the politicians' hot air had not advanced a step: Prussian conquest had unified Germany. The lesson was clear—might makes right.

Thus in German politics personal morality came to be divorced from reasons of state. That is to say that behavior such as duplicity and ruthlessness, which would not have been countenanced by political leaders in their social relations with others, was utilized by these same leaders in their political and governmental actions. Success was the only criterion for judging political actions. Power politics was the order of the day. And this approach would yield its greatest divi-

---

[1]For a text of the amendments to the Basic Law and statements by Kurt Kiesinger and Willy Brandt, see "Special Report," *Inter Nationes* (Bad Godesberg, 1968). The amendments were approved in the Bundestag by a vote of 384 to 100, and unanimously in the Bundesrat.

dends when supported by a military spirit that valued order, authority, and unquestioning obedience to one's superiors.

Yet all this is not to say that the German political tradition is one of arbitrary government. For another fundamental German value is legalism. Many Germans have been firmly convinced that order requires an all-encompassing set of rules. These rules are not to be the product of extensive popular discussion, but are to be the result of detailed study by experts. And since these rules are formulated by those who have the knowledge and training necessary for this task, naturally the rules should be followed. The good citizen does not seek to participate in the process of making the rules but wants only to be told what the rules are so that he or she can observe them.[2]

Thus the democratic political process had little prestige or attraction for most Germans. The ideal rather was the hierarchical, orderly system of the Empire. Bureaucrats were seen as the true superiors of society, in part because of their education and honesty, in part because the government bureaucracy historically had been staffed in Germany by the nobility. As late as 1951 almost a majority—45 percent—of those polled in Germany said that the time of the Empire was the best period in recent Germany history.

A legacy of such political values did not augur well for the durability of the Weimar Republic, no matter how attractive its constitution appeared to be to democrats. Although World War I had shattered Germany's autocratic system, the Germans' basic political values had not been transformed. Germany got a democratic republic primarily because the victors insisted that it must have one. And the Weimar system proved to be neither sufficiently long-lived nor effective to encourage support for democratic values. Under Hitler Germany reverted to a political system embodying values even more thoroughly authoritarian than those of the Empire.

Nazism was more than just exaggerated nationalism or anti-Semitism or a reaction to defeat and to Weimar. These were a part of the picture, to be sure, but only a part of it. Some of the ideas on which the Nazi movement was built went back at least 100 years. They depicted a past golden age when the German people (the mystical *Volk*) lived in harmony and happiness, partly because they were superior to other people and partly because they were close to the soil. The Industrial Revolution and its consequences—big cities, modern ways, and those who had brought this about (Jews)—uprooted the *Volk* and corrupted many of them. The doctrines associated with this point of view were formulated and propagated by several generations of teachers and students.

In promising Germany a new glory and telling Germans that they were a superior people, Hitler was arguing that Germany had a destiny, a *Kultur* mission. *Kultur* could be advanced, he proclaimed, only by superior races subjugating

---

[2]See the discussion in Gabriel Almond and Sidney Verba, *The Civic Culture* (Boston: Little, Brown, 1965), pp. 126–35, 321–23.

inferior ones. Much of this was not new, for German thinkers long had talked of the importance of a *Kulturstaat*. In their view democracies were concerned with mediocrity, not greatness. Emphasizing popular participation and politics was dealing with the trivial; philosophy, *Kultur*—these were the truly profound matters. *Kultur* was not the same as civilization; it did not involve the sophistication of degenerate French society. Instead it expressed primitive, pure *Volk* mores. These mores attained their validity by conforming to and expressing the forces of nature, the vital life forces. These subconscious, mystical forces can be felt in the blood by all those who are racially pure. (So, if all this does not make much sense to you, you know what your problem is.)

The stereotypical German is a very rational, calculating, unemotional person. He or she is seen as being very methodical and disciplined. What is not so widely understood is that this is only one stream or theme in German culture. There is as well a wild, romantic, undisciplined strain in the German tradition. And it was to this tradition that Hitler and the Nazis were returning.

In yet another way Nazi ideology drew upon a traditional theme in German thought. German political thinking long had tended to personify the state, to make it of considerably greater importance than the individual. Hegel, for example, one of Germany's foremost political philosophers from the early 19th century, had interpreted the course of history as the progressive revelation of the *Weltgeist* ("World Spirit"). This revelation, he maintained, was made visible not in individuals but in nations. And, of course, the highest revelation of the World Spirit was in the Prussian state.

Because the Nazi ideas were often set forth in philosophical and quasi-scientific language, they gained a certain amount of acceptance in respectable academic circles and were embraced by right-wing political groups. But significantly these ideas did not become a serious political force until they were wedded with the genius of Adolf Hitler and the disciplined organization of the Nazi party. Even then they might not have become a powerful political force if it had not been for the combination of other circumstances (the economic crisis, the legacy of defeat, the ex-army officers unable to adjust to civilian life, the debt-ridden peasants, and the alleged communist threat), which Hitler could and did exploit to the fullest.

Given that Nazi values did draw upon the German past in a way that the democratic values of Weimar did not, many people were concerned after World War II that there would be no democratic value consensus to support and make viable the present democratic system in Germany. Because democratic institutions failed to take root in Germany and autocratic leaders directed the country in aggression twice in the first half of the century, many observers claimed to detect a basic flaw in the German national character.

National character, however, is a very dubious concept. True, liberal institutions, emphasizing the dignity of the individual and popular control of the government, did not take hold in Germany. But part of the explanation may be that the speed with which it became a powerful industrial nation precluded this. In

Britain, and other West European countries where democracy fared better, industrialization was slower and was largely the work of private entrepreneurs. In Germany, on the other hand, liberal institutions not only were not given time to take root, but also had to combat a statist tradition derived from governmental direction of industrialization.

Moreover, when industrialization came, feudalism had not yet been swept aside. The aristocracy was still a power in the 19th century. The bourgeoisie had gained little headway and was excluded from public life. All this began to change, but the middle class was becoming influential long before it had learned to shoulder any political or social responsibilities. The failure of democracy in Germany is far too complex to be explained away by the phrase "national character."

Without necessarily accepting the national character approach, the Allied occupation authorities after World War II understood that the lesson of Weimar taught that merely seeing that Germany got a democratic constitution was not sufficient. At least basic values, if not character, had to be transformed as well. Thus they tried to implement programs of denazification and demilitarization. The first of these proved to be impossible as originally conceived; the second had to be revised once conflict with the Soviet Union convinced the Western powers that a strong Germany was needed to buttress the alliance against communism.

The denazification program had two related objectives: (1) to acquaint the Germans with the horrors of the Nazi era, thereby also inculcating the moral values of a free way of life; and (2) to remove from positions in public and semipublic office, as well as from positions of responsibility in important private undertakings, all persons who had been more than nominal participants in Nazi party activities. The latter objective could be attained only partially. Examining millions of dossiers was not an easy task. Moreover, the conclusion was reached soon that most cases demanded individual consideration. Most important, perhaps, too many Germans who had had Nazi connections were simply indispensable to the running of the country. Thus at times lesser offenders were punished while some who had been more closely associated with Nazism were given influential positions. Such apparent arbitrariness called the program into question. Nonetheless, it did succeed in removing a number of persons with Nazi connections from the judiciary, the communications media, teaching, and the civil service. The program, on a more positive note, reinstated many pre-Hitler trade union leaders to their former positions.

Efforts directed toward the first objective probably were more successful. The German educational system was revamped and steps were taken to ensure that future German citizens were presented with a more objective and truthful account of their country's history than had been typical under both the Empire and Weimar. While this was not the only factor, it certainly played a part in the clear transformation of German political values that has occurred in the last third of a century.

FIGURE 18-1   Aspects of Nation of Which One Is Proud

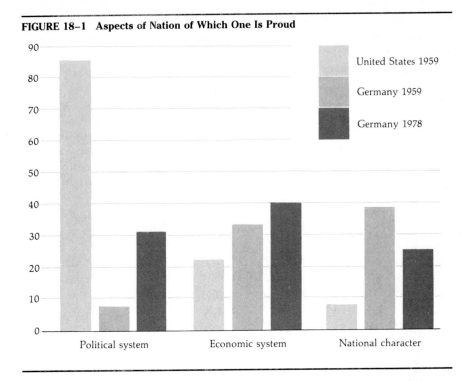

Figure 18-1 presents a portion of this fundamental shift.[3] German pride in their political system has increased considerably, and no longer do they regard their characteristics as a people as the main thing of which they can be proud. While even this new pride in the political system fails to approach the American level in 1959 (given American experiences of the 1960s and 70s, that pride clearly has declined), David Conradt cautions against regarding it as dangerously low. He argues that commitment need not be emotional, but can be based on a rational assessment of an extended period of effective performance. Thus even when the system encounters temporary problems, people are not disillusioned. (You may not love your old car, but after 15 years of good service you aren't going to junk it just because a tire goes flat.) For example, although during the recessions in the mid-1960s and the mid-1970s support for the Government declined, this did not reduce support for the democratic system. Additional evidence of long-term commitment to democracy regardless of short-term difficulties is the fact that in 1962 well over a quarter of those having unfavorable

---

[3]Much of the following draws upon David P. Conradt, "Changing German Political Culture," in The *Civic Culture Revisited* Gabriel Almond and Sidney Verba, eds. (Boston: Little, Brown, 1980), and Conradt, *The German Polity* (New York: Longman, 1978), p. 49.

views of the parliament's performance believed that no parliament was needed at all; 10 years later only 6 percent with unfavorable views believed that parliament could be abolished.

The growth in support for the political system is remarkable. When Germans were asked in 1951 when their country had been best off, virtually no one mentioned under the existing system, while 45 percent said the Empire and 42 percent were willing to select prewar Nazi Germany, despite the oppression of those years. By 1970, however, an overwhelming 81 percent chose the Bonn Republic and only 5 percent each cited the Empire and the prewar Nazi period.

Nonetheless, Germans are not very effusive about the freedom their political system provides. Americans tend to think that they are more free than are the citizens in any other country except for Canada (a compliment that the Canadians return to Americans). Slightly more Germans, however, think that Canadians, Americans, Britons, French, and Italians have a great deal of freedom than think that they themselves do.[4] Even so, two fifths of the Germans think they have a great deal of freedom. And only 7 percent thought that the country was ruled by a dictator. (That a fifth of the Britons and of the Canadians thought their countries were so ruled suggests that political conflict, or at least the level of political rhetoric, is a bit more bitter in countries usually thought to have a more bland politics than does Germany.)

As for attitudes toward democracy, by the end of the 1960s three quarters of the Germans polled regarded it as the best form of government. Furthermore, support for various specific aspects of democracy is strong. Whereas in 1950, 25 percent thought it would be best for the country to have only one party, by the later 1970s this had dropped to only 6 percent. In 1953 only a bare majority—55 percent—thought that they could freely express their political views; by the start of the 1970s, 84 percent saw no reason to be careful about what they said about politics. In 1952 only a quarter of the respondents polled said they were interested in politics, while in 1977 half were. Furthermore, other responses indicate that those expressing an interest in politics are more likely to support democracy than are those who are uninterested.

Given the German reputation for discipline some people may worry that the country never will be fully reconciled to democracy, which is a rather messy system with a great variety of interests seeking their own goals from which, rather than from a group of expert scholars, emerge the laws. How do the Germans feel about those actions labeled unconventional political participation? (At this point you may want to turn back to Chapter 2, where we discussed British support for these.) Remarkably, Germans differ little from Britons in this regard. Substantial majorities approve of petitions and lawful demonstrations, but reject other unconventional tactics. Virtually no one approves of damaging property or personal violence for political purposes, and only a ninth accepts the relatively harmless step of blocking traffic. But exactly the same is true of Britons. The major difference between the two peoples, and even this hardly is major, is

[4]*Gallup Political Index*, 281 (January 1984), pp. 11, 13.

that while 47 percent of the British accept boycotts for political purposes, only 25 percent of the Germans do. Thus the Germans do not appear to be any more rigid in their reaction to political dissent than are the British and, equally important, do not believe that they need to resort to the disruptive political tactics that were common during the Weimar Republic. Although demonstrations in Germany increased in 1980 by over a third compared to the previous year, reaching nearly 4,500, yet the proportion of these that were violent—little over 3 percent—changed hardly at all.

Interestingly, German attitudes toward unconventional political behavior do not vary a great deal by age. The sharpest difference is for demonstrations—70 percent of those 16 to 25 see them as a legitimate political tactic, while only 47 percent of those 40 to 50 do so. Focusing on the political attitudes of young Germans is worthwhile because clearly part of what is involved in Germany's growing acceptance of democracy and the Bonn political system is the dying off of older generations so that increasingly the population is composed of people who know only the Federal Republic firsthand. By 1986 one had to be nearly 40 to have lived under any other political system and to be well over 50 to have any real memory of the prewar Nazi period.

Surveys of the attitudes of young Germans provide mixed results. On the positive side, in the mid-1970s the percent of Germans under 30 who felt that nothing could be done about an unjust national law was lower than in either the United States or Britain. In other words, young Germans were less likely to feel powerless or politically ineffective. Although 90 percent of Germans 14 to 20 believed that "having good friends" was what made life worth living, yet "living in freedom" showed up well also—mentioned by 85 percent. Younger Germans attached considerably greater importance to free speech and political participation and less importance to economic security and domestic order than did older Germans.[5]

This helps to account for the marked reaction among young people to the government's campaign against radicals in the public service in the mid-1970s. The result was a considerable decline among young, better-educated, and politically active Germans in believing that one could voice political views freely. We are not talking here of a small, inconsequential group. The inhibited feelings among these young people were largely responsible for reducing the proportion of the total population that felt they could speak freely from 84 percent in 1971 to 73 percent at the end of 1976. This appears to have been only a temporary decline, since by the end of 1983 only a 10th (about the same as in the United States) of the Germans felt that anybody who criticizes the Government is severely punished.[6]

Feeling inhibited to discuss politics had a broader impact on the political attitudes of German youth. In 1978 a sample of Germans 14 to 24 were given a list

---

[5]Ronald Inglehart, "The Silent Revolution in Europe: Intergenerational Change in Post-Industrial Societies," *American Political Science Review* 65 (December 1971), pp. 991–1017.

[6]*Gallup Political Index*, no. 281, p. 11.

of nine interest areas and were asked to check those that appealed most to them. Politics not only got less than majority support, but came at the bottom of the list. Furthermore, whereas a decade earlier a quarter of this age group said that they frequently were involved in politics, now hardly 10 percent said so. Thirty-five percent were completely uninterested, compared with only 7 percent in 1968. Perhaps most bothersome, 40 percent in 1978 agreed with the sentence, "If everyone wants to decide and have his say, nothing ever gets done. Someone has to decide." One wonders in the German context whether that merely is support for social reality or a desire for a strong leader who ignores democratic processes.

Here again the negative effects appear to have been temporary. Subsequent evidence indicates that German young people are once again becoming involved in politics. Opposition in Germany to deploying American cruise missiles there may have had some benefit in helping to cure youthful political lethargy. Whereas in 1979 only 8 percent of Germans 14 to 21 had taken part in demonstrations, by 1983, 20 percent had.[7] And the proportion who had helped to collect signatures on petitions and participated in political discussions rose from 18 to 30 percent. Furthermore, three fifths of the German youth said they were willing to join up with others to push for their ideas about the right kind of life—just the type of democratic activism that appeals to Americans.

Despite much support for democracy among all ages in Germany, lingering, although certainly declining, support for Hitler is somewhat disquieting. In 1955 nearly half of the respondents in a poll agreed that Hitler would have been one of Germany's greatest statesmen had World War II not occurred. Since 16 percent didn't know, those disagreeing were only 36 percent. While by 1967, 52 percent now disagreed, yet that a third still could so regard him is shocking. More reassuring is a 1978 poll that found only 7 percent willing to say that they would vote for "a man like Adolf Hitler." But why, in heaven's name, would anyone want to? Here again a generational difference could be seen. While 12 percent of those over 50 would vote for someone like Hitler, only 5 percent of those 20 to 49 would.

So we come back again to the point that, although the evidence does not all point in the same direction, what is happening among young Germans is crucial for democracy's future and, on balance, encouraging. Two thirds of German young people are reasonably satisfied with democracy in Germany and 15 percent are very satisfied.[8] Only 15 percent are unsatisfied. But once again we have to qualify this positive result a bit. Among university students more than a quarter are not satisfied with German democracy and nearly two fifths of the unemployed youth aren't satisfied.

---

[7]Hans-Joachim Veen, "How the Young Really Look at Life," *German Comments*, no. 4 (October 1984), pp. 65–66, 72.

[8]Ibid., p. 65.

Nonetheless, the important point is that German youth are being socialized differently than in the past. The responses of parents and students to a variety of opinion-survey questions indicate that the old stereotype of authoritarian training in the German family and at the schools no longer is typical. In terms of thinking for themselves and being encouraged to be independent, German youth are being raised little differently, or even more openly, than are American and British youth. And the educational system is doing a much better job of producing the social equality familiar to Americans than is the British system.

While a tenth of German teenagers go to private schools—a higher proportion than in Britain—they do not become a power elite as tends to happen in Britain. And within the state-supported school system selectivity is not as great in Germany as in Britain. In some laender, particularly in the south, students qualify for the *gymnasium* (the prestigious academically oriented school) through exams taken at about 10 or 12 years old. In other laender, students are admitted on primary school teachers' recommendations. In part because teachers want to avoid being sued by irate parents, about half of every class is recommended for entry. The social effects of selectivity are weakened further because a third of the Germans who go on to universities come from the less prestigious *realschulen* and *hauptschulen*. Furthermore, about a quarter of Germans go to university, about twice as many as in Britain.

The effect of all this is that in Germany those who rise to positions of power tend to have had an educational experience fairly common to the population at large, and as parents have children who are experiencing that typical educational process. Unlike Britain, the educational system does not socialize the elite into a set of values differing considerably from those of the bulk of the population. And a sense of sharp class differences and resentments is not fostered. The unifying effects of a common educational experience, as Americans should know, cannot be overemphasized. German basic political values of the present and the future seem well able to support a democratic political system.

BIBLIOGRAPHICAL NOTE

Parts of Edward McWhinney, *Constitutionalism in Germany and the Federal Constitutional Court* (Leyden: Sythoff, 1962), and S. Rosenne, *Constitutionalism in Germany and the Federal Constitutional Court* (New York: Oceana Publications, 1962), deal with German constitutionalism. For background on the provisions of the present Basic Law, see John Golay, *The Founding of the Federal Republic of Germany* (Chicago: University of Chicago Press, 1958).

Important historical studies of German political values include Fritz Stern, *The Politics of Cultural Despair: A Study in the Rise of the Germanic Ideology* (Berkeley: University of California Press, 1961), and two books by George Mosse, *The Crisis of German Ideology: Intellectual Origins of the Third Reich* (New York: Grosset & Dunlap, 1964); and *Nazi Culture: Intellectual, Cultural and Social Life in the Third Reich* (New York: Grosset & Dunlap, 1966). Also interesting are Peter Viereck, *Metapolitics: The Roots of the Nazi Mind* (New York: Capricorn, 1961), and Peter Gay, *Weimar Culture: The Outsider as Insider* (New York: Harper & Row, 1968). An excellent novel by Richard

Hughes, *The Fox in the Attic* (New York: New American Library, 1961), skillfully captures the feeling and values of the Weimar period and compares and contrasts these with life in Britain in the same period.

Concise, comprehensive, and focused on precisely the key topics, the Conradt contribution to *The Civic Culture Revisited*, cited in Footnote 3, is absolutely essential reading for anyone interested in German political values. Kendall Baker, Russell Dalton, and Kai Hildebrandt, *Germany Transformed: Political Culture and the New Politics* (Cambridge, Mass.: Harvard University Press, 1981) examines values in the context of electoral politics in the late 1970s.

19

Individual and Group Political Activity

THE ELECTORAL SYSTEM

In devising their present electoral system, the Germans were of two minds. On the one hand, like many other Europeans, they were attracted by the seeming justice or fairness of proportional representation. It somehow seems only proper that a party's share of the seats in the legislature should correspond closely to its share of the popular vote—a result that occurs only by accident under the Anglo-American single-member, simple-plurality system. Yet they also were aware that proportional representation (PR) is widely thought to have significant defects. And for the Germans this was not just a matter of abstract belief, since the experience of the Weimar Republic seemed to many clear proof that PR affects the party system quite negatively. So the Germans endeavored to devise a hybrid system as a compromise. This is why the electoral system we are about to examine is so complex. The Germans wanted a system that would secure electoral justice but would not fractionalize the party system, that would avoid the depersonalized representation—the lack of contact between legislator and voter—involved in pure PR, and would provide some obstacle to the development of extreme, antidemocratic parties.

Under a PR electoral system each constituency returns several members to the legislature. Thus any given voter is not represented by a single legislator. You might think that this improves upon the American system. But it means that no one legislator is responsible for a given constituency, and thus the several representatives can pass the buck among themselves. No single representative need feel a special responsibility for the area. Nor need he or she make much ef-

FIGURE 19–1   Sample Ballot for a German National Election

Stimmzettel

für die Wahl zum Deutschen Bundestag im Wahlkreis 127 Schwalm-Eder

am 5. Oktober 1980

Sie haben 2 Stimmen

hier 1 Stimme
für die Wahl
eines Wahlkreisabgeordneten
(Erststimme)

hier 1 Stimme
für die Wahl
einer Landesliste (Partei)
(Zweitstimme)

---

1   Dr. Kreutzmann, Heinz
Parl. Staatssekretär
Borken (Hessen)   Sozialdemo-
Kellerwaldstraße 7   **SPD**   kratische Partei
                            Deutschlands

◯   **SPD**   **Sozialdemokratische Partei Deutschlands**   **1**
Leber, Matthöfer, Jahn,
Frau Dr. Timm, Zander

---

2   Jagoda, Bernhard
Obersekretär a.D.
Schwalmstadt-Treysa   **CDU**   Christlich Demo-
Am Weißen Stein 31   kratische Union
                            Deutschlands

◯   **CDU**   **Christlich Demokratische Union Deutschlands**   **2**
Dr. Dregger, Zink, Dr. Schwarz-
Schilling, Frau Geier, Haase

---

3   Wilke, Otto
Elektromeister
Diemelsee-Adorf   **F.D.P.**   Freie
Bredelarer Straße 1   Demokratische
                            Partei

◯   **F.D.P.**   **Freie Demokratische Partei**   **3**
Mischnick, von Schoeler,
Hoffie, Wurbs, Dr. Prinz zu
Solms-Hohensolms-Lich

---

4   Funk, Peter
Werkzeugmacher
Baunatal 6   **DKP**   Deutsche
Triftweg 6   Kommunistische
                    Partei

◯   **DKP**   **Deutsche Kommunistische Partei**   **4**
Mayer, Knopf, Frau Dr. Weber,
Funk, Frau Schuster

---

5   Keller, Gerhard
Zivildienstleistender   DIE GRÜNEN
Frielendorf 2   **GRÜNE**
Friedhofsweg 30

◯   **GRÜNE**   DIE GRÜNEN   **5**
Frau Ibbeken, Hecker, Horacek,
Kerschgens, Kuhnert

◯   **EAP**   **Europäische Arbeiterpartei**   **6**
Frau Liebig, Haßmann, Stalleicher,
Frau Kaestner, Stalla

◯   **KBW**   **Kommunistischer Bund Westdeutschland**   **7**
Schmierer, Frau Mönich,
Frau Eckardt, Dresler, Lang

◯   **NPD**   **Nationaldemokratische Partei Deutschlands**   **8**
Philipp, Brandl, Sturtz,
Lauck, Bauer

◯   **V**   VOLKSFRONT   **9**
Gotz, Taufertshöfer, König,
Riebe, Frau Weißert

fort to respond to the needs and views of the constituents. So long as a representative satisfies the local party leaders, he or she can be certain that his or her name will continue to be placed near the top of the party's slate of candidates. Under PR that is sufficient to ensure election, if the party is of any size at all. A representative has little incentive to be a good constituency person, circulating widely in the district and seeking to serve the voters.

To avoid this defect, the German electoral system has an element of the single member, simple plurality system. The country is divided into 248 constituencies, each of which returns one representative.[1] The boundary lines are drawn on the basis of the number of qualified electors in each constituency, with the requirement that no constituency's electorate may be more than one third above or below the national average. The candidate in each district receiving the greatest number of votes—regardless of whether this is a majority—is elected, just as in the United States.

These electoral procedures, however, are used to select only half of the membership of the lower house of the national legislature. The other half is elected from land party lists and thus represents an entire land rather than a single-member constituency. Each German voter gets to vote twice—once for a specific candidate to represent the local district and once for a party from whose list of candidates the top ones will represent the entire land. A sample ballot for a German election appears in Figure 19–1.

The complicated part of the system is that the votes cast on the party-list side of the ballot (the right-hand side in Figure 19–1) determine the party strengths for the *entire* legislature and not just for half the membership. Even though half the members are elected in single-member, simple-plurality constituencies, the *entire* system is PR. All the votes cast for the SPD party list (to use that party as an example) in each of the 10 German laender are added together to produce a national total vote. This total is used in calculating how many of the total 496 seats in the legislature are to go to the SPD.

Students of elections have devised a number of formulae for deciding how legislative seats are to be allocated to parties. Some of these methods tend to favor small parties—the highest remainder system, for example. The *d'Hondt* method (named after its devisor) used in Germany is a highest-average system, that tends to favor large parties. Each party's total vote is divided by the number of seats it already has won plus one. The party with the highest average is given the next seat, and the process continues round after round until all the seats have been allocated. A hypothetical example should clarify the process.

Assume that five members are to be elected, and that the voters have cast their ballots as follows:

---

[1] The best explanation of the electoral law is Uwe Kitzinger, "The West German Electoral Law," *Parliamentary Affairs* 11 (Spring 1958), pp. 220–37.

Party	Votes	Percent
A	52,000	26
B	36,000	18
C	34,000	17
D	32,000	16
E	24,000	12
F	22,000	11
	200,000	

On the first round no party has any seats, so the total vote of each is divided by 1. Party A has the highest average and wins a seat. A's votes must not be divided by 2 (1 seat won plus 1), and thus its average becomes 26,000. This places it between parties D and E. Since no party other than A has been allocated a seat, their votes still are divided only by 1. Thus party B is highest with 36,000 and is given the second seat. Now its total vote, like that of party A, but unlike those of parties C, D, E, and F, which have yet to win a seat, is divided by 2 (1 seat won plus 1), and it drops to the bottom of the pack with an average of 18,000. Party C wins the third seat and party D the fourth one. By this point the votes for parties A, B, C, and D are being divided by 2 but those of parties E and F are still divided only by 1 since they have yet to gain a seat. Nonetheless, party A's average—26,000—is higher than party E's—24,000—so the fifth seat goes to party A.

Thus all seats have been allocated and A has received 2, B, C, and D 1 each, and E and F none, despite the fact that each of the latter two received more than a tenth of the vote. If there had been a sixth seat to allocate, it would have gone to party E, which topped the list after five rounds were completed. Party A, whose total now is divided by 3 (2 won plus 1), has an average of 17,677. Thus were more seats to be allocated, it would have to wait not only for parties E and F to win their first seat each, but for party B to gain a second seat before it was awarded its third one.

For German national elections this process must go through 496 rounds—until all the seats in the legislature have been allocated. At that point each party's total representation in the legislature will have been determined. But each party's strength must be allocated to the 10 laender. That is, we now know that the SPD has won, say for example, 200 seats, but how many of those are from, say, Lower Saxony? The whole process described above is repeated for each party separately for as many rounds as the total number of seats to which it is entitled.

Only at this point do we finally know that the SPD is entitled to 27 seats, for example, in Hesse. Now comes the complicated part (now?!). The number of single member seats that the SPD already has won in a particular land is subtracted from the number to which it is entitled there. The difference is the number of candidates from the top of the SPD land list of candidates who will be declared elected from that land in addition to those SPD candidates who won single member seats. So, if the calculations show that the SPD is entitled to 27 seats in Hesse and it has won 15 single member seats there, then the first 12 names on its party list for Hesse will be elected. (Unless, as is permissible, some of these 12 had been candidates for a single member district and were elected there. In that case they would not be counted when the top 12 were selected.)

Those of you who are still with us at this point and who like to stump your teachers with "what if" questions, no doubt now want to ask what if a party wins *more* single member seats than the *total* number of seats to which it is entitled in a given land. This is extremely unusual, but does happen from time to time. The lucky party simply keeps the extra seats—you hardly can disqualify somebody who has been properly elected. Thus the total seats in the legislature may vary slightly from one election to the next. The SPD got an extra seat in 1980 by winning one more single member seat in Schleswig-Holstein than it was entitled to under the PR calculation, given the size of its vote there. In 1983 it received two extra seats, one in Bremen and the other in Hamburg.

But there is an even more unusual feature. Although the number of single member seats for each land is determined before the election and although half of the total membership of the legislature is elected from these seats, in any given land the number of candidates elected from the party lists may be greater or smaller than the number of single member constituencies. The reason is that a land's total representation is a function of the share of the total national party vote that each of that land's parties receives. That is, a land's representation is affected by whether voter turnout in that land is markedly above or below the turnout nationally. In effect, abstaining is voting to reduce your land's representation in the national legislature.

Voting for a minor party has the same effect. In order to avoid the splintering effects of PR upon the party system, the Germans have modified the electoral system to hamper minor parties. A party must win 5 percent of the total national vote or three of the single member constituencies to be allowed to share in the proportional allocation of seats.

If a party wins two single member seats and 4.9 percent of the vote nationally, it gets only the two seats. Should it win three seats and 4.9 percent, it gains 24 seats (4.9 percent of 496). If it fails to win any seats, but polls 5 percent of the vote, then it gains 25 seats. Thus, at this marginal point, winning one more constituency or another 0.1 percent of the national vote is worth about two dozen additional seats. In effect, the Germans were saying to minor parties that they must either have generalized support throughout the country at something more than a minimal level or have concentrated strength in some areas sufficient to outpoll other parties. Such parties would be accepted as reasonable contenders for representation; others would be regarded as detrimental to the party system and thus not entitled to representation.

The point of this detailed discussion of Germany's electoral system is to clarify our initial statement of the goals of the Bonn Republic's founders. Since the electoral system allocates to parties a share of the total seats in the legislature roughly equal to their share of the popular vote, the system is deemed fair. Since it allows each elector to vote for a single candidate to be the district's representative, it contains an element of personal representation and concern. And insofar as it establishes a hurdle that minor parties must clear before they are represented in Parliament, it avoids the fractionalization of the party system frequently associated with PR. The system is complex, but it has done a good job in achieving the conflicting goals sought of it.

The German electoral system provides a unique opportunity to study the effect of candidates' personality upon voting since each voter can vote twice—once for a candidate and once for a party. Some people might regard a particular party's candidate in a given election as especially capable and articulate, even though they usually did not support that party. Such voters might decide to depart from their usual party loyalty to vote for such an appealing candidate. During the 1950s in the United States many people who normally thought of themselves as Democrats nonetheless voted for the Republican presidential candidate, Eisenhower, because they agreed with millions of others, "I Like Ike." Unlike American voters, German voters are not faced with having to choose between their party and an especially attractive opposition party candidate. They can vote for such a candidate on one side of ballot and still vote for their party on the other half. Furthermore, since it is the party list vote and not the candidate vote that determines partisan strength in the Bundestag, they can split their vote in this sense without helping the opposition party at all. Their vote for the individual candidate will aid only him or her and not that party.

Apparently, even the Germans themselves have taken awhile to understand fully what is involved in the ticket splitting that is possible under their electoral system. For a time after the SPD and the FDP formed a coalition Government and the FDP appeared to be dropping dangerously near the 5 percent barrier, the idea was that SPD voters would "lend" their party-list vote to the FDP to prevent it from being eliminated from the national legislature. Only eventually did it dawn on the SPD that since it is the *party-list vote* and not the single-member constituency vote that determines a party's strength in the legislature, "lending" its vote to the FDP was voting to reduce its own strength. Thus in 1976 Chancellor Schmidt urged Christian Democrats, FDP supporters, and undecideds to split their ticket, voting for their party's individual candidate and "giving me your *Zweitstimme*" (party list vote, see Figure 19–1). Schmidt did not go on to explain that, given the way the calculations are made, Christian Democrats who did this would be cutting their party's strength in the legislature and increasing that of the SPD. Thus the request was in fact much less reasonable than it sounded.

Regardless of whether the German voters figured this out, ticket splitting is relatively uncommon. Ninety percent or more of the voters who vote for a Christian Democratic or SPD candidate on the left-hand side of the ballot vote for his or her party on the right-hand side.[2] More of the people who vote for FDP candidates, however, tend to desert the party on the party-list side of the ballot. Only about two thirds to three fourths of them vote the same way on both sides of the ballot. A substantial proportion—nearly 40 percent in 1969 and 1976 and nearly two thirds in 1972—of the party-list votes that the FDP receives comes from voters who had voted for the candidate of some other party on the single member side of the ballot.

Parties that concentrate their support primarily in certain areas will win most of their seats by electing representatives in the single-member constituencies. Parties with support spread fairly evenly throughout much of the country may not be sufficiently strong in any given area to elect individual candidates. Nonetheless, their total national vote may be substantial, in which case they would obtain a fair number of representatives in the legislature from their various party lists.

The success of Germany's two main parties along these lines in the last eight elections reveals an interesting pattern, as shown in Table 19–1. Initially the Christian Democrats won the great bulk of their seats in the single-member districts, doing considerably better in their regard than did the Social Democrats. At the end of the 1960s this pattern reversed, and by 1972 was almost exactly the opposite of what it had been 10 years earlier. In the mid-1970s another shift occurred; the two leading political forces won about the same share of their representation in single-member seats. Finally in 1983 the pattern altered once more, returning almost to what it had been in 1957.

While the relationship is not perfect, these proportions are affected by the main political forces' relative strengths in popular support. When the two parties are fairly close in their share of the vote, then the share of representation in single-member seats is fairly even or the Social Democrats' share is larger. When the Christian Democrats have a big lead over their opponents in the popular vote, then they get the great bulk of their representation by winning individual constituencies and the Social Democrats get theirs through the land lists. Since 1983 was the worst result for the Social Democrats in 20 years, the marked change in the figures for that election are not surprising.

TABLE 19–1   Percent of Each Party's Total Representation Won in Single Member Constituencies

	1957	1961	1965	1969	1972	1976	1980	1983
Christian Democrats	72	64	63	50	43	55	54	74
Social Democrats	27	48	46	57	66	53	58	35

---

[2]David P. Conradt, "The 1976 Campaign and Election: An Overview," in *Germany at the Polls: The Bundestag Election of 1976,* Karl Cerny ed. (Washington, D.C.: American Enterprise Institute, 1978). p. 33. Although unusual even currently, ticket splitting is more than twice as common as it was 20 years earlier.

In addition to examining the way in which the parties gain their seats, it is important to consider the impact of the electoral system on party strengths. If the Bundestag had been composed only of the single-member-constituency representatives in 1972, then the Social Democrats would have dominated it by holding 61 percent of the total membership instead of having only 46 percent, as actually was the case.[3] With an electoral system of only single-member constituencies, the Christian Democrats in 1976 would have had 54 percent of the seats; instead, they just failed to get a majority with 49 percent. The electoral system permitted the Social Democrats, in coalition with the Free Democrats, to remain in power and prevented the Christian Democrats' return to office. Without PR, 1983 would have been an unmitigated disaster for the SPD. It won only 27 percent of the single-member seats, but the electoral system gave it 39 percent of the legislature's members.

The parties with the biggest stake in the present electoral system, however, are the FDP and the Greens. Were the PR aspect of the system to be eliminated, both would be banished from the legislature, since they are unable to elect anyone in a single-member constituency—all of their members in the legislature are elected from the party lists under PR.

Given relative stability of public opinion, PR tends to stabilize party strengths in the legislature. The Social Democrats' share of the popular vote dropped only 3 percentage points from 1972 to 1976, and thus, under the German electoral system, their share of the seats in the Bundestag dropped by only 3 percentage points. Had there been only single-member districts, however, their legislative strength would have fallen by 15 percentage points from 61 percent of the seats to 46 percent. Thus to some extent PR makes elections a bit less of a gamble for parties.

In addition to the 5 percent barrier, newly formed small parties face another obstacle. A party with fewer than five seats in the national legislature or in the land legislatures must obtain the signatures of 0.1 percent of the eligible voters in a given land to place its party-list candidates on the ballot there.

Germany does not use primary elections. The signatures of 200 voters in a district are enough to get one's name on the ballot. Nonetheless, the overwhelming majority of the candidates are not independents, but party nominees. Candidates for single-member constituencies are selected either by all the party members in that constituency or by a special nominating committee elected by the members. The land party lists are drawn up by land nominating conventions. National party leaders have some influence in this process, but local and land party organizations will not accept orders. Placement on the land list is crucial since those near the top of a leading party's list are certain to be elected,

---

[3]These figures and the ones in the rest of this paragraph are not inconsistent with Table 19–1. A party with 100 seats might have won 50 in single-member districts, and thus would have 50 percent in the table. But 50 seats would be only about 20 percent of the total number of single-member seats. This paragraph and the previous one focus on two different aspects of party representation.

while those far down on the list have little hope. Thus adverse placement on the list can end a politician's career. Conversely, the German electoral system can provide candidates a safety net. About two thirds of the Christian Democrat and SPD candidates for single-member constituencies also are included on the party list. Assuming they have been able to obtain a good position on the list, they can be certain to be returned to the legislature even if they are defeated in the single-member constituency.

National party leaders were denied the power to draw up party candidate lists because it was felt that this would have given them excessive power. But, although the process of candidate selection is decentralized, it does not involve mass participation. The size of the group making the selection often is only 100 or 200 for single-member seats, quite small compared with the number of people making the choice in American primaries even when turnout is low. This does not mean that incumbents wishing to run again can count on automatic nomination. Increasingly at the single-member-constituency level, as well as at the land level, nominations occasion strong factional fights, especially in the SPD, given the changing nature of its members.

In addition to dispensing with primary elections, Germany does not have by-elections or interim elections. Should a member of the legislature die or retire, he or she is replaced by the next person on his or her party's land list, regardless of whether the member being replaced had been elected from the list or from a single-member constituency.

Candidates must be at least 18 years old. They are not required to live in the land they represent, as is the case in the United States, but most in fact do.

The age at which one can vote is 18 also. The government assumes the reponsibility for seeing that voters are registered. Lists of eligible voters are posted well in advance of an election so that any errors can be corrected. Voter turnout in Germany is quite high. Only in the first postwar election in 1949 did it fall below 80 percent. During the 1970s it reached a high of 91 percent, and in both 1980 and 1983 it was almost as good at 89 percent. Elections are held on Sunday so that voting will not conflict with jobs for most people.

German political campaigns are relatively long—two or three months instead of the few weeks common in France and Britain. Elections must occur within 60 days of the legislature being dissolved. Since German elections usually occur at regular four-year intervals, the date of the election is known and parties can begin their campaign activities well before the official 60 days. The 1983 election was an exception because the legislature did not serve its full term. Furthermore, since the date was early in March, the parties could not get their campaigns underway until after the Christmas and New Year holidays.

The publicly directed television networks give the parties free air time. A series of two-and-a-half minute spots coming after the evening news are allocated to parties on the basis of their strength in the national legislature. At the close of the last three elections a face-to-face debate among the four principal parties' (the Greens were excluded in 1983 because they were not yet represented in the legislature) top leaders has been telecast. The 1980 one, although shorter than the previous one, lasted over three hours. Apparently, the fact that nearly as many people (84 percent) watched the debate as voted encouraged extending it to four hours in 1983.

Assessing the impact of these debates on voting is difficult. Some observers felt that Hans-Dietrich Genscher, leader of the FDP and foreign minister and vice chancellor in the coalition with the SPD, emerged with the best image in 1980. He managed to appear reasonable, while the other three participants were throwing mud and calling each other names, like "Führer type." Again in 1983 Genscher seemed to have the best TV manner, making effective responses and posing penetrating questions. Franz-Josef Strauss, CSU, seemed—as always—too aggressive and Helmut Kohl, CDU, perhaps as a result, too passive and inarticulate. Hans-Jochen Vogel, SPD, projected intelligence and dignity, although attempting to reap sympathy by pointing out that the current party situation (the FDP had abandoned the Social Democrats for the Christian Democrats in 1982) put him at a three-to-one disadvantage in the cross-questioning.

In 1980 for the first time since 1969 the four leading parties signed an agreement for a "fair" campaign. The parties pledged themselves "to conduct a fair and nonpolemical election campaign." Among other things, they agreed to "desist from personal disparagement or insult in any form" and "not spread any disparaging allegations about other parties." A joint arbitration body was set up to investigate any complaints about violation of the agreement. Its powers were limited, however, to publicity. Although some instances were referred to the arbitration body, the agreement does not seem to have had any significant impact on campaign tactics. At the close of the 1983 campaign there was some talk of libel suits being filed because some people took exception to what opponents had said about them or their parties, but, then, if anyone is as litigious as Americans, it is Germans.

More important than the agreement's portions on campaign practices were its provisions on campaign spending. The electoral law does not limit campaign spending. Constantly rising expenditures had produced the previous agreements in the 1960s. But when these were not renewed in the 1970s, spending rose again—about $90 million by the leading parties in 1972. This was an enormous sum, even by American standards.

To reduce spending the parties in 1980 agreed to limits on certain activities. Although these limits were not as detailed as those in the agreements in the 1960s, still they did bar any radio or TV advertising and restricted poster advertising to 20 days from September 1 (the election was on October 5). The latter limitation did not apply, however, to advertising at the regional or local level. Furthermore, each party agreed that its campaign spending would not exceed stated levels. These were: SPD, $18 million; CDU, $16 million; CSU, slightly more than $4 million; and FDP, $3.6 million. Thus campaign spending would be less than half of what it had been in 1972.

For 1983 both the SPD and the CDU spent about $12.25 million, the FDP $5.5 million, the CSU $2.5 million, and the Greens only something over $0.5

million. Campaign spending did not decline as much as these figures suggest. The exchange rate of the German mark to the U.S. dollar had declined by about 10 percent between 1980 and 1983, so the dollar amounts would have declined even had spending remained at the same level. The parties did spend less in 1983, however, because the campaign was not as long as usual.

Regardless of whether the total is well over $40 million or $30 million, the sum is sizable; you might wonder where the German parties get the money to live in this style. Although the Basic Law requires parties to account for the sources of their income, this provision was not implemented by appropriate legislation until 1967. The Social Democrats had voluntarily published figures on income and expenditure, but the CDU and FDP had not. The SPD therefore pushed for the enactment of legislation that would force a public accounting, a move that was successfully resisted for a long time by the other two parties.

The 1967 legislation stipulates that donations to a political party, or to one or more of its regional associations, which exceed about $6,200 annually by an individual, must be reported. Similarly, legally constituted bodies that contribute about $62,000 or more must also be included in the party's report. Parties must publish the names and addresses of such donors. Personal donations up to about $550 per year are tax deductible.

The 1954 income tax law had permitted taxpayers to deduct political contributions, whatever their size. When the Federal Constitutional Court declared this law unconstitutional in 1958, the Christian Democrats' income was cut. Thus they became more interested in alternate means of party finance than they had been. As a result, Germany began an interesting experiment in governmental subsidies to parties. The national government gave grants to parties in proportion to their number of seats in the national legislature. Other levels of government made similar grants. Eventually, governmental subsidies of one type or another accounted for about 60 percent of party income.

Then in July 1966 the Federal Constitutional Court restricted this program. It held that government could not finance party activities designed to mold public opinion but could help only in "necessary expenses of a reasonable election campaign." Furthermore, this help had to be extended even to those parties that did not have seats in the Bundestag. As a result of this decision the Christian Democrats had to release 40 percent of the salaried staff at central headquarters. The decision was less of a blow to the Social Democrats, since their large number of dues-paying members gave them a substantial income. But since they hardly were rolling in money, they, as well as the Christian Democrats, felt a need to devise a party-subsidy law that would meet all constitutional tests.

The result was the Political Parties Act of 1967, which provided that all parties that polled 2.5 percent of the total vote or more in the previous election would be paid a set sum per vote. The Court still was not satisfied; it ruled that parties getting as little as 0.5 percent of the vote must receive payment. The result of this decision was that in the 1969 election the neonazi party received $400,000 from the national government to help pay its campaign expenses.

As the law now stands, any party obtaining 0.5 percent or more of the party-list vote (right-hand side of the ballot) in any constituency in the election for the national legislature qualifies for the subsidy. In the case of individual candidates (where there is no party list offered) 10 percent of the vote cast on the left-hand side of the ballot in a given constituency is required. The total subsidy to be provided is 3.5 DM (about $1.10) for every eligible voter. Each qualifying party is due a share of the total sum equal to its proportion of the party list vote, while qualifying individual candidates receive 3.5 DM for each vote they obtained.

Although these sums are referred to as reimbursements, they actually are more than this. Parties are entitled to the sums for which they qualify regardless of whether they spent that much during the election campaign. Thus because the 1983 campaign was shorter than usual, all the parties except the FDP made a profit at the taxpayers' expense out of the election. Both the SPD and the CDU qualified for about $11.5 million more in public subsidies than they actually spent on the campaign, the CSU $4.25 million more, and the Greens $3 million more. Only the FDP came up short, spending over $0.5 million more than its share of the votes earned it.

THE ROLE OF INTEREST GROUPS

As in other democracies, interest groups are very much a part of the political process in Germany. Initially, the public tended to distrust them. Nevertheless, interest groups developed rapidly and sought to exert their influence on political parties both in and out of Government. The principal categories of interest groups are religious, business, and labor. One might add to this environmentalist and antinuclear groups, but they are attempting to transform themselves into a political party.

There is no established church in Germany, but there never has been any formal separation of church and state, either. Consequently, the state collects religious taxes and pays the clergy and church educators. In theory, each baptized German belongs to some church and, unless he or she officially declares to have left it, is taxed for its support. The church groups were particularly important in the chaos of 1945 because they appeared to be the only solid institutions left. Allied occupation authorities often asked church leaders to take jobs in local government. Subsequently, many of them became influential in party circles, especially in the CDU. The activities of Roman Catholic groups and organizations are usually to be found on the side of the CDU. From their point of view, the SPD is suspect, because in its origins it was Marxist, materialist, and godless. The FDP, because of its secular attitude, was not much better. Some CDU supporters have been unhappy about Catholic activity on behalf of the CDU, fearing that the CDU would become solely a Catholic party. Moreover, many liberals in the CDU pointed out that the SPD had changed its outlook considerably and that Christians should be able to find a home in the SPD.

During the 1960s and 1970s the political activity of the Catholic Church declined and became virtually negligible. The 1980 campaign, however, saw a surprising change. Two Sundays before the election priests read to their worshipers a pastoral letter from the bishops warning about the "dangerously high level" of the national debt and the threat of government intrusion in the citizens' lives. For the clergy to condemn easier divorce and abortion, as they had done some years earlier, is one thing, but to comment on questions not related to the family or morals is another. Chancellor Schmidt, responding in his usual style, commented: "I've not heard of a theological chair of state financing and, so far as I know, there's nothing about the subject in either the Old or New Testament."

The day before the letter was read Strauss had asserted that after the election the SPD, if it won, would stop government collection of the church tax for the Catholic Church. Schmidt termed this a "a malicious and unbelievable defamation" and set a deadline for a retraction by Strauss. When this was not forthcoming, the SPD labeled Strauss a "liar." So much for the agreement on personal disparagement and insult!

The whole affair may not have done the Catholic Church much good, to say nothing of the Christian Democrats. A poll found that only 31 percent of Catholics agreed with the substance of the bishops' letter, and only 25 percent felt that it was nonpartisan. Even apart from this incident the influence of the Church appeared to be declining since the proportion of Catholics regularly attending church had fallen in a quarter of a century from about half to less than a third.

Labor is active primarily through the German Federation of Trade Unions, which has a membership of approximately 7.5 million. About 40 percent of the German workers are organized, about the same as in Britain. Most trade union officials (certainly a large majority), are card-carrying Social Democrats. In the immediate postwar years labor union sympathy for the SPD was open. Since 1957, however, a formal neutrality in politics has been the rule. While the preponderant majority of labor votes is cast for the SPD, labor demands generally are made in nonpolitical terms. German trade unions are owners or part owners of a number of businesses, including banks, cooperatives, breweries, hotels, insurance companies, and publishing houses. The fourth largest bank in Germany is owned by the unions, as is a large construction company that has been active in building low-cost and middle-income housing throughout Germany.

The Federation of Germany Industry is the most powerful organization in the business field. Nearly 90 percent of all industrial and commercial firms belong to it. In politics it has been openly pro-CDU. It has promoted some business leaders for elective office.

A number of business firms set up sponsors' associations, which served as a channel of funds to the Christian Democrats and the FDP. Many employers, especially large corporations, contributed to these associations. The law permitted tax exemptions for firms making such contributions.

The Hesse SPD challenged the constitutionality of the tax exemption granted to a sponsor association formed to collect money from a number of large firms in industry, banking, trade, and insurance. In 1958 the Federal Constitutional Court voided the statute that had authorized the exemption. It held that by granting well-to-do citizens a privileged status, the law violated "the basic right of citizens to equality." While the decision reduced the importance of the sponsors' associations, the Christian Democrats and FDP continue to receive funds from trade associations, organizations similar to those that exist in the United States.

Even before the decision, however, those administering the political funds were dissatisfied about the way the system was working. Once a party received support from a sponsor association, its partners in the coalition also demanded funds. Moreover, nearly half of the business community was uncooperative. Many businessmen were doubtful about the results, because they found Bundestag members more interested in their party's popularity than in the contributors of funds. Yet the desire to keep the Social Democrats out kept the checks coming in.

The SPD cannot expect contributions from large corporations, but it has managed to sell expensive advertising space in its publications to certain businesses, notably breweries and department stores.

The German Farmers' Association has been the principal voice for the farmers. Usually it has favored the CDU, although, paradoxically, its influence on governmental policy may well have increased while the SPD/FDP coalition was in power. To maintain the support of the right wing of the FDP. Josef Ertl, a Bavarian farmer and conservative FDP member of the Bundestag, was appointed minister of food, agriculture, and forestry. As such he won a considerable reputation as a champion of the farmers' interests. (See Figure 19–2 for the center spread in the FDP's 1976 campaign pamphlet highlighting Ertl and agricultural policy.) The Common Agricultural Policy of the EEC is a major source of support for European farmers. Despite the costs of this program and its effect upon food prices, Ertl fought tenaciously against any changes, including even those favored by the German Government, that would be adverse to farmers.

The techniques and methods that interest groups utilize are varied. Since ministerial officials draft legislation, interest groups have tended to go to them more often than to Bundestag members or to the ministers. In this respect, their work has been facilitated by the fact that advisory bodies of experts have been set up in a number of ministries. In these advisory bodies are to be found representatives of interest groups, providing a natural point of contact with officials of the ministries. Moreover, at times ministers have been unsure about proposed legislation, and hence have not wanted to take the responsibility of advocating it without knowing what the public reaction would be. Consequently, they have authorized their associates to try out the proposed legislation on the interest groups concerned. In this way, interest groups often have been able to act as a more effective check on the Government than have the members of Parliament.

FIGURE 19–2   FDP Campaign Pamphlet

Landwirtschaft.

In sieben Jahren haben Josef Ertl und Liberale mehr für unsere Landwirte getan als andere in 20 Jahren zuvor:

Seit 1969 steigen die Einkommen der Bauern im Durchschnitt der Jahre wie die Einkommen in der übrigen Wirtschaft: ca. 11%.

Unsere Landwirtschaft behauptet sich immer stärker im europäischen Wettbewerb: Die Ausfuhr deutscher Agrarprodukte hat 1975 die Zehn-Milliarden-Mark-Grenze überschritten.

Seit 1969 wurden auf dem Land über 600.000 neue Arbeitsplätze geschaffen und 125.000 Wohnhausmodernisierungen gefördert: der ländliche Raum ist attraktiver geworden.

Ein verbessertes Bildungsangebot führt zu größerer Chancengleichheit für die Jugend auf dem Lande.

Das Bauen im Außenbereich wird für Landwirte durch die Reform des Bundesbaugesetzes wesentlich erleichtert.

Josef Ertl, F.D.P.
Bundesminister für Ernährung, Landwirtschaft und Forsten

Die F.D.P. sichert das Eigentum an Grund und Boden.

Tierschutz-, Wald- und Naturschutzgesetz helfen zur Erhaltung unseres natürlichen Lebensraums und der Erholungslandschaft.

Eine gezielte Förderung für Voll-, Zu- und Nebenerwerbsbetriebe wird eingeführt. Jeder zehnte Betrieb erhielt in den letzten sieben Jahren die notwendige Hilfe. Neu:

Die Förderung der Landwirtschaft in Berggebieten und besonders benachteiligten Regionen.

Der landwirtschaftliche Strukturwandel geht jetzt ohne soziale Härten von statten:

– Altershilfe und Landabgaberente werden jährlich an die allgemeine Einkommensentwicklung angepaßt. Der Staat zahlt dafür 1976 = 1,5 Mrd. DM.

– Seit 1972 gibt es die berufsständische Krankenkasse. Den Beitrag für die Altenteiler zahlt der Bund. 1976 = 710 Millionen DM.

– Zusatzversorgung für landwirtschaftliche Arbeitnehmer, Waisenrente: insgesamt 2,8 Mrd. DM stehen 1976 für die Agrarsozialpolitik zur Verfügung. 1969 waren es 850 Mill. DM.

Although individual members of the legislature cannot be the source of legislation, interest groups do not ignore Parliament. In the Bundestag the interest groups have concentrated on committees; they have sought to increase the number of committees so as to permit greater specialization and in this way be certain to be represented by their friends on issues of importance to them. Members of the Bundestag usually are assigned to committees on the basis of special competence in the topic with which the committee is dealing. More often than not, these expert legislators have, or have had, some association with an interest group. Thus an interest group, in some senses, is represented by its own people. This provides a channel for focusing influence upon the bureaucracy should it prove to be unresponsive.

Finally, interest groups have sought the paid services of civil servants for periods of time. German law permits civil servants to take leave and return to their posts later. Consequently, interest groups have been able to prevail upon civil servants to join them for a time in a full-time paid capacity. One does not need much imagination to visualize the value to a group of a qualified civil servant who knows the inside of the regulatory process affecting that group.

The political parties, of course, seek to harmonize group interests with party principles. Where this can be done, no serious problem arises. Where this cannot be done, parties seek to play off one interest against another. Sometimes, however, the result is division in party ranks. The most important struggle takes place not when votes are taken in the Bundestag but, rather, when new proposals are being debated in the ministries and existing measures are being implemented, as well as when legislation is being hammered out in committees.

BIBLIOGRAPHICAL NOTE

The American Enterprise Institute series of electoral studies includes a book on the 1976 German election (cited in Footnote 2) with another one, dealing with the 1980 election, under the same editor in process. Max Kaase and Klaus von Beyme, eds., *Elections & Parties* (London: Sage Publications, 1978), also contains information on the 1976 election.

For studies of interest groups, see the following: Gerard Braunthal, *The Federation of German Industry in Politics* (Ithaca, N.Y.: Cornell University Press, 1965); Karl Deutsch and Lewis Edinger, *Germany Rejoins the Powers: Mass Opinion, Interest Groups and Elites in Contemporary German Foreign Policy* (Stanford, Calif.: Stanford University Press, 1959); and William Safran, *Veto Group Politics: the Case of Health Insurance Reform in West Germany* (San Francisco: Chandler, 1967).

20

Policy Alternatives

AN EVOLVING PARTY SYSTEM

Traditionally, German parties stressed ideology and doctrine. In part this was because, as explained in Chapter 17, during the Empire under the virtually personal rule of the kaiser and his chancellor, parties had little influence on government policy. Taking a moderate stand in an attempt to gain increased popular support was largely pointless; the chancellor ran the country as he wished regardless of party strengths in the parliament. Parties had little opportunity to attempt to put their policies into effect; they could not be distinguished on the grounds of what they had done. Thus, they developed very rigid, unrealistic doctrines that served to distinguish them sharply from each other.

Parties of this type are termed *Weltanschauung* parties. Literally translated, this means "world view." These parties presented all-embracing philosophical outlooks; they offered the voters not just alternative sets of policies, as do American parties, but a comprehensive political faith. When any new issue arose, this faith would determine the party's position on that question. Thus, its policies and doctrines were to be an integrated whole, intellectually satisfying to its supporters.

Weltanschauung parties tended to be totalitarian in a special sense. It is not that they were against liberty or support dictatorship. Instead, it was that they failed to recognize any distinction between public life and private life; everything was party life. Such parties formed a wide variety of auxiliary groups dealing with sports, hobbies, adult education, and the like, so that a connection between a party and its supporters could be maintained even during social and recreational time.

369

The impact of these factors on the party system should be obvious—they help to fractionalize the party system. A party that stresses ideology and doctrine is likely to have a rather narrow appeal. The more comprehensive a faith it presents, the fewer will be the number of people willing to accept all its views. And insofar as it is a faith and not just a set of policies that is being presented, one is forced to accept everything or seek another party. Only true believers are welcomed into *Weltanschauung* parties. Thus, each party appeals to only a limited segment of the electorate, and a multiparty system is the likely result.

During the Empire, German parties ranged from the Conservative party on the right, which was mainly interested in protecting Prussia's privileged position and the welfare of the great landowners, to the Social Democratic party on the left, which espoused a radical reconstruction of the economic system and the establishment of parliamentary democracy. In between were the Center party, which was really a conservative Catholic party, often cooperating with the Conservatives; the National Liberals, a party of industrial leaders with a sizable middle-class following and a program of political reform that would alter Prussia's favored position; and the Progressives, a free trade party which emphasized the desirability of inaugurating a genuine parliamentary system.

As already noted, these parties could talk but did not have real control over policy. Even when the old political system was crumbling in the closing years of World War I, they were unable to grasp power. The Social Democrats had become the largest party in the Reichstag in 1912, but were ill-suited to govern. They refused to enter any Cabinet unless the entire political system were reformed to transfer power from the old social elite more broadly to the people. This position combined with the party's internationalism made many Germans regard it as disloyal or unpatriotic. Nonetheless, in 1914 the Social Democrats in the Reichstag voted to support finances for the war and agreed not to oppose the Government during the conflict.

The next year, however, made increasingly clear that Germany was engaged in a war of conquest. Therefore, some Social Democratic legislators refused to continue financing the war effort, thus splitting the party. The majority of the Social Democrats in the Reichstag believed they were bound by their previous commitment. Also they feared a political backlash: if voting against military finances divided the nation and caused Germany to lose the war, the public would blame the Social Democrats for the defeat. Thus they found themselves in a situation similar to that of Americans who opposed the Vietnam war, except that defeat in World War I would be a major catastrophe. How can you refuse to support your country's soldiers when they are dying in battle? But how can you support even your own country in what you believe to be aggression?

Thus although the Social Democrats always were the largest party during the Weimar Republic until displaced by the Nazis in 1932, they had, in a sense, been fatally weakened by the experiences of World War I. Neither they nor any other party ever was able to gain a majority of the legislative seats to enact an effective program. Compounding the problem was the strength of the antidemocratic parties. On the left was the Communist party, patterned after the Russian model and consistently hostile to the Republic, which gained a tenth to a seventh of the seats in the Reichstag during Weimar. On the right the German National People's party was the focus for reaction and opposition to Weimar in the early years, rising to a fifth of the seats. Just as it waned the Nazi party (National Socialist German Workers party or NSDAP) erupted.

In the center of the political spectrum were the Catholic Center party and the German Democratic party. The supporters of the Center party were drawn from virtually all social strata. This plus its moderate policies made it an influential participant in most Cabinets. The Democratic party, formerly the Progressives, strongly supported the Republic. Like many other liberal parties in Europe, however, it was declining rapidly into insignificance.

The Social Democrats were of key importance. Although in theory a Marxist party, in practice they were much more moderate. Their leaders headed coalition Cabinets for about three years and participated in several others. Given more time, an effective party system might have evolved in Weimar Germany. Before that could happen the Nazis transformed the party system, outlawing all parties but their own to produce a totalitarian one-party system.

The Western occupation authorities began authorizing party activities on the local level only a few months after the defeat of Nazi Germany. The following year they extended permission to the land level. Parties suspected of Nazi leanings, however, were barred. The occupation authorities did not attempt to force the Anglo-American two-party system upon the Germans. When the party licensing procedure was halted—1948 in the American zone and 1950 in the British and French zones—31 parties had been approved. Anyone would have guessed that the Germany party system would resume its traditional multiparty form with doctrinaire, limited-appeal parties of the *Weltanschauung* type.

But as we have already said, "Bonn is not Weimar." The Basic Law, while providing that parties are free to organize, also declared that parties which, "according to their aims and the conduct of their members, seek to impair or abolish the libertarian democratic basic order or to jeopardize the existence of the Federal Republic of Germany are unconstitutional." The Constitutional Court, upon petition of the Cabinet or of either house of the legislature, rules on this question. It banned a neo-Nazi party and a Communist party. Both subsequently reappeared under new names. These parties have had such limited support, however, that taking them to the Court again hardly seemed worthwhile. Thus it would be hard to argue that the constitution is responsible for any fundamental change in the party system.

Nonetheless, the Germany party system clearly has been in the process of a fundamental change in the last third of a century (see Figure 20–1). In the first postwar election, 1949, 11 parties elected deputies to the Bundestag with no one party approaching a majority of the popular vote or seats. The two leading parties, the Social Democrats and the Christian Democrats, received 60 percent of the vote and two thirds of the seats. Four years later the Christian Democrats,

FIGURE 20–1   Two Leading Parties' Share of the Vote in Post-World War II German Elections

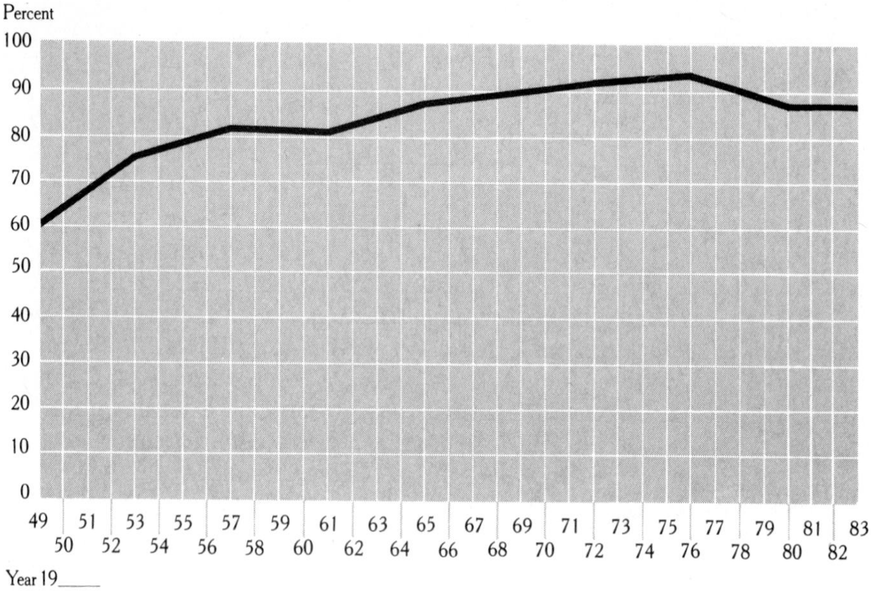

Percent

Note: In all cases the two parties are the CSU/CSU and the SPD. Except for 1972, the CDU/CSU always has been the larger.

with 45 percent of the vote, got half of the seats, and the number of parties with seats in the Bundestag was halved. In the next election the Christian Democrats gained further support to win half of the popular vote. This unprecedented accomplishment had been totally unexpected less than a decade before.

At the same time as this advance of the Christian Democrats, the Social Democrats were making steady, although less spectacular, gains. Thus, in the 1976 election the Christian Democrats and the Social Democrats received 91 percent of the votes and seats. And only one other party, the Free Democrats, was able to elect anyone to the Bundestag. While in 1980 and 1983 the two leading parties' combined total vote slipped back to 87 percent, the current party system clearly differs from the traditional German one.

Although the trend has been toward a two-party system, Germany's party system still differs from that of the United States and even of Britain. The electoral system with its 5 percent barrier (which we discussed in the previous chapter) has helped to discourage small splinter parties, but it is only part of the reason for the significant change that has occurred. Some observers have suggested that Konrad Adenauer's domineering role in his long tenure as chancellor encouraged his opponents to support the only significant opposition party, the Social Democrats. His success, at the same time, brought additional supporters to the Christian Democrats. Other analysts have pointed out that the old causes of faction—class lines and a dominant Prussia—were no longer a fact of political life in Germany. And a potential new source of faction—the refugees and expellees—quickly disappeared with the successful integration of these elements in German society. And some have argued that the experience of the Nazi regime soured the Germans on political ideologies.

Whatever the reason, a crucial change has occurred transforming German parties and their leaders. Compared to Weimar *Weltanschauung* parties, the leading parties in the Bonn Republic have been moderate, less dogmatic, and more willing to compromise. As a result, current German parties have succeeded more than did Weimar parties in building diverse followings. The sectional, limited appeal party, typical of Weimar, is not the norm in the Bonn Republic. The more moderate and pragmatic nature of political conflict in contemporary Germany is a very favorable development for the future of a viable democratic system there.

THE LEADING PARTIES

The oldest party in Germany, in existence for well over a century, is the SPD or Social Democratic party. During the 1930s, when the party was suppressed by the Nazis, its leaders went underground or into exile. In 1945 the party was revived to become first the major opposition party and then, in 1969, the major governing party.

In contrast to the SPD, the Christian Democratic Union/Christian Social Union (CDU/CSU) is a postwar product. A Catholic Center party had been active in German politics down through the Weimar Republic, but the Christian Democrats are not direct descendants of that party. The CDU/CSU was intended to be a union of all Christians, not just Catholics, since Protestants as well had suffered under the Nazis, and Christians of both types were opposed to communist advance after World War II. The party's first leader, Konrad Adenauer, although a Catholic, opposed clericalism. The fact that his successor, Ludwig Erhard, was a Protestant helped to further the party's nondenominational image. As we will clarify when we discuss party organization, the Christian Democrats are something of an alliance between the CSU, which operates only in Bavaria, and the CDU, which exists in the rest of the country. We will use the initials CD to refer to the entire organization except in those instances in which we need to distinguish between the main party and its southern affiliate.

The other parties represented in the Bundestag also are postwar creations. Although like the CDU something of an heir to an earlier political tradition, the Free Democrats (FDP) were formed in 1948 by the merger of four separate regional parties sharing similar liberal views. The Greens are even more recent, not being organized until 1980 and electing members to the national legislature only in 1983.

Doctrines and Policies

Although the SPD originated in the 19th century as a Marxist party, it already had begun to lose some of its extreme views around the turn of the century. The party came to accept parliamentary democracy and gradual, evolutionary reform. When its left wing split off to form the Communist party after World War I, the party became still more moderate. The party's transformation into a contemporary social democratic party was not completed, however, until well into the Bonn Republic. In large measure this delay was due to the influence of Kurt Schumacher, the party's first leader after World War II. Schumacher had been a socialist for too long to be willing to consider any revision of basic party doctrine. Thus, for example, in keeping with traditional party policy the SPD opposed German rearmament and membership in NATO. Schumacher scorned Adenauer as "the Chancellor of the Allies" for advocating these measures.

Schumacher's death in 1952, combined with the failure of the SPD to expand its electoral support as rapidly as the CDU, encouraged a reassessment of party policy during the 1950s. This process culminated in a major revision of party policy in 1959. This new basic program of the SPD usually is referred to as the Bad Godesberg Program after the name of the town where the party met to approve the program.[1]

The Bad Godesberg Program reversed the three main policy themes or doctrines that traditionally were associated with the SPD—socialism, pacifism, and anticlericalism. The aim was to project an image of a moderate, nondogmatic party. Thus, in economic matters the program did not talk of such traditional socialist policies as total state planning or class struggle. Instead, free competition was, incredibly, said to be one of the "essential conditions of a social democratic economic policy." The SPD explained that it favored "a free market wherever free competition really exists." "Efficient small and medium-sized enterprises are to be strengthened to enable them to prevail in competition with large-scale enterprises." This is about as socialist as Teddy Roosevelt's trust-busting was.

The traditional remedy of public ownership was not ignored entirely. Where there were natural monopolies, as in the supply of electricity, public ownership would be necessary. And government-owned industries might be useful competitors to keep private concerns from so dominating the economy as to abridge freedom. But the program went on to warn that "every concentration of economic power, even in the hands of the state, harbours dangers." While conservatives might observe that concentrated economic power would be a danger especially, rather than even, in the hands of the state, yet they would agree that

---

[1] The text of the Bad Godesberg Program appears in William Andrews, ed., *European Political Institutions*, 2d ed. (Princeton, N.J.: Van Nostrand Reinhold, 1966), pp. 187–98. *Bad* is not a term of evaluation and is pronounced as though it were spelled "bahd."

this represents a new attitude by socialists toward government economic action. To guard against the danger, the SPD indicated that it wanted to avoid a centralized bureaucracy. Thus any government-owned business should be run by governing boards representing workers and consumers. In any event, government ownership was viewed as a last resort that, apparently unfortunately, might be required in some cases, but which the true socialist would resist with great effort. The aim should be not to abolish the capitalist system but to correct its abuses—a goal that perhaps even the head of General Motors might be willing to accept. The party's slogan in the 1960s was the innocuous: "As much competition as possible—as much planning as necessary."

Given Marx's view on religion—the opiate of the people—it hardly is surprising that socialist parties traditionally have been anticlerical. This disposition has been reinforced in Europe by the highly conservative social and economic stance of the Church at most times and its active involvement in politics. In Germany this hostility has been directed at least as much against the Lutheran Church, which as the dominant Protestant faith almost has been an established church, as against the Catholic Church.

Reversing all this, the Bad Godesberg Program revealed that socialism was "rooted in Christian ethics, humanism, and classical philosophy." Had there been many Moslems in Germany at the time, that religion probably would have been included as a source as well. Contrary to what some may have thought, the SPD emphasized that it "does not proclaim ultimate truths . . . out of respect for the individual's choice in these matters of conscience." And just in case someone still had not gotten the point, the program proclaimed that "freedom to preach the gospel must be protected." The party did stop short of changing its name to Christian Socialists.

Finally, the party changed its stance on military matters. It gave firm support to military preparations essential for national defense. The year after the Bad Godesberg conference, the SPD defense spokesman in the Bundestag carried this reversal in policy to the next stage by formally announcing the party's acceptance of German membership in NATO.

Thus the SPD became more of a social democratic or social welfare party than a pure socialist party. It is more progressive or reformist than the other parties; it sees a larger role for the government in ensuring that everyone is cared for adequately.

Although one might expect the CD to have a religious *Weltanschauung*, the party has not developed a well-thought-out and unified program. A community of religious views does not guarantee agreement on political issues and the CD, appealing to both Catholics and Protestants, lacks even religious consensus. Thus, its Christian orientation has amounted to little more than acceptance of the traditional values of Western civilization and vague references to the dignity of humans and divine moral law.

Just as compromise of contrasting religious views has produced a vague policy, so also compromise between different economic groups has resulted in ambiguous stands. Since the party offers a political home to Christian trade unionists as well as to big industry and finance, it has been forced to favor policies attractive to both. In the immediate postwar years, the CD advocated, especially in industrial areas, nationalization of basic industries. But as the German recovery progressed, this part of the program was toned down or dropped altogether. In areas where the working-class vote was inconsequential, the party was more a free enterprise party from the beginning.

The CD's goal was a "social-minded market economy," that is, free enterprise tempered by social conscience. In the early and mid-1960s the party enacted laws designed to promote widespread ownership of stocks and securities, particularly among lower- and middle-income groups. Tax and other inducements were offered to both employers and employees as a means of encouraging more and more people to invest in the economy.

For the first 20 years of the CD's existence one person, Adenauer, was the party leader, and for 14 of those years he also served as chancellor of Germany. Thus to a considerable extent he came to embody the CD's policy. Its objectives did not need to be elaborated any further than to urge continued support for Adenauer's direction of Germany's affairs. A graphic example of this is the party's appeal in the 1957 election. Their posters were pictures of Adenauer's head with the simple exhortation "No Experiments."

In foreign policy Adenauer sought to make Germany once again an acceptable member of the international community and an influential member of the Western alliance. Although he negotiated with the Soviet Union, he took a hard and, some thought, excessively inflexible line on relations with communist countries. In keeping with this tradition the CD has been quite skeptical of the *Ostpolitik* policy launched under SPD Chancellor Willy Brandt. It fears that too much has been conceded to the Russians, East Germans, and Poles for too little or too-uncertain returns.

In addition to emphasizing their doubts about *Ostpolitik*, the CD in the 1976 election attacked the SPD for mismanaging the economy and running up a large budget deficit. They attempted to paint the SPD as dangerous radicals by telling the electorate that the choice was between "Freedom or Socialism." The SPD response had a certain irony since their campaign featured a virtual remake of the CD's 1957 Adenauer poster. A picture of Chancellor Helmut Schmidt—who had held the office for two years and had served in several other top positions—carried the caption, "Experience Is What Counts." (See Figure 20–2 for SPD stickers emphasizing that Schmidt must remain chancellor.) As for *Ostpolitik* indicating that the SPD was soft on communism, the SPD retorted that the Christian Democrats were warmongers. To vote for the SPD, they said, was to "Vote for Peace."

In 1980 the election again was fought primarily on foreign policy and defense issues. The SPD argued that détente—contacts between East and West aimed at gradually developing cooperation and understanding—was successful and had made peace in Europe safer. Chancellor Schmidt was concerned that the Soviet military buildup had destroyed the military balance between East and West. Thus

FIGURE 20–2   SPD Campaign Stickers

he made certain that the SPD remained firmly committed to its policy of accepting medium-range United States nuclear missiles based in Germany. But to satisfy the left wing of his party this policy was coupled with a policy of negotiating with the Soviet Union to reduce the number of missiles on each side. This was in keeping with the SPD declaration that "there is no acceptable alternative to d'etente."

The Christian Democrats charged Schmidt's Government with having neglected Germany's defense strength and with being an unreliable member of NATO. Again they objected to unnecessary concessions to the Russians. They maintained that, while they recognized the need to live with Eastern Europe as it was, this need not involve any moral or intellectual concessions.

Whatever the policy differences, what the election really came down to was the familiar German electoral appeal that changing leaders was risky, especially given the uncertain international situation of 1980. This became even more of a personality issue than usual because of the individual whom the Christian Democrats had selected to offer as their candidate for chancellor. Franz Josef Strauss long had led the CSU, the Bavarian affiliate of the CDU. Although Strauss never had led the national Christian Democratic organization, he had overshadowed most of those who had.

Although Strauss was well known nationally, that did not make him a strong candidate for chancellor because many Germans, both without and within the CDU, were highly suspicious of him. Although for many he has great personal magnetism, yet others fear his erratic behavior and errors of judgment. In 1962, for example, while serving as minister of defense, Strauss ordered the police to raid the offices of the newsmagazine *Der Spiegel* ostensibly to search for improperly obtained classified military information, but really to silence its criticisms of the Government's defense policies. For many people this incident was evidence of Strauss' lack of commitment to democratic values. The fear was not that he was a potential dictator, but that were he to become chancellor he would govern even more high-handedly than did de Gaulle in France.

Strauss' capacity for mischief seems unlimited. In 1972 on the vote to ratify the treaties with the Soviet Union and Poland, which were part of the SPD's *Ostpolitik*, the national Christian Democratic leader, Rainer Barzel, wanted his party to vote in favor to demonstrate that Germany was united in trying to close the books on the past and establish normal relations with countries that had suffered Nazi aggression in World War II. Strong opposition from Strauss, however, forced Barzel to instruct the Christian Democrat members of the Bundestag to abstain on the vote.

Some observers felt that in 1980 the Christian Democrats finally decided to let Strauss have a chance at winning an election in order to shut him up. If he actually managed to make the party a winner, that would be fine, but if they lost, at least they would not have to contend with his attempts to dominate the party. So despite the controversy he arouses, he was selected as their candidate for chancellor. For the most part Strauss ran a very circumspect campaign. Nonetheless, he may well have been the real issue, since polls showed that almost twice as many voters wanted Schmidt to remain chancellor as wanted Strauss to become chancellor.

Despite Schmidt's victory over Strauss, his Government soon ran into trouble. Economic recession put many Germans out of work; by mid-1982, unemployment was the worst that it had been in post-World War II Germany since

record-keeping began in 1950. The SPD favored a large public investment project to create jobs, but its coalition partner, the FDP, opposed this. The Economics Minister, from the FDP, proposed to stimulate the economy with tax
cuts, but this required extensive cuts in welfare, which enraged Schmidt and the
SPD. Thus the FDP switched to the CD, putting Schmidt out of office and
making Helmut Kohl of the CDU Chancellor.

Schmidt had been having trouble in the SPD over nuclear weapons; many
Germans had come to oppose siting U.S. nuclear missiles in Germany regardless of what happened in the Geneva negotiations. Schmidt urged all SPD members to boycott a peace march against the missiles in October 1981, but 55 of his
party's members in the legislature defied him and endorsed the march. Furthermore, SPD chairman and former Chancellor Willy Brandt did not support him.
Feeling increasingly repudiated, Schmidt declined to lead the SPD in the 1983
election, although ostensibly retiring for health reasons.

The SPD Executive selected Hans-Jochen Vogel as its candidate for chancellor. Unable to make the familiar argument that the voters should stick with the
existing Chancellor, the SPD (as can be seen from Figure 20–3) almost seemed
to be claiming the Vogel *was* Chancellor.

The title of the campaign paper in Figure 20–3 is significant—"In the German Interest." The SPD was arguing that Germany should not be subservient to
the United States and that the Government should not hesitate to stand up for
Germany's national interests—here was a new nationalism on the left of the political spectrum. Specifically on the key issue of the missiles, Vogel hedged. He
did not oppose them outright, but still tried to win the support of those who did
by saying that as Chancellor he would do everything possible to make their siting in Germany unnecessary. Eventually, some months after the election, the
SPD did reject the missiles, and Brandt said that the failure of the negotiations
in Geneva was not because of Russian intransigence, but due to U.S. determination to deploy the missiles and to reject any compromise offered by the Russians. The SPD still supports German membership in NATO, but "In the German Interest" clearly has moved the party some distance from the CD in foreign
policy and back in the direction of what the SPD had been in the Schumacher
years.

The economy had continued to worsen under Kohl—unemployment went
over 2 million for the first time and eventually rose to 2.5 million. But this could
be blamed on the policies of the Schmidt Government. The CD offered an austerity program to propel growth, which could reduce unemployment; the CDU
urged electors to vote in favor of economic recovery. Vogel responded that full
employment could not be obtained by growth alone and other action, such as
cutting the hours in the workweek and providing public sector jobs for young
people to give them industrial and technological training, was needed.

Although Kohl had been in office for only half a year, the CDU did not pass
up the opportunity (as Figure 20–4 shows) to tell Germans that they now had an
affable fellow as Chancellor (much nicer than that abrasive Herr Schmidt) and

FIGURE 20–3   SPD 1983 Campaign Literature

Im deutschen Interesse

Die wichtigsten Punkte aus dem Regierungsprogramm von Bundeskanzler Hans-Jochen Vogel.

Die Regierungsmannschaft von Hans-Jochen Vogel. Von links nach rechts: Hans-Jürgen Krupp, Anke Fuchs, Klaus Meyer-Abich, Egon Bahr, Volker Hauff, Horst Ehmke, Eva Rühmkorf, Willy Brandt (Parteivorsitzender), Hans-Jochen Vogel, Hans-Jürgen Wischnewski, Manfred Lahnstein, Herta Däubler-Gmelin, Jürgen Schmude, Heinz Westphal und Hans Apel.

Ein neuer Bundeskanzler: Hans-Jochen Vogel

Hans-Jochen Vogel besucht im Januar 1983 Parteichef Juri Andropow in Moskau.

Die deutschen Sozialdemokraten haben auf ihrem Wahlparteitag in Dortmund den Willen und die Bereitschaft bekundet, mit Hans-Jochen Vogel als Bundeskanzler nach der Wahl am 6. März erneut Regierungsverantwortung für die Bundesrepublik zu übernehmen. In ihrem Wahlprogramm und mit einem Sofortprogramm für die ersten 100 Tage einer sozialdemokratisch geführten Bundesregierung hat die SPD konkrete Schritte zur Überwindung der Arbeitslosigkeit, zur Wiederherstellung sozialer Gerechtigkeit, zu einschneidenden Umweltschutzmaßnahmen und zu einer sofortigen Abrüstungsinitiative angekündigt. Mit ihrem Kanzlerkandidaten Hans-Jochen Vogel kämpft die SPD um die politische Führung, weil sie überzeugt ist, daß nur eine kompetente Regierung die deutschen Interessen entschieden vertritt und das Vertrauen der Menschen besitzt, den Frieden im Innern und nach außen bewahren und sichern kann.

Hans-Jochen Vogel hat versprochen, unverzüglich nach seiner Wahl zum Bundeskanzler eine persönliche Initiative zur Förderung der Genfer Verhandlungen über die Mittelstreckenraketen mit dem Ziel zu ergreifen, daß es dort zu einer einvernehmlichen Regelung kommt, „die die Aufstellung neuer Systeme auf dem Boden der Bundesrepublik entbehrlich macht". Die SPD steht unverrückbar an der Seite ihrer westlichen Verbündeten, aber sie verwechselt Bündnistreue nicht mit Vasallentreue. Sie will im deutschen Interesse das jetzt Mögliche unternehmen, damit das Wettrüsten eingedämmt und verträgliche Regelungen gefunden werden, die den Frieden sicherer machen.

Ein Sofortprogramm für Arbeit und Beschäftigung steht an der Spitze der Vorhaben der SPD. Eine von Hans-Jochen Vogel geführte Bundesregierung wird einen nationalen Solidarpakt gegen die Arbeitslosigkeit anbieten und auch international auf den Abschluß eines Beschäftigungspaktes dringen. Die finanziellen Lasten zur Überwindung der Arbeitslosigkeit sollen wieder gerechter verteilt werden, unter anderem durch eine Ergänzungsabgabe zur Einkommensteuer für die Besserverdienenden und durch die Beschneidung ungerechter Vorteile für Wohlhabende, die sich Steuerspar-Modelle im großen Stil leisten können.

Unter Hans-Jochen Vogel wird die Bundesregierung dafür sorgen, daß künftig wieder von sozialer Gerechtigkeit im Land gesprochen werden kann: viele von der Übergangsregierung Kohl verfügten Gesetzesänderungen werden korrigiert oder rückgängig gemacht, vor allem die Verschlechterung des sozialen Mietrechts, der Abbau der BAföG-Leistungen und die Selbstbeteiligung der Versicherten bei Krankenhausaufenthalten und Kuren. Zur Rettung des Waldes will Hans-Jochen Vogel ein Notprogramm in Angriff nehmen.

Die SPD wendet sich in diesem Wahlkampf ausdrücklich an die Frauen. „Sie spüren", so das Wahlprogramm, „daß sie die eigentlichen Verlierer in einem CDU/CSU-Staat sein würden. Vieles würde zurückgedreht werden, was in den letzten Jahren als neue Lebenschancen für Frauen erreicht wurde."

Hans-Jochen Vogel erklärte auf dem Wahlparteitag der SPD in Dortmund, die Sozialdemokratie erstrebe die Regierungsverantwortung nicht deswegen, weil sie die Führer der Union für politische Verbrecher und ihre Anhänger für unanständig halte. Solche Vorwürfe, die der Generalsekretär der Union an die Adresse der SPD gerichtet hatte, seien schlimme Töne, die an eine schlimme Zeit erinnerten. Für seine Partei begründete Hans-Jochen Vogel den politischen Führungsanspruch der SPD mit den Worten: „Wir erstreben Regierungsverantwortung, weil nach unserer Überzeugung unsere Politik dem Frieden, der Gerechtigkeit und der sozialen Qualität unseres Volkes besser dient als die Politik unserer Gegner. Weil unsere Politik im deutschen Interesse liegt."

Hans-Jochen Vogel besucht im Januar 1983 US-Präsident Ronald Reagan im Weißen Haus.

FIGURE 20–4   CDU 1983 Campaign Literature

should stick with him. Thus leader personality continued to be a factor in electoral politics.

As for the CSU, it stressed (see Figure 20–5) that 13 years of socialism (that is, SPD Chancellors from October 1969 to October 1982) were more than enough. Clearly, demonstrators in the streets were too much for the conservative wing of the Christian Democrats that wanted to bring back order to Germany.

Although the policy differences between the CD and the SPD in 1983 were greater than they had been in 1980, the parties still were not poles apart. The choice was not between Marxist socialism and laissez-faire capitalism, but between social welfare or welfare capitalism. Policies have converged to the extent that elections can turn on leader personality and the advisability of switching horses. In such circumstances the Free Democrats have a difficult time staking out a distinctive position.

Some shifts in FDP policies over the years have added to the problem by blurring its image somewhat. The FDP's original aim was to appeal to those who disliked socialism but also opposed religious values in politics. It emphasized the need for political, religious, and economic freedom. Gradually by the early 1960s it had come to stress the last of these most and had moved to the right on the political spectrum. This shift halted in 1966 when the party withdrew from its coalition with the CD. Since then, the FDP has sought to present a more liberal and reform-minded image. As the only party in the Bundestag in opposition to the Grand Coalition of the CD and the SPD in the late 1960s, the FDP offered energetic and constructive criticism of the Government. After the 1969 elections it joined the SPD in a coalition government.

That alliance endured for well over a decade. The FDP is more middle-of-the-road than the SPD, but the policy differences between them were mainly matters of degree. The most marked disagreement concerned industrial relations. The FDP tends to be rather unsympathetic to trade unions. The two parties differed on extending the system of worker participation in the management of private industry. Although the SPD was able to pass legislation doing this, the FDP forced a significant concession denying unions and workers complete equality with management on the directing boards of German industry. The FDP argues that it is not antiworker; it regards participation in shopfloor decisions as important as in management and wants to be certain that workers who are not union members are not denied a voice at that level.

As already mentioned, the SPD/FDP coalition finally collapsed over economic policy and government spending for welfare benefits. In 1983 the FDP did not emphasize its issue positions as much as it did its role in the system—that of a balancer between the two large parties. The FDP argued that only by electing some of its candidates to the legislature could the electorate be certain of denying the Christian Democrats a majority and thus keeping Strauss from having a strong voice in national government. As noted in the previous chapter, the Free Democrats never elect any of their individual candidates, gaining all of their representation through the party lists. Recognizing that, the FDP explicitly campaigned for the electorate's "second vote" (see Figure 20–6) so that it would not be shut out of the legislature.

And indeed the FDP has shown an ability to check some of the more conservative of the CD's desires. The Free Democrats blocked revising the liberal abortion law, restricting immigration of foreign workers' dependents, and prohibiting demonstrators from wearing masks. They also prevented the CD plan

FIGURE 20–5   CSU 1983 Campaign Poster

Nach 13 Jahren Sozialismus

Wir sind in tiefer Sorge um unser Vaterland:
Millionen Arbeitslose, geplünderte Kassen, die
Wirtschaft in der Krise, der Sozialstaat in Gefahr.
Die Regierungspolitik von CDU und CSU
wird Deutschland wieder in Ordnung bringen.
Mit Verantwortung, Tatkraft und Vernunft.

Am 6. März wird ein neuer Bundestag gewählt.
Wählen Sie eine sichere Zukunft. **CSU**

FIGURE 20–6   FDP 1983 Campaign Leaflet

to grant amnesty to those people who had broken the tax law through financial contributions to parties.

The Greens have no difficulty in being distinguished from the other parties. At times they seem to go out of their way to shock the sensibilities of conservative Germans—wearing casual clothes, long hair, and beads in the national legislature and putting pots of flowers on their desks in the chamber. As the name suggests, the party grew out of environmental concerns. The SPD has tried to straddle the issue. On the one hand it wants to give German coal precedence over nuclear energy, while on the other it accepted limited use of nuclear energy subject to precise safeguards. But it wants to try to "make it possible to dispense with nuclear energy ultimately." The CD firmly states that "the peaceful use of nuclear energy is essential for maintaining energy supplies." They favor use of "nuclear energy to the extent necessary with the appropriate disposal of nuclear waste and strict safety precautions. But they will not allow problems of safety and waste disposal to be used as a pretext for obstructing the use of nuclear energy where such problems have been solved." The Greens are opposed firmly to nuclear energy—in contrast to the major parties—and also take other environmental stands, such as opposition to enlargement of airports.

In addition to environmentalists, the Greens also include pacifists and those seeking a vehicle for rejecting American missiles in Germany and for adopting neutralism. The SPD came to reject Schmidt's position on missiles largely because it feared losing a substantial portion of the left-wing vote to the burgeoning Greens. Thus the Greens have played a role in sharpening the contrasts between the German parties.

Supporters and Strengths

Religion and occupation have considerable influence on voting behavior in Germany. In general, Catholics vote for Christian Democrats and workers for the SPD. These two characteristics interact in an interesting way. While two thirds to four fifths of the Protestant workers vote for the SPD, only a half or less of the Catholic workers do. In fact, white-collar employees who are Protestants are much more likely to support the SPD than are Catholic workers. On the other hand, those who are self-employed, even if they are Protestant, vote predominantly for the Christian Democrats. The Catholic self-employed, naturally, are overwhelmingly committed to the CD.

Comparing Figure 20–7 with Figure 20–8 will give you a better picture of the effect on party strengths. The SPD is strongest in the "city-states" of Bremen

FIGURE 20–7   Major Party Victories in National Elections

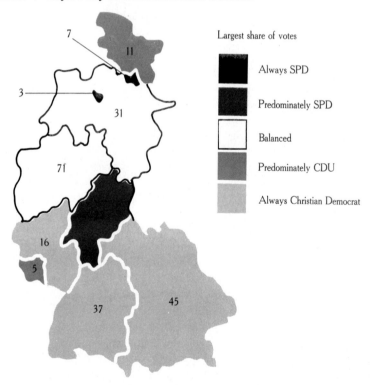

Largest share of votes

Always SPD

Predominately SPD

Balanced

Predominately CDU

Always Christian Democrat

Note: The number is the single-member seats each land has in the Bundestag.

FIGURE 20–8   Percent Catholic of Population, by Land

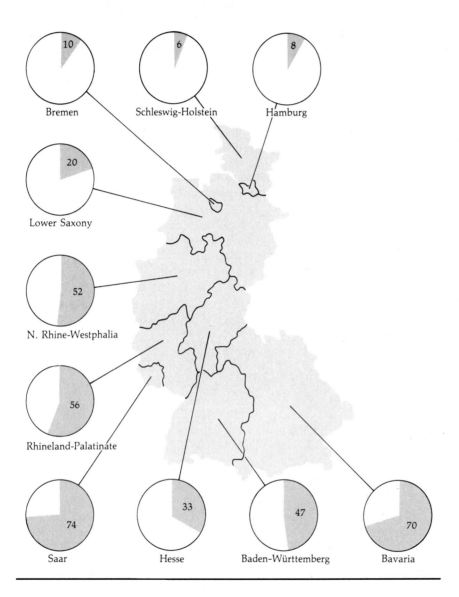

and Hamburg. Not only do these urban, industrial laender contain a large number of workers, but also relatively few Catholics live there. Germany has other
industrial areas, but, except for the Saar, the laender are sufficiently large to encompass rural areas as well. Thus in most laender the impact of the working-
class vote is diluted. As for the Saar, not only is it not totally industrial, but it

has the highest proportion of Catholics of any land. Thus the limited success of the SPD there is understandable. The other side of the coin is Schleswig-Holstein. Much of this land is the rural, agrarian area that the Christian Democrats usually could expect to dominate overwhelmingly. The fact that the SPD has enjoyed some electoral successes here is related to the land having the lowest proportion of Catholics.

Although Christian Democratic strength has not been confined to laender where Catholics predominate, yet religion obviously has been an element in their appeal. The religious composition of Bavaria and Rhineland-Palatinate, along with having the highest proportion of the work force engaged in agriculture, helps to explain the Christian Democrats' dominance in those two laender. CSU control of Bavaria (the party regularly gets about 60 percent of the vote there in national elections) is especially important, since this land is the second largest and returns almost one fifth of the members of the national legislature.

In discussing party doctrines, we noted that the Christian Democrats have not stressed religious views. Unlike the Center party in the Weimar Republic, they were trying to appeal to Protestants as well as Catholics. But these efforts to be a secular party have succeeded only partially. Voting support for the Christian Democrats comes disproportionately from Catholics. The positive aspect of this Catholic connection is the diverse class support that it gives the Christian Democrats. Were it not for its religious appeal the party would lose much of the support it has gained among workers and thus would be a middle- and upper-class party.

As Figure 20-9 shows, a substantial portion of the Christian Democrats' support comes from workers. Just as is true for the British Conservatives, the party would have little hope of ever winning an election were it not able to win over a portion of the social class that would seem to be the natural clientele for its opponents. The remarkable aspect in Figure 20-9 is the shift that it reveals in the nature of the SPD. Early in the Bonn Republic the SPD was overwhelmingly a working-class party. Now it has become only slightly so.

As the service sector of the German economy has expanded, the number of white-collar workers has increased so that in the 1980s they have come to outnumber the industrial workers. Thus Brandt's argument that the SPD should continue to concentrate on expanding its support among the new middle class would seem to be well grounded in the demographics of German society. He also sees this strategy as a means of heading off the Greens, who are strong among the well-educated middle class.

Nonetheless, this effort seems to have been counterproductive in 1983. By appealing to the interest of left-of-center white-collar workers, the SPD lost substantial numbers of skilled manual workers who had voted for them in the past. These workers are in some ways rather conservative and did not appreciate the SPD's apparent effort to cozy up to the Greens, especially when this seemed to involve approval of protest demonstrations and a weakening of support for the Western alliance. The political shift is rather like that which diverted

FIGURE 20–9   Class Composition of Population and Party Clienteles

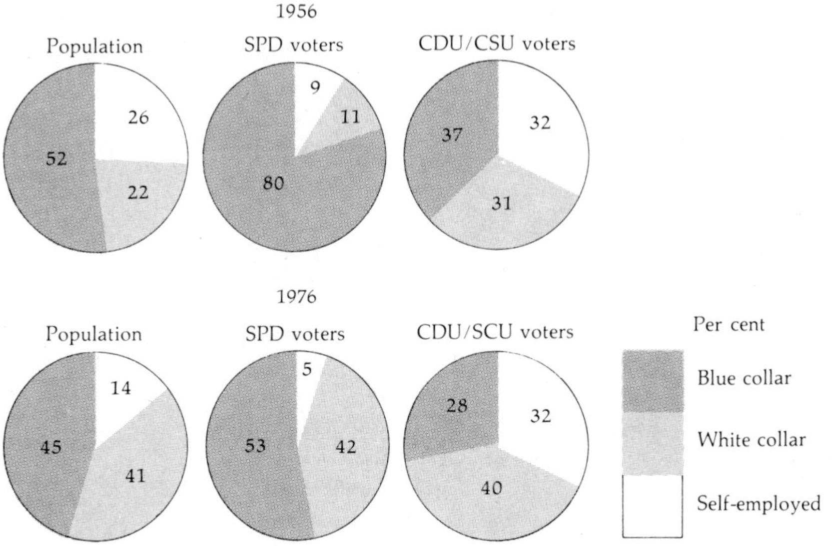

1956

Population   SPD voters   CDU/CSU voters

Population: 26, 52, 22

SPD voters: 9, 11, 80

CDU/CSU voters: 32, 37, 31

1976

Population   SPD voters   CDU/SCU voters

Population: 14, 45, 41

SPD voters: 5, 53, 42

CDU/SCU voters: 28, 32, 40

Per cent

Blue collar

White collar

Self-employed

many manual workers away from the Democratic party in the United States and to support for President Reagan. Thus the SPD lost some 2 million voters to the CD, while winning only about 150,000 away from them. Nor did the SPD change in policy prevent losses to the Greens, since about three quarters of a million of its former voters went in that direction.

About the only positive achievement of the SPD's 1983 campaign was to do better than any other party with young people. Well over a third of those voting for the first time supported the SPD, with less than a third going to the CD and less than a quarter to the Greens. Even so, for a party as new and small as the Greens to get this much of the youth vote and for the SPD to be only 5 percentage points ahead of the CD among this group suggests that the SPD did not do nearly as well as it should have done among this segment of the electorate.

The Free Democrats' main source of support has been the urban, Protestant middle class. Business and professional people who feel that the CDU is too dominated by big business prefer to vote FDP. The party also has received some support from large farmers. Over the years its support has tended to shift from the self-employed, however, to white-collar workers and civil servants. Especially while in coalition with the SPD it became more attractive to liberals, intellectuals, and students.

To some extent the FDP's appeal for voters is more negative than positive. People vote for it not so much because they like it as because they have some lingering suspicions of either the Christian Democrats or the Social Democrats. A 1980 poll found that 54 percent of those interviewed wanted more than two parties to have seats in the national legislature; only 21 percent felt that only the SPD and the CD would be enough. And 65 percent of those who favored more than two wanted only the FDP to be added.

For the first two decades of the Bonn Republic, the CD was the dominant Government party. Although, as Table 20–1 shows, it won only eight seats more than the SPD in the first election, it formed the Government. The next two elections the Christian Democrats gained considerable ground, mainly at the expense of minor parties, which fell by the wayside. The vagueness of the party's doctrines and the appeal of Adenauer enabled the CD to construct a broad coalition of diverse supporters. This culminated in the party's winning half of the popular vote in 1957, an event unique in German political history. Then, during the 1960s, the party lost a little ground, dropping back to about where it had been in 1953. From 1966 to 1969 the Christian Democrats had to share power in the Grand Coalition with their chief rivals, the SPD. From 1969 to 1982 the CD had to watch the SPD run the country in coalition with the FDP.

The Christian Democrats were able to return to power when the FDP switched sides in 1982. The CD solidified their hold on office with an electoral victory in 1983. Actually, the party did no better than it had seven years earlier, but the SPD's loss of support and the entry of the Greens into the legislature enabled the CD to remain in office with FDP support.

Early in the Bonn Republic, the SPD was hurt by the division of Germany into two countries. What is now East Germany includes many areas that formerly were SPD strongholds, in part because that section of Germany was much more heavily Protestant than what is now West Germany. Had East Germany been part of the Bonn Republic the SPD almost certainly would have been the largest party initially, as it had been at various times in both Imperial

TABLE 20–1   Election Results in the Bonn Republic

	1949		1953		1957		1961		1965	
	Percent	*Seats*	*Percent*	*Seats*	*Percent*	*Seats*	*Percent*	*Seats*	*Percent*	*Seats*
CDU/CSU	31	139	45	243	50	270	45	242	48	245
SPD	29	131	29	151	32	169	36	190	39	202
FDP	12	52	10	48	8	41	13	67	10	49
Others	28	80	17	45	10	17	6	0	4	0

	1969		1972		1976		1980		1983	
	Percent	*Seats*	*Percent*	*Seats*	*Percent*	*Seats*	*Percent*	*Seats*	*Percent*	*Seats*
CDU/CSU	46	242	45	225	49	243	45	226	49	244
SPD	43	224	46	230	43	214	43	218	38	193
FDP	6	30	8	41	8	39	11	53	7	34
Greens							2	0	6	27
Others	5	0	1	0	1	0	1	0	1	0

and Weimar Germany. As it was, had the Russians not objected to considering West Berlin a part of West Germany, the SPD would have been the strongest party in the Bundestag in 1949, since the delegation from West Berlin was overwhelmingly Socialist.

The SPD's failure to expand its support at the same rate as the CD appeared to condemn it perpetually to the role of Opposition party. By the late 1950s the party almost had convinced itself that it never could hope to win more than a third of the popular vote. This mood of resignation or futility helped those who wanted to modernize the party's doctrines to carry out the revisions of the Bad Godesberg Program. Since all else apparently had failed to bring success, party members were more willing to consider changing the party's image.

A single factor is unlikely to be the only cause of a major change in party fortunes, for in any democracy the voters eventually become dissatisfied with the party in power and decide that it is time for a change. And the CDU was unlikely once Adenauer had passed from the scene, to find another leader of his abilities and electoral appeal. Nonetheless, in the 10 years leading up to the Bad Godesberg Program the SPD vote increased by only 3 percentage points, while the following decade saw a gain of 11 percentage points. By the early 1970s the SPD not only had become the dominant party in the Government coalition, but had managed to win a slightly greater share of the popular vote than did the Christian Democrats.

That success, however, proved to be the high-water mark. The SPD subsequently slipped back to what seemed to have become its regular 43 percent of the vote. This level of support proved not to be firm in 1983, however, as the SPD dropped 5 percentage points to its worst result in 22 years.

In turning its back (in effect) on Schmidt the party did itself considerable harm. Nearly half of the voters in 1983 preferred someone other than Vogel or Kohl—the main parties' candidates—as Chancellor.[2] Using a scale of 1 (low) to 11 to express their support, voters gave Schmidt an average rank of 7.8, Kohl 6.9, and Vogel 6.2. Similarly on the question of competency, Schmidt received an average of 8.2, Kohl 7.5, and Vogel 6.7. Even among SPD supporters, Schmidt fared better than Vogel, the party's actual candidate, with an average ranking of about 10 on support and competency compared to only about 9 on each for Vogel.

The FDP also suffered from self-inflicted wounds. Many of its supporters were alienated by the shift in support from the SPD to the CD, especially since the party had pledged in the 1980 election that it would remain in coalition with the SPD for the entire four-year legislative period. Many FDP voters agreed with Schmidt's cry that he had been betrayed. The party lost about a third of its vote and suffered its second worst result in the entire Bonn Republic. About the only comfort was the fact that it had managed to clear the 5 percent hurdle and

---

[2]Werner Kaltefleiter, "Eine kritische Wahl," *aus politik und zeit geschichte*, B 14/83 (April 9, 1983), pp. 9–10.

thus wasn't eliminated from the legislature entirely, which had seem a distinct possibility only a few months before the election.

But having cleared the hurdle, the FDP benefited from the electoral system. In Britain the Alliance between the Social Democrats and the Liberals gained a share of the vote three and one half times greater than that obtained by the FDP in national elections only a few months apart in 1983. Yet the Alliance received only 23 seats in a 650-seat legislature, while the FDP was awarded 34 in a 498-seat one. (Why does the Alliance scream foul?)

In some senses the biggest victors in 1983 were the Greens. They added 4 percentage points to their share of the vote in the previous election and cleared the 5 percent barrier. While they didn't overtake the FDP, as it had appeared for awhile they might, still the party was little more than half a million votes behind the Free Democrats.

As explained in the previous chapter, parties in Germany receive substantial financial assistance from the government, ostensibly to cover the costs of election campaigns, but in fact as a subsidy to regular operations. The parties are not permitted to obtain in a single payment the entire sum for which they qualify. In the second year after the election they can draw only 10 percent of the total, in the third year only 15 percent, and in the election year only 35 percent. Thus the significance of public financial support of the parties varies from one year to another. The figures in Table 20–2 are for 1981—a year after a national election, when the governmental subsidy would be likely to be at its lowest. At that point each of the parties received about a seventh of their income from the government. In another year—even a nonelection one—the proportion might be as high as a fifth.

The Table indicates that the CSU and the FDP do not do nearly as well as the large parties in financing themselves from membership dues and the FDP is inordinately dependent upon gifts to meet its expenses. While the CSU operates only in Bavaria and the FDP does throughout the country, yet the CSU had a total income nearly half again as large—about $15 million compared to $11 million. In this particular year the two largest parties each had the same income, about $55 million. And their patterns of income had much more in common with each other than with the two smaller parties. The somewhat bigger SPD membership managed to offset the CDU advantage in gifts.

TABLE 20–2   Sources of Party Income in 1981 (Percent)

	Members' dues	Government subsidies	Parliamentary party contributions	Gifts	Loans	Other
SPD	57	15	13	7	2	7
CDU	43	12	14	17	9	5
CSU	25	12	11	22	27	4
FDP	21	14	9	43	3	9

Some people are concerned that the German subsidy system makes parties too dependent on the government; they worry that the program could be abused. And some wonder whether even the present law, as revised by the Court's requirements, puts minor parties at an impossible disadvantage. Major parties are rewarded financially at such a level that new contenders for public support seem not to have a chance. The Greens, however, hardly seem to have been hurt by the subsidy system in fighting the 1983 election; they were able to mount a successful campaign on very little money, and as a result made a substantial profit, which can help to finance their operations until the next election.

In any event, recent developments have made concerns about the government subsidy program much less pressing than those involving another aspect of party finances, an aspect that should have been unnecessary under the German system. The whole idea of the subsidy system is to help keep parties from being dependent upon wealthy special interests for financial support and to prevent one major party from having substantially greater resources than the other. The impact of gifts to parties was to be minimized.

Under German law, individuals can deduct from their income tax gifts to parties of no more than about $600. Any gift that a party receives in excess of about $6,500 must be made public. The parties have devised various dodges around these requirements. Since the tax-deduction limit is higher for nonprofit foundations, the parties have created such organizations; the CDU, for example, has the Konrad Adenauer Foundation. Such foundations simply are a means of channeling money to the parties without being subject to the intended provisions of the tax law. Furthermore, many firms will commission some subsidiary of a party to write a research report or provide some consulting service. The payment, of course, then passes through the subsidiary to the party. Note that in all this we are talking of party, not personal, corruption. Individuals are not being bought or paid off.

The biggest of these illicit party financial dealings is the Flick affair. In 1975 the Flick industrial conglomerate wanted tax concessions on its sale of shares it owned in Daimler-Benz. These were worth nearly $1 billion and would incur a tax of $125 million. But the tax would not have to be paid if the money from the sale of shares was invested in operations "particularly beneficial for the national economy." The idea behind this provision in the law was to encourage businesses to invest, thus stimulating the economy and creating jobs. Flick wanted a ruling that its investments, some of which were in other businesses that it owned, met the criterion.

So far, no particular problem. Flick got the ruling and everyone seemed happy. But in November 1983, after two years of investigation the public prosecutor said that Otto Lambsdorff, the FDP Economics Minister in the SPD/FDP coalition who had continued in this capacity in the new CD/FDP coalition, was suspected of having received from Flick a gift for his party of nearly $50,000. The gift, presumably, helped to encourage Lambsdorff to support a favorable ruling for Flick on the tax concession. Parliament, Lambsdorff himself agreeing, voted to lift his immunity from suit. And eventually in June 1984 he resigned from the Government because formal charges had been brought and he would have to stand trial.

But this was only the start of a tale that has mushroomed to incredible proportions. In October 1984 a Green member of the legislature was ejected from the chamber for referring to rumors circulating about how Kohl came to be leader of the CDU. Ranier Barzel, now the presiding officer of the legislature, had led the CDU in the early 1970s. Because of his failure to drive the SPD from office, he was pushed aside for a new leader, Helmut Kohl. The story was that he was persuaded to resign because over the next several years Flick would pay about $750,000 to a law firm with which Barzel was associated—and the money would go to him. While it would be hard to believe that Barzel's legal advice could be worth this much even over a period of several years, he denied any wrongdoing. While no violation of law was established, Barzel quickly resigned as the legislature's presiding office to avoid any further examination of the matter.

At this point a legislative committee decided that it had better look into the matter. It questioned leaders from all parties—Kohl, Strauss, Genscher, Brandt, Schmidt, and others—except, of course, the Greens, who, naturally, loved every minute of it. Flick supposedly had given about $16 million to various parties in the 1970s. Most of this had gone to the CDU. A Flick official had kept a list of the payments, however, and on it appeared the names of important people from every party. Kohl admitted to the committee that he had asked Flick for money for the CDU, but denied that he promised to exert any influence on the tax-concession question in return. He also maintained that in the late 1970s they gave the CDU through him only about $50,000, rather than the nearly $250,000 that had been rumored. Although just how he knew the sum is unclear, since he had said earlier that he received payment in the form of cash in envelopes, which he did not open, but passed on to the CDU treasurer.

It will be some time before all this is sorted out and prosecutions, where warrented, run their course. The German public appears to be shaken over what it regards as pervasive corruption. Legislators report that when they hold public meetings in their constituencies, the first thing asked when the session is opened for questions is, "How much did Flick pay you?"

Flick is only part of the party finance question. It was discovered in 1984 that the FDP had received an anonymous contribution of nearly $2 million in 1983. This was at a time when the law limited anonymous gifts to about $400. Only when the matter became public did the former leader of the party reveal that he obtained the money from a businessman who wanted to help prevent the FDP from going bankrupt.

Until January 1984, businesses were not entitled legally to tax deductions for contributions to parties, although many apparently claimed such. Now the law makes parties charitable institutions, so some tax relief can be claimed. As for those who violated the law prior to then by claiming deductions, they apparently will not be prosecuted.

By not being willing to finance themselves with membership support and substantial public subsidies, the parties, except for the Greens, who have not received such gifts, have damaged their standing with the public. This seems to verify the rather self-righteous, moralizing image that the Greens like to strike on the basis of their opposition to nuclear weapons. As for the Greens' finances, some claim that a portion of their money comes from the Soviet Union. Whether this is true or simply the established parties' effort to call into question the financial purity of the Greens as well is unclear.

Party Organization and Power Structure

Although highly centralized and hierarchically structured, the SPD, having developed as a traditional working-class party, also emphasizes mass membership—that is, dues-paying, card-carrying adherents as distinct from verbal or electoral supporters. The SPD has seen itself as more of a movement of the working class than a political party. It has actively sought a large membership and has maintained that the rank and file were to participate fully in making party decisions.

The restoration of political freedom after World War II helped the party's membership shoot up to nearly 900,000. But as the Germans became fully involved in rebuilding their nation and their personal lives, political interest waned and membership declined to only a half million. In the 1950s and most of the 1960s membership increased slightly year by year until the SPD victory in the 1969 election produced another spurt. Party membership was rather stable at about 1 million for a time, but in the 1980s has fallen below three quarters of a million.

As for member participation in decision making, the SPD holds a rank-and-file convention every two years plus extraordinary conferences as needed. The conference elects the executive, which wields the real power. The party rules make it responsible for "the control of the party," "conducting the party's business," and guiding "the fundamental attitude of the party organs." Since the executive meets only once a month, the party business is administered on a day-to-day basis by the Managing Committee, composed of the two party chairmen and four or five paid party officials from the executive. Thus this organ also exercises considerable influence on party policy.

In one regard the SPD's structure differs significantly from its form during the Empire and the Weimar Republic—the party no longer is connected officially with the trade unions. In order to get a united union movement, trade union leaders decided to avoid any party affiliations such as had been the practice in Germany and still exist in Britain. Thus, both Christian and socialist trade unionists could belong to the same organization. Nonetheless, most trade union leaders favor the SPD and actively assist the party even though their unions are not associated formally with it. This probably is one of the reasons why a separate Federation of Christian Trade Unions was formed in 1955. Despite this division of the unions on religious lines the German Federation of Trade Unions remains formally unconnected with the SPD.

Although not directly related to this structural change, the SPD also has ceased to be a trade union party in another way. In the 1950s two thirds of the SPD members were working class and 9 out of 10 had only a primary education. By the mid-1970s half the party's members were white-collar employees and only two fifths were blue collar. At the same time a substantial number of young people joined the party.

These two developments have produced considerable internal strains. Traditionally, the SPD's stress on intraparty democracy was more talk than reality. The leadershp tended to dominate party elections and perpetuate itself in power. Furthermore, its control over the party decision-making process enabled it to get its policies endorsed. In fact, one of the classic studies of party organization, which concluded that all parties were oligarchies, was based to a considerable extent upon the way in which the SPD operated in the early part of the 20th century.[3]

But the young people and middle-class persons who entered the SPD in the late 1960s and 1970s wanted to participate fully. Furthermore, they tended to be more left wing than the working-class members. Thus the Jusos, the SPD youth organization, frequently criticized the party leadership for being too moderate and for failing to implement more radical measures on government ownership of industry and redistribution of wealth. Subsequent complaints were that the Government's efforts to deal with terrorism had gone so far that they jeopardized civil liberties and that Schmidt's willingness to accept U.S. nuclear missiles in Germany undermined detente. Schmidt threatened to resign in mid-1981 unless the party's left wing stopped trying to overturn the Government's commitment on the missiles. As explained above, the party ultimately did repudiate Schmidt's position.

The old Michels picture of automatic leadership domination clearly has changed along with the change in the party's members. Despite having been the party's candidate for Chancellor in 1983 and subsequently its leader in the legislature, Vogel is not a power in the party. Willy Brandt, Chancellor from 1969 to 1974 and still party chairman, is the most influential figure now that Schmidt is gone. But his desire to turn the party to the left and win the support of those who otherwise might favor the Greens is challenged by many on the right wing of the party. And since Brandt is into his 70s, he can't be expected to hold his position for a great deal longer. Thus the SPD seems about ready to acquire a new generation of leaders and the direction in which they take the party will have considerable impact on its strength and nature for a good many years.

---

[3]Robert Michels, *Political Parties,* trans. Eden and Cedar Paul (New York: Dover, 1959); first published in 1915.

The Christian Democrats lack a mass membership tradition. Thus although the party constitution provides for a number of organs similar to those in the SPD, the organization of the Christian Democrats during their 20 years in power tended to resemble that of American parties—a relatively loose grouping of a number of land parties, which were themselves little more than electoral machines with little regular membership activity. Party membership never totaled much more than a third of a million.

Once they lost control of the Government, however, the Christian Democrats transformed themselves into a mass membership party. Toward the close of the 1970s they had reached 800,000 members. While they declined somewhat in the 1980s—only about 735,000 in 1984—they did a better job than did the SPD in retaining members. Thus in party membership they actually pulled ahead of the traditional mass party. Furthermore, at the grass-roots level the party developed its organization to the point that it was about as active and effective as that of the SPD. Nonetheless, the Christian Democrats have not faced the same pressures for membership participation in party policymaking as having occurred in the SPD, and regional party leaders continue to be important.

The most pronounced, although not only, case of regionalism concerns Bavaria. In this land the Christian Democrats are known as the Christian Social Union. The CDU does not run any candidates in Bavaria, while the CSU contests elections only there, leaving the rest of Germany to the CDU. The CSU is a separate party organization. Under the electoral law, for example, the votes received by the CSU are not combined with those for the CDU to determine a single total of Christian Democratic seats in the Bundestag. Although the CSU and CDU work together closely in the Bundestag, yet the CSU has its own set of party officers and frequently caucuses separately from the rest of the Christian Democrats, who have been elected under the CDU label.

The size of Bavaria and the extent of the CSU's domination there give Strauss a strong power base. The CSU usually holds about one fifth of the total Christian Democratic strength in the national legislature. In 6 of 10 national elections, the CSU, running candidates only in Bavaria, has polled more votes than has the FDP, operating on a national basis. The CDU is unable to match in any of the laender it contests the CSU performance in Bavaria. In 1983 the CDU did best in Baden-Wurttemberg with under 53 percent of the vote, compared to the CSU's 59.5 percent in Bavaria.

For some time Strauss toyed with the idea of expanding the CSU beyond the borders of Bavaria to organize the party and run candidates in the rest of Germany. He argued that this would drive the SPD from power because the CSU candidates would mobilize the votes of those who supported minor parties or abstained because the CDU candidates were not sufficiently conservative. Thus the total Christian Democratic vote and strength in the national legislature would be increased. The CDU leaders feared that all that would happen would be that the CSU candidates would drain votes away from the CDU candidates without tapping any significant new sources of support. The plan really was a means of strengthening the CSU at the expense of the CDU.

Following the 1976 election Strauss indicated that the CSU would not form a joint group with the CDU in the Bundestag, as it always had done in the past, and that he would move ahead with plans for expanding the CSU to all of Germany because Helmut Kohl, the national CDU leader, had cost the Christian Democrats the 1976 elections by not taking a sufficiently hard line against socialism. Kohl responded that the CDU was beginning plans to establish itself in Bavaria, thus challenging the CSU for the Christian Democratic vote there. Perhaps it was this threat that drove Strauss back into line. At the last minute Strauss changed his mind and the CSU and CDU formed their usual joint legislative group.

In an effort to unify the Christian Democrats, Helmut Kohl indicated in 1979 that he would not be a candidate for chancellor in the next year's elections. He intended that his successor should be Ernst Albrecht, the minister president of Lower Saxony. A CDU/CSU combined strategy committee was unable to agree on Albrecht or anyone else as a candidate, however, and recommended that the Christian Democrats in the national legislature suggest someone. They made their selection by secret ballot, voting 135 to 102 for Strauss over Albrecht. Since over 80 CDU legislators would have had to vote for Strauss to produce this total, he clearly had support outside of Bavaria. Thus Strauss became the Christian Democratic candidate for chancellor in the 1980 election, with the results that we have discussed.

Once Kohl became Chancellor he was able to deny Strauss the only Cabinet positions likely to interest him—foreign affairs, economics, and defense. So Strauss decided to remain in Bavaria, but periodically he emerges from the forest and growls. Whether this weakens Kohl's control of the Christian Democrats in unclear. Kohl's working style seems to be a good bit like that of President Reagan's—a cheerful image, little interest in details, and a lot of delegation of authority to subordinates. Many complain about Kohl's weak leadership, and yet he clearly has been successful. Since he is only in his mid-50s, he would seem likely to be a power in the party for years to come.

The Free Democrats have been dominated by a small group of leaders. Genscher became chairman of the party in 1974 after six years as deputy chairman. While his hold on the party seemed quite firm, his switch of coalition partners from the Social Democrats to the Christian Democrats weakened his support. Thus in November 1982 he was reelected chairman with only 56 percent of the vote compared to 90 percent two years earlier. Recognizing his loss of support, Genscher ultimately indicated that he did not plan to lead the party beyond 1986. But he soon was pressured to resign even before then, and in February 1985 Martin Bangemann, who had replaced Lambsdorff as Economics Minister, became chairman. How the party will operate under him remains to be seen.

As an amalgam of several diverse groups, the Greens are rather loosely organized, even at the Parliamentary level. Less than a year after the Greens entered the national legislature, one of its legislators withdrew from the group in disgust with its ineffective functioning. (He also was concerned about the Greens growing anti-Americanism and Communist influence.) Paradoxically, this ineffectiveness was due in part to very tight organization.

Although the Greens have few members—only about 32,000—the party is determined that they shall run the party and the leaders shall have no power at all. Any Green elected to a public office who begins to develop some skills in public speaking is branded immediately by many party members as an elitist. To keep their leaders cut down to size the Greens require that their members in the national legislature turn over to the party about three fourths of their salary and the majority of their tax-free expense allowance. Even more important is their rotation principle. Greens elected to the national legislature are not permitted by the party to serve a full term. After two years they must relinquish the seat to a party-designated backup. The only exception is if the legislator can win an exemption from 70 percent of his or her local Green party. But even such a prominent leader as Petra Kelly—perhaps the best-known Green in Germany—was unable to get this level of support from her local party to remain in the legislature.[4]

The Greens are divided sharply on a basic question of strategy having crucial organizational implications. Some Greens (known as "realists") want to function like other parties—try to elect members of national and land legislatures and participate in coalitions with other parties as a means of implementing some of their policies even at the cost of having to accept some measures they dislike. Other Greens ("fundamentalists") denounce this approach as an elitist thirst for the perquisites of office. They wish to demonstrate their moral purity by refusing all compromise. Furthermore, they believe that demonstrations in the streets are more effective than electoral politics (and besides don't require hard work on boring details). Clearly the organizational structure needed to mobilize thousands of people for a weekend protest march differs from that required to elect someone to office and then retain contact with the electors so as to represent their views in the legislature. In terms of popular support the Greens clearly are a political force to be reckoned with, but given their organization and clashing views on party function it is unlikely that they will be anything other than a negative force.

OTHER PARTIES

Although several parties in addition to the Christian Democrats, SPD, and FDP won seats in the national legislature in the first few elections of the Bonn Republic, by the start of the 1960s they were unable to win even one as Table 20–1 shows. The most successful was the Refugee party, which in 1953 won 27 seats

---

[4]After failing to be exempted, Kelly indicated that she would serve the entire term anyway, but would not be a candidate in the next election. Ultimately the national party permitted her and three other deputies to serve their full terms.

in the national legislature. Four years later, however, it failed to win any and eventually merged with another minor party. As we explained in a previous chapter, the German government implemented an extensive program to assist the refugees and integrate them into society. Thus a party specifically for them came to seem unnecessary.

A communist party polled 6 percent of the vote and 15 seats in the first election, but in the next election declined to 2 percent and no seats. In 1956 the Federal Constitutional Court, acting on the request of the Cabinet, banned the party in accordance with the Basic Law's prohibition of antidemocratic parties. While this decision was sound legally, many doubted its political wisdom because it seemed to give the communists a chance to claim that they were being persecuted and that the government feared free discussion of ideas.

Late in 1968 a new communist party (a direct heir of the banned one) was organized. The DKP has attempted to present an image of a reformist but nonradical party. Perhaps fearing another ban, the DKP chairman stated publicly that the goals of the party conformed to the tenets of the Basic Law. In five national elections since it was formed, this most recent version of the Communist party never has polled even 1 percent of the popular vote, and in 1980 and 1983 it had only 0.2 percent. It would appear that the Berlin wall and the heavily patrolled boundary between East and West Germany hardly are good advertisements for communism.

At the other end of the political spectrum are the neonazis. The first version of such a party gained less than 2 percent of the vote and five legislative seats in the first national election. It was superseded by another such party, which was banned in 1952 by the Federal Constitutional Court. Another extreme right party was formed in 1964—the National Democratic party (NPD). By 1968 the NPD had elected a combined total of 62 members in 7 of the 10 land legislatures. For the 1969 national elections the party nominated more than 400 candidates and gained more than 4 percent of the vote. But the 5-percent barrier of the electoral law kept the NPD out of the national legislature. The party's support rapidly collapsed in the 1970s. It now has only about 8,000 members, and in the 1980 and 1983 elections received only 0.2 percent of the vote. Thus the brief scare in the late 1960s that a new nazi party was rising to power can be seen as an unnecessary concern.

Thus the German party system of the Bonn Republic clearly differs from that of Weimar. Depending on how you consider the CSU, Germany has a four- or five-party system with two clearly predominating. Furthermore, the parties able to gain representation in the national legislature make neither narrow sectional appeals nor dogmatic ideological ones. The party system makes a major contribution to healthy democracy in Germany.

BIBLIOGRAPHICAL NOTE

Recent books on German parties include Gordon Smith, *Democracy in Western Germany: Parties and Politics in the Federal Republic* (New York: Holmes & Meier, 1980), and Max Kaase and Klaus von Beyme, eds., *Elections & Parties* (London: Sage Publications, 1978). Although the latter book focuses on the 1976 election, it discusses patterns of party support more broadly. Useful works on the SPD include Douglas Chalmers, *The Social Democratic Party of Germany* (New Haven, Conn.: Yale University Press, 1964), and Harold Schellenger, Jr., *The SPD in the Bonn Republic: A Socialist Party Modernizes* (The Hague: Martinus Nijhoff, 1968).

21

The Legislative System

THE COMPOSITION OF THE HOUSES OF PARLIAMENT

Like virtually every other country, Germany has a bicameral legislature. The lower house, the Bundestag, is composed of 496 members, elected by the procedures discussed in Chapter 19. Their term of office is four years, unless the Bundestag is dissolved early, which has occurred only in 1972 and 1983. In addition 22 delegates are chosen from West Berlin. Instead of being popularly elected by the West Berliners, they are selected by the legislature for West Berlin. They are not permitted to vote in regular sessions of the Bundestag on legislative matters or in the election of the chancellor. They can participate fully in debates on bills, however, and do have a vote in the Bundestag's committees. This peculiar situation is due to the fact that the Soviet Union refuses to recognize West Berlin as a part of the Federal Republic of Germany.

The upper house, the Bundesrat, is to provide a federal component in the legislature, just as the American Senate is. In implementing the federal principle, Germany has gone beyond even the United States. American senators do represent their respective states, but, since 1913, have been elected by the people of those states. Thus, they do not really represent the constituent governmental units of the federal system. They did so more nearly prior to 1913, when they were selected by state legislature. In Germany members of the Bundesrat clearly represent the land governments, since they are chosen by the executive branch of those governments. A comparable practice in the United States would be for the governor of a state, in consultation with his or her executive associates, to appoint the two United States Senators from that state. Such a procedure insures that the views of the state governments are considered in the national legislative process. Thus it can be argued that "states' opinions," if not "states' rights," have been carried a step further in Germany than in the United States.

The Bundesrat members usually are members of the Cabinet of their land government and hence play a dual national and local role. The Bundesrat has no set term, and its members continue to serve so long as their land governments send them to the national legislature. Each German land has from three to five members in the Bundesrat depending upon the land's population. West Berlin is permitted to send four "observers" to the Bundesrat. Although they are allowed to vote in the chamber's regular sessions, this is only advisory, since the votes are not counted with those of the representatives from the other German laender. Aside from the delegates from West Berlin, the total membership of the Bundesrat is 41. The seating arrangement is alphabetical by land delegation.

The party composition of the Bundesrat depends upon the political-party control in each of the laender. The duputies from each land vote in a bloc as instructed by their land governments. To the extent that the Bundesrat is important in national politics, therefore, it is incumbent upon the national parties to seek control of land governments. In actual practice, land election campaigns frequently have been dominated by national issues rather than matters of land concern. Thus, paradoxically, making the Bundesrat a more federal body than the American Senate has resulted in nationalizing land politics—that is, reducing the importance of purely regional and local political questions.

German law permits civil servants to take leave of absence from their government employment to serve in an elective office and later return to their civil service position without any loss of status. In fact, only recently did the Federal Constitutional Court bar civil servants from continuing to draw their civil service pay while serving in the legislature. So you will not be surprised to learn that usually about 40 percent of the Bundestag members are civil servants. That figure may be a bit misleading, since about a third of this group are school and university teachers, who typically have civil service status.

About a sixth of the members are professional people—such as doctors and lawyers—with an equal number managerial staff in private industry. Somewhat smaller than either of these two groups are officials of political parties, trade unions, or interest groups—relatively equally divided among these three. About a tenth are self-employed, a group that includes farmers. Only about 5 percent of the members are manual workers. On the other hand, about two thirds belong to trade unions.

Although a woman served as the presiding officer of the Bundestag from 1972 to 1976, women are grossly unrepresented. Less than a 10th of the members are women, a proportion no better than it was a quarter century ago.

The educational level of the members has risen over the years. Whereas formerly only about half had university degrees, now about three fourths do. Level of education varies among the parties. While the Christian Democratic and FDP members are fairly similar in this regard, about twice as many SPD members lack any higher education as do members of other parties. And about twice as many SPD members did not finish either secondary or vocational school compared to members of other parties.

The average age of Bundestag members has not varied much over the years. The high was 52.5 for the period 1957–60, and the low was 46.6 for 1972–76. The average age now is about 47. Age is affected in party by membership turnover. In 1969 and again in 1972 about a third of the members elected were serving for the first time. Turnover has declined in recent elections, however, with only about a fifth or a quarter of the Bundestag being new members.

Salaries for Bundestag members are generous. Until 1976 the salary was tax-exempt, but in November 1975 the Federal Constitutional Court ruled that members must pay tax on it. To compensate members for this change, the salary was almost doubled in 1977 to $3,400 a month. At the exchange rates prevailing in mid-1984 the annual salary was about $33,000, in addition to which legislators received a tax-free expense allowance of nearly $20,000. They also were allowed free rail and air travel and were given more than $500 a month to hire part-time clerical or research assistants.

ORGANIZATIONAL STRUCTURE

As do other legislative bodies, the Bundestag and the Bundesrat have standing orders of procedure, presiding officers, committees, and established modes of doing business. Because of the basic differences between the two bodies, notably the absence of a significant role for political parties in the Bundesrat, the organization of the two bodies is somewhat dissimilar.

The physical arrangement of the Bundestag chamber has produced some controversy. This might seem to you to be a trivial matter, but you may recall the discussion in Britain after World War II about the rebuilding of the House of Commons chamber, and Winston Churchill's views on the importance of the size and shape of the chamber. For the first several years the Bundestag met in a lecture-hall-type chamber—since Bonn never had been the capital of Germany, there were no government buildings there and the legislature used facilities that had belonged to a teachers' college. Members of the Cabinet sat on a raised platform at the front of the hall. Members wishing to speak had to leave their seats and go to a rostrum at the front of the chamber.

In 1961 the Bundestag decided to remodel the chamber to have the Government parties on one side facing the opposition parties on the other—like the British House of Commons. This would enable members to speak from their seats. The Cabinet was to have a special area on the majority side. This was a major change because Germany never had had such a legislative chamber under any previous political system.

Perhaps this explains why the vote in favor of this action was so close. But because it was and because plans also were under way to build a huge parliament building, the exact plans for the chamber were left to be determined later.

A new building for the legislature was completed, but this contains only offices for Bundestag members. In the end the Bundestag chamber was remodeled only slightly and the arrangements did not break with tradition. (See Figure 21-1.)

At the front of the chamber to the presiding officer's left are long desks where the chancellor and the Cabinet sit. Originally these seats were raised above floor level. But in 1969 as a symbolic gesture they were lowered to the same level as the members' seats to avoid any suggestion that the executive was looking down on the legislature. To the presiding officer's right are another series of long desks, where members of the upper house are permitted to sit as spectators during debates.

The Bundestag members sit at desks arranged in a fan shape—in keeping with traditional German practice, but also similar to the American Congress. Although the word *Hinterbankler* (backbencher) is used in Germany, it is a misleading term. Apart from the first row of seats, which are reserved for parliamentary leaders so that they can get to the speaker's rostrum quickly, seating arrangements are not related to status. The Christian Democrats allocate their seats according to land, the SPD alphabetically, and the FDP by drawing lots. Even these assignments are flexible. Since in most cases many members will be absent at any given time, many seats are vacant. So members simply sit wherever they wish. As the subject being debated changes, the people occupying the front row also change so that those most expert on the new subject can be near the rostrum.

The presiding officer of the Bundestag is known as the president, elected by the members by secret ballot. Although the SPD/FDP coalition was in power from 1969 to 1982, the president of the Bundestag was an SPD member only from 1972 to 1976. Since then the position has been held by either the CDU or

FIGURE 21-1   The Bundestag in Session

the CSU. Unlike the Speaker of the House of Commons, the president does not separate himself or herself entirely from any party membership.

The president's authority covers maintaining order during sessions and protecting the rights and prerogatives of Bundestag members. He or she can exclude unruly members from sessions of the Bundestag for up to 30 days. Assisting the president are four vice presidents and a number of recording secretaries, also elected by the Bundestag from among its members.

The key organizational unit of the Bundestag is the party group or *Fraktion*. Usually all the deputies of a given party, the SPD, for example, combine to form a *Fraktion*. Standing orders provide that a group must number at least 5 percent of the Bundestag total membership (including the delegates from West Berlin) to qualify as a *Fraktion*. Thus individual deputies belonging to no party or those representing small parties will not have much influence in the legislative process. The rule is another example of the steps the Germans have taken to hamper small parties to avoid the splintering of the party system that helped to weaken the Weimar Republic.

In the first Bundestag, elected in 1949, the Communist party just qualified as a *Fraktion*, while the Center party and the Union for Economic Reconstruction both fell short. By 1961 the provision was of little practical importance because the FDP was the only party other than the SPD and the Christian Democrats able to elect anyone to the Bundestag and it easily met the requirement. Following the 1983 election, however, the rule again became important. The Greens had 28 members—27 deputies plus a delegate from Berlin. As noted already, one deputy soon resigned from the group. Thus a loss of only two more members would deprive the Greens of *Fraktion* status.

Only *Fraktionen* are entitled to committee assignments and are permitted to introduce legislation. Furthermore, debate time is allotted to *Fraktionen* on the basis of their relative strength in the Bundestag. The *Fraktionen* in turn decide which of their members are to receive the committee posts allocated to the party group and which of their members are to be granted what segment of the debate time given the group. Hence, despite Article 38 of the Basic Law, which states that deputies are "not bound by orders and instructions and are subject only to their conscience," they can exert influence only if they belong to a *Fraktion*.

An important power center is the Council of Elders, a type of steering committee. It is a permanent committee of 28 members, composed of the Bundestag president (who presides over the Council as well), the vice presidents, and representatives designated by each *Fraktion* in proportion to its strength in the Bundestag. The Council of Elders meets weekly to set the agenda for the Bundestag and determine the time to be allowed for debating each subject. It is responsible for securing cooperation among the *Fraktionen* to facilitate the work of the Bundestag. The Council of Elders also appoints the presiding officer of the various legislative committees. While the Bundestag can override any of the decisions of the Council of Elders, this rarely occurs.

The Bundestag has 20 permanent committees, 17 of which are specialist-subject-matter committees. They range in size from 17 to 33 members, with 27 being the typical number. Each *Fraktion* is represented in proportion to its strength in the Bundestag. In an interesting departure from American practice, committee heads are allocated among all the parties according to their legislative strength. Thus, for example, in the 1983–87 Bundestag the Christian Democrats headed 10 committees, the SPD 8, and the FDP and the Greens 1 each. In contrast to the situation on the floor of the Bundestag, in committes representatives from West Berlin not only can participate fully, but have the right to vote as well.

Committees are empowered to summon Government ministers for questioning as well as to call expert witnesses to testify about proposed bills. Not uncommonly, a committee will invite civil servants from the relevant government department and representatives from various laender and the Bundesrat to attend its sessions so expert advice will be available if needed. No public record of committee votes is kept, which may help to produce greater flexibility in party positions and a spirit of compromise. Although the committees have powers of administrative surveillance, they function mainly to scrutinize proposed legislation and revise it as necessary.

The Bundestag performs most of its significant legislative work in committee. Without trying to claim that committees operate with complete objectivity, unsullied by any political considerations, we would suggest that the German tradition of legalism does affect the way in which the committees function. As one student of the German parliament summed it up:

> The Bundestag committee system is substantially a continuation of earlier German parliamentary traditions—a range of specialized committees of legislation, manned to ensure proportional party representation and expected to relieve the floor of the house of most of the burden of argument about legislative proposals. . . . There is the emphasis on specialized knowledge or experience as a desirable and indeed necessary qualification for active participation in committee work. . . . There is the widely diffused respect for expert opinion that inclines members to listen respectfully to civil servant advisers as well as outside "experts" summoned as witnesses at public hearings.[1]

Most of the Bundestag committee work is done in full committee since subcommittees are rather rare. Some other types of committees, however, have been created from time to time. Special committees may be created to deal with a specific issue likely to be of only temporary importance. Once the committee has finished its work it ceases to exist. Such committees can deal with a particular bill, as well as gather information. Investigatory committees are established to look into matters of malfeasance or improprieties in government. Neither of these two types of committees is as important as the permanent legislative committees.

The importance of parties and legislative committees means that the Bundestag spends less time in regular sessions than do most legislative bodies. In a typi-

---

[1]Neville Johnson, "Committees in the West German Bundestag," in *Committees in Legislatures: A Comparative Analysis*, eds. John D. Lees and Malcolm Shaw (Durham, N.C.: Duke University Press, 1979), p. 141.

cal week Monday and Tuesday are devoted to various party meetings with only Wednesday, Thursday, and Friday reserved for Bundestag sessions and committee work. Thus the Bundestag averages only about 60 meetings a year, and even these meetings may last for much less than a full day. The Bundestag may sit for little more than 300 hours in a typical year, which is little more than a quarter of the time that the U.S. Senate spends in such meetings. Nonetheless, in part because of extensive committee work, the German legislature passes 350 to 500 bills in a typical year.

Like the lower house, the Bundesrat does the bulk of its work in committee. It has only 13 committees with each of the 10 laender being represented equally. West Berlin is permitted to send an observer to each committee, but this person is not allowed to vote. The presiding officer of the Bundesrat, known as the president, is elected annually. The practice is to select a new president each year, rotating the office so that over a period of years each of the laender will have held the presiding officer's chair. (The Bundesrat can be seen in session in Figure 21–2.)

POWERS AND PROCEDURES

Legislative powers are divided between the central government and the governments of the laender. The constitution specifies that in some areas the central government has exclusive jurisdiction, while in others there is concurrent authority. The central government has exclusive legislative power (Article 73) in such matters as foreign affairs, citizenship, freedom of movement (passports, immigration, and so on), fiscal regulations (currency, money, coinage, and so

FIGURE 21–2   The Bundesrat in Session

on), customs and tariffs, posts and telecommunications, national railroads and air traffic, the legal status of persons in the service of the central government, industrial property rights (patents, and so on), cooperation of the national government and the laender in the field of criminal police, and in matters concerning the protection of the constitution. In the areas of exclusive national power, the laender can legislate only if, and insofar as, they are expressly so empowered by law by the central government.

The constitution sets forth a long list (Article 74) of matters that fall in the realm of concurrent powers, matters over which the laender are empowered to legislate as long as, and insofar as, the central government does not use its legislative power. The constitution stipulates, however, that the central government can act in these areas only insofar as national regulation is needed because the laender cannot act effectively or because action by one or more laender would injure the interests of the other laender or the nation as a whole. Finally, Article 75 lists several matters for which the central government may issue general directives, but must leave detailed control to the laender. Other articles round out the division of powers between the central government and the laender. Significantly, education and cultural affairs are left primarily to the laender.

Bills may be initiated by legislators or by the Government. They may start in either house except that Government sponsored bills must begin in the Bundesrat, which sends them to the Bundestag via the Cabinet. In this way, the Bundestag knows the views of the Bundesrat, which is to say the land Governments, on the Cabinet's proposals as well as the Cabinet's reaction to the Bundesrat's position. Bills which orginate in the Bundesrat are submitted to the Bundestag via the Cabinet, which must attach a statement of its views on the proposal.

The process of passing a bill from this point on can be clarified by referring to Figure 21-3. The diagram assumes that the bill is being proposed by the Government, since that is by far the most common situation. You should start on the left with the Government and trace the solid line to the right as far as it will go. Thus you will see what happens to a bill depending upon what each of the two legislative chambers does and this, in turn, will help you understand their relative power.

Turning to the diagram, then, the Government introduces the bill in the Bundesrat, which considers it in a committee and within three weeks sends it back to the Government along with its reaction. The Government adds its comments on the Bundesrat's position and sends the bill to the Bundestag.

Like many legislatures, the Bundestag considers a bill on three readings. Germany follows the American, rather than the British, practice of sending a bill to committee after first reading instead of after second reading. In the Bundestag, however, first reading can involve a short debate in which the parties state their general views on the proposed legislation.

Committees consider bills in great detail. Six months to a year or more may elapse before the bill comes back to the Bundestag. Although the Government has a controlling majority on each committee, it normally does not simply force

FIGURE 21–3   **West German Legislative Procedure**

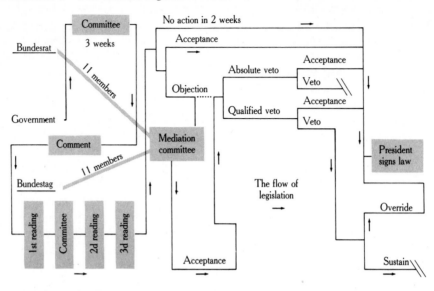

its legislation through. It will concede some points to opponents in an effort to get agreement. The German Cabinet compromises much more frequently during committee stage than does the British Cabinet. Some Cabinet ministers have close contact with some committees. Should the Cabinet have eliminated some aspect of a bill that they want restored, they may take their case to their legislative allies on the committee.

When a bill comes back from committee it is accompanied by a detailed report, usually written by the committee's staff, explaining the need for the bill, the main points discussed by the committee and the views of both its majority and minority, and why changes (if any) needed to be made in the bill as originally proposed. Since this report has the aura of having been written by those who are experts in the substance of the bill and in legal drafting, it carries considerable weight with the Bundestag.

Second reading provides an opportunity to discuss the detailed provisions of the bill and to consider amendments, although its general principles may be debated as well. Discussion on third reading is confined largely to a general debate of the main features of the bill, although amendments are in order if supported by at least 15 deputies. In urgent circumstances, all three readings of a bill can take place in a single day, provided that the members agree unanimously.

Rules prevent filibustering during debates. On third reading a member may speak no more than one hour unless the Bundestag votes him or her additional time. On the motion of 30 members closure can be voted upon, and debate is ended if a majority votes to do so. This rarely is necessary, however, since the debate in the Bundestag tends to be too limited rather than too lengthy. In the 1961–65 Bundestag only 40 percent of the members ever spoke at all, and only 6 percent spoke more than three times. One third of all the speeches made by Christian Democrats were made by only 8 percent of their members, and over half of the speeches made by Socialists were made by only 11 percent of their members. Over 60 percent of all the bills passed by that Bundestag went through all three readings without being debated at all. And of those that were debated, almost one quarter were discussed for less than 10 minutes. Less than 6 percent of the bills enacted were debated on the floor of the Bundestag for more than three hours.[2]

New rules, intended to make Bundestag debates more worthwhile, went into effect in the fall of 1980. These were aimed at eliminating lengthy set speeches— more of the give-and-take characteristic of the House of Commons was the hope—and giving the opposition members a larger role rather than leaving the last word always with the Government. The main speaker from each *Fraktion* now is limited to no more than 45 minutes, and other speakers from the same *Fraktion* may not exceed 15 minutes. When a member of the Government is speaking, any Bundestag member who disagrees with what is being said can be recognized immediately and speak for up to 20 minutes explaining why he or she disagrees. Also, when a *Fraktion* or any group of 26 members requests it, the presiding officer can grant "short-talk" time, in which interested speakers can talk for five minutes each. It is too soon to know how much impact these changes will have on traditional German parliamentary behavior, but they are moves toward making it more lively and useful.

Voting in the Bundestag is by a show of hands or by standing. In case of doubt, a division—similar to British practice—in which members file through doors past counting clerks is employed. If as many as 50 members request it in advance, a roll-call vote is taken. Once bills have passed the Bundestag, they go to the Bundesrat, and this brings us back again to Figure 21–3 and the upper right-hand portion.

When a bill reaches the Bundesrat, it usually is sent to a committee. The entire chamber (only 41 people) considers the committee's comments in a single reading of the bill. Voting is by roll call of the laender, with each land having from three to five votes according to population. A land may not split its votes, but must cast all the same way. If the Bundesrat accepts the bill or fails to act within two weeks, the bill goes to the president of the Republic.

Should the Bundesrat oppose a bill, however, the process becomes more complicated. A Mediation Committee has been established to work out agreements when the Bundesrat disagrees with the Bundestag. Unlike conference committees in the U.S. Congress, which are set up for particular bills as the

---

[2]Wilhelm Hennis, "Reform of the Bundestag: The Case for General Debate," in *Modern Parliaments: Change or Decline?* ed. Gerhard Loewenberg (Chicago: Aldine-Atherton, 1971), pp. 75, 78.

need arises, the Mediation Committee is permanent. It is composed of 11 members from each house of the German parliament. Aside from ministers of the national government, no one else is permitted to attend its meetings except by express decision of the Committee. In order to provide continuity, the standing orders permit no more than four changes of membership during the existence of a single Bundestag.

In contrast with procedures in the Bundesrat itself, Bundesrat members on the Mediation Committee are not bound by instructions from their respective land Governments on how to vote. The record of the Mediation Committee, judged by its ability to work out acceptable compromises, has been impressive. During the first four legislatures (1949-65), 256 bills were submitted to it, and in only 21 cases did the legislature not pass the bill in the form that the Mediation Committee had suggested.[3]

Thus Figure 21-3 shows Bundestag acceptance of the Mediation Committee report, since that is by far the typical situation. (Should the Bundestag not accept the report, the position would be the same as for the step we are about to discuss.) Now the bill returns to the Bundesrat once again. (The dotted line by the word *objection* in Figure 21-3 means that the Bundesrat may act upon a bill to which it objects without referring it to the Mediation Committee. Thus that step in the legislative process may be avoided.)

At this point, as you can see, there are two possibilities, because the Bundesrat has two kinds of vetoes. In matters affecting the interests of the laender, the approval of the Bundesrat is required for a bill to become law; should it not assent, the bill is dead. An example of such a bill is one providing, as frequently is the case in Germany, that a portion of the revenue raised by a tax is to go directly to the laender. Bills on administrative matters affecting the laender also are subject to absolute veto. Since most federal law in Germany is administered by the laender, this includes a great number of bills. In all, somewhat more than half of all the bills considered by the legislature are subject to the absolute veto of the Bundesrat—must have its approval to become law.

On all other bills—those not involving the interests of the laender—Bundesrat approval is not required. If it objects, the Bundestag can override it and pass the bill anyway. Thus in these cases the Bundesrat has only a qualified veto. Here again two possibilities exist (not separately distinguished in Figure 21-3). If the Bundesrat has rejected the bill by a simple majority, a majority in favor of it in the Bundestag is sufficient to override. But should the Bundesrat have voted against the bill by a two-thirds margin or greater, the Bundestag must vote for it by at least two thirds.

When the Bundesrat has a qualified veto it may, and usually does, call the Mediation Committee rather than vote against the bill. When the Bundesrat has an absolute veto, the Government or the Bundestag also can call the committee. Either way, the arrangement worked out by the Mediation Committee usually

---

[3]Alfred Grosser, *Germany in Our Time* (New York: Praeger Publishers, 1970), p. 126.

has included a good deal of what the Bundesrat wanted. Recall also that the Government's legislative proposals must go to the Bundesrat for comment before they are introduced into the Bundestag. This means that typically the Government consults with the Bundesrat when bills are being drafted in order to avoid adverse comments from the Bundesrat when the proposals are submitted to the Bundestag. One way or another, the Bundesrat, which is to say land Governments, plays an important role in the national legislative process.

The constitution provides that the national government must keep the Bundesrat informed of the conduct of affairs. In order to do this, the Ministry of Bundesrat and Laender Affairs was created, although informing the Bundesrat is not its only task. Approximately once a week, the minister meets the permanent representatives from the laender and tells them about Cabinet policies. Since he or she usually attends Bundesrat meetings and remains in close touch with its members, he or she is in a position to convey back to Cabinet colleagues the views of the land representatives. Given the variety of means, then, that the Bundesrat has for influencing legislative output, it is not surprising that it has made little use of its power to initiate legislation.

The Bundesrat is one of the world's strongest upper houses. It helps to make the German legislature a significant element in the policy process, and to balance the distribution of power between the executive and the legislature. It also, as earlier mentioned in the chapter, gives a national political significance to land elections. For example, although the SPD/FDP coalition maintained its control of the national government in the 1976 election, the Christian Democrats controlled enough land Governments (land elections are held separately from national ones, and at a variety of times) to have a 26–15 lead in the Bundesrat. Thus the land election in Hesse in October 1978 produced considerable interest. If the Christian Democrats managed to drive the SPD/FDP Government of Hesse from office, then Hesse's four votes in the Bundesrat would swing into opposition and the Christian Democrats would have had a 30–11 majority in the upper house. This would have put them over the crucial two thirds (27) of the Bundesrat. The result would have been to have made every veto of the Bundesrat an absolute one, since the national SPD/FDP Government, while having a majority in the Bundestag, was nowhere near a two-thirds majority. Thus it would have been unable to override any of the vetoes of the Bundesrat. As it turned out, the Christian Democrats did not come to power in Hesse, so the Government did not have to deal with this problem. But you can see why land elections can have considerable importance for national politics.

Even though the SPD/FDP Government did not have to contend with an immoveable obstacle to its program in the upper house, it still had to face a hostile majority there. Thus, for example, in May 1982 the Bundesrat defeated part of the Government's job-creation program to alleviate unemployment by voting against a 1 percentage point increase in the Value-Added Tax. In subsequent negotiations, the Government agreed to accept this defeat in return for the Bundesrat's acceptance of its proposed program of grants to firms for new plant and equipment investment, which would provide new jobs. With the return to power of the Christian Democrats in 1982 the problems of a negative majority in the Bundesrat, of course, ceased to exist.

Traditionally, Germans have tended to regard the legislative process as an activity that brings legal expertise to bear on a proposed statute so that it will be properly worded. Thus, extensive discussion of the general principles involved in a bill by those lacking legal knowledge has not been regarded as useful. You will have noticed at several points in the chapter that the German preoccupation with expertise in the legislative process has continued into the Bonn Republic. It is as though the Germans regard legislating as a legal rather than a political activity.

Add to this attitude the fact that typically various deals or compromises have been worked out among the concerned interests during the committee stage of a bill, and you can understand why extensive discussion of bills on the floor of the Bundestag has seemed superfluous. As we saw in the British section, if you look only at changes in the provisions of a bill, then floor debate is superfluous in the House of Commons also. Bills rarely are modified in any significant way because of what is said in the debates.

But what the British understand and the Germans have not fully grasped, is the importance of debate and discussion in the legislature as a means to legitimate the policy output of the government. People are much more willing to accept distasteful rules and regulations if they feel that the various alternatives have been considered fully and that the particular point of view they favor has had a chance to be heard. Related to this legitimating function of the legislature is its educative function. Through debates on the principles of legislation, a parliament has the opportunity to air the most prominent views on the leading public issues of the day. Even limited reports in popular newspapers of such debates help to educate and inform the citizens. The Bundestag, however, apparently regards performance of this function as either unnecessary or unimportant. To this extent, there remains something of an elitist orientation to the German political process.

The Bundestag still lacks an imaginative and aggressive group of well-educated and politcally trained members who realize that their chief task is to depict and explain things as they are and, in the process, to win the people's support for future policies. Many energetic members spend much time on committee work and in trying to compete with the bureaucrats in mastering details. And while this is not to be deplored, it often has been done at the expense of debating the main issues of policy. The German legislature does what it does well, but it leaves undone some important functions of legislatures in democratic systems.

BIBLIOGRAPHICAL NOTE

The standard study of the German legislature is Gerhard Loewenberg, *Parliament in the German Political System* (Ithaca, N.Y.: Cornell University Press, 1966). For committees, see the Johnson paper cited in Footnote 1. The role of the upper house is explained in Edward Pinney, *Federalism, Bureaucracy and Party Politics in Western Germany: The Role of the Bundesrat* (Chapel Hill: University of North Carolina Press, 1963).

22

Policymaking Structures

Germany follows the traditional parliamentary pattern of having a dual executive—that is, both a head of state and a head of Government. The head of state, whose position largely is ceremonial, is known as the president. The head of Government, who is the equivalent of a prime minister, is called the chancellor.

THE ROLE OF THE PRESIDENT

Contrary to practice under Weimar, the president is not popularly elected. This is to help restrict the president to only a ceremonial role; a president cannot claim to embody the popular will as fully as does parliament. The president is chosen instead by a body known as the Federal Assembly, which is composed of the members of the Bundestag plus an equal number of persons chosen by proportional representation by the legislatures of the laender.[1] Any German qualified to vote who is at least 40 years old is eligible for the office. Unlike the American Presidential Electoral College, the Federal Assembly does meet as a group to cast their ballots for president. But debate or campaign speeches before the voting are not allowed. An absolute majority is required for election on the first and, if necessary, second ballots. On the third ballot a plurality suffices, so that the election cannot drag on interminably.

Only in 1969 did a presidential election go to the third ballot. Theodor Heuss was elected on the second ballot in 1949 and was reelected five years later virtu-

---

[1]Representatives from West Berlin participate fully in the Federal Assembly.

ally unanimously on the first ballot. The second president, Heinrich Luebke, also was elected on the second ballot and reelected by a substantial margin on the first ballot. The third president, Gustav Heinemann, outpolled his opponent by only six votes on the decisive third ballot. Walter Scheel, elected in 1974, not only became the first president to be elected for the first time on the first ballot, but received more votes—530—than any other president had on first being elected to the office.

Scheel proved to be quite popular in office, yet he was not reelected to a second term. By the time his term expired the Christian Democrats had made sufficient gains at the land level (remember, half of the electoral college is chosen by the land legislatures) that they had a clear majority in the Federal Assembly. Despite the fact that the office is largely ceremonial, it has some political power (as we will see in a moment) and there is nothing ceremonial, nor nonpolitical, about elections for the office. Since Scheel recognized that he had no chance of being reelected, he refused to stand for a second term. At the last minute before the election the SPD offered as a token candidate Annemarie Renger, who had been Bundestag president from 1972 to 1976.

The Christian Democratic candidate was Karl Carstens, president of the Bundestag at the time. He received 528 votes on the first ballot, nine more than the required absolute majority. Carstens' election caused a bit of controversy because he had been a nominal member of the Nazi party as a young man. This would appear to be carrying the sins of the past a bit far inasmuch as Scheel also had been a nominal member of the party, and few had raised any questions at the time of his election.

Despite the political nature of presidential elections, the office has rotated among the leading parties as though it were on a fixed cycle. Heuss was a Free Democrat, Luebke a Christian Democrat, and Heinemann a Social Democrat. Heinemann's party affiliations were a bit out of the ordinary, however. Originally a member of the CDU, he had resigned in 1950 to oppose the party's policy of rearming Germany. For a time he headed a somewhat neutralist splinter group before joining the SPD. With Scheel the office was again held by a Free Democrat and Carstens was a Christian Democrat.

Carstens' presidency produced the first real divided control of the executive. For the first 30 years of the Bonn Republic, with one exception, the president always came from a party that was part of the governing coalition. The exception was at the end of Heuss' term from 1957 to 1959, when the FDP had left the coalition. This had made little difference since Heuss believed the president should be nonpartisan. Also, although he had been active in the FDP, he was a university professor and not really a politician. With the election of Carstens in May 1979, however, Germany did have an active politician as president who came from a party not part of the governing coalition. Carstens discharged his functions, however, in a ceremonial, rather than a political, fashion. While during his term the Government lacked an ally that it might otherwise have expected to have, his presidency did not produce any conflict between the two segments of the executive.

When Carstens decided not to seek reelection, the cycle of rotation of the presidency among the parties was broken, since his successor also was a Christian Democrat. Richard von Weizsäcker won a record first-ballot victory—832 votes compared with only 68 for the only other candidate (the remaining electors abstained). Von Weizsäcker comes from the liberal wing of the CDU and, thus, was supported even by the leaders of the SPD, who in any event recognized that they lacked the votes in the Federal Assembly to elect the president.

The president serves for five years and may be reelected only once. He or she must, upon election, resign from other public offices and from offices in profit-making organizations. He or she may not be a member of the Bundestag or of the legislature in one of the laender and may not practice a profession while in office. President Heuss took these limitations so seriously and was so determined to a symbol of unity for all Germans that he resigned his membership in the FDP after his election.

The president may be impeached for "willful violation of the Basic Law or any other Federal law." A vote by one quarter of either house of the legislature is sufficient to introduce the motion for impeachment. Then a two-thirds vote is required to bring the president to trial. The case is heard before the Federal Constitutional Court, which decides whether the president is guilty and, therefore, removable from office.

Germany has no vice president. Should the office of president fall vacant, the president of the Bundesrat serves the remainder of the term. The holder of this position also performs many of the president's functions when the president is out of the country or incapacitated by illness.

In 1949, when the constitutional drafters were drawing up the Basic Law, Germany clearly could not go back to having a kaiser, a monarchical head of state. The Weimar experience with a popularly elected president having fairly extensive powers had not been very attractive either. Yet the ingrained tradition of the parliamentary system was to have a head of government who was the product of the interplay of political forces and a head of state who was to some extent above the political battle and symbolized the people as a nation. So the drafters of the Basic law attempted to create a nonpolitical, symbolic head of state—a ceremonial presidency.

Unlike the situation in the Weimar Republic, the president cannot dismiss the chancellor or authorize the use of any emergency powers. All his or her political acts, except for designating the chancellor, must be countersigned by the chancellor or another appropriate minister. Nonetheless, the president does have some discretion of action, and the powers of the office are ambiguous to some extent.

After each Bundestag election the president offers a candidate for chancellor to the Bundestag. If no party has a majority, there is some choice in this selection. Should one party have a majority or clearly predominate, however, the president has little alternative but to choose the leader of that party. Thus, the simplification of the German party system has tended to reduce the president's discretion in these matters.

If the president's nominee gains an absolute majority, then he or she becomes chancellor. But if this does not happen, then the Bundestag may elect anyone chancellor by an absolute majority. Should it fail to do so within two weeks, then it can choose a chancellor by a plurality. But at that point the president has an option. He or she may accept the Bundestag's choice as chancellor or may call for new Parliamentary elections.

The point of these provisions is that the president cannot force his or her choice for chancellor upon an unwilling Bundestag. But at the same time the Germans want to be certain that the chancellor has fairly broad support. If this is not clearly the case, the president has the opportunity to call the electorate into the process. Thus far in Germany, these provisions have not been necessary. The president's nominee always has received an absolute majority. But in 1949 the vote was close. Adenauer had not a single vote to spare even when three votes were counted that had his name on them rather than "aye," which was the proper vote on the motion of whether he should become chancellor.

In the 1961 elections the chancellor's party failed to win a majority and had to make considerable concessions to the Free Democrats, with which it had been in coalition, in order to stay in power. Obviously, the president must, as in other parliamentary states, have due regard for the political complexion of the legislature when designating the head of the Government. In 1961, he waited until an agreement had been reached between the strongest party and its coalition partner, thus ratifying the informal choice that the leaders of the majority in the Bundestag had already made.

Among the ambiguities of the president's power is the matter of a veto. The Basic Law does not give this power, but does say that the president must sign laws before they are effective. The signature was expected to be automatic and simply indicate formally that the law had been passed. President Heuss, however, withheld his signature in some cases. He questioned, for example, whether a particular tax law that had been passed by the Bundestag alone needed as well the approval of the Bundesrat. When the Federal Constitutional Court ruled passage by both houses was required, Heuss refused to sign the bill and as a result it was not enacted. While this is not exactly a veto, it did have the effect of killing the bill.

Although the point in question was one of correct constitutional procedures, there was a substantive issue also. The Government and a majority of the Bundestag had favored the tax law on its merits. In blocking it, the president was becoming involved in politics. And to the extent that this was true, he would be less able to discharge his ceremonial role, for to do the latter successfully he must appear above politics so as not to repel the supporters of any party. One of the main duties of a ceremonial leader is to be a symbol of national unity.

Whatever the apparent role conflicts in this action, it has proved not to be an isolated incident. In subsequent cases when it was unclear whether the Bundesrat had a qualified or an absolute veto, the Government looked to the president. The precedent has been established that the president will sign a bill opposed by the Bundesrat only if convinced that Bundesrat approval was not necessary—that it did not have an absolute veto.

While this is an important area of discretion for the president, it may make the power of the office sound greater than it is. In some senses the president's signature on a law is no more than an advisory opinion indicating the president's belief that Bundesrat approval was unnecessary. The signature does not legally settle the question. Should the law be challenged in the Federal Constitutional Court, the Court may rule that the law is invalid because it required Bundesrat approval, despite the fact that the president's signature indicated a contrary opinion. Clearly, the president's discretion is limited and the power to withhold a signature should not be equated with the American president's veto power.

Nonetheless, the office of president in Germany is not unimportant. Under Heuss the presidency acquired considerable prestige. He proved to be human and accessible, combining dignity and an unassuming manner. He was ready and willing to participate in all activities that in his opinion served to advance the intellectual and political interests of his country. Luebke was not as capable or effective a president, in part because toward the close of his second term questions were raised about some of his activities during World War II and whether he had compromised with the Nazis. The election of his successor was held a few months early so that he could leave office sooner. Heinemann, on the other hand, despite serving for only a single term, performed the ceremonial functions well, particularly in his contacts with other countries.

Scheel was the most highly experienced politician to hold the office. He was the leader of the FDP, foreign minister, and vice chancellor when he was elected. He indicated a desire to expand the president's influence by exercising the office's limited powers fully. While he certainly was an active, highly visible president, he did not transform the president's role. Carstens' presidency conformed to the now-traditional ceremonial role.

Basically, then, the influence of the president, like that of the British monarch, depends upon the qualifications and initiative he or she possesses, and the prevailing political circumstances. Heuss said that the President "may not . . . take part in the practical decisions of day-to-day politics, but he is permitted to help in improving the atmosphere and facilitating the putting into effect of certain quite simple, reasonable, and generally accepted points of view." At times the president may be influential. Nonetheless, the chancellor, like the British prime minister, need not accept the advice of the head of state; the chancellor, not the president, is the key maker of policy.

CHANCELLOR DEMOCRACY

France has seen a shift in power from the Council of Ministers to the president as it moved from the Third and Fourth Republics to the Fifth. Similarly, in Germany the distribution of power within the executive branch in the Bonn Republic is different from that in Weimar. The shift, however, has been in the opposite direction—from the president to the chancellor. As we noted in Chapter 14, the power shift in France is not just a matter of altering the constitution, but also of the personality of the first president of the Fifth Republic. In Germany, as well, the personality of the first chancellor, in addition to the changes in the constitution, affected significantly the present powers of the office. Just as the Fifth Republic sometimes has been referred to as the de Gaulle Republic, so also the Federal Republic of Germany has been labeled chancellor democracy.

While we already have explained, in discussing the president's functions, the process by which the chancellor is chosen, an interesting sidelight should be added. Although West Berlin participates fully in electing the president, the votes of its representatives to the Bundestag do not count in selecting the chancellor. Were this not true, the history of the Bonn Republic might have taken a very different course. Counting the West Berlin representatives in 1949 would have made the SPD, rather than the Christian Democrats, the largest party. Thus they might have been able to form a coalition, and the Christian Democratic domination of politics in the first two decades of the Bonn Republic might not have occurred.

In the mid-1960s the Germans attempted to change the rules and count the votes for chancellor of West Berlin representatives the same as those of the other representatives. The United States, on behalf of the three occupying powers, vetoed this.[2] Thus, although Germany is a sovereign nation, the victors in World War II retain a certain control over its domestic political procedures.

Once chosen, the chancellor selects Cabinet colleagues, whose formal appointments are signed by the president. Members of the Cabinet may be, and usually are, members of the Bundestag. Cabinets have varied from 15 to 20 members. The president may advise the chancellor on these appointments, but, as the first chancellor demonstrated, such advice easily can be ignored.

The Basic law requires the chancellor to appoint a deputy. For about the first 20 years the office was little more than a figurehead. In part this was because Chancellor Konrad Adenauer was so dominant during this period. In 1966 when the Grand Coalition between the Christian Democrats and the SPD was formed, however, the SPD leader, Willy Brandt, was given the position. Subsequently, when the SPD and the DFP formed the governing coalition, the office went to the FDP—first Walter Scheel and, when he had been elected president, Hans-Dietrich Genscher. The position has come to be known as vice chancellor. The political situation, rather than constitutional provisions, have made the office significant.

The Basic Law strengthens the executive by providing that the Bundestag may not increase expenditures or taxes over what the Cabinet wants. This corresponds to the control over finance long exercised by the British Cabinet and,

---

[2]See Alfred Grosser, *Germany in Our Time* (New York: Praeger Publishers, 1970), pp. 94–95, for the convoluted German response that managed to count the votes of the West Berlin representatives without counting them.

more recently, by the French Council of Ministers. The Cabinet or its ministers may issue decrees having the force of law, but only when statutes already in effect, which the decrees must cite, so authorize. Moreover, the decree power may not be used by the central government to avoid the constitutional requirement of Bundesrat consent for certain types of legislation. In these areas, decrees by the central government or its ministers require the approval of the Bundesrat.

The Basic Law says little about emergency powers (such powers should not be confused with the "legislative emergency" discussed in the next portion of this chapter) other than giving the Government the power to nationalize the laender police should imminent danger threaten the democratic political system. As we explained in Chapter 18, in the late 1960s after protracted discussion, a series of amendments to the Basic Law gave the Government emergency powers, subject to detailed safeguards and legislative control. Under these provisions—which have yet to be used—the Government can obtain extraordinary power to deal with the labor market, transportation and communication, and supplies of food, water, fuel, and industrial materials.

The German Cabinet is intended to be a very formal body with elaborate operating rules. These specify the number of ministers needed for a quorum and require formal votes to reach decisions. When the Cabinet is divided, the majority is to rule except in some key instances. On financial matters, for example, the chancellor and the finance minister are allowed to have their way even if the rest of the Cabinet is opposed. All this differs considerably from the practice in Britain, where the Cabinet is governed by informal procedures that have grown up over the years, rather than by written rules, and where the prime minister normally ascertains the sense of the meeting by going around the table to "collect the voices" rather than calling for a formal vote.

Despite the German Cabinet's elaborate rules for joint decision making, collective responsibility for Government policy has been limited. The Basic Law makes the chancellor alone, not the entire Cabinet, responsible to the Bundestag. Furthermore, Article 65 says that the chancellor "determines, and is responsible for, general policy." Adenauer interpreted this provision to mean that he did not need to consult the Cabinet in making policy. He regarded the Cabinet as a board of experts whose role was to assist him only on his request. Should he so desire, he might consult them for information on which to base *his* decisions, but this might not be necessary, since he established a system of research committees responsible to him alone. Thus, when he presented his proposals to the Cabinet, he would have the weight of independent, expert opinion on his side. Although at times he used his ministers, the net result was that his personal research network tended to make his position stronger than that of the rest of the Cabinet and, thereby, reduced the ministers' authority.

Adenauer did not hesitate to criticize publicly his Cabinet colleagues when he disagreed with the positions they had taken in speeches. On the other hand, he was reluctant to dismiss even inefficient ministers if they were loyal to him personally. He tended to relate to his Cabinet in much the same way as an American president treats his Cabinet. Again this contrasts sharply with British practice, where the prime minister, although *primus*, still remains *inter pares*. This contrast is the more remarkable because Germany, like Britain, is a parliamentary, not a presidential, system.

Further aiding Adenauer in dominating the Government was the Federal Chancellery, provided for by the Cabinet's standing orders. The Chancellery's administrative staff performs primarily two types of functions. First, it issues relevant instructions, in the chancellor's name, to all ministries and thus decides many important matters before they reach the Cabinet. Second, it acts as coordinators by settling many disputes between ministries. Only those disputes that it cannot resolve go to the Cabinet for settlement. The head of the Chancellery, titled a state secretary, is the personal appointee of the chancellor. During the Adenauer period this state secretary was, in a sense, second in command and more powerful than any one of Adenauer's Cabinet colleagues.

In November 1984 Chancellor Kohl created a new position of head of the Chancellery and appointed to it a politician, also giving him a seat in the Cabinet. Kohl declared that experience had shown that coordinating three parties (the CDU, the CSU, and the FDP) required someone of Cabinet rank, who also had a seat in the Bundestag. While Kohl did not say so, his move responded to those who had criticized the ineffectiveness of the state secretary who had been in charge of the Chancellery staff, since under the new arrangement his power would be curtailed. Shifting power to someone fully attuned to political and electoral considerations was intended to ensure that the Chancellor gained the full power benefit of a staff of nearly 500 people making up the German equivalent of the Executive Office of the U.S. President.

The Chancellery is located in the building that looks like reversed capital E's in Figure 22–1 in the lower right-hand corner. The low, white buildings in the

FIGURE 22–1   Governmental Complex, Bonn, West Germany

center of the picture are the meeting chambers for the Bundestag and the Bundesrat. Connected to this building is an earlier legislative office building, while the high rise just above it is the more recently constructed office building.

After serving as chancellor for the first 14 years of the Bonn Republic, Adenauer resigned in October 1963 at the age of 87. His retirement was part of the price exacted by the Free Democrats for joining the Christian Democrats in coalition after the 1961 election. Adenauer's dominance had been such that some students of the German political system felt that calling it a parliamentary system failed to convey its true power distribution. Thus the label "chancellor democracy" was devised to do this.

Chancellor democracy had its pragmatic merits. Adenauer faced the problem of holding a number of diverse elements together in the CDU. He did a good job of mediating among all the groups. Although he was criticized for apparently not wishing to offend any major one of them, he hardly was playing merely a passive role. He prevented any one group from dominating the CDU and thus narrowing its appeal, which would have been unfortunate for the development of the German party system.

He exercised his powers cleverly and carefully built up his personal prestige. Though he exploited to the limit the opportunities that the constitution provided, he rarely was charged with violating it. Adenauer's prestige was enhanced considerably by his handling of foreign affairs, especially in the early years of the new regime when he was its sole spokesperson. Even his opponents admit that in those years he won considerable international position and prestige for his country by knowing when to be patient and when to display firmness and tenacity. In brief, he was imaginative, flexible, and statesmanlike in the pursuit of Germany's national interest.

Most important, by providing a stable and effective government, Adenauer demonstrated that democracy and authority are not mutually exclusive. In this way he contributed significantly to the German acceptance of democracy, a considerable accomplishment in a nation lacking a democratic tradition. He was given considerable credit for the rapid economic recovery and general prosperity, which stood in sharp contrast to the ruinous inflation of the early Weimar period and to the subsequent economic collapse. In short, Adenauer's strong leadership and clear-cut policies, together with the attendant prosperity, gave the Germans reason to believe that democracy could be a success. Had his political style been more democratic, his historical contribution to German democracy would not have been as great. Clearly, he possessed the attributes appropriate to the times.

Neither Ludwig Erhard nor Kurt Kiesinger, the Christian Democrats who followed Adenauer as chancellor, proved to be strong leaders. Erhard was hampered by the fact that, through most of his three years as chancellor, Adenauer remained the leader of the CDU and sought to prove that Erhard was less able than he himself had been. Furthermore, because some people had been alienated by Adenauer's arrogance, Erhard sought to be more congenial and to consult his colleagues more adequately in decision making. As a result, he was derided for being a "rubber lion." (The term conjures up an image of a helium-inflated balloon in a Thanksgiving Day parade, an image in keeping with Erhard's physical appearance.)

Nonetheless, during his time as chancellor relations improved with the opposition Social Democrats and the Bundestag generally. In his first official statement as chancellor, he said: "I regard the opposition as a necessary element of full standing in a parliamentary democracy and hope that our discussion and disputes, which are bound to arise, may be conducted in this spirit." In addition, Erhard stressed the importance of popular participation and public opinion in a democratic society.

Erhard's inability to deal with economic recession in Germany in 1966, however, forced him to resign. He found himself unable to marshal the necessary political support to make decisions and implement them. His failure to deal with an economic crisis seemed particularly damning, since he had been minister of economics under Adenauer. He had been identified closely with the CDU's social market economy and with the economic miracle of Germany's recovery. Thus, it seemed to some that his policies had failed in the long run. Furthermore, if he could devise no solution for a problem in the area of his supposed expertise, how could he be expected to deal adequately with problems in other areas?

The Government formed to replace Erhard's carried the CDU's acceptance of the SPD a step further, to a stage that Adenauer would not have countenanced. The new chancellor, Kiesinger, formed a Government that included both the CDU and the SPD—an arrangement labeled the Grand Coalition. (This coalition was formed to secure the agreement of both major parties on the steps required to deal with the economic problems Germany encountered in 1966.) The leader of the SPD, Brandt, became vice chancellor and foreign minister. Since Kiesinger often had to accept the views of the rival party to maintain the coalition, he did not appear, during his almost three years in office, to be as dominant as Adenauer had been.

By the time of the 1969 election the more liberal wing of the Free Democrats had gained control of the party and took it into coalition with the SPD. During almost five years as the Bonn Republic's first Social Democratic chancellor, Brandt demonstrated that he preferred to reach decisions more collectively than did Adenauer and to discharge the responsibilities of chancellor in a more democratic style. Nonetheless, Brandt's prominence within the Government and the SPD was such that no one thought of him as a weak chancellor. His authority was enhanced considerably when he was awarded the Nobel Peace Prize in 1971 in recognition of his efforts to improve relations between Germany and Russia and Eastern Europe through *Ostpolitik*.

Only a few years after the Nobel prize, Brandt resigned as chancellor because a high-ranking official in his Chancellery proved to be an East German spy. Brandt accepted the blame for not having prevented the spy from seeing secret documents. He also felt that he no longer could be effective in improving relations between East and West Germany. There also is some indication that his SPD colleagues pressured him to resign because they feared that he might become an electoral liability. The voters might come to believe the Christian Democrats' charge that the SPD was too gullible in its dealings with the Communists. The key point is that despite Brandt's sources of strength, he still was driven from the chancellor's office, just as Erhard had been, although for different reasons, six years earlier. The German chancellor is powerful, but remains accountable.

With Helmut Schmidt, the chancellor from 1974 to 1982, Germany almost came full circle back to the Adenauer style. Schmidt had a reputation for bluntly speaking his mind regardless of the consequences and for pursuing his own goals without much consultation with others. His detractors called him Schmidt-Schnauze—big-mouth Schmidt or Schmidt, the lip. Nonetheless, since the SPD could remain in office only with the support of the FDP, Schmidt had to compromise at times and pay some attention to views expressed in the Cabinet. This was especially true from 1976 to 1980 when the SPD and FDP together had only 10 seats more in the Bundestag than did the Christian Democrats. Not infrequently, Schmidt had to use de Gaulle's tactic of threatening that he would resign unless his colleagues and followers went along with his views. The basic difference between Brandt and Schmidt probably was more one of style than of power. Brandt at times seemed rather apologetic about his power and gave the impression that he would like to do something to make it possible for you to agree with him. Schmidt, on the other hand, was quite willing to lead and expected you to agree with him.

Helmut Kohl of the CDU, chancellor since October 1982, is the opposite of Schmidt in almost every way. Schmidt is short; Kohl the size of a fullback. Schmidt is biting and sarcastic; Kohl is folksy, almost jolly. Schmidt is quite knowledgeable about economics; Kohl knows little about the subject. Schmidt is an intellectual; Kohl is not and prefers to embrace with little questioning such traditional values as the family and hard work. Some observers wonder whether the CDU has returned to the days of Erhard. Kohl seems to bumble along from one mishap to another, exerting little leadership. Critics have referred to him as *Kanzler Tunix*—Chancellor Do-Nothing. He dislikes disagreement among his Cabinet colleagues, but instead of deciding which course the Government will adopt, simply shouts at them to agree among themselves. Yet despite all this, Kohl somehow seems to emerge on top and to remain in public favor because he is a nice man. This should not seem too strange to you, since you may have heard something about the Teflon Presidency. Kohl either is more skilled that he generally is credited to be or he is extraordinarily lucky.

Although the doctrine of individual ministerial responsibility is not a tradition in Germany as it is in Britain, instances of it have occurred. For example, in June 1978 Werner Maihofer resigned as minister of the interior. He accepted responsibility for the failure of the police to act quickly enough on a tip that might have saved the life of an industrialist who had been kidnapped by terrorists and was eventually killed. He also took the blame for the practice of border police of making lists of people who entered Germany carrying copies of left-wing publications, even though he apparently did not know that this was being done. This was not a completely clear example of individual responsibility because it also had a partisan political aspect. Some people felt that Maihofer's apparent ineffectiveness had contributed to the poor showing of his party—the FDP—in a couple of land elections at the time. Thus in resigning he was serving as a political sacrifice and not just acknowledging administrative failures.

Another incident earlier the same year provides a stronger example since it involves not only undesirable administrative action but also the relation between a minister and the legislature. Defense Minister Georg Leber resigned because he discovered that the military counter-intelligence had bugged more telephones than he had told the Bundestag in the previous week's debate. Thus he was inadvertently guilty of misleading the Bundestag in addition to being in charge of an organization that had acted improperly. He accepted responsibility "to protect the armed forces from any harm that might befall them in consequence of political disputes about the incident." This probably is a fuller practice of individual responsibility than now would occur in Britain under similar circumstances.

A more recent precedent points in the opposite direction, however, and also reveals something about Kohl's method of operation. Defence minister Manfred Wörner late in 1983 dismissed Germany's third-ranking general from his post as one of two NATO European deputy commanders on the basis of information from military counterintelligence that the general was a homosexual and, therefore, a security risk. This, apparently, was a case of mistaken identity. Wörner eventually had to admit that incorrect statements had been made and that the information passed on to him could not be verified. He admitted that he had been gullible and had made mistakes in dismissing the general. Thus the general was rehabilitated and reinstated. (He did not return to active duty because by the time he was cleared he was within a month of the time for his scheduled retirement.)

On the one hand, Kohl was angry that the debacle made his Government look incompetent. On the other hand, Wörner had informed him from the start and Kohl did not ask a single question about the matter. While Wörner offered to resign, Kohl did not accept this. He said that for the minister to admit mistakes and offer an apology was sufficient. Thus the general was cleared and the minister was spared the embarrassment of resigning—and Kohl had shown that he could be nice to everyone. (Guess who came out of the Bavarian woods during this affair and indicated that he was available to be defense minister, an offer that may have influenced Kohl to keep Wörner.)

LEGISLATIVE-EXECUTIVE RELATIONS

Legislative leadership is in the Cabinet's hands. About four fifths of all bills are initiated by the Cabinet. In the early years of the Bonn Republic many bills were introduced by individual members. But since such bills are less than half as likely to pass as are those introduced by the Government, their number has declined considerably. Furthermore, the Government was available to draft bills experienced civil servants with detailed legal training, whose services are not available to the Bundestag.

Although in contrast to the U.S. Congress all members of a party in the Bundestag tend to vote together as a group, party cohesion in Germany has not reached the level it attained in Britain in the 1950s. The period 1976–80 is particularly interesting in this regard because the SPD/FDP Government had only 10 seats more than the Christian Democratic opposition; only a small defection could kill bills that the Government wanted to pass. Nonetheless, a handful of left-wing SPD members did not hesitate to vote against Government legislation or abstain. Thus in June 1977 a tax-increase bill passed by only two votes, and in February the following year antiterrorist legislation—a major Government proposal—passed by only a single vote.

Shortly before the beginning of the 1980 election campaign the Government was defeated on two bills, although they were not of major significance. A revolt among FDP members killed a bill dealing with control of traffic noise (the FDP, worried about the possible challenge from the environmentalist Greens in the election, were trying to show that they wanted even stronger action), and dissenting votes by left-wing SPD members killed a bill regulating the way in which conscientious objectors could establish their refusal to serve in the military (they felt the requirements were too stringent, while the Christian Democrats felt they were too lenient). While such action may not seem anything out of the ordinary to Americans, it would have been unheard of in the British parliamentary system until relatively recently.

Thus the German legislature, despite being part of a parliamentary system, plays a larger role in the policymaking process than does the British Parliament. What, then, of the main function of the House of Commons—calling the Government to account; what is the role of the German legislature in this regard? As we saw in the previous chapter, debates on the floor of the Bundestag do not serve this purpose very effectively.

The procedures for questioning ministers, however, have been strengthened. At first only one hour a month was set aside for questions, and written notice well in advance was required. But since 1960 the procedure has been more like the British practice. Now deputies question ministers at the start of each meeting of the Bundestag; they need give notice of their questions only three days in advance (in exceptional circumstances only one day). In addition, supplementary questions may be asked from the floor. Should the normal question hour be inadequate to deal with all inquiries, other question sessions can be scheduled. Deputies are limited to three questions a week. Unfortunately, they may not question the chancellor.

In 1965 the Bundestag initiated a new procedure of a topical hour. The aim was to discourage ministers from making statements to the press and television before discussing a subject with the Bundestag. If 30 members so request, the Government is required to make a statement to the Bundestag on a specified subject. Should only 15 make the request, then the Bundestag votes to determine whether a statement will be required. Statements come immediately after the question period. They are followed by an hour-long debate on the topic, with each speaker limited to five minutes.

While questions and statements are useful in enforcing accountability, the most important means is the distinctive characteristic of a parliamentary system—the ability of the legislature to vote the executive out of office. Since executive instability was regarded as one of the defects of the Weimar Republic, the drafters of the Basic Law tried to devise a system that would entrench the chancellor to some extent without abandoning the parliamentary system for the American separation-of-powers system. The result is a procedure known as the constructive vote of no confidence.

The underlying idea is to prevent a negative majority, of, say, the extreme left and the extreme right, from voting a Government out of office when all they can agree upon is that they do not like what the Government has been doing. Therefore, in Germany a chancellor defeated in the Bundestag, even by an absolute majority, is not required to resign. The only way the Bundestag can force a chancellor from office is to elect a successor by an absolute majority. This means that the Government's opponents must agree upon what they want to have in place of the existing Government before they can get a change.

No attempt was made to pass a constructive vote of no confidence until April 1972, when the Christian Democrats tried to remove Brandt from office. They thought they could succeed because some FDP deputies had defected from the SPD/FDP coalition. Since the vote is a secret ballot, they hoped that even more deputies might desert the governing coalition. But only 247 deputies voted for Barzel, the CDU leader, two short of the number required to put him in office. Rumors were heard, but never substantiated, that a couple of waivers were paid not to vote against Brandt.

Ten years later the Christian Democrats tried again. On this occasion the FDP as a party had formally withdrawn from the coalition. The vote was 256 for Kohl, 235 for Schmidt, and 4 abstentions (2 SPD deputies were ill and did not participate). Thus Kohl had seven votes more than he needed and replaced Schmidt as chancellor.

A chancellor may seek to mobilize support by making an issue a matter of confidence. When this is done, 48 hours must elapse before the vote is taken, just as is true for the constructive vote of no confidence. Chancellors have called for such votes on only three occasions, and only one of these was for the purpose of mobilizing support. In February 1982 Schmidt asked for a vote of confidence in support of his Government's program to combat unemployment. He was attempting to whip the FDP into line and did get a 269–226 victory. But before the year was out the FDP had deserted the coalition.

When a chancellor asks for a vote of confidence and fails to obtain an absolute majority, he may request the president to dissolve the Bundestag and call an election. This is the only way an election can be called before the Bundestag has served its full time. This is why elections in Germany tend to occur regularly at four-year intervals even though the country, unlike the United States, has a parliamentary system. The German chancellor lacks the maneuverability of the British prime minister in seeking to schedule elections at a time when the public opinion polls indicate that the Government parties are popular.

Despite the clear language of the Basic Law that failure to obtain an absolute majority is sufficient to permit a request for elections, the prevailing interpretation has come to be that a chancellor must actually be *defeated* in a request for a vote of confidence to be able to ask the president to dissolve the Bundestag. Although the Christian Democrats had failed to replace Brandt in 1972, as explained above, the defections of some of the FDP meant that the Government had lost its majority and had no more votes in the Bundestag than did the Opposition.

Thus Brandt decided to ask for a vote of confidence with the deliberate intention of losing. The danger in this strategy was that should the Christian Democrats elect someone chancellor before the president had responded to Brandt's request to dissolve the Bundestag, the elections would not occur and the Christian Democrats would take over the Government. Nonetheless, the SPD took the risk and had some of their deputies withhold their votes, deliberately defeating Brandt, so that an election could be called early. The Christian Democrats did not try to elect one of their members chancellor before the president had called an election of the Bundestag.

After Kohl became chancellor under the constructive vote of no confidence, the matter came up again. Kohl wanted to have elections more than a year and a half early in order to get popular approval of the steps his Government had begun taking since replacing Schmidt's Government. So, for only the third time in the Bonn Republic's history, he called for a vote of confidence in December 1982, with the deliberate intention like Brandt 10 years earlier of losing so that elections could be called. And he duly was defeated—8 votes for, 218 against, and 248 abstentions.

Now if you have been reading carefully, you will have noticed that we have said the chancellor may *request* the president to dissolve the Bundestag and call an election. The Basic Law says that the president may do this; it doesn't say that he must. This is one of those ambiguities about the president's powers, like the requirement that he sign the laws. President Carstens had some doubts about the propriety of what chancellor Kohl had done (despite the fact that they both came from the same party). The argument was that what Brandt had done in 1972 was permissible because a vote on the budget—always a key element in any Government's program—had produced a tie, 247 for and 247 against. Thus it was not clear whether his Government could control the legislature, and elections to resolve a possible stalemate were in order. In 1982, however, Kohl's Government clearly did control the Bundestag and his defeat on the motion of confidence was for the purpose of calling elections early, not to resolve a potential legislative deadlock. Carsten consulted with the leaders of all the parties and having established that they all favored earlier elections did grant Kohl's request to dissolve the Bundestag. Clearly the president felt that he had discretionary power in this matter.

Even this did not entirely settle the matter because four deputies took the matter to the Federal Constitutional Court, seeking a ruling that holding the election was illegal. In mid-February 1983, as the election campaign was moving into its final stages, the Court dismissed the suit by a vote of 6–2. The majority argued, a bit tendentiously, that while deliberately losing a vote was improper, dissent within the FDP was such that the Government could not tell whether it firmly controlled the Bundestag. Thus Kohl's maneuver was acceptable and the elections were legal. The main thing to be said in favor of such an argument is that the FDP had divided 34 to 18, with 2 abstentions, on the question of whether to support Kohl on the constructive vote of no confidence in October. Even allowing for the FDP dissidents, however, Kohl clearly had a working, if narrow, majority in the Bundestag.

Although these complicated procedures are intended to insulate the chancellor and ensure Cabinet stability, yet (contrary to widespread German belief) laws can't provide ironclad guarantees. In 1966 the SPD and the FDP carried a motion in the Bundestag calling on Chancellor Erhard to ask for a vote of confidence. They knew that he would lose such a vote, since, with the withdrawal of the FDP from the coalition with the Christian Democrats (seems like those folks are always deserting somebody, doesn't it?), he no longer had a majority in the Bundestag. Once he lost the vote, they would demand new Bundestag elections, which they expected to win.

Erhard refused to play this game and ignored their motion. Unfortunately for him, however, his own Christian Democrats no longer wanted him as chancellor either. The day after the SPD/FDP motion passed, the Christian Democrats in the Bundestag met and elected a successor to Erhard. Thus, although he had not been voted out of office by the Bundestag, he had no choice but to resign as chancellor. The Grand Coalition between the Christian Democrats and the SPD came into office. Thus the chancellor and the political composition of the Government changed by procedures not provided for in the Basic Law.

Although the vote-of-confidence procedures have been used only three times and the constructive-vote-of-no-confidence provisions have come into play only twice, they have not been unimportant the rest of the time. The entrenched position of the chancellor has facilitated flexibility in party discipline in the Bundestag. Bills that the Government did not favor have been passed and the Government did not fall, as might well have occurred under the British parliamentary system. The German system makes it quite clear that matters of confidence in the Government and passage of legislation are two separate things, a distinction that the British lost sight of in the 1950s and only recently have begun to regain.

On the other hand, a government serves little purpose in remaining in office if all of its bills are defeated in the legislature. And while the Germans have devised a procedure to give the chancellor an entrenched position, the constructive-vote-of-no-confidence provisions did not deal with the problem of enabling the Government to get its legislative program through the Bundestag. A deadlock could develop if the Bundestag would not support the chancellor, but could not agree upon a successor, while the chancellor felt that the political situation was inappropriate for calling an election. In that case he or she might resign because of an inability to get a legislative program through the Bundestag, and the whole purpose of the constructive vote of no confidence to secure executive stability would be destroyed.

Therefore, Article 81 of the Basic Law provided for a "legislative emergency" (do not confuse this with the emergency powers given to the Cabinet by the constitutional amendments of the late 1960s, which we discussed above and in Chapter 18). You can best understand the procedures involved by referring to Figure 22–2 and tracing the line from left to right to ascertain the various outcomes depending upon the choices made. As we already have seen, if the Government is defeated on a vote in the Bundestag, the Bundestag may select a new chancellor by an absolute majority. Alternatively, the Government may ask for a vote of confidence on the bill, and if it wins an absolute majority the bill passes and goes on to become law (assuming Bundesrat agreement). If the Government fails to receive an absolute majority on the vote of confidence, it may

FIGURE 22–2   West German Legislative-Emergency Procedure

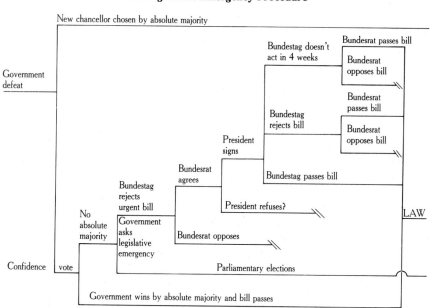

call for Bundestag elections. Should it choose not to do this, then Article 81's legislative-emergency provisions can be used.

The Government labels the bill urgent in a last attempt to persuade the Bundestag to pass it. If the Bundestag votes against the bill anyway, then the Government may ask for a declaration of legislative emergency. If the Bundesrat opposes this, the matter is killed. But if it agrees, the request goes to the president. How much discretion the president has is one of those ambiguities in presidential powers noted earlier in this chapter. By saying that he or she *may* declare a legislative emergency, the Basic Law seems to imply that he or she could decline to do so. If the president signs the declaration, then an obstructionist Bundestag may be bypassed in the legislative process. Any bill that it rejects or fails to act upon within four weeks becomes law anyway, if the Bundesrat approves it. This means that 21 people, a majority of the Bundesrat, can enact a law. The legislative emergency remains in effect for six months unless the Bundestag elects a new chancellor.

One of the safeguards on this procedure is that once the emergency expires another one cannot be declared until elections are held. Article 81 is intended to be simply a temporary aid and, if it does not solve existing problems in a few months, the voters must be asked to sort things out between the chancellor and the Bundestag. Furthermore, during the period of legislative emergency the Basic Law cannot be amended, repealed, or suspended.

Admittedly this is a very complex procedure. But it must be understood as part of the German's effort to correct the deficiencies of the Weimar Republic so that this time democracy could survive. The search for executive stability through the constructive vote of no confidence necessitated some procedure like that of Article 81. At the same time, because abuse of emergency powers in Article 48 of the Weimar constitution had helped to undermine democracy, safeguards had to be written into the Basic Law. All this has made the provisions very complicated.

This is a perfect example of what it means to respond legalistically to pressing problems. The drafters of the Basic Law, operating within traditional German governmental values, believed that a viable democracy could be produced if only the governing law—constitution—were drawn up properly and contained all the right provisions. Few understood that this was more a political than a constitutional or legal question. And this is why Article 81, which has not been used to this point, is likely to remain vestigial. The important development has been the simplification of the party system. The fact that two leading, near-majority parties have emerged means that the circumstances for which Article 81 was drawn up are unlikely to arise. Deadlocks such as it envisioned may occur in fractionalized party systems, but not in the concentrated system that has developed in Germany, especially given the country's tradition of party discipline.

The Basic Law does not provide for a motion of censure, as distinct from a vote of confidence. Nonetheless, in June 1977 the Christian Democrats introduced in the Bundestag the first such motion in the history of the Bonn Republic. They did not seek a vote on a motion of confidence because they did not believe that they had any chance of defeating Chancellor Schmidt on such a vote. But they hoped that they could win over enough FDP or SPD members on a motion of censure to pass it. Thus they could embarrass Schmidt politically. But this would have been the only effect, since Schmidt would have remained in office even if it had passed (which it did not). The fact that under the provisions of the constructive vote of no confidence, even a chancellor censured by the Bundestag can continue as chancellor indicates the extent to which the office has been entrenched in the Bonn Republic to avoid the instability of Weimar.

Germany, like France, seems to have solved the traditional European political problem of executive instability without departing from a democratic framework, as too often has occurred with past such solutions. Interestingly, the two countries have achieved this result in differing ways. France has strengthened that part of the executive that is not responsible to the legislature (nor much to anyone else), while Germany has entrenched the one that is responsible. Furthermore, the legislature has not been downgraded as much in Germany as in France. Despite the Adenauer tradition, Governments in Germany have had to make some concessions, have had to seek some consensus in carrying out their programs. In both countries developments in the party system have been at least as important as institutional reform in explaining the success of their current political systems in dealing with long-standing defects in the political process.

BIBLIOGRAPHICAL NOTE

There are no books in English dealing exclusively with the German executive. Klaus Bolling, *Republic in Suspense: Politics, Parties and Personalities in Postwar Germany* (New York: Praeger Publishers, 1964), contains much valuable commentary on executive leadership. The folowing biographies are a source of some information: Terence Prittie, *Adenauer* (London: Stacy, 1971); Rudolf Augstein, *Konrad Adenauer* (London: Secker & Warburg, 1964); and Hermann Bolesch and Hans Leicht, *Willy Brandt: A Protrait of the German Chancellor* (Tubingen: Erdmann, 1971). See also Konrad Adenauer, *Memoirs* (Chicago: Regnery/Gateway, 1966).

23

Policy-Implementing Structures

Increasing governmental activity in the economic and social fields has made administration more vast and complicated in virtually every country. Even apart from this trend, however, administration long has been a significant element in the German political system. The Germans very early established a systematically organized civil service as one of the twin pillars on which the state rested. The other was the army. Administration in Germany differs from that of Britain and France because Germany is a federal system and vests some significant powers in the laender.

STAFFING AND ORGANIZING THE BUREAUCRACY

The German civil service in the 19th century earned the reputation of being competent, incorruptible, and objective. Since recruitment was based on expert training and knowledge, and since higher education generally was unavailable to the lower classes, membership in the higher civil service tended to be limited to the sons of the upper classes. Furthermore, civil servants who expressed liberal or democratic views endangered their positions. Consequently, the civil service developed into a conservative class system. But precisely because of their prestigious background, civil servants were looked up to by the general population. The high-level civil servant seemed to typify all that was best in German national character. Added to this was the orderliness of the bureaucratic system itself, another quality attractive to most Germans. Thus, in general, the Germans were willing to allow the bureaucrat to exercise great power.

432

During Weimar, an attempt was made to liberalize recruitment to the civil service, with some decline in quality as a result. In the Nazi period, civil servants whose loyalty to the new order was in question were removed. Recruitment also was controlled carefully. The net result of the Nazi period was also a decline in quality. At the end of the World War II, there was an attempt to denazify the service and to rebuild it. After the somewhat uncertain period of the first postwar years, the general quality and competence of the service has improved.

The present status of the civil service is regulated by the Federal Civil Service Act (1961).[1] This law sets up three classes in the civil service. These are the higher service, the intermediate service, and the ordinary service. In order to qualify for the higher service, a person must have a university education and have passed the initial examination, which is followed by three years' experience in the service and the passing of a second examination. The intermediate service requires a secondary education (or its equivalent), plus three years in the service and the passing of the intermediate service examination. The ordinary service requires an elementary school education or its equivalent and an apprenticeship period.

Traditionally, legal training was required to qualify one for the higher civil service. Under the present law this has been broadened to include degrees in economics and political science. The class composition of the civil service has been broadened somewhat also. Yet most recruits still are sons either of the wealthy or of civil servants. Contributing to a continuation of the class bias is the fact that few civil servants are promoted to the top positions from lower ranks. Entry into the higher civil service normally is directly at that level. Thus, only those with the proper education (and the German educational system tends to be biased toward the upper classes) can secure the top positions.

The Federal Personnel Committee regulates conditions of service and appointment. Its members are chosen from different branches of the bureaucracy as well as from nominees of the trade unions, including the civil servants' union. Working closely with the Personnel Committee are the personnel committees of the laender. Grievances are handled by councils set up for such purposes. Civil servants may belong to trade unions, but have no right to strike.

Germany was the first nation to accept responsibility for the wrongful acts of officials while performing their official duties. Part of the reason may have been that state ownership of various enterprises occurred earlier in Prussia than in most other countries. In any case, the present constitution acknowledges this legal responsibility and authorizes administrative courts, similar to those in France, to deal with such cases.

An interesting innovation was the Bundestag's creation, when the new German army was established, of the post of defense commissioner. The commissioner is elected by the Bundestag to investigate all complaints about possible

---

[1]For partial text, see John C. Lane and James K. Pollock, *Source Materials on the Government and Politics of Germany* (Ann Arbor, Mich.: George Wahr, 1964), pp. 114–16.

violation of the basic rights of soldiers or of the principles of internal leadership in the military forces. The commissioner has access to pertinent papers and other necessary information and may refer complaints to appropriate sources for settlement. The Bundestag intends the commissioner to serve as a watchdog guarding against the development of antidemocratic sentiments in the military. The defense commissioner has served in several instances to alert the Bundestag to practices that it wants to eliminate.[2]

How much political activity to permit by those who are governmental employees is an important question in every political system. The constraints and the reason for them vary considerably from one country to another. In the United States, as you know, civil servants' political activity is limited to protect them from the venal politicians, who would otherwise force civil servants, if they wanted to keep their jobs, to contribute money and time to the politicians' reelection campaigns. The British, as we have seen, also constrain bureaucrats' political activity, but not because they fear abuse by the politicians. Their concern is the reverse: the possibility that politicians might believe that civil servants who disliked the politicians' party might sabotage its policies. Civil servants are required to be neutral so that they can be trusted to serve whatever party currently is in power.

The continental political systems follow another pattern for yet other reasons. There the typical belief is that civil servants are better educated, more intelligent than politicians and, obviously, should run the country. Thus civil servants are permitted, indeed almost encouraged, to be active in politics, even for national offices. German civil servants are required by law to be servants of the people, not of any political party, and to carry out their tasks impartially. But Germany, like France, has not drawn a sharp line between political and administrative service of the government. Civil servants may enter national politics freely without resigning their office. Those who are successful simply take a leave of absence. When they cease to be members of the Bundestag, they are reinstated in the civil service. Moreover, nothing prevents a civil servant from participating actively in politics on the land or on the local level. In most cases, however, those elected to a land assembly take a leave of absence, but with the right of reinstatement. Because of this right, and hence the very real possibility of going back, civil servants tend to continue their official associations.

Also blurring the line between politician and civil servant was some ministers' practice of sending bureaucrats to address the Bundestag in their place or to respond during the question period. In addition, they often asked bureaucrats to participate in committee decisions and even to sign unpopular orders. Such deliberately fostered confusion made it difficult to distinguish clearly between the responsibility of ministers and that of civil servants. Because some

---

[2]Klaus Bolling, *Republic in Suspense: West Germany Today* (New York: Praeger Publishers, 1964), pp. 184–85. See also Lane and Pollock, *Source Materials on the Government and Politics of Germany,* pp. 127–28, and Walter Stahl, *Politics of Postwar Germany* (New York: Praeger Publishers, 1963), pp. 260 ff.

ministers failed to consider themselves accountable, the public at times centered its fire on the civil servants.

In 1967, however, partly as a result of the negotiations that led to the Grand Coalition, the situation was altered by the creation of parliamentary state secretaries in the larger ministries. These appointees, who are similar to junior ministers in Britain, must be members of the Bundestag. Their primary duty is to stand in for ministers at Bundestag question time, a practice that makes for an element of ministerial responsibility. In turn, the career civil servants have become a little like the permanent secretaries in Britain in that they do not become involved in party politics.

While orthodox political activity by civil servants supporting mainstream parties may be permitted or even encouraged, the situation differs considerably for those whose political views are less acceptable. In 1972 the national government and the heads of the laender agreed on a standard procedure to keep extremists out of government jobs. While one might agree with the goal, the way in which the procedure has been interpreted and implemented raises serious questions. The stringency with which this Extremists' Decree has been applied has varied with the political composition of the area—the Christian Democratic—controlled laender being more zealous.

The Decree established a national office—the Office for the Protection of the Constitution—to screen applicants for government jobs. Land governments send enquiries to the Office to see whether it has any information in its files about people who have applied for, or hold, land jobs. Bavaria, the home of the CSU, has been most active in using the Office—averaging nearly 25,000 enquiries a year during the 1970s. The teachers' union has complained about arbitrary administration of the Decree. For example, in one land, applicants for teaching positions were questioned because they rented rooms in the same house as did a Communist. Elsewhere applicants for government jobs were questioned for having stood on a left-wing ticket in university student elections, for having handed out political leaflets, and for signing a candidate's nomination papers. After one is interviewed for what the authorities regard as questionable activity, months go by before one is informed whether government employment will be permitted. The delay is caused by the large number of enquiries that the Office has to process. The Decree applies not just to teachers or what Americans would consider regular civil servants, but even low-level railway and postal employees are screened. Train engineers and postal clerks have been fired for belonging to the Communist party.

Only a relatively small proportion of those applying for government jobs were denied them under this screening program and even fewer were dismissed from employment. Nonetheless, the thought of a governmental agency keeping extensive files on citizens' political activities is disquieting. Few would deny that the Decree had a negative effect upon free political discussion in Germany, especially among young people. The German governments seem ultimately to have realized this and have administered the program much more leniently in the

1980s. In many places routine checks no longer are made. While in part the program was due to the SPD's efforts to defend itself from any attack that it was soft on communism, it also was a product of Germans' sensitivity about their nation's political history. The Soviet Union enjoys proclaiming periodically that former Nazis continue to hold positions of influence in West Germany because the Germans really did not disapprove of what they did in the 1930s and 1940s. While there is little foundation for such charges, Germans' guilt over their past seems to require them to respond with excessive zeal just to prove themselves.

The German civil service has been criticized for being unimaginative, authoritarian, and enslaved by routine and rules—charges that do not sound too different from what one hears in most countries about bureaucrats. Traditionally, however, Germans have differed from Americans in their views of the civil service. In the United States most people tend to regard the bureaucrat as aloof and see the politician as the defender of their interests. For Germans the politician was remote, while the bureaucrat was seen as sympathetic to the average person's problems.

The traditional German view seems to be changing, however. In a 1979 poll 80 percent said that civil servants were cumbersome and slow and 60 percent said that bureaucracy was too large and unattuned to people's needs. We can only speculate, but it seems unlikely that the German civil service has deteriorated. More plausible is the explanation that Germans have come to expect a more responsive government. Challenging the traditional sacrosanct position of the civil service is one more evidence of the health of the contemporary German democracy.

German ministries are headed by political appointees and staffed by permanent civil servants. The political minister in charge usually appoints one state secretary *(Staatssekretar),* although some departments have two.[3] The state secretary is the equivalent of the British permanent head of the department. Although state secretaries usually are promoted from the ranks of the higher civil service, the law permits the chancellor to appoint a few without any restrictions.

THE ROLE OF THE LAENDER IN NATIONAL ADMINISTRATION

The term *civil servant* in Germany includes such diverse occupations as meter reader, railway conductor, and teacher—all of these are considered employees, and thus representatives, of the state. Furthermore, in Germany most administrators are state- and local-government employees, rather than national government ones. Instead of being way off somewhere in the capital city, they are nearby and in contact with the population.

Except for defense, railways, and the post office, the national government in Germany employs only about 10 percent of the total number of civil servants.

---

[3]The term *Staatssekretar* is used also to denote the highest rank in the civil service.

About one third of all administrators work for local governments, and over half are employed by the laender. National ministry staffs number only about 100,000 persons. Of these more than 8,000 are in the higher civil service. They occupy the top positions in each department and include the chief secretaries, bureau chiefs, and immediate staffs.

German ministries have little administrative machinery of their own. For the most part, the actual implementation of the law is left to the bureaucracy of the laender. The constitution provides that the laender "execute the federal laws as matters of their own concern insofar as this Basic Law does not otherwise provide or permit." Even where land and national government ministries exist side by side, the national ones are concerned chiefly with drafting uniform legislation and in seeing that the administration by the laender conforms with the statutes and the constitution. National ministry offices usually are small and compact, with supervisory offices in the major cities. The bulk of detailed administrative activity occurs in the counties and municipalities under the direction of the land governments.

You will recall from Chapter 21 that Bundesrat members are both legislators and executives. They participate in the national legislative process, but also serve in Governments of their respective laender, where they direct implementation not only of the laws passed by their land legislatures, but also those passed by the national legislature. Thus they administer laws that they themselves have helped to pass or, alternatively, have voted unsuccessfully to defeat.

Unlike Britain and France, Germany is a federal system. This means that there is a division of powers between the national and constituent units of government that cannot be altered unilaterally. In Chapter 21 we discussed this division of powers, noting that only a few areas were the exclusive province of the national government. Residuary or reserve powers rest with the laender. These are relatively few, the most important being education and cultural affairs. The great bulk of governmental powers are concurrent—either the national or the land governments can legislate in these areas. Should there be any conflict, the national government's action would take precedence.

These provisions give the national government such extensive powers that some observers have questioned whether Germany is anything more than a quasi-federal system. The national government appears to be by far the most dominant element of the system. Evaluating German federalism just by looking at the distribution of legislative power, however, is not adequate. Unlike the American states, the German laender play a major role in administering laws passed by the national legislature. And in implementing these laws land administrators have a fair amount of discretion.

This immediately raises the question of how diversity bordering on chaos can be avoided and how national–state conflict can be resolved. Clearly, the national government of the United States would have been naive to leave the racial integration of the public schools in the hands of the relevant state officials in many Southern states. The national government in Germany can issue administrative regulations that are binding upon land administrators. But these require the approval of the Bundesrat, which means that at least half of the land governments must agree. The national government also can send its agents to investigate the quality of land administration. Should this be deficient, the national government can demand improvement and compliance. But again this requires the agreement of the Bundesrat. Given the ample opportunity for input from the laender in the national legislative process, as discussed in Chapter 21, conflict over administrative matters rarely comes to this point.

BIBLIOGRAPHICAL NOTE

The following are useful on various aspects of German administration: Gordon Craig, *From Bismarck to Adenauer: Aspects of German Statecraft* (Baltimore: The Johns Hopkins Press, 1958); Herbert Jacob, *German Administration Since Bismarck* (New Haven, Conn.: Yale University Press, 1963); Edward L. Pinney, *Federalism, Bureaucracy, and Party Politics in Western Germany* (Chapel Hill: University of North Carolina Press, 1963); Roger H. Wells, *The States in West German Federalism: A Study in Federal-State Relations,* 1949–1960 (New York: Bookman Associates, 1961); and Hans-Joachim Arndt, *West Germany: Politics of Nonplanning* (Syracuse, N.Y.: Syracuse University Press, 1967).

24

The Judicial Structure

The German judicial system, as are the systems in other continental countries, is similar to the French pattern. The law is code law instead of case law, although precedent has become increasingly important in Germany. Moreover, the judiciary is identified with the state more than in Britain or the United States. This is largely a matter of emphasis, for courts everywhere are in a sense instruments of the state. In Britain and the United States, however, they are viewed as protectors of the individual, both from private and governmental actions. In Germany and in other continental countries, on the other hand, they are viewed as dispensers of justice, seeing to it that justice is done from the point of view of society at large, with less concern for the individual person. Finally, court procedure under the Roman law system, as already discussed in part Three on France, differs from the Anglo-American pattern.

JUDGES AND COURT ORGANIZATION

Although Germany did not become a democratic state until after World War I, the German courts gained considerable independence as early as the first quarter of the 19th century. The Prussian consitution of 1850 had even proclaimed the rule-of-law principle, including the idea that courts were free of executive influence. As in the higher civil service, judicial positions were open only to university graduates (typically law degrees), a qualification that only the sons of the wealthy could hope to meet. This meant that judges were drawn from the conservative strata of society. It is not surprising, therefore, that most German judges developed a conservative political orientation, which became particularly evident in the Weimar and Nazi periods, when they did not seem to grasp the nature of the Nazi movement.

As in France, the Germany judiciary is supervised by the Ministry of Justice. Judges are recruited from law school graduates who seek a judicial career. They must first spend some three to four years in probationary and preparatory service, following which they must satisfactorily pass a final examination. Appointments are made by the minister of justice, who is assisted by nominating committees at both the national and land levels. The nominating committees are selected by the respective legislatures. Promotion is through seniority and merit, and is handled by the minister of justice and a committee of judges.

Judges are independent, but they must not violate the principles of the constitution. They hold their positions during good behavior, and may only be removed by their fellow judges through procedures regulated by law.

Judicial procedure in Germany is much like that in France, with the judge dominating the proceedings. It is his or her job to ascertain the truth, and to this end to admit or exclude evidence. As in France, the rules of evidence are relatively flexible. And again as in France, there are pretrial investigations, with the accused seldom released on bail, although pretrial detention is reviewed periodically. In case of acquittal, however, the defendant may seek indemnification for the detention prior to the trial. The Basic Law abolishes the death penalty.

The Germans have tried to prevent a person's financial situation from being an obstacle to obtaining justice. Under a 1980 law a single person with a net monthly income of about $380 or less can take a case to court free of charge— the government pays for the lawyer. A person with two dependents can make up to about $700 a month and still qualify for free legal aid. Some assistance is available for those who earn more than this, but those exceeding an upper limit (about $1,100 a month for singles) are eligible only in special hardship cases. People whose income exceeds the limits for assistance are permitted to pay legal costs in installments geared to their income.

Another 1980 law provided assistance when a lawsuit was not involved. It enabled low-income citizens to obtain legal advice regardless of whether they went to court.

Although Germany is a federal system, its land and national court systems do not parallel and partially overlap each other as is true in the United States. Instead there is a single integrated system of regular courts. The three lower levels of the court system are all land courts. As is the practice for administrative matters, the land courts are used to try federal as well as land cases. Thus, virtually all cases in Germany start in a land court. The top level courts are national courts. Uniformity is obtained despite this structure by the fact that all courts are regulated by national codes, both as to procedure and as to the bulk of the substantive law that they apply. Moreover, all legal judgments and instruments are applicable throughout the nation. The law does not vary from state to state, as is so often true in the United States.

At the bottom of the court hierarchy are the local courts *(Amtsgerichte)*, presided over by a single judge. In the smaller places he or she hears all types of small civil suits and minor criminal actions. In larger towns, the court may have several sections or categories of cases, each presided over by a single judge. In both instances the judge is joined by two lay assessors, and in certain criminal cases a second judge is added. The assessors are chosen by lot from lists of local inhabitants. An American-type jury is not used.

Standing above the local courts are the district or provincial courts *(Landgerichte),* serving both as courts of original jurisdiction and as courts of appeal. They are divided into sections, or chambers, some concerned with appeals and others with original jurisdiction. On the civil side there is usually a section that hears appeals cases and another section that hears those original cases over which local courts lack jurisdiction. On the criminal side there are two appeals sections (little chamber and big chamber) and two original jurisdiction sections. One of the original jurisdiction sections is also called the big chamber, and the other the assize court, which tries the more grave criminal cases, such as murder.

All sections of the district court have three judges, except the little chamber, which has one judge and two lay assessors. The judges in the big chambers are also assisted by two lay assessors. The assize court, however, has a six-member jury, which votes jointly with the three judges. Although decisions are reached by majority vote, the judges exercise preponderant influence.

The superior courts *(Oberlandesgerichte)* have two sections, civil and criminal. The civil section, staffed by three judges, reviews judgments of district courts and may alter them. The criminal section has a little and a big chamber; the little chamber has three judges and the big has five. These decide points of law; they do not try cases but may order retrial in a lower court.

Decisions of the superior courts may be appealed to the Federal High Court *(Bundesgerichtshof),* which has approximately 100 judges. It is divided into sections of five judges each, some dealing with civil matters and others with criminal. The Federal High Court must review all cases submitted to it. Consequently, most of its work is concerned with appeals, and hence its major function is to insure uniformity of legal interpretation among the courts of the laender. Because some crimes are exclusively national, however, there is a criminal section that has original jurisdiction over them. An example of this would be cases of treason. The judges for this court are selected by the minister of justice in connection with land legal officials and an equal number of members of the Bundestag. The Federal High Court is the final court—even in cases of treason, which originate there—unless a constitutional issue is raised. In that situation the case goes to the Federal Constitutional Court, which we discuss in the next section.

As in France, the government accepts liability for the wrongful acts of its officials while performing their official duties. Unlike the situation in France, however, claims against individual officials, as well as salary and other pecuniary claims of civil servants, go to the ordinary courts. But judgments are handed down against the state and not against the offending officials. The bulk of claims against public authorities, as well as conflicts between them, are heard, however, in separate administrative courts.

The German administrative court system is extremely elaborate and complex. Special courts concentrate on such matters as labor relations, commercial disputes, tax disputes, and social security cases. Because of the large number of pension cases, Germany has 49 social welfare courts organized at three levels to deal with this subject. Tax courts operate at two levels—11 at the regional level to hear the cases originally and a Federal Financial Court for appeals.

Perhaps the most important elements in this system are the general-purpose administrative courts. These are intended to protect citizens against governmental officials who they feel are infringing on their rights by arbitrary or unfair action or by refusing to act when they should. The system consists of 31 administrative courts, 10 superior administrative courts for appeals, and the Federal Administrative Court to hear cases involving the constitution.

A citizen with a complaint appeals first to the agency responsible for the action or inaction involved. If the response is not satisfactory and fails to settle the matter, then he or she may go to an administrative court. At neither this level nor the appeal level is a lawyer needed; the citizen can argue his or her own case. Only in the Federal Administrative Court must lawyers be used.

Since at times citizens may learn about administrative actions only when it is too late for satisfactory redress, government agencies must warn citizens. That is, whenever some intended action might infringe on citizen rights, the agency planning to act must tell the citizens of this and that they have a right to protest. Failure to do this can be sufficient grounds for an administrative court to void governmental action.

The matters dealt with by the administrative courts do not involve abstract rights or fundamental civil liberties so much as they concern people's day-to-day relations with the government. Whether somebody gets a liquor license or a building permit is not a basic question of democracy. Yet such matters are important to the individuals involved, and fair treatment by government is a right. The administrative court system helps Germans fight back on a more equal basis with government and defend themselves from arbitrary action.

BASIC RIGHTS AND THE CONSTITUTIONAL COURT

Remembering what had happened to their basic rights under the Nazis, the Germans were anxious to provide all possible legal safeguards against losing them again. The first section of the constitution, consisting of 19 articles, deals with the people's rights in a detailed fashion. At the outset the constitution declares that the "dignity of man is inviolable" and that it is "the duty of all state authority" to "respect and protect it." The enumerated basic rights are said to "bind the legislature, the executive and the judiciary."

Elsewhere, the constitution forbids extraordinary courts, double jeopardy, and retroactive laws. The right of habeas corpus is also preserved. The police may not hold a person longer than the end of the day following arrest unless he or she is charged with a crime. The judge's decision in a habeas corpus proceeding is subject to appeal to higher courts. Also, provision is made against mental and physical ill treatment of detained persons. And due process and the equal protection of the laws are declared to be part of the consitutional order.

Aware of how the guaranteed rights of free speech, free press, and free assembly were abused by both the Nazis and the Communists during the Weimar Republic so as to subvert democracy and destroy these rights, the framers of the Basic Law sought to shield the political system from the abuse of freedom. Article 9 prohibits associations whose aims and activites are in conflict with criminal laws or are directed against the constitutional order. Article 18 asserts that "whoever abuses freedom of expression of opinion, in particular freedom of the press, freedom of teaching, freedom of assembly, freedom of association, the secrecy of mail, posts and telecommunications, the right of property, or the right of asylum, in order to attack the free democratic basic order, forfeits these basic rights."

In order to defend the liberties specified in the Basic Law, the Germans, although lacking a tradition of judicial review, readily accepted American insistence upon it. A Federal Constitutional Court was established, and experience over more than a third of a century indicates that the Germans have taken to these procedures quite readily. Not only is the Federal Constitutional Court generally accepted, but similar courts function extensively at the land level to review land legislation.

The Federal Court consists of two panels of eight judges each. To be eligible for appointment one must at least be 40 and of proven legal ability. But one need not have made a career as a judge; a legal degree is sufficient. Thus although more than 40 percent of the appointees to the Constitutional Court have been judges, more than a quarter have been civil servants with most of the rest being professors or lawyers. Appointees serve a 12-year term and cannot be reappointed.

The minister of justice maintains a list of potential nominees to the Court. Included are the top judges and others suggested by the Federal Government, a land Government, or a party in the Bundestag. The Bundesrat and the Bundestag alternate in filling vacancies on the Court from this list. For this purpose the Bundestag appoints a 12-person committee whose political composition is the same as that of the house itself. Eight votes are required to select a judge. The Bundesrat makes the selection itself with a two-thirds vote required for appointment.

Again, it is interesting to note from an American standpoint the extent of influence given to the laender in this matter. The laender have a chance to suggest possible judges and half the time actually appoint the judge to the Court. As in the United States, the Court has as one of its duties the settling of disputes between the national and land governments. The procedure used for selecting the personnel of the Court in Germany gives the laender an opportunity to defend what they conceive to be their vital interests by selecting judges sympathetic to their views. This is not to suggest that the judges of the Federal Constitutional

Court are biased. But obviously approaches to interpreting and applying a constitution differ from one judge to another—some are strict constructionists and others are more liberal. And in Germany the laender have some opportunity to get judges with the orientation they prefer onto the Court. Thus the German laender are less likely than the American states to see the highest court in the land as being a hostile element of another level of government. The Federal Constitutional Court is more likely to be regarded as an impartial arbiter.

One panel or senate of the Constitutional Court deals with questions of the violation of civil liberties and constitutional rights, while the other senate hears all the other cases within the Court's jurisdiction. Examples of these would be conflicts between two or more laender or between a land and the national government. Although the first senate deals only with cases of one general type, it has had the heavier work load.

The Court has three types of jurisdiction—concrete, abstract, and constitutional complaint. In concrete jurisdiction the Court considers an actual case that raises a question of constitutionality. This is the way that the American Supreme Court operates. If it is claimed in a case in the regular court system that the Basic Law has been violated, the case goes to the Federal Constitutional Court. Should it be a violation of a land constitution that is claimed, the case goes to the constitutional court of the appropriate land.

Under abstract jurisdiction, it is possible for the Court to rule on a constitutional question when there is no actual case before it. As noted in the discussion of the form of judicial review practiced in France, this is a procedure that the U.S. Supreme Court has refused to follow. In Germany, however, the Federal Government, a land Government, or one third of the total membership of the Bundestag can request that the Court rule on the constitutional validity of a law before that law actually is implemented or, should it be in effect already, before any case has arisen questioning the law. The comments, made in Chapter 16 on the appropriateness of this procedure in a code law system, are relevant here as well.

Unfortunately, whatever party is in Opposition in the Bundestag has tended to use this power as a political weapon. When legislation that it strongly opposes passes, it seeks to thwart the majority by moving a political conflict into a legal forum and getting the Court to throw out the law. As the German newspaper *Sueddeutsche Zeitung* commented,

> There is no longer almost any law of great political, economic or social significance that goes into effect without checking by the highest court. In principle, there is nothing to complain about this, although the growing danger is not to be overlooked, that political decisions in the final analysis have to be made by judges on the Constitutional Court. In this manner, there comes an element of insecurity in the application of laws, particularly, to the degree that they affect economic life.

The constitutional complaint is similar to abstract jurisdiction but broader in scope. Anyone in Germany can challenge any law on the grounds that it infringes rights guaranteed by the Basic Law. There are no court costs for this procedure, and the challenger need not even hire a lawyer unless he or she wishes to do so. Thus in Germany when someone says, "I'll fight it all the way to the Supreme Court," it is not quite the idle threat that it is in the United States.

Constitutional complaints are far and away the great bulk of the matters brought to the Constitutional Court. More than 4,000 were filed in 1983 alone, bringing the total since the Court was founded in September 1951 to more than 58,000. Given the Germans' litigious nature, the procedure would get totally out of hand unless some limits were imposed.

The Court can charge someone it feels has abused the right to appeal to it $385. It rarely does this, however, so as not to discourage people from seeking to defend their rights. Normally, one must go through the regular court system before getting to the Constitutional Court. Furthermore, the Court has a screening committee, which can reject a request to hear a case. The committee does not examine the evidence but simply checks whether due process was observed and whether the decision of a lower court conformed with constitutional principles. About 98 percent of the constitutional complaints are not heard by the Court, having been rejected for lack of legal merit. When a complaint is brought, the law in question is suspended and not enforced until the Court decides on the merit of the complaint.

Despite the effort to make the constitutional complaint work load manageable, the Court still gets cases that by any reasonable standards would seem to be ruled out by the principle *de minimis non curat lex*—the law is not concerned with trifles. For example, a man fined $20 for riding his bicycle through a pedestrian zone complained to the Court on the grounds that not all available witnesses had been heard. (As a result the Court raised the limit for complaints it would accept to those involving a fine of $30 or more.) A pet owner complained that his constitutional rights had been violated when the city of Hamburg doubled the annual tax on dogs to $90. (The highest court in the country spends its time on this sort of stuff?) Some people think the Court gets so many complaints because lawyers collect $190 for filing them regardless of their merits.

Nonetheless, whatever the problems with the procedure, about 1.5 percent of all the complaints filed have resulted in overturning a law, regulation, or previous court decision. To that extent, rights that would have been infringed in some way have been protected. And some of the cases involved have been far from trivial. In 1983, on the complaint of two lawyers the Court prohibited the national census only two weeks before it was to have been taken. The Court agreed with their contention that insufficient safeguards had been provided to prevent data abuse. The danger was that individual rights to privacy could be violated because the census form was so constructed that each person providing data could be specifically identified.

Previous chapters in this section have noted, as relevant, various important decisions of the Court, so there is no need to discuss a long list of cases here. One additional important decision is worth mention, however. In 1983 Kohl's Government had enacted a so-called forced loan. Single taxpayers earning more than about $16,000 and couples earning more than about $32,000 were required to pay a surtax of 5 percent on the tax due the government through 1985. This sum would be repaid to them, but not until 1990 and then without any interest. The aim was to raise money to fund a government program of housing construction to stimulate economic recovery. The Court ruled that the government had no constitutional basis for such a surtax. The government was forced to stop collecting it and to reimburse taxpayers for the more than $600 million it already had collected. In this case, as in all others at the national or land level, whenever a law is declared unconstitutional, it is automatically repealed.

The Court is empowered to rule on petitions by the Cabinet or the Bundestag that a political party be banned because it seeks to overthrow the established democratic order. Under this power a neonazi and a communist party were declared illegal. The Court also has ruled, however, that a person cannot be punished for membership in, and service to, a banned political party at a time before the party was prohibited.

What the Germans have sought to do is to strike a viable balance between liberty and license. On the one hand, they wish to protect basic liberties from the violation they suffered under the Nazis. Yet they also want to avoid the Weimar situation where freedom was used in an abusive fashion so as to undermine the democratic system. Thus they have included in the Basic Law provisions aimed at protecting the state from those who would seek to subvert it. In the end these concerns interrelate, for those who seek to destroy the democratic order would abolish individual liberties were they to succeed.

Sometimes, as in the case of the Extremists' Decree mentioned in the previous chapter, the government seems to have gone too far in the direction of trying to defend against those who might subvert liberty. Another such instance is the Kohl Government's measure against protestors. In part reacting to peace and antimissile demonstrators, the Government had the law changed to allow arrest of passive onlookers at demonstrations who failed to disperse when told to do so by the police. Thus one's right simply to move about in public was being curtailed, to say nothing of the limitation on the right of political assembly. The FDP did manage to secure a compromise provision that anyone arrested for failing to disperse could avoid conviction by proving that he or she had been trying to calm the demonstrators. While this perhaps made the law a bit less harsh, still many objected that it had the effect of shifting the burden of proof from the government to the individual—you had to prove that you should be exempted from the law rather than the government having to prove that it should be applied to you.

It is precisely because the country's history makes Germans especially sensitive to the balance and tensions between liberty and license that a constitutional court is especially important. Such a court cannot guarantee that liberties always will be protected from subversive forces, but it can make the rise of a dictator more difficult. It also can play a major role in educating the public to the importance of basic freedoms and provide them with a means of defense in those instances when the government goes too far in trying to control those who it fears might be a threat to liberty. It can contribute significantly to the establishment of a tradition of liberal democracy and to a conviction that citizens are secure in the exercise of their basic rights. It is to obtain these goals that the Federal Constitutional Court is willing to listen to citizens who want to complain about the doubling of the dog license fee.

Every country has to live with its past—the American treatment of the Indian is nothing of which to be proud, for example. But there comes a point at which the children should no longer have to answer for the sins of the fathers. The bulk of those who ran the Nazi state are now in their late 70s or older, if still alive. Only Germans over 40 had even been born when Hitler committed suicide. German genes do not carry some character flaw that is passed on from generation to generation. Nazi rule of Germany was appalling, but it is to be explained in the context of the history and traditions of the times. No people can break totally with this past and have a completely new beginning. We have seen at various points in this part of the book that current German government and politics are influenced by German tradition. The influence of history is even more obvious; the Germans have made strenuous efforts to ensure that the nightmare does not happen again. Perhaps because of their past they are more conscious than many other countries of potential threats to freedom and the need to defend liberty. They have constructed and established a remarkably successful political system. The democratic traditions that they lacked in the past are now being built. Indeed, Bonn most certainly is not Weimar.

BIBLIOGRAPHICAL NOTE

On the German judicial structure see Wolfgang Heyde, *The Administration of Justice in the Federal Republic of Germany* (Bonn: 1971). For the operation of the Federal Constitutional Court, see Donald Kommers, *Judicial Politics in West Germany* (Beverly Hills, Calif.: Sage, 1976).

PART FIVE

PROSPECTS FOR EUROPEAN DEMOCRACY

25

Durability and Change: Western European Democracies in Crisis?

Before examining the communist political system in the Soviet Union, we need to sum up the democratic political systems of Britain, France, and Germany. In this way we shall see some of the attributes that these systems have in common, as well as some of the major problems that confront them. The fact that they all face serious economic problems, which at times seem insoluble, may make radical solutions that would alter the basic structure of the systems themselves seem more attractive.

ACCOUNTABILITY AND CONCENTRATION OF POWER

We analyzed Britain first for the good reason that American scholars long regarded Britain as the model for all things good politically. If only American government and politics could be more like the British, we all would be better off, they said. France and Germany had had troubled histories and hardly could be considered models of democracy. Britain offered a standard of excellence against which these two countries and others could be compared to ascertain the shortcomings of their political systems. Thus, because of the longevity and stability of the British political system, we began with Britain as a model of parliamentary democracy, and then went on to France and Germany as alternates to or variations on the themes we found in the British political system.

A recurrent theme in the chapters on Britain was accountability or responsibility. A second theme often touched on, although not so explicitly noted, was concentration of power. The essence of the British political process can be summarized in terms of the way these two themes relate to each other.

Concentrated power easily can be a great danger, as will become quite clear in Part Six when we analyze the Soviet Union as an archetypal dictatorial system. But in a political culture like Britain's with a traditional deep respect for democratic values, concentrated power can be an asset, for it means that responsibility is focused as well. In dictatorial systems this is irrelevant, for they provide no way of enforcing responsibility—the leaders are not accountable to the people. But in Britain they are.

So long as accountability is maintained, the British have been content to allow political leaders to exercise political power relatively unencumbered, for *the* limitation on power is not a written constitution, but accountability. Nor does a system of checks and balances like that in the United States defend freedoms.

The power structure of British government can be understood only in terms of the presence of accountability. Neither the monarch nor the House of Lords is accountable, and thus can't be allowed to exercise any real power. The judiciary is somewhat more accountable, since its members are appointed by the Government and can be removed by Parliament, but it is subject to little control. Thus its power, too, must be circumscribed; British courts lack the power exercised by American ones.

The civil service clearly does exercise power at its upper levels and thus must be accountable. A special means of achieving this must be devised, however; one that will not jeopardize the benefits of efficiency and merit selection. Thus the British have developed the doctrines of the political neutrality of the civil service and of ministerial responsibility. The nationalized industries also are centers of power and must be accountable. In this case the problem is to avoid losing the advantages of commercial efficiency. The public corporation is an attempt to satisfy the demands of both efficiency and accountability.

The key structure in this system, in the traditional view, is Parliament. The people cannot by themselves call all the government's officials to account. The job is too vast; it requires full-time effort. Therefore, the task is delegated to elected legislative representatives. These representatives are accountable directly to the people with everything else accountable to the representatives. British parties, unified and cohesive, help to clarify where responsibility lies and thus to aid the electorate in calling their representatives to account.

The Cabinet wields considerable power. Therefore, it is essential that it be accountable. This explains why the Government must keep Parliament informed of its plans and actions, why these must be debated fully there, why the existence of an official Opposition is essential, why the Opposition is consulted in planning the Commons' agenda, why the Government allows time for censure debates, why the Government submits daily to questioning of its actions and policies.

These are devices to make the Government more accountable and responsive to the people. And here we return again to the matter of concentrated power. Government may be accountable to the people, be subject to their control and yet not be very responsive to their desires because power is too fractionalized, is concentrated insufficiently to permit carrying out the people's wishes or meeting their needs.

This was the problem in Third and Fourth Republic France and, not infrequently, has seemed to be the problem in the United States—government has not been very responsive. In those French systems the voters decided who would represent them in the legislature. In the United States we decide this and, as well, who will be the chief executive. But given the normal diffusion of power in these systems, the electorate has not been able to decide who really is in charge. Therefore, it has been unable to know where to place the blame for failures or inaction. The result is a general malaise that, clearly in France, but perhaps also in the United States, lowers commitment to the political system.

In Britain the voters were thought to have the power to determine who would govern. And should they decide that the party currently entrusted with this power was doing a bad job, then at the next election they could sweep them from office and get a change in policy. No other rascals need be turned out, no other strongholds of power assaulted. The party in power had no excuse for failure because the domestic power structure contained no obstacles to thwart a Government from carrying out its program.

While this summary of the virtues that the British political system long has been thought to possess remains true to some extent, yet this picture increasingly has come to be recognized as highly idealized. The atrophy of the doctrine of ministerial responsibility has weakened the accountability of both the political leader and the top bureaucrat. The cautious attitude of the civil service militates against utilizing new methods and knowledge that may be essential to coping with contemporary problems. The device of the public corporation has not ensured properly the responsibility of nationalized industries to Parliament. Nor, despite British membership, does Parliament have effective control over the decisions taken in the European Economic Community.

Most grave of all, Parliament's ability to control the Cabinet is seriously in doubt. Cohesive parties do focus responsibility. But precisely because British parties are highly disciplined—unified in their Parliamentary voting with little crossing of party lines—the ability of Parliament to call the executive to account has declined considerably. To some extent the function of calling the executive to account has been thrown back upon the people, to be exercised only once every four or five years by those with only modest knowledge of and interest in politics, rather than being performed daily by the politically aware in Parliament, as was the case in the 19th century. During the 1970s, not only experts on politics but even average Britons increasingly came to feel that the activity of the House of Commons was neither effective nor very important.

Accountability and concentration of power can serve as useful themes in analyzing the French political system as well. The basic problem for much of the Third and Fourth Republics was diffused power. No single party could command a majority in Parliament. Often not even a coalition of parties could do so. Opposition similarly was fractionalized. Thus, although Governments often were defeated in the legislature, no alternative Government existed—that is, no majority party or group with alternative coherent policies existed. Political groups combined readily to oust a Government, but could not agree upon what should be done thereafter. The legislature was unable to formulate policies. Affairs drifted on until problems reached crisis proportions before the system was galvanized into brief action.

Instead of seeking accountability, one of the basic rules of the game in this political system was to avoid responsibility at all costs. De Gaulle was determined to transform this situation in the Fifth Republic. So successful was de Gaulle in bringing strong leadership to France that many people felt that the executive had become too dominant in the policy process. Such concerns hardly were unique to France. In the late 1960s and early 1970s a good deal was heard in the United States about an imperial presidency. We have noted previously that some students of the British political system believe that system is becoming presidential, that the prime minister overshadows the rest of the Government. Few would disagree, however, that during the decade 1958–68 de Gaulle dominated French government and politics far more than other democratic leaders did their countries' political system.

De Gaulle was not inclined to involve Parliament and the parties in the tasks of governing. People held positions of responsibility in the Government because they enjoyed his confidence, not because they represented powerful groups in parliament. In some ways his system resembled Germany under the Second Empire, a period that, as we have seen, did little to nurture the values essential to parliamentary democracy. De Gaulle was little interested in the political competition normal to a democracy; he refused to lead any political party. Often he seemed to be concerned only with lofty principles, expecting the administrative apparatus to devise the means of achieving them. The public seemed content to let him shoulder the nation's burdens and attempt to devise miraculous solutions for nearly insoluble problems. The opposition parties assailed de Gaulle but offered little in the way of coherent alternative programs.

The Fourth Republic, like the Third, was criticized for engendering popular apathy. People were unaware, or, worse, indifferent to political crises. De Gaulle's style of governing prevented the Fifth Republic from doing much to remedy this. Reliance on de Gaulle seems to have given people even less of a sense of participation and involvement in the political process. This continued under de Gaulle's successors. Politics aroused little interest because the possibility of change seemed so small; the same political forces had controlled the government for nearly a quarter of a century, and it appeared that they always would do so. An immediate result of the victory of Mitterrand and the Socialists was an upsurge of enthusiasm and interest in politics—along with not a little anxiety on the part of others—now that change clearly was possible. The people were not helpless; they could obtain a major shift, if they so desired. But when that change in partisan control of the Government failed to solve France's economic problems instantaneously, disillusion quickly set in. The French, looking for another messiah, felt they had been cheated.

De Gaulle's principal bequest to France was strong and stable executive leadership. As we explained, this may have been due not so much to changes in the government structure as to changes in the party system. These two clearly are intertwined, however. We pointed out that the results of the 1981 French legislative elections could be interpreted as the triumph of the institutions. The change in control of the levers of power in France has not been accompanied by a return to the political system of the Fourth Republic. The fractionalized party system that weakened the executive in the Fourth Republic has been avoided, and in President Mitterrand France has a person not content to be a political cipher. Thus while de Gaulle would not share some of Mitterrand's views—but remember de Gaulle was more nationalist than conservative, so the disagreement would not be as great as one might expect at first thought—the results of the 1981 elections might not worry him all that much. His political system has survived.

In Germany a dominant personality began to bring strong, stable leadership a decade earlier than in France. Konrad Adenauer, like de Gaulle, often was irritating and unlikable. Both were arrogant and high-handed. Despite their elite orientations, however, neither was an authoritarian at heart. Both were dedicated to molding their countries into strong, yet free, nations. Adenauer's domination of German democracy during its formative years was precisely the style of government that was needed. The belief that equated democracy with weak leadership, as had been true in the Weimar Republic, had to be laid to rest. As a paternalistic figure, Adenauer was attractive to many Germans, especially in a period of considerable economic and political uncertainty. When all else was in doubt, he provided a rock of stability. One could have democracy *and* a strong leader with a sense of purpose. Under Weimar the Germans had been forced to choose between these; under Bonn they could have both.

Germany's political achievements are not based on Adenauer's contribution alone, great as that may be. The Bonn Basic Law contains a more democratically attractive solution to the problem of excessive executive turnover than does that of the French Fifth Republic. The German executive is entrenched, but, unlike the French chief executive, remains responsible and accountable.

That Germany has departed further than has France from a fractionalized party system is even more significant. The concentration of political forces makes avoiding weak, deadlocked Governments easier. In contrast to Weimar the main parties no longer are narrow sectional organizations, but broad groupings of diverse interests. Ideology matters less in German politics today than it does in French. In France old conflicts and attitudes can continue to affect political behavior even when they have ceased to be very relevant to contemporary affairs. In Germany this is less likely to occur.

The assertion that initially was little more than whistling in the dark has become true beyond doubt—Bonn is not Weimar. The Weimar Republic lasted less than a decade and a half before being replaced by a monomaniac's nightmarish vision, which was highly attractive to many and terrified few. The Bonn Republic has lasted three times as long as Weimar.

Thus we see in Britain a political system many of whose traditionally claimed virtues seem more illusory than real; in France a political system of apparent, but not fully proven, durability that has purchased executive stability and leadership at the price of legislative inconsequence; and in Germany a well-rooted political system with a reasonable balance between executive and legislature but which is not very effective in legitimation because of its apparent aloofness from the citizens. Each of these systems has its virtues, each its defects. Each has lessons to teach Americans, but none provides a model to be copied in toto.

THE ECONOMIC DILEMMA

Whatever the defects and virtues of political systems on paper, their success depends, of course, upon how they actually function, how effective they are in coping with the problems nations face. Their policy output greatly influences citizens' ratings. Few can doubt that economic success is the overriding reason for the health of German democracy today. Within a generation Germany went from desolation to recovery to prosperity as one of the major economic powers of the world. Unlike Weimar, Bonn's problems of unemployment and inflation have not been excessive by the standard of other countries' current experience. The incredible inflation of Weimar, when restaurant meals literally changed in price while they were being eaten, has not been repeated. While Germany has had considerable outside help in recovering economically, its people rightly can feel that their industriousness and abilities were the major factor in rebuilding the country.

Had the Bonn Republic not been successful economically, commitment to the democratic political system would be considerably weaker. As we noted in Chapter 17, one of the reasons few people cared to defend the Weimar Republic from its attackers was its inability to deal with Germany's economic problems. Inflation, unemployment, and economic despair were so prevalent that people were ready for almost any change, thinking, incorrectly, that nothing could be worse than the situation in which they found themselves at the moment. Thus, the prosperity of Bonn created an opportunity for democracy to take root. Had things gone wrong economically, democracy never would have had a chance in contemporary Germany, despite all the efforts to draft a democratic constitution. The Weimar experience had demonstrated the futility of relying on legal defenses alone.

France, also, has done well economically since the end of World War II. Despite the Fourth Republic's political inadequacies, France made substantial economic gains during the 1950s. Had this not been true, the system probably would have collapsed even sooner than it did.

Under the Fifth Republic the economy did even better. France was converted to a belief in growth and material progress, to a commitment to efficiency and economic modernization. The stress which French leaders placed on these in the 1960s and 1970s resulted in a dramatic rise in industrial production and a mushrooming in the total value of exports. Rhetoric was supported by government-facilitated capital grants, tax exemptions, and interest rate subsidies. Unfortunately, the resulting surpluses in the French balance of trade were not used to reduce the gap between the rich and the poor, which remained larger in France than in most Western industrialized nations. The unemployed and older civil servants were the principal sufferers.

While France and Germany strengthened their economies, Britain did not. After being told by Prime Minister Macmillan in 1959 that they never had had it so good (which was more true than Harold Wilson's response that they never had been had so good), Britain experienced a couple of decades of economic stagnation or even regression. Speculating about what difference the prosperity of Germany or France would have made to Britain is interesting. We have evaluated the British political system more qualifiedly, more guardedly than do traditional writers. Almost all of Britain's problems and danger points, the dissatisfaction and anxieties of her citizens, can be traced to a malfunctioning economy. Had Britain, like Germany, had an economic miracle, we could have repeated unhesitatingly the traditional praise of its political system. The impact of Britain's poor economic record has required us to be as concerned to point out political shortcomings as to identify political virtues.

When in the 1970s OPEC oil countries escalated the price of an essential energy resource, all Western industrial powers experienced soaring inflation. At one point in Britain the rate surpassed 20 percent a year. The feeling began to grow that neither a Labour nor a Conservative Government could do anything to solve Britain's economic problems and halt inflation. Many people began to wonder whether interest groups had attained such positions of influence in the British political process that controlling wage demands of the trade unions had become impossible. Government, Parliament, parties—all appeared to many Britons to be ineffective. Given their traditional positive attitudes toward their political system, we hesitate to assert that sizable numbers of Britons became alienated politically. Nonetheless, disenchantment certainly was widespread. The discontents generated by current political issues contributed to this negative mood.

Conditions were not as bad in Britain as they might have been, however, because at this time the country was developing its gas and oil reserves in the North Sea. This energy bonus, whose existence hadn't even been known not too many years earlier, meant that the British economy was not battered by the rapidly rising petroleum prices of the 1970s. By 1980 Britain was able to produce virtually all of the oil it needed and the great bulk of the gas. France and Germany lacked such resources. As a result the English disease proved to be contagious—both these countries came to experience what the British had lived with for two decades. Growth and productivity rates fell; declining tax revenues forced public spending cuts; inflation worsened, although never reaching the rates it had in Britain.

Something, of course, had to be done. It appeared, however, that Western democracies were caught in a cruel dilemma—the trade-off for lower rates of inflation was higher rates of unemployment, rates every bit as intolerable as the level of inflation had been. In Britain unemployment began to rival what it had been during the worldwide depression of the 1930s in numbers of people out of work, if not in percent of the work force lacking jobs. The scars over the deep wounds the 1930s experience had inflicted were reopened and, having been reinfected, began to fester once more. By the mid-1980s more than 3.3 million were out of work in Britain. In France the number climbed past 2 million, while in Germany it surpassed 2.6 million.

Tied up with the unemployment problem—in terms of demagoguery, if not reality—is the status in these three countries of various minorities, racial, religious, and ethnic. In discussing tolerance in Britain we mentioned the hostility that has developed to immigration by West Indians, Pakistanis, and Indians. As unemployment worsened, urban riots broke out in several British cities and continued night after night. White youths attacked blacks and Asians; Asian youths mobilized in aggressive self-defense. Black youths fought with police in anger at constantly being suspected of petty thefts. Looting and vandalism made some streets look as they had during the German bombing of England in World War II.

Some favored respressive steps. But others felt these dealt more with symptoms than causes. Former Prime Minister Edward Heath criticized his own Conservative party's Government, saying, "If you have half a million young people hanging around on the streets all day you will have a massive increase in juvenile crime. Of course you will get racial tension when you have young blacks with less chance of getting jobs." In his view the problem was that the British people "lack any indication of whether there is any better sort of life for them at the end of these incomprehensible [economic] policies" being pursued by the Thatcher Government.

As we noted in the German section, the country experienced labor shortages, particularly in the lower-paid, more menial occupations, as its economy expanded in the 1960s. Thus immigrants willing to clean the streets, dig graves, collect garbage, and perform other manual tasks at cheap wages were welcome. The typical *gastarbeiter* (guest worker) was an Italian, Yugoslav, or, especially, a Turk. Turks, as they began to be joined by their dependents, became the largest group of foreigners in Germany at 1.5 million. Although Germany stopped recruiting guest workers outside EEC countries in 1973, their numbers remain significant—about 10 percent of the entire German work force and about 20 percent of all manual workers.

Most of these workers are covered by government health and pension programs, but they cannot vote. Although they are intended to be only temporary residents, many have brought their families to join them. Thus they are producing a second generation of immigrant workers, whose social, economic, and political integration is a problem, especially in a time of economic contraction.

In France, for the same reasons as in Germany, the pattern was similar except that the immigrant workers came mainly from North Africa (especially Algeria), Portugal, Spain, and Italy, and made up a slightly small segment of the work force. We noted how in France the leader of the Gaullist party began in the mid-1980s to compete with a neofascist party for the anti-immigrant vote. Such maneuvers have not been limited to that end of the political spectrum, however. During the 1981 elections the leader of the Communist party, Georges Marchais, advocated action to protect the jobs of French workers from immigrants in terms that certainly were provincial, if not outright racist. Apparently, regardless of what Marx said, not all workers are brothers.

Thus in all three countries animosity toward people of different customs, language, and color is having a political impact. The level of popular concern may well be highest in Germany. Gallup asked people in all three countries how they regarded certain characteristics of the country in getting ready for the coming years.[1] In all three, only about a quarter of the respondents saw immigrant workers as a strength. In Britain half and in France a bit more regarded them as a weakness. In Germany 70 percent so labeled the *gastarbeiter*. (Interestingly, Americans responded to this question virtually the same way as did Germans. So you would do well not to denounce them for intolerance.) Another poll found that two thirds of the Germans want the immigrant workers to go home and 90 percent want them to be banned from bringing their dependents to Germany. A so-called National Democratic party is seeking political support on the basis of opposition to immigration.

To blame immigrant workers for unemployment is incorrect, totally apart from the point that France, Germany, and Britain deliberately recruited them in the first place. The problem is that Europe has not developed a job market in new technological areas as well as have the United States and Japan. From the mid-1970s to the mid-1980s total employment fell in Europe by 3 million—new jobs aren't being created. But what has affected the thinking of many workers is the fact that 1984 was the 12th straight year in which unemployment had increased in Europe.

The typical responses of many left-of-center parties to high unemployment are policies that can be called vulgar Keynesianism—that is, ever higher government spending to stimulate the economy and create jobs. Ever-expanding government means, of course, expanding taxes. In the 24 OECD countries taxes averaged 27 percent of gross domestic product (GDP) in 1965, grew to 32 percent in 1974, and reached 37 percent in 1982. While Americans may think they are highly taxed, this is not so, relatively speaking. The share of GDP going to taxes in the United States was only 31 percent in 1982. Germany was right at the OECD average, while in Britain taxes took 40 percent of GDP and in France 44 percent. Such high taxes tend to mean that profit margins are small and businesses have little to invest to stimulate the economy and produce new jobs.

So what has been the political impact of the developments we have been discussing? In 1979 the Conservatives under Margaret Thatcher drove Labour from office in Britain. The next year in the United States Ronald Reagan drove Jimmy Carter out of office. In 1983 the Christian Democrats won confirmation

---

[1]*Gallup Political Index,* No. 285 (May 1984), p. 39.

of their recent snatching of power, while the SPD suffered its worse defeat in nearly a quarter of a century. A few months later Thatcher was reconfirmed in office, while Labour collapsed to its worse performance in three quarters of a century. In 1984 Reagan was reconfirmed in office with a larger electoral vote than any previous candidate had obtained.

The only exception to all this would appear to be France, with Mitterrand's victory in 1981 quickly followed by the Socialists' triumph in the legislative elections. But within a year this supposed reform Government was enacting economic policies as conservative as those of its predecessor, the right-wing parties were doing well in local elections, and the Socialists were anticipating a disaster in the 1986 legislative elections.

Thus the electorate in major Western democracies seems to have made a decisive swing to the right. And yet there is little real sentiment for an end to the welfare state. Asked whether, in order to give their country a better chance to be among the countries that count in the world 30 years from now, they would be content with less social benefits, only 7 percent of the French consented, 12 percent of the Germans, and 15 percent of the British.[2] (Americans were more willing to make such a sacrifice, but even in the United States only a third would do so.) And that, of course, is the problem. People want lower taxes, but they also want a full range of public services and benefits. They expect the government to see that anyone who wants a job can find one and that at the same time inflation is kept at a moderate rate. Since no one knows how to do all this, dissatisfaction is common in all these countries.

THE MARXIST ALTERNATIVE

The failure of democratic governments to solve their countries' economic problems provides greater credibility to alternative, radical solutions. When prices no longer respond to changes in supply and demand in the way we have come to expect, when economic growth stagnates at the same time as inflation soars, when unemployment and inflation rise together, then prevailing economic knowledge appears to be in error. The appeals of parties advocating extensive government ownership and control of the economy come to seem worth closer examination.

Democratic political systems originated and developed at a time when the free enterprise economic system was flourishing. Then few people were attracted to a political philosophy that advocated complete government control of the economy. But the role of government in democracies has changed considerably in the 20th century. A century ago governments gave little priority to public policies providing direct services to individuals; today governments spend 30 to 45 percent of their countries' Gross National Product. Furthermore, governments found that relying on Adam Smith's unseen hand to regulate the economy

---

[2]Ibid.

was too costly; economic problems such as unemployment, inflation, and balance of international trade required government action. Thus today fiscal policy is not just a matter of raising enough taxes to pay for government expenditures; the problem differs from that faced by Charles I in Britain and Louis XIV in France. Fiscal policy is a tool for regulating the economy, along with monetary policy, which involves interest rates and money supply. Democratic governments not only intervene in the economy through these measures, but also often own and operate various economic enterprises ranging from railroads (fairly common) to the manufacture of matches (unique to France).

Thus whereas a century ago communist economic doctrine seemed totally different from prevailing capitalistic practice, now, to some, it seems to be a matter merely of going a bit farther in a direction already embarked upon. But if communism was to have any hope of appealing to people in West European democracies it would have to jettison the rigidities of the Soviet system. It would have to reject violence as a means of obtaining power, accept competition among various parties, and relinquish office if voted out of power. Thus whatever its economic policies, it would have to accept political democracy.

The attempt of West European communist parties to make these changes in their doctrines and policies was called *Eurocommunism,* a term first used by a Yugoslav journalist. This is fitting since it was the Yugoslav leader Marshal Josip Tito who gave the first practical demonstration of alternate forms of communism. Tito was expelled from the Cominform, the international communist organization, in June 1948 for refusing to accept the Soviet Union as the model for political and economic development. While Tito certainly was building a communist state in Yugoslavia, he wanted to do it in his own way. Thus, in essence, he was denying that the leaders of the Soviet Union were entitled to be the sole interpreters of Marxist ideology and how it should be implemented in practice.

In June 1956 Palmiro Togliatti, the leader of the Italian Communist party, said, "The Soviet model should no longer be obligatory. . . the complex of the system is becoming polycentric, and in the communist movement itself one can no longer speak of a single guide."[3] This was the origin of the doctrine of polycentrism—the true parent (although it is an Italian idea, we resist calling it the godfather) of Eurocommunism.

Togliatti did not want to abandon Marx, because he felt that Marx's analysis, despite its age, remained basically correct. Class struggle and exploitation continued to be useful concepts in understanding the political process. But Marx, who, after all, wrote *The Communist Manifesto* almost a quarter of a century before Italy was unified into a single nation, could offer little guidance for specific policies in Togliatti's Italy. Furthermore, since few, if any, of the leaders of the Soviet Union had been in Italy or had much knowledge of the political and economic situation there, their advice on practical implementation of commu-

---

[3]Quoted in Stanley Henig and John Pinder, eds., *European Political Parties* (London: Allen & Unwin, 1969), p. 206, n. 1.

nist doctrine was of little worth. Thus they must permit the PCI to decide for itself how best to pursue the goals of communism in Italy.

That Togliatti should have been the one to develop and propagate such a doctrine is surprising. During the period of Fascist control of Italy he had lived in exile in the Soviet Union, returning home in the spring of 1944 to build the PCI into a major postwar political force. He had been one of the early leaders of the Comintern. And in 1949 he condemned Tito. Immediately after World War II the PCI was regarded widely as perhaps the most extreme communist party in Western Europe. It was well armed from helping to drive the Nazis from Italy during the war and many thought in the late 1940s that it might try to seize control of the government by force. In 1956 it approved the Soviet Union's crushing of the Hungarians' revolt against their communist government. Nonetheless, even a party such as this soon began to want to run its own affairs without instructions, to say nothing of control, from Moscow.

Diversity within international communism posed a number of contrasting challenges. It challenged electorates in Western Europe to assess whether communist parties truly supported democracy. It challenged the parties themselves to demonstrate that they could revise their political and economic doctrines, and democratize their party power structures. It challenged the foreign and defense policies of the West, for should these changes be only cosmetic, should they be only a trick, being taken in by them could have serious, perhaps fatal, consequences. It also challenged the Soviet Union and its allies for if West European communist parties really were becoming committed to Western democracy, then the Soviet Union would lose its most loyal supporters in these countries. Indeed, as we pointed out in Chapter 12, the French Communists shifted from defending the actions of the Soviet Union at home and abroad to criticizing it, particularly treatment of political dissidents and intervention in other communist countries. The ultimate challenge of diversity to the Soviet Union was that it might prove contagious and infect Soviet satellite states in Eastern Europe. Thus all the European gains for communism might be lost. These were the challenges posed by Eurocommunism.

The French Communists were the least willing to accept Eurocommunism. The Italian Communists, a larger party than the French, under Enrico Berlinguer, and the Spanish Communists, a smaller party than the French, under Santiago Carrillo, were the driving forces for Eurocommunism in the late 1970s. However reluctantly and for whatever reasons, as we discussed in Chapter 12, the French Communists eventually did profess to accept Eurocommunism. But like many repentant sinners, the PCF proved to be a backslider. Although the party claimed to reject any model of communism that does not support national autonomy, democracy, and the absence of monopoly power by any party, yet it was less willing than it had been a few years earlier to cooperate with the French Socialists or with the Italian and Spanish Communists. Furthermore, it returned to defending the international actions of the Soviet Union, as with the invasion and occupation of Afghanistan in 1979–80.

So why did President Mitterrand give 4 of the 44 positions in his second Government to Communists?[4] The Socialists had a working majority in the National Assembly and did not need Communist votes to keep their prime minister in office; as for President Mitterrand himself, the National Assembly cannot vote him out. The Communists were admitted to the Government only after accepting a detailed agreement. They pledged "flawless" support for the Socialists' two-year plan to reduce unemployment and expand productivity, not only in Parliament, but also at the local level and in factories themselves. They limited their demands for government ownership to those industrial groups which the Socialists already had planned to take over. As for foreign policy the Communists were forced to sign a Government declaration calling for Soviet withdrawal from Afghanistan and supporting a balance of forces in Europe, which is to say that the new NATO medium-range nuclear missiles are needed. The Communists even had to accept the Socialists' position that the Soviet Union should stay out of the internal affairs of Poland. Thus, by including Communists in his Government, Mitterrand had demonstrated that he could make them jump through the hoops. A further advantage was that the agreement would help to prevent the Communists from trying to stir up troubles for the Government with the trade unions.

But what was the price for this? Not very great. The three ministries—transportation, health, and job training—had nothing to do with French security—internal or external—or foreign policy. The latter ministry, in fact, did not even exist until the second Government was formed. The fourth position given to the Communists was minister delegate to the prime minister (a second-level Government position) for civil service and administrative reforms. In the first Government this had been a third-level Government post. Furthermore, it was not an independent ministry, but an office responsible to the prime minister. These were not exactly the power bases from which one stages a coup against a government.

By way of comparison, the last time (1947) that Communists held positions in the French Government, at a time when the party was much stronger than in 1981, it had the position of vice premier plus four ministries, including defense. (Mitterrand was a minister in that Government.) The Communists did not subvert French democracy then, nor could they do so in the 1980s. As for the possibility that Communist ministers might have access to top secret material, the French foreign minister explained, "The structure of our government is like that of a big company. The messenger boy is not informed of what the management is up to." Eventually the company found that it didn't even need a messenger boy—when Fabius became Prime Minister in 1984 the Communists left the

---

[4]The first Government that Prime Minister Pierre Mauroy formed for Mitterrand was only a one-month interim one lasting from Mitterrand's assumption of office until the legislative elections. Following those elections a new Government was formed that made a few other changes in addition to admitting Communists for the first time.

Government because they were unable to block the economic policies he intended to implement.

Even the renovated Marxism of Eurocommunism has had little appeal to the electorates in France, Germany, and Britain. In so far as the left has raised a serious challenge in these countries it has come from the antimissile peace movement. Hundreds of thousands of Germans have turned out to demonstrate against the placement of cruise and Pershing 2 nuclear missiles in their country. And a handful of terrorists have engaged in a few bombings. Most significant, the SPD now opposes the missiles. Yet Kohl's Government seems to have lost little support for firmly accepting the missiles.

In Britain the Campaign for Nuclear Disarmament once again is able to mobilize large demonstrations as it did in the 1960s. Labour has opposed not only the siting of U.S. missiles in Britain as part of NATO's defense effort, but also wants Britain to give up its nuclear weapons regardless of whether it can obtain any concession from the Soviet Union in return. Yet here again the Government's popularity seems to have been little affected by the missile issue.

As for France, Mitterrand and the Socialists are committed to nuclear weapons as staunchly as are the more conservative Governments of Britain and Germany. De Gaulle developed a *force de frappe,* a nuclear striking force, independent of any controls by other countries as a matter of national pride. Mitterrand has not hesitated to maintain this force. The U.S./NATO missile issue does not arise in France, since the country has remained outside the alliance's military command (although still an adherent to the treaty) ever since de Gaulle took it out to demonstrate national independence. But were such missiles to be located in France, few demonstrations would be likely. In France few people raise any objections to nuclear weapons.

SYMBOL, SUBSTANCE, AND INSTITUTIONALIZATION

Thus economic policy affects popular attitudes toward government much more than does foreign policy. One exception to this should be noted, however. In April 1982 Argentina invaded the Falkland Islands, a British possession, off its coast in the south Atlantic. Despite the incredible logistics problems involved, Margaret Thatcher immediately sent a naval task force to recapture the Falklands. When this action quickly succeeded in defeating Argentina with modest British casualties, Thatcher's popularity soared and Britons had a new sense of pride and self-confidence—it was like the old days of the Empire when much of the map was red. The feeling was like that which many Americans had as President Reagan proclaimed that America was back and standing tall. The Falklands factor was one element in Thatcher's reelection triumph.

That is to say that analysis of popular attitudes toward government must take account of symbolic gratifications as well as substantive output. Furthermore, this chapter has concentrated mainly on current problem areas. We have not looked at other areas where the record is better—the unquestionably significant rise in living standards and the provision of health care and welfare benefits, for example. Nor have we been able to provide a historical dimension by looking at successful processing of policy problems over some period of time. Thus we should conclude on a rather more positive note with a few comments about the institutional structure of these countries apart from any specific policy difficulties of the moment.

British political structures are highly institutionalized and durable. Although tradition is immensely important in the British system, the system is neither rigid nor brittle. The British have shown great talent in adapting old institutions to new functions, in shifting power and reforming society in generally acceptable, nondislocative ways. They have demonstrated knowledge that one who wants to retain the legitimacy of a political system must recognize that limits exist to the role of rationality in politics. It is wiser, although intellectually less satisfying, to allow for sentiment and tradition by means of piecemeal reform than to implement major structural changes recommended mainly by their abstract intellectual brilliance and the demands of some that all problems must be solved at once.

While the British have not solved their past fundamental political problems at a single stroke with an elaborate logical plan, they have evolved piecemeal responses tested by experience. This approach frustrates the impatient and frightens the anxious, but it has proven to be extremely successful. It would be a rash person who would argue now that this procedure should be abandoned as ineffective. The British genius for adaptability has not run out.

As for France, more than most countries, it seems always to be either on the verge of a crisis or at some major fork in the road. The Fifth Republic has coped with a number of the country's basic problems. In some instances these seem to have been disposed of permanently, but in other instances the solution may be only temporary. The current system of government continues the administrative tradition of strong executive rule. But France's competing tradition of Assembly government also has a long history. The Mitterrand Government has a chance to redress the balance somewhat toward that latter tradition without abandoning the positive institutional reforms of the Fifth Republic. In so doing and by showing that the system does allow for change in the wielders of political power, it can give France the durable, widely accepted as legitimate, political system that it so long has lacked.

The high expectations aroused by the Weimar Republic and the deep revulsion produced by what followed it have made many people cautious in their evaluation of the Bonn Basic Law and the current German political system. Nonetheless, Germany clearly has made a success of the Bonn Republic. Policy problems remain, of course, but democracy has taken root and a new political tradition of supportive values is being created.

Responses to a Gallup poll question help to make the point of these comments. People were asked how they felt about their country's political institutions in getting the country ready for the coming years. In Germany 57 percent regarded these institutions as a strength and little more than a third felt they were a weakness. In Britain nearly as many—51 percent—regarded them as a strength and only a quarter felt them to be a weakness. But in France only a third saw them as a strength and close to half—45 percent—believed they were a weakness. The net balance is slightly more positive in Britain than in Germany, while in France the Fifth Republic, despite its achievements, still does not seem firmly institutionalized.

These three major European democracies vary from each other in many respects. Yet all of them are alike fundamentally in being democracies. However the principle may be qualified in practice, in each of them the governing political power is responsible to the people. Those who wish to control that power both can and must compete for it openly, with the electorate deciding to whom the victory goes. Each system has its inadequacies and shortcomings, but, nonetheless, more often than not lives up to its ideals. This situation contrasts sharply with that prevailing in the Soviet Union. Our analysis of the Soviet Union in the final part of this book should help to clarify the fundamental differences between that system and democracies and, by showing how communism operates in practice, provide a basis for evaluating that policy alternative.

BIBLIOGRAPHICAL NOTE

The last couple of decades have seen an outpouring of doom-and-gloom literature about the British political system. For an unemotional, informed discussion of Britain's policy problems, see William Gwyn and Richard Rose, eds., *Britain: Progress and Decline* (New Orleans: Tulane University Press, 1980). Lest you think that nothing ever changes in Britain, see Frank Stacey, *British Government 1966-1975: Years of Reform* (Oxford: Oxford University Press, 1975), for a discussion of the many reforms implemented and attempted. Jock Bruce-Gardyne and Nigel Lawson, *The Power Game* (London: Macmillan, 1976), provides case studies of a few policy decisions, along with a final chapter offering a good overview of the distribution of power in the British system.

Two recent studies of comparative public policy in Europe are Charles Andrain, *Politics and Economic Policy in Western Democracies* (North Scituate, Mass.: Duxbury Press, 1980), and *European Politics: Political Economy and Policy Making in Western Democracies* (New York: St. Martin's Press, 1980). For a comparative study of the effect of government's growth on effectiveness and consent, see Richard Rose, *Understanding Big Government: The Programme Approach* (London: Sage Publications, 1984).

A good deal has been written in the last few years about Eurocommunism. Useful titles include the following ones: Neil McInnes, *Euro-Communism, The Washington Papers,* vol. 4, no. 37 (Beverly Hills and London: Sage Publications, 1976); Roy Godson and Stephen Haseler, *"Eurocommunism": Implications for East and West* (New York: St. Martin's Press, 1978); Bernard Brown, ed., *Eurocommunism and Eurosocialism: The left Confronts Modernity* (New York: Cyrco Press, 1979); David Childs, *Eurocommunism, Origins, Problems, and Perspectives* (London: Croom Helm, 1980).

26

Europe as a Community

In the previous chapter we compared and contrasted the three largest nations in Western Europe, stressing their basic similarities as democracies despite their many political and institutional differences. While this explicitly comparative treatment differed from the country-by-country approach that we used in the previous parts of this book, we still examined the countries as separate governmental systems. Before contrasting these countries with the Soviet Union, we need to devote some time to thinking about European countries collectively—as an *international* political system.

This is essential because one of the most remarkable achievements of European democracies in the last quarter of a century is their development of cross-national ties going well beyond mere ad hoc cooperation or even traditional alliances. Not only is this accomplishment significant in itself, but it also tells us a great deal about the adaptability of the West European democracies and their ability to respond to problems even when such responses require freeing themselves from the dead hand of history to set off in new directions. This chapter considers Europe as a community by discussing the organization popularly known as the EEC (European Economic Community) or the Common Market.

THE GENESIS OF UNITY

Throughout history many wars have been fought across large geographical areas; however, most have *not* been global conflicts. This is because during most of human history people in one part of the world were not aware that other people existed in another part of the world. Even when they learned of such people, they lacked the logistic ability to transport and supply sizable armies across oceans. In modern times (that is, post-Renaissance) the growth of technology and, even more important, of bureaucratic structures—which made possible systematic taxation and administration—began to greatly increase the scope and destructive capacity of war.

In 1618 a rebellion in Bohemia led to a religious and political struggle that quickly spread to involve all of Europe. The next 30 years saw a series of wars. The Germanic areas of central Europe, the principal battleground, were so devastated that some scholars estimate the population was reduced by more than half. The next half century produced only a variety of local wars, none of which involved all of Europe.

But the first decade and a half of the 18th century had to endure the war of the Spanish Succession, a conflict that was even more wide-spread than the Thirty Years' War had been, since fighting erupted in North America as well as in Europe. This international dimension was even more prevalent in a later conflict in the second half of the century. The Seven Years' War (from 1756 to 1763) was international in scope because it determined whether the British or the French would be the chief colonial power in North America and India.

Although the destructive capacity and geographical scope of war were expanding drastically, conflict remained limited in some senses. Battles tended to be fought by relatively small armies of professionals, men who made a career out of military service. Since men with the requisite skills and experience were hard to find, commanders often tried to avoid battle so as not to squander scarce manpower. Thus wars frequently were as much matters of maneuver as they were of combat. As for the citizens, provided that they were not so unlucky as to happen to be in the path of an army, they could live largely in disregard of any war their country happened to be fighting.

All this changed with the Napoleonic wars at the start of the 19th century. Armies were now composed of the population at large. With the mobilization of the citizen-soldier vast military forces were called into being and death and destruction reached new heights. With the defeat of Napoleon at Waterloo the wars for the rest of the 19th century remained relatively limited despite the rapid growth of industrial and technological development. The American Civil War provided extensive evidence of how total war had become, but this conflict was geographically limited.

In 1914 conflict in the Balkans spread—rather like the Thirty Years' War three centuries earlier—throughout Europe in a conflict eventually known to history as World War I. The fighting spilled over from Europe into Asia Minor and the Middle East; the combatants included troops from North America and the South Pacific; and an Asian nation—Japan—was one of the belligerents. And just over 20 years after this international conflict ended, another conflagration truly enveloped the entire world with fighting not only in Europe but also in Asia and Africa. This, the most destructive and wide-spread conflict in history, well merited the label World War II.

This brief historical summary may seem to be rather provincial in globe terms—the focus is clearly upon Europe, as though European countries and peoples are the only ones that have mattered. But the reason for this focus is that the principal conflicts of the last three centuries—especially those of the current century—have tended to be between European nations and increasingly have tended to spread from Europe to encompass a global battleground. Many of the political leaders of Europe were haunted by this knowledge as they surveyed in 1945 the ruins of their continent—cities in rubble, millions of homeless refugees, obliterated industry. The problems of Western Europe which we discussed in the previous chapter were as nothing compared to those of 1945, a time when few could envision how the masses of Europe would be able to obtain the food, clothing, and shelter they needed for survival and a time when the victorious countries were almost as badly off as were the vanquished.

The political leaders of Europe saw all this and vowed that it would never happen again. For the first time they perceived the past three centuries of international conflict as a *civil war,* as battles occurring *within* a single political unit: Europe. Of course, Europe was not really a single political unit, but their idea was to make it such. They felt that the national rivalries that had produced three centuries of intermittent warfare which, increasingly, tended to spread throughout the world, could no longer be tolerated. The rivalry which they regarded as most pernicious was that between France and Germany—three times (1870, 1914, and 1939) in less than a century these nations had fought each other. The only solution appeared to be to bind the economies of these two rivals so closely together that it would be impossible for them to fight each other again. And it was this that the political leaders of Western Europe set out to do as they rebuilt their continent in the middle of the 20th century.

Thus it was that common disasters and common fears galvanized European political leaders. Yet they also shared common ideals, sought positive goals. They saw European union as a desirable goal in itself for they felt it could provide a new political faith to replace discredited nationalism and might well also counteract the strong appeal which Communism exerted in Western Europe immediately after World War II. They also saw European union as a means of revitalizing European culture and thus of resisting the cultural (that is to say the uncultured) pressure of the United States. Some would also argue that many of these key leaders also shared a religious faith. Christian Democracy was at its zenith as a political movement in the immediate postwar period. At times the foreign ministers of the six countries most fully involved in working for union all shared a Catholic background.

The roll call of the key leaders in this process is extensive, but if any one person deserves to be called the founder of European unity it is Jean Monnet (pronounced as though it were spelled John Mo nay). Monnet was a French bureaucrat who also had been an international civil servant. While he is often thought of as an idealist and a visionary, he was also a practical man of affairs who gave European unity a concrete beginning.

In May 1948, 750 delegates from many European countries had met to discuss union. They founded the European Movement and passed many resolutions, which, a year later, led to 10 countries creating the Council of Europe. This apparent success, however, did little more than point out the fundamental division which existed between those interested in uniting Europe. On the one hand there were those—mainly the British, the Swiss, and the Scandinavians—who favored a cooperative approach. Union would be limited to a few unessential functions. While consultation between nations was expected to be regular, decisions would be taken only by unanimous vote and even then would not be binding. No organization would be created to implement, to say nothing of enforce, decisions. Opposed to this was the supranational approach, which was willing to pool sovereignty, thus limiting national independence to some extent. The new postwar constitutions of France, Germany, and Italy all specifically provided for such national limitation in order to further European unity. Under this approach supranational organs wielding some independent power would be created. In other words, union was seen as a first step toward a United States of Europe, to develop eventually into a federal system. Thus just as the United States is composed of many states with certain powers plus a central government with independent powers, so a single political system would come to exist in Europe composed of such states as France, Germany, and others along with a separate central government.

The supranationalists quickly became disillusioned with the Council of Europe. While it provided a handy forum for cross-national contacts and discussions, it produced little action. The supranationalists decided that a new beginning was necessary. Despite being idealistic, they were sufficiently realistic to recognize that centuries of separate development made complete union of European nations impossible—the conflicts of the past, the different languages and customs, and the diverse political structures simply would not allow the creation of a single nation. Instead they opted for a strategy which became known as functional federalism—union would be sought on a limited sector-by-sector or function-by-function basis.

In 1950 the French Foreign Minister Robert Schuman called for the pooling of all European coal and steel markets into one single market. All existing national tariffs and quotas would be eliminated, as would be cartels and price-fixing. Here was a plan that might hope to merge key French and German industrial capacity so that military conflict between them would be unlikely. While this proposal was known as the Schuman Plan, the person who actually formulated it was Monnet. Only five other countries—Germany, Italy, the Netherlands, Belgium, and Luxembourg—were willing to join with France in this merger. Thus in 1952 they established the European Coal and Steel Community (ECSC). The key aspect of this agreement was that the ECSC would have a supranational structure—although only to a limited extent the members had agreed, nonetheless, to limit their national sovereignty. An executive body (called the High Authority, and presided over by Monnet as the first ECSC

President) was set up to administer the agreement, a parliament (the Assembly) was created mainly as a forum for consultative discussion, and a Court of Justice was empowered to settle disputes over the implementing of the agreement.

In March 1957 the process of functional federalism was carried much further as treaties were signed in Rome by the six members of the ECSC to create two new communities, the European Atomic Energy Community (Euratom) and the European Economic Community (Common Market). By the end of that year the governments of all six countries had ratified the treaties and the organizations began to function in the beginning of 1958. While the three communities originally had distinct executive bodies (since the powers varied from one organization to the other) eventually they were merged into a single executive. The three communities became a single European Community.

The British regarded all this as impractical nonsense. Talk and some cooperation was fine, but nations had diverged too greatly over the centuries to be able to pool sovereignty even to a limited degree. Furthermore, the British traditionally had held aloof from the continent, getting involved in European affairs only when necessary to preserve a balance of power—to prevent any one country from being predominant. And finally, the British felt that France, Germany, and Italy were unreliable—they were unstable political systems with little, or at best dubious, commitment to democracy. In short, union was, as the British would put it, a nonstarter.

But while the British could disdain the ECSC, treating the Common Market in the same way was risky. The key policy of the EEC was to eliminate all internal trade barriers—those between members—but to constuct a common barrier against nonmembers. Thus, should the Common Market by sheer good fortune just happen to succeed, Britain would be looking in from the outside with its nose pressed against the window. It could well be cut off from a major market for its products if the EEC's external tariff hampered British businesses from competing with goods produced by enterprises within the EEC. Clearly, some alternative had to be devised to ensure that Britain had a market, for only if it could sell manufactured goods abroad in volume could it afford to import the food and raw materials that it lacked at home.

Therefore, Britain decided to form its own trade organization, but one lacking any hint of the EEC's supranationalism. The result was the European Free Trade Assocation (EFTA) composed of Britain and six other countries on the periphery of the EEC. Launched in 1960, EFTA sought to remove trade barriers between its members, but to do so entirely by voluntary cooperation. EFTA lacked the elaborate structure of the European Communities—no consultative assembly, no court to settle disputes, and, most important, no supranational executive. The governing body simply provided a means for regular meetings of representatives from the member governments to discuss trade policy and other relevant matters.

While EFTA was intended to link at least some European countries to Britain and keep it from being left in the lurch should any EEC success entice others to think of joining the six countries in the Common Market, Britain itself tried to jump ship when HMS EFTA had hardly left port. Only about a year after EFTA had begun to function Britain opened negotiations with the EEC for membership. Naturally, the British always had assumed that if and whenever they decided to cast their lot with the EEC they would be welcomed with open arms—it would not even be a matter of the prodigal having arrived home, but of the messiah having arrived to show his people the true way into the future. Little did they count on the hostility of President de Gaulle of France.

Once France had fallen to the Nazis in World War II, de Gaulle had been given a base of operation in London and had been consulted regularly throughout the struggle to free Europe. But there is no loathing like that produced by being forced to accept charity, especially when the recipient is ordinately proud. De Gaulle now saw an opportunity to spite the British. Therefore in January 1963 de Gaulle proclaimed that France would block Britain from membership because it was insufficiently European. As often was true of de Gaulle's high-handed actions, this charge was not totally imaginary. As already explained Britain's traditional policy had been to remain as aloof as possible from continental affairs. It did regard itself as being more advanced politically than were the nations of the continent. And it did feel that it possessed a special relationship with the United States that the other nations lacked. De Gaulle's dislike of the United States was even greater than his dislike of Britain and he was not about to allow a British Trojan horse into the EEC to permit U.S. influence over its operation.

In 1967 Britain once again applied for membership and once again the following year de Gaulle said no. Eventually de Gaulle died and Britain tried once more, this time succeeding. Thus at the start of 1973 Britain, along with Denmark and Ireland, joined the EEC.

Greece, which had been an associate of the EEC for some years became a full member in 1981. The European Community expanded again in 1986 to include Spain and Portugal, thus becoming an organization of 12 nations and 320 million people—double its original size. Thus the movement for European unity clearly has proved viable, yet this success has been achieved only by departing from the original vision of its founders, as will become clear in the next section.

COMMUNITY INSTITUTIONS

The European Community's structure is composed of four principal institutions. The Commission is headquartered in Brussels, Belgium, the Council of Ministers in Luxembourg, and the Court of Justice in Strasbourg, France. As for the European Parliament, while it holds a plenary session in Strasbourg about once a month, its committees meet in Brussels, and its staff is located in Luxembourg. Yes, that is a ridiculous arrangement, but everybody wanted to be sure that they got their share of the money to be spent locally to accommodate the various insititutions.

The Commission has 14 members—two each from the four largest countries and one from each of the other six. (These figures and those mentioned elsewhere in this section are as of the end of 1985. The accession of Spain and Portugal to the Community in 1986 increased the numbers.) Commissioners serve four-year simultaneous terms, but may be reappointed. While the presiding officer technically is merely president of the Commission, he sometimes is referred to as president of the European Community. All of the Commissioners, including the president, are appointed by general consent of the member states. While all must agree on these appointments, the established practice is to allow each country to designate whomever they wish to fill their position(s) on the Commission. Nonetheless, once appointed, commissioners are supposed to be independent of their country and to seek the general welfare of the Community as a whole. Thus the Commission is intended to be a Community institution.

In contrast to this is the Council of Ministers, which is intended to represent the member state governments, each of which is given one representative. In a sense the Council is not so much a single institution as it is a collection of separate bodies. Depending upon the subject to be discusssed, various groups of specialist ministers from each of the member states meet. The most important such gathering is that of the foreign ministers from each nation, since they are empowered to act on any subject. Given the nature of membership in these various groups, members of the Council of Ministers have no fixed term and change whenever their governments wish to send someone else. Related to the Council is Coreper, the meeting of ambassadors to the European Community from each of the member states. These ambassadors also serve at the pleasure of their home government.

Perhaps the most visible, but the least powerful of the Community's institutions is the European Parliament. Composed of 434 members, allocated as indicated in Table 26–1, the Parliament conducts business in seven languages (to increase to nine with membership of Spain and Portugal) by means of simultaneous translation. Serving nonoverlapping five-year terms, MEPs (Members of the European Parliament) or Euro-MPs were originally chosen by appointment. Typically parties in the parliaments of the member states decided who would represent their country.

In 1979, however, the first international elections were held. Voters throughout Europe went to the polls to elect directly their country's representatives in the European Parliament. Turnout exceeded 60 percent, with 111 million peo-

TABLE 26–1 National Representation in the European Parliament

Britain	81	Belgium	24
France	81	Greece	24
Germany	81	Denmark	16
Italy	81	Ireland	15
Netherlands	25	Luxembourg	6

ple voting. Every country used proportional representation except Britain, which clung to its traditional procedure of single-member, simple plurality voting.

Turnout remained at nearly the same level for the next elections in 1984, although once again varying a good deal from country to country. More than three fourths of the electors cast their vote in Belgium, Luxembourg, Italy, and Greece, while half to two thirds did so in Denmark, France, Germany, Ireland, and the Netherlands. In Britain, however, only a third bothered to participate. The election results, which did not vary dramatically from those of five years earlier, appear in Table 26–2. The center-right groups—the Christian Democrats, European Democrats (British and Danish Conservatives), the Liberals, and the Progressive Democrats (French Gaullists and Irish Fianna Fail) continued to hold a majority, albeit a now narrow one. The key thing to notice about these strengths is that they are cross-national partisan groupings—the representatives from one country have joined with those of similar political outlook from another, rather than sticking together in distinct national delegations. Thus in at least one regard, the European Parliament functions as a supranational political institution rather than a meeting place of separate national delegations.

The Parliament's powers are primarily consultative. In addition it can direct questions to the Commission and the Council of Ministers. It is empowered as well to reject the Community's budget by a two-thirds vote. Furthermore, it can vote the entire Commission out of office, also by a two-thirds vote. While the latter never has occurred, the Parliament has rejected the budget twice.

The Court of Justice has 11 members appointed by general consent among the member states for six-year terms; appointments can be renewed. Cases reach the Court in a variety of ways. One member state may charge another with violating the European Community's basic Treaty, but this rarely happens. More commonly the Commission will charge a member with violating the Treaty or a member will file a complaint against the Commission or the Council. Also the various institutions of the Community—the Parliament, the Commission, or the Council—may seek to overturn the action of one another. Most interesting from a supranational perspective is the fact that in some limited circum-

TABLE 26–2   Result of 1984 Election for the European Parliament

Political group	Seats	Change
Socialists	132	+ 8
Christian Democrats	109	− 8
European Democrats	50	− 13
Communists	42	− 6
Liberals	32	− 7
Progressive Democrats	29	+ 7
Others	40	+ 19

stances private individuals may bring suit against the Commission or the Council in the Court.

While the Court can condemn violations of Community law by the member states, it lacks any means of implementing its decisions—it has no means of imposing its sanctions. The situation is even more true than it was early in American history when President Andrew Jackson said of a Supreme Court decision that he disliked, "John Marshall has made his decision, now let him enforce it." Nonetheless, only once has a member state suggested that it might defy a decision of the Court and even in that case it decided in the end upon partial compliance.

In addition to its power to decide actual cases, the Court also provides advisory opinions. Either the Council or the Commission can ask it to indicate whether an international agreement being considered by the Community is compatible with the basic Treaty. Even more important, judges in the various member states can seek advisory opinions on the proper interpretation of Community law when such questions arise in the trials being held in their courts. When such a request is made the Court's opinion is binding upon the judge who requested it.

By the end of 1984 nearly 5,000 actions had been brought to the Court, nearly two fifths of them, however, were matters of limited importance since they were proceedings involving the staff of the institutions. Like most courts, the Court of Justice moves fairly ponderously—about 1,000 of these actions had not yet been settled and still were pending. Nonetheless, the Court has made many significant decisions. Perhaps the most important has been its holding that Community law takes precedence over conflicting national law. Thus just as the supremacy clause of the American Constitution limits the powers of the state governments, so the actions of the Community can limit the member states—that is to say that their sovereignty, long regarded as the hallmark of national independence, is limited.

From this description it would appear that the Community is quite similar to the American federal system—a governmental system divided into three branches, executive, legislative, and judicial, with a central government predominant over the constituent governments. Were that the case, then those who wanted a supranational Europe would have triumphed. To see why they have not, we need to look more closely at the system in operation.

The basic decision-making procedure is for the Commission to submit a proposal to Coreper. After extensive discussion, the ambassadors recommend to the Council what action should be taken. The Council may issue directives, which are binding upon member states concerning the goals to be obtained, but allow each country to decide upon the means to achieve these ends, or regulations, which expand the provisions of the Treaty and apply directly in each country just as though they were laws passed by the national legislature. The Council must consult with Parliament before acting, but it is entirely free to ignore any views Parliament voices. Nonetheless, Parliament is not without influence. In fact, about two thirds of all its suggestions for changes in proposed Community laws have been accepted to some extent. Furthermore, a decision by the Court has suggested that Parliament may be able to hold the Council to ransom. If Parliament withholds its opinion on a proposed directive or regulation, the Council is barred from acting—only when Parliament has given an opinion, thus exercising its right to be consulted, can the Council issue a rule, even if it totally ignores Parliament's advice concerning the content of the rule. To this point Parliament has been quite cautious about exercising this apparent veto power which those who drew up the Treaty did not intend for it to have.

Parliament's role in the budget process is rather complicated. The Commission proposes a budget, which the Council then revises before sending it on to Parliament. After discussing it, Parliament returns it to the Council for further revision before it returns to Parliament for final action. About three fourths of a typical Community budget is spending directly required by the Treaty. In these matters Parliament's power to make changes is quite limited. But in the case of spending for programs established without specific Treaty authorization, Parliament has more power. Each year the Commission sets a ceiling on how much Parliament can increase the spending in this portion of the budget. Should the Council disagree with these increases, it can reject them only by a weighted, rather than a simple, majority vote. The problem from the Parliament's standpoint is that in the end it must vote on the budget as a whole. Thus if it has failed to persuade the Council to accept its changes, it has no further weapon but to vote the entire budget down. This is not very satisfactory since typically the Parliament is trying to get the Council to agree to larger expenditures and if the budget is voted down then spending simply continues at the same level as in the previous year. What all this means is that the Council really is the law-making body for the Community.

Furthermore, the Council is the chief executive—it instructs the Commission on how to administer the Community. The relationship has altered considerably from what it was under the ECSC. The High Authority of the ECSC could act directly upon coal and steel firms in the member states without having to go through their national governments. It could issue binding, detailed decisions, fine companies for noncompliance, and tax. And it acted on the basis of majority vote—there was no national vote.

The merger of the separate commissions of the three communities changed this. Now the bulk of the Commission's business was EEC, rather than ECSC, matters. The EEC Commission had not been given as much supranational power as the High Authority of the ECSC had. While in the ECSC the High Authority had made decisions and the Council of Ministers served as a harmonizing link with the member states rather than as a policymaker, in the EEC the Council of Ministers made the decisions and the Commission simply had the job of implementing them. While the EEC did have supranational powers, they were lodged, unlike the situation in the ECSC, in a body—the Council of Ministers— that was intergovernmental, not supranational. The result was something of a halfway house between the cooperative approach which the British had favored for European unity and the supranational approach more popular with many continental political leaders, such as Monnet.

Such a result was not inevitable, despite the institutional changes in the EEC compared to the ECSC. In the early days of the EEC the Commission, whatever its powers, did tend to function as the key institution following the precedent established by the High Authority in the ECSC. In the mid-1960s, however, the Commission came up against that immoveable object—Charles de Gaulle. Two changes were at issue. The Treaty had provided that after a transitional period the Council of Ministers would move to weighted majority, and even at times simple majority, voting. Whatever else de Gaulle may have thought about the British, he was even more adamant than they in being unwilling to relinquish any national sovereignty. Thus he was not about to accept a voting procedure which could result in France being forced to implement a decision that he opposed. To make matters worse the Commission miscalculated by choosing this time to push for a plan that would make the Community even more supranational than the Treaty had provided. Sizable sums were being raised for the Community from the common external tariff and the Commission proposed that this Community income should be controlled by the Parliament. The red flag had been waved in front of the bull, who, naturally, charged.

Using a tactic which he had found to be quite effective in French politics, de Gaulle picked up his marbles and went home—France boycotted EEC meetings until such time as everyone else would come to their senses, that is, see things as de Gaulle did. The EEC and the process of economic integration ground to a standstill. The "compromise" which eventually resolved this stalemate was that any thought of Parliament controlling Community resources was abandoned and majority voting went out the window as well. Henceforth it was accepted that on matters of vital interest to any member state, action could be taken only by unanimity—a national veto had been restored.

Increasingly the practice has come to be that unanimity is required for everything, not just for vital interests. As a result although the Commission retains the power of formulating proposals for action, it has lost considerable power to the Council of Ministers (which in practice means to Coreper). Facilitating this shift has been the change in the composition of the Commission. Increasingly its members have tended to become people who have been active in their country's partisan politics prior to their appointment. This is not to say that they are hostile to the idea of European unity, but simply to note that they are rather more the products of political patronage and may well anticipate returning to domestic politics following their term on the Commission. Such Commissioners are likely to have greater difficulty than did their predecessors in functioning primarily as Community officers rather than as national representatives.

Important as these matters are, however, one might argue that the key concern should be substance rather than form. Regardless of how the institutions of European unity have developed and the extent to which they have fallen short of the supranational vision of the founders, what actually has been accomplished, what are the achievements of the European Community?

POLICIES AND SUBSTANTIVE ACHIEVEMENTS

The movement for European unity had two goals, one visionary and the other practical. One hope was to construct a single governmental system—a United States of Europe. The other was so to meld the economies of France and Germany that another war between them would be impossible. While the first of these is now regarded as having been a mirage, considerable progress has been made toward accomplishing the second; political links that only a generation ago would have been thought impossible *have* been established between European nations.

No one now believes that in the foreseeable future Europe will become a single federal system similar to the United States. Nonetheless, some progress toward political unity has been made. The various cabinet ministers of the member states of the European Community maintain regular contacts with each other. And at the very highest level, the European Council brings the prime ministers and the presidents together with the President of the Commission three times each year to discuss matters of common concern. Senior foreign policy civil servants from each of the member states meet together every month. Each country's foreign office is linked directly by special telex to its counterpart in every other member state and messages frequently are exchanged as the members try to coordinate their international actions. At the UN the ambassadors from each of the 10 countries meet together to seek mutually agreeable positions on the topics being considered.

Furthermore, it begins to appear that the aura of de Gaulle is finally dissipating. In 1982 Britain opposed the prices which were proposed to be guaranteed to Community farmers under the Common Agricultural Policy; Britain was exercising what had come to be called a "veto." For the first time in 16 years the other members refused to abide by the practice that had originated to persuade de Gaulle to end the French boycott of EEC functions. The other nine members voted to implement the proposal despite British objections. In keeping with this precedent, the possibility of some form of majority voting in the Council of Ministers was being discussed actively in mid-1985. None of this was supranationalism, but was a move in the direction of further limiting national sovereignty.

As for the economic goal, it is important to understand that the Treaty of Rome, like the American Constitution, is a framework document. It specifies procedures and some goals, but it leaves to subsequent legislation and policies putting flesh upon the bones. The aim was to create a customs union, a single domestic market. To do this required eliminating all unfair advantages—such as cartels and subsidies to industry and agriculture—that producers enjoyed in one country but not in another. A common policy for agriculture and for transportation was to be established. And people, enterprises, and investment funds were to be free to move within the Community wherever economic opportunities were available.

The customs union has been achieved. Tariff and quota barriers to trade between countries within the Community have been eliminated and all of them apply a common tariff to goods imported from outside the Community—to that extent the Community is a single market just as the United States is. This market is giant; the EEC accounts for one third of the world's exports, more than the United States and Japan combined. Furthermore, exports are much more important to the Community's economies. One fourth of the total gross domestic product for all the countries of the Community derives from exports—three times as great as is the proportion for the United States. And while prior to the formation of the Common Market the EEC countries did a third of their trading with each other, now they do over half.

These accomplishments must be qualified, however, by the Community's tendency to move toward protectionism in the 1980s—protectionism not only toward the outside world, but between the member states themselves. While economic barriers to internal trade have been eliminated, other obstacles remain. Technical product standards, for example, have not been harmonized and at times deliberately are drafted in such a way as to give domestic producers an advantage over producers in other Community countries. Excessive paperwork at times discourages trade from one Community country to another. Also all of the member state governments have been guilty of giving domestic producers subsidies prohibited by the Community regulations. In 1982 the Commission instituted action against member states for 140 violations, nearly a third of them by France. Progress toward a common transportation policy has been so limited that 60 percent of the Community's commercial traffic still needs separate licensing for each boundary crossed within the Community.

Yet here again some evidence, or at least hope, of progress exists. In May 1985 in a case brought by the European Parliament the Court of Justice found that the Community's transportation ministers had violated the treaty by failing to develop the policies and programs they were required to do. Many hope that this decision will help to prod the ministers into action. In a somewhat related action, half the Community—the Benelux countries, France, and Germany—had decided that for the 1985 tourist season their citizens may travel across each other's borders without having to go through customs.

It also is true that many unfair trading practices have been abolished. EEC antimonopoly regulations take precedence over the laws of the member states—another example of a supranational aspect of the EEC. The Commission is empowered to investigate cases of apparent price-fixing or of unfair price-cutting. Furthermore, when it finds evidence of such violations, it not only prosecutes but also judges. It has fined more than 100 companies for violations. Its jurisdiction extends not just to companies headquartered within the Community but also to foreign firms such as IBM and Pioneer, the Japanese electronics company (both of which have been fined) which do business within the Community. As for those companies which believe they have been penalized improperly, their only recource is to appeal to the Court of Justice.

While a customs union would help to bind the French and German economies together, to merge them fully would require monetary and economic union as well. The visionary view was that the Community members eventually would merge their separate currencies into a single monetary unity—francs, lira, deutsche marks, pounds, and so forth would give way to a Eurodollar or some such entity. No one now expects that to happen. Nonetheless, all Community members except Greece and Britain participate in the European Monetary System. The EMS requires the central banks of each member to work together closely so that the exchange rates between these currencies will not diverge greatly from existing levels. Capital can move more freely within the Community than in the past, although France and Italy retain exchange controls. Also the Community has established a special fund to provide loans to member states experiencing balance-of-payments problems. The idea is to try to solve these problems within the Community rather than having to rely on an external agency like the International Monetary Fund. The Community is more likely to understand the reasons for any problems its members face and to formulate more acceptable conditions for agreeing to loan the funds needed. Beyond these measures, however, each member state tends to have its own distinct policies of economic management—monetary and fiscal policy remains a national, rather than a Community, matter.

The EEC's budget is too small to have any significant impact on fiscal policy within the Community. Community spending equals only about 3 percent of the total spending by all governments of the member states. Nonetheless, the fact that there is any Community budget at all, that it has independent revenues of its own, is a supranational element. Over half of its funds come from Value Added Taxes (VAT). This tax, widely used in Europe for some time, collects a portion of the amount by which the value of a good is increased at each stage in the productive process. Each member state decides for itself what the rate for VAT will be within its boundaries and on which goods it will be levied. Regardless of these decisions, however, each member must pass on to the Community a specified share, usually about one percent, of all the revenues it raises through VAT. The other primary source of Community funds—a third of the total—is customs duties. As already noted, the EEC has a common external tariff which all members must apply to goods imported from outside the Community. The duties collected are passed on to the Community, which reimburses the member states for the cost of collection.

Given the limited progress toward a common transportation policy, economic union has developed primarily in the coal and steel industry and in agriculture—in other areas economic policy tends to be made separately by the member states. Economic unity in coal and steel is the heritage, of course, of the ECSC, the first of the communities and the one providing for the greatest measure of supranationalism. As for agriculture, it consumes two thirds of Community spending. Next in importance, although a considerable distance behind, is regional policy, accounting for 10 percent. The Community provides grants and loans for enterprise in depressed areas throughout its territory. These sums are too limited, however, to have dramatic impact on national policymaking. Despite the large portion of the budget going to agriculture, spending for this purpose has declined relatively. In 1970, 90 percent of the budget was spent for agriculture.

Because it has been quite contentious and involves special interests with considerable muscle, the Common Agricultural Policy (CAP) deserves further discussion. Many countries aid agriculture—the argument being that the weather is so uncertain that even efficient producers can be destroyed—but they do so in a variety of ways. The basic procedure in the Community is to guarantee farmers high prices.

Each spring the agriculture ministers from the member states meet to set prices for various farm products. Should prices drop below this level when farmers actually sell their output, the Community steps in and buys as much as is necessary to bring the price up to the established level. This system would be undercut if food produced more efficiently (for lower prices) outside the Community were allowed to enter. So the Community imposes a levy on cheap imports to bring their price up to the level established for farmers within the EEC.

What this means is that food is relatively high-priced within the EEC—the consumer is disadvantaged. The price of butter and beef within the Community, for example, is 50 percent higher than world prices and sugar is 33 percent higher. Secondly, farmers in other countries, such as the United States and Australia, object vigorously to being denied the market that their productive efficiency would gain them were it not for the Community's import levy. What angers such farmers even more is the Community's policy of subsidizing its farmers' exports of food. EEC farmers can afford to sell at the lower world prices only if they receive payments from the Community to make up the difference between those prices and the established EEC price. So far as non-Community farmers (and their governments) are concerned, this is unfair dumping of surplus EEC production, which reduces the sales they otherwise would be able to make in world markets.

This charge has some validity. As we have seen, if the EEC farmers can't sell their products at the established price, the Community must buy what they offer for sale; the CAP encourages overproduction. Better to have this surplus sold somewhere, thinks the Commission, than for the EEC to have to stockpile it. The latter, as a matter of fact, is exactly what the Community has had to do in some cases. Community farmers produce about 25 percent more butter than Community residents consume. The Community has had to buy so much surplus butter that people have referred to the existence of a butter mountain. Similarly, there has been concern about a wine lake. The only way to avoid creating such geographical monstrosities is to subsidize sales to the rest of the world.

But why, you may ask, when it irritates the rest of the world and penalizes Community consumers would the EEC follow such a policy. It is time to tell you one of the facts of life: In all Western democracies one of the most powerful special interest groups are the farmers. No one, certainly no politican seeking reelection, wants to offend the farmers. (Note that President Reagan posed as the farmers' friend until after he was reelected.) Community dairy farmers have benefited most from the CAP—about a third of its spending is for milk products. Grains and meats receive a sixth each.

Further complicating the problem are the contrasting interests of the member states. If one wanted to summarize the basic bargain at the heart of the EEC, one could say, without excessively simplifying, that German industry was to be assisted at the price of helping French agriculture (or vice versa). That is, unless each country got its special advantage the whole deal was off. (This is what the idealism of Monnet had given way to by the latter part of the 1950s.) France accounts for more than a quarter of EEC agricultural output, with Italy at a fifth and Germany a bit lower than this.

Another bit of relevant information is the proportion of the workforce involved in agriculture. Greece is exceptional with 30 percent of its workers on the farm, while both Ireland and Italy are high with 19 and 13 percent respectively. Denmark and France at 8 percent have a sufficient amount of people involved in agriculture for their governments to take a special interest in them. Even Germany at 6 percent surpasses the United States and only Britain and Belgium at 3 percent are comparable to the United States. Add to this the fact that national farm spending in France almost equals that of Britain, Italy, and Germany combined. Clearly special interests are at work here.

Typically Britain and Germany are net contributors to the budget, while the other members are net recipients of funds. Britain's problem is that it imports a good bit of its food from outside the Community as a result of traditional trading links with members of the British Commonwealth such as Canada, Australia, and New Zealand. As we have seen, when these imports enter Britain, the Community levy is imposed upon them to bring their prices up to the established price. Britain then is obligated to transfer these funds to the Community. Furthermore, since so few British workers are farmers, Britain gets relatively few, even less than Germany, of the benefits of CAP spending.

Set this against the fact that in recent years Britain has not been as prosperous or as economically successful as the majority of EEC members and you can see why the British feel that their financial contributions to the EEC are not commensurate with their ability to pay nor equitable compared to the contributions of other members. This has led to some horrendous battles at European Council meetings. Prime Minister Margaret Thatcher has pounded the table and demanded that the Community give me "my money back." (She's not called the Iron Lady for nothing.) While the other members have groused that it just went to show Britain's lack of commitment to European unity stretching on back as far as its refusal to join up at the start of the process, they have quieted her down by giving some refunds. But these have simply been palliatives, rather than permanent, long-term solutions. As we noted earlier, when Britain sought in 1982 to reform the Community budget and the CAP, the other members overrode its opposition.

You should not think that it is only the British who can be beastly. Josef Ertl, long-term German agricultural minister, spared no effort to reassure his country's farmers that he would defend their stake in the CAP (see Chapter 19). When he retired from office, his successor, Ignaz Kiechle, quickly sought to demonstrate that someone from the CSU could look after German farmers just as successfully as had someone from the FDP. In 1985 when the other members wanted to reduce farm prices, Kiechle blocked them, despite the fact that German Chancellor Helmut Kohl strongly had been urging majority voting in the Council of Ministers.

Thus progress toward economic union has occurred in that the Community does have a common agricultural policy. Whether that policy is a good one is another matter. Clearly some reform is necessary, yet vested interests—both national and occupational—make accomplishing this difficult.

While all this is important, in some ways it misses the essential point. What matters is not so much the price of milk as the change in attitudes. Whatever its specific policy problems and its lack of progress toward supranationalism, Europe *is* a community to an extent undreamed of a generation ago. France and Germany do not anticipate as they did only a decade and a half after World War I, fighting each other again. Their citizens move across their borders to attend concerts and other entertainment events with no more thought, perhaps even less, than Americans and Canadians do in North America. The Maginot and Siegfried lines mentality—the fortifications set up to defend France and Germany from each other a half century ago—has disappeared. While the haggling over the CAP was not what he had in mind, Monnet doubtless would be pleased to see what the process he launched has achieved in a third of a century.

BIBLIOGRAPHICAL NOTE

Michael Palmer, Deputy Director General of the European Parliament explains the workings of that body in *The European Parliament* (Oxford: Pergamon Press, 1981). The extensive appendices include, among other items, the names, partisan affiliations, and committee assignments of all the members of the first directly elected Parliament. The Delegation of the Commission of the European Communities, located in Washington, D.C., publishes a variety of materials on the organization. Perhaps most useful for keeping up to date on current developments is the bi-monthly magazine *Europe*. The British news weekly *The Economist* regularly follows Community affairs in addition to providing a brief monthly summary of key events.

PART SIX

THE SOVIET UNION

27

The Setting of Soviet Politics

The U.S.S.R. (Union of Soviet Socialist Republics), no less than other nations, is conditioned by the past, by her geography, by her people, and by her political and social heritage. While a detailed examination of that past is beyond the scope of this book, the authors believe that even a cursory survey of the past will contribute to an understanding of the country and its political system. In this chapter we shall be concerned with presenting a few basic facts about the country's physical setting, its ethnic diversity, and its heritage of political autocracy. In the next chapter we shall consider the changing foundations of Russian politics in the decades before the Communist seizure of power. In this way, the Communist effort to impose a revolutionary system on the country can be viewed in the appropriate context, and the modifications in that system can be seen, in part at least, as the result of a need to compromise with social forces that have their roots in the past.

THE PHYSICAL SETTING

The present territories of the Soviet Union constitute about one sixth of the inhabited land surface of the world, or about 8.5 million square miles. This represents an area as large as the United States, Canada, and Mexico combined. It stretches from the Baltic Sea to the Pacific Ocean and from the Arctic to the frontiers of Iran, Afghanistan, and China. Much of the area was acquired in a rapid expansion to the Pacific. Russia's march eastward across Siberia was as rapid as America's westward march to the other side of the Pacific.

The country is divided into 15 republics. By far the largest is the Russian Soviet Federated Socialist Republic (RSFSR), accounting for approximately three fourths of the nation's total area and over one half of its population. It stretches from the Baltic to the Bering Sea. The other republics, in order of the size of their population, are: Ukraine, Kazak, Uzbek, Belorussia, Georgia, Azerbaijan, Lithuania, Moldavia, Latvia, Kirghiz, Tadzhik, Armenia, Turkmen, and Estonia.

Nearly all of the area of the Soviet Union is north of the 50th parallel (that is, north of the United States), although the most southerly parts reach below the 40th. For all its continental nature, it is largely landlocked except for the Arctic. It has the longest and perhaps the most useless coastline in the world. All seas and rivers are frozen part of the year. The great rivers flow to locked seas. The only ice-free port, prior to the acquisition of Königsberg, Memel, and Liepãja (Lepaya) was Murmansk. Vladivostok is kept open year-round with icebreakers.

For the most part, the Soviet Union has a cold climate, which is to be attributed more to its continental position, away from the moderating effect of oceans, than to its northerly latitude. There are extremes, nevertheless, ranging from the frigid Arctic to the intense heat of the deserts of Central Asia, with some areas having moderate to semitropical climates. Generally speaking, however, large areas of the country are unsuited for agriculture, and the amount of new land that can be opened up is limited. Summers are brief; frosts occur late in the spring and early in the autumn. Conditions for the planting of winter wheat or rye are not favorable because of the intense cold and poor snow cover. Moreover, the quality of many of the soils is poor, and irrigation possibilities are limited. Because of variations and unreliability in rainfall, even the more favored regions experience great uncertainties.

One of the most striking geographical facts about the U.S.S.R. is the immense Russian Plain. Across this plain flow a number of great rivers that have been important avenues of transport, commerce, and conquest. The low watersheds and short portages between the rivers have made it possible to connect them with canals. There are more than 180,000 miles of navigable rivers, although winter freezing prevents year-round use. The Volga is the most important single river, carrying half the country's total river freight. It drops less than 1,000 feet in some 2,300 miles. The great rivers of Siberia are of considerably less value, since they flow north into the frozen Arctic. Mountains in the Soviet Union are for the most part to be found along the periphery. The Urals, a low, eroded chain, are the one exception.

The importance of the rivers as arteries of commerce ought not, however, to be overemphasized, for the railroads still carry the bulk of the freight traffic. Roads are a rarity in the countryside, with mud prevailing for several months of the year. Although more than twice the area of the United States, the Soviet

Union has 0.25 million miles of paved roads, compared to 4 million miles in the United States. Moreover, the peasants do not own their own cars or trucks.

From the Arctic southward, there are five zones, each with a characteristic soil and vegetation. The tundra of the far north, with the subsoil perpetually frozen, does not provide much vegetation or opportunity for its development. Gradually, it merges into the forest zone, which covers nearly half of the total area of the Soviet Union. It is the largest forested area in the world and contains a mixture of trees. South of the forest zone is the famous steppe region of Russia, extending from the western boundaries all the way to the Altai Moutains in the east, an area that is, on the whole, rich but often lacking ample rainfall. The semidesert and desert zone lies partly in southeast European Russia and in areas of central Asia. The smallest, as well as the most southern, of the five main zones is the subtropical. It covers some 190,000 square miles along the Black Seacoast, the Caspian Seacoast, the Crimea, southern Transcaucasia, and the mountains of central Asia. Vegetation in the seacoast areas is extremely thick because of the humus soil and heavy rainfall. Central Asia, with its mild winters and hot summers, has sometimes been referred to as the Imperial Valley of the U.S.S.R.

In natural resources, the Soviet Union is perhaps the richest nation in the world. She has all the raw materials necessary to contemporary civilization, although there is reason to believe she does not have all that she needs of each. These resources are scattered widely, although some areas seem particularly well endowed. The Ural Mountain range has a variety of minerals; the Ukraine has coal and iron ore; the mountains of central Asia and the Far East have many of the rare metals, including uranium; there has been an abundance of oil; Siberia has iron ore reserves greater than the United States, Britain, and France combined; and the natural gas fields of western Siberia are said to be the largest in the world. The supplies of timber are large, although for the most part considerably removed from the principal population centers. Similarly, there is a great hydroelectric potential, which is only partially developed. Because so much remains unexplored, it is possible that the Soviet endowment in natural resources may prove richer than present estimates indicate. Some studies have concluded, however, that the U.S.S.R. will face an energy problem in the years ahead.

The population of the Soviet Union, according to 1981 estimates, is about 275 million, most of it concentrated in European Russia, and more than half (60 percent) of it is in urban areas. Well over 90 percent have never spent a day of their lives outside their country and probably never will if present regime restrictions continue. There are more than 100 distinct and different ethnic groups represented in this total, although the number of major groups is considerably smaller. More significant, however, is the fact that almost three fourths of the population is Slavic, making for a greater ethnic unity than is sometimes supposed, although this does not mean that political unity necessarily follows.

Numerically, women predominate in the Soviet Union, making up 54 percent of the population. This disproportion stems in part from large losses in World

War II, but it is perhaps even more attributable to the purges conducted over several decades by the Soviet regime. One serious study concludes that over 20 million deaths were caused by Stalin's terror.[1]

The Russian Slavs are subdivided into three main groups. The most numerous are the Great Russians, who account for one half of the total population.[2] The Ukrainians, sometimes called Little Russians, number over 40 million. The White Russians (Belorussians), not to be confused with the political White Russians (as opposed to the Red), number over 9 million. In addition, there are Slav minorities, chiefly Poles, Czechs, and Bulgarians. Traditionally, most Russian Slavs have been Orthodox Christians, although the Uniate Church, which had a connection with Rome and which for the most part was to be found in the Ukraine, was not insignificant. Protestant sects made little headway in Russia, with the exception of the Baptists, whose actual membership is not known but is estimated to number more than 200,000.

The second largest ethnic group in the U.S.S.R. is the Turkic or Turko-Tartar people, who number around 30 million. Predominantly Moslem, they are in the main the descendants of the Asiatic warriors who were led westward by Genghis Khan and Tamerlane in the 13th and 14th centuries. In this group are to be found the Uzbeks and the Kazaks of central Asia, the Kazan and Crimean Tartars, the Azerbaijanis of the Transcaucasus, the Kirgiz peoples who live in central Asia along the Chinese frontier, and the Yakuts in eastern Siberia.

In the third largest ethnic group are the Transcaucasian peoples, who number some 8 million. Prominent among these are the Georgians, the Azerbaijani, and the Armenians, together with smaller but closely related groups. They are of mixed religious affiliation, although preponderantly Christian at the time of the Revolution in 1917.

A fourth and final major ethnic group, the Finno-Ugrian, is linguistically and ethnically related to the Hungarians, the Turks, and the Finns. They number about 5 million. These peoples are mostly Estonians, Udmurts, Chuvash, Finns, and Karelians.

In addition to the main divisions already listed, the 1970 census reported more than 2 million Jews living in the U.S.S.R. Most of these are scattered, although some are concentrated in the special Jewish autonomous region known as Birobidjan. One of the larger national minorities, the Germans, about 1.5 million strong, lived on the Volga but were relocated to Siberia during World War II.[3]

It has been popular in some circles to explain the behavior of the Soviet regime, as well as its very existence, in terms of traits to be found in the Russian

---

[1] Robert Conquest, *The Greater Terror: Stalin's Purge of the Thirties* (New York: Macmillan, 1968).

[2] The first mention of Slavs seems to have been made in the sixth century. There is no agreement on the root meaning of the word *Slav*. In certain West European languages, it is synonymous with "slave." In the languages of the Slavic peoples, however, the word means "praiseworthy" or "choicest."

[3] Soviet policies toward religion and national minorities will be treated in subsequent chapters.

character.[4] There is no doubt that certain characteristics or traits tend to stand out more in some people than in others. Efforts to relate the collective behavior of peoples who are today gathered together in nations to traits of national character ought not be minimized. At present, however, the state of knowledge in this area is insufficient to justify firm conclusions.

The Russians have on occasion been depicted as loving or at least easily accepting authority.[5] It is true that they have often appeared to put up with a lot. On the other hand, they have at times demonstrated an independence of mind, a boldness of spirit, and outright resistance. The more one looks into the matter, the more one becomes convinced of the inevitable complexity and indecisiveness of national character. While certain traits may offer clues to a people's collective behavior, it is impossible to assign such traits any specific or precise weight.

Traits do not originate in something called the national makeup of a people but in the historical experience of those people. Human actions frequently are reactions to conditions of life that reach back into the past. The legacy of history, economic and social dislocations, the flow of new ideas, and cataclysmic events such as wars—all play their part in shaping a nation's future as well as the attitudes of the people toward that future and toward their ultimate destiny.

LONG HISTORY OF POLITICAL AUTOCRACY

It has often been pointed out that Russia's geographic vastness, coupled with the building of the Russian state largely in isolation from the West, resulted in a physical and a psychological separation from the influences that in Western Europe served to do away with, or at least to modify, political autocracy. The influences of the Renaissance, the Reformation, and the Counter-Reformation simply did not penetrate Russia. And Western liberal-democratic ideas of the 17th and 18th centuries did not make any significant inroads until the 19th century, and then in limited and often perverted form. It is noteworthy that throughout Russia's long political past no institutions that could limit or channel autocratic power took root. Isolation from the West, however, may have been only one factor, because institutions that might have shared power were created (for example, Zemsky Sobor, Senate, State Council), but they did not succeed in assuming a role comparable to that of similar institutions in the countries of Western Europe.

Russia's long pre-Soviet history may, for the sake of convenience, be divided into four periods. The first is the pre-Mongolian period or the time of Kievan

---

[4]For example, see Edward Crankshaw. "Russia in Europe: The Conflict of Values," *International Affairs,* October 1946, pp. 501–10. See also Joseph K. Folsom and Nikander Strelsky, "Russian Values and Character—A Preliminary Exploration," *American Sociological Review* 9 (June 1944), pp. 296–307.

[5]See Geoffrey Gorer and John Rickman, *The People of Great Russia: A Psychological Study* (New York: W. W. Norton, 1962).

Russia, dating from the ninth century to about 1240. The second phase is the era of Tartar rule or the Mongolian period, which lasted nearly 250 years. The third period represents the resurrection of the Russian state, the rule of Ivan IV (the Terrible or the Dreaded), and the Time of Troubles, an era covering some 130 years. The fourth period represents the rule of the Romanov dynasty (1613 to 1917). This somewhat arbitrary division of Russian history provides a mere chronological framework, although a convenient one, within which Russia's development and expansion can be viewed.

One of the outstanding features of Russia's long history is her growth and expansion into a great empire. This was far from a steady and firm development, for there were many setbacks. Although Russia of the Kiev period was strong enough to maintain and preserve the nation for some 400 years, she was considerably smaller and weaker than the Russia of later epochs. The ruling princes of that period were powerful, but a great deal less so than the later tsars.

The epoch of Tartar rule, and particularly its disruption, was accompanied by the growing predominance of Moscow. With the division of Russia into many principalities during the Mongol period, the princes of the Moscow area gained in power, mainly by obeying the Tartars and through their friendship with church leaders, which resulted in Moscow's becoming the spiritual capital of Russia.[6] Gradually, Moscow gained a powerful economic hold over the small rival principalities. In 1340, the Khan singled out the Moscow prince as the Great Prince, making other princes subordinate to him. The succession of princes of Moscow, whose power and domain grew in comparison to the other principalities, provided a unifying force once the Tartar yoke was loosened. By the 16th century Moscow had become the political capital of Russia.

The unification of Russia in the post-Mongolian period was in no small part the work of Ivan IV. His official rule dates from 1533 to 1584, although, in effect, others ruled for him in the early years, since he came to power as a child, when Russia was in considerable turmoil due to quarrels among the princes for supreme control. By his determination and utter ruthlessness he became a powerful ruler and succeeded in unifying his country. With his death in 1584, however, Russia entered the Time of Troubles, a period of strife, palace intrigue, and civil war—a period that also witnessed the attempt of the king of Poland to make himself tsar of Russia. This era came to an end with the election of the first Romanov as tsar in 1613.

The rule of the Romanovs, spanning some 300 years, was the period of Russia's greatest expansion and the era of her rise to a position of power among the nations. But most of Russia's achievements as a nation in this period were associated with a few of her rulers. Clearly predominant is Peter the First (the Great), although the works of Catherine the Second (the Great) and Alexander the Second also stand out. Peter, who ruled between 1682 and 1721, set out to

---

[6]Russia had accepted Christianity in the 10th century.

Europeanize Russia within his lifetime. Russia was to be westernized deliberately and expeditiously in order that she might become a powerful nation. He brought Russia to Europe by building a new capital on the swamps where the Neva River flows into the Baltic, which he called St. Petersburg, later to be called Petrograd and now Leningrad. He traveled to France, Holland, Denmark, England, and Austria, and everywhere he went he gathered information and recruited artisans to build industry in Russia.[7] All of Russia's resources were harnessed to the building of a powerful westernized nation. Even the church, with the creation of the Holy Synod, was brought under state control.

Some 40 years elapsed after Peter's death—years characterized by uncertainty, intrigue, and palace revolutions—before Catherine II came to the throne. She is regarded as a follower of Peter in that she sought to carry out his westernization policies. During her reign (1762-96), the Russian empire was enlarged and solidified. The non-Russian nationalities, however, constituted an internal weakness that was to plague Russia's rulers and that the Communists were to exploit at a much later date.

Although the Russian empire continued to grow, it was not until Russia's involvement in the Napoleonic Wars that it acquired the status of a first-rate power. From that time on it was to play a significant role in European affairs.

"The heart and core of the old Russian state was the autocracy, born under the Mongols, cradled in the Muscovite period, and reaching maturity in modern times."[8] This is a succinct and apt depiction of Russia's political past under the tsars, although subsequent sections of this chapter will refer to some challenges to the autocracy and to attempts to modify it.

A few cursory observations about the development of autocracy in Russia may suggest the futility of seeking an easy explanation for its existence. One need but mention such things as the vast and interminable Russian Plain, which at one and the same time presented no barriers to foreign invaders and was conducive to free movement of people away from the center. In such circumstances, it was virtually impossible to maintain a compact, homogeneous nation without autocratic authority. Moreover, these factors, together with Russia's geographic vastness, combined to produce a country in large part isolated from the rest of the world. This was especially true during the period of Tartar rule, when "the new Russia of the backwoods (the Moscow area) . . . was thus politically cut off from Europe."[9] And isolation certainly played a part at a later date in keeping out moderating influences and liberal ideas that flourished in Europe and tended to modify the more objectionable aspects of European autocracy.

---

[7]It may be argued that this was an inauspicious beginning, for it set the pattern of state intervention in the development of the economy, which at a later date tended to prevent the development of an energetic and imaginative system of free enterprise.

[8]S. R. Tompkins, *Russia Through the Ages* (New York: Prentice-Hall, 1940), p. 1.

[9]Bernard Pares, *A History of Russia* (New York: Alfred A. Knopf, 1926), p. 73.

A noted historian has suggested that "it was not because of any alleged innate sympathy of the Russian soul to autocracy that the Tsardom of Moscow came into being but out of the stern necessity of organizing a military force sufficient to overthrow the Mongol yoke and then of securing control of a territory vast enough for strategic defense. . . . Political freedom was sacrificed for national survival."[10] Another historian has asserted that tsarist autocracy was accepted as a necessary evil, in preference to the autocracy of the Polish nobles or other foreign rulers.[11]

There is some disagreement as to which of the Moscow princes was the first to assume the title of tsar (caesar), but it is most often associated with Ivan IV (the Terrible or the Dreaded).[12] The beginning of autocratic rule in Russia is often associated with him. It was during his reign that the *Oprichnina,* a forerunner of the modern secret police, was established. It was also during his rule that slavery was introduced and a new nobility created. Ironically enough, it was during his reign that the *Zemsky Sobor* was established. This assembly gained in power during the Time of Troubles (1584–1613); in 1598 it elected Boris Godunov tsar and in 1613 elected the first Romanov, whose descendants were the ruling family until 1917.[13]

Other tsars who have stood out in Russian history for the most part continued in the traditions of Ivan IV, although their autocratic rule was not always accompanied by the degree of ruthlessness and brutality that is associated with Ivan and Peter I. Moreover, those who are known for their liberalization policies, such as Alexander II, did not accept limitations on their absolute power. Even the weaker tsars did not willingly accept limitations on their autocratic authority.

The Russian Orthodox Church, over the years, became the most vocal defender in Russia of tsarist absolutism. Christianity was accepted in the 10th century by the Russian ruler, Vladimir. Since the parent body was the Eastern Church, the Russian Church was from the beginning under the nominal control of the patriarch at Constantinople. In time, the Moscow princes gained influence in the selection of the Russian metropolitan, the head of the Russian Church. With the fall of Constantinople to the Turks in 1453, or about the time the Mongol domination ended in Russia, the Russian Church was completely severed from its Byzantine ties. Thereafter, the church fought for the unity and independence of the Russian Metropolitanate.[14]

---

[10]George Vernadsky, *A History of Russia: Kievan Russia,* vol. 2 (New Haven, Conn.: Yale University Press, 1948), p. 17.

[11]Edward Crankshaw, *Russia and the Russians* (New York: Macmillan, 1949), p. 52.

[12]D. S. Mirsky, in *Russia: A Social History*, C. J. Seligman, ed. (London, 1931), p. 137, and M. T. Florinsky, *Toward An Understanding of the U.S.S.R.* (New York: Macmillan, 1939), p. 7. However, Pares, *A History of Russia*, p. 89, and Tompkins, *Russia Through the Ages,* p. 110, assert that Ivan III was the first official tsar.

[13]No *Sobors* were held between 1654 and 1682, and after 1698 no *Sobors* were ever summoned.

[14]Vladimir had from the beginning "made use of the higher clergy as counselors," and "the priests, as the only literate persons, were invaluable for civil purposes; for the keeping of records . . . for embassies and for other public services." See Pares, *A History of Russia,* p. 30. The priests also brought a system of law to Russia.

With the establishment of the Holy Synod during the reign of Peter I, the Church came under state control. The new princes of the Church, especially the Ukrainian prelates, not only became subservient but also labored long to produce learned vindications of the new secular authority. "Thus, with the approval of the higher clergy, the Russian theocratic monarchy was transformed into a secular absolutism of the western type."[15]

The fact that most European countries had accepted Christianity from the Western Church (Rome) made the West appear hostile to the Russians. This helped to make the Orthodox Church an ally of Russian nationalism. Hostile actions of Western countries came to be viewed by the Russian Church as attacks upon Holy Russia, the true interpreter and defender of Christ.

It was not until the late 19th century, however, that a full-blown exposition of the Russian version of the divine right of kings doctrine was produced. Its author was Pobiedonostsev, the former tutor of Alexander III and procurator-general of the Holy Synod. Not only did he defend tsarist autocracy in terms of divine origin of the tsar's authority, but in addition, he argued that Russia could be saved from the corrupting influence of foreign ideas only by a complete autocracy of state and church.

During the long history of Russian autocracy the most persistent issue was serfdom. Popular concern with political, legal, and other reforms was important, especially in the 19th century, but clearly secondary. The main preoccupation seemed to center on the injustices of serfdom and the crying need for a solution.

It was during the reign of the Romanovs that serfdom became a firm and fixed institution. Land grants that had been made to the service gentry in payment for military service included the peasants who lived on the land. Many of these, however, made successful escapes to the more remote regions of Russia. In 1646, all squires who owned land were required to register it, together with the names of each of their peasants. These and their future descendants became legally attached to the land. Serfdom became hereditary. A code in 1649 confirmed serfdom as a state institution. By 1675, the sale of serfs apart from land, although illegal, had become so widespread that it received legal sanction. Moreover, punishment for escape and for aiding fugitives became increasingly harsh.

But serfdom was more than an economic and social problem, with its legacy of economic backwardness, poverty, illiteracy, and human indignity. It was also a political problem in that it engendered attitudes of suspicion and distrust toward political authority and the agents of that authority. Serfdom was but the most notable symbol of Russia's peasant heritage, a heritage with which even the Soviet leaders have had to contend.

Despite a growing awareness of the acute nature of the problem of serfdom, and despite studies ordered by various rulers, no really significant step was taken

---

[15]Mirsky, in *Russia*, Seligman, p. 184.

to deal with it until the reign of Alexander II. What was done from time to time, even under Alexander II, left much more undone. It is a simple unadulterated fact that no tsarist regime found an acceptable solution to the most acute problem of Russian society.

Russian autocracy, along with serfdom, did not go unchallenged indefinitely. Protests took several forms. In the earlier years they consisted chiefly of limited peasant revolts, along with two revolts of major proportions led by nonpeasants, which attracted considerable support. In the 19th century the protests were mainly political and literary, although limited peasant uprisings continued to take place.

The first of the major rebellions was led by a type of freebooter, a Don Cossack by the name of Stenka Razin. The rebellion continued for four years (1667–71), but in the end it was suppressed and Razin was executed. A hundred years later (1773–74) another major rebellion broke out that for a time gained considerable headway, even threatening St. Petersburg. It too was brutally put down and its leader, Emilian Pugachev, executed. For the most part these were unorganized, spontaneous reactions against the oppressions of serfdom and the government's tax and other policies. Besides drawing support from the peasants, these revolts attracted outlaws and other elements that sought to profit from participating in them.

The first major political protest against tsarist autocracy is most frequently referred to as the Decembrist Revolt.[16] During the Napoleonic wars, Russian soldiers had seen something of Europe and had absorbed some disturbing ideas. The result of these new ideas was a liberal movement which contributed to the uprising that occurred in December 1825, after the death of Alexander I. It was led by officers of the guard regiments, some of whom had been in France after the defeat of Napoleon. They formed outside the Council of State, shouting for "Constantine and Constitution." Constantine was a brother of Alexander and in line for the throne, except that he had abdicated his right years earlier, although this fact was kept secret. Upon Alexander's death, Constantine proclaimed his younger brother Nicholas as tsar. Certain regiments refused to take the oath to Nicholas, who thereupon opened his regime with a ruthless suppression of the Decembrists. The Decembrist uprising was not a peasant revolt. It was lead by the nobles and a few liberals, loosely organized in secret societies. Although they lacked a coherent political program, they did talk of republicanism and of free speech. And they all agreed that serfdom was a crying injustice.

The intellectual atmosphere that helped make the Decembrist uprising possible was but the beginning of a literary protest against the evils of tsarism. This protest was to gain momentum during the 19th century—a century that produced Russia's greatest writers. Among these are Pushkin, Lermontov, Gogol, Herzen, Turgenev, Chekhov, Dostoyevsky, and Tolstoy. Most of these became

---

[16]See A. G. Mazour, *The First Russian Revolution, 1825* (Berkeley: University of California Press, 1937).

absorbed with contemporary political and philosophical problems, much to the dislike of the ruling group. Censorship and imprisonment awaited those who advocated change. Gradually, however, they acquired boldness and experience, managing to circumvent the censors and to increase their popular following.

Nicholas I had inadvertently contributed to the rise of a generation of revolutionary writers. During his reign, the reorganization of the universities revealed the lack of competent instructors. Promising young intellectuals were encouraged to travel and to study abroad. Many of these went to Germany and upon their return were brimming over with ideas they had acquired from Hegel, Fichte, Schelling, and other philosophers and writers.

One result of the 19th-century Russian intellectual activity was the development of a cleavage between those who saw Russia's future in Western ideas and ways of doing things and those who believed in indigenous solutions to Russia's problems. These schools of thought came to be known as Westernizers and Slavophiles. After the reforms of Alexander II, this controversy tended to die down. As Alexander's regime moved on, however, a period of reaction set in, in part motivated by the Polish revolt and the various attempts on the tsar's life. The disillusionment with some of his reforms and the recall of Russian students from abroad contributed to the renewed spread of revolutionary doctrines.

The intellectual protest against tsarism and the evils of serfdom was but the forerunner of political activity in its various forms. New ideas and new political doctrines took root and were disseminated. Political organizations were being established, and political programs formulated. These and related questions will be discussed in subsequent pages. Suffice it to say at this point that these developments are but another indication that autocracy was being challenged, and, as we now know, the end of its long history was approaching.

BIBLIOGRAPHICAL NOTE

Among the studies that discuss the characteristics of the Russian people, some of the more informative are: Raymond A. Bauer, *Nine Soviet Portraits* (New York: John Wiley & Sons, 1955); Clyde M. Kluckhohn, Raymond A. Bauer, and Alex Inkeles, *The Soviet System: Cultural, Psychological and Social Themes* (Cambridge, Mass.: Harvard University Press, 1956); Sir John Maynard, *Russia in Flux,* edited and abridged by S. Haden Guest from *Russia in Flux and The Russian Peasant and Other Studies* (New York: Macmillan, 1948); Klaus Mehnert, *Soviet Man and His World* (New York: Praeger Publishers, 1962) and *The Russians and Their Favorite Books* (Stanford, Calif., Hoover Institution Press, 1983).

Among excellent contemporary journalistic accounts are: Robert G. Kaiser, *Russia: The People and the Power* (New York: Pocket Books, 1976 and 1984); Kevin Klose, *Russia and the Russians: Inside the Closed Society* (New York: W. W. Norton, 1984); Andrea Lee, *Russian Journal* (London: Faber, 1982); David K. Shipler, *Russia: Broken Idols, Solemn Dreams* (New York: Times Books, 1983); and Hedrick Smith, *The Russians* (New York: Quadrangle Books/New York Times, 1976 and 1983).

28

The Changing Foundations of Russian Politics

STEPS TOWARD REFORM

From what has been said above, it should not be assumed that tsarist Russia took no steps toward reform. Although the various reforms in the end proved insufficient, many of them gave considerable promise at the time of their adoption. In a way, many of them can be looked upon as truly great advances, particularly those taken by Alexander II. Unfortunately, however, many of the promising reforms either were nullified by succeeding rulers or were not carried forward. Others, although significant, fell short of what Russian conditions demanded.

Russia at the beginning of the 19th century was a country of contrasts, a phenomenon that prevails today. It had attained the position of first-rate power on the continent, and yet it was one of the most backward countries in the world. As the century wore on, however, the weaknesses became predominant. This was to become glaringly evident at the time of the Crimean War and later during the Russo-Japanese War at the outset of the 20th century.

Economically and socially, Russia was a picture of backwardness at the beginning of the 19th century. Although the small gentry class lived relatively well, the serfs were living in poverty and their number was increasing. Moreover, the serfs were virtual outcasts. There was mass illiteracy. Non-Russian nationalities, especially the Jews, were oppressed. Nowhere in the social or economic picture could one point to progress.

Politically, Russia entered the 19th century no less backward. There was no semblance of self-government or even a widespread discussion of it. The church and state were united behind the tsar-autocrat. The tradition of absolutism and authority characterized the Russian political scene. The first two tsars of the 19th century were brothers who ruled for 54 years, a period divided almost equally between them. Steps toward reform during their reigns were so few and so lacking in their approach to Russia's basic problems that there is a danger of overemphasizing them.

Alexander I (1801–25) was primarily interested in foreign affairs, which occupied most of his attention. He seems to have favored the establishment of a constitutional monarchy, but only one of several projected constitutional reforms ever came into effect, and it was only partially realized. A State Council established in 1810 possessed only advisory powers. Its existence, therefore, constituted no effective limitation on autocracy.

Nicholas I (1825–55) is regarded by many historians as the most reactionary among the tsars. He came close to establishing a police state. His Russification program among the non-Russian nationalities was symbolized by the concept "one flag, one government, one church, one people." He ordered the opening of new schools to prove that the people did not want to go to school. When he was proved wrong, severe limitations were imposed on what was to be taught. Chairs of history and philosophy were considered dangerous. Many writers were placed under house arrest. Moreover, censorship generally became more stringent. His reign could appropriately be described as one long rearguard reaction against new ideas.

Some reforms, however, were inaugurated during the rule of Nicholas I. The most notable among these was the codification of the laws under the direction of Count Speransky, who had been responsible for the 1810 reforms establishing the State Council. Speransky completed his monumental task of codification of the laws in 1833.

The most promising steps toward reform were those that were taken by Alexander II (1855–81). These included: emancipation of the serfs (1861); reorganization of the institution of local government, the *Zemstvo* (1864); reform of the judiciary (1864); budget reforms (1862); reorganization of municipal government (1870); and the introduction of conscription on a nonclass basis (1874). Moreover, at the time of his assassination (1881) he had approved the project of Count M. T. Loris-Melikov for the creation of an advisory council to work with the State Council.

The emancipation of the serfs was hailed as a great and courageous act, which earned for Alexander the title of tsar-liberator. The emancipation, however, was only partial, and it was qualified. The state undertook to buy only one half of the land from the squires that was to be given to the peasants, who would be given 49 years in which to pay for the land. The village assembly, the *Mir,* was given the responsibility of collecting the payments. Until all the payments were made, the peasant could not consider himself an owner of any part of the land. As time progressed, the peasants found the redemption payments an almost unbearable burden. At the same time, it was becoming increasingly evident that the lands originally purchased were proving insufficient for the number of peasants needing land. The liberation had been a great step forward, but other steps had to be taken if the peasant problem was to be dealt with successfully.

The reform of the *Zemstvo* was at least in part the consequence of the emancipation of the peasants. Earlier, the landlords had governed the local community, but now the newly liberated peasants wanted some voice in local affairs. The reorganization of the *Zemstvo* provided that the local government assembly be elected on a nonclass basis. Similarly, prior to the liberation the landowners had dispensed justice. In the changed circumstances, this could hardly be continued. Among the reforms in the judiciary was the introduction of juries and lawyers.

Among the other reforms, the requirement that the nobility serve in the army also seemed to recognize the greater equality acquired by the peasant. Some reforms, like the granting of a considerable amount of self-government to the universities (1863) and making the budget public for the first time in Russian history, were of a more general nature.

None of these reforms, be it noted, limited the autocratic powers of the tsar. They did, however, teach the people something of local self-government, and they gave them some real hopes for the complete extinction of serfdom.

It should be noted that Alexander, as well as others who sought reform, labored under severe handicaps. The nobility was determined to defend its economic interests. And the peasantry, in whose innate political virtues the intelligentsia reposed such unjustified confidence, was something less than capable of assuming its newly acquired reponsibilities. Moreover, Alexander had to rely on an unenlightened and often inept bureaucracy to carry out his policies. As a consequence some of his messages "never arrived," and others were "not understood." In the light of such circumstances, it is perhaps surprising that considerable progress was achieved.

The assassination of Alexander II doomed the prospects of further reform, and ushered in a period of reaction. Even the Loris-Melikov proposal, prepared during his reign as a modest concession to public opinion, was never promulgated. The new tsar, Alexander III, agreed with his antireform advisors. Among the most influential of these was his former tutor, Pobiedonostsev, who was now procurator-general of the holy synod. Although the official retreat was fairly general, it was most felt in education and the press. The university autonomy, gained under Alexander II, was revoked. Student clubs were banned. A number of measures further restricted newspapers and their editors. A program of intensified Russification was begun. A new set of officials, called rural chiefs, was introduced to direct the work of the locally elected institutions of government.

Extraordinary measures, ostensibly designed to deal with revolutionary organizations and their activities, enabled the political police, the *Okhrana*, to exercise far-reaching oppressive powers.

Economically, however, Russia experienced considerable growth during the latter half of the 19th century. Industrialization moved along at an increasing rate. Cities and towns grew apace, as did the number of their inhabitants. The most notable achievement in the transportation field was the building of the trans-Siberian railway.

BEGINNINGS OF CONSTITUTIONALISM

In 1900, Russia was a stronghold of absolutism. By contrast, in the United States, England, and a number of Western European countries the democratic system was widely accepted. Democratic ideas were spread elsewhere. Even in Germany and Austria, democratic institutions were making some inroads.

Although political activities among Russian citizens were limited in 1900, a political ferment was in the making. The political movements that could function openly, and that therefore were not regarded as a threat to the government, were few. The most important of these were the *Narodniki* (populists), an intelligentsia-led revolutionary group that sought to enlist the support of the peasantry by "going to the people." Their movement had begun in the early 1870s. Much to their dismay, "the youthful agitators discovered that they could not arouse the people's 'pent-up revolutionary energy' . . . [some] were stoned out of the villages and turned over to the tsarist police by the indignant peasants. The first waves of the go-to-the-people movement had broken against the wall of popular indifference and police repression."[1]

These failures tended to turn many of the youthful revolutionaries toward more and more direct action. The result was a split, out of which two rival organizations emerged, the terroristic *Narodnaya Volya* (the people's will) and the antiterrorist *Chernyi Peredel* (the black partition), a defender of the *Narodniki* tradition. One of the great movers in the *Chernyi Peredel* was George Plekhanov, who was to become one of the leading Russian Marxist theoreticians. By 1900, the *Chernyi Peredel* was a respectable organization.

A number of other political organizations were formed in secret and continued to function underground. Among these were: the agrarian Social Revolutionaries, whose ideas were a combination of Marxism and the teachings of the Utopian Socialists; the *Kadets* (constitutional democrats), made up primarily of the liberal and moderate intelligentsia, which desired the gradual and peaceful displacement of autocracy by a constitutional form of government; and the Social Democrats, who were the Russian exponents of Marxism.[2]

---

[1]Leopold H. Haimson, *The Russian Marxists and the Origins of Bolshevism* (Cambridge, Mass.: Harvard University Press, 1955), pp. 13–14.

[2]Marxian ideas are discussed in detail in Chapter 29.

The Russian Marxists emerged from the underground revolutionary ferment in the 1880s. Many of those who had been identified with *Narodnaya Volya* and *Chernyi Peredel* were converted to Marxism. Despite police repression, the Marxian movement continued to grow and to remain active, although underground. The Russian Social Democrats were far from united, as exemplified by their split in 1903 into the Bolshevik and Menshevik wings.

The political ferment that flourished in the years around the turn of the century was given a considerable impetus by the evils stemming from industrialization, which came to Russia at a considerably later date than it did to the Western European nations. When it did come, industrialization came in a rush and brought about evils that have accompanied industrialization elsewhere (poor working conditions, long hours, inadequate pay, no organization to speak for the worker), except that it produced them more precipitously. Neither society nor the industrial owners were in a position to cope with these conditions, nor did they seem to feel any particular responsibility for doing so, although there was some progress toward efficient and enlightened management prior to the revolution. The growth of industrial enterprises, the rapid increase in the number of industrial workers, the great increase in the population of the cities and towns, together with the evils associated with industrialization everywhere—all occurred in Russia at a time when fresh Marxian ideas were attracting a large audience in European countries.

In 1905, a revolution was triggered by the disastrous consequences of the Russo-Japanese War (1904–5). Previously, the protest against autocracy was, in the main, by individuals and small groups. In 1905, however, the Russian masses were moved to action on a large scale. To the impact of an unsuccessful foreign war were added the consequences of domestic hard times and the constant urgings of revolutionary parties, working in part through the *Zemstvos*.

The *Zemstvos*—the local government assemblies whose work the government had in many ways sought to impede—had gained considerable respect and popularity among the people. Among other things, they had done much in the field of public health and education and they had organized relief during the famines in 1901–3. In November 1904 the first all-Russian Congress of *Zemstvos* met in St. Petersburg. It put forward a number of demands, including the recognition and guarantee of civil liberties, the elimination of class and racial discriminations, and the establishment of a representative assembly with real legislative powers.

The situation was made more acute by the massacre of several hundreds of peaceful petitioners, led by Father Gapon, who on Sunday, September 22, 1905, moved toward the Winter Palace, carrying portraits of the tsar and singing religious and patriotic songs, to present the grievances of the workers and to ask for the tsar's intervention and help. The immediate result was an increase in tensions, which found expression most frequently in strikes. Disturbances continued throughout the summer, aggravated by the returning soldiers after the formal conclusion of the war at the end of August.

The tsar's promise in June to a joint deputation of the *Zemstvos* and munici- pal councils that he would call together a national assembly, "as soon as possi- ble," to set up a new regime in which the public was invited to participate had not quelled the disorders. When it was announced in August that the projected legislature—the *Duma*—would be elected on the basis of a narrow franchise and that it would have only consultative powers, the growing unrest spread to the Baltic provinces and the Caucasus. The situation continued to deteriorate, culminating in a general strike in October.

In the face of these conditions, Nicholas gave in. Although martial law was the tsar's reply to the revolution, he simultaneously proclaimed a moderate con- stitution, providing for a national legislature, the *Duma*, which was to be elected on the basis of universal manhood suffrage. It was to have legislative initiative and the right to pass on projects submitted by the tsar.[3] A bill of rights guaran- teed the freedoms of speech, assembly, and conscience. A cabinet of ministers was made responsible to the *Duma*. The proclamation embodying these conces- sions by Nicholas came to be known as the October Manifesto. Count Witte, who had a considerable hand in convincing the tsar to grant the constitution, was made the first responsible prime minister. Russia, at least in theory, became a constitutional monarchy.

In this new-found freedom, the pre-1905 secret societies blossomed forth into political parties. The most active of these were the Social Revolutionaries, the Kadets (Constitutional Democrats), and the Russian Social Democrats, who about this time had split into the Bolshevik and Menshevik wings. All of these parties sponsored an exceptionally active discussion of current political, social, and economic problems. They held meetings, published newspapers and political tracts, and in other ways sought to propagate their programs and points of view.

Russia's political experience under the constitutional monarchy is not easy to evaluate. The legislative beginnings were not auspicious, partly because of a lack of experience on the part of the participants. More important, however, is the fact that a number of the tsar's acts were clearly in violation of the constitu- tion. In the midst of the uncertainties came World War I, which was to loom so large in the destiny of tsarism and Russia's future.

The first *Duma* convened in 1906, but was dismissed after a brief period of less than three months, most of which time had been spent in conflict with the government. It was dominated by the Kadets, "who devoted their full energy to expounding the indignation and disappointment experienced by the country at large at the inadequate reform and demanding a constitution on the English and the American pattern."[4] It thus earned the name "the *Duma* of the National In- dignation." Count Witte was dismissed as prime minister and replaced by Peter

---

[3]See Serge L. Levitsky, "Legislative Initiative in the Russian Duma," *American Slavic and East European Re- view* 15 (October 1956), pp. 313–24.

[4]Edmund A. Walsh, *The Fall of the Russian Empire* (Boston: Little, Brown, 1928), p. 85.

Stolypin, who, until his assassination in September 1911, ruled the country with an iron hand.

The second, and newly elected, *Duma* was convened in March 1907. It met a similar fate after an existence of less than four months. Unlike its predecessor, it contained a strong group of Social Democrats, who had boycotted the first elections and who accounted, in part, for its hostile and revolutionary attitude. It achieved nothing in a parliamentary or legislative sense. When the *Duma* refused to consent to the arrest and trial of 16 Social Democratic members, who were charged with conspiracy and sedition, it was dissolved.

A third *Duma* was elected in the same year, but only after the electoral law had been changed without even consulting the *Duma,* as the constitution provided. The revised electoral law did away with universal manhood suffrage. Some of the non-Russian nationalities were disfranchised, and severe limitations were put on the electoral rights of the peasantry. The whole electoral procedure was involved and complex. Thus, by a clever manipulation of the electoral regulations, the Government was able to manage the election of a conservative *Duma*, dominated by the propertied classes and the large landholders. It served its full term.

During the period of the third *Duma,* the Government introduced two significant reforms. One was the law calling for a gradual introduction of compulsory education for all children in the primary grades, a clear departure from past policies. The second important law introduced the Stolypin land reforms (1906–10), the completion of which was prevented by the outbreak of the war. Stolypin's aim was to free many peasants from their bondage to the *Mir* and to make them free farmers. While this policy was attacked as discriminating in favor of the relatively well-to-do peasants, it was, in fact, designed to create a group of free peasants who would feel that they had a vested interest in the established order so that they would defend it.

The fourth and the last *Duma* convened in 1912. Like the third, it was conservative and docile. For a brief period during the war, it rose to a position of leadership simply because its members were appalled by the decay in the government and because they sensed the approaching doom of tsarism.

The period of the *Duma* (1906–17), while representing a significant step toward democratic government left much to be desired. The tsar, as noted above, was far from being a constitutional monarch—that is, above politics. Not only did he from time to time exercise real political power, but, in addition, he violated the constitutional rights of the *Duma*. Also, he elevated the State Council, an administrative body, to the position of an upper house. Moreover, administrative officials were often found abusing the emergency powers still on the statute books. More important perhaps is the fact that the *Duma* really never acquired many of the essential powers associated with a true parliamentary legislature. For example, it never gained a really effective control of finance; and its power to call ministers to account and to vote them out of office if need be was not recognized in practice.

WORLD WAR I AND THE DISINTEGRATION OF THE OLD ORDER

A noted historian has said that Russia by 1914 was making such progress in the economic, social, and political realms that in another 10 years "the possibility of a revolution in Russia would have been very slight."[5] Russian industry, in all its branches, experienced a remarkable and a sustained upsurge in the final decade of the past century and in the pre-1914 years of this one. During the same period, no other nation approached Russia's economic growth rate. While workers were limited in what they could do to improve their lot, their economic position was nevertheless improving. Westernization and modernization reached also into the countryside. In brief, social and economic change, although creating problems in its wake, was proceeding at a rapid rate. But the promise of this period was cut short as the nation plunged into war in 1914. This is not to suggest, however, that Russia could have stayed out of the war once it came, for vital national interests were at stake.

The initial reaction of the people to the declaration of war was favorable and even enthusiastic. The German declaration of war aroused the people to a high sense of unity and dedication in carrying out their duties. This lasted for a long time. Moreover, despite tremendous losses and lack of equipment, the Russian soldiers fought well. It is now generally agreed that the efforts of the Russians saved France from collapse in the west. When news of reverses at the front became known at home, however—particularly news of shortages of military supplies, news of bungling and inefficiency, together with a seemingly general ineptitude—the mood of the people seemed to change.

The attitude of the people was influenced in part by conditions on the home front. There was a feeling that much of the bungling was due to inept administrative personnel and to the ministers in charge. The influence of Rasputin, a self-appointed "man of God," on the domestic scene is not to be underestimated. His influence was in large part due to the tsaritsa's belief that Rasputin could cure her son, the heir to the throne, of hemophilia. Because he seemingly had certain magic healing powers, the tsaritsa looked upon him as a man sent by God, and abided by his advice in the political and military realms. Constantly, she urged Nicholas to follow the advice he was getting from Rasputin. Historians do not agree on the extent of this influence, but many Russians noted the removal of able men whom the tsar had appointed in the summer of 1915. After several plots on his life, Rasputin was finally killed in December 1916.

The regime's answer to popular dissatisfaction with the way things were going in the military as well as in the domestic field was to send Nicholas to the front to take personal command of the army. Aside from the fact that Nicholas had no military training, his departure for the front resulted in his being politi-

[5]George Vernadsky, *A History of Russia* (New York: New Home Library edition, 1944), p. 214.

cally isolated. The Bolsheviks, for their part, were spreading defeatist propaganda and making the most of a revolutionary situation.

It was at this time that the *Duma* requested the appointment of a responsible cabinet and the inauguration of much-needed reforms. Army commanders, *Zemstvos,* and the general public joined in the *Duma's* request for the appointment of a responsible cabinet. But the tsarist regime seemed to have been oblivious to any danger.

The beginning of the collapse of tsarism came in the form of food riots in the capital in March 1917. Actually, food was not in short supply, but the distribution was bad and people had to wait long hours in queues to get their rations. Troops of the Petrograd garrison were asked to put down the disorders, but they refused to do so, and in a day or two went over to the side of the rioters. Thus, the revolution and the collapse of tsarism came without much bloodshed.

The *Duma* leaders, who were witnessing the collapse, finally asked for the tsar's abdication. When asked, he abdicated in favor of his brother, who refused to become tsar unless the position were offered by a constituent assembly. In these circumstances, the *Duma* leaders (liberals and moderate socialists) created a provisional government, and thereby made the revolution complete.

The *Duma* leaders realized that they did not possess the authority to create a new government, but nevertheless proceeded to do so because they were convinced that it would be done by the leaders of the Petrograd Soviet of Workers' Deputies, which had come into existence even before the tsar's abdication was announced. Indeed, the Soviet, whose name was soon changed to include soldiers' as well as workers' deputies, lost no time in challenging the provisional government, and in a few months was to become the vehicle for the Bolshevik seizure of power.

Once established, the provisional government faced two basic decisions. The first had to do with the question of war—whether to continue it or to make a separate peace with Germany. The second was the question of domestic reform—whether it should be initiated or postponed. The government decided to carry on with the war and to put off reform until a later date. These decisions were to contribute to its downfall. In themselves, they would not have been disastrous if the government had possessed real authority. From the beginning, however, it was to be harassed by the Soviets of Workers' and Soldiers' Deputies that were springing up throughout the country.

It was on the home front that things began to deteriorate first. The first decree of the provisional government, among other things, had proclaimed a general amnesty; established freedom of speech and press, the right to strike, the right of universal suffrage; and had declared for a summoning of a constituent assembly. These freedoms permitted the socialist parties to begin agitating anew. Many of their leaders who had been imprisoned on various charges in 1915 were released by the provisional government. Since the land problem was not yet solved and since the army was composed mainly of peasants, the demoralizing effect of this socialist propaganda was disastrous. But it must not be forgotten, however, that the offensives of 1917 on the Austrian and Rumanian fronts, although successful in their initial stages, were a serious drain on the resources of the provisional government, and hence contributed to its weakening.

On the same day that the provisional government had issued its first decree, under pressure of the Petrograd Soviet, the Soviet issued its famous Order Number 1, which "was the principal agency in the destruction of the Russian army."[6] Under this order, soldiers' committees were to be set up in each military detachment, and all weapons were to be under their control and not that of the officers. Moreover, each detachment was to obey the political decisions of the Soviet and only those orders of the military commission of the state *Duma* that did not contradict the orders of the Soviet. Since the collapse of the Russian army came after the Revolution, not before, it could be said that the collapse was the result of the Revolution, but that would be an oversimplification, for the Revolution was in part made possible by reverses at the front and the impact of these reverses on the domestic scene.[7]

It is obvious, therefore, that from the first days of the Revolution there were two governments in Petrograd—the provisional government and the Soviet of Workers' and Soldiers' Deputies. The struggle for power between them was to continue from the spring of 1917 until the Bolshevik seizure of power in the fall of 1917. Initially, the Bolsheviks were skeptical of the Soviet. In any case, they were a minority in the soviets of Petrograd and Moscow, as well as elsewhere. Moreover, the Petrograd Soviet was, in their opinion, too friendly toward the provisional government. When it was clear, however, that the soviets were following a course increasingly independent of the provisional government, and with Lenin's agitation in favor of a seizure of power, the Bolsheviks began working inside the soviets in pursuit of their aims. After a time, they succeeded in winning a majority of the delegates, first in the Petrograd Soviet and then in the Moscow Soviet. Subsequently, upon Lenin's urgings, the Bolsheviks were instrumental in having the Petrograd and Moscow soviets establish "military revolutionary committees," which were to be instruments for the seizure of power.

Meanwhile, the First Congress of Soviets was held in June 1917. At this Congress the Bolsheviks and their allies had but a scant fraction of the total number of delegates.[8] The Social Revolutionaries had by far the largest number of delegates, with the Mensheviks next. Despite their lack of strength, the Bolsheviks proposed that the soviets should seize power. This proposal was defeated, mainly by being ignored. Shortly after the Congress had adjourned, the Bolsheviks became the leaders of the abortive July insurrection, which resulted in the arrest of many of their prominent leaders. Lenin, however, succeeded in escaping to

---

[6]Vernadsky, *A History of Russia*, p. 236.

[7]See John Shelton Curtiss, *The Russian Revolutions of 1917* (New York: Van Nostrand Reinhold, 1957), pp. 29 ff.

[8]Curtiss, *The Russian Revolutions of 1917*, p. 41, says that the Bolsheviks and their allies had 137 out of 1,090 delegates.

Finland, from where he attempted to direct the second layer of leaders in their agitation and their work of organizing the workers and soldiers.

Simultaneously, the provisional government resumed the war effort with the launching of the July offensive. Initially a success, the offensive ended in failure. This failure and the growing inflation, plus the Soviet-inspired demands for reform and withdrawal from the war, resulted in increasing difficulties on the home front. More and more workers were becoming Bolshevik followers. The peasants, too, were becoming increasingly restive. At the same time, some of the national minorities were getting restless, partly because of the provisional government's failure to enunciate a nationality policy.

A radical effort to deal with the situation on the home front took place in September. This was the famous Kornilov affair. General Kornilov, the commander-in-chief of the army, was persuaded by his advisors and by emissaries of Alexander Kerensky, head of the provisional government, to bring a detachment of troops to Petrograd in order to put an end to the inimical activities of the Soviet. His mission, however, was subsequently viewed by Kerensky as an attempt to seize power. Thereupon, Kerensky appointed himself supreme commander and sought to dismiss Kornilov, who refused to be dismissed and marched on Petrograd. Kerensky appealed to the Soviet for help. Spurred on by the Bolsheviks, who otherwise detested the provisional government, the Soviet responded to Kerensky's call to fight a common battle against Kornilov. The net result was Kornilov's defeat and arrest, as well as a strengthening of the Soviet in its struggle wih the provisional government.[9]

THE BOLSHEVIK SEIZURE OF POWER

After the Kornilov affair, the growing strength of the soviets throughout the country was accompanied by an increase of Bolshevik power and influence inside the most important soviets—those of Petrograd and Moscow. The Bolshevik party had at the beginning of 1917 some 30,000 members. By October, the number had jumped to 200,000. Their strength was also reflected in their gaining control of factory committees and of some trade unions. But most importantly, they gained majorities in the Moscow and Petrograd soviets, and were soon to gain control over others.

In spite of their growing strength, the majority of Bolshevik leaders were not optimistic. Lenin was the exception. From nearby Finland, he urged preparation for an immediate uprising. Bolshevik leaders in Petrograd did not believe that power could be held, even if they were successful in seizing it in the capital. As if in desperation, Lenin returned to Petrograd in disguise (in late October) to urge acceptance of his position personally. Within a few days, he succeeded in winning over to his position all except two of the important Bolshevik leaders.

---

[9]For Kerensky's latest reflections on the situation, see his *Russia and History's Turning Point* (New York: Duell, Sloan & Pearce, 1965).

Employing the military revolutionary committees of the Petrograd and Moscow soviets, Lenin and his collaborators prepared to seize power on the eve of the meeting of the Second Congress of Soviets. In the night (November 6–7), they seized the important buildings (palace, railway stations, and telephone and telegraph centers) in Petrograd and in Moscow, and arrested the members of the provisional government who had not succeeded in fleeing. The next day (November 8), they appeared before the Second Congress of Soviets with the request that their actions be endorsed. This the congress did, vesting power in a Council of People's Commissars, headed by Lenin.

Although in power, the Bolsheviks and their allies permitted the elections for the Constituent Assembly to be held. These had been scheduled by the provisional government, after considerable prodding by the Bolsheviks and their allies in the Soviets. In one sense, the results were disastrous for the Bolsheviks, for they received a relatively small portion of the delegates. In view of the party's small membership, however, polling one fourth of the total vote could be interpreted as a moderate success. The Social Revolutionaries won a majority. Nevertheless, the Bolsheviks permitted the Constituent Assembly to convene in January in 1918. When they were convinced that the Assembly would not do their bidding, the Bolsheviks disbanded it with force after its first day in session. The Assembly was never to be heard from again.

Once in power, the Bolsheviks were forced to deal with several problems if they were to consolidate their authority. In the foreign realm, they had to liquidate the war with Germany and the Allied intervention that was to follow. Domestically, they had to liquidate the tsarist system and to build one of their own. Moreover, they had to embark upon the building of a new society.

The Bolsheviks, who had clamored for an end to the war, had little choice but to make peace at almost any price. At Brest-Litovsk in March 1918, they signed such a peace, with great losses of territory.[10] The signing of a separate peace by Russia was viewed by the Allies as little short of treasonous. The first thought in Allied circles, even before they could know the nature of the new Russian government, was how to prevent Allied munitions and their matériel that had been sent to Russia from falling into the hands of the Germans.

The Allied landing of marines at Murmansk in the early part of 1918 was the beginning of an Allied effort to deal with the consequences of the Russian withdrawal from the war. Later this move was to acquire the label "Allied Intervention," and the Bolsheviks as well as many non-Bolsheviks were to ascribe to it a purely political motive. Although there was no political motive initially, within a brief period after its inception the intervention did acquire a political motive.

As opposition to the Bolshevik regime developed into a civil war, with many troops and officers of the old Russian army forming units to fight the hastily or-

---

[10]See John W. Wheeler-Bennett, *The Forgotten Peace: Brest-Litovsk, March 1918* (New York: St. Martin's Press, 1939). See also George F. Kennan, *Soviet-American Relations, 1917–1920: Russia Leaves the War* (Princeton, N.J.: Princeton University Press, 1956).

ganized Red Army, some Allied assistance to the anti-Bolsheviks was forthcoming. Additional Allied troops (although the total was never great) were landed in European Russia and in Siberia. In Siberia some Allied forces were much more concerned with watching the Japanese than with any attempt to overthrow the new Bolshevik regime. A comprehensive study, however, concludes that the intervention in Siberia was directed at neither the Japanese nor the Bolsheviks, but against the Germans.[11] It was believed in the West that a large number of German (Austrian) prisoners in Siberia were given arms by the Bolsheviks (at Germany's bidding) and that they were about to take large parts of Siberia.[12]

Although one ought not to underestimate the psychological impact on the Bolsheviks of the intervention, particularly when one remembers that Allied troops were landed in Russia as late as January 1919, one cannot overlook the fact that the Allied victory in November 1918 really knocked the heart out of the intervention. Allied troops, aware of the original intent of the intervention, soon became restive and had to be withdrawn. If one looks at the intervention with a balanced view, it is difficult to escape the conclusion that while it was a political fiasco it was, at least partially, a military success because it "played its part in stopping the flow of German troops from east to west."[13]

One needs also to remember the so-called American intervention in the years 1921–23, which was primarily a mission of mercy and good will. It took the form of the American Relief Administration, a private organization that responded to the urgent appeal of the Russians. Later, the U.S. Congress joined in by appropriating millions of dollars. This intervention saved millions of Soviet citizens from starvation.

Closely related to the intervention was the civil war that was precipitated by the Bolshevik revolution. Although Bolshevik intentions and aims had been well advertised, their strength had been consistently underestimated by the provisional government. Having awakened to the rude realities of the situation, the opponents of the Bolsheviks rallied around certain tsarist army generals who organized fighting forces to challenge the new regime. In the end, although they fought for approximately three years, they could not reverse the tide.

In the meantime, the newly formed regime was occupied with the task of liquidating the tsarist political order and building one of its own. Smashing the old order was easier than building a new one, for Marxian theory had provided virtually no guideposts for the new order. Lenin had said that it had to be a dictatorship of the toiling masses, but he had not worked out any detailed plan. There was much improvising to meet the demands of the moment. The Red Army had been hastily organized to meet the threat to the regime posed by the

[11]Christopher Lasch, "American Intervention in Siberia: A Reinterpretation," *Political Science Quarterly* 77 (June 1962), pp. 205–23.
[12]Ibid.
[13]Sir Edmund Ironside, *Archangel, 1918–19* (London: Constable, 1953), p. 220.

civil war and the intervention. Equally hastily, the new regime organized a security police, first known as the Cheka—the so-called extraordinary commission for combating counterrevolution, sabotage, and dereliction of duty.

The Red Army and the secret police were initially conceived as instruments to guard against the revival of the old order, although, as time was to prove, the new regime came more and more to be based on force and terror. While the one-party state was not immediately instituted, the Bolsheviks lost no time in beginning the liquidation of other political parties, even those that had initially collaborated with them. Moreover, the problem of organizing a competent and loyal bureaucracy did not prove so easy as Lenin had predicted.

The overriding consideration in all of the new regime's efforts was the vast and complex problem of building the new society. One economic and social system had to be displaced by another.[14] The initial period of the attempted rapid transformation has come to be known as war communism (1918–21). In this period, the efforts of the workers to run factories and of the government to force the peasants to deliver their produce to government-owned enterprises were soon recognized as failures.

This initial period was followed by a compromise with capitalism or, as described by some Soviet spokesmen, a strategic retreat. This was the period of the so-called New Economic Policy, which was to terminate about 1928 with the launching of the new "socialist offensive" in agriculture and the beginning of the era of successive five-year plans. This was also the period of Lenin's death and the first major struggle for power.[15]

BIBLIOGRAPHICAL NOTE

Among the general histories that may serve as an introduction are: J. D. Clarkson, *A History of Russia* (New York: Random House, 1961); N. V. Riasanovsky, *A History of Russia,* 3d ed. (London: Oxford University Press, 1977); and Hugh Seton-Watson, *The Russian Empire, 1801–1917* (Oxford: Clarendon Press, 1967).

Bertram D. Wolfe, *Three Who Made a Revolution,* rev. ed. (Boston: Beacon Press, 1955), is a valuable discussion of the events leading up to the Revolution, while Edward Halett Carr, *A History of Soviet Russia* (New York: Macmillan, vol. 1, 1951; vol. 2, 1952; vol. 3, 1953; vol. 4, 1954), is a scholarly treatment of post-Revolutionary events. See also Robert V. Daniels, *Red October: The Bolshevik Revolution of 1917* (New York: Charles Scribner's Sons, 1968); Leonard Shapiro, *The Russian Revolution of 1917: The Origins of Modern Communism* (New York: Basic Books, 1984); and Adam B. Ulam, *The Bolsheviks: The Intellectual and Political History of the Triumph of Communism in Russia* (New York: Macmillan, 1965).

---

[14]For a perceptive discussion of the major problems that the Bolshevik leaders had to face in this regard, see Barrington Moore, Jr., *Soviet Politics—The Dilemma of Power* (Cambridge, Mass.: Harvard University Press, 1950), p. 85 ff.

[15]See Chapter 29.

29

Expression of Collective Interest: Marxism

The ideological foundations of the Soviet political system are to be found in the writings of Karl Marx, Friedrich Engels, V. I. Lenin, and other Marxists. As the word *Marxist* suggests, the common body of doctrine is known as Marxism or, in the Russian version, Marxism-Leninism. It is necessary to have a working knowledge of this body of doctrine if one is to understand the Soviet system. What follows is designed, understandably, to provide a summary only of the most essential elements of that doctrine.

HISTORICAL DEVELOPMENT OF SOCIALIST IDEAS

All socialists agree in the desirability of securing a fairer and more satisfactory apportionment of wealth and economic opportunity through some substantial limitation on the private ownership of property. This idea is not new; its historical roots can be found in the Old Testament. In different epochs, however, the arguments in its behalf have varied and the emphases and motivations of its proponents have not been the same.

Early socialism was motivated by religious and moralistic considerations. Each person was viewed as equal in the sight of God and therefore entitled to share relatively equally in the fruits of this earth. In the early modern period (about 1500), socialism became a combination of social revolt and religious zeal. Even as increasing importance was being attributed to economic life through the development of trade and commerce, socialistic ideas were, for the most part, still utopian, idealistic, and visionary. The primary motivation among the pioneers of socialism was an urgent desire to get people to realize the good, rather than the bad, that is in them.

Although all beginnings are more or less relative, especially in the field of social history, the year 1848 may be viewed as the birth year of modern socialism. The Industrial Revolution had by the 19th century considerably altered the economic order in the West. Large-scale industry had developed, and with it a large class of propertyless wage earners, the proletariat. These developments were accompanied by evils (inadequate housing, poor sanitation, poor working conditions, long hours of work, absence of safety measures, and so forth) that came in the wake of the industrialization of modern society. In 1848 Karl Marx and Friedrich Engels published the *Communist Manifesto,* which not only sought to explain these evils but, in addition, to put forth a program of why and how they were going to pass from the scene.

Marxism is often described as scientific socialism. It is, in part, the result of two converging developments—modern science and the Industrial Revolution and its attendant consequences. While there is no effort here to pass judgment on modern science, its development enabled Marx to say, in effect: let us not be led down the mythical paths of the past if we are to explain social phenomena; let us put society under the microscope in order that we might get a scientific answer to the question of what makes it tick. Modern science had pointed the way to a mundane and realistic approach to the study of society.

Society itself had provided many of the tangible and visible factors that would enter into the analysis. There was the development of steam and machinery, with the replacement of manpower by steam power. There was discovery, exploration, and commerce. There was the trading merchant class, the bourgeoisie, which rose to a position of dominance. There was the proletariat. There were the glaring evils accompanying this economic and social revolution.

Since these evils had their gravest impact upon the proletariat, it is perhaps not unusual that socialism, since about the time of the publication of the *Communist Manifesto,* should have concerned itself primarily with the interest of hand laborers in industrial society. This will become even more apparent as we comprehend the nature of the Marxian analysis concerning the rise and development of capitalism, as well as its projection of the impending future evolution of capitalist society.

Before setting forth the basic ideas of Marx, however, it is well to be clear about the meaning of the terms *socialism* and *communism,* for when they are used in different contexts they have considerably varied meanings. Historically, over the past hundred years or so, they have come to be associated with different means of approaching a similar goal. The word *communism* came into use in 1840. From 1840 to 1872 it came to imply revolutionary action aimed at the violent overthrow of capitalistic society. *Socialism,* on the other hand, was employed to designate constitutional activities aimed at the reform of the economic system through national control of the means of production. Between 1872 and 1917, however, the two terms became more or less synonymous, or, more precisely, the term *communism* was dropped. Within 25 years of the writing of the *Communist Manifesto,* its authors were referring to themselves as socialists or social democrats. With the seizure of power in Russia by the Bolsheviks, the old distinctions were revived and even accentuated. In more recent years, the degree to which the economy should come under collective ownership or direction has also tended to distinguish communists and socialists.

As employed by the Russians and their allies, the term *socialism* is frequently used to designate a stage in the transition from capitalism to the new society. It is the period in which the government has taken over the economy but one in which the ultimate stage of development has not been reached, the ultimate stage being communism—a classless and stateless society.

The term *communism* has been used to designate the Marxian doctrine, particularly as it has been modified and applied by the Russians. This has perhaps been done more frequently by non-Russians, although the Russians have also used the term quite extensively to signify the same thing. The Russians seem to prefer to use "socialism" or "Marxism-Leninism" when referring to the doctrinal ideology on which their system is based. Non-Russian socialists, even when they accept the Marxian analysis, prefer not to call the Russian system socialist, whereas Russian leaders do not recognize any system but their own as truly socialist. The Russians, however, use the term *communist* freely when talking of their party and party leaders.

As employed in the pages that follow, unless otherwise indicated explicitly or in context, the term *socialism* will refer to the ideology or doctrine as expounded by Marx and other Marxists. When speaking of the political and economic system built up by the Russians, it will be more appropriate to speak of Communism or Bolshevism. The important thing to note, however, is that the reader should be aware of the different ways in which the terms *socialism* and *communism* are used. The person using the terms, on the other hand, ought to make it quite clear how they are being used.

MARXISM AS A MATERIALISTIC CONCEPTION OF HISTORY

By far the greatest part of Marxian writings can be said to consist of an interpretation of capitalism. To be sure, Marx and his disciples concerned themselves about the establishment and the nature of the future society. But the bulk of their literary output deals with the laws of social evolution, and particularly with the factors governing the rise of the bourgeoisie, the modern capitalist class, and its "inevitable" demise. Therefore, Marxism is, first of all, an interpretation of capitalist society, in other words, an effort to define its place in the spectrum of long-range social development.

Different philosophers have sought an answer to the question of what is the moving force in history. Some have found it to be the will of God; others became convinced that the culture cycle was the law of history. Marx, on the other hand, concluded that on the basis of his researches societies rise and develop along a well-established path—the path of dialectical materialism.

The word *dialectics* was employed originally in ancient Greece to refer to a method of argument or disputation. A logical presentation of a point of view, or thesis, would provoke an opposition, or an antithesis. As a result of such a clash of views, the opinions of the disputing parties underwent a change, with the result that something new, higher, or more profound developed—a synthesis. There was a negation of the old and the creation of the new. Marx contended that the dialectic was at work in the social order, that each social order provoked or created an inner opposition. The result was a new and better society, which itself would become the new thesis and, in turn, create a new opposition, and so forth and so on.

What is the moving force in the dialectic process? Earlier, the German philosopher Hegel had argued in favor of the dialectic process, but he believed ideas to be the moving force in that process. Marx, on the other hand, concluded that the material factors in life were primary and all-important. They were the original force, while ideas, art, religion, philosophy, forms of political organization, and so forth, were but derivative forces. They were not even autonomous forces, but were dependent upon the material conditions of any given society.

According to the materialistic conception of history,[1] people make history by trying to satisfy their needs, which are originally imposed by nature but later modified by the artificial environment. These needs (food, clothing, shelter) are satisfied by people's productivity, which consists of extracting things from nature, in working them up, and in adapting them to their needs.

The productive forces (scientific and technical know-how) that people have at their disposal to satisfy their needs will determine all of their social relations. "The organization of any given society is determined by the state of its productive forces" (Plekhanov). In other words, "occupational activities determine the fundamental modes of social behavior and in this behavior are formed ideas, attitudes, and habits which express themselves in other fields of culture" (Marx and Engels). It follows, therefore, that as the nature of the productive forces changes, the organization of society will also change. For example, the change in the state of the productive forces under capitalism resulted in the building of urban communities, with the consequent need for urban services (garbage collection, fire protection, and so forth). This, in turn, required a change in the organization of society so as to bring about these services. Urban local government with which we are familiar would have been unthinkable 2,000 years ago, for the state of the productive forces then available created no need for it.

---

[1]One of the clearest expositions of the materialistic conception of history is to be found in a brief essay by one of the earliest Russian Marxists. George Plekhanov, "The Materialist Conception of History," originally published in 1897.

Moreover, the Marxists argue, the prevalent mode of economic production in any society gives rise to definite interests, which are essentially antagonistic, thus dividing society into classes. These interests become expressed in law. "All positive law is a defense of some definite interest" (Plekhanov). For example, at a time when horses were domesticated and economically useful (for hunting or transport), the owners of horses needed a law against horse stealing. But all interests cannot be protected equally, for they are in fundamental conflict. The net result of the conflict of interests between antagonistic classes is a state organization (government, law, and so on) whose function is to protect the interests of the dominant group or class. The state is therefore an organization of class domination, an organ of oppression of one class by another.[2]

When new productive forces evolve, the existing social institutions—government among them—do not permit their proper utilization. In the end, the class struggle becomes more and more acute and logically can only be resolved by revolution. Thus, revolution is the inevitable result of the contradiction between the new scientific and technical know-how and the inability of social institutions to bring about the creative potentialities that the new forces of production offer.

To substantiate their theory, Marx and his followers cited historical examples, the most notable being the feudal system, which was overthrown when it stood in the way of the proper utilization of the new productive forces (the Industrial Revolution) of bourgeois capitalism. Capitalist society, therefore, was not only a necessary step in social evolution, but also a beneficial one in relation to the past. In relation to the future, however, it is an evil that will be destroyed.

The basic law of social development, according to the Marxists, has been stated above. But what are the proofs of its operation in capitalist society? First and foremost, not unlike the societies that preceded it, capitalism creates within itself an inner opposition. Just as feudalism created an inner opposition, bringing forth the bourgeoisie to destroy it, so the bourgeoisie bring forth the modern wage-earning class, the proletariat, which is to overthrow bourgeois society. Capitalism brings forth the proletariat because it needs it to operate the factories and other means of production. But it exploits the propertyless wage earners, for they cannot buy back all that they have produced. They do not get paid for all that they do; some is held back.[3]

Second, the position of the worker gets worse as time goes on. The rich get richer and the poor get poorer. Economic power tends to centralize, and wealth accumulates in large fortunes. This centralization of wealth robs the proletariat of purchasing power, which results in crises—overproduction, unemployment, economic depressions, and panics. These crises, Marx was convinced, would

---

[2]While Engels did not disagree with this analysis, he did concede that there were brief periods when the warring classes were so nearly equally balanced that the power of the state for the moment assumed a certain independence in relation to both.

[3]This is Marxian labor theory of value—that is, labor produced capital as well as the actual goods of consumption. This idea was not original with Marx.

destroy the entire capitalist system, for not only does the lot of the workers become more and more unbearable but, in addition, the ranks of the proletariat are greatly enlarged by more and more of the bourgeoisie being pushed out and forced to make a living as wage earners. Thus, revolution becomes imminent as capitalism ripens.

Finally, bourgeois society is doomed, for it has not done away with class antagonisms but has established new classes, new conditions of oppression, new forms of struggle in place of the old.[4] While the "history of all hitherto existing society is the history of class struggles,"[5] earlier societies had many classes. "In ancient Rome we have patricians, knights, plebians, slaves; in the Middle Ages, feudal lords, vassals, guild-masters, journeymen, apprentices, serfs."[6] The epoch of the bourgeoisie, however, has simplified the struggle. Instead of many classes, there are only two, the bourgeoisie and the proletariat.

Moreover, as Plekhanov was to suggest, the evolution of bourgeois society would result in a more enlightened proletariat, and hence one ready to revolt.[7] There is an immense difference, he observed, between being conscious of the restrictiveness of laws and consciously striving to abolish this restrictiveness. Where people do not strive to abolish old institutions and to create new ones, there the way for the new system has not been properly prepared by the economics (the productive forces) of the society. But as science and technology reduce ignorance, people will better understand natural phenomena. As a consequence, they will better understand social and economic phenomena. When they do they will revolt.

V. I. Lenin, who was to become the leader of the Bolshevik Revolution, is the immediate doctrinal authority for the Russian Communists, as well as for many other Marxists. The Russian Communists almost always speak of Marxism-Leninism when referring to the ideological doctrine by which they profess to be guided. Although other Russian Marxists, notably George Plekhanov, preceded Lenin in laying the doctrinal foundations for Russian Marxism, Lenin has come to be regarded by the Russian Communists as the true interpreter of Marx.

Lenin made two principal contributions to Marxism. The first adds to the analysis of capitalism, while the second concerns the question of techniques for the overthrow of bourgeois society.

Lenin condemned capitalism for all the evils Marx had attributed to it, and he added others. In its later stages of development, capitalism, because of its monopoly controls, fostered scarcity at home. The reduced domestic buying power sent capitalists in search of markets abroad, which led to imperialism. Consequently, capitalism produced competing imperialistic ventures by the capitalist countries, thus leading to war.[8] At the same time, the state machinery

[4]*Communist Manifesto* (New York: International Publishers edition, 1932), p. 9.
[5]Ibid.
[6]Ibid.
[7]*Essays in Historical Materialism* (New York: International Publishers edition, 1940), pp. 36–37.
[8]See his *Imperialism, the Highest Stage of Capitalism* (originally published in 1916).

was strengthened, with a notable growth of the bureaucracy and the military. Simultaneously, repressive measures against the proletariat were on the increase.[9]

Closely related to this idea was Lenin's argument that the proletarian revolution did not need to wait until society had gone through the evils of the capitalist phase, although this was contrary to his earlier thinking on the subject. The peasantry, he said, could be allied with the industrial workers to bring about the revolution. In his change in outlook, he may have been guided by his desire to consummate the proletarian revolution in Russia, which was still a backward country and not yet developed as a bourgeois society. The Russian peasantry, because of the lingering evils of serfdom, was, in his "more mature opinion," ready to join with the workers in seeking power.

Lenin's other contribution was his development of the concept of the professional revolutionary. Marx had viewed the proletarian revolution as inevitable. Lenin accepted Marx's analysis but was more insistent upon the need for leadership to bring it about. Marx and Engels paid little attention to the idea of a communist political party. Lenin, on the other hand, talked constantly about the need of a party of professional revolutionaries, and devoted more than 20 years to building that kind of party. While Marx and Lenin agreed that capitalism prepares the way for the revolution, Lenin was somewhat skeptical about the proletariat's rising spontaneously. Consequently, he argued that a small, tightly organized party of dedicated and trained revolutionaries was needed. These people would lead the proletariat in its successful revolution.

MARXISM AS A POSITIVE PROGRAM

Although Marxists are first of all preoccupied with an interpretation of capitalism, they utilize this interpretation as the foundation upon which their positive program rests. Unlike other philosophers who have sought to explain the world, the Marxists also seek to change it. Once their analysis of the existing order is made they see two tasks confronting the proletariat. First is the seizure of political power, or converting their potential superiority into an actual one. Second, once political power is secured, the proletariat must go about the task of building the new economic and social order.

Marx argued that while history produces a revolutionary situation, it would be necessary for the proletariat and history to work together. The proletariat must have a program whose function is to show the workers how they can achieve political power. In democratic countries, they should organize politically to win the battle of democracy. In countries where the democratic process was forbidden to them, they should use organized force. Thus, Marx's program was at once both evolutionary and revolutionary.

Lenin, who was impatient to witness the revolution in Russia, placed a greater emphasis on action. Every step in the real movement is more important than a

---

[9]*State and Revolution* (New York: International Publishers edition, 1932), p. 29; originally published in August, 1917.

dozen programs, he declared. Moreover, he insisted that it was impossible to win by democratic means so long as the bourgeoisie commanded the army and the police. He frequently emphasized that unless revolutionary theory is combined with revolutionary practice, it is not Marxism but opportunism.[10] "The replacement of the bourgeois by the proletarian state is impossible without a violent revolution."[11]

Lenin, moreover, was much more preoccupied than Marx with the form of the new political authority once political power had been captured. While asserting that the bourgeois state must be destroyed root and branch, Lenin insisted that the communists would for a time need the state. This new workers' state would function during the period of transition from capitalism to communism. Its functions would be to suppress the bourgeoisie and to build socialism. It would be a dictatorship of the proletariat. So as not to leave any of his followers in doubt, Lenin declared: "He who recognizes *only* the class struggle is not yet a Marxist. . . . A Marxist is one who *extends* the acceptance of class struggle to the acceptance of the dictatorship of the proletariat."[12]

The dictatorship of the proletariat would do away with the bourgeoisie by nationalizing capital—that is, by seizing all income-producing property, including natural resources as well as capital industries. Those who sought to resist would be liquidated. Nothing must stand in the way of the new proletarian authority "to abolish all exploitation," to crush "the resistance of the exploiters," and to guide the masses " in the work of organizing the socialist economy."[13]

The gains from the productive property, now in state hands, would accrue to the entire community and be distributed by public authority. Presumably there would be private property in income, although this could not be invested for the purpose of making a profit. Although there are contradictory statements among Marxists as to the relative equality of reward, Marx and Engels in the *Communist Manifesto* asserted that the ultimate objective was a society in which everyone would contribute "according to his ability" and in turn be rewarded "according to his need." Lenin, although speaking of immediate aims, was more specific when he talked of paying workingmen's wages to managers, technicians, bookkeepers, and government officials.[14]

As conceived by Marx, however, the dictatorship of the proletariat would not be a dictatorship of one person or a few. As he envisioned it, the proletarian state would be a dictatorship of the majority (proletariat) over the minority (bourgeoisie), and hence in reality a democracy.

[10]See V. Adoratsky, *Dialectical Materialism* (New York: International Publishers, 1934), especially chap. 6.
[11]*State and Revolution,* p. 20.
[12]Ibid., p. 30. Italics his.
[13]Ibid., pp. 22–23.
[14]Ibid., p. 43.

MARXISM AS THE CLASSLESS, STATELESS SOCIETY

The struggle between the capitalists and the proletarians, according to Marx and his followers, represents the last historic clash between classes. With the abolition of private ownership of the means of production, the basis for the existence of classes will disapper. Everyone will be in the same "class," or more correctly, classes will disappear, for the concept of class has no meaning unless there are two or more of them.[15]

Since the state is the oppressive instrument of the dominant class, according to Marxian theory, there will be no need for it in a classless society. Therefore, the state will "wither away," but Marxists have not been too precise as to how soon this would take place. In 1918, Lenin thought of the transition period in terms of "ten years or perhaps more." A year or two later, he admitted that perhaps he had been overly optimistic, and for a time dwelt on the need for strengthening the state in the transition period. But he does not seem to have departed from his assertion in *State and Revolution* that what the proletariat needs is "only a state which is withering away, i.e., *a state which is so constituted that it begins to wither away immediately.*"[16] *In any case, irrespective of the time it took, Lenin expected the withering away of the state to be progressive and continous.*

Assuming the disappearance of classes and the withering away of the state, it still remains to be asked how the classless society will be organized and how it is to function without state authority. Here the Marxists are even more vague than in the matter of the duration of the dictatorship of the proletariat. Somehow, all production would be concentrated in the hands of vast associations of the whole people. The administrative functions normally associated with the state would become part and parcel of the productive process. Presumably, the people would choose representatives who would determine the basic policies to be pursued. They would plan the utilization of the material resources for the good of all. In essence, everyone would be a member of a cooperative commonwealth of the world in which cooperation would take the place of compulsion. The profit motive would give way to the service motive, and people would do the right thing because it was the right thing to do.

If the classless, stateless society seems utopian and unrealistic, the Marxists would be the first to deny it, on paper at least. "We are not Utopians," said Lenin, "and we do not in the least deny the possibility and inevitability of excesses on the part of *individual* persons, nor the need to suppress *such* excesses. But . . . no special machinery. . . is needed for this; this will be done by the armed people itself, as simply and as readily as any crowd of civilized people, even in

---

[15]In 1957 the Chinese Communist leader, Mao Tse-tung, revised Marxian doctrine to the extent of admitting that "contradictions" existed in China, that there were differences between the communist government and the people. The Russians, however, have denied that such contradictions exist in the Soviet Union.

[16]Page 22.

modern society, parts a pair of combatants or does not allow a woman to be outraged."[17] In practice, of course, the Russians have yet to produce any evidence of the withering away of the state, although they are now at the end of the seventh decade of the dictatorship of the proletariat.

CRITIQUE OF MARXISM

The foregoing discussion of Marxian theory is far from being exhaustive. Our main aim has been to concentrate on those aspects of the theory that would be most meaningful to a student of Soviet politics and government. Similarly, an extensive evaluation of that theory is beyond our scope here. Yet some critical analysis seems in order.

Unquestionably, Marxist writings have had an important impact on the world. There are elements of truth in these writings, else they could not have had such influence. However erroneous he may have been with respect to his predictions of future developments or however naive he may have been with respect to a future communist system, Marx did contribute to man's knowledge about the past. By tracing social and especially political institutions to their materialistic or economic bases, he at least called our attention to the importance of materialistic factors, although most of us would not agree that they were always the decisive ones. Moreover, his exposition of the conflict between the proletariat and the bourgeoisie gave us an added insight into social relationships. And his demonstration of some of the instabilities of capitalism has contributed to more meaningful insights with respect to the workings of a free enterprise economy. Finally, because of his many assertions, other researchers have been challenged to probe deeper, in order that they might contribute to a better understanding of our social order.

First among the criticisms that might be made of Marx's theories concerns the basic assumption that materialistic forces are primary in the shaping of all human development, that all other forces are derivative and secondary. The findings of most modern social scientists indicate that society is much more complex than the Marxian formula assumes. There is evidence that ideas and other considerations do motivate people, quite independently of materialistic forces. Moreover, Marx did not say that technical changes (inventions, and so on) were governed by materialistic forces alone. Why, it might be asked, does creativity in human affairs have to be limited to the technical sphere?

A second criticism that might be made of Marx's analysis is that the consequences of the Industrial Revolution that he saw are not to be associated with capitalism alone.[18] The Industrial Revolution, whether engineered by private enterprise or by the state, as in Russia, creates new social classes. State-initiated

---

[17] *State and Revolution,* p. 75.

[18] See the series of articles by Hugh Seton-Watson in the *Manchester Guardian Weekly,* January 28, February 4, 11, and 18, 1954, under the general title, "Some Myths of Marxism."

industrialization produces an industrial working class, while the bureaucracy, sometime euphemistically referred to by the Russians as the "toiling intelligentsia," becomes the ruling class.[19] The plight of the workers under state-engineered industrialization, in the sense that they are materially exploited and emotionally disoriented, is not unlike that of the Western European workers during the early capitalist period. Exploitation of the workers, therefore, is not the result of capitalism or of socialism but of the early stages of the Industrial Revolution.

Third, Marx did not foresee that when the Industrial Revolution had run its course the lot of the worker would improve and a certain social balance would be achieved. The position of the proletariat improved for several reasons. Free speech and a free press, by making possible a thorough discussion of workers' grievances, aroused the social conscience of the educated people. In addition, workers were able to organize in unions and thus push their demands. Moreover, they gained the right to choose members of legislative bodies and were influential in securing legislative enactments favorable to them. Without denying the great influence that capitalism wielded, it can be seen that political liberty and representative institutions enabled Western democracy to evolve a system characterized by a considerable balance among social classes.

Another defect in Marxian theory lies in its underestimation of the strength and flexibility of capitalism. Instead of impoverishing the middle class and driving more and more of its members into the ranks of the proletariat, capitalism has enabled the middle class to become more prosperous and to grow in numbers. Moreover, it had demonstrated a remarkable ability to adjust to public regulation of some of its important activities. By making concessions, it has provided untold opportunities for the middle class and for the workers, demonstrating a dynamic flexibility.

In their revolutionary appeal for unity among workers of the world, Marx and his followers underestimated the strength of the appeals of nationalism. National loyalties have proved to be stronger than loyalties to class, something that is true of the capitalist class as well as of the proletariat.

Finally, the Marxists erred in their assumption that workers would act, and act rationally, in given circumstances. Studies in the political behavior of human beings indicate that people are often exceedingly irrational in their political choices. More important, perhaps, is the fact that people are seldom moved to action. Thus, Marx was wrong when he assumed the revolutionary character of the workers, as well as when he assumed that they would act rationally in support of their class interest.

As Djilas has written, "Marx became a Communist first and founded Communist doctrine afterward. . . . [He] searched the British Museum for objective

---

[19]See Milovan Djilas, *The New Class* (New York: Praeger Publishers, 1957). For an excellent recent critique of Marxian theories, see his *The Unperfect Society: Beyond the New Class* (New York: Harcourt Brace Jovanovich, 1969).

laws that would justify his prophetic zeal."[20] Elsewhere, he was written that "Communist ideas did not spring forth from the working class," and that "Communists have never anywhere fully understood the working class."[21] And as Robert Wesson has said, what distinguished Marx and other socialists was his proclivity for revolution, which explains much of the success of his doctrines.[22]

With respect to the Soviet Union, Marxism, or Marxism-Leninism, has meant whatever the Soviet leaders have chosen to have it mean. In the first place, the men who set up the dictatorship, aside from a few educated Marxists such an Lenin, could not have known much about Marxism. Many peasant lads, like Nikita Khrushchev, who joined the party in 1918, were barely literate. Second, Soviet Communist leaders, including Lenin, Stalin, Khrushchev, and their successors, have never hesitated to revise Marxist postulates when it was thought necessary to defend certain policies or programs. By and large, the Soviet leaders have been guided by the cardinal aim—the abolition of private property. To achieve this, they have found it necessary to strengthen the state and, in the process, to protect the interest of the dominant class—the party apparatus.

Stalin's main contribution to Marxism-Leninism is the idea of "socialism in one country." When the Bolshevik revolution was not followed by similar revolutions elsewhere, Stalin saw in the outside world a threat to the Soviet system (the so-called capitalist encirclement). To meet this threat, Stalin believed that the Soviet state had to be strengthened, and this could be done, in his opinion, only by a rapid transformation of the Soviet economic system. This required forced industrialization, which in turn called for collectivization of agriculture in order that the new proletariat be fed. Marx had stressed the importance of the proletariat. Lenin had put greater emphasis on the party. Stalin sought to merge the party and the state so as to make the Soviet Union the chief instrument of proletarian revolutions.

From the notion of "socialism in one country" flowed certain other ideas. The dictatorship of the proletariat had to be viewed as the dictatorship of the one-party state. This dictatorship had to be strengthened in the so-called transition period, and especially the army and the police as guardians of that dictatorship. Moreover, the period of this dictatorship was to be relatively long, during which the economic and cultural prerequisites for "socialist victory" were to be created. These ideas led to the destruction of all opposition and to the strengthening of the monolithic character of the regime. The withering away of the state was, for all practical purposes, forgotten.

Stalin's idea of "socialism in one country" had other interesting implications and consequences. For example, revolutionary movements in foreign countries would be staged or called off depending upon whether Soviet foreign policy was

---

[20]*The Unperfect Society,* p. 116.

[21]See his articles in the *New York Times,* July 31, August 1, 2, 1972.

[22]Robert G. Wesson, *Why Marxism?: The Continuing Success of a Failed Theory* (New York: Basic Books, 1976), p. 25.

furthered thereby. Similarly, in order to increase labor productivity Stalin introduced significant wage differentials and worker-discipline legislation. Moreover, he departed from Lenin's emphasis on internationalism, stressing the achievements of the Russian state, claiming Russian firsts in inventions, and elevating heroes of tsarist Russia to positions of veneration. Although a member of a minority nationality (Georgian), Stalin became more Russian than the Russians.

Khrushchev, although not much of a theorist, advanced three ideas to which reference should be made. Allegedly correcting Stalin's errors, he in effect revised Lenin when he asserted that war between the communist and noncommunist camps was not inevitable. Similarly, he revised Lenin when he proclaimed that it was possible for proletarian revolutions to be achieved by nonviolent means. More interesting than either one of these notions were his observations on the withering away of the state, which revised Marx as well as Lenin. Instead of being the last stage in political development prior to the establishment of the classless and stateless society, the dictatorship of the proletariat gives way to the "state of all the people." Instead of ceasing to exist, the state apparently dissolves itself slowly into organized society. In this organized society, the Communist party will replace the government, and therefore its role will become even more important than in the past.

Ironically, at the very time that economic stagnation was most evident in the post-Khrushchev years, there were ideological discussions revolving around the concept of "mature socialism." Perhaps anticipating a revision of the 1961 Party Program (to eliminate its unfounded claims and disproved projections), General Secretary Chernenko in 1984 indicated that Soviet society was merely at the "beginning" of a "historically protracted period—the stage of developed socialism," and spoke of "improving developed socialism." "Communism" was therefore far off in the future.

In the foreign policy realm, note should be made of the so-called Brezhnev doctrine, the essence of which is that the Soviet Union has the right to intervene in the affairs of any communist state when the communist political order is threatened from within or without. This doctrine was proclaimed as a way of justifying the Soviet invasion of Czechoslovakia in August 1968, but it may also have unpredictable implications for the future.

MARXISM: RELEVANCE OF THE IDEOLOGY

At one time Marxism was an understandable human response to poorly understood, rapid, and threatening change that came in the wake of the Industrial Revolution. Today, however, Marxism has nothing to say about most of the great problems facing the world—the danger of nuclear war, the population explosion, the depletion of renewable energy resources, and the various threats to the environment. Moreover, there is some question about the relevance of Marxian ideas even in the system that purports to be based on those ideas.

Among the so-called experts there is some disagreement about the role of ideology in the Soviet system. A few maintain that it is a body of "ceremonial political functions," a type of Sunday creed to which most communists pay lip service. A much larger group contends that ideology is a guide to action, a type of instruction manual of pragmatically extracted precepts from Marxist teachings, which permits the greatest flexibility in the practical implementation of fundamentally inflexible principles. This means that each Marxist-Leninist postulate expresses the position of the Communist party concerning some specific question at a particular time. When a goal is reached or circumstances change, the postulate loses validity, and the party's ideological position can be changed. Thus, adherence to traditional concepts can be interpreted as faithfulness to the party line or as dogmatism. Readiness to modify such concepts can be interpreted as revisionism or as creative Marxism. Similarly, peaceful coexistence can be "a form of the class struggle on a worldwide scale" or "downright capitulation." As a guide to action, therefore, ideology is viewed less as a collection of dogmas and more as an instrument of communication and leadership.

Other experts, while agreeing that ideology as a guide to action assists the leaders in coping with practical needs, whether economic or political, maintain (correctly, in the opinion of this writer) that ideology has an influence on policy beyond these needs. As a guide to action, Marxist-Leninist teachings are utilized to enhance and extend the role and power of the Soviet Communist party, but these teachings also reflect the party's world outlook. In this ideology are found most of the basic teachings of Marx: the class struggle, the overthrow of capitalism, and the establishment of a system of social (collectivist) production. Ideology in the Soviet Union is thus "a continuous process resulting from the interplay of Communist theory and practice, affected at times—perhaps continually—by the interests of ruling groups, by Communist internecine struggles and by the personal characteristics of dictators, but with a logic of its own."[23]

In spite of the fact that most of Marx's predictions have been falsified by history, Soviet leaders continue to spout the old arid formulas. In any conflict between ideology and power, however, the former always gives way.

It is interesting to note that many Marxists outside the Soviet Union have recently found comfort in Marx's earlier writings, especially those dealing with the concept of alienation; that is, people were alienated because their work was sold. The ideal society of those early writings was one in which it was possible for a person "to do one thing today and another tomorrow, to hunt in the morning, fish in the afternoon, rear cattle in the evening, criticize after dinner . . . without ever becoming hunter, fisherman, shepherd or critic."[24] Thus, alienation would disappear only when the division of labor had given way and when people worked for the fun of it. As Wesson has pointed out, "the naivete of this

---

[23]C. Olgin, "What Is Soviet Ideology?", *Bulletin: Institute for the Study of the USSR* 11 (November 1964) p. 9.
[24]Cited in Wesson, *Why Marxism?*, p. 15.

nostalgic dream is striking. But the idea has had a remarkable appeal for many modern readers."[25] It is not surprising, however, that Marxism-Leninism in the Soviet Union has no room for the concept of alienation.

BIBLIOGRAPHICAL NOTE

There are several editions of Marx's writings; among them, one of the more convenient brief collections is *Capital, The Communist Manifesto, and Other Writings* (New York: Modern Library, 1932). Among Lenin's numerous works, several deserve mention: *What Is to Be Done; Two Tactics of Social Democracy; Imperialism: The Highest Stage of Capitalism;* and *The State and Revolution.*

Analyses and critiques of Marxism include those of H.B. Acton, *The Illusion of the Epoch: Marxism-Leninism as a Philosophical Creed* (London: Cohen & West, 1955); Sidney Hook, *Marx and the Marxists* (Princeton, N.J.: Van Nostrand Reinhold, 1955); John Plamenatz, *German Marxism and Russian Communism* (London: Longmans, Green, 1954).

Especially interesting are two books already cited: one by a one-time Marxist (and one-time member of the Politburo of the Yugoslav Communist party), Milovan Djilas, *The Unperfect Society;* the other by Robert G. Wesson, *Why Marxism?* A truly monumental survey of Marxism has been done by a one-time Polish communist, Leszek Kolakowski, *Main Currents of Marxism,* 3 vol. (New Haven, Conn.: Yale University Press, 1978).

---

[25]Ibid.

30

The Communist Party and Its Role

The Communist party is the driving force in the Soviet system. It is the dictatorship, not really *of* the proletariat, but *over* the proletariat and over all other groups in Soviet society. It has a complete monopoly of political power; no competing groups or influences are tolerated. The Soviet "Government" is not a government in the Western sense, for it is not an autonomous force. It cannot function independently of the party. As Stalin once said, "Not a single important political or organizational question is decided without direction from the party." The party makes the decisions, while the governmental apparatus serves as the party's agent to carry out these decisions.

In any study of the Soviet system, therefore, the key role of the Communist party must remain in the foreground, but, as a subsequent chapter will show, this role is not confined to the spheres of economics and politics. Every phase of human endeavor is within the scope of its all-embracing authority and concern.

BACKGROUND OF RUSSIAN COMMUNIST PARTY

The early Russian Marxists, as did those in Western Europe, thought of themselves as social democrats and initially called their party the Russian Social Democratic Labor party. As a consequence of internal quarrels, the faction that was to gain dominance called itself the Russian Social Democratic party (B).[1] In 1918, they changed the name to Russian Communist party (B), and in 1925 it

---

[1] The "B" stood for Bolsheviks; for discussion of Mensheviks and Bolsheviks see below.

became the All Union Communist party (B). After the 19th Party Congress in 1952, the official name became the Communist Party of the Soviet Union (CPSU).

Russian Marxism grew out of a split in the *Narodnik* (populist) organization, referred to in Chapter 28. The *Narodnik* movement was initiated by intellectuals who hoped and expected the peasantry to be responsive to their agitation—that is, to their explanations of the peasants' plight and their suggested remedies. When the peasantry proved unresponsive, and indeed hostile, many of the *Narodniki* turned more and more to direct action and violence. They acted through an organization called *Narodnaya Volya* (the people's will). Those who opposed violence established a rival organization, called the *Chernyi Peredel* (the black partition). Subsequently, leaders of the latter group, such as George Plekhanov, became convinced that the peasantry was a nonrevolutionary, conservative, and indifferent element. After searching for a new faith, they embraced Marxism, and founded the first Russian Marxist organization, called the Emancipation of Labor.

Declaring its disillusionment with the peasantry, this group, under the intellectual leadership of Plekhanov, declared that the revolutionary movement in Russia could triumph only if it were based on the working class. This constituted a break with the important *Narodnik* idea, which they had once shared, that Russia could skip the capitalist phase of development. Plekhanov and his cohorts were in effect saying that Russia was launched on the course of capitalist development, which would produce the working class, and which in turn would overthrow Russian bourgeois society.

Marxism, however, meant different things to many Russians who professed to be Marxists.[2] Some equated it with industrial development, others with traditional trade unionism, still others with idealistic reforms and opportunism. Plekhanov and his pupil, V. I. Lenin, viewing themselves as orthodox Marxists, sought in the 1890s to defend the orthodox Marxist analysis and particularly to reassert its revolutionary content. They agreed with the *Communist Manifesto* that the proletarian revolution would come in the wake of capitalist development. Because Russia was industrially backward, they believed that the initial task was to facilitate a bourgeois-democratic revolution in Russia. While Plekhanov remained loyal to his position to the end, Lenin was to find it increasingly inconvenient, for it got in the way of his activist bent. Other Russian Marxists were to find themselves similarly divided.

The Russian Social Democratic Labour party, founded in 1898, developed a split of major proportions at its second congress, held in London in 1903.[3] Out of

---

[2] See Leopold H. Haimson, *The Russian Marxists and the Origins of Bolshevism* (Cambridge, Mass.: Harvard University Press, 1955).

[3] The first congress had met secretly at Minsk, but the principal participants were arrested before anything could be done beyond the appointment of the Central Committee and the decision to publish a party organ. The second congress had to be held abroad; originally it convened in Brussels, but soon it transferred to London for fear of police pressure.

it emerged two distinct groups of Russian Marxists, the result of a split that had been in the making for several years. The groups came to be known as Mensheviks and Bolsheviks. These words are derived from the Russian words *Menshe* and *Bolshe,* meaning less and more, respectively. The split between the Mensheviks (or minority men) and the Bolsheviks (or majority men) continued to widen in the years ahead, leading to their complete and formal separation in 1912.

The Mensheviks and Bolsheviks found themselves divided on two primary and several subsidiary questions. The first of the major questions concerned the political implications of Russia's industrial backwardness. The Mensheviks, led by Plekhanov, held to the orthodox view that socialism would come to Russia only after the bourgeois-democratic revolution, and this was to be a long-term affair. The opposite view, often identified with Leon Trotsky, originally a Menshevik, held that the capitalist class was not strong enough to bring forth the bourgeois revolution. Hence, the proletariat should bring on the revolution and keep it going (in "permanence") until the proletarian revolution should be completed. This would mean telescoping two revolutions into one. While continuing to pay lip service to the orthodox doctrine, Lenin and the Bolsheviks were in spirit close to the latter group. Subsequently, Lenin was to add his own contribution to Bolshevik theory by suggesting an alliance with the peasantry so as to give the proletariat a broader base. By the tactical combination of the proletariat with the peasantry to complete the democratic revolution, and subsequently with the village poor to bring on the proletarian revolution, industrial backwardness, in Lenin's view (and later Stalin's) could actually be turned to the advantage of socialism.

The second major question in the split among the Russian Social Democrats involved the nature of the party. Lenin, as leader of what was to become the Bolshevik faction, argued for a relatively small, closed party of carefully selected and dedicated revolutionaries. This would be a disciplined organization run from the center. While sympathizers would be encouraged, they would not be members of the party. The leaders of what was to become the Menshevik faction, on the other hand, argued for a broadly based party that would admit all who believed in its program. Such a party would of necessity have to accord some voice to the rank and file. Moreover, such a party would collaborate with other parliamentary parties when it was in its interest to do so, something that was anathema to Lenin. Although initially in a minority, Lenin, through tactical maneuvers, gained a majority of the delegates for his side. In the years ahead, he did all in his power to consolidate his position of leadership and to rebuff all challenges to his authority.

The definitive split in 1912 resulted in no small part from Lenin's precarious hold on the leading committees, which he was afraid he could not maintain, and therefore directed the formation of a separate Bolshevik organization with a separate central committee. The Bolsheviks, however, resisted his suggestion that they call themselves Communists, a name they adopted only after their seizure of power.

The collapse of tsarism and the establishment of the bourgeois-democratic provisional government seemed to favor the Menshevik position. The gains of the Bolsheviks, however, and particularly their seizure of power in November 1917, irrevocably settled the argument in favor of the Bolsheviks, at least insofar as Russia was concerned. The Menshevik arguments were answered by revolutionary action. The events of 1917, for all practical purposes, resolved the Bolshevik–Menshevik controversy in favor of the Bolsheviks. The Mensheviks, as well as others, continued an uneasy and harassed existence as opposition parties until the end of the civil war, when the Bolsheviks put an end to opposition groups.

The history of Russian Marxism in the early part of this century, and particularly the history of what transpired in 1917, has provided us with the major clue to Bolshevik success. In no small measure, their success may be attributed to the elasticity of their tactics. Their firm dedication to the goal of achieving political power was certainly important. Perhaps other political groups were equally dedicated to their respective goals, but they had none of the ingenuity or the willingness of the Bolsheviks to alter their methods, to change their positions, or to take seemingly contradictory positions when doing so would advance them toward their objective.

Lenin, for the most part, was the master tactician in all Bolshevik maneuvers. The elasticity of his tactics enabled him to bring the peasants into his theories because he believed that their discontent could be channeled to Bolshevik ends. Similarly, he was convinced that the discontent among the non-Russian nationalities could be harnessed in the interests of the proletarian revolution. His changes in attitude as to whether or not the Bolsheviks should participate in the Soviets, whether they should take part in the Duma elections, and so forth, further confirmed his influence on Bolshevik tactical elasticity. Lenin's dedication to this principle has by and large been observed by his party successors.

BOLSHEVIK CONCEPT OF PARTY

Out of this factious and discordant background and out of the experience of governing in subsequent years, the Bolsheviks developed a concept of party that embraces certain definite characteristics. In the main, these characteristics are identified with questions concerning what the party is supposed to be and what it is supposed to do. The answers to these questions have not varied materially during the period of Soviet rule.

The early formative years gave the party an indelible cast. That cast was in the nature of a monolithic revolutionary elite. Lenin was especially insistent upon the elitist principle: only the most qualified and dedicated persons should be permitted membership. They all must be of one mind, or at least capable of accepting iron discipline and obedience once the party line had been handed down. No deviations were to be permitted; in other words, no internal factions could exist. The party was to speak with one voice and to act as one unit. Sympathizers (fellow travelers) were encouraged to cooperate and to lend themselves to party ends, but they would not be permitted to become encumbrances on the party's disciplined and monolithic machine.

All of these ideas, predicated upon the assumption that the party would be the instrument for the seizure of political power in the name of the proletariat, were reinforced under the leadership of Lenin's successor, Joseph Stalin. By comparison with Stalin, Lenin's intolerance of disagreement and compromise was mild indeed. Rigidity in the interpretation of the party line increased constantly during Stalin's reign. Slightly varying points of view became known as major and treasonous deviations, which were punished with increasing severity.

Stalin's successors, although making certain modifications in the Soviet system, have not departed from basic Bolshevik tenets concerning the nature of the Communist party. It continues to be viewed as a monolithic, highly centralized, and disciplined organization. There has been no suggestion that factions be permitted within the party or that top leaders of the party be subject to criticism any more than they have been in the past.

The Soviets have described the Communist party as the most conscious segment of the working class, whose role it is to lead and to speak for the proletariat. As the all-wise and only true defender and expounder of socialism, the party is supposed to know what needs to be done during the period of transition from capitalism to communism. Since no one else can be trusted with this task, the party becomes not only the source of all initiative, but also the all-wise judge of human actions and motivations and of good and evil. Moreover, the party not only assumes the role of guarding and protecting the interests of the proletariat against all other movements that would seek the favor of the proletariat but, in addition, prevents the formation or operation of any group whose aim is to appeal to any segment of society for support.

In other words, the party is the main, if not the sole, instrument for the totalitarian remaking of society. The party organization is charged with facilitating the execution and acceptance of the policies of the party's high command. Moreover, it must from time to time assimilate into its ranks various individuals, while at the same time making sure that their devotion to the party is unquestioned, so that the party may continue to be a trustworthy instrument of its leaders. The party, in short, operates as a machine of the party leadership for the total reconstruction of society.

The Bolsheviks have often defended their totalitarian dictatorship by arguing that democracy prevails inside the party. They have said that until the party takes a position on a certain question, party members are free to discuss and debate the various aspects of that question. Moreover, they have asserted that even after the party line has been established, rank-and-file members, as well as those at the top, are encouraged to engage in criticism and self-criticism.

In practice, as a subsequent section of this chapter will show, dissent within party ranks was discouraged from the outset, and progressively repressed until it came to an end. The criticism that remains today is a controlled criticism, directed from the top. The lesser figures in the party and their work are the invariable objects of this criticism. On occasion, a more prominent figure is accorded the "opportunity" of indulging in self-criticism, admitting his sins, and bringing down wrath upon his own shoulders. But high party leaders, as well as party policies, are immune from criticism from below unless for some reason these leaders decide that a change is needed and that it would be facilitated by controlled and directed criticism.

But even controlled criticism does not assert that the party erred in a given situation. As a general rule, the criticism centers on bureaucratic inefficiency, venality, and outright refusal to carry out assigned tasks. Sometimes governmental officials are charged with being unimaginative, slow, and inept in adapting party policies to the circumstances at hand. Other times they are accused of misinterpreting party directives. Such criticism, the leaders hope, will have the effect of diverting attention from them as well as from the party when things go wrong.

Party leaders who die or are removed from office may be subject to criticism. This has been true even of top leaders such as Stalin and Khrushchev. But the contention is always made that their misdeeds are not the fault of the party. In the downgrading of Stalin, for example, it was even asserted that other party leaders had no choice but to carry out his evil directives. The system that permits or enables a personal dictator to arise is seemingly never at fault.

ORGANIZATIONAL STRUCTURE AND AUTHORITY WITHIN THE PARTY

The Soviet Communists have by and large adhered to Lenin's precept that the party should be kept relatively small. The party has grown numerically, but for the most part this has been a controlled growth. The years of World War II were somewhat of an exception. Because casualties among party comrades were particularly high, recruitment policies were liberalized, with the result that by the end of the war the party membership nearly doubled. New members were often taken in more because of their contribution to the war effort than for their knowledge of and dedication to Marxism-Leninism. In 1984 party membership totaled over 18 million, including candidates for membership. Most of the candidates are among the 42 million members of the *Komsomol* (Communist youth organization). In a total population of some 275 million, the Communist party is still a relatively small and select organization, comprising about 9 percent of the adult population. In absolute numbers, of course, 18 million constitutes a sizable organizational force.

In the light of Marxian theory, one might expect to find the Communist party the party of the proletariat. Soviet industrial workers, however, while constituting an important core of the party membership, are by no means in a majority. In fact, they account for approximately 40 percent of the total. The rural areas account for something less than a fifth of the total, although Soviet statistics in this area are exceedingly meager.[4] The remainder is made up from the "toiling

---

[4]Soviet authorities have admitted that as late as 1958 some collective farms had no party units, while on others they were small and weak.

intelligentsia," or the bureaucracy, which, together with the workers, enables the party to retain its predominantly urban character.

The really important development in party membership is to be found in the shift in emphasis from the workers to the technical and administrative intelligentsia. Party membership among the workers and among farmers has been in relative decline, while among the growing class of technicians, factory managers, engineers, and party and government bureaucrats, party membership has been on the increase. This has had the effect of raising the intellectual level of the party membership. It has also resulted in the wielding of an increasing influence by the new Soviet administrative and intellectual elite, with a corresponding decline in the influence of the workers and the farmers. It is interesting in this connection that Khrushchev in 1961 observed that in time there would be no need to divide party members into workers, farmers, and white-collar workers.

At least two things need to be noted about social composition. First, a person's social background is based on the category listed at the time of an individual's recruitment into the party. Thus, one-time party head Brezhnev was listed as a worker. Moreover, in recent years junior office workers were transferred to the category of workers. Second, workers and peasants are represented only nominally in positions of real political influence.

For a long time rank-and-file representation in the party of various nationalities favored the Slavs, especially the Great Russians. This was especially true in Stalin's time. In recent years, however, there has been a considerable redressing of the balance, with the avowed aim of bringing the percentage of party membership among the non-Russian nationalities up to that of the Russian Soviet Federated Socialist Republic (RSFSR). While this goal has in a large measure been realized, the Great Russians still seem to enjoy a disproportionate representation in the party's top leadership groups.

From time to time party ranks are purged of "undesirables."[5] The Russian Communists have looked upon the purge as a rational and desirable way of keeping the ranks pure by cleaning out the undesirable elements. This is in conformity with the Leninist notion that the party should be a monolithic organism. The need for the purge presupposes that the rigid process for admission to the party is not foolproof, that some persons will get in who should have been excluded. At the 24th Party Congress in 1971, Brezhnev announced that party membership cards would be recalled and new cards issued on the basis of meritorious behavior and performance. This exchange of party cards began in March 1973, and represented a mild purge of undesirables from the party ranks, resulting in the expulsion of some 347,000.

In the struggles for power within the party, however, the concept of the purge was broadened to include mass expulsions and a large-scale liquidation of party

---

[5]For an excellent work on the purge as a technique of Soviet totalitarianism, see Zbigniew K. Brzezinski, *The Permanent Purge: Politics in Soviet Totalitarianism* (Cambridge, Mass.: Harvard University Press, 1956).

leaders at all levels.[6] Purges to this end could hardly be defended as merely a cleaning out of persons of doubtful dedication to Marxism-Leninism, for some of Lenin's most devoted followers perished in the purges.

Where the penalty is mere expulsion, on the other hand, many members deliberately become undesirable, for being thrown out is by and large the only way out of the party. Once a person becomes a party member he dares not give thought to leaving the party on his own volition. To leave, or to suggest leaving, is tantamount to treason. Yet some persons have found it difficult to continue living a lie—that is, to pretend to believe the party's propaganda. The way out for some of these people is expulsion, which can sometimes be induced by failure to pay dues, attend meetings, or perform assigned tasks. Excessive consumption of alcohol may also produce undesirables, and hence candidates for expulsion.

Ostensibly, the Communist party is organized on the basis of the principle of democratic centralism. This means, as Soviet spokesmen have explained it, that the party is a pyramidal organization. At the bottom are some 390,000 primary units, once called cells. Above these are several layers of intermediate bodies; each layer has fewer units until the top is reached, where there is one supreme party organization. This setup is allegedly democratic because, in theory at least, members of the lower units in the pyramid elect persons to the unit above, and these, in turn, are responsible to those who elected them. The centralist aspect is to be found in that it is incumbent upon the lower layers to obey the directives and to carry out the orders of the units above them.

In Soviet practice, however, the accent has been on centralism. First of all, the elective principle has been largely meaningless, for so often members have been co-opted—that is, named by someone above, a practice admitted by the Soviets, although in the form of a criticism. Second, the leaders at the very top, so long as they stick together, are in no danger of being ousted, and they in turn can virtually dictate the selection of those immediately below. These, in turn, because they have the confidence of the top leaders, can dictate the selection of those below them, and so on down the line. The one possible exception involves local party secretaries, some of whom have been ousted after the introduction of the practice of voting for each member of the local committee individually and by secret ballot. Secretaries of city and district committees must be approved by committees of higher units, which sometimes means that approval from top leaders is necessary. Finally, the practice of ruthlessly punishing dissenters has discouraged members from questioning the adequacy of individuals whom they have "elected."

Moreover, party rules protect members of the executive bodies at all levels from disciplinary action by the respective primary organization to which they

---

[6]The struggle for power within the party is discussed in a subsequent section of this chapter. Milovan Djilas says that Stalin's tyranny "devoured . . . some seven hundred thousand Communist party members." See *The Unperfect Society: Beyond the New Class* (New York: Harcourt Brace Jovanovich, 1969), pp. 150–51.

belong. Punishment can be inflicted only if a two-thirds majority of the executive body concerned, meeting in plenary session, gives its consent. In this way the leaders run no risk, if indeed one ever existed, of being embarrassed by a "defeat in their own precinct."

Democratic centralism, as theoretically conceived, operated only at the beginning—while the Bolshevik party was in the process of organization. Even then the leaders were in large measure self-appointed, reaching the top through ability and the force of their personalities. Once the top group was fairly well established, the members of that group, and not those below, determined who should join them in positions of leadership. From that time on, democracy gave way to centralism and to authority.

The party congress, according to party rules, is the supreme organ of the party. In practice it is anything but that. Prior to 1971 it was supposed to meet at least once every four years. In fact, between 1939 and 1952 no congresses were held. Since 1952 there have been seven congresses: 1956, 1959, 1961, 1966, 1971, 1976, and 1981. At the 1971 congress the rules were changed to require a meeting every five years to coincide with the introduction of new five-year plans.

Aside from the infrequency of their meetings, which, in any event, last but a few days, congresses are handicapped by their sheer size; recent ones have had several thousand delegates. Moreover, their proceedings give every outward indication of being carefully prepared in advance, with no dissenting debate and all debate being taken unanimously. Party congresses are, in reality, huge manifestations or rallies of the party faithful who merely sit, perhaps also listen to, and applaud the party leaders. Conversely, the congresses provide a platform for the leaders to extol their alleged accomplishments, to call for renewed efforts on behalf of old or new goals, and to proclaim changes in the party line.

Far more important than the party congress is the Central Committee, ostensibly elected by the congress and meeting at least once every six months. Its membership has been characterized by large turnovers from one congress to another. The greatest turnovers ocurred in the 1930s, after the great purges, but more recent changes have been quite extensive. At the 20th Party Congress in 1956, for example, 133 members were elected, over a third of them for the first time, while of the 112 candidate members over half were chosen for the first time. At the 22nd Party Congress in 1961, the membership of the Central Committee was increased to 175 members and 155 candidate members. Among these the holdovers constituted approximately 37 percent. These large turnovers have not resulted from actions freely taken by the respective congresses, for no one is elected to the Central Committee unless his name is proposed by the top leadership of the party. Succeeding party congresses have increased the size of the Central Committee. In 1981 there were 319 members and 151 candidates. Although the turnover rate was low in the post-Khrushchev years, signs point to a larger turnover after the projected party congress in 1986. The vigorous shakeup of party personnel that was initiated in the Andropov era, and the new party program that was being drafted in 1984 and 1985 seemed to presage such an outcome.

The Central Committee is charged with directing the work of the party between congresses, and its powers, at least on paper, are extensive. Aside from its authority to manage party resources, appoint editors, and set up various party institutions, the Central Committee "directs the work of central government bodies and social organizations of working people through the party groups in them." While basic directives are issued in the name of the Central Committee, in actuality these functions are performed by and under the direction of the Politburo (or policy bureau) and the Secretariat (discussed below). While the Central Committee was relatively important in the 1920s, it rarely met during the latter years of Stalin's rule and, according to one-time party secretary Khrushchev, it was never called into session during World War II.[7] In more recent years, the Central Committee has held fairly regular sessions. There is no evidence, however, to suggest that it has seriously impeded the proposals or programs of the recognized leader or leaders. Because many of its members are prominent in the governmental bureaucracy, in science and technology, in the military, and in the cultural field, the Central Committee serves as a link between the party elite represented in the Politburo and the Secretariat and the important scientific-technical-administrative apparatus that supervises the operation of the Soviet system.

For most, if not all, of the Soviet period, the most powerful party body has been the Politburo (between 1952 and 1966 known as the Presidium), which has generally numbered about a dozen men. In 1952 it was merged with the Orgburo (organizational bureau), making it a body of 25 members and 11 candidates. After Stalin's death in 1953, its membership was cut to its former size. In recent years its size has fluctuated between 10 and 15 members and 6 to 9 candidates. In 1985 it numbered 12 full members and 6 candidates. As the group that is supposed to direct the work of the Central Committee between its plenary meetings, the Politburo is the supreme policymaking body in all spheres of Soviet life. Although elected by the Central Committee, Politburo members are chosen only upon recommendation by the Politburo—a recommendation that in the past originated with the recognized leader.

The Secretariat is a type of management board of the party apparatus. In recent years it has consisted of 5 to 12 secretaries (several of whom are also members of the Politburo) who are chosen by the Central Committee in much the same way as the members of the Politburo. With a staff of approximately 100,000 full-time party professionals, the Secretariat is charged with directing the current work of the party. This means that it selects personnel for positions of responsibility in various parts of the Soviet system, and that it verifies fulfillment of party decisions in all fields—political, economic, social, propaganda, and so on. In this way, the Secretariat not only serves to implement policies but is at the same time the eyes and ears of the Politburo.

In the Politburo and in the Secretariat there is a broad division of labor. These general areas of responsibility include foreign affairs, heavy industry, ag-

[7] *New York Times,* June 5, 1956.

riculture, party affairs, agitation and propaganda, political administration of the armed forces, and other spheres of activity with which the party is concerned.[8] Because of their intimate association with the party, state, military, and police apparatus, the members of the Secretariat are now thought to be in a position to exercise a decisive influence in the Politburo on all matters of high policy.[9] But in the end the Politburo decides.

Although party rules have emphasized the principle of collective leadership, the general tendency in the Soviet system has been toward one-man rule. This was true in Lenin's day, but much more so after Stalin consolidated his power in the late 1920s. It was Stalin's position as general secretary of the party and his determination to use that position to the utmost that enabled him to rise to a position of unquestioned ascendancy. Nikita Khrushchev, although never using the title of general secretary (merely first secretary), was able to rise to one-man leadership in a brief span of time. His successor, Leonid Brezhnev, also assumed the title of first secretary, but the party Congress in 1966 restored the title general secretary.[10]

One other organ of the Central Committee, the Control Committee, deserves mention. Its task is to check on members to see that party discipline is observed, that its rules and its program are loyally adhered to, and, in case of violations, to punish the guilty. In addition, it passes on appeals from disciplinary actions of the central committees of the republics.

It is important to note that most of the men who have reached the top of the party hierarchy in recent years have spent most of their lives in administrative and organizational work. Most of the men in the Secretariat and in the Politburo have had long careers in the party apparatus. Some of the men at the top have been consistently identified with a single area of competence, while others have had responsibilities in a number of fields. Most of them were graduated from institutions of higher learning, and a majority have only narrow, highly specialized technical training.

In the 1985 Central Committee the situation was not too different. Almost half (42 percent) of its full membership was made up of men whose primary background was work in the party apparatus. The next largest group (31 percent) represents men who had devoted most of their adult years to the state bureaucracy. The third largest group had primarily a military background. In view of these facts, it is perhaps not surprising to find that approximately 85 percent of Central Committee members whose careers have centered in the state bureaucracy have had a technical-scientific education, while 78 percent of members whose careers have been primarily in the party apparatus have had such

---

[8]See Figure 30–1. For an excellent discussion of the various reorganizations of the Secretariat, see Merle Fainsod, *How Russia Is Ruled,* rev. ed. (Cambridge, Mass.: Harvard University Press, 1963), pp. 190–208.

[9]Abdurakhman Avtorkhanov, "The General Implications," *Bulletin: Institute for the Study of the USSR 11* (December 1964), p. 15. See also Leonard Schapiro, *The Communist Party of the Soviet Union* (New York: Random House, 1960), pp. 563, 580.

[10]For a discussion of one-man rule versus collective leadership, see the subsequent sections of this chapter.

FIGURE 30–1 Organization of the Secretariat

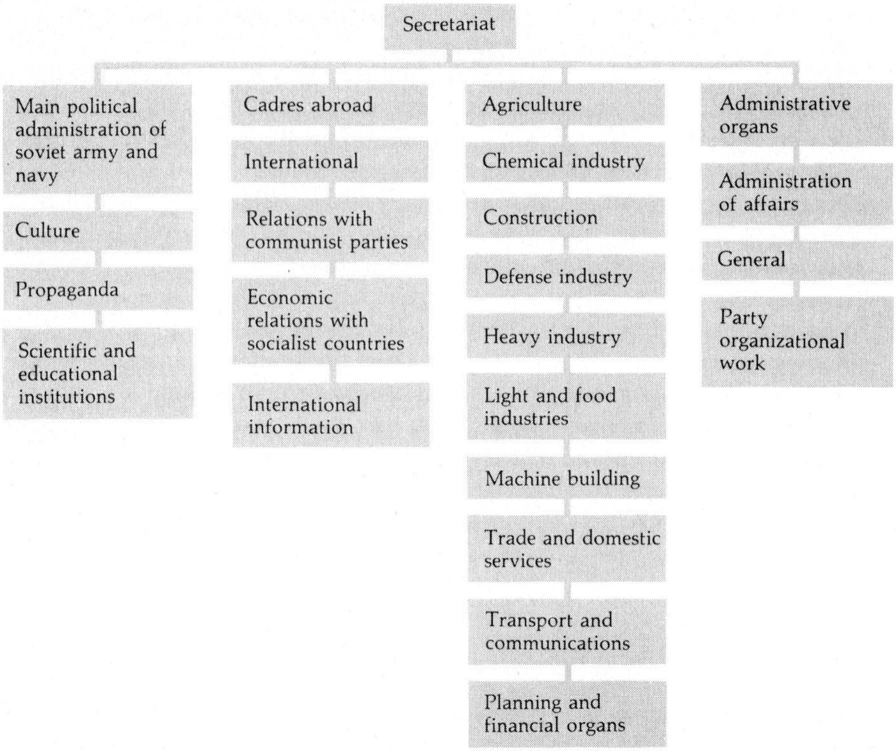

```
                            Secretariat

Main political        Cadres abroad        Agriculture          Administrative
administration of                                               organs
soviet army and       International        Chemical industry
navy                                                            Administration
                      Relations with       Construction         of affairs
Culture               communist parties
                                           Defense industry     General
Propaganda            Economic
                      relations with       Heavy industry       Party
Scientific and        socialist                                 organizational
educational           countries                                 work
institutions                               Light and food
                      International         industries
                      information
                                           Machine building

                                           Trade and domestic
                                           services

                                           Transport and
                                           communications

                                           Planning and
                                           financial organs
```

specialized training. Some 9 percent have had no higher education, while the remainder have had military or general educational training. Women make up less than 3 percent of the committee membership.

Some observers have suggested that younger party members are unhappy about the power exercised by the older generation. The group that controls the majority part of the party's apparatus in Moscow, for example, tends (on the average) to be about 60 years of age, with an average of 40 years of tenure in the party. In 1985 the average age of Politburo members was 68. Both government and party leaders in the provinces average from 50 to 55 years of age. These facts are particularly telling when we note that about one half of the 18 million party members are only now approaching 40, with an average tenure of 10 years in the party. This younger group has few representatives in the higher organs of party power.

The party governing bodies at the national level, as the above suggests, are by all odds the most important. Each republic except the largest, the RSFSR, has governing bodies that correspond to those on the national level. In almost every instance the name of the institutions are the same: congress, central committee, and so forth. Below the national level, however, the executive of party committees is called a bureau instead of a politburo. Party organizations below the national level are subservient to the national organization of the party, where all the important decisions are made as well as many of lesser significance.

The party organizations of the various subdivisions of the RSFSR report directly to the governing bodies of the national party. The desire of certain leaders in the RSFSR to establish a separate organization for their republic led to the celebrated Leningrad case, following World War II. The result was the purge and liquidation of a number of party leaders, including one Politburo member. In 1956 the 20th Party Congress established a special Bureau of RSFSR Affairs in the Central Committee, but this was abolished in 1966.

The first duty of party organizations in the republics is to see to it that the decrees and instructions emanating from the Central Committee in Moscow are carried out. The Central Committee seeks to ensure that this will be done (1) by specifying in great detail the duties of party organizations at all levels, and (2) by providing extensive controls in the party apparatus from top to bottom.

The bureaucratic apparatus of the party is vast, although the exact number of individuals engaged in full-time paid party work remains a secret. Various estimates have run from 100,000 to 500,000, with the first figure probably being more accurate as of this writing.[11] After 1956 there was a conscious effort to reduce the number of full-time party functionaries, but reliable statistics are lacking. The number of part-time unpaid party workers has, however, increased considerably.

The initial core of *apparatchiki* (men of the apparatus) emerged from the Bolshevik pre-tsarist conspiratorial underground organization. Stalin's rise to supreme power can in large part be attributed to his close association with this group. In the early years of the Soviet regime, his chief party work was in the Orgburo, which constituted his first base of operations. From that position, he built, shaped, and controlled the party's bureaucratic apparatus. It was in connection with this work that in 1922 he was named to the post of the general secretary, a position that has come to be regarded as that of unchallenged supreme authority in the party.[12]

The party's bureaucratic machine serves to make the authority of the dictatorship effective. As the long arm of the dictatorship, operating under the respective sections of the party Secretariat, it handles the detailed work of the party. It transmits directives and orders, supervises local party organizations, checks on fulfillment of tasks, assigns personnel, calls party secretaries to render an accounting of their work, and reports its observations to the appropriate party leaders in Moscow. Figure 30–1 depicts the main organization of the Secretariat

---

[11]See Schapiro, *The Communist Party of the Soviet Union,* pp. 572–73.

[12]For an excellent summary of the growth of the party apparatus, see Fainsod, *How Russia Is Ruled,* chap. 6.

of the Central Committee into various departments. It must be noted, however, that changes in the organization of the Secretariat have been made periodically and these have not always been publicized. Because of this fact, no scheme such as the one above can be up to date.[13]

In November 1962, the Central Committee approved a proposal by the party's first secretary, Khrushchev, to reorganize the party structure into two hierarchies, one to be concerned with agriculture and the other with industry. The resulting hierarchies of party committees would be coordinated for the first time at the republic level, where only one central committee and only one politburo existed. The avowed reason for this reorganization was to make more effective the party's control function—that is, in seeing to it that the policies and programs of the top leadership were carried out. This scheme did not produce the desired results and was probably a major reason for Khrushchev's ouster. In any case, his successors declared it a failure and abandoned it, going back to the territorial principle of organization.

THE STRUGGLE FOR POWER WITHIN THE PARTY

In the writings of Marx, Lenin, and other Marxian theorists, there is the presumption that unity of purpose would characterize the dictatorship of the proletariat. The Russian experience has demonstrated, however, that irreconcilable differences arose. This should not have been too surprising in view of the ideological splintering that has prevailed during the past century in the whole socialist movement, including its Soviet component. Uncompromising from the outset, the leaders of the Bolshevik faction, once in power, were determined not to tolerate factions inside the party. To this end, they embarked upon a course of cleansing the party, which in turn led to the physical liquidation of party dissidents, high and low. In the end, the purge was transformed into mass terror under Stalin; the unity of the dictatorship of the proletariat became the unity of the graveyard. Under Khrushchev and his successors the purge was continued, but it has been largely bloodless.

Lenin remained the unquestioned leader of the young Communist regime until his death in 1924, but he laid the psychological basis for purging party ranks, which was to become the decisive instrument in the struggle for power within the party. His utter rejection of compromise and his equating of disobedience in party ranks with treason left room in the party only for those who unquestioningly accepted the party's course as it was defined by the leader. During Lenin's lifetime, however, the purge of party ranks meant no more than expulsion from the party.[14] More frequently, discipline took the form of transferring

---

[13]For a detailed depiction, see Abdurakhman Avtorkhanov, *The Communist Party Apparatus* (New York: Meridian Books, 1968), pp. 201–6.

[14]The outbreak at Kronstadt in March 1921 among the Red Navy sailors, one-time supporters of the Bolshevik revolution who demanded, among other things, civil liberties and the end of the party dictatorship, was nevertheless crushed with armed force. This cannot, however, be viewed as a party purge.

the person to work in more remote regions of the country. But the groundwork for more severe measures was laid in his lifetime.

In the initial years of Lenin's rule, some party members believed that a certain amount of opposition within the party was possible. In 1920 a group calling itself Democratic Centralists appeared at the Ninth Congress of the party and, among other things, accused the Leninist Central Committee of being a "small handful of party oligarchs" who were exiling comrades because of their "deviant views." Simultaneously, party rank and file unrest developed into the so-called Workers' Opposition, which demanded that industry be controlled and managed by the trade unions.[15]

Lenin's answer to the Democratic Centralists and the Workers' Opposition, his one-time supporters who were turning against the regime, was to get the 10th Party Congress (1921) to declare these and similar groups dissolved and to prohibit the formation of groups that were critical of the general line of the Central Committee. Moreover, he insisted on a proviso, kept secret for a time, which in effect forbade agitation against the party line even by leading members of the party. Although Lenin on occasion employed threats that clearly implied physical violence, he did not punish dissenters with anything more severe than expulsion from the party. But his suppression of all opposition within the party inevitably led to resolving struggles for power by force and violence.

In his position as general secretary of the party, Stalin had laid the basis for consolidation of power in his hands. This consolidation proceeded slowly. For a time, while Lenin lay dying and for two or three years thereafter, power seemed to be shared by a triumvirate in the Politburo, composed of Stalin, Lev Kamenev, and Gregory Zinoviev, who had banded together to keep Trotsky from succeeding Lenin. In response to Trotsky's open criticism of the state of things, Stalin's two cohorts demanded firm action (including arrest) against Trotsky, while Stalin appeared to be moderate and restrained. Gradually, Trotsky was removed from one position and then another until he had no power left.

In the meantime, differences between Stalin and his two cohorts had been developing. But Stalin had been preparing for a showdown. As general secretary, he was building a faithful machine of party workers who would increasingly control delegations to party congresses. Second, he was forging a coalition in the Politburo against Kamenev and Zinoviev, which included Nikolai Bukharin, Aleksei Rykov, and Mikhail Tomsky. Step by step, Stalin was able to isolate Kamenev and Zinoviev to such an extent that they abjectly confessed their errors and promised to abide by party discipline. But they were expelled from their positions and from the party, although they were later readmitted.

Once the so-called leftist deviationists (Kamenev et al.) were subdued, Stalin borrowed their program (collectivization of agriculture and intensive industrialization) and introduced it as Soviet policy. The so-called rightists (Bukharin et al.) became restive. Stalin alleged that he had discovered a plot of the right-wing

---

[15]For an excellent summary of party opposition under Lenin, see Fainsod, *How Russia is Ruled,* pp. 141–48.

group to consolidate forces with the remnants of the leftist faction. Under Stalin's attack, Bukharin, Tomsky, and Rykov capitulated; they confessed their sins and asked to be permitted to do battle against all deviations from the general line of the party. But they were soon removed from the important positions they had held.

At the beginning of 1934 Stalin could boast of complete victory. "The anti-Leninist Trotskyite group has been defeated and scattered. . . . The anti-Leninist group of the right deviationists has been defeated and scattered . . . the party today is united as it has never been before."[16] Thus, in his struggle for absolute power, Stalin narrowed the margin of permissible dissent for the opposition until it disappeared.[17]

Throughout the period when he was consolidating his power, Stalin and his henchmen repeatedly declared that the need of purging party ranks increased after the proletariat had gained power. Power, they said, tended to attract opportunists, many of whom were able to conceal their real motives. Moreover, the bourgeoisie had not accepted defeat and was instead resorting to all sorts of vicious means in an effort to undermine the Soviet system. The opportunists in the party became convenient and ready tools of the class enemy. Therefore, said the Stalinists, the party had to be vigilant against the wrecking activities of these elements.

The road of repression moved from expulsion to arrest and imprisonment in the late 1920s and early 1930s. By the mid-1930s it had led to the extermination of the old Bolsheviks and to mass terror. A most revealing document concerning the Great Purge of the 1930s is the speech of the one-time party secretary, Nikita S. Khrushchev, to a closed session of the 20th Party Congress in February 1956.[18] Although questions remain, Khrushchev's speech provided many previously unknown details of a purge whose main features have long been known.

The Great Purge ostensibly had its origin in the assassination in December 1934 of the Leningrad party secretary, Sergei M. Kirov, by a fellow communist. The circumstances surrounding his assassination remain vague, or, to use Khrushchev's words, "inexplicable and mysterious." Khrushchev clearly asserts that there are grounds for believing that the killer was aided by people inside the secret police, and he asserts that the leaders of the secret police in Leningrad, after being given light sentences for their negligence, were shot in 1937 "in order to cover the traces of the organizers of Kirov's killing." This would seem clearly to implicate Stalin.

---

[16]Stalin, *Problems of Leninism,* pp. 515–16.

[17]For a more detailed discussion of Stalin's consolidation of power, see Fainsod, *How Russia Is Ruled,* pp. 148–60. See also Brzezinski, *The Permanent Purge,* especially chaps. 3 and 4.

[18]For a purported text, see *New York Times,* June 5, 1956. See also text published by the *New Leader* under the title, *The Crimes of the Stalin Era,* and annotated by Boris I. Nicolaevsky. See also Bertram D. Wolfe, *Khrushchev and Stalin's Ghost* (New York: Praeger Publishers, 1957), and Roy A. Medvedev, *Let History Judge: The Origins and Consequences of Stalinism* (New York: Alfred A. Knopf, 1971).

In any case, "the next four years claimed victims in the hundreds of thousands."[19] Trotsky had been exiled, but Kamenev, Zinoviev, Bukharin, Rykov, and countless of their alleged followers paid the supreme penalty. The blood bath also engulfed other important party figures and many more lesser ones. Tomsky committed suicide, as did a number of lesser figures. Many who excaped liquidation were sent to camps in Siberia, from which few returned. Expulsions from the party were on a mass scale. One fifth of the total membership was expelled; in the Ukraine one out of four was turned out.

The Great Purge also devoured many officers of the Red Army. Among those who perished was the chief of staff, Marshal Tukhachevsky. A number of generals and many lesser officers shared his fate.

Scarcely a segment of Soviet society remained unscathed. Many of those who perished, both inside and outside party ranks, were innocent, even by Stalin's admission. But since the infallible Stalin could not be responsible, the liquidation of innocent people was attributed to "enemies of the people," who had infiltrated party and police ranks. In any event, a momentary halt to the purge was called, while many of these purgers were purged. In the meantime, Stalin continued to liquidate those who became suspect, but at a somewhat slower pace and with less attendant publicity.

Originally, the purge was associated with the difficulty of coordinating communists in the making of policy. Lenin's answer was the authoritarian formula, which under Stalin developed into an unbridled liquidation of all opposition or competition in matters of policy determination within the party. Simultaneously, the party purge provided an opportunity for the regime to sweep away all opposition, party and nonparty, real and imagined.

In the absence of institutional or other limitations on the dictatorship, the purge gained momentum. As it progressed it created the impression of a huge and continuing conspiracy against the regime, suggesting the need of extending the purge. This intensified already existing tensions and uncertainties. Fear bred fear. Had not a temporary halt been called, the purge might very well have consumed the system.

After a brief lull, during which many of the purgers lost their lives, the purge was resumed. Perhaps what we have come to refer to as "the purges" should be characterized as the violent eruptions of a purging process that is in continuous operation. Professor Brzezinski, in his cogently written book, concludes that the purge has become a permanent institution.[20] In his opinion, it serves to release or absorb tensions, conflicts, and struggles for power within the system. It

---

[19]Fainsod, *How Russia Is Ruled,* p. 150.

[20]Brzezinski, *The Permanent Purge,* see especially pp. 168–75. Other and different views of the purges are to be found in such works as Isaac Deutscher, *Russia in Transition and Other Essays* (New York: Coward-McCann, 1957); George Fischer, *Soviet Opposition to Stalin: A Case Study in World War II* (Cambridge, Mass.: Harvard University Press, 1952); and Robert Conquest, *The Great Terror: Stalin's Purge of the Thirties* (New York: Macmillan, 1968).

facilitates the circulation of elites in a monolithic system where competition and free choice do not prevail. Moreover, it provides a way of maintaining revolutionary fervor by periodically weeding out corrupt and careerist elements.

Nikita Khrushchev's ascendancy to supreme power in the years after Stalin's death (1953), as well as his ouster in 1964, may have opened a new chapter in the struggle for power within the Communist party. Khrushchev's rise to a position of unquestioned leadership was somewhat reminiscent of Stalin's.[21] Within a month of the former dictator's death, he was the senior secretary of the party and not long thereafter was made first secretary. Almost simultaneously came the execution of Lavrenti Beria, Stalin's head of the secret police, and a number of his associates. Using his position as first secretary, Khrushchev asserted his leadership by assuming the role of the party's spokesman in the Central Committee and by becoming head of the government. At the same time, he sought to disassociate himself from the evils of the Stalin regime, primarily through his denunciation of the former dictator's misdeeds in a speech (discussed below) to a closed session of the party congress in February 1956. Moreover, he moved to discredit his principal rivals, Stalin's and his one-time associates in the Politburo. He was challenged briefly in 1957, but succeeded in outmaneuvering his foes and removing them from the party Presidium (Politburo) and the Central Committee. The "collective leadership" was dissolved.

By the end of 1958 Khrushchev's leadership was beyond challenge. While condemning Stalin's personality cult and extolling collective leadership, he had built a personality cult of his own. He had achieved primacy without much bloodshed, it is true, and to a degree persuasion replaced preventive terror. Following the 21st Party Congress in January 1959, however, Khrushchev launched a widespread purge of the party and governmental apparatus. He set the stage for the new purge by telling the congress that changes in the party hierarchy were necessary in order to make better use of young party members, to free old members from excessive burdens, and to replace those officials "who have remained behind the times."

In October 1964 Khrushchev was replaced by some of the same men whom he had placed in positions of responsibility. The change resembled a palace revolution. An established Communist dictator was toppled for the first time as a result of a high-level plot on the part of his associates. Perhaps one of the consequences of the Khrushchev era may be that struggles for power at the top levels can take place without the danger of participants losing their heads. And it may be that the ouster of Khrushchev signified the replacement of a personal autocracy by a bureaucratic oligarchy, even though such a development would be contrary to past Soviet history. If that should be the case, however, the problem of extending intraparty democracy will still remain. But predictions are hazardous.

---

[21]For a detailed discussion of Khrushchev's struggle for power, see Fainsod, *How Russia Is Ruled*, pp. 161–75.

The overthrow of Khrushchev did not seem to be based on fundamental disagreements concerning the party's domestic and foreign policies. Rather, the disagreements seemed to involve the methods by which these policies were executed, as well as Khrushchev's general style of leadership. At the same time, Khrushchev became a convenient scapegoat for the political and economic failures of the system.

Leonid Brezhnev seemed to have moved to the position of "first among equals" a little more slowly than Khrushchev before him. By 1980, however, the Soviet press had dropped all references to "collective leadership." Brezhnev became general secretary of the party in 1966 and his power and influence were constantly on the ascendant, despite periods of apparent ill health in later years. The celebration of his 70th birthday in December 1976 and his elevation in June 1977 to the presidency (chairman of the Presidium) of the Soviet Union gave ample proof of his primacy in the Soviet system.

The deterioration of Brezhnev's health (by 1979) ushered in a "succession crisis" that had not run its course six years later. Brezhnev died in 1982 at age 76, and was succeeded by the ailing Yuri Andropov, who died in 1984 at age 69. He was succeeded by another member of the old guard, Konstantin Chernenko, who passed from the scene in 1985 at age 73. He was replaced by a relative youngster, Mikhail S. Gorbachev (b. 1931), which seemed to signify the beginning of an era of greater leadership stability. As in the case of his predecessors, Gorbachev is Russian.

THE DOWNGRADING OF STALIN AND ITS MEANING

After the death of Stalin in March 1953, his successors set about downgrading their former hero. Their efforts were by and large imperceptible until December 1953, when they liquidated Lavrenti Beria, for many years head of the secret police under Stalin. The first direct and extended criticism of Stalin was presented by Khrushchev at a closed meeting of the 20th Party Congress in February 1956. Although the Soviets did not publish it, a purported text was released by the United States.[22] In this speech, Khrushchev paid Stalin a tribute for his role in the Bolshevik revolution and civil war and for his fight to build a socialist society in the U.S.S.R. But most of the speech was devoted to a criticism of his shortcomings and the grave consequences that ensued from them.

The principal criticism of Stalin, in the Khrushchev speech, centered on the so-called cult-of-personality charge. Stalin had become a personal dictator. Unlike Lenin, he did not tolerate collegiality in leadership or in the work of the party and government. He ignored his colleagues in the Central Committee and even those in the Politburo. Often he did not even bother to inform them of important decisions he had made. The cult of one-man rule, said Khrushchev, was contrary to the Leninist principle of collective leadership.

---

[22]See *New York Times,* June 5, 1956.

Moreover, the development of the cult of personality, according to Khrushchev, was promoted by Stalin himself, for he took an active part in the campaign of praise. Unlike Lenin, he was not a modest man. By taking credit for the achievements of the collective, Stalin arrogated to himself the attributes of an infallible superman. Stalin's vanity resulted in the establishment of many "monuments to the living" in the form of huge statues, busts, portraits, Stalin prizes, and so on. All of this, said Khrushchev, was foreign to Marxism-Leninism.

More serious than the un-Leninist nature of the cult of personality were its dire consequences. It was the "source of a whole series of exceedingly serious and grave perversions of party principles, of party democracy, of revolutionary legality." Whoever opposed Stalin's concept of leadership or attempted to argue against it met with moral and physical annihilation. The result of Stalin's arbitrariness was the killing of countless thousands of innocent party comrades.

In describing the fabrications against his party comrades who perished, Khrushchev dealt in the main with the principal personalities—those who had achieved high positions.[23] In addition to citing individual cases by name, he reported that "of the 139 members and candidates of the party's Central Committee who were elected at the 17th Party Congress, 98 or 70 percent, were arrested and shot." And more than a majority of the nearly 2,000 delegates to that Congress were arrested.

Stalin originated the concept "enemy of the people," which "made possible the usage of the most cruel repression . . . against anyone who in any way disagreed with Stalin, against those who were only suspect of hostile intent." Many of those who in 1937–38 were branded "as 'enemies' were actually never enemies, spies, wreckers, and so on, but were always honest Communists." Many were shot without trial, but trials were not too significant anyway, for convictions were made on the basis of confessions, which "were gained with the help of cruel and inhuman tortures."

Arbitrary behavior by one person, said Khrushchev, encouraged and permitted arbitrariness in others.

Khrushchev, however, did not criticize Stalin's struggle against dissident factions within the party. On the contrary, he praised his fight against the left deviationists (Trotsky, Kamenev, Zinoviev) and against Bukharin and other representatives of the right. Even Lenin had criticized the actions of Kamenev and Zinoviev, but, said Khrushchev, there was no suggestion on Lenin's part that they should be arrested and certainly no thought of shooting them.

The second major criticism in Khrushchev's speech, although he did not dwell on it, was aimed at Stalin's theory of the class struggle during the period of the dictatorship of the proletariat. The terror of the middle and late 1930s was defended by Stalin as a necessary retaliation against the class enemy. The

---

[23]At one point, he made reference to over 7,000 persons who, upon investigation after Stalin's death, were posthumously rehabilitated. See also Footnote 6, above.

use of extreme measures against the class enemy is perfectly justifiable and right, said Khrushchev. But, he added, this repression came after socialism was fundamentally constructed and the exploiting classes generally liquidated. It came at a time when "there were no serious reasons for the use of extraordinary mass terror." And in any case, he added, this terror was not directed at the defeated exploiting classes, "but against the honest workers of the party and the Soviet state."

The third major criticism was directed at Stalin's role in World War II. In the postwar years, he was pictured as a "military genius" who was single-handedly responsible for the success of the Soviet armed forces. This, according to Khrushchev, was far from the truth. Initially, he said, Stalin was not alert to the many warnings from foreign and Soviet sources that Germany would attack the Soviet Union. The failure to heed these warnings and to prepare for the attack had disastrous military consequences for the Soviet armed forces. Moreover, the earlier liquidations of the cream of the army's officer corps had left the Soviet Union in a weakened position. Second, the military reverses in the early part of the war immobilized Stalin. He ceased to lead. He was convinced that all was lost, that everything Lenin had built lost in a brief period of time. Only when other Soviet leaders told him what must be done did he resume leadership.

When he did resume command of the war effort, however, he often hampered it. He interfered with field commanders, to the detriment of the army. Even urgent pleas from the front by Khrushchev and others for orders that would save the situation were ignored. He even refused to come to the telephone to talk to Khrushchev, who was desperately calling from the front. The net result was huge losses to the Soviet army.

In addition, Khrushchev criticized Stalin's wartime policy of deporting and exiling minority populations (such as the Volga Germans) who were near the front. This resettling was indiscriminate. Even Communist party members and their leaders among these nationalities were deported and exiled with the rest.

The successors of Stalin, by their criticism of a man theretofore depicted as infallible, set in motion forces that were difficult to control. Their criticism of Stalin reverberated around the world, and within a brief period of time produced crises at home and abroad.[24] The most immediate impact of the criticism of Stalin was the ideological crises in communist parties in the noncommunist countries. French, Italian, American, and other communists suddenly discovered that their hero had feet of clay and worse. For years they had been engaged in perpetrating a hoax. And this on the authority of Moscow itself! This was not easy to take, for it was perhaps the rudest shock experienced by the foreign apologists of the Soviet Union. Some left their respective parties. Some asked where Khrushchev and his colleagues had been when all the evil deeds were being done. Others fell in with the new party line without outward questioning.

---

[24]This analysis is in part based on A. Avtorkhanov, "Current Soviet Political Problems," *Bulletin: Institute for the Study of the U.S.S.R.* 4 (January 1957), pp. 3–14.

Fellow travelers, although not all, fell by the wayside in great numbers. But the crisis was not to end there.

The way had been prepared for the ideological crisis in the world communist movement by Khrushchev's revision of Lenin in his opening address to the party congress. By declaring that there were various roads to socialism (that is, by declaring that force and violence was not necessarily the only means, that war is not inevitable, and so forth), he appeared to be revising Stalin, but in effect he was revising Lenin also. This was far too flexible an interpretation for many comrades in the various communist parties, and some openly declared that such flexibility would deprive them of the very thing that distinguished them from other workers' parties. The theoretical revision of Lenin and the personal condemnation of Stalin were bound to keep the world communist movement in a certain amount of ideological turmoil.

The crisis in communist ranks was not confined to party comrades in the noncommunist world. The beginning of a series of political crises in Eastern Europe followed quickly on the heels of Khrushchev's declaration about "different roads to socialism" and his revelations of the abuses under Stalin's rule. The restiveness of the satellite countries exploded in the autumn of 1956 into a full-blown revolt in Hungary, together with more peaceful changes in Poland. In both instances the revolt was against domestic Stalinists and, by implication at least, against Russia's Stalinist methods in dealing with the satellites. The Hungarian revolution soon assumed a general anticommunist character. It was phenomenally successful until crushed by Soviet troops that were sent into Hungary for that purpose. Open Soviet intervention in Eastern Europe came again with the invasion of Czechoslovakia in August 1968, because of an avowed desire of the Czechoslovak regime to follow the path of a more humane communism.

The events in Hungary served to make more acute the psychological crisis that had been developing inside the Soviet Union in the wake of Khrushchev's revelations about Stalin. The Soviet rulers took note of unrest among their own students and workers some time before the blowups in Poland and Hungary. After the Hungarian revolt had occurred, Soviet citizens were warned in the party press about their criticism of the party and the government, while "hiding behind the slogan of the struggle against the cult of the individual." University students were seemingly most vocal, and Khrushchev was moved to tell the dissatisfied: "If you do not like our methods, then go to work and others will come to study in your place."[25]

In assessing the Khrushchev denunciation of the cult of Stalin, Avtorkhanov notes three main contradictions in it. The first is practical: Stalin's methods were declared to have been illegal and not in the best interests of the party, and yet it would have been impossible to maintain the communist system without them. The second is theoretical: Stalin's theory of the class struggle during the

---

[25]*Pravda,* November 10, 1956.

period of the dictatorship of the proletariat was denounced; yet, these theories were indispensable in justifying communist practice. The third contradiction is moral: Stalin's treachery, suspiciousness, and hypocrisy were depicted as personal traits, whereas these qualities are an essential feature of the communist system. It should be noted, however, that some scholars accept the first two points but not the third.

The various crises which followed in the wake of the criticism of Stalin could not but put a strain on the collective leadership. Suggestions to this effect were met with evasive denials until July 1957, when it was revealed that such old Bolsheviks as Molotov, Kaganovich, and Malenkov, as well as other members of the top leadership, had been removed from their posts because of their deviationism—that is, their attempt to oppose party policies as conceived by Khrushchev and his collaborators. Attacks upon this "antiparty group" were repeated several times. At the 21st Party Congress, the names of several other former party leaders were added to the antiparty roster, along with a demand for an explanation of their parts in the plot. At the 22d Party Congress in October 1961, Khrushchev, as well as his collaborators, returned to the attack, with further revelations concerning the crimes of the Stalin era. This time he portrayed the members of the antiparty group as accomplices of Stalin. It remains to be seen if one day his name may also be associated with those crimes.

Apparently disturbed by erosion of discipline caused by de-Stalinzation, Khrushchev's successors have allowed a partial rehabilitation of Stalin. Thus, while allowing some criticism of certain aspects of Stalinism, including the Stalinist aspects of Khrushchev's leadership, they have intensified repressive measures against writers and intellectuals who present a severely negative portrayal of Stalin. And several pieces have been published that present at least some aspects of his rule in a positive light. It would be hazardous to guess how far this rehabilitation will go.

Younger party members, better educated than their elders, display some evidence of a critical stance. Their right to questions and to criticize is very much on the agenda. They are more inclined to ask for explanations than to accept commands. The response of the leadership has been to appeal for unity, while at the same time hinting that those who express criticism from unprincipled positions (that is, disagreeing with the official party line) might have to be purged from party ranks.

BIBLIOGRAPHICAL NOTE

On the history of the party, see Leonard Schapiro, *The Communist Party of the Soviet Union* (New York: Random House, 1960). More recent useful works include Seweryn Bialer, *Stalin's Successors: Leadership, Stability, and Change in the Soviet Union* (Cambridge and New York: Cambridge University Press, 1980); George W. Breslaur, *Khrushchev and Brezhnev as Leaders: Building Authority in Soviet Politics* (Winchester, Mass.: Allen & Unwin, 1982); Ronald J. Hill and Peter Frank, *The Soviet Communist Party,* 2d ed. (Winchester, Mass.: Allen & Unwin, 1983); John Lowenhardt, *The*

Soviet Politburo (New York: St. Martin's Press, 1982); Roy Medvedev, *All Stalin's Men* (Garden City, N.Y.: Anchor Press/Doubleday Publishing, 1984); Michael Waller, *Democratic Centralism: An Historical Commentary* (New York: St. Martin's Press, 1981); Michael Voslensky, *Nomenklatura: The Soviet Ruling Class* (Garden City, N.Y.: Doubleday Publishing, 1984).

Much valuable information may be gleaned from the two volumes of *Khrushchev Remembers* (Boston: Little, Brown, 1970, 1974), as well as from Roy A. Medvedev, *Let History Judge: The Origins and Consequences of Stalinism* (New York: Vantage Books, 1971).

31

Policymaking Structures: Governmental Institutions

Since the party is the decision-making body in the Soviet system, government is mostly a matter of administration. Governmental forms, as well as the whole fabric of organizational and institutional life in the Soviet Union, constitute the administrative apparatus for implementing party policies and party aims. An appreciation of this basic fact is indispensable to an understanding of the Soviet system. All else is secondary. Soviet governmental forms, as well as the theories that ostensibly govern their functions and powers, must ever be viewed as subordinate to the party hierarchy.

DUALISM OF PARTY AND GOVERNMENT

Formally, the party and government structures are separate and independent.[1] Organizationally, they are similar except at the lowest level. They are in the nature of twin pyramids or dual hierarchies. The governmental hierarchy parallels that of the party (described in Chapter 30) in that the Supreme Soviet of the U.S.S.R. corresponds to the party congress, the Presidium of the Supreme Soviet resembles the party Central Committee, and the Council of Minis-

---

[1]The governmental and party changes announced immediately after Stalin's death in March 1953 were, however, allegedly decided upon at a *joint* meeting of the party's Central Committee, the Council of Ministers of the U.S.S.R., and the Presidium of the Supreme Soviet of the U.S.S.R.

FIGURE 31–1 **Intersecting Pyramids of Party and Government Organization**

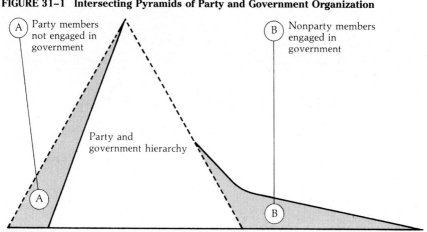

ters is similar to the party Politburo. A governmental hierarchy corresponding to that of the central government exists in each one of the union republics. At the lowest level, governmental powers are vested in a soviet of working peoples' deputies, whose executive and administrative organ is the executive committee.

In theory, authority is wielded by the constitutionally established governmental bodies. In practice, however, party predominance is guaranteed by the existence of the party pyramid, which parallels the governmental structure at every level, and by the knowledge of all those in the governmental hierarchy that their basic task is to carry out party policy. Party and nonparty individuals in government offices are aware of and consult with party officials at their respective levels of authority. No governmental decision of any consequence is made except upon order or approval from competent party officials.

As implied above, party predominance is also guaranteed by an interlocking directorate of party members who simultaneously hold governmental and party posts. Party members who occupy governmental positions but do not serve as party officials are nonetheless aware that they are primarily engaged in performing tasks pursuant to party decisions. Nonparty governmental employees are for the most part to be found in lesser jobs, but they, too, realize that the governmental structure is but an appendage of the party.

The Soviet constitution of 1977, to be discussed below, even more than its predecessor (the so-called Stalin constitution of 1936) openly recognizes the predominant position of the party. The preamble speaks of the party as the "vanguard of the whole people" and Article 6 says that it "is the *leading and guiding force of Soviet society and the nucleus of its political system, of all state and public organizations.*"[2]

---

[2]Italics added.

BUILDING A GOVERNMENTAL STRUCTURE

When the Bolsheviks seized power, they had little idea of how to organize the dictatorship of the proletariat. There was no ready-made Marxian blueprint for a governmental organization in a workers' state. Lenin, to be sure, had gone a long way toward developing the idea of the dictatorship of the proletariat, but he had not gone beyond generalities. Consequently, Bolshevik efforts to fashion a governmental structure were largely a matter of trial and error.

The soviets (councils) of workers' and soldiers' deputies that arose in 1917[3] were to become the pattern for the Bolshevik organization of the state. Initially the Bolsheviks had frowned upon participating in the soviets, for the soviets appeared to be cooperating with the provisional government. The soviets, in any case, were under the firm control of the non-Bolshevik revolutionary parties, a fact not calculated to induce Bolshevik cooperation. Before long, as noted in Chapter 28, the Bolsheviks saw in the soviets the one potential instrument for the seizure of power. After having served this purpose, the soviets became the organizational pattern for the Bolshevik state, and governing bodies at national, local, and intermediate levels became known as soviets.

The soviets under the Communist regime differ markedly from their earlier prototypes. Initially, they were loosely organized democratic bodies. Members of several different revolutionary parties engaged in free and vigorous debate. Decisions were reached by majority vote. There was no attempt to suppress minority opinion. Once the Bolsheviks had taken over, however, they were determined to make of the soviets monolithic organizations. The more moderate revolutionary groups soon withdrew, for they were not anxious merely to serve Bolshevik ends. By the summer of 1918, all non-Bolshevik representatives had withdrawn or been expelled, leaving the Bolsheviks in complete control.

The Bolshevik approach to a constitution is entirely different from that to which we have been accustomed. Constitutionalism in the West has been identified with limited government. Initially, it constituted a way of curbing and regulating the powers of kings and other monarchs. Once this was done, the next step was to deny certain powers to the new democratic governments, in accordance with the consent of the governed, and to provide procedural safeguards in the exercise of those limited powers that were granted to popular governmental authorities. This view of constitutionalism is foreign to the Soviet leaders, for their constitution neither imposes limitations upon government nor provides for meaningful procedural safeguards against the abuse of authority.

If the Soviet constitution does not serve the purposes normally associated with constitutions in the West, why, it may be asked, did the Soviets bother with a constitution at all? There would seem to be at least two main reasons. First, a constitution makes the governmental-administrative structure explicit, providing for a smoother operation of the bureaucracy. Second, a fundamental law

---

[3]These were patterned on the short-lived Petrograd Soviet of 1905.

that stressed the rights of workers and peasants and proclaimed their participation in the government would serve Communist propaganda objectives at home and abroad.

In the early months of the Bolshevik regime there was no constitution. When they had seized power, the Bolshevik leaders went to the Second All-Russian Congress of Soviets, which was then in session, with a resolution decreeing a temporary government, bearing the name "Council of Peoples' Commissars." The resolution was adopted, including the naming of Bolsheviks to all leading posts in the government. This government was to last until the convocation of the Constituent Assembly, which had been promised by the provisional government. The Bolsheviks set the election for November 25, 1917, but, as noted earlier, the outcome was not favorable to the Bolsheviks. Nevertheless, they permitted the Constituent Assembly to convene in January 1918, but when they realized that it was not susceptible to manipulation by them, they disbanded it by force after it had been in session only one day.

A Bolshevik-framed declaration, setting forth the basic principles for the organization of the new state, which the Constituent Assembly refused to adopt, served as the basic law of the Russian state until the formal adoption of a constitution in July 1918.[4] The constitution, adopted by the Fifth All-Russian Congress of Soviets, provided a governmental structure for the Russian Soviet Federated Socialist Republic (RSFSR), by far the largest of the present 15 soviet republics. For the most part, this constitution ratified the evolving structure of soviets, setting forth specific provisions concerning the composition and powers of soviets and their central executive committees, the organization of the Council of People's Commissars, the powers of the central and local governments, and electoral rights. The revolutionary functions of the constitution were said to embrace the establishment of a dictatorship of the urban and rural proletariat (including the poorest peasantry), the establishment of socialism, and the suppression of the bourgeoisie and exploitation.

By 1921, under Bolshevik guidance, socialist soviet republics had been set up in Belorussia, the Ukraine, and Transcaucasia, which had entered into a treaty relationship with RSFSR. In 1922 a Union of Soviet Socialist Republics was created, and in 1923 the constitution was revised to reflect this change.[5] The new constitution, formally ratified by the Congress of Soviets in January 1924, followed closely the RSFSR model of 1918. All powers of any significance were vested in the central government, leaving the union republics exceedingly little authority.

By 1936 the number of soviet republics had grown to 11.[6] In addition, a drastic social and economic transformation had taken place in the years 1929–35. A

---

[4]This declaration, in effect, became the preamble of the constitution. For texts of the declaration and the constitution, see James H. Meisel and Edward S. Kozera, *Materials for the Study of the Soviet System* (Ann Arbor, Mich: George Wahr Publishing Co., 1950), pp. 57, 79.

[5]For text, see Meisel and Kozera, *Materials for the Study of the Soviet System,* p. 152 ff.

[6]The Uzbek, Turkmen, Kazak, Kirgiz, and Tadjik republics were added, while Transcaucasia was divided into three republics—Georgia, Armenia, and Azerbaijan.

new constitution was needed, said Stalin, in order to bring the fundamental law into conformity with those changes. Allegedly, classes had been abolished and society transformed. Therefore, it was possible to introduce universal suffrage, direct and secret elections, and to eliminate inequality between workers and peasants. But, said Stalin, the new constitution "preserves unchanged the present leading position of the Communist party," which provided "democracy for the working people, that is, democracy for all."[7]

The widespread discussion throughout the Soviet Union of the draft of the 1936 constitution, and particularly the publicity surrounding this discussion that the Soviet leaders purveyed abroad, suggests that foreign (as well as domestic) propaganda may have been the dominant motive behind the new constitution. Soviet leaders, anxious to find allies among the capitalist democracies against the nazi, fascist, and Japanese threat, were eager to demonstrate that the 1936 constitution was proof of an evolving democratic system that enjoyed the support of the Soviet peoples. Therefore, there existed a common bond between the capitalist democracies and the Soviet Union in the face of the fascist threat.

In the post-Stalin period a new constitution was promised for several years. First, Khrushchev announced the appointment of a large committee to draft the new constitution. After his downfall in 1964 little was heard of the project until Brezhnev made known that he had reconstituted the committee. There were some expectations that it would be ready for consideration at the party congress in 1971, but at that time Brezhnev announced only that a new constitution was in preparation. Those expecting a new constitution were again disappointed when at the party congress in 1976 Brezhnev simply reported that work was continuing on it. Finally, in June 1977 a draft of the new constitution was published, with the aim of having the formal adoption coincide with the 60th anniversary of Soviet power in November 1977.

The 1977 constitution differs little from the 1936 one. The preamble declares that the Soviet Union is no longer a dictatorship of the proletariat but a "state of the whole people," a formulation first put forth by Khrushchev. Second, the new constitution makes the exercise of basic rights much more dependent upon the fulfillment of duties. Third, the organization and operation of the economy is spelled out more fully. Fourth, the formal executive is augmented with the creation of a vice presidency. Finally, there is a chapter (new) on foreign policy.

GOVERNMENTAL STRUCTURE: FEDERALISM AND ELECTIONS

The governmental forms through which the party dictatorship is exercised resemble those to be found in a democracy, at least superficially. There is great emphasis on "popularly elected" legislative assemblies (soviets), which choose their respective executives and to which these executives are supposedly responsible. Moreover, the Soviet Union claims to be a federal state, with a distribu-

---

[7]"On the New Constitution," in *Problems of Leninism,* pp. 578–79.

tion of governmental powers between the central government and the 15 republics. These governmental forms, upon closer examination, will stand revealed as a type of democratic facade behind which the party dictatorship functions. At the same time, something of the party's tactics in the operation of that dictatorship will be brought into sharper focus.

Ostensibly, the U.S.S.R. is a federal state, formed on the basis of voluntary association of equal republics. Any impartial study of the Soviet system will reveal, however, that this is not the case. A governmental system cannot be called federal unless (1) the distribution of powers between the central government and its component subdivisions provides the subdivisions with some real substance of power, and (2) the central government is prevented from altering this distribution of powers through its actions alone. The Soviet system meets neither of these two tests, either in theory or in practice.

Moreover, the 1977 constitution seems to strengthen the central government further. Article 3, for example, says: "The Soviet state shall be organized and shall function in accordance with the principle of democratic centralism" (see previous chapter for discussion of this principle). In addition, this constitution, as the one before it, grants powers to the central government that are so all-embracing as to leave the republics with no real substance of power. Finally, as in the past, the power to amend the constitution is vested in the central government alone; the republics are not required to ratify amendments.

Yet ironically enough, the constitution asserts that each of the union republics has "the right freely to secede from the U.S.S.R." Moreover, it provides that each union republic has the right to enter into diplomatic relations with other countries. These are not the attributes of a federal state but of a confederation.

In practice, however, the Soviet Union is neither a federation nor a confederation. The republics have neither the powers usually associated with component units of a federation nor can they exercise the powers normally enjoyed by members of a confederation. None of the republics has been permitted to establish diplomatic relations with foreign countries. A British proposal in 1947 to exchange diplomatic representatives with the Ukraine was rejected. Additional Moscow disrespect for the "rights" of union republics was demonstrated when in 1956 the Karelo-Finnish Republic was abolished without any seeming effort to obtain its approval, although the constitution asserted that the boundaries of a union republic may not be altered without its consent. Again, it cannot too often be emphasized that the U.S.S.R. is a highly centralized dictatorship where authority is wielded by the leaders of the Communist party, a unitary organization. Moreover, it is a sound generalization that a one-party dictatorship is a poor place to look for federalism, to say nothing of a confederate arrangement.

The Soviet nationality policy is the basis for Moscow's claim to federalism. This policy, ostensibly one of autonomy, was based on the need to weld together the diverse fragments of the Russian empire that had fallen apart with the Revolution and that the Red Army was bringing into the fold. Lenin had sought to harness minority discontent to the aims of the Revolution; hence a departure from tsarist policy was imperative. The departure was in the direction of autonomy and it was an improvisation.

From the outset, however, it was evident that there would be no national autonomy in the realm of political power or in the matter of social or economic organization of society, although for some years that followed many continued to hope. In May 1918, Stalin, who was made chairman for nationalities when the Bolshevik government was established, stated that Soviet authorities were "for autonomy, but only for an autonomy where all power rests in the hands of the workers and peasants." In 1925 he depicted Soviet nationality policy goals as being "proletarian in content and national in form." During World War II, however, even the basic right of autonomous existence was violated when several nationalities were uprooted from the Caucasus because of alleged disloyalty.[8]

Similarly, it was made clear from the outset that the "right freely to secede" was meaningless. In 1920, Stalin reaffirmed the right, but at that stage of the revolution, he said, a demand for secession would be regarded as counterrevolutionary. Moreover, the history of Soviet nationality policy is replete with purges of party and nonparty "nationalists" in the Ukraine, Belorussia, Armenia, and several of the other non-Russian republics. Under Stalin, deliberate systematic efforts were made to eradicate "local chauvinism." Many of those who were purged were charged with harboring a desire to detach their respective republics from the Soviet Union, although the constitution presumably gave them this right.

What remained of the national autonomy, therefore, was largely linguistic and cultural. Soviet leaders, in their propaganda, made much of their policy of encouraging minority nationalities to advance themselves culturally through the use of their native language and through the development of their native cultural heritage. But the basic aim of the party leadership in Moscow was not cultural advancement for its own sake. Rather, they saw in the native language, educational system, and culture the means through which the party could more effectively sovietize the minority peoples. This takes on added significance when one remembers that these means could not be utilized by any other group to pursue a different or contrary aim.

Interestingly enough, an increasing number of Russians, from dissidents to holders of power, have come to believe that Russians are worse off than many other nationalities. They think that cultural expression among minority nationalities is tolerated more than among the Russians. Some Russian writers have organized to fight demolition of historic monuments, including churches. Moreover, they note the fact that nearly 500 valuable pieces of architecture were torn down in Moscow in the 1930s. They also point to the distortions of Russian

---

[8] In 1957 it was announced that five of the nationalities would be rehabilitated, and in 1965 it was announced that the Volga Germans had not really been disloyal.

classics. Some Russians see Marxism as a Western idea alien to all things Russian, and therefore tend to be drawn to the Russian Orthodox religion.

It is also of interest to note that after 1948 the Jews were not recognized as a minority, although an autonomous region (Birobidjan) was set aside by Stalin for Jewish colonization. Ironically enough, however, they are a minority even in Birobidjan. In the early years of the Soviet regime many of the leading communists were Jews, but Stalin purged most of them. In the last years of his life it was practically subversive to speak or write in Yiddish. Jewish schools, newspapers, and periodicals were closed down. Even Jewish prayer books were unobtainable. Articles in the official press were clearly derogatory.

Throughout the Khrushchev era and since, there has seemed to be an increasing harassment of Jews. More than a few anti-Semitic books and articles have been published, although some were critically reviewed in the Soviet press. Moreover, articles in the press emphasized that Jews were involved in a large share of the economic crimes committed by Soviet citizens. In addition, Soviet newspapers reported that a number of Jews were arrested on espionage charges, allegedly having given state secrets to Israeli diplomats. In August 1972, emigration taxes were imposed on Jews wishing to emigrate from the U.S.S.R., requiring them to reimburse the state for the cost of their education before they could obtain an exit visa. As United States–Soviet relations seemed to improve after 1973, these taxes seemed to have been quietly dropped, although the desire of Jews to emigrate continues to create all sorts of unpleasant difficulties (for example, loss of job, questioning by the police, difficulties for relatives, and so forth).

According to the constitution, all members of the various legislative bodies (the soviets) are elected "on the basis of universal, equal, and direct suffrage by secret ballot." If one goes beyond this formal proviso, however, any initial impressions of popular democracy are quickly dispelled. First of all, when the Soviet voters go to cast their ballots they find only one list of candidates; there is only one candidate for each office to be filled. There are no alternative candidates to vote for, although by invalidating the ballot the voters can in effect cast a vote against the official list.[9] In practice even this demonstration of opposition has become difficult, simply because Soviet election officials do not require voters to enter the voting booth before casting their ballots, and hence they destroy the secrecy of the ballot. To vote for the list, one need not mark the ballot, but one must do so if he or she is to invalidate it. Faced with the spectacle of certain voters openly demonstrating their loyalty to the regime, other voters, who may or may not be inclined to invalidate their ballots, are discouraged from entering the voting booth before casting their ballots. Moreover, many voters believe, rightly or wrongly, that the voting booth itself does not ensure secrecy, since the officials have ways of detecting those who invalidate their ballots. In

---

[9]According to the Soviet electoral law, an election is not valid unless the list receives at least 50 percent of all the votes cast.

view of these considerations, the reports that official lists receive more than 99 percent of the votes cast can better be understood.

Second, popular democracy is lacking in the nominating process. Soviet propagandists have defended the single list of candidates on the ground that these are chosen after long and thorough discussions, which allegedly characterize the nominating process. The right to nominate candidates is accorded to Communist party organizations, trade unions, cooperatives, youth organizations, and cultural societies. Since the Communist party is the sole guiding force in all of these associations, there is no possibility of a person's being nominated if he or she is in any way repugnant to the party. Prior to an election, meetings of voters are held to discuss the various nominees. It is here that the party's view of who should be the candidate is made amply clear. No one will take a position against the party, although it does not follow that the nominee will be a party member. Often the party finds its expedient, particularly in local soviets, to have nonparty candidates. These are nonetheless persons whom the party can trust.[10]

Finally, if need be, the Communists can control the results of elections, for they count the ballots. Who is to question the accuracy of the count? There are no challengers, no demands for a recount, no critical press, or political opposition to reveal irregularities. Even if 99 percent of the voters did not cast their ballots for the official list, as reported, the election officials could make it so.

That the party should be in complete control of the nominating and electoral process is perfectly consistent with the communist view that in their system only one program can exist. If no alternative to communism is to be tolerated, why permit the nomination or election of persons who may oppose communism? But then, the question may be asked: Why have elections at all? Why are they necessary; what purposes do they serve? Why is there such a determined effort to get all eligible voters to the polls?

An analysis of the Soviet system suggests that, from the communist point of view, the elections serve several purposes. They provide a plausible facade by means of which the regime can claim popular support, especially in its propaganda abroad. Moreover, they constitute a technique by which the regime hopes to instill in the broad masses a sense of involvement in communist undertakings. For those who do not cherish such an experience, their participation in communist elections serves to create a climate of futility, moral despair, and hopelessness. No one who hates communism can go through the symbolic approval of what he or she hates without a sense of personal degradation, of having destroyed one's own personal integrity. In addition, communist leaders find elections soul-satisfying, especially when they register such overwhelming majorities. The lesser communists, on the other hand, are afforded an opportunity by the elections to show their importance and to experience a feeling of power.

---

[10]In the Supreme Soviet of the U.S.S.R., the percentage of Communist party members and candidates approaches 72 percent, while in local soviets it falls below 50 percent.

The efforts of thousands, if not millions, of party workers are required during a national election campaign. Finally, elections provide an excellent peg on which to hang domestic propaganda messages. Periodically they furnish the regime with a convenient opportunity to praise itself, to explain away shortcomings, and to exhort the people to make new sacrifices.

Soviet leaders have admitted the propaganda function of their elections. One of them wrote openly: "The Soviet election system is a mighty instrument for further educating and organizing the masses politically, for further strengthening the bond between the state mechanism and the masses."[11] Similar statements are to be found in the Soviet press and in party pronouncements, especially in the days preceding an election.

GOVERNMENTAL STRUCTURE: LEGISLATIVE AND EXECUTIVE

The Supreme Soviet of the U.S.S.R. is a bicameral[12] body, consisting of a Soviet of Union and a Soviet of Nationalities. The Soviet of Union is chosen directly by the people in electoral areas on the basis of one deputy per 300,000 inhabitants. The Soviet of Nationalities is designed to represent nationalities, with deputies distributed as follows: 32 to each union republic, 11 to each autonomous republic, 5 to each autonomous region, and 1 to each national area. They are also directly elected. Each chamber has about 750 members. Both chambers are elected for five-year terms and are said to have equal powers.

The Supreme Soviet, according to the constitution, is the highest organ of state authority; it is the exclusive wielder of the legislative power of the central government. Despite these constitutional declarations the Supreme Soviet cannot qualify as a parliamentary body as that term is generally understood. This conclusion would be valid on the basis of any objective analysis of the Supreme Soviet's activities, even if one did not take into account the predominant role the Communist party plays in the Soviet system.

First of all, the Supreme Soviet is supposed to meet twice yearly. An examination of the record in several post-World War II years reveals that it met only once yearly in the years 1947–52, inclusive. More important, however, is the fact that each annual session averaged no more than five days. Could anyone seriously suggest that the Supreme Soviet, with a membership exceeding 1,500, would be capable of legislating in the vast areas of authority that the constitution theoretically grants it by sitting 5 or 10 days a year?

Moreover, a cursory examination of its activities during these brief sessions indicates that the Supreme Soviet engages in little deliberation or debate, to say nothing of dissent. The rank-and-file members play a simple role. They sit qui-

---

[11]Andrei Y. Vyshinsky, *The Law of the Soviet State* (New York: Macmillan, 1948), p. 772.
[12]Soviets of the republics and other subdivisions of the U.S.S.R. are unicameral.

etly while government and party leaders deliver a series of speeches, they applaud at the appropriate moments, and they cast unanimous votes for all government proposals. Unrehearsed and free debates are out of the question. The members are well rewarded, however. They receive a monthly salary approaching that of a skilled worker (this is in addition to what they receive in their regular jobs), plus free annual passes on all railway and water transport facilities. During the sessions of the Supreme Soviet they receive a liberal per diem.

From the Communist party point of view, this is perhaps as it should be. The Supreme Soviet, a large and unwieldy body, is the governmental counterpart of the party's congress. In both cases, these large gatherings serve essentially similar purposes. Their function is not to debate and discuss but to applaud and assent. In a 20-year period (1937–58), for example, the ministers enacted, through decrees and resolutions, some 390,000 pieces of "legislation," while the Supreme Soviet and its Presidium (discussed below) were passing some 7,000 laws, resolutions, and decrees. Moreover, many of the acts of the Supreme Soviet merely confirmed decisions already promulgated by its Presidium.

The Soviet Union may be said to have a dual executive, although a comparison with other countries in this respect would be misleading. There is the Presidium of the Supreme Soviet, a collegial executive body elected by the Supreme Soviet, which is a permanent nucleus of the Supreme Soviet. It consists of a president (formally, chairman), a first vice president, a secretary, 15 vice presidents (one for each of the union republics), and 21 members. It has become customary to elect the presidents of the presidia of the union republics to fill the vice presidential posts. Several top party leaders are always members. The president or chairman of the Presidium performs many of the functions of a formal executive in a parliamentary state. He receives credentials and letters of recall of diplomatic representatives, awards decorations, confers titles of honor, ratifies treaties, convenes sessions of the Supreme Soviet, exercises the right of pardon, and appoints and recalls diplomatic representatives. Decisions concerning these matters are made by the Presidium collectively, understandably on the initiative of the party.

At the same time, the Presidium is said to have powers that would make it correspond to a legislative body. In the interval between sessions of the Supreme Soviet, it performs many of the powers of the parent body. It has the power to issue decrees, to declare war, to order general or partial mobilization, to annul those decisions of the Council of Ministers of the U.S.S.R. and of the union republics that do not conform to law, to appoint and remove the higher commands of the armed forces, to proclaim martial law, and to appoint and remove ministers. The last is subject to confirmation by the Supreme Soviet. The Presidium also has the power to interpret the laws of the U.S.S.R. and to conduct nationwide polls (referenda) on its own initiative or on the demand of one of the union republics.

The Supreme Soviet also chooses the Council of Ministers, which is composed of the heads of the usual departments plus those ministries responsible for various parts of the economy.[13] The number of economic ministries was quite large at one time but was considerably reduced in 1957, when the Communist leadership decided to decentralize the actual implementation of party economic goals. Formally, the Council of Ministers is selected by the Supreme Soviet, but the real ministerial assignments are made by the party leaders. As might be expected, the Council of Ministers is engaged not so much in policy discussions as in the means of implementing policies already arrived at. Even the constitution refers to it as an "executive and administrative organ."

The Council of Ministers also has a "presidium," or a type of cabinet, consisting of the chairman of the Council of Ministers, his or her deputies, and personal appointees of the Council, in 1977 totaling 14. This body was not mentioned in the 1936 constitution, although even prior to 1953 there had been a "presidium" of the Council of Ministers and even a "bureau of the presidium," but without having been identified publicly. They were no doubt made necessary by the unwieldiness of the Council of Ministers, which by 1952 had exceeded 60. Although drastically reduced in the reforms of 1953 and 1957, it grew rapidly in the 1960s. As of 1985 there were 63 ministries and 22 state committees, whose chairmen have ministerial rank. These, plus the 15 chairmen of the councils of ministers of the union republics, who are ex officio members, and the 14 members of the presidium of the Council (allowing for four persons counted twice) make for a grand total of 110 who are entitled to sit as the Council of Ministers. The 1977 constitution, however, leaves the determination of ministries to future sessions of the Supreme Soviet.

The administrative powers of the ministers are vast and far-reaching. One can appreciate how far-reaching they are only if one bears in mind that in addition to the normal bureaucratic apparatus of a large industrial nation there is added a bureaucracy to direct and administer the whole economy of the country. In such circumstances it is inevitable that the Council of Ministers be the source of much rule making as well as legislative proposals. Apparently, the decentralization projected in 1957 was at least in part based on the sheer inability of the ministries in Moscow to direct and supervise this huge bureaucracy in minute detail.[14]

There are two types of ministries represented in the Council of Ministers— all-union and union-republic. All-union ministries are ministries of the central government that operate directly through their own bureaucracy down to the lowest level. Union-republic ministries, on the other hand, are said to function indirectly through corresponding ministries in the republics. Often in the past, however, they have exercised direct control over certain enterprises. Moreover, the union-republic ministries have occasionally controlled and directed the

[13]For a good account of the evolution of the Council of Ministers, see Julian Towster, *Political Power in the U.S.S.R., 1917–1947* (New York: Oxford University Press, 1948), pp. 272–76.
[14]For a discussion of the administration and the bureaucracy, see Chapter 32.

work of purely republic ministries, which are supposedly for the administration of the individual republics.

Although ministers are technically responsible to the Supreme Soviet and, in between its sessions, to the Presidium of the Supreme Soviet, they are really responsible solely to the top party leaders. Most top party leaders are, of course, members of the party Politburo, and many of them are also members of the Council of Ministers. There is no such thing as collective responsibility of the cabinet, nor are there any resignations of ministers as a group. There are no motions of censure, no political attacks on the ministers by the legislature, and no votes of confidence. As long as individuals remain acceptable to the top party leadership, they have no reason to fear dismissal.

GOVERNMENTAL STRUCTURE: JUDICIARY

The judicial system in a dictatorship cannot be a significant instrument for limiting the arbitrary acts of the wielders of political power. Rather than that, Soviet courts have often been told quite frankly that they are to act as faithful servants of the dictatorship. The insistence in the past upon the idea that the judges are independent and subject only to the law was intended precisely to exclude any thought of political independence. When the constitution says the contrary, it has been pointed out that the law spoken of is communist law, and this means communist law. Moreover, in the period of the extreme Stalinist period the secret police were not responsible to the courts or even to the law, even communist law. Reforms instituted after the death of Stalin were supposedly designed to establish "socialist legality." But it is well to remember that they do not point out that this did not mean they were going to protect the rights of individuals. To them "socialist legality" means that laws are to be obeyed by government agencies and by individuals alike. This does not mean, however, that the regime is bound by the law as defined and interpreted by the courts. In the last analysis Soviet courts are the servants of the party.

As a general rule, laws and the means of enforcing them are a direct reflection of the ideas and principles that dominate the society that produces them. In this respect, Soviet laws and Soviet courts faithfully reflect the Marxist-Leninist doctrine, upon which the Soviet system is based. This doctrine is not based on some abstract concept of justice; rather, it is seen as a product of the dominant class. Accordingly, Soviet leaders have never pretended that their law and their courts are the instruments of the state, and they are deliberately designed to strengthen and to defend the conquests of the proletarian revolution as these are interpreted by the top party leadership. In short, the primary objective of Soviet laws and Soviet courts is to preserve the Soviet regime and its achievements and to aid and protect the regime as it works to carry out its programs. Conversely, the Soviet judicial system is designed to crush those who constitute a barrier to these ends.

In view of these basic concepts and in the light of the party's extensive program in all fields of human endeavor, the need for a centralized, uniform, and disciplined judicial system becomes strikingly evident. That system must be studied and judged in this context, for to condemn it solely on the basis of the results and thereby leave the impression that it conceivably could come near our own standards of justice while remaining an integral part of the dictatorship would be misleading and meaningless. Soviet law and the Soviet judiciary cannot be studied apart from the political system they serve and whose instruments they are.

The provisions in the Soviet constitution concerning the rights and duties of Soviet citizens are completely in harmony with basic Soviet ideas about law and justice. Contrary to the belief of many persons, who apparently have not bothered to read the constitution of the U.S.S.R., Soviet citizens *are not* guaranteed the basic rights of free speech, press, and association in the way that these are secured for the citizens of democratic countries. Article 50 of the constitution defines these rights so narrowly as to make them meaningless in any true sense. Their guarantee is prefaced by the following clause: "In conformity with the interests of the working people, and in order to strengthen the socialist system." This is the identical formulation found in the 1936 constitution. Hence, these rights could not, even in theory, be said to guarantee a person the right to advocate anything except the socialist system. And the party is the all-wise judge of what that system is and what will or will not strengthen it.

Similarly, Article 51 states: "In conformity with the aims of building communism, citizens of the U.S.S.R. are guaranteed the right to unite in public organizations." It cites examples, such as trade unions, cultural and scientific societies, youth organizations, and others. It would be difficult, therefore to defend, even in theory, a right to any type of organizational life except that which accords with the party's wishes and desires.[15]

Moreover, several articles in the 1977 constitution further limit the exercise of basic rights. Article 39 says: "The exercise by citizens of rights and freedoms must not injure the interests of society and the state." Article 59 says: "Exercise of rights and freedoms shall be inseparable from the performance by citizens of their duties." And Article 62 states: "The citizen of the USSR shall be obliged to safeguard the interests of the Soviet state, to contribute to the strengthening of its might and prestige." In addition, Article 66 specifies that parents have an obligation to prepare children "for socially useful labor," and "to raise worthy members of the socialist society."

Other articles speak of the right to rest and leisure, to education, to housing, medical care, and to maintenance in old age. They also refer to equality of women and the equality of the races. The freedom to worship or to engage in antireligious propaganda is recognized, but there is no recognition to a right to

---

[15]For a discussion of how the Soviet regime utilizes its concept of civil rights to harness the masses to the dictatorship, see Chapter 33.

engage in propaganda in favor of religion. There is "the right to work," but there is not the right to stop working—that is, the right to strike. Moreover, the inviolability of homes and of the person is guaranteed, but the actions of Soviet authorities have frequently made a hollow mockery of this alleged guarantee.

The other declared duties of Soviet citizens include military service as an "honorable duty" and the defense of the U.S.S.R. as a "sacred duty." It is the duty of every citizen to abide by the constitution, to observe the laws, to maintain labor discipline, to safeguard and fortify public, socialist property as the sacred and inviolable foundation of the Soviet system.

Taken as a whole, therefore, the so-called Bill of Rights not only specifies the purposes for which certain "rights" are to be utilized but, in addition, asserts that the defense and furtherance of these purposes and aims are among the fundamental duties of Soviet citizens. What gain is there, many Soviet citizens might ask, in being given the right to speak, to write, to organize in order to defend a system they may not like? Or in being told that it is their duty to do so? Yet, in reality such is the Soviet Bill of Rights.

In the Soviet Union each republic has a court system, consisting of local and intermediate courts and a supreme court. In addition, there is the Supreme Court of the U.S.S.R., which is the highest court of the nation. Moreover, there are special tribunals, such as military courts. Some special tribunals have received little publicity, such as those in the concentration camps, and there may be others whose existence is known to only a limited number of people in the Soviet Union. On the other hand, the special transport courts, which had jurisdiction over crimes affecting railroads and waterways, were abolished in 1957.[16]

The basis of the Soviet judicial system is the people's court, established in each district and consisting of a popularly elected judge and two people's assessors, chosen at a general meeting of persons at their place of work, residence, or military unit. The judge, who is supposed to have legal training but often does not, is selected for a term of five years, while the assessors are chosen for two-year terms.[17] There are no juries. These courts exercise original jurisdiction in various kinds of civil cases and in minor criminal cases.

A variety of courts are to be found between the people's courts and the supreme courts of the republics. These are based on territories, areas, regions, autonomous regions, and autonomous republics. The judges of these courts, five in number, are elected for terms of five years by the soviets of the respective geographic units. All these courts have panels of people's assessors, but they are utilized only in cases of original jurisdiction, and not in appellate cases. All these courts may review cases originating in the people's courts, and they possess original jurisdiction in the more important civil and criminal cases.

---

[16]At the same time it was also announced that a "people assessor," a representative of the public, would in the future sit on military courts.

[17]Assessors at upper levels in the judiciary are selected by the respective soviet that appoints the professional judges.

The supreme court of each republic, consisting of five judges and a panel of assessors elected by the republic's supreme soviet for a term of five years, exercises both original and appellate jurisdiction. It has original jurisdiction in civil and criminal proceedings of major importance. It exercises a certain supervisory function over the courts below it and can set aside any of their verdicts. In 1957, the load of the supreme courts of the republics was increased when the Supreme Court of the Soviet Union was restricted largely to appellate functions.

The Supreme Court of the U.S.S.R. is elected by the Supreme Soviet for a term of five years. Presumably because it has been restricted mainly to appellate jurisdiction, its size was reduced in 1957. In 1970 it consisted of a chairman, 3 deputy chairmen, and 16 members, plus the 15 chairmen of the supreme courts of the union republics who serve exofficio. In addition, there were 45 assessors, who served when the court was exercising original jurisdiction in civil and criminal cases of exceptional significance. The 1977 constitution does not specify the exact number of members. The court rarely sits as one body; in the performance of its actual work it is divided into several colleges.

In addition to its other functions, the Supreme Court of the U.S.S.R. is charged by the constitution with the supervision of the judicial activities of all the judicial organs of the U.S.S.R. and of the Union Republics. This power has been exercised to ensure a centralized, uniform, and disciplined judiciary. The restoration in 1970 of a national ministry of justice signified additional central control over the court system.

In the late 1950s and in the 1960s extrajudicial institutions of law enforcement were considerably augmented. These in the main consist of (1) comrades' courts, (2) voluntary citizens' militia, and (3) children's commissions. The first have been in existence for a long time, but their jurisdiction and powers have been extended in recent years. The latter two are of relatively recent creation. All of them seem to be based on the assumption that direct public action is more effective in the case of certain offenders than the regular courts are.[18]

Comrades' courts may be created in places of residence (apartment building, collective farm, and so forth) or in places of work (factory, office, and so forth). The members are elected by the respective collective for a period of one year. The size of the court is not specified, except that the members choose a chairman, vice chairman, and secretary from among themselves. Comrades' courts concern themselves with violations of labor discipline, drunkenness and other improper social behavior, violations of apartment or dormitory regulations, petty theft, and similar offenses. Originally, they could impose reprimands and assess small fines. In 1965 they were empowered to impose fines up to approximately $55 and to demand full repayment on damaged property. They may also decide to transfer a case to the regular courts. Decisions of com-

---

[18]For an excellent account of crime and its study in the Soviet Union, see Peter Juviler in *Soviet Politics and Society in the 1970s,* eds. Henry W. Morton and Rudolf L. Tökés (New York: Free Press, 1974), pp. 200–38.

rades' courts may not ordinarily be reviewed by a court, although a trade union committee or the executive committee of the local soviet may suggest that the case be heard over again.

The voluntary citizens' militia, or public-order squads, came into being when the antiparasite laws were being passed. Initially, these public-order squads were designed to combat drunkenness, rowdyism, and other breaches of the peace by patrolling the streets, usually during the evening hours. They work under the guidance of party organizations as well as the police. A significant portion of their membership comes from the ranks of the Komsomol. There have been reports of many abuses of authority (beatings, invasions of privacy, and so forth) by the voluntary citizens' militia, but the Soviet authorities insist that the streets have been made safer.

Children's commissions handle lesser crimes or infractions by juveniles. These most frequently involve thieving and group violence (fist fights, malicious mischief, joyriding), as well as drunkenness and running away from home. A majority of juvenile crimes are apparently committed while the perpetrators are intoxicated. As a preventive measure, the Soviets have experimented with imposing evening curfews.

In the late 1950s and in the 1960s the Soviets experimented with another form of extrajudicial law enforcement—the so-called antiparasite tribunals, which were not really courts but mass meetings of the local population. The antiparasite laws provided for the exiling to more remote regions of the country persons who evaded socially useful work or who lived on unearned income. Sentences could be up to five years, with forced labor at the place of exile and possible confiscation of property not acquired by labor. In 1970 a new version of the antiparasite law was enacted that dropped the reference to exile but tightened up on other penalties, including a mandatory one- or two-year prison sentence or corrective labor. In effect, the duty to work was laid down as a legal obligation that the state would enforce. While some of the antiparasite laws may still be on the books, their enforcement seems to have been taken out of the hands of ad hoc gatherings of neighbors.

The prosecutor-general is vested with supreme advisory power to ensure the strict observance of the law by all ministries and institutions subordinated to them, as well as by officials and citizens of the U.S.S.R. generally (Article 163). Appointed by the Supreme Soviet for a period of five years, he or she in turn appoints the prosecutors-general of the republics, territories, regions, and autonomous regions, who serve for five years. Area, county, and city prosecutors are appointed for a like period by the prosecutors of the republics, subject to the approval of the prosecutor-general of the U.S.S.R.

The powers of the prosecutor-general in the enforcement of laws are vast. According to the constitution, all officials of his office are in no way subordinate to any local organs of authority. In discussing the judicial reforms in 1957, however, Soviet officials revealed that a "special council" of the Ministry of the Interior, which included the secret police, had existed and had given instructions to the courts. Ostensibly, the full powers of the prosecutor have been restored, and the court system has been divorced from the secret police.

Many Soviet judicial procedures have over the years come under considerable criticism in the democratic countries. Perhaps the most telling commentaries on these procedures, however, have been the admissions by Stalin's successors that many innocent persons were imprisoned or executed during the Stalin era. It is now alleged that some of the notorious judicial practices have been or are being abolished. It still remains to be seen, however, to what extent this will be done. In any case, it does not seem likely that Soviet judicial procedures will be modified to such an extent that they will meet democratic standards of justice.

One of the most repugnant of communist judicial practices stems from the absence of habeas corpus. The result is long pretrial incarceration and investigation. This period may last for months or even years, during which the imprisoned person may not be told why he or she is being held. Friends and close relatives may have no idea where the person may be or why. The 1961 RSFSR Code of Criminal Procedure empowers the prosecution to hold a suspect up to nine months without filing charges. According to the announced judicial reforms of 1957, the right of counsel was to be accorded at some stage in the pretrial investigation, but the legal codes adopted in December 1958 limit this right to minors. Moreover, the persons conducting investigations are to be less subject to the orders of the prosecutor than heretofore. While these reforms, if actually put into practice, may result in an improved situation for some unfortunate persons, they do not go to the heart of the problem. The absence of habeas corpus, particularly in a society where the public cannot know who is being held or for what period of time, continues to perpetuate fear and uncertainty.

Another repulsive practice, perhaps made partially possible by the absence of habeas corpus, is the forced confession, the sole basis of countless convictions. Long pretrial imprisonment has given the police authorities ample time to torture and to wear down victims to a point where they will sign anything. This has made possible the fabrication of a case against the accused that was false from beginning to end. Stalin's successors have admitted this, although the more specific references were to party comrades who were liquidated and not to the ordinary citizens, who must have received even less consideration. Allegedly, proof of guilt will in the future require more than a confession. While this may be a modest gain, depending upon what weight courts continue to give to confessions, it does not do away with long pretrial imprisonment or with the techniques for obtaining confessions. Nor does it forbid the use of such confessions in court.

The Soviet judicial system operates on the inquisitorial approach. In countries where democratic legislative bodies and a free press stand as guardians against the misuses of the judicial process, the inquisitorial approach has achieved high standards of justice. In the Soviet Union, however, it has made it possible for the judges to browbeat witnesses and to create an atmosphere of fear in the courtroom. The accused, who are obliged to take the stand and be grilled by the judge, often present a sorry spectacle. Even the so-called defense attorneys are often afraid to attempt a real defense, particularly in instances of the so-called crimes against the state. After the downgrading of Stalin, some Soviet jurists advocated the discarding of the presumption of guilt doctrine and the acceptance of the principle that a person is assumed to be innocent until proved guilty. While present statutes do not recognize this principle explicitly, they do state that the burden of proof rests on the prosecutor.[19]

In a somewhat similar situation are the ostensible guarantees to a public trial and to defense counsel. As in the past, the right to a public trial would not seem too meaningful, for the constitution permits legislation to deny it. Consequently, innumerable trials have been secret. It is possible, however, to overemphasize the value of public trials in the Soviet Union, for they have not been a barrier to miscarriages of justice. The right to defense counsel has in the past left much to be desired. By not being familiar with the case in the pretrial investigative period, defense attorneys have rarely had time to prepare a defense in the allotted time. Moreover, in certain types of cases neither the defense attorney's nor the defendant's presence was required for conviction. It still remains to be seen whether significant reforms are instituted in this area.

Also of concern to many students of the Soviet judicial system is the absence of any protection against double jeopardy. Acquittal does not prevent additional trials for the same alleged offense. Similarly, moderate sentences may be appealed to higher courts and stiffer penalties imposed. It is altogether possible for a person to receive a moderate sentence in the court of original jurisdiction, thereby conveying a favorable impression of the Soviet judicial system, only to have a much more stringent sentence imposed by an appellate court without this fact's becoming public knowledge. Now, however, appeals from acquittal or mild sentences must be made within a year. At least so the law states.

Two procedures, said to be abolished in 1957, were not even a part of Soviet law, and therefore all the more repugnant. One was the practice of holding a person in violation of the criminal code in cases of minor negligence and other administrative offenses not foreseen by the law. Administrative officials, usually in the Ministry of Interior, imposed penalties, some of which banished the person for several years. The second practice permitted the holding of a person in violation of the criminal code for crimes by analogy—that is, for acts that were analogous to illegal acts. These practices are allegedly no longer in existence. A similar procedure, also allegedly discarded, permitted punishment of relatives for crimes committed by their kin. The family of a soldier who deserted abroad, for example, was held collectively responsible for this act. A new type of offense has been added, however. Particularly dangerous state crimes committed against any other workers' state are now punishable under a new law.

---

[19]Harold J. Berman, *Justice in the U.S.S.R.: An Interpretation of Soviet Law,* rev. ed. (New York: Vintage Books, 1963), p. 71.

Reports of ... Soviet judicial practices must, however, be tempered with the ... always reserved the right to go outside the law if ... it. The setting up of the voluntary citizens' ... the ... by the Presidium of the Supreme Soviet in 1961 authorizing ... the death penalty for speculation in currency, are examples ...

It should also be ... noted that new laws can be made any time that the regime's leadership ... At the time of the 1958 reforms, for example, the "counterrevolutionary ... of "agitation or propaganda" against the Soviet system was ... punishable by up to seven years' imprisonment. And while the mass ... of the Stalin era have apparently been eliminated, it may be significant ... death penalty has been extended in recent years to several new ... crimes ... Among these are serious economic crimes, illegal ... large-scale bribery, and resistance to a police officer ... to death.

It is ... Soviet courts are not impartial in dispensing justice. Party members ... receive more lenient sentences than nonparty citizens. Moreover, ... has from time to time printed stories indicating ... been reluctant to bring party members to court at all. That ... party members exists cannot be questioned, but the extent ... far from clear.

Finally, ... where there is no free press as a guardian of people's ... judicial practices and procedures cannot ... have a serious impact upon the rulers ... corresponding emphasis upon secrecy, many odious practices ... without becoming known to the most astute observers ... to be the first prequisite for the type of judicial standard ... (See chapter 33 for a discussion of human rights ...)

THE ARMED ... SYSTEM

... headed instrument of the bourgeois state, and, ... but something had to be put in its place—an armed ... but since the party was to become all-powerful in the ... understandable that the army (armed forces) could ... force. New armed forces were established, but like ... they became the instrument of the prevailing political authority ...

It needs to be ... that the Communist party is regarded as the source of all ... authority. Any efforts to set up alternate or competing centers of ... and any questioning of the party's program, have been ... dangerous and treated as such. The army, like other institutions in the ... is supposed to be subservient to the party. It can have influence only to the extent that what it wants to do is also what the party wants to do. In the age of missiles and space technology, however, the technical specialist is in a position to exert considerable influence in the allocation of critical material and human resources. If the army ever achieved an independent status, the result would probably be a military dictatorship and not a dictatorship of the party.

The party's aim, of course, has been to produce the type of military man who will see no conflict between his role as a military man and his role as a party member. More than that, the party has sought to raise the political educational level of the military commanders, so that they will act as loyal party men. It should surprise no one that over 85 percent of the officer corps is made up of party members, and that the top command of the military forces is made up exclusively of party members. In other words, the military officer comes to this position imbued with the idea that the party is the most important part of the Soviet system and that he, as a party member and as a military man, owes his highest allegiance to the party. And the party, for all practical purposes, means the top leadership. Military men, therefore, are party comrades, and it would be unthinkable for them to challenge the authority of the party leaders in the hierarchy above them. To do so would be to challenge the Soviet system itself.

Nevertheless, the party has also developed other means of ensuring the loyalty of the armed forces. First of all, the officers in the armed forces live well, and rarely do they cherish the loss of the privileged positions they happen to occupy. Second, there is the authority of the superior officers, who are also trusted party leaders and upon whose good opinion promotion depends. In addition, the party's Central Committee has a special section whose responsibility is confined to political administration in the military forces, where the *zampolit* (deputy commander for political affairs), formerly political commissar, guards the party line. Moreover, the party organizations in the armed forces have independent chains of command. They report to the top party authorities and are not subject to the local party organization. Finally, the secret police operates within the military forces and, like the party organizations, is not subject to control by the local or regional party organizations.

As a result, loyalty in the armed forces has been maintained, although not without purges, some of which have been of considerable proportions. We do not know to what extent there was any serious attempt on the part of military men to overthrow the system, but we do know that they have expressed their displeasure with some decisions of the political leaders.

Khrushchev has revealed that there have been differences between the party leadership and certain highly placed officers. He has reported that one such officer made the party leaders uneasy, while another one criticized the party leadership in a private conversation with another officer.[20] He has also reported that

---

[20]*Khrushchev Remembers: The Last Testament* (Boston: Little, Brown, 1974), pp. 16–17.

Admiral N. G. Kuznetsov openly criticized the political leadership after its decision to put off building up the navy and to concentrate on the air force and missiles. For this he was relieved of his duties and demoted, even though this upset some military men, but, says Khrushchev, "we had to put an abrupt halt to any manifestation of Bonapartism among the military."[21] Khrushchev also reports that very early in his leadership he was made commander in chief of the armed forces, although this decision was not made public.[22] And in the Epilogue of his second volume, he warns that, while there is no military class in the Soviet Union, if "given a chance, some elements within the military might try to force a militarist policy on the government. Therefore the government must always keep a bit between the teeth of the military."[23]

There have been some indications, however, that political leaders have used the military leaders in their struggle for power within the party. In 1957, for example, when an effort was made in the party Presidium (later renamed Politburo) to oust Khrushchev, Minister of Defense Marshal Zhukov, who owed his appointment to Khrushchev, employed military aircraft in order to get members of the Central Committee to Moscow quickly, thus enabling Khrushchev to frustrate the efforts of his opponents in the Presidium. Thereupon Khrushchev ousted his foes and rewarded Zhukov by making him a full member of the Presidium—the first time a professional soldier achieved such a distinction. But Zhukov erred in thinking that he could curtail the work of party organizations in the military, and in a few months was ousted not only as minister of defense but also as a member of the Presidium and the Central Committee. Subsequently, the role of the party in the armed forces was strengthened through explicit orders and through a reaffirmation of the principle that the leadership of the military cannot be outside the control of the party. As long as the authority of the party dictatorship is maintained, therefore, it seems safe to conclude that the armed forces will be loyal to whichever leaders remain at the top of the political ladder.

BIBLIOGRAPHICAL NOTE

A general view of the structure of the Soviet government may be found in Frederick C. Barghoorn, *Politics in the U.S.S.R.,* 2d ed. (Boston: Little, Brown, 1972); Joseph L. Nogee, ed., *Man, State, and Society in the Soviet Union* (New York: Praeger Publishers, 1972); John R. Reshetar, Jr., *The Soviet Polity: Government and Politics of the U.S.S.R.,* 2d ed. (New York: Dodd, Mead, 1978); Michel Tatu, *Power in the Kremlin: From Khrushchev to Kosygin (New York: Viking Press, 1970).*

More recent works that deserve mention are: Archie Brown and Michael Kaser, eds., *The Soviet Union Since the Fall of Khrushchev* (New York: Free Press, 1975); Peter H. Juviler, *Revolutionary Law and Order: Politics and Social Change in the U.S.S.R.* (New

---

[21]Ibid., pp. 25–27.
[22]Ibid., p. 12.
[23]Ibid., pp. 540–41.

York: Free Press, 1976); Henry W. Morton and Rudolf L. Tökés, *Soviet Politics and Society in the 1970s* (New York: Free Press, 1974); Roy A. Medvedev, *On Socialist Democracy* (New York: Alfred A. Knopf, 1975).

Mention should also be made of: Jonathan R. Adelman, *Communist Armies in Politics* (Boulder, Colo.: Westview Press, 1982); Jeremy R. Azrael, ed., *Soviet Nationality Policies and Practices* (New York: Praeger Publishers, 1978); Stephen F. Cohen, Alexander Rabinowitch, and Robert Sharlet, *The Soviet Union Since Stalin* (Bloomington: Indiana University Press, 1980); Michael J. Deane, *Political Control of the Soviet Armed Forces: A Conflict of Interests* (New York: Crane, Russak, 1977); Everett M. Jacobs, ed., *Soviet Local Politics and Government* (Winchester, Mass.: Allen & Unwin, 1983); and Peter Vanneman, *The Supreme Soviet: Politics and the Legislative Process in the Soviet Political System* (Durham, N.C.: Duke University Press, 1977).

32

Policy-Implementing
Structures:
Administration

The Soviet state, more than any other political system known to human beings, is an administrative state. Soviet society is bureaucratized to the highest degree. Even the lives and daily decisions of individual Russians are guided by the decisions of the Communist party, as expressed in the all-embracing administrative system. A detailed treatment of this system is beyond the scope of this book. But it is important that its main features be examined, its formal organization depicted, and some of its major problems set forth.

NATURE OF SOVIET ADMINISTRATION

Prior to their seizure of power, the Bolsheviks, and especially Lenin, envisioned a new type of society without bureaucracy, police, or army. Anyone knowing the four rules of arithmetic, in Lenin's view, possessed the qualifications of an administrator. After the initial establishment of the new society, administration would need to be only a part-time affair. It was not long, however, before the Bolshevik leaders learned how indispensable was a highly organized bureaucracy to the orderly functioning of a modern state, especially a state bent on speeding industrialization and embarking upon large-scale social engineering. This became particularly evident when they started the U.S.S.R. down the path of successive five-year plans.

The scope and extent of public administration in the Soviet Union would be sizable under any political system. There is a huge territory to oversee, with varied climates, peoples, and problems to cope with. An authoritarian system, of whatever type, would need an extensive bureaucracy to make sure its edicts were obeyed and the empire held together. This is all the more true of a dictatorship that sets out to remake society and does not hesitate to run roughshod over anyone and everyone who might stand in the way.

Moreover, one can appreciate the size and scope of the Soviet bureaucracy if one keeps in mind the fact that virtually nothing in the U.S.S.R. occurs as a result of private enterprise. A notable exception are the private plots in agriculture, discussed below. The government runs or controls every form of economic activity—stores, factories, mines, farms, trains, ships, and all of the other things normally associated with private endeavor in other countries. In a broad sense, everyone works for the government.

The size and scope of the administrative machine becomes even more meaningful if one remembers that it is not merely a matter of a bureaucracy running the machinery of government it has inherited. Under its control nothing is supposed to happen by accident. Everything is planned and controlled. The bureaucracy not only runs things but, in addition, plans them and runs them according to the plans. Under such a system and in such a large country, the size and scope of the administrative apparatus must be large indeed.

In the Soviet Union, therefore, the administration works within the framework of the policy guidance that the party establishes. From the beginning, it was the party that had to determine what the factories should produce; how raw materials, manpower, and machinery were to be combined so as to realize the planned output; and how that output was to be distributed. As an arm of the party dictatorship, the Soviet bureaucracy has the task of building a communist society in accordance with the party blueprint. As such, the Soviet bureaucracy cannot be viewed as a nonpolitical and detached civil service. It is clearly partisan.

But the party does more than merely furnish policy guidance. It is constantly engaged in checking on the execution of its policies. The top political leaders must keep an eye on the bureaucrats, who have not been above falsifying records and engaging in a whole host of other "unsocialist" acts in order to receive material or political rewards from their superiors. The administrators all along the line have learned to expect the party's watchful eye, and to fear the attribution of political motives to some of their acts, with possible dire consequences, even when such motives may never have existed.

Simultaneously with checking on the fulfillment of its policies, the party is engaged in mobilizing popular support behind planned targets. This may range all the way from exhorting the workers to surpass planned output to urging a mass movement of people to an area where there is a manpower shortage; such exhortations very often are made without taking other circumstances into account, which may result in making matters worse. In short, the bureaucracy can expect to hear the party's voice at all stages of its operation.

As the above suggest, public administration in the Soviet Union is highly centralized, with control and direction from the center. The most important control agency is the party, which decides on the nature of all other controls. These controls have been altered so often that any description of them would soon be out of date. For example, the Ministry of State Control gave way in 1957 to the Commission of Soviet Control that, in turn, gave way to the State Control Commission in 1961. In 1962, Khrushchev reorganized the party into two hierarchies, one to check performance in agriculture and the other in industry. As a part of this reorganization, the State Control Commission was replaced by the Committee of Party and State Control. Khrushchev's successors abolished the dual hierarchy arrangement, and established a new control body—the People's Control Commission—which, however, has no jurisdiction over party affairs.

Other controls are exercised by the office of the state prosecutor and by the secret police. In addition, various ministries and the State Planning Commission perform control functions. Moreover, the party also makes use of advisory workers' committees and a corps of volunteer inspectors.

This multiplicity of controls must be viewed against the party's shifting standard of what meets or does not meet the requirements of theoretical dogma. What is perfectly acceptable today may turn out to be un-Marxian tomorrow. What supports the strategy of party leaders becomes an impediment when that strategy changes, and it has changed often during the life of the Soviet regime. When something does not produce the desired result, there are changes, often based on little more than the principle of trial and error, although the party leaders never admit this. In their words, each change is but another step toward the desired goal, a step that more appropriately corresponds to "the present stage of socialist development."

In their search for workable administrative arrangements, the party leaders have emphasized the desired objectives, usually to the exclusion of other considerations. To them, loyalty and adherence to party directives have been of the utmost importance. Efficiency is important, but secondary. The rights of individuals, on the other hand, are given little weight. The administrative machine, understandably, operates to achieve state-determined objectives and not to preserve abstract personal rights.

FORMAL ADMINISTRATIVE ORGANIZATION

Superficially, at least, the Soviet administrative organization bears a certain resemblance to that found in most other countries. There are ministries—until 1946, the Soviet leaders avoided this bourgeois term—and bureaus, offices, missions, and others. There is a civil service to staff these various offices. Moreover, from time to time there have been changes and reorganizations in the administrative structure. In other ways, however, the Soviet administrative organization is unique, which will become evident from what follows.

As noted in an earlier chapter, there are three types of ministries in the Soviet Union—all-union ministries, union-republic ministries, and republic ministries. All-union ministries are national ministries that operate from Moscow through their own employees down to the local level. The line of responsibility is vertical. Union-republic ministries are those ministries that exist on the national level and on the republic level. In other words, the ministries in Moscow that operate through corresponding ministries in each of the republics are known as union-republic ministries. The line of responsibility, therefore, is both vertical and horizontal, although the vertical is more important. In both all-union and union-republic ministries, the final control rests in Moscow. Republic ministries on the other hand, are ministries that exist on the republic level, with no corresponding ministries at the national level. These are responsible to their respective republics, although they may be engaged in carrying out programs determined in Moscow.

The number of ministries in the various categories has changed a number of times. The number of all-union ministries was increased and decreased several times. At the time of Stalin's death, for example, there were 60, but two days later these were reduced to 25. Within a year, the number had increased to 46, and by 1956 it was up to 52. This number dropped sharply after the 1957 reorganization, discussed below, but by 1969 the number of ministers at the national level increased to about 90 and to about 110 in 1985. The 1977 constitution, unlike that of 1936, does not list the ministries by name, but merely provides that this will be done subsequently by legislative act.

In 1957 the Soviet Union underwent a sweeping reorganization of its industrial-administrative structure. Most of the all-union ministries in the economic sphere, as well as many union-republic industrial ministries, were abolished. In their place more than 100 regional economic councils were set up, corresponding to the number of economic regions into which the Soviet Union was divided. In most instances these regions coincided with the existing administrative and territorial divisions of the U.S.S.R. The regional councils, which were given authority to run the vast industrial empire, were, in theory, to be chosen by the governments of the respective republics, but Moscow retained a veto power over members of the councils as well as over council decisions.

In some circles this reorganization was referred to as decentralization of the Soviet economy. Soviet leaders, notably Khrushchev, insisted that it was, in effect, a more effective centralization. It was only the operative control that was being decentralized. Decisions concerning basic policy as well as planned targets were still to be made in Moscow. The regional councils and local authorities were merely to have more discretion in finding ways and means of carrying out basic economic directives. This meant that power once exercised by a departmental bureaucracy in Moscow had been transferred to the bureaucracy that was actually at the center of production. In addition, some of the powers previously exercised by ministries in Moscow had been transferred to local ministries and local party committees.

To insure basic control from the center, the functions (and to some degree the administrative apparatus) of the all-union ministries that were abolished were transferred to the reorganized State Planning Committee and to a whole host of other committees, which in a way resembled skeletal ministries. Most of the heads of the abolished ministries were made chairmen or deputy chairmen of these new committees, with the rank of minister of the U.S.S.R.

Less than a year after the 1957 reorganization went into effect, evidence began accumulating that all was not running smoothly. Complaints began appearing in the Soviet press that certain regional councils were putting local interests ahead of the national interest. After seeking to remedy the situation by providing bonuses for deliveries of goods to outside economic areas, the Soviet leaders found it necessary to resort to sterner measures. A decree was promulgated that made it a criminal offense to fail to deliver goods to other areas or to the government—a method of control that had been used in the past. Unless there was a valid excuse, the guilty would be subject to strict disciplinary measures or fines of up to three months of salary. Second offenders would be treated more harshly.

Further difficulties were evidenced by the fact that in 1960 a new agency, the Russian Council for the National Economy, was established. It was charged with coordinating the work of the 70 regional economic councils in the Russian republic (RSFSR). In 1962, a new reorganization divided the country into 17 major economic regions, each with a council to be concerned with the development of resources and with the coordination of planning and production among the management bodies under its jurisdiction. In 1963 the Supreme National Economic Council was established to coordinate the planning and management of industry on a nationwide basis. The authority of the regional councils was further reduced when in 1965 several state committees, notably in the defense field, were converted into full-fledged ministries and thus removed from the jurisdiction of the councils. By late 1965 the Soviet leaders had abolished the regional councils altogether, thus continuing the search for more efficient ways of organizing and operating a vast planned economy.

At the top of the formal administrative structure is the Council of Ministers of the U.S.S.R. During most of Stalin's reign this was a large and unwieldy body, which really never decided anything important as a body. Really effective power was exercised by a small group, sometimes referred to as the Presidium of the Council, which consisted of the chairman and the deputy chairmen of the Council. With the abolition of many national ministries, the Council initially decreased in size, but in more recent years the number of national ministries has again risen appreciably.

The Council of Ministers is the directing agency of the administrative machine. It is supposed to have the main responsibility in supervising the carrying out of the industrial plans. As such, it can overrule the councils of ministers of individual republics. It exercises wide decree powers in finance, taxation, pricing, and foreign trade. It is also empowered to issue decrees in the realm of military affairs, and it can promulgate measures to protect socialist property. Important decrees are often issued jointly with the Central Committee of the party. Sometimes there is a joint promulgation of decrees by the Council of Ministers and by the All-Union Council of Trade Unions. The All-Union Council has been empowered to issue binding decrees, especially in the labor legislation field, subject to approval by the Council of Ministers.

Centralized economic planning became an essential feature of the Soviet economy by 1921, although it is usually associated with the beginning of the era of the five-year plans. Established in 1921, *Gosplan* (State Planning Committee) did not come into prominence until the launching of the first five-year plan in 1928. That year also marked the consolidation of the Stalin dictatorship and the final abolition of private economic enterprise.

The principal aims of the five-year plans during Stalin's reign centered on the building of a heavy industry and the collectivization of agriculture. The former involved a series of successive drives to build new capital goods factories and plants at an ambitious rate. The latter was ostensibly aimed at increasing agricultural production by seeking to convert small and often scattered peasant holdings into large-scale mechanized units. These were monumental tasks, and in the industrialized sector there were some substantial gains, but the human and material costs in both were huge.

Centralized planning and direction are still the responsibility of *Gosplan,* which is to determine the direction and rate of economic development. It coordinates its efforts with those of planning committees in the respective republics, which in turn coordinate with various enterprise directors, as well as with the directors of the economic ministries.

The planning operation is an involved and complicated affair. It begins with the aims and goals of the party, transmitted via party and governmental channels from top to bottom. *Gosplan* and the subsidiary planning bodies at the republic, regional, and local levels must work out the detailed plans in collaboration with other governmental authorities as well as with economic ministries, regional officials, and individual enterprises. These plans involve not only planning for a set number of years but, in addition, planning for each year and each quarter of a year. The more detailed planning involves targets and timetables for each month.

The precise number of people in the Soviet bureaucracy is difficult to determine, mainly because there is some question as to who should be included. Should one include, for example, the people who work full time in the trade unions, the party apparatus, and the youth organizations? Depending upon how one conceives the bureaucracy, its estimated size runs from 10 to 15 million.

The vast army of civil servants is recruited under the watchful eye of the Communist party, which is the final judge in all personnel matters. The party's concern with personnel is understandable, for the highest duty of the bureaucracy is to carry out party policies. For years the party's concern with personnel was exercised through the Cadres Administration of its Central Committee and through similar party organizations at all levels of government. Now, however, individual ministries recruit people at the lower levels, usually from the universities, where they can prescribe certain courses, or from schools that are attached to certain ministries. But as one moves up the bureaucratic ladder, the transfer and movement of personnel is subject to increasing party control.

The government (party) can shift personnel at will. Although the 1940 decree on the compulsory transfer of personnel was repealed in 1956, the government can employ other coercive means to achieve the same end. For example, it can appeal to the trade unions, the party, or the youth organization to send its members to new industrial sites, the virgin lands, or elsewhere. Uncooperative persons can be expelled from these organizations, a circumstance fraught with serious practical consequences for the persons concerned, such as the loss of job, position of responsibility, or privileges attendant to membership. Moreover, the government can, and does, promulgate new decrees at will. And it can, and often does, act without the benefit of any legal sanction.

As the above paragraphs suggest, the bureaucracy is first of all responsible to the party. In actual practice, control of the bureaucracy is complicated. The People's Control Commission has vast powers to investigate and to institute measures of correction, to reprimand, and to dismiss. The Council of Ministers exercises powers in the same realm. The Presidium of the Supreme Soviet can modify and interpret decrees and decisions of administrative bodies. The police, the courts, and the prosecutor's office, to say nothing of the "volunteer" inspectors (who are publicly encouraged), exercise a type of cross control. Finally, there is the criticism and self-criticism voiced through the press, in editorials, or in letters to the editor. Despite the fact that the party ostensibly provides the necessary guidance, the nature of the control apparatus lends itself to confusion and abuse. And the Soviet press continues to assert that the work of the control organs is far from what it should be.

So as to deal more effectively with the large number of lawsuits between state economic enterprises, the Soviet leaders have established a system of so-called state arbitration tribunals. They have the power to summon witnesses, to request the submission of documents, to appoint expert examiners, and to issue decrees that must be obeyed. They are appointed by, and are subordinate to, the supreme executive bodies of the areas in which they function, and their decisions may be reversed or altered by these same executive bodies. The chief arbitrator is attached to the Council of Ministers of the U.S.S.R. He supervises the arbitration work of state arbitrators at all levels, and issues general instructions to them. He is also empowered to review their decisions.

In the settlement of disputes, the state arbitration tribunals are supposed to protect the "property rights and lawful interests of enterprises." At the same time they are to protect the basic concerns of the state by declaring invalid all contracts between enterprises that do not conform to Soviet law or that run counter to the plans of the State Planning Committee. Most of the disputes between economic enterprises concern alleged breaches of contract, which may involve late or nondelivery of goods, poor quality of goods, or their delivery in poor or damaged condition. Some disputes concern prices and terms of payment. Other disputes involve damage claims resulting from the delivery of allegedly defective materials or machines. Arbitration tribunals are also called upon to resolve precontract disputes, where enterprises are legally required to enter into contracts and yet cannot agree on the terms.

MANAGEMENT OF GOVERNMENT ENTERPRISES

Lenin believed that capitalism had simplified and routinized industrial methods to such an extent that socialized industry could be operated by anyone who could read and write. "The ability to observe and record and to make out receipts—this, with knowledge of the four rules of arithmetic, is all that is required." Soviet leaders were to learn the hard way, however, that the role of management was much more important than that.

For years the great problem in Soviet management was the lack of freedom to manage. The first phase in Soviet industrial management was characterized by the power of factory committees and the trade unions. They had to be consulted on virtually everything. But neither the factory committees nor the trade unions were trained to deal with problems of supply, manufacturing, and distribution. Consequently, Soviet industrial production dropped sharply. For a time, in the era of the New Economic Policy (NEP), many of the capitalist managers were called back. By the time the Soviet leaders were ready to launch the five-year plans (1928), they were convinced that the managerial concept must be accepted.

The philosophy behind the five-year plans was production at any cost. In order that nothing should interfere with the pursuit of the announced goals, the factory committees had to go. The five-day week and other labor gains also had to go, while the trade unions were made a part of the governmental machinery, with assigned roles to play. Their chief task now was to ride herd on their members in order that management might reach its assigned production quotas. To achieve the goals of the five-year plans, the managers needed to have the power to manage, and with minimum interference even from party organizations.

The purges of the 1930s, however, dealt the managerial concept a hard blow. Many old Bolsheviks who held high administrative or party posts were liquidated or displaced. Managers of various ranks were removed by the thousands, and many of them were shot or sent to slave labor camps. The net result was a widespread fear of making decisions. The safe way was to refer everything, even ridiculously minor matters, to Moscow. Soviet management was to suffer from this malady as long as Stalin lived. Since his passing, however, there have been indications that the new Soviet leaders have been engaged in restoring the power of management to the managers.

The acceptance of the importance of the managerial role was accompanied by a trend toward capitalist-type incentives. In the early years of the regime, when the trade unions sought to protect the workers, the five-day week was the rule, and there was a trend toward equality of wages. With the launching of the five-year plans, however, the previous trade union attitude was viewed as defensive and negative. Increasingly, the practice of rewarding people in proportion to their output became the rule of the Soviet society, receiving constitutional recognition in the fundamental law of 1936.

To the end that people would be rewarded "according to their work," the salaries of managers jumped phenomenally, for their work was regarded as much more important than that of the ordinary workers. In addition, managers were given bonuses for overfulfillment of planned goals, as well as compensation in kind, such as good apartments, special food, a radio, and even a private automobile. The work of engineers, technicians, and skilled laborers received similar recognition, with corresponding gradations in salary and rank.

Differentiation was also made even among the unskilled workers. Piece rates and production quotas were established for them, with increasing rewards for those who surpassed the so-called norm of production, which was raised steadily as more and more workers surpassed it. Those who consistently produced above the norm were designated as *stakhanovites* (shock workers), after a coal miner named Stakhanov whose work output was allegedly phenomenal. In setting wage scales in the Soviet Union, familiar capitalist principles, such as education, experience, and the arduousness, complexity, and exactness of work, are given weight. The net result is wider differentials and inequalities of reward than in the United States, where legal enactments and union activity have served to narrow the gap.

Those workers who are judged to be particularly deserving are awarded medals, trips to Moscow, special vacations, and other honors. Negatively, the capitalist type of reward was accompanied by rigid controls, applicable particularly in the case of the less cooperative worker. Movement from job to job became almost impossible. Absenteeism without an acceptable excuse was punished progressively in wages, ration coupons (during rationing), and, ultimately, in the loss of job and dwelling quarters. Drunkenness was also punishable.

The drift toward capitalist patterns of reward was not, however, accompanied by any visible trend toward a free market as a regulator of the economy. Production and distribution were determined by the plans, as were the costs and profits. The plans were enforced, for the most part, by changing the rate of the turnover tax, a type of sales tax, which is also the principal source of government revenue. By increasing or decreasing the rate, the government can effectively encourage or discourage certain types of economic activity. It could, for example, make shoes expensive and television sets inexpensive. In brief, this is the way the party's arbitrary decisions concerning the allocation of resources were carried out.

Under this system the preferences of the consumer were ignored. Moreover, the producing enterprise had no particular incentive to turn out quality goods. The result, all too often, was an accumulation of poor quality goods that went unsold. In order to remedy this situation and to combat a malaise in the economy, Moscow in 1965 announced a new set of economic reforms designed to shift considerable operational control to enterprise managers while keeping the system of centralized planning. Cautious approaches were made to the use of certain market mechanisms such as interest charges, profits, and consumer demands. The central planners continued to set basic targets, but most factories were to be given greater authority in carrying out the plans. It was reasoned by the leadership that requiring enterprises to pay interest on the money they borrow and permitting them to share in the profits would, in effect, reward those enterprises that made desirable goods at a reasonable price and punish those that turned out goods no one wanted. In this way, enterprises were encouraged to make an effort to discover what the consumer liked and desired. Similarly, the new system was to encourage managers to improve the efficiency of their operations.

This shift toward the employment of market mechanisms was associated with a Soviet economist, Liberman. He argued that enterprises would improve production, make better goods, and increase efficiency if they were charged interest on the money made available to them, provided they could also share in the profits. The implementation of his ideas initially led to modest successes, but serious problems remained. The government did not permit sufficient flexibility in prices, and suppliers often did not live up to their contracts, in terms of both delivery times and quality of goods. In addition, it began to appear that the leadership had second thoughts about the reforms, because of both opposition from central agencies and ministries and the apparent timidity of the managers themselves in exercising the promised new authority.

In 1973 and 1974 new rulings were issued, but the 1965 statute has not been officially amended or repealed. For all practical purposes, however, the 1965 reforms have been negated in practice. The attempt to utilize economic levers was handicapped from the outset by centrally determined prices and the ever-present detailed instructions from above. The appearance in January 1977 of a new journal, which was to deal with such problems as who is entitled to give directions to managers of production associations and enterprises, seems to focus on the need to regulate more precisely the legal position of various agencies connected with Soviet economic life.

As the Soviet industrial empire grew, the importance of the technical-administrative intelligentsia became more and more evident to the Soviet leaders. Increasingly, members of this group rose to higher and higher posts in the administrative hierarchy. During Stalin's dictatorship, however, they were sufficiently terrorized that they could not openly challenge party dictates, even when these were obviously faulty. By 1957, on the other hand, a number of them felt sufficiently secure to argue publicly against some of the theses put forward by party leaders. At the same time, the growing importance of the technical-administrative intelligentsia in the party membership was becoming evident.

Yet, during the Brezhnev years the party leaders seemed to be in full control of industrial developments at all levels. In the 1970s, party representatives in ministries were given increased powers to check on the work of the ministerial apparatus. In 1982 and 1983, Brezhnev's successor, Yuri Andropov, launched a campaign against favoritism in appointments and against the protection of incompetent and corrupt officials, which was supported by his successor, Konstantin Chernenko. Major corruption scandals were publicized and a number of highly placed officials were shot, while others received prison sentences. The new Soviet leader, Mikhail Gorbachev, seems equally determined to bring about reforms in the bureaucracy.

MANAGEMENT IN AGRICULTURE

Despite the revolutionary cry of "all land to the peasants," the Bolshevik leaders did not intend to promote private ownership of land. In the early years they attempted, in effect, to confiscate agricultural produce through compulsory deliveries, a practice highly resented by the peasants. During the NEP period, however, the peasants were free to produce and to sell. The more enterprising ones leased land and even hired labor, practices that led to the growth of a moderately well-to-do group of peasants, subsequently called kulaks. In 1929 the party leaders called a halt and embarked on a program to collectivize agriculture. Through heavy taxation, refusal of credit, making it illegal to own or lease farm machinery, and, in the final analysis, through physical liquidation of the recalcitrants, the regime conducted its farm revolution, which was virtually complete by 1932. The original plans had called for the collectivization of 15 to 20 percent of the land during the first five-year plan. At least in part because of peasant opposition, this figure was boosted to 75 and subsequently to 90 percent.

Some form of collective ownership and operation of agriculture was required by the Marxian doctrine, although the details were far from clear. Seemingly of more importance to the Soviet leaders was the promotion of greatly increased agricultural production, which was necessary to feed the growing industrial-urban population. This could be achieved by mechanization, but there was some question of how effectively machinery could be used on the small and often scattered pieces of land—hence the conclusion that mechanization would only be effective on large-scale agricultural units. Parenthetically, however, it might be noted that during the entire period of Stalin's dictatorship productivity per acre was not raised. Increased yields were achieved only by adding acreage.

Agricultural land in the Soviet Union is in the form of collective farms (kolkhoz) and state farms (sovkhoz). The state farms are government owned and operated; the workers on them are ordinary wage earners. The collective farms are also really government owned, but they resulted, in the main, from the merging of neighboring farms under rules set forth by the government. Hence, the people who live on them have a right, at least in theory, to their exclusive use. Under rules handed down by the government, the members of the kolkhoz divide the profits of their labor, which made for a very uncertain income. In more recent years the Soviet government established minimum earnings to go to each collective farmer. Moreover, in most instances the individual family dwelling was retained by the family, together with an adjoining household or garden plot of from one-half to three acres. The plot, theoretically, could be used as the family saw fit, but in practice the government could and does change the rules.

Over the years it became increasingly evident to the Soviet leaders that these private plots were occupying a large part of the time of the collective-farm members. Instead of planting a few vegetables and berries for the family table, the peasants were using these plots to grow major produce as well as to support the maximum livestock permitted (a cow and two calves, a pig, a few goats or sheep, and an unlimited number of poultry). Prior to World War II, the average member of a kolkhoz was earning approximately one half of his total income from these plots, a fairly good indication that collective farmers were not giving the collective effort a very high priority.

Soon after legalizing the private plot, the government began to hedge it in with restrictions designed to make it so costly that the peasant would ultimately abandon it. High taxes were imposed on produce from these plots. After World War II, the government increased compulsory deliveries on a portion of the produce, even requiring the delivery of milk, eggs, wool, and so forth, whether the farmer owned the livestock or not. Moreover, there was an attempt to reduce the size of the plots in 1950, during an amalgamation of small collective farms into larger ones. After a temporary relaxation in 1953–54, the regime returned to the attack. In 1956 it inaugurated a program designed to eliminate the private plots. In 1961 decrees urged consumer cooperatives to step up the purchase of surplus produce from the farmer, pointing to the elimination of the last remnants of a free market. By 1965, however, shortages in agricultural produce forced the government to encourage peasants to grow food on the private plots, and to sell the surplus at local markets, where supply and demand determine the price.

In the 1950s there were several developments indicating that the collective farm itself may be on the way out. A number of the smaller collective farms were amalgamated, with the result that the total number was reduced by more than one half. Almost simultaneously there was a move to promote the construction of *agrogorods* (agricultural cites), where the collective farmers would live, commuting to work. While this idea fell by the wayside after Khrushchev's rise to power, he nevertheless promoted the further merger of collectives as well as the creation of additional state farms at the expense of the collective farm idea. The 6 million acres of virgin land opened up in 1955, for example, were all organized on the state farm principle. Between 1966 and 1976 the number of collective farms dropped from approximately 36,000 to 29,000, while the number of state farms grew from about 12,000 to 18,000.

In the late 1970s the government seemed to be promoting a new version of the *agrogorods,* merging farms into gigantic agro-industrial associations. This could mean a resettlement of as much as 25 percent of the population. By bringing about an interfarm amalgamation, the government hope to provide off-season employment and some of the amenities of urban living for those living on the land.

Generally speaking, the government has in recent years increased its investment in agriculture, provided higher prices for farm produce, and demanded lower prices for consumer items that the farmer needs. While the net result has been an increase in the standard of living of farm families, many problems remain, to which reference will be made below.

Ostensibly, the members of each collective farm meet in an annual assembly and elect a management committee to run the affairs of the farm for the year. In actual practice, the Communist party by and large controls all such elections. In any case, the management committee must operate under the general laws dealing with collective farms and it must fit its operation into the overall agricultural plan.

In accordance with the general rules, applicable to all collective farms, the land, farm buildings, draft animals, and major tools are owned in common. Credit and other things furnished by the government must, of course, be paid for by the collective. Each able-bodied adult is required to put in a minimum number of days in the collective effort, which means about one half of his annual work time. But, in view of the fact that a large part of agricultural work is seasonal, this normally means much more than half time. Income to the peasant depended upon how well the collective farm did at the end of the year. Because of the understandable uncertainties in such a system of reward, the regime has in recent years sought ways to guarantee a minimum wage to the collective farmer.

Prior to 1958 the collective farms were not allowed to own the major agricultural machines. These were leased by the government through the Machine Tractor Stations (MTS), which were important instruments of political control. They also acted as effective collecting centers of agricultural produce, for each collective was obliged to sell a certain proportion of its produce at a low government-established price. In 1958, however, all of this was changed. Collective farms now own their own machinery. In place of the MTS there is now the Farm Machinery Association, whose job it is to sell and repair machines and to sell fertilizer and other farm needs. The practice of obligatory deliveries of farm produce at low prices has given way to a more realistic price system.

The day-to-day operation of a collective farm is under the direction of the manager or farm chairman. Assisting him or her is an administrative staff—bookkeepers, brigade leaders, watchmen, storekeepers, day and night guards, an agronomist, and the manager of the livestock unit. Obviously, by American standards Soviet collective farms are top-heavy with administrative personnel.

While there have been some improvements in Soviet agriculture in recent years, enormous problems remain. First of all, productivity is low, except for the private plots. The growth of agricultural production has barely kept pace with that of the population. In per capita terms, Soviet agriculture, with all its technological advancement, is scarcely more productive than the backward agriculture of pre-1914 Russia. The average Soviet farmer produces food for only 7 persons as compared to the American farmer who produces for 46 persons. The private plots, on the other hand, with less than 4 percent of all arable land, contribute about 25 percent of the Soviet Union's gross agricultural product (if we include meat and animal products from private livestock holdings). The private plots contribute 40 percent of the vegetable product in the largest republic, the RSFSR.

A second problem concerns hidden costs. At harvest time, for example, a large number of trucks, tractors, and personnel are "borrowed" or "commandeered" from industrial enterprises and/or the army. Moreover, there is inadequate machinery, and the problem of spare parts has not been resolved. For example, when milking machinery breaks down, there is an urgent need to employ milkers.

Third, there is a shortage of manpower, particularly those trained to operate agricultural machines. Only one youth in 20 wants to stay on the farm; 50 percent of farm labor consists of older women. One reason is that farm life is considered dull and boring. At certain times of the year there are no roads; mud cuts farms off from towns and even from one another. There are few diversions or entertainment, especially for the young.

Finally, the Soviet leaders seem to have realized that centrally controlled prices and procurement plans, as well as other forms of interference, have had an unfavorable impact on production. It remains to be seen, however, whether they can liberate themselves from old ways. Two recent developments would seem to be positive. The first of these is the experimentation with the so-called link system. In this system, 7 to 10 people, often members of the same family, are allocated certain lands and machinery, and they are paid according to their output. It is not uncommon for a link member to earn two or three times what a collective or state farm worker does. The other development concerns the assistance being given by the government to private plot production, but without advertising it openly. In order to increase milk and meat production, for example, the government will provide fodder for cows and pigs, and will even help the farmer in the marketing of his or her produce. It is necessary to emphasize that these are recent developments, which could be merely temporary concessions. (See also Chapter 34.)

SOME CONCLUSIONS ABOUT SOVIET ADMINISTRATION

It is difficult to evaluate the effectiveness of the Soviet administrative apparatus. First of all, the operations of the Soviet government are treated with such great secrecy that we are not sure just how much of the picture we do not see. Second, there is the matter of what yardstick should be used in passing judgment. And finally, we have no way of balancing the costs against what the Soviet citizen would be willing to pay for the services he or she receives. In spite of these difficulties, however, it is possible to make some reasonably sound observations about the administrative machine, based in large part on revelations in the Soviet press.

Contrary to Lenin's expressed hope that the organized state bureaucracy would dwindle and ultimately disappear, it has actually grown. There would seem to be several explanations for this trend. First of all, Stalin found in the bureaucracy the only firm foundation of his power. Under his rule, the Soviet regime operated on the premise that no one could be trusted including the more seasoned party members. Consequently, a system of checking and crosschecking required the services of countless people. Second, the sheer size of the country and the assumption that the party should direct or at least have its eye on all developments required a huge bureaucratic machine, often resulting in duplication and endless paper work. Finally, there has been a tendency toward overstaffing in government agencies, due in part to an inefficient distribution of manpower and in part to the growing tendency of people to prefer office employment to work on farms or in factories. Moreover, the shortage of qualified personnel in the earlier years of the regime encouraged establishments to recruit and to hang on to more people than they actually needed.

While there may be other reasons that would explain the growth of the bureaucratic apparatus, the essential fact remains that it has grown to considerable proportions. And equally important is the fact that this development is at variance with the promises of the regime when it came to power, a consideration that would seem of no small consequence to the citizen who pays the bill.

There is no clear-cut line of responsibility in the Soviet bureaucracy. Technically, responsibility is vertical to the Council of Ministers, which, in turn, is supposed to be responsible to the Supreme Soviet. In practice the picture is far from clear. The bureaucracy is, in the end, certainly responsible to the party but the party has set up various channels of control, with no clear lines of authority. The trade unions and local soviets are told, for example, not to interfere in the management of government enterprises. At the same time, they are told to assist enterprises and to oversee their work, creating a situation that often leads to a conflict in jurisdiction. Simultaneously, the *Komsomol* organizations are urged to be vigilant, and the secret police is expected to be ever watchful.

For the most part, it seems that the party wants it this way. By avoiding firm and set channels, the party leadership is able to skip intermediate control centers and to go directly to the lowest level if intervention seems necessary. Knowing this, and believing that party officials will ultimately hear about it, managers tend to take their problems to party committees rather than to the appropriate government agencies. One consequence of this is that there is an absence of a close working relationship up and down the bureaucratic ladder. Such a close relationship exists only with immediate superiors and immediate subordinates.

On the whole, however, the party is probably in a position of firmer control than it was a decade ago. This is especially true in agricultural management, where party organizations and party members have come to play a more decisive role. In industry, too, as state enterprises have expanded, so has the party.

Moreover, by institutionalizing the practice of frequent promotion, demotion, or transfer of local officials, the party seeks to minimize the opportunities for local arrangements that might be detrimental to its basic objectives.

The demands upon the administrative apparatus are such, and the bureaucratic restrictions so confining and often contradictory, that responsible administrators have found it necessary to go outside the law if they are to achieve what is expected of them. This means finding informal ways of bypassing technical bureaucratic requirements. More specifically, it involves asking for favors, which beget requests for favors in return. Sometimes it is necessary to falsify reports or to employ other means of concealing the real situation. Often the net result is a whole network of protective evasions, which the Soviet press has sometimes labeled "the building of family relationships."

Such extralegal arrangements are officially condemned, but despite its secret police and its other means of control, the regime has often seemed helpless to cope with them. Paradoxical as it may seem, the administrative apparatus, as it has grown, has to a certain extent been able to resist manipulation at the same time that it was becoming more and more indispensable to the Soviet dictatorship.

Since the people do not have any control over the administration, the absence of popular trust in it is not strange. This is particularly true when we remember that the Soviet regime has made countless promises that it has subsequently failed to fulfill. Even such solemn obligations as the repayment of loans made to the government have been broken. Soon after World War II, the government, without warning, proclaimed a currency reform, as a result of which the citizens received 1 ruble for every 10. A similar reform was promulgated in early 1961. Similarly, in 1957 it was announced that the government would postpone payment of state loans for 20 to 25 years. Moreover, no interest is to be paid on this money. This is all the more repugnant to the holders of government securities, for although their purchase was theoretically voluntary, almost no one could avoid "investing" less than one month's salary annually in these loans.

These are but some of the more obvious ways in which the Soviet administration has broken faith with its people. Reference has already been made elsewhere concerning arbitrary administrative acts, such as arrests and imprisonment. Various citizens of the U.S.S.R. could no doubt provide an endless catalog of administrative acts that have caused them to lose confidence in the regime. But the Soviet regime is not dependent upon popular support, and most of the available evidence suggests that popular support is not very high on the regime's list of desired goals or priorities.

SOME OBSERVATIONS ON THE SOVIET ECONOMIC REVOLUTION

Irrespective of what has been said in the foregoing about the Soviet system, one cannot deny that it has been able to produce some desired results. There has been an economic revolution in the Soviet Union. Through a series of successive five-year plans, the economy has in large measure been industrialized. The regime was ruthless in its takeover of the economy and in its direction. It appropriated the means of production and distribution. Nothing was permitted to stand in the way of the government's aims. As a result of the regime's determined and impatient approach, there has been considerable progress, particularly in those areas where the best talent and the best materials were allocated. Generally speaking, however, the trial-and-error method resulted in huge costs, both material and human. But the country was moved ahead, and this is what the leaders wanted.

The motivation behind the industrialization drive was largely political. There was a firm conviction that the economy should be exploited for political purposes, for example, to build a strong industrial and military state. The prolonged emphasis on the development of heavy industry and a large military establishment, together with the extremely low priority accorded to consumers' goods, was ample proof. Consequently, the building of socialism became a distinctly secondary consideration.

At the same time, the Soviet leaders had to provide incentives to those who were made responsible for the achievement of the regime's goals. To some extent, these persons, as loyal party functionaries, could be relied upon to carry out the party policies in any case. But social and economic inducements were seemingly more important. The managerial class was provided with better wages, better living quarters, bonuses, and increased opportunities for promotion and recognition. The method of positive and negative incentives was applied with considerable success.

Nevertheless, the economy is plagued with all sorts of difficulties. Resource allocation is a perennial problem; the Soviet press continues to report extensive supply failures. The rising costs of raw materials and the heavy military outlays are a strain. There is waste and inefficiency. Soviet managers have little propensity for risk-taking, and opt for prolonged maintenance over replacement and innovation. In an effort to improve productivity, the Soviets have engaged in the merging of enterprises into large associations, but this has not gone smoothly. Moreover, Moscow has been importing Western technology, but this is really a short-term solution.

In the consumer area inefficiency and inflexibility have been institutionalized, as evidenced by the long shopping lines. Unquestionably, the Soviet Union has one of the world's worst distribution and retail systems. Although there has been no publication of data on inventories in the retail trade since 1975, there are many indications that retail stores have suffered considerable losses through rejection of various products, especially clothing garments and shoes.

To a degree, failures in the consumer sector have been ameliorated by the "second economy," which is illegal or semilegal. It produces goods and services, various forms of repair, and secondhand items such as automobiles. The leaders accept this economy grudgingly because it eases some of the shortages that the official economy does not meet. It is interesting that failures in the consumer sector are accompanied by discussions and disagreements, which involve a fair amount of mutual recrimination—by customers, product designers, producers, suppliers, and administrators.

BIBLIOGRAPHICAL NOTE

Among the more useful of the numerous studies of Soviet economic policy are: Abram Bergson, ed., *Economic Trends in the Soviet Union* (Cambridge, Mass.: Harvard University Press, 1963); Philippe J. Bernard, *Planning in the Soviet Union* (New York: Pergamon Press, 1966); Marshall I. Goldman, *USSR in Crisis: The Failure of an Economic System* (New York: W. W. Norton, 1983); Alex Nove, *Political Economy and Soviet Socialism* (London: Allen & Unwin, 1979); Constantin A. Krylov, *The Soviet Economy: How It Really Works* (Lexington, Mass.: Lexington Books, 1979); Karl W. Ryavec, *Implementation of Soviet Economic Reforms: Political, Organizational, and Social Processes* (New York: Praeger Publishers, 1975).

Specialized studies of agricultural administration include: D. Gale Johnson and Karen McConnell, *Prospects for Soviet Agriculture in the 1980s* (Bloomington: Indiana University Press, 1983); Karl Eugen Wädekin, *The Private Sector in Soviet Agriculture* (Berkeley: University of California Press, 1973); Harry G. Shaffer, ed., *Soviet Agriculture: An Assessment of Its Contribution to Economic Development* (New York and London: Praeger Publishers, 1977).

Useful discussions of Soviet labor, trade unions, and industrial management are: Jeremy Azrael, *Managerial Power and Soviet Politics* (Cambridge, Mass.: Harvard University Press, 1966); Emily Clark Brown, *Soviet Trade Unions and Labor Relations* (Cambridge, Mass.: Harvard University Press, 1966); Arcadins Kahan and Blair A. Ruble, eds., *Industrial Labor in the U.S.S.R.* (New York: Pergamon Press, 1979); James R. Millar, *The ABCs of Soviet Socialism* (Urbana: University of Illinois Press, 1981).

Information on local administration is included in Jan S. Adams, *Citizen Inspectors in the Soviet Union: The People's Control Committee* (New York and London: Praeger Publishers, 1977); John A. Armstrong, *The Soviet Bureaucratic Elite: A Case Study of the Ukrainian Apparatus* (New York: Praeger Publishers, 1959); William Taubman, *Governing Soviet Cities: Bureaucratic Politics and Urban Development in the U.S.S.R.* (New York: Praeger Publishers, 1973).

An extensive treatment of the Soviet economy is to be found in the two-volume report of the Joint Committee of the U.S. Congress, *Soviet Economy in a Time of Change* (Washington, D.C.: U.S. Government Printing Office, 1979).

33

Policy-Implementing Structures: Instruments of Control

One of the most perplexing and, at the same time, one of the least adequately answered questions encountered by persons seeking to understand the workings of a communist regime concerns the methods and techniques by which the masses are mobilized to do the regime's bidding. Since the number of persons belonging to the Soviet Communist party does not exceed 9 percent of the adult population, how do they manipulate the other 90-odd percent? Part of the answer is to be found in the fact that Soviet leaders have never operated on the assumption that it is sufficient not to have people against you. They must be for you. It is not enough to prevent undesirable acts. It is essential that people act positively. It is imperative that the people do the things that the party wants done, even if these are deeply repugnant to the people who are forced to do them. Explaining how the party gets the masses to do its bidding is the task of this chapter.

FORCE AND FEAR

From the outset, the new Soviet regime employed the instruments of force and fear to compel obedience, a practice that has been copied by every other communist regime. Over the years these instruments were developed and applied with increasing refinement. And, although they were supplemented by various efforts at persuasion, behind each such effort there always lurked the possibility of a serious if not a frightful sanction.

Following Lenin's dictum that the communists should not be squeamish about spilling blood, the wielders of the new authority lost no time in imprisoning and executing their opponents, real or imagined, even though they had violated no law. Those considered most dangerous to the new regime were put out of the way, often without benefit of any type of trial. In the initial years, it was the "class enemy" (former owners of productive property and persons who had been associated with the tsarist regime) that felt the brunt of the terror. In subsequent years, however, the terror was to seep into all segments of society—workers, peasants, and even the Communist party.

Those who were not considered dangerous enough to warrant physical liquidation were imprisoned for varying terms. People were banished to concentration camps for years on a no more serious charge than that they were found to be "socially dangerous," although there was no definition of social danger. Proceedings against a person did not have to be public, nor was it necessary for him or her to be present or to be represented by counsel. In some cases, sentences of people sent to camps contained the proviso, "without privilege of correspondence." The authority to pass such judgments was vested in special boards of the secret police, and they were in no way bound by provisions of the criminal code, nor were they responsible to the courts. A 1983 law permits the authorities to lengthen prison sentences for malicious disobedience in prisons.

To take care of a vastly larger number of individuals whose loyalties were suspect, but who were not considered dangerous enough to liquidate or to imprison, the new Soviet regime created a secret police.[1] Initially it was known as the Cheka, extraordinary commission for combating espionage, counterrevolution, sabotage, and speculation, but subsequently it was known under a variety of initials (OGPU, NKVD, MVD), reflecting changes in name and, to some extent, changes in function. In August 1954, its powers allegedly curbed, the secret police became the Committee for State Security (KGB), and was made responsible to the Council of Ministers. Khrushchev's successors, however, seem to have enhanced the role of the KGB.

Agents of the secret police are to be found in all segments of Soviet society, in the offices, in the army, in schools, in recreational clubs, and in collective farms, but most people can only surmise as to the identity of the agents. They move about freely and are not subject to local control of any type.

People who are something less than enthusiastic about the regime are made aware of the existence of the secret police in a variety of ways. Some are asked

---

[1]See Simon Wolin and Robert M. Slusser, *The Soviet Secret Police* (New York: Praeger Publishers, 1957), Jonathan R. Adelman, *Terror and Communist Politics: The Role of the Secret Police in Communist States* (Boulder, Colo.: Westview Press, 1984); and Ronald Hingley, *The Russian Secret Police: Muscovite, Imperial Russian, and Soviet Political Security Operations* (New York: Simon & Schuster, 1971).

to report to the local office, where they may be questioned about remarks they or their associates have allegedly made. Or they may be asked to explain their absence from parades or other manifestations sponsored by the authorities. Or they may be held for a few hours or a day, with no hint as to the reason. Subsequent invitations to appear may follow, and one never knows when a more permanent stay may result.

When the authorities wish to be beyond intimidation, a person may be held for days or months, or even years, and without knowing the charge. Such imprisonment is usually accompanied by endless interrogation, particularly if a confession is desired. The methods used to extract confessions have been so adequately described in recent years that further comment would seem superfluous here. Suffice it to say that the methods of torture, mental as well as physical, have been systematically refined and developed. Once caught in the web, even high party dignitaries become helpless.[2]

In recent years there has been a notable increase in the regime's use of psychiatric hospitals to isolate and punish citizens who express unorthodox religious or political views. It is estimated that the number of persons declared insane without medical justification and confined in psychiatric wards without having been formally arrested or charged with any crime runs into the hundreds.

The tactics of secret police agents are many and varied. Often the agents are provocateurs, posing as enemies of the regime and urging the creation of antiregime organizations. When the desired persons have been implicated, the net closes and the agents become star witnesses in court, admitting all. At other times, they are placed in prison to talk about their "crimes," and in the process they learn as much as possible about the past activities of their cell mates, only to become more convincing witnesses at the trial.

Secret police agents cannot be everywhere at all times. Hence, there is need for a sizable net of informers if surveillance is to be reasonably complete. Wherever a few people come together, for work or pleasure, there is certain to be one or more secret police informers. Everyone knows they exist, although they are not known even to one another. Since people do not know who the informers are, they are led to suspect everyone, including close friends. The result is a general feeling of isolation and distrust.

Most informers are recruited, but there are those who volunteer, hoping thereby to build some good will with the authorities against the exigencies of more difficult times. Often enough the informers find that they are pitted against each other to ensure a thorough reporting job. Failure of one informer to report even a minor matter results in his or her integrity's being questioned. Once having begun to inform, the informer is at the mercy of the secret police. Even more onerous tasks are demanded, and should he or she hesitate, the ques-

---

[2] See Khrushchev's speech to the 20th Party Congress (February 24–25, 1956) for some notable examples (*New York Times,* June 5, 1956).

tion of changed loyalties immediately arises. Even past performances are examined for hidden and disloyal motives.

The end result of the techniques of force and fear is to eliminate or to cow and terrify all those who would be capable of offering an alternative to the Communists. The effect of the terror apparatus is made more frightful by virtue of the feeling that anyone could be next. It matters not whether the threat is real or not; it is sufficient that the people think so.

MOBILIZING PUBLIC OPINION

Supplementing force and fear in harnessing the masses to do the bidding of the dictatorship are a host of elaborately developed techniques for mobilizing and monopolizing public opinion. Unlike democratic governments, the Soviet regime is not interested in satisfying popular demands. But it knows that people will continue to do some thinking even if they cannot make their views known publicly. It is imperative, therefore, that the Soviet leaders learn something of the people's frame of mind so as to be able to channel their thinking more effectively along desired lines. In order to do this, the regime exercises complete and active control over the public opinion media and, in addition, seeks to exclude all competing influences.

The extent of the government's monopoly in the public opinion field cannot be appreciated unless one bears in mind that there are no privately owned newspapers or press agencies in the Soviet Union. There are no privately owned stocks of newsprint or printing presses. There are no privately owned movie theaters, film producing, or film importing enterprises. There are no privately owned or operated television or radio stations, or privately produced programs. There are no privately published or privately imported books. It is illegal to publish anything privately, even with a mimeograph machine. In short, Soviet citizens are not to attempt to spread their ideas except through channels the government provided. And the official censor guards the access to these channels.

Nevertheless, in the last few years there has been a great deal of underground private dissemination of typewritten or duplicated materials (*samizdat*, which means "self-published"). Perhaps the most notable of these has been the *Chronicle of Current Events*, a publication that has reported on the regime's restrictions on civil liberties and its persecution of dissidents.

In general, however, the government's control over the instrumentalities of public opinion enables the leaders to control what the public is to know. Visitors to the Soviet Union never fail to be astounded at the extent of popular ignorance about world events that are well known to people in the democratic world. Even Lenin's testament was not published in the Soviet Union until some time after Stalin's death, 30 years after its publication in the outside world. Moreover, ignorance is compounded by a great deal of misinformation that the regime regularly purveys.

From time to time, the party leaders' ideas as to what the public should know change, and history needs to be rewritten. For example, one-time Politburo member Lavrenti P. Beria was, like Orwell's Winston, "lifted clean out from the stream of history." After his execution in 1953, the official state publishing house supplied subscribers of the Soviet Encyclopedia with four pages on Friedrich Bergholtz and pictures of the Bering Sea, recommending that the four-page article on Beria and his picture in Volume 5 be cut out and replaced with this new material. Beria will never have existed! Stalin is barely mentioned in the new Soviet Encyclopedia. To the surprise of many, Nikita Khrushchev received the same treatment, and before his death in 1971 had become an "unperson."

Control over what the public can read or hear extends also to the outside world. The number of publications from noncommunist countries is pitifully small, and these are permitted to come in only after the most careful screening by the censorship. Foreign radio broadcasts, especially those from the United States, were jammed prior to 1963 by an array of Soviet transmitters. However, after a pause, jamming was reintroduced. In addition, Soviet citizens have not been free to travel outside their country except on official missions, a practice that was seemingly modified in a limited manner after 1956. Likewise, foreign visitors to the U.S.S.R. were pretty well excluded during the heyday of the Stalin era, and their contact with Soviet citizens was extremely dangerous to the latter. Since 1956 it has been much easier for foreigners to visit the Soviet Union and to talk with Soviet citizens, although the length of their stay and the areas they can visit have been rigidly limited.

The protective curtain against outside ideas has also been used to keep undesirable information about Soviet society from reaching the outside world. The few foreign news correspondents who have been permitted in the Soviet Union have not been permitted to gather news freely.[3] They have had to rely, for the most part, on official handouts. Moreover, until 1961 their dispatches had to be submitted to the censor, with no knowledge at the time of what was passed and what was deleted. More recently, the Soviets have permitted correspondents of foreign radio and television networks to broadcast from Moscow. In all cases, however, the government has felt free to expel correspondents if what they reported met with official displeasure. The representatives of one American network were even expelled because that network produced, in the United States, a television show that was regarded in Moscow as being "anti-Soviet propaganda." Although newsgathering in the Soviet Union is still not free, the outside world gets considerably more news from there than it did some years ago.

Owning and controlling the existing instrumentalities of public opinion, however, does not satisfy the Soviet authorities. They are determined that all segments of society should be involved in the regime's propaganda effort to create an atmosphere of assent for the party's aims and policies, and especially for

---

[3]See the books by Hedrick Smith, Kevin Klose, David K. Shipler, and Robert G. Kaiser, referred to in the Bibliographical Note to Chapter 27 for firsthand accounts of newsgathering in the Soviet Union.

its current programs. To this end the Soviet leaders have created a welter of new and different propaganda instruments.

These propaganda instruments are designed to reach groups and individuals who could normally avoid political polemics. Scientists, teachers, musicians, writers—all are given a propaganda outlet, which they are expected to utilize by way of praising the communist way of life and the opportunities it affords them. Writers who might have pleaded that it was inappropriate for them to contribute to clearly political papers, such as *Pravda,* the official organ of the Communist party, discovered that the regime had created a newspaper for writers alone, *The Literary Gazette.* Writers could be reminded that in tsarist days they were unable to find an outlet for their views. Now, the government has set up a special newspaper for them wherein they can write about the great opportunities for writers and artists in a communist society. Here was a means of expressing their gratitude. Here was an outlet for their views. Here were printing presses and stocks of newsprint—and here were party-furnished texts of what they should like to say. How much easier could it be!

Similarly, other groups in Soviet society are provided an outlet of their own. A biology professor, for example, cannot claim that it would be inappropriate for him or her to write in political journals. There is no need to. The government provides a special and dignified platform, a specially created newspaper for professors. And the party is generous in providing themes to write about. If the professor can demonstrate that official duties do not leave enough time, someone will be found to write a piece for him or her. The greater the professor's reputation the more important it is, from the regime's point of view, to have his or her name associated with the party's goals and programs. The same can be said of the scientists, musicians, actors, engineers, and others.

Members of some groups are more effectively involved by various public meetings. Engineers and other respected personnel in a plant or other economic enterprise are asked to take part in party-sponsored political meetings or other propaganda manifestations. If they cannot always be prevailed upon to give a speech or to take some other leading role, they are asked "just to sit on the platform." In this way the rank and file can observe a visual connection between party leaders and the respected persons in their enterprise. In other words, the regime does not want to leave uncommitted anyone in whom the rank and file could see a leadership alternative to the Communists.

Since everyone cannot be counted upon to read the party's program or even to listen to it over the radio and television, the Soviet leaders have developed face-to-face agitation to a fine art, a technique always regarded as paramount. It has been estimated that the Communist party enlists the part-time services of some 2 million persons in face-to-face agitation.[4] Formerly known as "Agita-

---

[4] See Alex Inkeles. *Public Opinion in Soviet Russia: A Study in Mass Persuasion* (Cambridge, Mass.: Harvard University Press 1950) and Paul Lendvai, *The Bureaucracy of Truth: How Communist Governments Manage the News* (Boulder, Colo.: Westview Press, 1981).

tors," they are now called "Politinformers." They speak to groups in factories or on collective farms. They visit homes and small gatherings of apartment dwellers. In this way no one can escape getting the party's propaganda message, perhaps in several different forms.

The primary responsibility for directing the Communist party's propaganda is vested in the Central Committee's agitation and propaganda section, commonly referred to as Agitprop. It must see to it that all propaganda outlets do their job. It issues directives and suggestions. And it furnishes various materials. Moreover, it sees to it that those who fail or falter are criticized for their shortcomings.

Twice a year (on the anniversary of the Bolshevik revolution and on May Day) Agitprop develops and the party issues officially a large number of slogans, which constitute the keynote of the party's policies for the coming months. They are the principal guideposts for the various propaganda outlets. These are modified by subsequent party declarations on various subjects. In the absence of official party declarations, the party's different official organs offer ample clues as to the current party line on any subject. And, of course, there are the confidential instructions from Agitprop.

One or two examples of the more detailed work of Agitprop may be instructive. The face-to-face agitation, for example, is systematically organized. At regular intervals, Agitprop publishes the *Agitator's Notebook,* which contains materials for speeches and themes to be stressed. Generally speaking, there are several brief articles, some dealing with domestic problems and some with foreign affairs. Thus the agitator is furnished a steady and current stream of propaganda materials. Moreover, the so-called letters to the editor, which are often depicted by Soviet leaders or their sympathizers as examples of freedom of expression in the Soviet Union, are for the most part organized and controlled by Agitprop or its agents. Closely related to the letter writers are the so-called worker, peasant, youth, and soldier correspondents, who are trained and paid for their contributions. The various newspaper staffs are instructed in how these correspondents are to be trained and how they are to go about their work. In editorial conferences with these correspondents, there is often a party representative to give advice and guidance. Sometimes the party calls conferences of correspondents to discuss the important themes to be dwelt upon. Hence, it is obvious that these correspondents and letter writers deal only with those topics deemed appropriate by the party. Their function is to help the regime mold public opinion, and not to express it as it actually exists.

This does not mean that ordinary persons do not write letters, because indeed they do. Most of the ones published, however, are fairly harmless from the regime's point of view. They deal with alcoholism, with the husbands' responsibility in helping working wives, whether more failing grades should be given in Soviet schools, and similar topics. There are letters that are critical, but these are more often than not anonymous, and they are usually not published. Periodically, secret police officials go through letters received by a newspaper, and some are taken away, usually the anonymous ones.

THE MASS ORGANIZATIONS

In addition to the instruments of force and fear and the techniques of persuasion, the Soviet leaders have developed numerous organizations through which everyone is involved, in one way or another, in helping to carry out the party's program. Whereas the instruments of force and fear are employed to destroy opposition and to instill fear, and whereas the public opinion media have been developed and organized to make sure the party's propaganda message gets to everyone in a variety of contexts, the numerous party-sponsored organizations are designed to harness the masses to the dictatorship by having them help the party to realize specific and concrete aims. All mass organizations have been referred to by Soviet leaders as "transmission belts," linking the party with the masses. Not only are people not allowed to oppose or to stand aside; they must actively assist in carrying out Communist party programs.

The most far-flung of the mass organizations are the soviets. Although they constitute the administrative apparatus for carrying out governmental policies, they are also the principal means by which mass participation in community activities is secured. The majority of the members of local soviets, unlike those at the top, are not members of the Communist party; hence, the idea of popular control in administration is conveyed. But, as noted in an earlier chapter, the soviets are organized on a pyramidal basis, with effective party control at all levels. Moreover, even the selection of nonparty members for local soviets is decided upon by the party.

Because they are a part of the governmental structures and therefore have the authority of the state behind them, the soviets reach out to include a large number of people. They have officially been depicted as "the mass organization of all toilers." Because they are so described, no citizen can refuse to help the soviets in carrying out their tasks.

Supplementing the soviets are the trade unions. Unlike those in democratic countries, Soviet trade unions are not expected to hold views that are essentially different from those of the employer. They were described by Stalin as "the mass organization of the proletariat, linking the party with the class primarily in the sphere of production." But in the Soviet Union the interests of the proletariat are not judged to be in conflict with the interests of any other group. Initially, the trade unions did conceive workers' interests more narrowly and sought to represent them as against the narrower interests of management. But within a brief period of time they were brought into line. The workers were depicted as being also the owners. If they should strike, therefore, they would be striking against themselves.

As are other organizations in a communist state, trade unions are organized in a pyramidal fashion, with authority being wielded by the All-Union Central Council of Trade Unions, which is at the apex of the pyramid. At the base of the pyramid is the factory committee, elected by the union in each factory. Between the base and the top are a number of intermediary committees at the district and republic level. Throughout the trade union organization, however, the real wielder of authority is the Communist party. In various enterprises, party control is achieved through the appointed director, the primary unit of the party, and the shop committee. The shop committee is nominally an agency of the trade union but, in the past at least, it has been more of an adjunct of management than a representative of the workers.

Therefore, the trade unions have in the main functioned as instruments of the party in seeking to attain higher production quotas, labor discipline, efficiency, and other regime goals. Beyond this, in actual practice their principal area of action has been in the social welfare field. They have been charged with the administration of social insurance and labor benefits. Interviews with Soviet workers who have left the U.S.S.R. show that they regard Soviet trade unions solely as instruments of the party and of factory management.

In 1957 the Soviet leaders took steps that indicated they wanted the trade union representation on the disputes commissions at least to uphold the legal rights of the workers. At the same time, they revealed that in the past a worker's complaint did not get much of a hearing, often none at all. Rights of appeal were narrowly limited. Often the union members of the disputes commissions had sided with the actions of management, even when they ran contrary to the law. While not suggesting that the trade unions defend traditional workers' rights, they were told that they should at least defend those legal rights which the workers in the Soviet Union do possess.

Mass organizations also embrace the youth. It has been evident for a long time that the Soviet leaders, although jealously guarding top leadership positions, have staked everything on youth. The future of communism is in their hands. Not only must the new leaders come from the youth but, in addition, new generations of supporters for the regime must be won there. The communist way of life cannot be perpetuated unless a steady stream of new adherents can be recruited who are enthusiastic enough to want to perpetuate it.

Consequently, the Soviet leaders have left no stone unturned to develop the most elaborate network of youth organizations.[5] These include the *Octobrists* for small children, the *Pioneers* for adolescents, and the *Komsomol* (union of Communist youth) for the young adults. All children are *Octobrists,* but there is progressive elimination as one goes up the ladder. The cream of the youth, from the party's point of view, is to be found in the *Komsomol,* which in turn is the principal recruiting ground for new party members. Similarly, leadership is from the top down. Party members lead the *Komsomols,* which in turn are responsible for work among *Pioneers,* while *Pioneers* are supposed to help the *Octobrists.* The party, of course, is the final judge in all matters of youth organization and action. The activities of these youth organizations are carefully planned and supervised. In the case of the *Octobrists* and *Pioneers,* it is mostly a matter of implanting attitudes, but in the case of the *Komsomols* there is more serious work to be done. Broadly speaking, the work of the *Komsomols* can be

---

[5]The Soviet schools, as devices for harnessing the masses to the dictatorship, are treated separately in a subsequent section of this chapter.

said to comprise four basic functions: (1) assisting in the ideological training of youth, (2) setting an example, by hard work, which will help the regime realize its economic aims, (3) helping the regime to spot trouble or disloyalty by maintaining a sharp lookout at all times, (4) assisting the regime in realizing its objectives in the armed forces. Moreover, *Komsomol* members are required to play an active role in the quasi-military civil defense agency (DOSAAF), which is directed by top-flight reserve officers of the Soviet armed forces. Here they are taught first aid, given shooting practice, trained to operate and manipulate parachutes, taught about guided missiles, and subjected to further political indoctrination. To achieve their varied goals, the *Komsomols,* some 42 million strong, have the unstinging support of the party, which spares no effort in their behalf. In order to realize the ideological tasks of the *Komsomols,* for example, special courses, schools, and study groups are organized. Here the youth study the history of the party, the biographies of Soviet leaders, and the works of Marx, Lenin, and others. In addition, over 200 youth newspapers and magazines are published with a total circulation of over 20 million copies.

Moreover, there are a number of other techniques designed to capture the youth for the regime. Among these are youth theaters, youth physical-culture centers, and youth homes and recreation centers. To the end that new generations must be won for communism, leisure as well as work time of young people is carefully planned, supervised, and directed by the Communist party.

But there are indications that all is not well in the *Komsomols.* Soviet newspapers continue to carry accounts of poor and unsatisfactory work in the youth organizations. The *Komsomolists* are negligent of their leadership duties among the *Pioneers.* Many of them are calculating careerists, using the *Komsomol* organization to advance personal ambitions and goals, being indifferent to everything that does not affect their careers. Many have fallen for bourgeois tastes in music, literature, art, dress, and manners. Many have not responded to special appeals to engage in various volunteer projects. Many who have completed their university or technical studies find ways of remaining in the larger urban centers and thus avoiding service in the more remote provinces. Many have raised embarrassing questions about the regime's promises and declared goals. Soviet leaders have spoken of "unhealthy moods among the youth," and official *Komsomol* newspapers have written of "ultrarevolutionary demagogues," "apolitical persons devoid of ideals," and "nihilists, carrying out a reappraisal of values."

While it would be difficult to speak of opposition to the regime among youth because it is impossible for opposition to organize or be manifested openly, it is possible, at least, to speak of a passive dislike for the regime.[6] There is a revulsion against the constant interference in the personal lives of young people.

---

[6]See Georgie Anne Geyer. *The Young Russians* (Homewood, Ill.: ETC Publications, 1975). For an earlier view of a former Soviet student, see David Burg, "Soviet Youth's Opposition to the Communist Regime," *Bulletin: Institute for the Study of the U.S.S.R. 4* (April and May 1957), pp. 41–47, 44–50. An excellent collection is Stephen F. Cohen, ed., *An End to Silence: Uncensored Opinion in the Soviet Union: from Roy Medvedev's Underground Magazine Political Diary* (New York and London: W. W. Norton, 1982).

There is dissatisfaction with the material state of things. There is a feeling of isolation and a yearning for contact with the outside world. Even among the privileged youth, the system of completely limiting the individual tends to produce moods of depression.

Bits of evidence stemming from informal gatherings in private homes, apparently not so hazardous as in Stalin times, reveal a general desire for political and spiritual freedom. Although political topics are for the most part studiously avoided, unorthodox views on other matters are frequently expressed. Further testimony of the yearning for freedom is provided by the fact that the names of several underground student magazines have found their way into the Soviet press. Far from creating new generations of unconditionally obedient robots, devoid of feelings and ideas, the Communist party may, in the long run, produce the exact opposite.

In the Khruschev years young *Komsomol* members were openly asking some difficult questions. They were asking what the society they were supposedly building will look like in the future. Having come face to face with the contradictions and injustices in the Soviet system, they were seeking an answer from their leaders as to the nature of the future society. Aware of the inequalities of the Soviet class structure, they wanted to know if communism would mean the end of these inequalities. The regime's answer was the new party program (1961), which reiterated many old promises and had the avowed goal of catching up with the United States in 10 years. By 1980, according to the program, Soviet citizens could look forward to certain free services, including most utilities, municipal transport, midday meals, education,[7] medicine, and rent-free housing. Within a decade of its inception, however, this program was conveniently "forgotten" and went unmentioned.

There are other bits of evidence of generation gap difficulties between the party leadership and the *Komsomol* membership. In 1968 a considerable shakeup of the *Komsomol* leadership took place. The extent to which changes were made is illustrated by the case of a man who had not been involved in *Komsomol* work for 10 years, and yet was elected secretary of a provincial *Komsomol* organization, directly in violation of *Komsomol* statutes. Moreover, the party leadership has stepped up its campaign against proponents of "bourgeois ideology," who are allegedly attempting to subvert the soviet intellectual community.

Writers and artists in the Soviet Union, too, cannot escape being mobilized. They are expected to develop and to utilize their talents in order that they may more effectively support the communist political system. There is no freedom to create except as the creation assists the party in mobilizing support for the regime. The Soviet bill of rights gives writers and artists the "right" to create, but only for the purpose of defending and strengthening the socialist system. And

---

[7]The 1936 constitution proclaimed education to be free, but shortly before World War II tuition charges were introduced for secondary and higher education. The 1977 constitution merely refers to the right of education.

the party leaders are the sole judges of what that system is and what strengthens it and what does not.

From time to time the party conducts a literary purge, during which certain works and their authors are severely criticized and the magazines that published their pieces are censured. Sometimes the authors are expelled from the Union of Soviet Writers, an organization that serves to keep would-be mavericks in line. During Stalin's reign, many writers also went to prison camps. The usual criticism is that literary and artistic works are ideologically harmful, apolitical, imitative of bourgeois Western concepts, or based on the notion of art for art's sake. In the Communist party's view, Soviet art, literature, music—in short, all forms of artistic expression—must serve to glorify the Soviet system, the Soviet leaders, and the domestic and foreign policies of the Soviet Union.

But the party does not simply wait to judge artistic and literary works in a sort of postaudit. Through its official organ *Pravda,* the *Literary Gazette,* and other media, the party frequently sets forth tasks for writers and artists. They are told to stress the efforts of workers and peasants in the realization of the current economic plan, or some other objective with which the party is currently concerned. Occasionally, the party bemoans the absence of a great poem, novel, opera, or other work depicting some Soviet scene, and calls for the production of such a work. In other words, great art or great literature is what contributes to the realization of whatever goals the Communist party is pursuing at any one time.

For those who live up to the party's expectations there are generous rewards. Artists of all types, but especially writers, actors, and singers, are held in high esteem by the regime and consequently receive considerable note in the press and other publicity media. Moreover, they are the highest paid people in Soviet society, which makes the material rewards perhaps more important than the recognition. Soviet writers and composers receive royalties, which means that some of them are millionaires. Actors and singers, if considered good, are given special engagements for extra pay, even though their regular salaries are high. Finally, the better artists have an opportunity to travel abroad, they have better clothes, and they have good housing, which is scarce everywhere. If an artist is willing to have his talents exploited for political purposes, therefore, he gets recognition from the regime and usually can be assured of excellent material rewards.

After Khrushchev's 1956 revelations of the crimes and abuses of the Stalin era, party publications called for an end to the narrow political approach to art. The Stalinist cult was held responsible for a debased cultural life. Certain writers who were sent to prison during the Stalin period were released, and some who had met a worse fate were posthumously "rehabilitated." Within a year a tremendous change had occurred in the Soviet literary and artistic output. No longer was there an effort to hide or to avoid the facts of Soviet life, including illegal arrests, the prison system, and the fate of former colleagues. In print, on canvas, and on the stage, Soviet artists and writers were presenting ambitious and greedy party officials and government bureaucrats as the villains of their pieces. Their heroes were simple people, often not even party members. Some writers, cautiously hopeful, were stressing the need for freedom of creative endeavor.

The victory in late 1956 of the anti-Stalinists in Poland, and more particularly the Hungarian Revolution, forced the Soviet leaders into a reappraisal of their new attitude toward art. Reportedly, there followed stormy sessions of writers' and artists' associations, where the political leaders sought to reassert the party line in the artistic and literary fields. The meeting of artists fell in line, adopting a resolution in which they promised to reflect in their works "the beauty and grandeur of Communist ideals," and pledged to combat the infiltration of alien influences. Reports of the meeting of writers, however, indicated that the party leadership was not too pleased with the results. the author of the most controversial work of fiction at that time (Vladimir Dudintsev, author of *Not by Bread Alone*), far from confessing his errors, defended his work, despite the fact that the party leadership was displeased with it.

In 1957, before he knew that his novel, *Doctor Zhivago*, could not be published in the Soviet Union, Boris Pasternak arranged for its publication outside Russia by an Italian publisher. The publisher, an alleged communist, refused to suspend publication when, as a consequence of the decision that it would not be published in the Soviet Union, he was asked to do so. The book was translated into several languages, and in 1958 Pasternak was awarded the Nobel prize in literature. Before Soviet authorities could act, Pasternak signified acceptance of the award, but subsequently declined when he was bitterly attacked in the Soviet press, expelled from the Union of Soviet Writers, and threatened with exile.

In the early 1960s there seemed to be room for optimism. The refreshing nature of Yevtushenko's and Voznesensky's poems, as well as those of other poets, and the forthright prose of Nekrasov and some of his colleagues gave rise to hopes of increasing relaxation. The publication of Alexander Solzhenitsyn's *One Day in the Life of Ivan Denisovich,* depicting life in one of Stalin's concentration camps, seemed to improve opportunities for critical realism. In 1963, however, Khrushchev made it clear that the party was on the side of those who insisted on maintaining ideological purity in the arts.

In the last years of the 1960s, the Soviet leaders appeared to be turning back the clock. First came the trial and imprisonment in 1966 of Andrei Sinyavsky and Yuli Daniel for having published works abroad under pseudonyms—works allegedly harmful to the Soviet regime. Then came the arrest and imprisonment of several other writers, seemingly for having protested the actions against Sinyavsky and Daniel, and in turn new protests generated new trials. And in 1966 an article was added to the Russian Republic Criminal Code making it a crime to spread "deliberate fabrications defaming to the Soviet state and Public order." This was ready-made to use against the dissidents.

The Soviet military invasion of Czechoslovakia in August 1968 brought further difficulties. Many important Soviet writers refused to fall in with the official party line. Scientists, educators, and other intellectuals also refused to lend support for the Soviet intervention. A few of the most outspoken protestors were brought to trial, again generating new protests.

There followed an increasing number of trials similar to those in the Stalin era (that is, no evidence for the defense permitted and no cross-examination of prosecution witnesses). Those who protested these proceedings were often arrested and tried themselves. The transcripts from some of these trials, circulated by *Samizdat*, reveal that many of the defendants spoke out even in court. For example, the writer Andrei Amalrik, tried and convicted in 1970, charged that his trial reflected "the cowardice of a regime that regards as a danger the spreading of any thought, any idea alien to its top bureaucrats." Before he served out his term he was sentenced to another three years by a labor-camp court. In 1976 he was given permission to leave (he died in an auto accident in Spain in 1980).

One of the most notable writers to protest against censorship and the restrictions on individual freedom is the 1970 Nobel Prize winner, Alexander Solzhenitsyn, who could no longer get his works published in the Soviet Union. His *The First Circle, Cancer Ward,* and *August 1914* were published in the West. In 1969 he was expelled from the Writers' Union, but answered back with a devastating criticism. Thereupon the regime intensified its public attacks on Solzhenitsyn, branding him a traitor and defaming his character and the conduct of his personal life, but the writer continued openly to condemn the government for its harassment and persecution of dissident intellectuals. Following the publication abroad in December 1973 of his accounts of Soviet concentration camps *(The Gulag Archipelago, 1918–1956),* he came under severe attack in the Soviet press, and in 1974 was expelled from his homeland.

Other writers who have voiced protests against or violated the government's censorship policies have found themselves expelled from the Writers' Union or removed from their positions with literary journals. And persons who defended the writer or editor under attack were often punished as well.

Clearly, censorship of creative literature has been more rigorous and more consistent under Brezhnev than under Khrushchev. In brief, there has been less cultural freedom, although there has been more freedom of discussion in the scientific-technological sphere, especially where the aim has been to improve the economic performance of the system. But economic reform can be closely linked to political reform, so that those who propose economic change need to be cautious.

In the light of these developments, the future of literary and artistic expression in the Soviet Union seems unclear. For a brief moment, at least, Soviet writers felt a release from the deadening conformity into which they had for years been forced by the Stalinist dictatorship. They were able to experience a modicum of creativity, which they had not known in the years before. Perhaps the tide cannot be completely reversed. Yet in May 1984, a joint resolution of the Council of Ministers and the Central Committee of the party asserted that leaders in the film industry were responsible for carrying out party decisions and called on them to produce films that "meet the demands of the contemporary stage in building Communism and to propagandize the Leninist foreign policy of the Soviet Union, actively exposing the aggressive course of imperialism, heightening the vigilance of the armed forces, and assisting military-patriotic education."

The mass organizations discussed in the preceding pages are the ones that seem to get the greatest attention from the Communist party, and are, therefore, perhaps the most important in helping realize specific and concrete tasks. But other organizations also have important roles to play. There are sports groups, an association of railway workers, an organization for war veterans, an association of collective farmers, reserve military organizations, and so on. All of these have their periodic meetings, at which they examine their problems, their past work, and in the end, inevitably pledge to do their utmost to come up to the expectations the party holds out for them.

The net result of the whole scheme of mass organizations is that nearly every person, at least in the cities, is caught up in the vortex of communist organizational life, often belonging to several organizations, each of which strives to bend him or her to fit the communist mold. The composition of each group may vary with changing occupational or avocational groupings, and the techniques may be altered by party edict, but the end is always and forever the same. The Soviet citizens, despite everything they can do, become entangled in the communist web. In addition to their regular jobs they find themselves going to meetings and conferences, taking part in parades or other manifestations, and being involved in one or more so-called voluntary projects. Physically, they find themselves exhausted and resenting the time spent at propaganda meetings. Psychologically, if they do not like the communist system, they see themselves compromised, involved as in a huge conspiracy, contributing to a perpetuation of the system, yet seeing no way out of the web in which they have become enmeshed.

DISSENT

In the 1970s, evidence of dissent grew, despite reprisals. It was provoked in part because the Brezhnev regime made it impossible to continue publication of criticism of the Stalin years, as well as by government reprisals against a few intellectuals who had protested the Soviet invasion of Czechoslovakia in 1968. In 1969 the Action Group for the Defense of Civil Rights in the U.S.S.R. was formed, but its leader, Pytor Yakir, was soon convicted on the charge of anti-Soviet activities and imprisoned. In 1970 another group, the Committee for Human Rights, was formed by two leading physicists, Andrei Sakharov and Valery Chalidze. Both groups, but especially the latter, attracted a number of notable writers, scientists, and other intellectuals.

The latter group was particularly active in seeking to monitor Soviet violations of that part of the Helsinki accords (signed in 1975) that deals with human rights and that gave the dissident movement unexpected new life. Most of the leaders of this group have been imprisoned; Sakharov was sent into internal exile in 1980, and in effect placed under house arrest. Chalidze, while on a trip to the United States in 1973, had his passport taken away by Soviet diplomats. The same thing happened to Zhores Medvedev in August 1973, while doing scholarly work in Great Britain. A well-known geneticist, Medvedev spent some time in 1970 in a psychiatric hospital because of his dissident views. This "treatment" has been meted out to a number of dissident intellectuals in recent years.

The employment of psychiatric hospitals to "treat" persons with dissident views suggests that Soviet authorities are substituting selective persecution for mass terror. It is interesting to note that even as the climate of repression has grown worse, the 1977 Soviet constitution could assert that "persecution for criticisms shall be prohibited" (Article 49). But even a cursory reading of the constitution as a whole provides ample evidence that the permitted criticism is narrowly defined, and that governmental authorities can easily interpret any criticism as anti-Soviet and therefore prohibited.

In the past several years repression of well-known intellectuals has continued apace. Prison, exile, and/or revocation of citizenship have been their rewards for expressions of dissent. During these years several Soviet artists defected while on trips abroad. After some 20 years of secret police repression, dissidence appeared to be reduced to negligible proportions.

What do the dissidents want? It is difficult to generalize, except that all of them want freedom that they now do not have. Some want greater freedom within the system, while others would like to replace the system. Some of them are religious and some not. Some believe in a socialist order and some do not. Artists and writers want freedom to create and do not like to be bound by the canons of "socialist realism." All of the dissidents seem concerned with problems facing Soviet society, as well as those facing other societies, and the impact of all of this on the international order. They would like to be able to travel freely, to discuss with citizens of other nations problems of common concern, and to do this without fear or government-directed hindrance.

The Soviet authorities are not sympathetic to these aspirations. Nor are non-dissidents free of troubles. In 1979 some of the Soviet Union's most prominent established writers—none of them could be regarded as a dissident—sought to publish a new literary magazine *(Metropol)*, which they hoped would relax tight state control over the arts. Despite the fact that the literary content was essentially apolitical, the authorities nullified this attempt to go outside the censorship channels. Not much seems to have changed in recent years.

SCHOOLS IN A STRAITJACKET

Along with the youth organizations, the Soviet Communist party looks upon the schools as the main instruments for shaping the new generations. Since the launching of the first Soviet earth satellite in 1957, the Soviet educational system has received a good deal of attention in the West from educators and political leaders alike. It is beyond the scope of this book, however, to examine the Soviet educational system in all its ramifications. We are primarily interested in it as an instrument in the hands of the party for molding new generations to fit the requirements of its political leaders.

As do all other institutions in the Soviet Union, the schools have a definite role to play. In addition to providing the type of training desired by the party, mostly professional and technical, the schools are supposed to turn out young citizens who will be enthusiastic supporters of the Soviet system. The attempt to reeducate older generations has not borne much fruit. Hence there is an urgent need, from the point of view of the party, to redouble the effort to guide young people along the desired path. Therefore, little is left to chance. All educational programs are carefully planned with definite political objectives at all levels.

As might be expected, there is a desire to get to children at an early age. The much-advertised nurseries, or day-care centers, where working mothers may leave their young ones, offer the first such opportunity. Here, in picture, song, and story, the young ones learn to glorify Soviet leaders and their achievements. In most instances the young one returns to the mother at the end of the day, although there are a growing number of centers that return the child to the parents only for the weekend.

Understandably, the party sets the educational goals of the Soviet schools and assigns important personnel to check on their realization. Basic directives are usually in the form of resolutions of the party's Central Committee, which may be spelled out in greater detail by the Council of Ministers. Key articles from the party press or in educational journals offer further guidance. In addition, there are the ministries of education in the republics. Moreover, important school officials (administrators and teachers) are party members and presumably familiar with the party line on education. Through all of these channels Soviet teachers are told, time and again, that all education must be based on the one and only true science, the science of Marxism-Leninism.

To this end textbooks and other teaching materials are expected to conform with increased emphasis on ideology as one moves up the educational ladder. Moreover, the general tone is set by the most important general reference work for all citizens, the Large Soviet Encyclopedia, which is regarded as the final authority and the undisputed source of information on all subjects. It was produced on the basis of a political directive that in 1949 declared that the second edition "should widely elucidate the world-historical victories of socialism . . . in the U.S.S.R. in the province of economics, science, culture, art." And "it must show the superiority of socialist culture over the culture of the capitalist world." All articles are thus written from the point of view of the Marxist-Leninist world outlook. This concept of an encyclopedia is foreign to the Western world, and foreign to the traditional concept of what an encyclopedia should be.

In their propaganda aimed at the outside world, Soviet leaders have expressed considerable pride in their educational system. Among other things, they have on innumerable occasions pointed to the banishment of illiteracy as one of their great achievements. While not denying this, an objective observer must also ask: What achievement is it if the purpose is to enslave the mind? What gain is it for an Armenian or a Ukrainian to have the party organ, *Pravda,* translated from the Russian into one of his own tongue? This is not to suggest that banishing illiteracy is not a desirable goal, but to point out that in the Soviet system it is not an unmixed blessing.

In their domestic output, in contrast to what is said about the educational system in propaganda destined for abroad, the Soviet leaders are frequently critical of the shortcomings of their schools. On the one hand, there are the material deficiencies, poor or inadequate physical facilities (necessitating double and even triple shifts), inadequate housing and work space for teachers, and the like. On the other hand, and seemingly more important, are the undesirable results. Too many students are receptive only to the type of learning that will get them into institutions of higher learning, while these institutions can admit and accommodate only a portion of them. Moreover, many of the university graduates are often pictured as ideologically unprepared, enamored of cosmopolitan views and tastes, and, in general, not possessing the ideological outlook the party leaders expect and desire.

In late 1958 and early 1959 the regime launched an organizational overhaul of the Soviet school system, which came to be known as the "Khrushchev School Reform." Its avowed goal was to channel only a relatively small proportion of young people toward higher education. The remainder were to be trained for a specific niche in the labor force, while giving them a modicum of general knowledge. In support of this plan, Khrushchev observed that it was unwise and unrealistic for so many young people to aspire to a higher education, particularly when many of them did so because they found the idea of manual labor repugnant.

The objectives of the Khrushchev School Reform were to be achieved through an eight-year compulsory school, followed by on-the-job training for two or three years. While for some, on-the-job training consisted mainly of going to school, 80 percent of the university admissions quota was reserved for persons with at least two years of work experience. While on the job, these youngsters would prepare themselves for institutions of higher learning through special classes, night schools, or correspondence courses. Under this plan, Soviet authorities would be able to determine at an earlier age than before who would go to the university, to the technical institutes, or to the mines and factories.

This aspect of the Khruschev School Reform was not enthusiastically received by a number of educators, who doubted the wisdom of interrupting the educational careers of promising students. It came under fire in the Soviet press soon after Khruschev's ouster in 1964, and in 1965 it was altered so that quotas would be in proportion to the number of applications received from high school graduates and from young workers.

In 1966 the Khruschev School Reform was abolished in all but name, leaving young people from industry at a severe disadvantage in competing for university places. In 1972 the party and government issued a joint decree calling for greater stress on combining traditional school subjects with production, including student excursions to factories and farms, as well as some work experience during the school year and during vacations. A 10-year program of compulsory school was set up, but shortages of school buildings, textbooks, qualified teachers, and other facilities have hindered achievement of this goal.

In 1984–85 new educational reforms were introduced, designed to stress increased vocational training and greater ideological awareness. In addition, there was a new emphasis on the teaching of Russian in non-Russian regions. The years of required schooling were increased to 11, with entry at age six instead of the previous seven.

There are great disparities as well as inequities in Soviet education. Some schools are blessed with good equipment and excellent instructors and others are not. Getting into the better schools depends in part in connections and favors. Children of the educated have a much better chance of making it to the university than children of workers or farmers. Only one out of seven graduates of secondary schools can get into institutions of higher learning, and if one gets expelled from one university it is impossible to get into another one. According to the Soviet census of 1970, fewer than half of all adults had gone beyond the seventh grade, and fewer than 6 percent had any education beyond the secondary level.[8]

ATTACK ON COMPETING INFLUENCES

In seeking to create the new socialist man, the Communist party found it necessary to combat those influences which ran counter to its ideological position. As noted earlier in this chapter, foreign influences were in large measure excluded by policies that came to be referred to collectively as the Iron Curtain. Domestically, at the time the Communists seized power, the family and the church were the most powerful influences in shaping new generations. Consequently, Soviet leaders lost no time in devising ways of eliminating or minimizing these influences.

Marxian theory had explained society and the nature of its development in a "scientific" way and without the need of a deity. Previous political systems, according to Marx, had made use of religion to enslave the people more effectively. Religion was an opiate that served to divert the worker from his earthly woes. It was, in essence, one tool in the hands of the bourgeoisie for keeping the proletariat in its place. In view of the close association of the then prevailing faith (the Russian Orthodox Church) with tsarist autocracy, this analysis must have

---

[8]An interesting study is by Susan Jacoby, *Inside Soviet Schools* (New York: Hill & Wang, 1974).

seemed plausible to many Russians. In the new society, said Marx and his followers, religion will be relegated to the museum.

Soviet leaders were unwilling, however, to wait for the day when the people would discard religion as no longer useful. Consequently, they embarked upon the task of destroying churches. Countless thousands of them were physically demolished, although a few of the more impressive ones were left standing. Most of the churches were stripped of their religious appurtenances, including gold-covered bibles, silver and gold crosses, the more impressive icons, robes, and other things of value. Many of these were placed in museums. In many instances, regime partisans prevented the use for religious purposes of the churches left standing. These gradually deteriorated over the years, although some have been refurbished since World War II. In most instances, however, they are not used for religious purposes, but are labeled as "architectural monuments." Their preservation at state expense is justified on the ground that they are examples of architecture of a certain period and therefore historically important to the nation. Some of the churches left standing were converted into atheistic museums.

The physical destruction of churches was accompanied by a corresponding attack upon the clergy. The more important ones were quickly liquidated unless they succeeded in escaping. Others were imprisoned or herded into labor camps. Those who were neither liquidated nor imprisoned were mocked and persecuted. All sorts of indignities were heaped upon them. Moreover, they were left without any means of support, for they were forbidden to plead for any type of aid for themselves or their churches. They were forced to rely on voluntary and usually surreptitious gifts.

The 1936 and 1977 Soviet constitutions proclaim freedom of religious worship, but the right to propagandize about religion is limited to those who are against it. As the regime evolved, new church leaders came into being, but these swore allegiance to the new regime. During World War II, Russian church leaders prayed for Stalin and for the victory of the Red Army. Since that time, the Russian Orthodox Church, as well as a few Protestant churches, have been able to function in a limited way. In many areas there are no churches or clergymen, and even in cities like Moscow and Leningrad, they are few and far between. A few synagogues have also been permitted, although during the latter years of Stalin's reign a calculated anti-Semitic policy—never identified as such—was in effect. As of 1985 there were only four seminaries for training Orthodox clergymen, and the number of new students who may enter each year is severely limited.

Religion is not regarded as a private affair in the Soviet Union. For members of the party and the *Komsomol* it cannot be, for both are dedicated to oppose actively all noncommunist ideological influences, especially on the young. Numerous visits to Russian churches by American tourists in recent years revealed an almost total absence of representatives of the high school and college generation. Women and older people tend to stand out in any church congregation, although there is a fair sprinkling of persons in their 30s and 40s, and some in their late 20s.

In the case of the youth, the party and *Komsomol* organizations have an active campaign of providing them with other things to do on Sundays and other religious holidays. There are special parades and manifestations, youth work projects, visits to libraries, museums, and historical places, as well as circuses and carnivals. Religious instruction for the young is not permitted, while youth publications attack religion in all of its manifestations. In brief, the party will endeavor to make sure that the church cannot compete successfully for the allegiance of the young. As a totalitarian and materialistic philosophy, communism cannot tolerate effective competition for people's minds from a spiritual force.

Moreover, by the time most youngsters reach adulthood they are made all too clearly aware that advancement in their society depends upon the party. The most desirable jobs, as well as promotions, are controlled by the party. Young persons soon learn that their attitude toward the party and its policies can be decisive. Consequently, they are not likely to jeopardize their future knowingly. And they know that if they go to church or if they become known as religious persons, these matters will be noted in their *dossiers,* or personnel files. In such circumstances, some jobs will certainly be closed and promotion in others impeded. Consequently, these are compelling reasons for avoiding even the appearance of being religious.

Finally, the party keeps a close watch on whatever religious activities are permitted. Official governmental councils for church affairs have been established to regulate the spiritual safety valve. There is something cruelly ironical in an avowed Communist's being the supervisor of the Orthodox hierarchy. Like other organizations in the Soviet system, churches are expected to serve communist propaganda purposes and to endorse the party's political decisions. From the regime's point of view, the basic battle has been won; only mopping-up operations remain, and the vestigial remnants of worship will eventually dwindle to nothing.

On the other hand, regime actions in recent years suggest a growing concern about religion. During the Khrushchev era, for example, antireligious activities were stepped up considerably. Additional churches, monasteries, and seminaries were closed or turned into museums. Many clergymen were arrested under pretexts of fraudulent manipulations, insanity, or the exploitation of believers. A retroactive income tax was imposed on all priests. Antireligious publications, antireligious lectures, and other antireligious activities were markedly multiplied. A special institute of atheism was established, and a course in atheism was introduced in the schools. Prizes were announced for literary and artistic works that most effectively conveyed antireligious messages. It is perhaps significant that while the struggle against religion in the early decades of the regime was carried on by semiliterate party agitators, in more recent years it was performed by scholars, scientists, writers, and poets, who were mobilized in the antireligious crusade.

In spite of this systematic attack, there are indications of rumblings beneath the surface. While it is not possible to speak of a religious revival, there is some evidence of hostility toward a system that does not regard religious attitudes as matters of personal and private concern.

In the early years of the new regime, youngsters were encouraged to inform on their parents as a means of discovering anticommunist sentiment. Many parents stood in fear of their children, and many went to prison because of them. As the years wore on, and particularly as young citizens came to realize the hollowness of the regime's claims and promises, and as they began to experience the same material fate, informing by children dropped off sharply. But by that time, the regime had consolidated its position, won many new recruits, and refined its techniques for controlling the masses.

At the same time, however, the number of the disaffected grew. To young fathers and mothers a great deal of the "old-fashioned nonsense" they had learned from their parents now seemed to make sense. Consequently, parental disillusionment with the regime has continued to be of constant concern to the Soviet leaders. Inevitably, children were hearing things in the family during their formative years which, in the opinion of the leaders, must be unlearned.

It is in the light of this situation that one must look at the party's intensive campaign among the young, in and out of school. It is in this light that one must, at least partially, view the use of boarding schools and the effort of the Soviet leaders to "reform" the family that does not do its job "correctly." Thus a 1969 law promises that the state will help with the "communist" upbringing of children but emphasizes that it is the parents' duty to perform this role. If the parents fail, the child may be transferred to a boarding school or adopted.

Aside from all the other things discussed in this chapter, as ways of influencing and controlling the people's minds, there are two primary means of countering family influence. One is to get hold of children as early as possible in their lives, and the other is to monopolize their waking hours or, negatively, to leave as few days and waking hours as possible in which children can be with their parents.

In contemplating the future, it should be noted that in recent years naked force and violence have been less in evidence than in the past. Some observers feel that former inmates of Soviet prisons, some of whom now occupy important governmental posts, give the society an inner toughness and constitute a substantial barrier against the rise of a new police terror system. Some even suggest that the day of the informer may be past, and that Soviet society is no longer controlled by fear. This does not mean, however, that the Soviet leaders have rejected force and violence as instruments of political control, or that they will not resort to them if less violent means fail to keep the people in line and thereby threaten the security of the regime and its leaders. Force and fear, along with persuasion, are ever present in varying combinations.

BIBLIOGRAPHICAL NOTE

An understanding of the extent to which force and fear are utilized under the Soviet system may be gained from F. Beck and W. Godin, *Russian Purge and the Extraction of Confession* (New York: Viking Press, 1951); Zbigniew Brzezinski, *The Permanent Purge, Politics in Soviet Totalitarianism* (Cambridge, Mass.; Harvard University Press, 1956); Iosif G. Dyadkin, *Unnatural Deaths in the U.S.S.R.: 1928–1954* (New Brunswick, N.J.: Transaction Books, 1983); Arthur Koestler, *Darkness at Noon* (New York: Macmillan, 1941); Nathan Leites and Elsa Bernaut, *Ritual of Liquidation, The Case of the Moscow Trials* (Glencoe Ill.: Free Press, 1954); and Ronald Hingley, *The Russian Secret Police: Muscovite, Imperial Russian, and Soviet Political Security Operations* (New York: Simon & Schuster, 1971). Of special importance is the three-volume account by Aleksandr I. Solzhenitsyn, *The Gulag Archipelago, 1918–1956* (New York: Harper & Row, 1973–78). Mention should also be made of Sidney Bloch and Peter Reddaway, *Psychiatric Terror: How Soviet Psychiatry Is Used to Suppress Dissent* (New York: Basic Books, 1977), and Harvey Fireside, *Soviet Psychoprisons* (New York: W. W. Norton, 1979).

Alex Inkeles, *Public Opinion in Soviet Russia: A Study in Mass Persuasion* (Cambridge, Mass.: Harvard University Press, 1950), is a pioneering study of the Russian use of the mass media and of their role in public opinion formation. Also see Alain Besancon, *The Rise of the Gulag: Intellectual Origins of Leninism* (New York: Seebury Press, 1981); Christel Lane, *The Rites of Rulers: Ritual in Industrial Society—the Soviet Case* (New York: Cambridge University Press, 1981), and Ellen Propper Mickiewicz, *Media and the Russian Public* (New York: Praeger Publishers, 1981). Insight into *Komsomol* activities may be gained from Ralph Talcott Fisher, Jr., *Pattern for Soviet Youth: A Study of the Congresses of the Komsomol, 1918–1954* (New York: Columbia University Press, 1959). See also William Taubman, *The View from Lenin Hills: Soviet Youth in Ferment* (New York: Coward-McCann, 1968), and Georgie Anne Geyer, *The Young Russians* (Homewood, Ill.: ETC Publications, 1975).

On dissent and dissenters, see the books by Hedrick Smith, Robert Kaiser, Kevin Klose, and David Shipler, cited in Chapter 27. See also Roy A. Medvedev, *On Soviet Dissent* (New York: Columbia University Press, 1980); Andrei D. Sakharov, *My Country and the World* (New York: Vintage Books, 1975); Aleksandr I. Solzhenitsyn, *Letter to the Soviet Leaders* (New York: Harper & Row, 1974); Alexander Solzhenitsyn et al, *From under the Rubble* (Boston: Little, Brown, 1974); Anatole Shub, *The New Russian Tragedy* (New York: W. W. Norton, 1969), and An Observer (George Feifer), *Message from Moscow* (New York: Vintage Books, 1971).

Also of interest are William C. Fletcher, *Soviet Believers: The Religious Sector of the Population* (Lawrence: The Regents Press of Kansas, 1981), and William E. Odom, *The Soviet Volunteers: Modernization and Bureaucracy in a Public Mass Organization* (Princeton, N. J.: Princeton University Press, 1973).

34

The Soviet Challenge

Because Western democratic political systems rest on popular approval, some people are apt to think of other political systems as having the consent of the majority of their respective peoples, at least at the time of their initial establishment. This is not true, however, of the Soviet or any other communist system. In no country has a majority voted freely in favor of communism, either before or after its inauguration. And yet the Soviet leaders (and their ideology) assert that all other countries must sooner or later go their way. This is the Soviet challenge, in its most elemental form, to the non-Soviet world. Although this chapter deals with the Soviet challenge, the reader should bear in mind the evolving challenge of other communist systems, notably that of China.

UNIVERSALITY OF THE CHALLENGE

All societies around the world are told, in effect, that the laws of historical development are pushing them inevitably toward revolution and the proletarian dictatorship. The all-embracing Marxian ideology not only professes to explain the basic laws of social development, and thereby to predict the shape of the future society but, in addition, it seeks to provide the instruments with which the transformation is to be brought about. In the hands of Soviet and other communist leaders, this ideology and the systems they have built constitute a type of declaration of war on the noncommunist world. Hence this world finds itself, whether it wishes it or not, in the midst of a life-and-death struggle.

There are three aspects to this struggle. The first is essentially domestic—that is, the challenge (or threat) that the Soviets will provide a viable political, economic, and social system that best meets the needs of the members of society and provides the greatest measure of social justice. Or, to put it in question form: Will they succeed in building a social order that, by its sheer success in meeting human and social problems, will constitute a powerful attraction and a persuasive argument for conscious imitation? As of 1985, the answer was an undeniable no.

The second aspect of the struggle—really a part of the first—is the challenge to the non-Soviet world to establish and maintain a social system (or systems) that will continue to be superior to anything that the Soviets may devise. By and large, this is a dual problem. On the one hand, there are the highly developed industrial nations, which have, in the main, established viable social systems, but which must be able to adjust to the changing needs of evolving industrial societies. On the other hand, there are the nonindustrialized nations, sometimes referred to as underdeveloped countries, which find themselves in varying degrees of economic and political development. The challenge to these two broad groups of non-Soviet nations, although related, is of considerably different magnitude for each.

The third aspect of the struggle concerns the militant effort of the Soviet leaders to utilize the power of the Soviet Union and her allies to alter the international status quo in their favor. To this end, they are employing a variety of means. Because of the nature of modern weapons of war, this aspect assumes major proportions, for it is here that the life and death of nations and peoples may hang in the balance.

HOW VIABLE A SOCIAL ORDER?

An evaluation of a changing social order must remain tentative. While Stalin was alive, an appraisal of Soviet society was less difficult. But gone are many of the rigidities of that era. Although many things remain as before, some changes are taking place, and any current estimate must take this into account. This is not to suggest that extraordinary departures are expected, but merely to call attention to the fact that Stalin's successors are less resistant to experimentation.

Without doubt, great strides have been made in the Soviet Union toward industrializing a backward nation. The rate of economic growth in the 1950s was particularly impressive, but it had slowed down considerably in the later 1970s. The world has witnessed dramatic proof of the achievements of Soviet science and technology. But progress has been uneven; some aspects of the economy have received much more attention than others. And the human and material costs have been high. The judgment of a one-time Soviet citizen is still valid: there has been considerable progress for those who survived. Also, there is a marked contrast between new buildings and equipment and the lack of proper maintenance.

Moreover, there is a marked contrast between the growth in industrial production and the slow pace in agriculture. In most food items, production per inhabitant is below that of 1913. In December 1958 Khrushchev admitted that "the agricultural situation was grave" and that some earlier Soviet agricultural statistics had been a "fraud" and a "deception"—an interesting description of official data by a Soviet leader. In the same year, he admitted that to produce a unit of milk the Soviet farmer put in three times as many man-hours as the American farmer. And in the case of wheat it was seven times the man-hours. In the ensuing years he continued to express dissatisfaction with the results of Soviet agriculture, frequently accompanying his declarations with changes in farm management. In 1963–64, in 1972–73, in 1975, and in subsequent years, the Soviet Union was forced to buy large quantities of wheat, mainly from the United States and Canada. Because of the huge purchases (19 million metric tons in 1972–73 and 13 million metric tons in 1975 from the United States alone), an agreement was reached in October 1975 that would enable them to buy 6 to 8 million metric tons per year over the next five years. Subsequently, purchase agreements were made for still larger shipments, but following the Soviet invasion of Afghanistan the United States in 1980 embargoed these additional purchases. President Reagan lifted the embargo in 1981.

On the whole, the Soviet Union has a low standard of living. Most, if not all, European countries have a higher one. This means that the Soviet rate of national economic growth has not been reflected in such consumer items as food, clothing, or housing. Rather, it is to be found in the buildup of capital goods industries and in the Soviet military establishment. It needs to be noted, however, that in the Khrushchev and Brezhnev years there was a far greater emphasis on consumer goods and services than in the preceding years, resulting in a higher standard of living, particularly in the urban areas. The rise in real incomes in the past decade, however, mostly benefited those who had been less well off, however, thus canceling out some of the improvement.

The boasts about surpassing the United States standard of living are not apt to materialize in the near future. Substantial increases in consumer items cannot be brought about without encouraging individual initiative, providing better living conditions, and increasing agricultural production. At present, the low agricultural output still ties up about one third of the Soviet labor force, which is in sharp contrast to the 4 or 5 percent of the U.S. labor force that produces large agricultural surpluses. Housing is far behind nations in the West, and medical services, while free, suffer from serious shortages of space, equipment, and drugs. For the privileged, however, there are special clinics and hospitals where care is excellent.

The low standard of living is coupled with an uneven distribution of consumer goods. The "new class," the privileged in communist society, gets the most of what there is to get. But within other groups in Soviet society (for example, the workers) there is also a large disparity in rewards. The gap between the low and high paid in virtually every group is greater than gaps within similar economic groups in the United States. In any event, and however else the Soviet Union may be described, it certainly is not an egalitarian society.

Moreover, the Soviet standard of living, such as it is, is in part dependent upon the work of many women. Although there are laws on the "protection of female labor," a substantial percentage of steam-furnace stokers, metal welders, blacksmiths, and stevedores are women. Moreover, they handle hot asphalt, lay bricks and stone, handle ties and rails in railway construction and repair, and unload coal, cement, and grain—to say nothing of their work as janitors, street cleaners, and farm workers. What may be even more important is the fact that the percentage of women in the Soviet labor force has increased over the years.

While uncertainties continue as to the ability of Soviet society to achieve a measure of balanced economic growth and to provide its citizens with an improving standard of living, no such uncertainties are to be found in the political realm. Barring a cataclysmic upheaval, the Soviet Union seems condemned indefinitely to dictatorial rule. The Communist party remains an all-powerful elite, and its leaders are determined to keep it that way. For the foreseeable future, therefore, there is no indication that the Soviet Union will be anything except a one-party dictatorship.

This means that whatever aspirations for political freedom the peoples of the Soviet Union may have—and there are various indications that such aspirations exist to some degree—will go unrealized. It means also that the secret police and other instruments of totalitarian control will continue to function. It seems ironic that an ideology whose avowed and declared purpose was to liberate people should produce the opposite. Over the past century and a half, man's personal liberty has increased in many countries, but in the Soviet Union, as in other communist states, it has become more restricted.

Nevertheless, certain contradictions beset the leaders of the U.S.S.R. On the one hand, they may be able to make concessions in a number of areas, but they will not be able to make them in the one significant area of giving people a voice in deciding who should govern. To do so would be to invite the people to replace them with someone else. This they can never do. Moreover, it is doubtful if they can even permit open and free criticism, for to do so would be to pave the way for the next step in the democratic process—that is, to throw out of power those leaders whose policies and programs are the bases of the criticism.

On the other hand, the leaders are beset with demands, particularly from young people, that there be a more realistic discussion of the nature of the future society. To the young people the single most intriguing aspect of communism is the promise that goods are to be distributed in conformity with the principal of "to each according to his needs." The young people, even the Communists among them, have come face to face with the contradictions and injustices of the Soviet system. The less fortunate, particularly, are anxious to know if there is going to be an end to the inequalities with which they are so familiar.

That the young people are asking questions and arriving at independent answers, even though they cannot voice their thoughts openly, suggests that they are unwilling to accept what they are told by their leaders. The leaders would rather not discuss such questions at all. But they know that whether they wish it or not, these discussions will "go on without us, without our intellectual influence." Consequently, they have attempted to provide answers. From the reactions their answers have provoked, however, they must know that the young people are far from satisfied.

The absence of the most significant freedom—political liberty—has its crucial implications for all other freedoms. As was pointed out in Chapter 33, a dictatorship of the modern totalitarian variety seems to need control over all aspects of human endeavor, and cannot, therefore, permit unbridled freedom in any area. From time to time it may be able to make some concessions. But without political freedom, people cannot feel secure in any of their other liberties.

The period of liberalization (1955–57) in literature and other forms of cultural expression is instructive in this regard, although far from conclusive. Subsequently, the all-powerful government was able to reimpose more rigid controls and to get pledges of reform and rededication from artist and literary associations. But it does not seem likely that the educated younger generation, which responded so favorably to the liberalization, will be easily reconciled to the Kremlin's reimposition of orthodoxy. The Soviet public, as one Soviet writer pointed out to an audience of critics, is tired of "the same steam shovel, the same dam, the same road." Moreover, for a time there was reason to believe that the Soviet leadership team would be forced to seek an accommodation with the increasing desire of writers and artists to be free of the fetters of socialist realism, but their actions have not given reason for much hope.

VIABILITY OF THE NON–SOVIET WORLD

What the above suggests is that Soviet society is far from being a viable social order. But viability is a relative matter. The crucial question, particularly in the long run, may be: Does the non-Soviet world present examples of a more viable social order or orders? In this respect it is difficult, if not impossible, to speak of the non-Soviet world, or even of the Western world, as if it were one. Many of the nations of the non-Soviet world vary a great deal from each other in their historical and cultural heritage, as well as in their political, economic, and social experience.

For the purposes of this discussion the countries of the non-Soviet world may be divided, although somewhat arbitrarily, into the industrialized or developed nations and the underdeveloped countries. It must be kept in mind, however, that some nations will not fit into either category or, rather, they will fit both categories partially. They are the countries that are either in transition or experiencing serious social crises.

For the most part, the countries in the first category (United States, Great Britain, France, Canada, Germany, Italy, Japan, Switzerland, Scandinavia, and the Low Countries) are sometimes referred to as the free nations. Most of them have experienced political freedom long enough to appreciate keenly what is at stake, what there is to lose. Most of them, too, have evolved in the direction of an improving standard of living for their peoples. They want to remain free, but some of them have serious economic problems.

There is some question, however, if even these nations are fully aware of the nature and extent of the communist challenge and what they must do to remain free. Certainly, there is some division among the peoples of these countries on this question. When the domestic communist party is weak or nonexistent, it is difficult for many inhabitants of the country to perceive the danger. Similarly, when the communist movement is gaining ground in another country, people who are somewhat removed from the scene do not become excited easily, especially if what is taking place is in little known areas and in countries that have only recently achieved their independence.

Most Western leaders have long believed that communist victories anywhere constituted a threat to the free world. They viewed such victories as enhancing the power of the Soviet Union and its allies, and thereby reducing the actual or potential area of the free world. This view was not shared by certain nations, sometimes labeled neutralist, whose leaders deliberately sought to avoid involvement in great power controversies. In recent years, as differences among communist states evolved, significant segments of opinion in democratic countries have questioned the earlier views of their leaders.

To meet the communist threat in various parts of the world, the major nations in the free world have embarked upon programs of economic and other aid, particularly to underdeveloped countries and especially to those which are seeking to establish or perpetuate democratic political systems. The hope is that such aid will help these countries to make the transition from backwardness to industrialization without sharp and violent political and social upheavals.

In many of these countries the situation is favorable to the Soviet Union. Among large segments of the people there is mass ignorance, backwardness, resentment of the wealth the West holds, and little or no experience with political freedom. There is great impatience to get things done; slow growth has few supporters. Moreover, their political leaders, often naïve and almost always ambitious, are attracted by the Soviet experiment in radical social and industrial engineering. They are impressed by the rapid transformation of peasant Russia into an industrial and military power.

Moreover, the Soviet Union has embarked upon its own aid program to certain underdeveloped countries. Because they need not account to an electorate, the Soviet leaders can dispense aid irrespective of cost. Even if they cannot win people over to their side, the Soviets can foment unrest or augment already existing trouble. Sometimes, however, the U.S.S.R.'s actions have helped the West by betraying Soviet bloc intentions. The ruthless suppression of the Hungarian Revolution in 1956 and the invasion of Czechoslovakia in 1968 and Afghanistan in 1979–80 are but three examples.

MILITANT SOVIET EFFORTS TO CHANGE THE STATUS QUO

The Soviet challenge to the non-Soviet world is made particularly acute by the militant campaign waged by the Soviet leaders and their allies to change the international status quo. Their violations of World War II agreements, which were designed to guarantee free and unfettered elections to the countries of Eastern Europe, are well known. And Korea and Vietnam are a matter of record. Just as there were some signs that Soviet foreign policy was becoming less militant came the invasion of Afghanistan.

While the objectives of Soviet foreign policy and the means for their implementation are in large measure dictated by the Marxist-Leninist world outlook, it would be a mistake to ignore the influence of historical and other factors that antedate the Soviet era. The Soviet leaders inherited tsarist Russia's geography, population, natural resources, and its drive to gain access to warm-water outlets to the sea. Although the Bolsheviks consented to great losses in territory in the German-imposed treaty of Brest-Litvosk, they waged a concerted and largely successful military campaign to regain the tsarist patrimony after Germany was defeated in the west. Among the first foreign policy ventures of the new regime, therefore, was the one to reclaim the fruits of tsarist expansionist policies. Soviet leaders may deny the influence of the tsarist inheritance on their foreign policies, but in this case actions speak louder than words.

Marxian theory tells the Soviet leaders that the world is in a process of conflict and change. This process, the same theory tells them, will lead to proletarian revolutions in all nation-states, and the overthrow of their capitalist social orders. Most Soviet leaders have been convinced, however, that this process needs assistance. Consequently, they have believed that one of the missions of the Soviet regime is to promote revolutions. In other words, world revolution is the maximum goal of Soviet foreign policy, the minimum goal being the survival of the U.S.S.R.

In pursuit of this goal (or goals) the Soviet leaders have utilized a variety of means. At varying times, they have employed espionage networks, infiltration, foreign trade, propaganda, domestic communist parties, the secret police, and such organizations as the Comintern and Cominform. And finally, they have utilized their military establishment. For them, war and diplomacy are two sides of the same coin, but they distinguish between just and unjust wars. Among the just wars are wars of liberation from colonialism and capitalism. By definition, any war engaged in by the Soviet Union would to them be a just war. By the same token, wars waged by capitalist countries, particularly the leading ones, would be unjust wars.

Soviet leaders have on many occasions insisted that Marxism teaches the inevitability of violence as the final arbiter in international affairs. They have no faith in the idea that communist and noncommunist states could exist side by side, with common legal principles or moral precepts regulating their relations. This, combined with the Marxian notion of the inevitability of proletarian revolutions, the Soviet doctrine of just and unjust wars, and the Kremlin's possession of nuclear and other capabilities, presents the remainder of the world with some unpleasant prospects.

In more recent years, however, the Soviet leaders have said that "peaceful coexistence is an objective necessity," a point of view not shared by their Chinese comrades.[1] Meanwhile, they have not hesitated to exploit the universal fear of war to gain some of their objectives without war.

It has been argued that once the Soviet regime achieves the basic objectives of communism at home, the need to foment revolutions will fade or disappear. A more persuasive argument, it seems, is that the preservation of the totalitarian system at home will be more difficult to justify as the objectives of communism at home are met. In order to continue exacting sacrifices and denying basic freedoms, the Soviet leaders will need to show that this is required in the interests of aiding the Soviet brand of Marxism to advance in the world at large, as well as of protecting the Soviet Union from dangerous ideas coming from the outside world.

From time to time, Soviet leaders have said that they believed in the coexistence of differing social systems. In Stalin's time, such expressions were meant for foreigners and not for the Soviet public. Moreover, such declarations did not speak of permanent coexistence, or of the conditions for its establishment and maintenance. On the contrary, a careful examination of those statements revealed that the basic condition would be the willingness of the non-Soviet world to yield to the Kremlin's world revolutionary objectives. Coexistence, from Stalin's point of view, was the time needed to achieve superiority—the period during which the Soviet Union would seek to destroy or weaken the military and political solidarity of the free world.

There is reason to believe that Stalin's successors have been forced to alter his concept of coexistence. Available evidence suggests that they do not accept nuclear war as a realistic means of achieving their objectives, although some experts are convinced that the Soviets are not above engaging in nuclear blackmail if they should find themselves in a favorable military position. Moreover, the new Soviet constitution has a section on foreign policy, which asserts that the Soviet Union supports "peaceful coexistence of states with different social systems," and pledges "noninterference in internal affairs" of other states (Articles 28 and 29). In the same place, however, the Soviet Union is pledged to support "the struggle of peoples for national liberation." In addition, the 1961 party program states that "Leninism teaches and historical experience confirms that the ruling classes do not yield their power voluntarily." And in their instructions to writers, the Soviet leaders have made it quite clear that political

---

[1] These and other differences in the communist camp are discussed below.

and military coexistence does not mean that there should be ideological coexistence.

The Soviet leaders have never tired of stressing the need to improve political indoctrination. This type of exhortation seemed to reach its zenith at the time of the 1980 summer Olympic games in Moscow, when the Soviet citizens were constantly called upon to increase their vigilance against foreign ideologies.

In this, as in other areas, the Soviet leaders have demonstrated that while they may be inflexible where goals are concerned, they are exceedingly flexible in strategy and tactics. They do not believe that their system can be safe so long as free nations exist as beacons of hope for those who live in tyranny. Yet if they reject nuclear conflict as a means to an end, they can be counted on to work harder in the exploitation of other instruments to reach the same goal. Therefore, it ill behooves a world that is tired of conflict to accept at face value the disarmingly attractive doctrine of peaceful coexistence. If it is to have any real meaning for the noncommunist world, peaceful coexistence, as a concept, will require further modification by the Communists so that it constitutes a genuine effort on both sides to reach a workable accommodation.

SOME OBSERVATIONS ON DÉTENTE

In the 1970s the Soviet Union has indicated a strong interest in improving relations with the West, especially the United States, seeking at least a relaxation of tensions, which came to bear the name "détente." The Soviet leaders even boasted in some conferences of communist states that détente has borne more fruit than the policy of confrontation. They have indicated a desire to improve trade relations with the West, openly recognizing that the Soviet Union is a long way behind in modern technology, especially in the computer field. Since they have little in the way of goods that the West needs, a relaxation of tensions would seem to require some demonstrated willingness to reach accords on disarmament or on other problems, but the Soviets have resisted. As of this writing (1985), disarmament discussions between the U.S.S.R. and the United States are moving along at a snail's pace.

The height of détente was represented by the agreements signed in Helsinki on August 1, 1975. These accords recognized the existing territorial boundaries in Europe, provided for mutual notification by NATO and Warsaw Pact nations of upcoming military exercises (including the invitation of observers), and committed the signatories to respect human rights and fundamental freedoms.

In 1976 and 1977 the "Public Group for Furthering the Implementation of the Helsinki Agreements in the USSR" reported that, from their observations, the Soviet government has not and does not intend to fulfill its obligations in the area of human rights. The group of Soviet citizens reported that the practice of psychiatric repression has neither been condemned nor stopped, and that there has been no improvement for those who want to emigrate. The Soviets have reacted to the unfavorable publicity given these reports in the West by insisting that since the Helsinki agreement also spoke of noninterference in internal affairs, other nations have no right to criticize anything that is happening in the Soviet Union. Moreover, as indicated in the previous chapter, most members of the above-mentioned group have been arrested on one charge or another, and all of them have been subject to persecution in varying degrees.

The rulers in the Kremlin seem to resent the fact that the human rights issue has become a stumbling block on the road to increased economic cooperation. For the foreseeable future, therefore, relations between the Soviet Union and the West are apt to be characterized by elements of conflict and cooperation. The Kremlin's difficulties are also compounded by the attitude of some communist parties in Western Europe, whose public attitude toward human rights is not to the liking of Moscow.

THE COMMUNIST CAMP

The seemingly monolithic nature of the communist camp in the early post-World War II years proved to be deceptive. The first open break came in 1948, with the public airing of differences between Yugoslavia and the Soviet Union. For a time a form of unity was reestablished with the "isolation" of Yugoslavia. After Stalin's death in 1953, and particularly after Khruschev's denunciation in 1956 of many of the actions of his predecessor, the bonds between Moscow and its Eastern European satellites began to loosen. While varying degrees of attachment to Moscow are to be found in these nations, signs of independence have been notably on the increase. In the main, however, most of the communist regimes in these countries, including Yugoslavia, support the Soviet Union in its basic approaches to foreign policy.

The Soviet invasion of Czechoslovakia in 1968, however, raised the question of whether the Soviet Union could ever put in order its relations with the East European states. Developments in Poland in the 1980s made the problem still more acute. The so-called Brezhnev Doctrine, enunciated in connection with the Czech invasion, asserts the right of the Soviet Union to intervene in the internal affairs of any other socialist state when socialism is threatened. Since the Soviet Union presumably decides when such a threat exists, the sovereignty of these states would seem to be in perpetual jeopardy. It might be interesting to speculate whether the Brezhnev Doctrine might at some time in the future be invoked to justify Soviet action against China.

The most acrimonious discord in the communist camp has involved the Soviet Union and China. Apparently, there are four major issues in dispute. The first concerns the question of leadership of the international communist movement. The Chinese have stressed the equality of communist states and they have accused the U.S.S.R. of "great power chauvinism." The Soviets have at least paid lip service to the principle of equality, but at the same time they have pointed out that power and responsibility cannot be separated. At a time when they believe that the communist camp must ultimately rely upon the power of the Soviet Union, the Kremlin leaders believe that the decisive voice should be theirs.

The second question at issue concerns the matter of revolutionary tactics and strategy. In the late 1960s and early 1970s the Chinese leaders wanted the communist camp to pursue global revolution; they stressed the point that communists should not be deterred by nuclear blackmail. The Moscow leaders, for their part, were convinced that their knowledge of what is possible in foreign affairs was superior to that of their comrades in Beijing. Since the mid-1970s, however, the Chinese leaders have demonstrated little interest in world revolution, and have sought to portray the Soviet Union as the greatest threat to world peace.

The third problem dividing Moscow and Beijing involves the nature and form of intrabloc assistance. The Chinese leaders have complained that the newer communist states, notably China, have not received sufficient aid or even the right type of aid from Moscow. They have criticized the Soviet leaders for their reluctance to provide massive aid for the Chinese industrialization program. And they have been critical of Soviet aid to such noncommunist states as Egypt. Moreover, they have charged that Moscow has used its aid to exert political pressure. To all these charges, the Soviet leaders have replied by citing statistics on the extent of their assistance (military and economic), made at great sacrifices to the people of the Soviet Union. In addition, the Kremlin has on occasion pointed out the uneconomic nature of certain plans of the newer communist regimes. Moreover, the Soviet leaders have made it quite clear that, in the current stage of development of their society, it is necessary to provide greater and greater material incentives to their people. In addition, they have maintained that it was their international duty to so build communism at home so as to provide their foreign comrades with an appealing example.

Finally, the Chinese leaders were critical of some of the consequences of de-Stalinization. They said that they saw the reemergence of capitalist forms in several of the smaller communist nations and in the U.S.S.R. itself. Liberalization, they feared, would lead to the liquidation of communism. In the late 1970s and early 1980s, however, China began experimenting with greater domestic liberalization than had the Soviet leaders, which seemed to nullify their earlier accusations against Moscow.

While the above would seem to be the major elements in the disagreement between China and the Soviet Union, there may be others. There have been heated disagreements over territorial boundaries. And Beijing has publicly suggested that the Kremlin rulers regard noncaucasians as something less than equal to the whites. Whatever else may be at issue, it should be noted that nationalism is still the great force of our age. Communist national states, not too much unlike noncommunist nations, are beset with different internal problems, and their views of their respective national interests are far from identical. Consequently, they have different ideological needs. In this atmosphere of diversity, the discord in the international communist camp is not likely to be resolved in the near future.

Moreover, the Soviet Union may one day have to confront the problem of the various nationalities in its own empire. Nationalism remains strong in the

Ukraine and in the Baltic republics, where some demonstrations and strikes have taken place in recent years. In addition, there have been indications of an aroused nationalism in Georgia and Armenia. On several occasions, Soviet leaders have demonstrated that they see the nationalities question as potentially dangerous. One of their more recent worries involves the spillover of Islamic fundamentalism into their Moslem republics, whose population is over 40 million. In any case, the leaders in their more rational moments must realize that time does not stand still and that change is the law of life.

BIBLIOGRAPHICAL NOTE

The attempt to evaluate the Soviet challenge on the international front may be facilitated by the following works: Vernon Aspaturian, *Process and Power in Soviet Foreign Policy* (Boston: Little, Brown, 1971); Louis Fischer, *Russia's Road from Peace to War: Soviet Foreign Relations, 1917–1941* (New York: Harper & Row, 1969); Vojtec Mastny, *Russia's Road to the Cold War: Diplomacy, Warfare, and the Politics of Communism, 1941–1945* (New York: Columbia University Press, 1979); Adam B. Ulam, *Expansion and Coexistence: The History of Soviet Foreign Policy, 1917–1967* (New York: Praeger Publishers, 1968); *The Rivals: America and Russia since World War II* (New York: Viking Press, 1971); and *Dangerous Relations: The Soviet Union in World Politics, 1970–1982* (New York: Oxford University Press, 1983).

The following more recent works are recommended: Shirin Akiner, *Islamic Peoples of the Soviet Union* (Boston: Rutledge & Kegan Paul, 1983); Lilvia Brucan, *The Post-Brezhnev Era: An Insider's View* (New York: Praeger Publishers, 1983); Harry Gelman, *The Brezhnev Politburo and the Decline of Detente* (Ithaca, N. Y.: Cornell University Press, 1984); Alexander George et. al, *Managing U.S.-Soviet Rivalry: Problems of Crisis Prevention* (Boulder, Colo.: Westview Press, 1983); William E. Griffith, *The Superpowers and Regional Tensions: The USSR, the United States, and Europe* (Lexington, Mass.: D. C. Heath, 1982); Richard Pipes, *Survival Is Not Enough: Soviet Realities and America's Future* (New York: Simon & Schuster, 1984); and Daniel Yergin, *Shattered Peace: The Origins of the Cold War and the National Security State* (Boston: Houghton Mifflin, 1977).

Also of interest are: Héléne Carrére d'Encausse, *Decline of an Empire: The Soviet Socialist Republics in Revolt,* translated from the French (New York: Newsweek, 1979); Anatoliy Golitsyn, *New Lies for Old: The Communist Strategy of Deception and Disinformation* (New York: Dodd, Mead, 1984); Paul Hollander, *Political Pilgrims: Travels of Western Intellectuals to the Soviet Union, China, and Cuba, 1928–1978* (New York: Oxford University Press, 1981); George Liska, *Russia and the Road to Appeasement: Cycles of East-West Conflict in War and Peace* (Baltimore: The Johns Hopkins Press, 1982); Harry Rositzke, *The KGB: The Eyes of Russia* (Garden City, N. Y.: Doubleday Publishing, 1981); and Richard H. Schultz and Roy S. Godson, *Dezinformatsia: Active Measures in Soviet Strategy* (New York: Pergamon Press, 1984).

Index

i

About the Authors

Alex N. Dragnich received his B.A. from the University of Washington and his M.A. and Ph.D. from the University of California, Berkeley. He joined the faculty of Vanderbilt University in 1950; served as chairman of the Political Science Department, and in 1978 became Professor Emeritus. In 1970, he received the Thomas Jefferson Award for "distinguished service to Vanderbilt through extraordinary contributions as a member of the faculty in the councils and government of the University." In 1947-50, he served as Cultural Attache and Public Affairs Officer in the American Embassy in Belgrade, and in 1959-60, he was Chester W. Nimitz Professor at the U.S. Naval War College.

Among his books, in addition to the present work, are *Tito's Promised Land: Yugoslavia* (1954); *Serbia, Nikola Pasic, and Yugoslavia* (1974); *The Development of Parliamentary Government in Serbia* (1978); *The First Yugoslavia: Search for a Viable Political System* (1983); and, as co-author, *The Saga of Kosovo: Focus on Serbian-Albanian Relations* (1984). He is the author of a number of journal articles. He served in a number of capacities in professional organizations, including that of president of the Southern Political Science Association. In 1979 he was the recipient of the Senior Scholar Award of the Southern Conference on Slavic studies.

Jorgen S. Rasmussen received his Ph.D. in political science from the University of Wisconsin-Madison in 1962. After teaching at the University of Arizona, Vanderbilt University, and Columbia University, he joined the faculty of Iowa State University in 1972, serving as chairman of the Department of Political Science from 1972 to 1976. In addition to this text, he has written two other books. His articles have appeared in many scholarly journals and edited volumes in the United States, Britain, and Canada. He has served as the Executive Secretary of the British Politics Group since its founding in 1974. His Iowa State position is a joint appointment in both Political Science and the College of Education, the latter responsibility including supervision of social studies practice teachers.

A Note on the Type

The text of this book was set in 10/12 Times Roman, a film version of the face designed by Stanley Morison, which was first used by *The Times* (of London) in 1932. Part of Morison's special intent for Times Roman was to create a face that was editorially neutral. It is an especially compact, attractive, and legible typeface, which has come to be seen as the "most important type design of the twentieth century."

It was composed by Carlisle Graphics, Dubuque, Iowa.

Printed by R. R. Donnelley & Sons, Crawfordsville, Indiana.

ISBN 0-534-10515-7

FORMER ISBN 0-256-03389-7

PHYSIOGRAPHY OF EUROPE

100 200 300 400 500 600 Kilometers
100 200 300 Miles

Meters
2000
1000
200
0
-200

RELIEF

ATLANTIC

OCEAN

NORWEGIAN

SEA

NORTH

SEA

SCANDINAVIAN

MOUNTAINS

KJÖLEN

PENINSULA

Gulf

Oslo

Stockholm

L. Vänern

Vättern

BA

SEA

Skagerrak

Kattegat

JUTLAND

Copenhagen

SHETLAND IS.

ORKNEY IS.

HEBRIDES

GRAMPIANS

SCOTTISH LOWLANDS

BRITISH

IRELAND

Dublin

IRISH CENTRAL PLAIN

IRISH SEA

PENNINE CHAIN

ISLES

MIDLANDS

CELTIC

SEA

SCILLY IS.

Thames R.

London

English Channel

BRITTANY

Paris

FRANCE

Loire R.

Seine R.

BAY OF

BISCAY

PLAIN OF

MASSIF

CENTRAL

CEVENNES

Garonne R.

IBERIAN

CANTABRIAN MTS.

Douro R.

SPANISH

Madrid

PLATEAU

Lisbon

Guadiana R.

PENINSULA

Tagus R.

Guadalquivir R.

SIERRA NEVADA

Strait of Gibraltar

Rabat

ATLAS MTS.

BALEARIC

SEA

IVIZA

MAJORCA

MINORCA

MEDITERRANEAN

Algiers

PYRENNES

Andorra

FRISIAN IS.

The Hague

IJSSELMEER

NORTH

Brussels

ARDENNES

Meuse R.

Rhine R.

Bonn

Luxembourg

VOSGES

JURA MTS.

Bern

Vaduz

Saône R.

Rhône R.

Rhône R.

Inn R.

ALPS

PLAIN OF

LOMBARDY

Po R.

Monte Carlo

CORSICA

The Vatican

Rome

SARDINIA

APENNINES

TYRRHENIAN

SEA

Elbe R.

Berlin

GERMAN

PI

HARZ

MTS.

Weser R.

Oder R.

Warta R.

Vistu

ERZ MTS.

SUDETEN MTS.

BOHEMIAN

PLAIN

Prague

BLACK

FOREST

BOHEMIAN

FOREST

Danube R.

Vienna

Budapest

PLA

HUN

Drava R.

Sava R.

Be

ISTRIA

DINARIC ALPS

ADRIATIC

SEA

Tiber R.

Tira

IONIAN

SEA

SICILY

Str. of Messina

MALTA

SEA